I0759412

The Soccer 100

The Soccer 100

Oliver Kay & James Horncastle
with The Athletic Soccer Staff

WILLIAM MORROW
An Imprint of HarperCollins*Publishers*

Without limiting the exclusive rights of any author, contributor or the publisher of this publication, any unauthorized use of this publication to train generative artificial intelligence (AI) technologies is expressly prohibited. HarperCollins also exercise their rights under Article 4(3) of the Digital Single Market Directive 2019/790 and expressly reserve this publication from the text and data mining exception.

THE SOCCER 100. Copyright © 2025 by The Athletic Media Company. All rights reserved. No part of this book may be used or reproduced in any manner whatsoever without written permission except in the case of brief quotations embodied in critical articles and reviews.
For information, address HarperCollins Publishers, 195 Broadway, New York, NY 10007. In Europe, HarperCollins Publishers, Macken House, 39/40 Mayor Street Upper, Dublin 1, D01 C9W8, Ireland.

HarperCollins books may be purchased for educational, business, or sales promotional use. For information, please email the Special Markets Department at SPsales@harpercollins.com.

hc.com

FIRST EDITION

Tables and graphs reproduced from originals by Will Jeanes / The Athletic

Library of Congress Cataloging-in-Publication Data has been applied for.

ISBN 978-0-06-341267-5

Printed in the United States of America

25 26 27 28 29 LBC 5 4 3 2 1

Contents

Foreword

By Mauricio Pochettino

My love of football began on my family's farm in Murphy, a small town in Santa Fe province in Argentina, about 230 miles inland from Buenos Aires.

Only about four thousand people live in Murphy but, like everywhere else in Argentina, it is football mad. It is the number one passion. Normally one of the first birthday presents you receive is a *pelota*, a ball. It was the only thing I wanted to play with. Before you learn to run, you start to touch the ball with your feet. Then you start to play with your friends, your brothers, your brothers' friends—on the field, in the street—and, slowly, you learn to play football.

It's a difficult sport to explain. Why? Because you play with your feet. In basketball, American football, baseball, rugby, tennis, almost every other sport, it's about using your hands. In football, everything happens with your feet. You learn to control the *pelota* and you run with it, making fast actions, almost like you are dancing with it. As you grow up, you learn how to pass the ball, how to time it right, put the right amount of weight on the pass—and how to take the ball from the opponent.

It's by far the most popular sport in the world. It is played in every country, every city, every town, every village. You don't need money to play football. You just need a ball and a patch of grass or sand or concrete.

And you don't need a specific physical profile to play it. You can be tall or short, you can have long legs or not, you can have big muscles or not. We can talk about the importance of a certain physical profile, but some of the greatest players in history—I would argue the two greatest in history, both of them from Argentina—were usually the smallest players on the pitch.

When *The Athletic* asked me to contribute this foreword, they explained the concept of this book about the 100 greatest male footballers of all time. My first thought was, "Wow! How can you limit this to 100?" We are talking about a sport played in every country. I could name 100 great footballers from Argentina alone.

One of my most vivid early memories, aged six, is of Argentina winning the World Cup in 1978. I watched it on a small black-and-white television. I couldn't take my eyes off it. Mario Kempes was my first football hero, along with others like Daniel Passarella, Osvaldo Ardiles, Ricardo Villa, and the goalkeeper Ubaldo Fillol. These were my heroes, the ones I looked up to and decided I wanted to emulate.

But as I grew older, the footballer I really idolized was Diego Maradona. I had his poster on my bedroom wall. But it was more than that. Every boy of my generation in Argentina regarded Maradona as a superhero.

By the time of the 1986 World Cup in Mexico, I was 14, starting out as a footballer and getting a real feel for and understanding of the sport. I remember every Argentina game at that tournament so clearly. Best of all I remember Maradona's two goals in the quarter-final against England—the 'Hand of God' for the first and the amazing zigzag dribble for the second. A crowd of 500 of us in Murphy watched on a big screen as Maradona led us to victory over West Germany in the final to become world champions again. Afterward we all went into the main square to celebrate together, and everyone was chanting Maradona's name.

Seven years later I was a young player at Newell's Old Boys, in the nearby city of Rosario, when our coach, Jorge Solari, told us there was a possibility to sign Maradona from Sevilla. At that time, I didn't believe it was serious because Maradona was like someone from another planet.

But a few weeks later the coach said Maradona really was coming. He also said I should call him to welcome him to the club. He gave me Maradona's cell phone number. I was starting to wonder whether the whole thing was a joke. I was sitting with my girlfriend Karina, now my wife, in a very small apartment in Rosario, staring at the old landline phone. I remember saying to her, "What do I say? '*Hola*, Diego. This is Mauricio.' And he will say, 'Mauricio?! Who is Mauricio?!'"

I decided I would call him. He was in a car on the motorway from Buenos Aires to Rosario. The phone rang.

"*Si?*"

"*Hola* Diego. Sorry to disturb you. I am one of your new teammates at Newell's Old Boys."

"Oh, thank you. Which teammate?"

"Mauricio Pochettino."

And he said, "Oh, Poche! Thank you for calling me. I'm so happy to be joining Newell's Old Boys. You're a very good player, very strong. I hope you don't kick me in training . . ."

I couldn't believe it. Maradona knew who I was!

That was a different era. Back then you and your teammates lived in each other's pockets. We would be on a bus, on the way to a game, all watching the same match or the same movie on a VHS tape on a small TV, laughing at the same jokes, all connected to each other.

I even shared a bedroom with him when we traveled to away games. You would think the great Maradona would have a room to himself, but no, there he was, sleeping away in the next bed. It didn't seem real. The first few times, I honestly couldn't sleep. Maradona is sleeping in the next bed!

And, look, this was a difficult stage of his career—he was 32, he had some personal difficulties at the time and he was no longer the same explosive Maradona who had inspired Argentina to World Cup glory in 1986—but his ability with the ball was incredible. In training, we were watching in disbelief. He played only five games for Newell's but, for that short time, my teammates and I knew we were in the company of true, eternal greatness.

• • •

What sets the greatest players apart?

Of course technical quality is one part of it. But there's also a different kind of charisma that the best players have on the pitch. Even when you watch young kids playing, you can sometimes see one kid has a totally different energy the other kids don't have. It's the same at elite level: certain players are on a totally different level. Even at that stage of his career, Maradona was like that.

With the great players, you see it in the way they touch the ball, the way they pass the ball, the way they control it. With some players, the ball bounces off them. But with Maradona or Lionel Messi, it's like the ball is connected to them. Watching them in motion, it's as if you see the ball smiling, like it knows: "This guy will treat me well. This guy is going to give me love." The ball never looked happier than when it was at the feet of Maradona or Messi.

I was blessed with the opportunity to play in Europe, in Spain and France, and to play for my country, including at the Copa América in 1999 and the World Cup in 2002. With Argentina, I played with guys like Javier Zanetti, Diego Simeone, Juan Sebastián Verón, Pablo Aimar, Juan Román Riquelme, Ariel Ortega, Hernán Crespo, Gabriel Batistuta . . . At Paris Saint-Germain I played with Ronaldinho and Jay-Jay Okocha, who were two of the most spectacularly gifted, most joyous footballers I ever saw. They played with smiles on their faces. Ronaldinho played like he was dancing, like samba. Another one was Iván de la Peña at Espanyol. He doesn't have the profile of some of the others I mentioned, but he was a genius, another of those players who made the ball smile.

Then there are the ones I played against.

At Espanyol we used to come up against the Real Madrid *galácticos* side of Luís Figo, Zinédine Zidane, Roberto Carlos, David Beckham, Raúl and the Brazilian striker Ronaldo, or the Barcelona team of Xavi Hernández, Andrés Iniesta, and Rivaldo. Toward the end of my playing career at Espanyol I played against a very young Messi. It was only a brief encounter, but even at that stage, everyone was so excited about his potential, particularly in Argentina.

My coaching career has allowed me to work with so many wonderful players. It is hard to pick out just a few, but I worked with Harry Kane and Son Heung-min at Tottenham Hotspur and Messi, Neymar, Sergio Ramos and Kylian Mbappé at PSG. I would like to mention another two who, like De la Peña, rarely receive the recognition but who were two extraordinary players: Mousa Dembélé at Tottenham and Marco Verratti at PSG. Again, they made the ball smile.

To coach Messi was a privilege. Before that, I had admired him from a distance—even from the opposition dugout—and thought he was the best player I had seen since Maradona. But then to work closely with him, on the training pitch with him for 90 minutes or two hours every day, was an amazing experience. He has the most incredible technique, but also he has this ability to read exactly what is happening on the pitch and what the team needs him to do.

The other thing he shares with Maradona is that special mentality and special energy I talked about. The talent is unbelievable, but so is the motivation. They are different characters off the pitch—Maradona more extrovert, Messi more of an introvert—but they have that same force of personality on the pitch. When they are on the ball, the energy changes.

I mentioned Ronaldinho, who played like he was dancing samba. That to me is a characteristic of the Brazilian people and Brazilian football. They like to play with a smile. In Argentina, it's more . . . we say *grinta*, which is something like "grit" in English. Maradona and Messi were both born with the type of talent you might see once in a generation if you are lucky. But that talent is underpinned by *grinta*.

It can't be a coincidence that so many of the greatest players have come from South America, particularly from Brazil, Argentina, and Uruguay.

One thing is the nature: the physical attributes, coordination, and technical ability you are born with. The other thing is the way we are nurtured. There are some who have one or two ingredients to be a great football player, but I always feel the perfect equation includes passion plus necessity. To be a great football player, you have to *need* it—the way Pelé needed it, the way Maradona needed it growing up in Villa Fiorito in a poor area of Buenos Aires, when they were playing football to survive, or to find a way to put food on the table for their family. When you add passion and necessity, that is when you have all the ingredients to "cook" a football player.

Maybe the changing social environment means that fewer people feel the necessity that builds that kind of fighting spirit. In the more affluent nations, that brings challenges when it comes to developing players. But great talents keep emerging. Look at, for example, Yamine Lamal, who at the time of writing is emerging at Barcelona as one of the best players in the world while still a teenager.

• • •

For me, it's hard to rank footballers.

From my perspective, there are two number ones: Maradona and Messi. Someone from Brazil would have Pelé as number one, so that makes three number ones. Perhaps someone from the Netherlands would have Johan Cruyff as number one. Some people prefer Cristiano Ronaldo, another all-time great, to Messi.

I am not old enough to have seen Pelé or Cruyff, but, just looking at Maradona and Messi, it's so hard to put one of them above the other. Each was the best in his own era. Each of them did things that were out of this world.

If I have to choose just one, I am probably more on the side of Maradona, partly because of what he means to every *argentino,* particularly among my generation, and partly because the environment of playing football 40 years ago was so difficult. Messi has been an absolutely incredible player—and I know this better than almost anyone—but among my generation, particularly in Argentina, it is hard to imagine there could ever be a better footballer than Maradona.

I don't envy *The Athletic*'s writers in trying to pick a top three, never mind a top five, never mind a top 10, never mind a top 100. Some of my favorites will not make the list, I'm sure.

But I look forward to seeing which players have made it and reading about them. I look forward to seeing which player comes out on top—and I don't think I'm biased in suggesting it should be a fellow *argentino*.

And I look forward to thinking that all over the world, another generation of footballers will soon be starting to take their first steps, receiving their first *pelotas*, opening their eyes to the world of football and not yet knowing quite how far their dreams might take them.

Mauricio Pochettino began his playing career with Newell's Old Boys in his native Argentina. The center-half played in Europe with Espanyol, Paris Saint-Germain, and Bordeaux, and gained 20 caps for his country, featuring in the 2002 World Cup. As a manager, he has coached Espanyol and Southampton, and enjoyed a five-year stint with Tottenham Hotspur, taking the London club to the 2019 Champions League final. He won Ligue 1 with PSG in 2022, spent a season with Chelsea, and, in September 2024, was appointed head coach of the United States national team.

Introduction

By Oliver Kay

In the summer of 1981, six years old and bitten hard by the football bug, I used my pocket money to buy a book from a rummage sale.

I never knew the book's title. By the time I got my hands on it, it had lost its cover.

But turning its dog-eared pages, causing its spine to creak horribly, felt like entering another world. Besides a chronicle of every World Cup from 1930 to 1974, it contained a list of the greatest players of all time. It was dominated by British players, some of them familiar, but sprinkled among them were exotic names I had never seen before, legendary players from far-off lands.

Some had evocative nicknames: Lev Yashin, an acrobatic Soviet goalkeeper dressed in black from head to toe, was the "Black Spider"; Ferenc Puskás, the scourge of goalkeepers and defenses all over Europe, was the "Galloping Major"; the name Garrincha, a mesmerizingly gifted Brazilian who had been born with a defective spine and crooked legs, meant "Little Bird."

Greatest of all, the book said, was another Brazilian: Edson Arantes do Nascimento, known universally as Pelé, who had started out kicking a grapefruit around the streets of São Paulo. He had won the World Cup three times, the first of them as a 17-year-old, and ended up scoring more than 1,000 goals in his career. His nickname? "The King."

That treasured book fell apart in the end. My old football magazines and sticker albums usually went the same way, having been read from cover to cover again and again and again. I was desperate to cram my young brain with knowledge about football and footballers. And . . . what else was there to do? Football was hardly ever on television.

More than four decades later, the world is very different for sports fans. The opportunities to immerse yourself in sport seem boundless. There are TV sports stations offering wall-to-wall coverage. There are dedicated sports websites like *The Athletic*. There are social media outlets where athletes can communicate with their fans at the push of a button. Video-streaming platforms offer instant access to just about any goal of the hundreds that Lionel Messi and Cristiano Ronaldo have scored in their careers.

But has something been lost? With so much attention and energy focused on the here and now, are we losing a connection with those stories and those great names whose contributions have reverberated through the game's history?

That is what *The Soccer 100* is about. It is a celebration of 100 of the greatest players in the sport's history.

In an ideal world, that last part would read "the 100 greatest players in the sport's history"—and perhaps it will be marketed as such—but deep down, we know it cannot possibly be that.

Football has been played professionally for a century and a half. It is played and followed in every corner of the world. Comparing players in different positions, across different eras, is fraught with difficulty. How do you even begin to rank players whose careers and skill sets are as diverse as Giacinto Facchetti, Gordon Banks, Gerd Müller, Zinédine Zidane, and Neymar?

Data was not our friend here. Comparing eras is made so much harder by changes in tactical trends, competition formats, and even the world map. The proliferation of fixtures, many against small countries, has seen so many long-standing international appearance and goal records topple over recent years. Puskás, Eusébio, Müller, and the rest never got the opportunity to rack up goals against Lithuania, Andorra, San Marino, and the like.

There might be an algorithm that could take appearances, goals, and trophies won into account, but any such appraisal would be as flawed as it was dull. On paper, Diego Maradona's goalscoring record does not look spectacular, but anyone who watched him in his prime—indeed, anyone who has taken five minutes to watch some of those goals on YouTube—knows he scaled heights rarely, if ever, reached before or since.

We decided to put it down to a vote among 10 of our most experienced football writers and editors. We started by proposing every great player we could think of, even if that meant trawling the history books and previous lists of this nature. We then cast a vote where each of us proposed our top 100, in order, with points awarded for each ranking position. We put the results into a spreadsheet, looked at them . . . and gasped: "How is *he* below *him*?" Seconds later, another gasp: "How is *he* not in the top 100?"

We debated whether it might, on reflection, be worth deciding the rankings by committee instead. But no, we stuck with the original vote, putting our various gripes to one side, and went off to write the stories of 100 men who have left an indelible impression on the game.

And yes, they're all men. Women's football is booming, its popularity growing by the year, and it is hoped that in time we will produce a book about Mia Hamm, Marta, Aitana Bonmatí, and the greatest players in the women's game. But this one is about the men's game, a companion to *The Baseball 100*, *The Football 100*, and *The Basketball 100*.

Similarly, the selection very much concentrated on what these players delivered on the pitch. Some in their number have courted controversy off it—wealth and fame have brought their own pitfalls—but this was never designed to be an assessment of their characters. Rather, it is an appreciation of their quality as footballers and the brilliance they provided on the biggest stage.

All of this brings us to our top 100 and the need for us to apologize to some wonderful players who did not make the cut.

The long list extended to hundreds of players, any one of whom would have been a worthy inclusion in this book. But we could have turned this into *The Soccer 200*—and left the rankings out of it, in the interests of diplomacy—and it would still have upset people.

The difficulty was outlined by John Hollinger in *The Basketball 100* when he pointed out that "if we're covering more than 75 years' worth of players, more or less, and only naming 100, that's basically one player a year."

Consider football's longer history, its global reach and the depth and richness of the game's culture in so many countries across the world—and the task becomes even harder.

There was discomfort when we realized only three players from Africa, one from North America, and none at all from Asia or Oceania had made our top 100.

We briefly wondered whether there was a case for putting the voting process to one side in pursuit of a wider geographical spread. Landon Donovan (USA), Abedi Pelé (Ghana), Harry Kewell (Australia), and Son Heung-min (South Korea) are players of global renown, but selecting players on geographical grounds would have been against the spirit of the exercise and there were more contentious omissions than theirs.

Some of the game's first real stars, such as the Argentinian forward José Manuel Moreno and the prolific Austrian-Czechoslovakian striker Josef Bican, fell by the wayside. It is gratifying that Dixie Dean, Giuseppe Meazza, and Matthias Sindelar made it since their stories, written by Michael Walker, James Horncastle, and Mark Critchley, respectively, are among the most compelling in the book.

Inevitably, there is a slant toward the modern era, but it does not seem to extend to the modern day. Two of our top five are still playing at the time of writing (albeit in the twilight of their glorious careers . . . yes, you know the two), but only one other current player made our top 30. It probably says something about the difficulty of evaluating contemporary players that he, Kylian Mbappé, might have been ranked lower had our ballot been held a few months later after a difficult start to his Real Madrid career.

The only other current players who made *The Soccer 100* are well into their thirties. In time, the likes of Virgil van Dijk and Rodri might earn the kind of reverence that has been bestowed on Luka Modrić and Karim Benzema toward the end of their careers. So might, for example, Erling Haaland, Vinícius Júnior, or Lamine Yamal in years to come, but you never can tell.

As for English football's "golden generation" of the 2000s, only one of them makes *The Soccer 100*. David Beckham is one of the most famous athletes on the planet. But among the top 100 footballers of all time? Sorry, Becks.

There are 15 Brazilians among our selection, more than any other nation, but arguably there could have been at least another five. There was no place for Sergio Ramos, the defensive linchpin of the Real Madrid team that dominated the Champions League in the 2010s. We could not find room for either Spain's celebrated Luis Suárez or his Uruguayan namesake; there was an argument for including both.

There is something particularly enduring about that generation of athletes who lit up a world emerging from the darkness of global conflict: Wilt Chamberlain in basketball, Willie Mays in baseball, Rocky Marciano and Sugar Ray Robinson in boxing. The same is true of football: Alfredo Di Stéfano, Puskás, Yashin, names that cropped up in the sports press and then, very occasionally, appeared in grainy footage on television screens as international competitions began to gain prominence.

Their greatness is set in stone. The Fédération Internationale de Football Association (FIFA), the game's global governing body, have named annual awards in honor of Yashin (best male goalkeeper) and Puskás (best goal). EA Sports' long-running football franchise allows gamers to play with an "Ultimate Team" featuring the likes of Yashin, Puskás, Eusébio, and Pelé (though not Maradona, for licensing reasons).

Such tributes bring a degree of name recognition that might otherwise be lost, but with them comes a danger that they are reduced to a mere reference point. Tim Spiers's chapter on Yashin brings the goalkeeper's story to life in a way that, frankly, an "Ultimate Team" rating of 92 and an augmented-reality animation of him cannot begin to.

Rather than a series of profiles, we wanted to tell the players' stories in a more varied way. Jack Lang wrote about Garrincha's signature move; Phil Hay explored Johan Cruyff's genius through the eyes of Swedish defender Jan Olsson, the man on the wrong end of the Cruyff Turn; Sarah Shephard focused on the "otherness" of Sócrates, the chain-smoking Brazilian medic; Michael Cox microanalyzed Maradona's brilliance through the prism of a career-defining performance against England at the 1986 World Cup; Daniel Taylor went to the Portuguese island of Madeira to learn more about its favorite son, Cristiano Ronaldo; Nick Miller wrote about the goal for Santos against Flamengo in 2011 that announced Neymar as Brazil's newest *fenómeno*.

We were lucky enough to interview some of our subjects. I spoke with Kenny Dalglish. Greg O'Keeffe went to Denmark to meet Michael Laudrup. Felipe Cárdenas had an audience with Mario Kempes, the Argentinian goalscoring hero of the 1978 World Cup. Adam Crafton recalled a riotous afternoon in the company of Zlatan Ibrahimović. George Caulkin wrote from the heart about Alan Shearer, once his idol, now a close friend.

It's not all sweetness and light. I wrote about how the Munich air tragedy hung over Sir Bobby Charlton throughout his illustrious career; Jacob Whitehead explored the trauma that overshadowed Marco van Basten's goalscoring exploits in his own mind, if nobody else's; Mark Critchley dug deep in search of the truth about Sindelar, whose death in 1939, as a symbol of the Austrian resistance movement, has been a source of intrigue for decades.

That is the thing. This book is about the stories. The rankings? Not so much, we hope. To quote Joe Posnanski in *The Baseball 100*, "I don't care about the rankings. Every one of these players has a fascinating story—about persistence, about confidence, about pure talent, about amazing moments, about the lengths people will go to to become quote-unquote 'great.'"

• • •

Can there ever be a definitive verdict on the greatest footballer of them all? Even during Pelé's prime, some would argue for Di Stéfano, Puskás, Garrincha, or, later, Franz Beckenbauer or Cruyff. Maradona scaled breathtaking heights with Argentina and Napoli in the 1980s, but his career was pockmarked by controversies and ultimately curtailed by a self-destructive nature. It's complicated.

For all the fluctuations and contentious omissions from this list, though, the selections higher up were more settled. There was a clear top 20, a clear top 12, and a clear top six of (and let's keep them in chronological order to avoid any spoilers): Di Stéfano, Pelé, Cruyff, Maradona, Cristiano Ronaldo, and Messi. To return to an earlier point, these names are set in stone.

It was never going to be a unanimous choice, but for *The Soccer 100*, we settled on a No. 1, a choice that reflects not just greatness but sustained greatness: era-defining greatness, jaw-dropping greatness, the type of greatness that can leave you feeling like you are watching football from another dimension.

Again, it comes back to something Posnanski wrote in *The Baseball 100*, this time about his No. 1, Mays. "To watch him play, to read the stories about how he played, to look at his glorious statistics, to hear what people say about him is to be reminded why we love this odd and ancient game in the first place," he wrote. "Willie Mays has always made kids feel like grown-ups and grown-ups feel like kids. In the end, isn't that the whole point of baseball?"

Posnanski could easily be writing about football there. He could certainly be writing about Messi, Ronaldo (either version), Maradona, Cruyff, Pelé, or so many others featured in this book.

And yes, that is the whole point of sport. It can feel like such a serious business these days, compromised by political and commercial interests, but at its heart, it is still the same old game we fell in love with, illuminated by comic-book heroes, ordinary people with the power to do extraordinary things. This book is about them.

The Soccer 100

100.

Uwe Seeler

Seeler was a craftsman of a goalscorer who could receive the ball nearly anywhere and fashion a shooting chance.

"Uns Uwe, loyal und bescheiden—der Größte aller Zeiten."

By Seb Stafford-Bloor

It is the autumn of 2024 in Hamburg.

The pale sun glints on the River Elbe as it flows beneath the dock cranes and out toward the North Sea. It's a high-culture city, home today to media companies and a symphony hall that is the envy of the rest of Germany, but it still thinks of itself as a tough, working-class town.

Its football club, Hamburger SV, is a fallen giant. A six-time German champion and a European Cup winner in 1983, they have been mired in the second division—the 2.Bundesliga—for the better part of a decade and are on their seventh attempt to climb out.

In suburbia, brown leaves flutter down from the trees and line the pavements. After HSV's 2–2 home draw with Paderborn, my brother-in-law is hacking away at one of his garden hedges.

Clunk. Clunk. Clunk. The team's form weighs heavily on him and the garden is where he goes to shed that frustration—today with an enormous pair of shears.

That garden is where I learned much of my German; the good words and the bad. It's why I'm most fluent in my second language when talking about porous defenses, wasteful forwards, and coaches who promise to learn from defeats and setbacks but never, ever do.

But it's also where I first learned about Uwe Seeler and what he means to the city.

For the watching world, Seeler's career has been condensed into two moments, both against England. He captained the West Germany team that lost 4–2 to Sir Alf Ramsey's side in the 1966 World Cup final. Among the most famous images from that day are two of Seeler. In the first he is tenderly embracing Gordon Banks at full time. Two great players, one genuine show of respect.

The other, more poignantly, sees him devastated by defeat and being consoled by a local police officer on his way toward the Wembley tunnel.

Four years later, he would be a thorn in England's side, scoring the equalizer as West Germany recovered a two-goal deficit to derail Ramsey's defending champions 3–2 in the World Cup quarterfinal.

It was an astonishing goal. Like something from the future. Retreating to meet Karl-Heinz Schnellinger's driven cross, he somehow managed to redirect a header back across Peter Bonetti and into the England net. The footage is grainy now and that helps imbue it with mystery. Where did the angle or the power even come from?

So, that is Seeler to the rest of the world. But not in Hamburg—his Hamburg—because that is very different. Seeler is HSV's immortal. He scored 496 goals for the club from 1954 to 1972, 340 more than any other player in history.

Within those goals lies the essence of the player. Right foot, left foot, with power and artistry. Somewhere online there is a compilation set to smooth but playful jazz, and the range of abilities it shows—even today—is astonishing.

Seeler was a craftsman of a goalscorer who could receive the ball nearly anywhere and fashion a shooting chance. He was just 5'7" and had the stocky body and round face of someone other than a world-class athlete. But his repertoire was extraordinary: diving headers, falling volleys, thumping shots. Seeler, in the true, traditional sense, could do absolutely everything and could beat goalkeepers with subtlety, surprise, and booming power.

He played for HSV for his entire career. He also lived in Hamburg's northern districts for the rest of his life. When he died in July 2022, his hometown fell into mourning. Outside the Volksparkstadion, there is a bronze statue of his right foot and flowers and candles decorated it for months.

In the stadium itself, the ultras said goodbye with a vast tifo, reading: "Uns Uwe, loyal und bescheiden—der Größte aller Zeiten." (Our Uwe, loyal and humble—the greatest of all time.)

Linguists will note the grammatical error—*uns*, not *unser*—but that is a deliberate invocation of regional dialect for a player truly of the north. And that matters because Seeler's goals gave him prestige, significance, and medals. His 88th-minute winner against Cologne in 1960 gave HSV their first national title in more than three decades, but his symbolism, humanity, and heritage have prevented his legend from dimming.

My brother-in-law has finished with his hedges and we're now watching his robotic lawn mower prowl the grass.

"What you have to understand is that it was not just him. Seeler is Seeler. His goals—everything—sure. But his dad played for us, so did his brother. Their family is HSV."

It's true. Uwe's father, Erwin, played for the club between 1939 and 1948. Dieter, his older brother, was a HSV player from 1955 to 1965. Uwe and Dieter's sister, Gertrud, was a member of the club's handball section when she was a child, too. Their grandfather was a barman who worked on the city's docks, taking the lineage right to the banks of the Elbe and to Hamburg's industrial heart.

It matters, too, that Uwe never strayed from those roots. German football only truly professionalized in 1963 when the Bundesliga began. Before then, while players could top up their income with off-contract payments made in clever, clandestine ways, wages were limited. Even when German football entered its professional era, players could only earn a pittance compared to what was on offer in countries that were less suspicious of money's influence.

"At that time, he could have left. Okay, yes, players could earn a bit of money," my brother-in-law says, mimicking an under-the-table gesture. "But Seeler could have been a rich man in Italy or Austria. Do you know the story about the university?"

The story about the university is an essential part of the Seeler parable. In 1961, he was offered a fantastic amount of money to join Helenio Herrera's Inter Milan. The figures are unreliable, but at a time when his wages were officially capped at 400 deutsche mark a month, Herrera's Inter were reportedly willing to pay him DM 150,000 a year, in addition to a DM 500,000 signing bonus.

To call that potentially life-changing is an understatement. Still, Seeler was not for turning and, according to local legend, his resistance was partly inspired by a letter received from the dean of Hamburg University, emphasizing his worth to the local community.

"If you manage to withstand this temptation," the dean wrote, "that would be a radiant signal, giving people cause to reflect on their ways."

Seeler stayed and scored goals for another decade. Money be damned.

"Imagine a player doing that today," chuckles my brother-in-law as his mower trundles past.

Player name: Uwe Seeler
Born: November 5, 1936
Died: July 21, 2022 (aged 85)
Position: Striker
Debut: 1954
Main teams: Hamburger SV (1954–72); West Germany (1954–70)
Career highlights: One of just five men to score at four or more World Cups, doing so in the 1958, 1962, 1966, and 1970 editions. Hamburg's record goalscorer.

99.

Javier Zanetti

At his best, Zanetti turned his respective flank into a dark alley in a bad neighborhood.

Trophies, triumphs, and tireless hard work

By Carl Anka

There are dozens of statistics we can use to articulate the brilliance of Javier Zanetti. His longevity lends itself to fascinating and faintly hilarious tidbits. After all, there are very few footballers who played with both the Brazilian Ronaldo and Lionel Messi.

However, the most straightforward way to explain Zanetti is by relaying the following story. After exchanging vows with his wife, Paula, Zanetti asked if he could go for a quick run before the wedding reception as he wanted to keep on top of his cardio work.

In the player's autobiography, *Giocare da Uomo* (Play Like a Man), Paula describes herself instinctively laughing at the request before realizing her husband had packed a change of clothes and running trainers and was actually serious about going for a jog.

She gave her blessing and off he went.

"If I got angry every time Javier went training," she wrote, "then I would have had a sour face on every day since I was 14 years old."

This story can go a long way toward answering any footballing question about the Argentinian.

How did he manage the shift from right-back to left-back after the arrival of Maicon at Inter Milan in 2006? Because this is a man so dedicated to his craft that he went jogging on his wedding day.

How did he bounce back after being snubbed by José Pékerman and Diego Maradona for Argentina's World Cup squad in 2006 and 2010? Because this is a man so dedicated to his craft that he went jogging on his wedding day.

What made him so much of a constant at Inter Milan that 17—*seventeen*—different full-time head coaches decided they couldn't do without him? *Because this is a man so dedicated to his craft that he went jogging on his wedding day.*

And so on. Zanetti's relentless pursuit of physical precision made him one of the best full-backs the world had ever seen and his intensity and industry kept him there for the best part of a decade. His willingness to embrace hard work owes a debt to an early rejection from his first club, Independiente, due to his perceived scrawniness as a 16-year-old back in 1989.

The teenage Zanetti would then spend two years working as a bricklayer in Dock Sud—one of the toughest areas of Buenos Aires—along with his father, Rodolfo. If money was tight, he took on additional shifts selling milk in the local neighborhood.

"I liked my father's work," Zanetti would later recall in his book.

"But above all, I liked the idea of doing something concrete and useful. Building a house is a metaphor that I like, it's at the core of my life philosophy: starting from the bottom and reaching the top."

It took a few more years before Zanetti reached the heights of top European club football, but, once he arrived, he stayed at that summit longer than anyone thought possible. The full-back/defensive midfielder played 1,102 games over his professional career, making him one of the most experienced outfielders of all time. He could, and probably should, have earned more than his 145 caps for Argentina, too. Those controversial snubs by Pékerman and Maradona cost the man of many monikers—*El Tractor, Pupi, La Bandiera,* and *El Capitano*—more opportunities with the national side.

Argentina's loss was Inter Milan's gain. Although Zanetti spent three years playing in his homeland for Talleres, in the second tier, and Banfield, he belongs to the Italian powerhouse. He was the club's first signing after Massimo Moratti stepped in as chairman in 1995. Players of the caliber of Ronaldo, Christian Vieri, and Alvaro Recoba would come and go through the Moratti years. There were trophies, triumphs, and chaotic periods, too. Yet Zanetti was a constant. The true great of the era.

He arrived at the club as a willowy 22-year-old with his shoes in a plastic bag. He departed with five *Scudetti,* four Coppa Italia wins, a quartet of Italian Super Cups, a Champions League, a UEFA Cup, and a Club World Cup winner's medal. Of his 19 years at San Siro, he spent 15 as Inter's captain. His was a stabilizing presence that no manager could do without. He was a shield against the many forces of entropy that swirled around the club.

Zanetti's unflashy nature, coupled with Serie A's array of talented defenders, meant he often went overlooked during awards season. Yes, he was not an eye-catching, buccaneering full-back in the same vein as Cafu. He did not go about his defensive duties with the same graceful artistry as Paolo Maldini. Rather, Zanetti was a man who relished the hard work of defending and his relentless training helped set a standard for friends, teammates, and fans alike.

To Zanetti, good things require hard work and sacrifice, but if you properly apply yourself with consistency and effort, then anything is possible.

Make no mistake, he was not a defensive clogger, hacking wingers to pieces to make tackles. Zanetti received only two red cards in his professional career. He remained a gentleman duellist.

At his best, Zanetti turned his respective flank into a dark alley in a bad neighborhood. Wingers walking through there were likely to lose possession, their temper, or both trying to beat the dogged Argentinian. Everything Zanetti did was done with precision and discipline.

Partway through the 2008–09 season, José Mourinho moved the Argentinian into defensive midfield following an injury crisis. Player and manager weathered the storm and ended that season celebrating the club's 17th Serie A title. A season later, Zanetti started in midfield in the Champions League final and cried as the final whistle confirmed his side as victors. Of Zanetti's 16 trophies at Inter, 15 of them came with him wearing the armband. The other—the 1998 UEFA Cup—saw him score a rare goal in the final against Lazio.

He was also—crucially—a gentleman. Away from football, he formed the Leoni di Potrero Foundation to support children with social isolation problems. Another charitable group, Fundación Pupi, helps children from low-income families in his native Argentina. Zanetti saw football as a job; a role that must be taken seriously. He also saw it as a means of delivering a ray of happiness and joy to others and worked to cultivate it wherever he could.

His final match in San Siro was on May 10, 2014, against Lazio. Manager Walter Mazzarri brought him on for Jonathan Moreira early in the second half and there was palpable excitement every time he was near the ball, the home crowd doing everything possible to savor their long-standing hero. Then, just as the game approached its final moments, the matchday camera focused on Zanetti.

He was looking at one of the stadium clocks, trying to work out how many seconds he had left on the pitch. You can watch him drinking it all in as his time at the club ticks down. A career well spent; 19 years of hard work where the rewards were worth all that running.

Upon his retirement, Inter Milan retired Zanetti's No. 4 and named him vice president. Who else could compare?

The scrawny boy who became a hero. A defensive workhorse who regularly outperformed stallions.

Player name: Javier Adelmar Zanetti
Born: August 10, 1973
Position: Right-back, left-back, defensive midfielder
Debut: 1992
Main teams: Talleres (1992–93), Banfield (1993–95), Inter Milan (1995–2014); Argentina (1994–2011)
Career highlights: Captained Inter Milan to the treble in 2009–10. Won Serie A five times.

98.

Kevin Keegan

Keegan was the darling of the Kop and, for a while, also carried England's hopes.

"My Ballon d'Or trophy? I doubt Cristiano would use it as a doorstop."

By Daniel Taylor

It's when you go up the stairs of Kevin Keegan's house and into his trophy room that you are reminded of how the sport has changed since the days when he was, by some distance, the superstar of European football.

A few years ago, while collaborating with him on his autobiography, he gave me a personal tour and, as you can imagine for a man of his achievements, his trophy cabinets were filled with all sorts of nostalgic memories.

There were all his medals from those triumphant years when he was the talisman of a Liverpool side at the forefront of English football.

Other trophies came from his three-year spell as one of the first English footballers to show it was possible to flourish on foreign soil, winning the Bundesliga title with Hamburg and making himself one of the most popular players there has ever been in the German league.

I was allowed to hold the Golden Boot he won as the First Division's leading scorer in 1981–82 when he was wearing the colors of Southampton. There was even a pair of the old Pirelli slippers from the days when Keegan, like no other footballer of his generation, had commercial deals coming out of his ears.

But there were also two trophies that, over time, had discolored through age. One was turning a shade of seaweed green and it came as a surprise, on closer inspection, to discover that these rather unremarkable specimens were actually his Ballon d'Or awards, from 1978 and 1979.

What stuck in the mind was that Keegan, the ultimate team player, seemed remarkably unmoved to have won the award twice. It was, he said, an obvious honor, but he was never obsessed with individual awards and maybe it was also true that, in his days as a player, there was not so much gravitas given to the Ballon d'Or as in the years when Lionel Messi and Cristiano Ronaldo were competing for a much more glamorous trophy.

"For my first one, a guy wandered onto the pitch—I can't even remember who it was—to hand me the trophy before a game somewhere," Keegan told me. "I shook his hand, put it in my bag, and lugged it home with the rest of my stuff. It never weighed a great deal, like a trophy from a pub darts competition, and it rattles now whenever it is lifted because a bolt has come loose and is floating inside the wooden base.

"The metal is discolored and you can even see the glue where the plaque has been fixed on. I had it valued once and the guy took one look before telling me it was worth a tenner. I doubt Cristiano would use it as a doorstop."

Modesty aside, Keegan remains the only Englishman to have won the Ballon d'Or on two occasions. Messi has eight, Ronaldo five, and there are three players—Johan Cruyff, Michel Platini, and Marco van Basten—on three wins apiece. Keegan is in the next bracket with Alfredo Di Stéfano, Franz Beckenbauer, Karl-Heinz Rummenigge, and the Brazilian Ronaldo.

By his own admission, the miner's son from Doncaster was the "least naturally talented player on the list. I didn't float like Cruyff. I never had the grace of Pelé or the moves of Maradona."

Yet there is also a reasonable argument that Keegan ought to have had a hat trick of successes by winning the same award in 1977 too—the year he bid farewell to Liverpool by helping Bob Paisley's team win the European Cup against Borussia Mönchengladbach in Rome.

Keegan scored 20 goals for Liverpool that season and, of the 25 countries voting for the Ballon d'Or winner, 11 picked him in first place, whereas only seven selected Allan Simonsen of Mönchengladbach, the eventual winner.

How did Simonsen get the award? That was because of the scoring system at the time. Simonsen had seven runner-up votes, as opposed to Keegan's three, and the Denmark international gained extra points by being nominated in third position three times.

"Nobody bothered telling me at the time, which was probably another measure of how different things were back then, and the truth is that I was never obsessed with personal glory anyway," was Keegan's verdict in his 2018 autobiography, *My Life in Football*. "For me, it was the team medals that counted the most."

There were plenty of them in a career that began with the teenage Keegan being rejected by Doncaster Rovers, his local club, for being too small before finally getting his chance amid the puddles and potholes of lowly Scunthorpe United.

When Liverpool caught wind of his talent, it led to a whirlwind six years at Anfield in which he won three league titles, an FA Cup, the European Cup, and two UEFA Cups, becoming the darling of the Kop.

For a while, Keegan also carried England's hopes, winning 63 caps in what was a frustratingly bleak period for the national team. He had the most famous perm in football, copied by fans up and down the country.

Then, having helped Hamburg win their first title since 1960, he scored 26 top-division goals in one of his two seasons with Southampton and achieved a lifelong ambition when Newcastle United, then of the division below, fired their Cupid's arrow in his direction.

Newcastle were the team Keegan's father had supported and so began a love affair that still exists to this day.

The local newspaper in Newcastle responded to his signing with a front-page headline that simply read "Here he is!" and, always the showman, when Keegan left the club two years later, it was in a helicopter, still in his kit, waving goodbye from the St. James' Park pitch directly after his farewell match.

He returned, twice, to become the club's manager, and it is never easy, unless you saw it close-up, to put into words the adulation he received, and continues to receive, from the Newcastle public. Jack Charlton, one of England's 1966 World Cup winners, summed it up best as another native of the Northeast.

"If Kevin Keegan fell into the Tyne," he said, "he'd come up with a salmon in his mouth."

Player name: Kevin Keegan
Born: February 14, 1951
Position: Forward
Debut: 1968
Main teams: Scunthorpe United (1968–71), Liverpool (1971–77), Hamburger SV (1977–80), Southampton (1980–82), Newcastle United (1982–84); England (1972–82)
Career highlights: Won the European Cup in 1976–77. Won the Ballon d'Or in 1978 and 1979, the only Englishman to win the award more than once.

97.

Gunnar Nordahl

Nordahl remains, at the time of writing, the third-highest scorer in almost 100 years of Serie A.

The firefighter who blazed a trail to Milan

By Oliver Kay

Growing up in the small Swedish town of Degerfors, Johanna Reimers could not help noticing that her grandfather was a big deal.

"When you were walking through the town with him, you would never be alone," she says. "Everyone would stop him and ask for photos and autographs."

She knew her grandfather had another identity: Gunnar Nordahl, a former professional footballer who had played for Sweden and then joined AC Milan. His home was an Aladdin's cave of newspaper cuttings, photographs, trophies, and medals. Reimers, her brother, and her sister would explore his treasure trove with a sense of wonder.

But the extent of his reputation and fame only truly began to dawn on her after he died in 1995. "His funeral was at a really small church outside Norrköping," Reimers says. "We went there as a family and we got there and . . . it was a full house, cameras everywhere, people from all over the world. That's when we really began to realize what a big star he had been."

There was another dawning when Reimers, by now a sports journalist, moved to Italy in the early 2010s to report on another Swedish center-forward who had joined Milan.

Zlatan Ibrahimović was a superstar—and, unlike Nordahl, never made light of that fact—but it was gently put to him by the Italian sportswriters in his introductory press conference that he was following in the footsteps of football royalty, such was the reverence in which Nordahl was still held more than 60 years after he joined Milan.

"And it was so strange but so nice," Reimers says, "to sit there and hear people talk about how respected Gunnar still was and to be able to find out more of that side of my family's history."

Ibrahimović is Sweden's record goalscorer, one of the greatest players of the modern era, but even in Italy, where he excelled for Juventus and both Milan clubs, his legacy cannot match that of Nordahl, who is Milan's all-time record goalscorer, the third-highest in Serie A history, and the top-scoring non-Italian in the top division.

It is all the more remarkable when you consider Nordahl did not move to Italy until he was 27. He had spent the previous decade playing in Sweden, scoring goals at an absurd rate for Hörnefors IF, Degerfors IF, and IFK Norrköping while working as a firefighter.

The turning point of his career was the football tournament at the 1948 Olympics in London. Nordahl scored seven goals in an outstanding Sweden team that also featured Gunnar Gren and Nils Liedholm, who were to follow him to Milan, and his older brothers Bertil and Knut, the latter of whom went on to join Roma. Sweden won the gold medal, beating Yugoslavia 3–1 in the final.

On the back of that success, Nordahl was offered a transfer to Italy. Moving was not a straightforward decision because it would mean the end of his international career, given that the Sweden national team had a strict amateur-only policy, but he concluded it was an opportunity he could not refuse.

"He chose to go because of the money, basically," Reimers said. "He could have stayed in Sweden as an amateur and continued as a firefighter, but he wanted to go and try to make a good living for the future of his family."

That would only be the case if Nordahl was successful in Milan. It was a gamble as he set off for Italy by rail in January 1949—likewise for Milan, plucking a center-forward from the relative backwater of Swedish football—but one that paid off handsomely for both parties over the next seven years.

Nordahl was an immediate success, scoring 16 goals in his first 15 games for Milan. He was a powerful, brutally effective, clinical center-forward built like a heavyweight boxer. The Italian press soon nicknamed him *Il Bisonte* ("the bison") or, in honor of his previous trade, *Il Pompiere* ("the fireman").

The available footage of Nordahl throws up few surprises. He has the direct, square-shouldered running style that was common among center-forwards of that era, but what stands out is his finishing prowess. Predominantly right-footed, he was equally confident lashing the ball past an opposition goalkeeper with his left or rising above opposition defenders to score with a perfectly placed header.

There isn't much subtlety or finesse. Those qualities came from his former Sweden teammates Gren and Liedholm, who arrived in Milan in the summer of 1949. They were very different players—Gren an incisive inside-right, Nordahl a bustling center-forward, Liedholm a playmaker with a supreme understanding of time and space. But they combined to wonderful effect as Milan won the Scudetto in 1950–51, their first in 44 years. Together they were known as Gre-No-Li (Gren-Nordahl-Liedholm).

Nordahl's pomp came before the "door bolt" ethos of *catenaccio* took an unyielding grip on Italian football, but his strike rate was extreme, winning the *Capocannoniere* award as the league's leading scorer in five of his first six full seasons in Milan.

He remains, at the time of writing, the third-highest scorer in almost 100 years of Serie A, behind Silvio Piola, the star of the league's early years, and former Roma captain Francesco Totti. But Piola's 274 goals came in 537 appearances for several clubs, primarily Lazio; Totti's 250 goals came in 619 appearances; Nordahl's total of 225 goals (210 for Milan, 15 for Roma) came in just 291 games.

Nordahl's legacy might have been even greater had the timing been better.

He was a few weeks short of his 34th birthday, in his final season at Milan, when the European Cup was launched in 1955–56. They reached the semifinal, only to be beaten 5–4 on aggregate by the great Real Madrid side who went on to dominate the first five years of the competition. Nordahl scored a hat trick when Milan beat Lille 5–0 in the 1951 final of the Latin Cup, which at the time was the most prestigious European tournament, but legacy-wise it is not quite the same.

"And the thing he was really sad about was that he never played in the World Cup," Reimers says. "He really wanted to have done that, but going to Italy meant he couldn't play for Sweden anymore. He always hoped it would change. They changed the rules before we hosted the World Cup in 1958, but by then he was much older [36] and had some injuries and he couldn't be on the team."

With a 37-year-old Gren and a 35-year-old Liedholm in their ranks, Sweden reached the final of that World Cup on home soil, where they were beaten 5–2 by a Pelé-inspired Brazil. For someone who had built an illustrious career on being in the right place at the right time, Nordahl was unfortunate that the opposite applied to his international career.

But his legacy in Sweden and Milan endures.

"He changed the course of Swedish football by breaking the ground for so many players to be able to go abroad and play football professionally," Reimers says. "Before that, it was just amateur football; you couldn't play football and make money. But he went abroad and showed people in Sweden that, no, actually you can do both."

Player name: Nils Gunnar Nordahl
Born: October 19, 1921
Died: September 15, 1995 (aged 73)
Position: Striker
Debut: 1937
Main teams: Hörnefors IF (1937–40), Degerfors IF (1940–44), IFK Norrköping (1944–49), AC Milan (1949–56), Roma (1956–58), Karlstad BK (1959–60); Sweden (1942–48)
Career highlights: AC Milan's all-time top scorer with 221 goals in 268 games. He scored 43 goals in 33 games for Sweden. Won the Olympic Gold medal in 1948, scoring seven goals in four matches.

96.
Alan Shearer

At his peak, Shearer had everything: pace, power, aerial ability, dynamism.

The striker who came home

By George Caulkin

For the record, Alan Shearer would like it known that he is very much alive, if no longer kicking. This is the thought—vaguely peculiar if taken out of context—that comes to him when he walks up the hill from the center of Newcastle upon Tyne to St. James' Park and sees his own likeness, cast from metal and perched on a plinth, glaring down at him. Glaring has always been part of his skill set.

"I have to pinch myself, in more ways than one," he says. "I have to remind myself I'm not dead yet. That's when you usually get a statue, isn't it? No matter how many times I look at it, it still feels surreal, but

I'm incredibly proud and very grateful. It's a weird thing because I'd like to think I'm pretty normal."

Also for the record: Despite his own caveat, Shearer's normality never stretched to football, except in the sense of making genius a matter of routine. Asked to list his qualities as a player, he again retreats to the humdrum. "Honest, hardworking, loved scoring a goal," he says, which in no way encapsulates the obsession, his drive, the will to win, the numbers, his impact, the brutality of his art, the glare that melted defenders and officials.

After one of his goals, Sir Alex Ferguson, then the Manchester United manager, told reporters that Shearer "hit it as if he meant to kill it," which feels like the perfect description of his essence as a No. 9. He was a classic, all-around center-forward with narrow eyes, dynamite in his boots, a single objective, and murderous intent.

Nobody has done it more in the modern era. Shearer's 260 goals in the Premier League are a record (before the competition was renamed and repurposed in 1992, there were another 23 goals in the top division for Southampton), which leaves him 47 clear of Harry Kane in second place.

At his peak, he had everything: pace, power, aerial ability, dynamism. His instinct for goal was uncanny, but he was not the kind of striker who lurked around the penalty area and offered little else. He could run the channels. He could hold the ball up and bring others into play. As he grew older and injuries nagged at his body, he became increasingly adept at buying his team time, winning free kicks, and defending set pieces.

Yet goals were his currency, his addiction. "It was pure," he says. "It was something almost indescribable and I got hooked from a very early age. The first time I did it, I wanted it more and more and the more I did it, the more I had to do it again. Nothing was going to stop me.

"It's the biggest rush ever, a few seconds of lose-yourself giddiness, a magical drug that takes hold of you and doesn't ever relent. You always want more. And there's the counterpoint, too: When I missed, it lingered. It festered. I might have looked and sounded controlled, but I'd get home and wouldn't sleep."

Shearer is a living statue because that drug fed his normality. He had left Newcastle, his hometown, as a teenager, traveling to Southampton at the other end of the country in search of a career. By the time he returned to Tyneside for a world-record fee of £15 million in 1996, joining from Blackburn Rovers where he won the Premier League, he called himself "only a sheet-metal worker's son from Newcastle."

Shearer's father was also called Alan. His mother, Anne, worked as a home help for the local council. "There wasn't a lot of spare cash flying around," Shearer told *The Athletic*. "They kept an empty whisky bottle in the lounge and they would gradually fill it with loose change, which was how they could afford to buy me new football boots or shirts, how they paid for school clothes for Karen, my sister. I'll never forget them emptying that penny jar."

In Southampton's dressing room, surrounded by men when he was still a boy, Shearer turned that normality into his superpower. His thirst for goals would not slake itself. "I probably had a better attitude towards graft and commitment than other people," he says. "I tried harder than most, I guess. I don't think anyone could outwork me or want it more than I did. And that was my strength."

The effect was astonishing. On his full debut as a professional at the age of 17 years and 240 days, Shearer became the youngest player to score a hat trick in England's elite division, but it was when he left for Blackburn, linking up with Kenny Dalglish, one of his early heroes, that he truly blossomed. His £3.6 million fee was then a record for a British club.

His four-year spell at Ewood Park, where Dalglish constructed a team that took on Ferguson's mighty Manchester United, was breathtaking. In the final three seasons, he scored 31, 34, and 31 league goals, the focal point of a team built with two wingers and made to get the best out of him. Blackburn finished fourth, second, and first in the Premier League during his time at the club.

By 1996, when England reached the semifinals of the European

Championship and Shearer, who won 63 caps, claimed the Golden Boot, the biggest clubs in Europe were knocking. Not yet 26, Blackburn offered him the player-manager's role. Ferguson courted him and Shearer listened but, in the end, the pull of home was undeniable.

This, too, was not normal. It was an era when Newcastle United were upwardly mobile—under the management of Kevin Keegan, Shearer's other idol, they had just been pipped to the title by Ferguson's side—but their recent history told a depressing tale of selling their best talent, not buying it. Beating Manchester United to anything was more or less unheard-of. It still is.

Shearer is not an overtly emotional man, but this was a moment that stirred huge emotion. Nor was he a romantic kind of player—too powerful, too brutal, too much hitting it like he meant to kill it—but it could only be a romantic story. Ferocious and forever ours.

Keegan left soon afterward, but Shearer stayed for a decade, reaching a couple of FA Cup finals, falling out with Ruud Gullit, surging again under Sir Bobby Robson, playing and scoring in the Champions League, suffering and recovering from devastating injuries and firing in goals, always goals, until he surpassed "Wor" Jackie Milburn's total as Newcastle's record goalscorer.

Manchester United won the lot and Newcastle, infamously, won nothing. "I don't regret it," Shearer says. "Why would I? How could I? It was all I ever wanted. It's what I worked for. It means everything."

When Shearer's statue was unveiled in September 2016, its right arm held aloft in perpetual celebration, it was on a patch of ground not owned by the club just outside St James'. It had been paid for by the family of Freddy Shepherd, Newcastle's former chairman, a reflection of the sourness and strained relationships that were a feature under the ownership of Mike Ashley, for whom Shearer briefly served as interim manager and then never heard from again.

Since Ashley's departure, the statue has been moved and now stands at a corner of the Gallowgate End beside one of Sir Bobby, the eternal enthusiast who, like Shearer, came home to Newcastle and performed miracles when he got there. For all their contrasting personalities, both represent the best of the club they supported and the city they adored, strong men of purpose, conviction, and principle who believed in work and gave everything of themselves.

Unlike Robson, Shearer did not have to wait until death for his statue, but making the abnormal normal has long been a theme. One more for the record: There has been nobody better.

Player name: Alan Shearer

Born: August 13, 1970

Position: Striker

Debut: 1988

Main teams: Southampton (1988–92), Blackburn Rovers (1992–96), Newcastle United (1996–2006); England (1992–2000)

Career highlights: Scored a record 260 goals in the Premier League and 283 overall in the English top flight—the fifth most in history. Top scorer at Euro 1996 as England reached the semifinals on home soil.

95.

Hugo Sánchez

Sánchez's celebrations were performance art.

The showman who opened the door to North American players in Europe

By Felipe Cárdenas

Stardom at Real Madrid can be fleeting. There is no light brighter than the one that shines at the Estadio Santiago Bernabéu and Hugo Sánchez understood that perhaps better than anyone. The former Mexican international, considered the best player his country has ever produced, became a goalscoring icon at La Casa Blanca.

Sánchez was a five-time winner of La Liga's Pichichi Trophy, awarded to the division's top scorer. In addition to his consistency as a clinical center-forward, Sánchez became known for his elite athleticism and often acrobatic finishes. His famous *chilena*, or bicycle kick, was a trademark that defied belief, but one he performed with ease.

However far he was from goal and whether he had time to settle the ball or not, he would invariably score with a spectacular mid-air volley. Famously two-footed, Sánchez's left foot produced his most impressive goals. His scissor kick against Logroñes in 1988 at the Bernabéu appeared on every highlights' tape that kids grew up watching in the 1990s. His tally of similar goals for Real Madrid ran into double figures.

The striker may be most associated with Real Madrid, but Sánchez actually won his first league-scoring accolade while across the capital with Atlético Madrid in 1984–85. There were three successive Pichichis after his move to Real Madrid, with five in six years overall. His final award came in 1989–90 after a 38-goal season, every one of them scored with a one-touch finish.

That glorious blend of volleys, textbook headers, and simple tap-ins were all part of Sánchez's prolific appetite. It would be over two decades before Cristiano Ronaldo beat Sánchez's 38 goals with his own 40-goal season in 2010–11.

Even Sánchez's celebrations were performance art. He would race to a corner flag and spring into a front flip, followed by a two-fisted celebration similar to a bullfighter acknowledging praise from an adoring audience. This was a sophisticated showman who never took his success in Europe for granted.

"I'm going to share a comment that was directed at me when I arrived in Spain," Sánchez told this correspondent in 2022. "'Hey Hugo, you've come here as a young player. You have to learn and you have to teach because you've been brought to a foreign country and you're taking a job away from somebody who is local. If you're going to take that job away from him, you have to show why you're better. You have to show your quality.'"

For Sánchez, though, fame at Real Madrid came with a price. During his first 11 years in Spain, including that stint at Atlético, he overcame the stigma in Europe that follows players from North America. To this day, their talent and football culture are questioned.

In his case, he had to prove that a Mexican striker could excel at the highest level when there was nearly no proof of concept to which he could point.

Sánchez has claimed to have been the victim of racial abuse in Spain, classist insults, and nationalistic vitriol that continue to plague football today. In 2023, he spoke about why he empathizes with current Real Madrid star Vinícius Júnior. The Brazilian winger has been targeted by racist insults during his time in the Spanish capital.

"What I went through is similar to what Vinícius is experiencing today," Sánchez told ESPN. "The good thing is that they focus on the good players. I'll never forget what fans in Gijón yelled at me. I was also the type of player who would kick harder after being kicked. I drove defenders crazy."

Sánchez, who had about as many nicknames as a prizefighter, was the first Mexican footballer to become a global star. He was first known as *el Niño de Oro*, "the Golden Boy," in 1972. Four years later, he became an Olympian and would later sign as an 18-year-old with Mexican side Pumas UNAM, a popular Mexico City–based club that's part of the National Autonomous University of Mexico. He would eventually graduate from the university's school of dentistry.

After starring for Pumas as a youngster, a brief stint with the San Diego Sockers of the now-defunct North American Soccer League was preceded by his longevity in Spain. There the nicknames matured. *El Señor Gol*, *El Macho*, and *El Penta Pichichi* were monikers bestowed upon a player who had established himself as a dominant force at the world's biggest club.

"One of the things I learned in Spain and in Europe is that if you don't prioritize your sporting responsibilities, you won't win titles, and if you don't win titles, you won't make money," said Sánchez. "That was the Real Madrid mentality. For me, they're the best club of all time and they're rich because they've won so many titles and because they concern themselves with the sporting side of the business first."

From a young age, Sánchez wanted to become the best striker

in the world. His family supported his sporting ambitions but also stressed the importance of formal education. The 1970 World Cup in Mexico, where Pelé lifted his third world title with Brazil, changed Sánchez's aspirations.

"My interest in football began during that World Cup," he said. "I was [almost] 12 and that was when I first became enthusiastic about wanting to represent my country and wear the Mexico national team shirt. That's when my dreams began."

He was just 19 when he made his first World Cup squad in 1978. He would make 58 appearances and score 29 goals in an international career that spanned 21 years, but the national team was more a source of frustration than satisfaction for Sánchez. Mexico failed to qualify for the 1982 World Cup at a time when he was nearing his peak.

Sánchez was his country's star at the 1986 tournament held in his homeland, but the home side lost to West Germany in a penalty shootout at the quarterfinal stage. The striker scored just once in the tournament. He made one appearance at the 1994 World Cup in the United States at the age of 35 and retired from international football in 1998, his involvement since limited to an 18-month stint as national team manager, in which he lost the 2007 CONCACAF Gold Cup final to the United States.

He is now an outspoken and often controversial pundit with ESPN, but he is still a figure most associated with the high standards of Real Madrid. Only six players have scored more than his 208 goals in 282 appearances for Los Blancos, a tally that made him a club great at a time when Mexican footballers were rarely visible in Europe.

The striker with the spring in his step and a penchant for manic celebrations was a pioneer.

Player name: Hugo Sánchez Márquez
Born: July 11, 1958
Position: Striker
Debut: 1976
Main teams: Pumas UNAM (1976–82), Atlético Madrid (1981–82 on loan, 1982–85), Real Madrid (1985–92), América (1992–93), Rayo Vallecano (1993–94), Atlante (1994–95), Linz (1995–96); Mexico (1977–98)
Career highlights: Won La Liga five times with Real Madrid—for whom he scored 208 goals in 282 appearances—and the Mexican Primera División twice with Pumas UNAM.

94.

Gareth Bale

Bale won the Champions League five times at Real Madrid but was more appreciated by his national team.

Why was Wales's talisman not cherished by Real Madrid?

By Stuart James

Five Champions League winners' medals, three La Liga titles, more than 100 goals, a contender for the best goal scored in a European Cup final, and another, in a Copa del Rey final against Barcelona, that makes you rub your eyes in disbelief every time you watch it.

Yet if Gareth Bale returned to Real Madrid and was paraded on the pitch at halftime, it's hard to know what sort of reception the Welshman would receive. That's not to say there would be whistles—Bale knows that feeling at the Bernabéu—but it's hard to imagine the red carpet being rolled out for a man whose relationship with Real Madrid was complex, to say the least.

Signed in 2013 from Tottenham Hotspur for £85 million—a world-record transfer fee at the time—Bale produced match-defining moments of jaw-dropping brilliance for Real Madrid.

How many players could cover 59 meters in seven seconds with a ball at their feet and run off the pitch and back on again before scoring the way Bale did against Barcelona in that Copa del Rey final? And what about *that* extraordinary overhead kick against Liverpool in the 2018 Champions League final?

But Real Madrid wanted more. More from Bale as a player and more from him as a personality.

"The thing in Madrid is that they expect you to be this *galáctico*," Bale said, referring to the term that was associated with superstars such as David Beckham, Luís Figo, and Cristiano Ronaldo. "They expect you to do all the same things they've seen other players do. And I probably wasn't the same as most of them. I liked to keep myself to myself, whereas a lot of people like to go out and not necessarily show off, but kind of build their brand in a certain way. I was never really like that. I wanted to play football, then go home and be a normal person."

In many ways, Bale felt like an outsider at Real Madrid—someone who was never going to dance to the tune of the Spanish media or conform to what anyone thought he should be off the pitch, which caused issues.

His love of golf became a four-iron to beat him with at times. A spate of injuries—ankle, calf, adductor—did not help. Teammates talked about him not socializing with them—going out late for dinner was never his thing—and there was also the fact Bale rarely spoke Spanish.

From a football point of view, Bale's favorite language was Welsh. Nothing gave him greater enjoyment than playing for the country he first represented as a 16-year-old at Southampton. "Cut him in half and dragons fall out," Gwyn Morris, Bale's former physical education teacher at Whitchurch High School in Cardiff, once told me.

Bale played 111 times for Wales, becoming their most-capped player, and scored 41 goals, breaking a record previously held by Ian Rush. "But it wasn't just the goals; it was the timing of the goals and the stages," Chris Gunter, Bale's former Wales teammate, says. "Welsh football wouldn't look how it does now without that goal against Andorra."

Gunter is talking about the late free kick that spared Wales embarrassment against Andorra and, ultimately, set them on the path to qualification for Euro 2016, where Bale inspired his country to a memorable run to the semifinals in their first major tournament since 1958. Playing with a mixture of freedom, confidence, and pride, Bale was in his element that summer in France.

"He was winning Champions Leagues but was at his happiest, I think, when he was playing for Wales," Gunter says. "I don't know if that was partly because there was huge pressure at Madrid where all the eyes were on him. But when he came to Wales, he would definitely have enjoyed it more and been more relaxed. And that's his character—he doesn't need to play for the best team. His enjoyment would come from playing football and just doing it with his mates."

If Wales came first, Madrid came second. Or maybe third. "Wales, golf, and Madrid—in that order" was a phrase that Predrag Mijatović, the former Real Madrid player and sporting director, coined for Bale on a Spanish radio show one night. Those words ended up on a flag that the Wales players held up, grinning from ear to ear, after qualifying for Euro 2020. Bale was center stage, laughing as much as anyone. It was a joke, but a joke that went down badly in Madrid.

Not that Bale was going to lose any sleep over it. By late 2019, relations were so bad that it was hard to escape the feeling he was past caring. Zinédine Zidane, back at Real Madrid in his second spell as manager, had made his thoughts clear on Bale at a press conference four months earlier. "If Gareth Bale leaves tomorrow, so much the better for everyone," he said.

That kind of narrative was familiar. "We continue to measure Bale based on his price," Jorge Valdano, the former Real Madrid player, sporting director, and coach, told Onda Cero's *El Transistor* program in 2018. "His price tag has created a fantasy that he is a world superstar. But the last five years don't correspond to what Real Madrid paid for him, even if every season he is applauded for scoring the goal of the year."

For context, Bale scored 106 goals for Real Madrid and registered 67 assists. Three of the goals were in Champions League finals (there was also a penalty in the shootout victory over Atlético Madrid in 2016), not forgetting that remarkable solo effort that won Real Madrid the Copa del Rey in his first season at the club. Bale wasn't delivering Cristiano Ronaldo numbers, but he could hardly be described as a failure.

At the end of the 2017–18 season, following his Champions League final double after he came off the bench against Liverpool, Bale said he needed to consider his future. In hindsight, it would have been in everyone's best interests if he had left that summer. Instead, it was another four years (one of them spent on loan at Tottenham) before an unhappy marriage was over.

A move to Los Angeles FC followed in 2022 and, in typical Bale fashion, so did success. Introduced as a substitute in the MLS Cup, Bale scored a dramatic and emphatic extra-time header to force the game into a penalty shootout that LAFC went on to win.

Yet there would be no happy ending at the World Cup in Qatar later that same month, where Wales were eliminated in the group stage and Bale looked unrecognizable from the player who had almost single-handedly won games for his country for more than a decade.

The sense that his time may be up was confirmed the following January, when he announced his retirement from football at the age of 33. In a statement on their website, Real Madrid listed the 19 trophies Bale won at the Bernabéu and described him as "a true legend of the club and the world game."

Such recognition felt belated, but his true value was always cherished back in Wales.

Player name: Gareth Bale
Born: July 16, 1989
Position: Winger, forward, left-back
Debut: 2006
Main teams: Southampton (2006–07), Tottenham Hotspur (2007–13), Real Madrid (2013–22), Los Angeles FC (2022); Wales (2006–22)
Career highlights: Wales's best player at Euro 2016 as they reached the semifinals in their first appearance at a major tournament since the 1958 World Cup. Won the Champions League five times, playing in four of the finals, and scored one of the best goals in the competition's history in the 2018 showpiece.

93.

Giacinto Facchetti

A towering player, Facchetti's threat did not actually come from the air.

The goalscoring left-back and Inter Milan's worst-kept secret

By James Horncastle

As Inter Milan celebrated winning the treble in 2010, an unprecedented feat for an Italian club, Esteban Cambiasso, the glistening and bald midfielder, emerged from the dressing room at the Bernabéu a changed man.

Cambiasso had replaced the Inter jersey he wore on the night for another one. It was thick, woolen, and vintage. On the back, the white number wasn't his own. It was a 3 rather than a 19.

The shirt belonged to a different era. It belonged to the Inter great Giacinto Facchetti. He had pulled it on in Vienna in 1964. The occasion was Inter's first European Cup final against a Real Madrid team that still featured Ferenc Puskás, Alfredo Di Stéfano, and Paco Gento. Madrid had won the first five editions of the competition. Other Italian teams, Fiorentina and Inter's rivals AC Milan, had tried and failed to take the trophy off them.

It meant Inter needed to be truly great. In Vienna that night, they ascended to mythical status in the pantheon of Serie A's best teams. They became the Grande Inter. It was Facchetti who set up Sandro Mazzola's opening goal in a 3–1 win. He was yet to become captain of the side. That honor continued to belong to Armando Picchi. But Facchetti was, as they say, *di fascia*. The double entendre alluded to his position out-wide as a game-changing left-back and the word for *armband*.

Facchetti was only nominally a defender. In 1965, when Inter sought to retain the European Cup, he completed an epic comeback against Liverpool in the semifinals. Inter had lost the first leg 3–1 at Anfield. At San Siro a week later, Mario Corso executed one of his trademark *foglia morta* free kicks, the trajectory of which imitated an autumn leaf falling to the ground. Joaquín Peiró then picked the pocket of Liverpool goalkeeper Tommy Lawrence, sneaking up behind him on a restart and nicking the ball, controversially, as he attempted a drop kick.

Facchetti finished the job in style. Mazzola found Corso between the lines and he played a first-time through-ball with the outside of his foot to the onrushing Facchetti, who drilled it home. "That was Inter in those days," Mazzola remarked to *Gazzetta dello Sport*. "They often pulled off the impossible."

The goal epitomized Facchetti.

He was born in Treviglio, closer to Bergamo than Lombardy's regional capital Milan, and started out as a forward for his hometown team. When Facchetti tried out for Inter, the recruiter casting his eye over the wannabe footballers was none other than Giuseppe Meazza, the Italian goalscorer after whom San Siro was later named.

Meazza never suppressed Facchetti's instincts as he came through the ranks at Inter, but by the time he broke into the first team, his chances of playing as a No. 9 were minimal. Antonio Valentín Angelillo was coming to the end of his time at the club, but he was too prolific and too fondly thought of by Inter's owner, Angelo Moratti, who used to invite him around for Christmas. When Inter replaced him, they were true to their name and went international, signing Gerry Hitchens and then Jair.

Milan, as a city, was about to innovate a style of play that not only dominated Europe for the next decade but became synonymous with Italian football until the late 1980s. And even then it was hard to shake. Facchetti emerged as the age of *catenaccio* began. It has gone down in history as a time of lockdown defenses and rare forays forward. The mentality was clean sheet first, score second.

Facchetti was the fly in the ointment of that narrative.

Helenio Herrera, the proto-Mourinho coach of the Grande Inter, did more than opportunistically send Facchetti up front when Inter needed to rescue a point from the jaws of defeat. Reserved off the pitch, Facchetti was outgoing on it. He was a *fluidificante*, a marauding full-back, and his combinations with Inter's attacking players made them a slicker, more unpredictable proposition.

His pace and timing meant he was difficult to track. Before becoming a footballer, Facchetti ran the 70-meter sprint in nine seconds flat. Nothing special by today's standards, but fast enough in 1958 for the Italian Athletics Federation to ask the teenage Facchetti to choose spikes over studs.

Taciturn, the only noise Facchetti made was the whoosh as he galloped up the pitch. A towering player, Facchetti's threat did not come from the air. His game wasn't limited to heading in Corso's delectable deliveries. A deadly finisher, he struck the ball true. Facchetti scored 59 times in Serie A, the most by a defender. The 10 he managed in 1965–66 was a single-season record for a defensive role until Daniel Passarella scored 11 for Fiorentina in 1985–86.

Italy's most influential columnist at the time, Gianni Brera, referred to Facchetti as "my private center-forward." It was Inter's worst-kept secret that their backup striker was their full-back. Facchetti's rear-wheel drive granted Inter the traction to win four league titles and it could have easily been six had they not lost a playoff to Bologna in 1964 and messed up on the final day in 1967. A one-club man, he won two of Inter's three European Cups as well as the Intercontinental Cup twice.

There were ups and downs with Italy. Facchetti was in the team when the *Azzurri*, the Italian national side, suffered the embarrassment of losing to North Korea at the 1966 World Cup. Two years later, he found redemption, lifting Italy's first European Championship as captain. More memorable was his participation in the Game of the Century—the epic World Cup semifinal in 1970 against West Germany when the *Azzurri* prevailed 4–3 in extra time only to lose, exhausted, to Pelé's Brazil upon their return to the Azteca four days later.

The expectation when Facchetti hung up his boots in 1978 was that he would stay on as an executive. Instead, a role upstairs was a long time coming. When Angelo Moratti's son Massimo bought the club back into the family's hands in 1995, the first thing he did was make Facchetti an honorary president.

Affectionately, Moratti still called him "Cipe." It was an old nickname, one that had stuck ever since Herrera mistook Facchetti for another player, Cipelletti, in one of his first training sessions.

Facchetti passed away in the autumn of 2006, just as the *Calciopoli* scandal—when executives from clubs and Italian footballing bodies were found to have influenced referees to favor certain teams over the 2004–05 and 2005–06 seasons—handed Inter their first league title in 17 years and inaugurated a period of dominance not seen since the 1960s. When Cambiasso pulled on Facchetti's jersey at the Bernabéu in 2010, the club came full circle.

The Grande Inter had returned.

Player name: Giacinto Facchetti
Born: July 18, 1942
Died: September 4, 2006 (aged 64)
Position: Left-back
Debut: 1961
Main teams: Inter Milan (1961–78); Italy (1963–77)
Career highlights: Instrumental in Inter Milan's *catenaccio* system, which they used when winning the European Cup in 1964 and 1965. Captained Italy to victory at Euro 1968 and to the final of the 1970 World Cup.

92.
Eric Cantona

Cantona had a transformative effect at Old Trafford.

Le Roi who made a good Manchester United team great

By Carl Anka

Eric Cantona is on this list because of what he achieved at Manchester United. This book prides itself on honesty, integrity, and proper fact-checking, so we'll set our stall early here.

If you were to ask a French journalist about Cantona's impact, they would likely paint him as a maverick figure who burned brightly but briefly. Ask a Premier League viewer and they'll likely call Cantona one of the "early greats," but then say his accolades have been surpassed.

Ask a Leeds United fan about Cantona and expect their eyeballs to widen before they liken him to Judas. Ask Henri Michel or Michel

Platini about him and they may offer a weary sigh and smile, like a lecturer reminiscing about a brilliant but lazy student who eventually figured it out years after school.

But ask a Manchester United fan about Cantona and expect a response on par with those who still believe in Santa Claus.

Cantona spent five years at Manchester United, a spell that included a 250-day suspension for his "kung-fu kick" on a Crystal Palace fan following a red card at Selhurst Park, before retiring at age 30. The inadvertent inflationary pressure of Lionel Messi and Cristiano Ronaldo on the value of goals and assists means several attackers in this list of 100 greats—in particular those who peaked in the early 1990s—can now look quaint in comparison. Cantona's 64 league goals in 143 games for United is a more than respectable return.

Still, a disappointing international career and a relatively modest return in European competition means the Frenchman stands on an uneasy pedestal for some. He is one of the greatest "you had to be there" footballers of the past 40 years, which means a small cottage industry has crept up online as people attempt to "dispel the myth of Cantona."

But things snap into place when you rewatch games from his Old Trafford heyday. Cantona's emergence at United is a stunning case of bottled lightning. A footballing maverick landing in the right club, with the right manager, at the perfect time.

The Frenchman's career was in a tailspin before arriving in England. Cantona was fond of having "physical debates" with authority figures with whom he disagreed. In 1991, while playing for Nîmes, he incurred a ban for throwing the ball at the referee, prompting then-French national team coach Platini to recommend Cantona leave for England. He would sign for Leeds United at the start of 1992, initially on loan, and help the Yorkshire club win the league title at Manchester United's expense.

Yet it was the subsequent campaign, the Premier League's inaugural season of 1992–93, when the Frenchman became the footballing cult hero we now know and recognize. The story varies as to who on Leeds's staff called Old Trafford to enquire about the availability of their Republic of Ireland full-back Denis Irwin, but the chairman, Martin Edwards, and manager Sir Alex Ferguson responded by asking for Cantona. One thing led to another and Manchester United signed the Frenchman in November 1992 for a fee of £1.2 million.

The club, and the Premier League at large, would never be the same again.

Cantona's goalscoring prowess and eye as a creative talent bolstered the side's attack and pushed them from good to great. His work rate and approach to training helped United stay there. The Frenchman is commonly cited as a positive influence on the famed "Class of '92"—Cantona set a standard to which the future of the club would strive.

"If you read the papers or listen to the television commentators, we seem to be awash with 'world-class' footballers," wrote Ferguson in his 2015 book, *Leading: Learning from Life and My Years at Manchester United*. "I don't mean to demean or criticise any of the great or very good footballers who played for me during my 26-year career at United, but there were only four who were world-class: Cantona, [Ryan] Giggs, Ronaldo, and [Paul] Scholes."

Would Giggs and Scholes have reached their heights without the influence of Cantona? Would Ronaldo have made the leap from good to great without the lessons passed on by Giggs and Scholes? One Manchester United great often helps another and the club's Premier League era of dominance begins with Cantona.

Non-United fans may roll their eyes at the mythologizing, but his five years at United yielded a tremendous playing return: four Premier League titles and two FA Cup victories. The second half of the 1995–96 season represented his apex. After returning from his eight-month suspension in October, he scored key goals against Arsenal, Tottenham Hotspur, and pacesetters Newcastle United to take his team to the summit of English football once again.

Standing 6'2" with a boxer's build and a tremendous first touch, he was a sturdy combatant yet a silky-smooth creator. His lack of outright pace meant he found it difficult against more organized defenses in European competition. Still, Cantona is an excellent early prototype for modern-day Premier League attackers who can drop deep, create space, and link up with teammates before crashing the penalty area and scoring for themselves.

He peaked at one of the biggest football clubs in the world just at the precise moment their fandom was about to go global, but Cantona's emergence also benefited the development of the Premier League. At a time when broadcasters, sponsors, and other interested parties needed recognizable protagonists to make their new competition stand out, here was an attacking footballer who quoted poetry and thrived between the lines while most teams continued with a rigid 4-4-2.

His chip against Sunderland in December 1996 burns bright to this day. Recall that snaking dribble past multiple defenders before a powerful drive into space. Then, rather than shooting at goal with gusto, he delicately lifts the ball over Lionel Perez. For a brief spell, Cantona was among the Premier League's leading arguments that football could be art. It is little surprise that he has spent his post-playing career making music, films, and documentaries that cover folk heroes. To many people, he is one.

It also helped that Cantona's fondness for poetry and verse stood him out to an English media class used to talking to footballers of a different ilk. The Frenchman was one of several talented footballers in his homeland with a passing knowledge of Antonin Artaud. In Manchester, he stood out: like a well-traveled friend you make in your teenage years who introduces you to foreign films and music.

There's a reason United fans of a certain age still turn up the collars on their shirt when having a kickabout. Cantona's artistry endures, even when memories of his playing record fade.

Player name: Eric Cantona

Born: May 24, 1966

Position: Forward

Debut: 1983

Main teams: Auxerre (1983–88), Marseille (1988–91), Bordeaux (loan, 1989), Montpellier (loan, 1989–90), Nîmes (1991–92), Leeds United (1992), Manchester United (1992–97); France (1987–95)

Career highlights: Cantona was one of the key players in Manchester United's enormous success in the 1990s, winning the Premier League four times and the FA Cup twice.

91.

Patrick Vieira

Vieira was a colossus who stamped his authority across midfield.

The man-mountain upon whom the Invincibles were built

By Jordan Campbell

The scene was the London Palladium in late 2021 and, up on the stage, Arsène Wenger and David Dein were fielding questions from an Arsenal-centric audience. The latest query flung up from the floor was a request for the former manager and the club's ex–vice chairman to pinpoint which signing, pound for pound, had furthest exceeded expectations.

There was technically a pool of 450 potential answers, but both men snapped back with the same single name. Fittingly, it was a midfielder they considered to be two players in one: Patrick Vieira.

"When I arrived, I was not known and everyone said: 'Who is this guy?'" said Wenger, reflecting briefly on his arrival from Japanese football in 1996. "So when Patrick came at the same time—he was the first player I signed—maybe it convinced people that, 'Okay, he doesn't know what he is doing, but at least he brings good players.'"

Vieira arrived as a 20-year-old who had played five times the previous season for AC Milan, which is why Arsenal were able to acquire him for just £3.5 million. Nine years, 405 appearances, and seven major honors later, the Frenchman left as the symbol of Wenger's golden era at Arsenal; a player who straddled two distinct chapters either side of the millennium.

He integrated seamlessly into a team that had been successful, winning a domestic cup double in 1993 and the European Cup Winners' Cup in 1994, but one that was perceived to lack beauty. Wenger inherited a constrictive team built on a regimented defensive structure, cemented by George Graham in the previous decade. "Boring, boring Arsenal" was how they were christened but, after a stellar debut from the bench against Sheffield Wednesday, Vieira's dynamism started to tip the scales.

In the transition from Old Testament to New, as the Premier League's sophisticated style and foreign influence became dominant, Vieira's role evolved in line with Wenger's growing obsession with technical superiority. Initially, it had been his formidable partnership with compatriot Emmanuel Petit that laid the foundations to win the 1997–98 title. He retained his destructive instincts throughout his time at the club but later, when flanked by Brazilian holding midfielder Gilberto Silva, marauding forward became frequent.

It was illustrative of a team that had been unshackled, one Vieira led to history by going the full league season unbeaten in 2003–04. That version of Wenger's Arsenal played with futuristic imagination and fluidity; polished with the artistry of Thierry Henry, Dennis Bergkamp, and Robert Pires, but stitched together by Vieira's combativeness and incision.

Henry, with his irresistible dribbling and finishing, was the natural poster boy of the Invincibles team, but Vieira is the name opponents cite most often as the player who left an indelible impression.

Lining up in the cramped tunnel at Highbury, barely wide enough to fit shoulder to shoulder, the World Cup winner had the ability to emasculate.

"I was captain at Leeds and I'm walking to the front of the line where Vieira is ready to go and he's absolutely massive," Dominic Matteo, once of Liverpool and Leeds United, told *The Athletic*. "It can get into your head before you've kicked a ball. I can still see Vieira leaving a bit on Eirik Bakke in the tunnel before we lost 5–0 at Highbury. I didn't play in the first game at Elland Road that season, but something must have gone on between them. Vieira hadn't forgotten.

"He was waiting for Bakke and, as soon as he saw him, he barged straight through him, a bit like: 'I'm right here, don't think I've let it go.'"

It did not help that they could see *and* smell his war paint. His red jersey would be a deep maroon, soaked by the Vicks VapoRub he would smother over his chest before kickoff. It became iconic, a facade of exertion worn by a player whose on-pitch persona was coolness personified—until something triggered the red mist.

Vieira's mettle reinforced a pretty Arsenal team with the minerals to compete. He believes they would have won more if they had been nastier, but Cesc Fàbregas, speaking to *The Rest Is Football* podcast, described how Vieira, like clockwork, would land a heavy challenge on a teammate in the final training session before a big game.

"It was to create a moment of tension for everyone to feel that, in 24 hours, we had a war," said Fàbregas. "The presence that he had inside the pitch is something I have not seen from many players."

Only after spending 90 minutes in Vieira's orbit could you appreciate the true force and ubiquity of his presence.

"Vieira gave as good as he got," said former Leeds and Newcastle United midfielder Lee Bowyer. "The thought back then was that you could get in the face of some of the foreign players as they wouldn't like it, but he was physical and enjoyed that side of the game, so you knew you were in for a battle.

"With Vieira, whenever you felt like you had got away from him, he'd slide and stretch that long leg out and get a toe on the ball. You'd think: 'How have you done that? I thought I was gone!' When he was in possession, he'd use his wingspan to hold you off and that's when you felt how strong he was."

Vieira went on to spend a year at Juventus, three and a half at Inter Milan, and 18 months at Manchester City before he retired in 2011, but it was the final five years of his Arsenal spell, particularly after assuming the captaincy in 2002, that captured his peak.

Teams would regularly put three players against Arsenal's two in the center of the pitch, but Vieira was an equalizer.

He bullied opponents physically and won back possession. He had retractable limbs that activated anytime someone tried to run past him. He broke up play effortlessly, stepping in to intercept as if he had been sent a signal in advance. His ability to glide across the ground and make late runs into the box, which invariably ended with him dinking the ball over the goalkeeper, made him one part brawn, one part finesse. It was that powerful running that saw him score the opening goal at White Hart Lane on the day Arsenal won the league at the home of their rivals Tottenham in 2004.

The sheer stature of Vieira at 6'4" meant the primary focus was on his destructive capacity, but therein lay his deceptive brilliance. Vieira's footwork in tight areas was that of a much smaller man. Combined with his strapping physique, it formed a force field around him and the ball. He would lure his opponents in and had so many different, instinctive ways of escaping pressure.

His other familiar move was *La Croqueta*, made famous by Michael Laudrup, a double-tap skill that saw the ball shifted from one foot onto the other just as a tackle arrived. If the ball was played to the wrong side, he would plant his body, spin, and drag it all in one motion to send the onrushing opponent chasing thin air. When the ball broke loose, his huge stride meant he was invariably first on the scene. Even with one knee on the ground, he could circle like a protractor and escape through an impossible gap.

"I loved playing against Vieira but, man, what a player," said Alex

Rae, who confronted the Frenchman while playing for Sunderland and Wolves.

"He gave you the feeling that you had half a chance because he was so graceful and didn't panic on the ball. The amount of times it would pitch up about four foot and you'd fancy yourself to get a nibble only for him to flick it over your head was incredible. You thought you had him, but you soon realized you never did."

Vieira made opponents feel as if gravity was his servant. He was the ultimate box-to-box midfielder, but his skill set was so broad that, in today's game of specialist roles, to confine him would feel like a dilution of his talent.

It is that variety that has made distilling Vieira's majesty a challenge for current broadcasters. In attempting to convey the competitive spirit of Vieira in bite-size form, younger audiences are continually fed a black-and-white vignette of the Frenchman feuding with his Manchester United counterpart Roy Keane.

Their series of contests as captains of the two dominant teams in England between 1996 and 2005 remains the most ferocious individual rivalry the Premier League has produced. It was vicious, unforgiving, and deeply personal, with both players viewing every duel as a microcosm of a wider war.

There were times they did not even make it out of the tunnel before the sparring began, most notably in 2005 when Vieira made a beeline for Gary Neville as he headed into the dressing room at the end of the warm-up to warn that he was coming after him if he got heavy-handed with his teammates again. Keane took exception to it. "I'll see you out there."

In defining the rivals by wrapping their identities up in each other, however, it dumbs both down. Certainly, it paints a broad-brush version of Vieira and reduces him to his most brutish form.

This is a player who won three Premier League titles, four FA Cups, was named in the PFA team of the year six times, and won player of the year in 2000–2001 over his nine years at Arsenal.

Yes, his temper overspilled often in his early years in England—his eight Premier League red cards is the joint-most alongside Richard

Dunne and Duncan Ferguson—but to project him through this single prism whitewashes the eclectic nature of his game. There is a reason Keane had such begrudging respect for the Frenchman.

Former Manchester United goalkeeper Peter Schmeichel even went as far as to say Arsenal were 25 percent weaker when Vieira was not in the team. Those who competed against him in his pomp would put that number even higher.

Player name: Patrick Vieira
Born: June 23, 1976
Position: Midfielder
Debut: 1993
Main teams: AS Cannes (1993–95), AC Milan (1995–96), Arsenal (1996–2005), Juventus (2005–06), Inter Milan (2006–10), Manchester City (2010–11); France (1997–2009)
Career highlights: Won the World Cup on home soil in 1998 and Euro 2000 with France. Captained Arsenal to their "Invincible" title-winning season in 2003–04, one of eight league titles amassed over his career.

90.

Tostão

Eduardo Gonçalves de Andrade, better known as Tostão and seen here with Pelé, is one of the greatest footballers Brazil has ever produced.

A ballet dancer in the middle of a riot

By Jack Lang

These doubtful, uncertain times in my professional life allowed me to look at things from a much more human standpoint. We must go searching for good things, human things, and not be like the twentieth-century man, stuck in the age of ambition, hate, machinery, and lovelessness."

It reads like the quote from a continental philosopher; a nice little chunk of Herbert Marcuse, perhaps. Those familiar with the writing of Dr. Eduardo Gonçalves de Andrade, however, will not be surprised in the slightest that the words flowed from his mind.

Gonçalves de Andrade, better known as Tostão, is one of the greatest footballers Brazil has ever produced. He has also spent the past 30 years constructing a reputation as one of the country's best newspaper columnists, mixing perceptive analysis of his favorite sport with dollops of culture, wit, and nostalgia. Plus, on occasion, righteous asides about the ills of modern society.

It would be easy to look at those contrasting figures—the sprightly playmaker and the aging wordsmith—and fail to spot a through-line. Yet the two are one and the same. The quote above does not come from one of Tostão's recent columns, but from April 1970.

He was 23 at the time. He was always a man apart.

A *tostão* was a little coin, the smallest denomination of the currency used in colonial and imperial Brazil. It was no longer in circulation by the time Tostão was born, in January 1947, but the name lived on in a popular idiom. Something with no perceived value was said to be "not worth even a *tostão*."

There was no value judgment attached to the nickname—Tostão just happened to be the tiniest kid in his neighborhood—but it came to seem slightly prophetic.

Tostão was, by any reasonable metric, a sensational footballer. He was lithe, skillful, and subtle, a ballet dancer in the middle of a riot. He created countless goals and scored plenty, too, despite not being an out-and-out forward. It is testament to his ability as a finisher that he remains the top scorer in the history of Cruzeiro.

Yet there was always an element of self-doubt. When a newspaper labelled Tostão "The New King"—a clear reference to Pelé—after Cruzeiro dismantled Santos 9–4 over two legs in the final of the 1966 Brazilian championship, he was overcome by embarrassment. "I felt like a charlatan," he later said.

Even hindsight didn't soften his self-assessment. "I practically only used my left foot, I couldn't head the ball—I did so with my eyes shut—I was slow over medium and long distances," he wrote in 1997. "My long-range shooting was poor, while my technical and physical limitations (and lack of pace) meant I couldn't keep up with my speed of thought. My mind told my body what it wanted it to do, but my body often didn't obey."

Anyone who watched Tostão in his pomp will view this as a gross exaggeration. Either way, he committed to overcoming his perceived shortcomings by focusing on his strengths: his movement, his anticipation, his uncanny ability to knit the play together in crowded areas.

"Jean-Claude Killy, the famous French skier, used to train mentally with a stopwatch and would say that he managed almost the same time when it came to the actual race," he wrote. "I trained the moves mentally, constantly picturing game situations in my mind's eye."

Although those efforts bore fruit for Cruzeiro, it took time for Tostão to establish himself for the Brazil national team. He first broke into the squad as a teenager—he made one appearance at the 1966 World Cup, scoring in the 3–1 defeat by Hungary—but was viewed as Pelé's deputy for the best part of three years thereafter, only making the occasional start.

It was under iconoclastic coach João Saldanha, very much a kindred spirit, that Tostão really came to the fore, scoring 10 goals in 19 days as Brazil secured their place at the 1970 World Cup. His understanding with Pelé, which verged on the telepathic, augured well for the tournament in Mexico.

Tostão, though, would have to do things the hard way. First came a nasty eye injury, sustained when an opposition defender clobbered the ball into his face at close range. The blow detached Tostão's retina and the damage was so severe that he had to travel to Houston to undergo surgery.

His race to be fit for the World Cup gripped Brazil. National newspapers squeezed fresh quotes out of his eye surgeon at every opportunity, publishing them next to the latest photos of Tostão keeping fit in the gym. On April 12, 1970, the front page of the *Jornal do Brasil* carried a headline about the launch of Apollo 13—and a picture of Tostão having his eye examined.

He eventually made it, but by the time he joined the pretournament training camp, Saldanha was gone, having rubbed Brazil's military regime up the wrong way one time too many.

The new coach, Mário Zagallo, was not initially sold on Tostão. With so much creativity already in the side, he favored a classic No. 9, someone who could compete with defenders physically and push them deeper. "I wasn't the center-forward he wanted," Tostão wrote.

Support came from senior teammates. Gérson and Pelé stated his case to Zagallo, who agreed to a compromise. He could play if he occupied the center-backs and did not constantly drop back into his more natural withdrawn role. Tostão agreed.

His World Cup was a masterpiece of self-sacrifice. Tostão only scored in one match. In others, including the final against Italy, he committed to the game plan so totally that moments of individual brilliance were few and far between. "Younger people must watch the final and think, 'That Tostão wasn't up to much,'" he said in an interview in 2017.

It's not that there were no eye-catching moments. There was the wriggly dribble that led to Jairzinho's winner against England and a crafty goal against Peru. But Tostão's main responsibilities were to his teammates. He was there to bounce short passes off, to create gaps with selfless runs, to manipulate the opposition defense. "I played for the collective," he said recently. "I was a good support actor."

The best supporting evidence for that claim is the place that the 1970 side holds in the hearts of football fans. Brazil did not just win the World Cup, they enchanted people with their attacking play. That Pelé, Jairzinho, and Roberto Rivellino scored 14 goals between them is testament to the contribution of the team's egoless No. 9. Even the final, emblematic goal of Brazil's campaign bore Tostão's fingerprints. It was he who chased back to win the ball deep inside his own half, kick-starting a flowing move that culminated in Carlos Alberto's finish.

"He facilitated the work of others," Gérson said. "His intelligence far exceeded that of a normal player. That was his genius."

When Tostão was forced to retire three years later due to lingering complications with his eye, it felt like that genius—or at least a decent portion of it—was going to go to waste. Instead, it was simply diverted. Tostão walked away from football, went to medical school, and worked as a doctor for over a decade.

Then, when he could no longer resist the siren song of his first love, the glory and the agony, the beauty and the beastliness, he picked up his pen.

Player name: Eduardo Gonçalves de Andrade (Tostão)
Born: January 25, 1947
Position: Forward, attacking midfielder
Debut: 1962
Main teams: América Mineiro (1962–63), Cruzeiro (1963–72), Vasco da Gama (1972–73); Brazil (1966–72)
Career highlights: Won the World Cup in 1970 as part of a brilliant Brazil team.

89.
Marcel Desailly

Desailly sees red in the World Cup final of 1998.

A red card, antidoping duties, and a World Cup triumph

By Liam Twomey

As he strode downcast toward the Stade de France tunnel, still processing the reality of being sent off in the 68th minute of the biggest match of his life, Marcel Desailly had no idea his World Cup final was about to take another unwelcome turn.

Out of sight of the pitch, he was quickly intercepted by a FIFA official and corralled into a room with no television screens. There have been better circumstances for a footballer to find out they have been selected for antidoping control testing.

A pair of Zinédine Zidane headers had given France a 2–0 advantage over a lackluster Brazil led by a mysteriously listless Ronaldo, but there was no telling what might happen in the time that remained. Desailly had charged upfield from a defensive corner kick and lunged rashly into Cafu, hoping to achieve a lucky rebound and a chance to score a World Cup final goal. Instead, he received a second yellow card and the immediate knowledge that if catastrophe struck, he would be the scapegoat.

Now this. Not helping was torment enough. Not watching was unbearable.

"That's when I took a big risk," Desailly recalled in a 2018 column for *The Guardian*. "I made a huge scene! Telling them that I couldn't possibly stay there! I barged my way out of the room in spite of the FIFA guy doing his best to explain that I wasn't allowed to leave until I had 'fulfilled my duties,' so to speak. By then, though, I was past caring! It didn't matter what might happen to me. I had to know what was happening in the game."

Desailly found a screen near the tunnel where he watched 10-man France comfortably hold Brazil at bay until Emmanuel Petit surged forward to make it 3–0 in the 93rd minute. He ran back onto the pitch at the final whistle to partake in the celebrations and lifted the World Cup trophy. Then he returned to the room and "fulfilled his duties."

Any other ending would have felt like a cruel disservice to Desailly, one of the most dominant and decorated footballers of his generation. On the eve of the tournament, he had told the French press that this would be his finest hour. France captain Didier Deschamps, his closest friend in football since their time as teenagers at Nantes, added that Desailly was at the peak of his powers—a serious claim for anyone lucky enough to watch him play in the 1990s.

There was a time in the middle of the decade when no Champions League final could happen without him. His first of three consecutive appearances in May 1993, shutting down a faded Marco van Basten alongside match-winning goalscorer Basile Boli as an upstart Marseille side upset the great AC Milan in Munich, created a footballing earthquake. The Italian giants, at the urging of their CEO Ariedo Braida, signed him six months later.

No club in Europe had less need for a top defender than Milan, whose regular starting back four of Mauro Tassotti, Alessandro Costacurta, Franco Baresi, and Paolo Maldini belonged in the Pantheon. So, instead, Desailly was shifted into central midfield alongside Demetrio Albertini, tasked with breaking up opposition moves and initiating attacks.

"Marcel was a special partner," Maldini said of Desailly to *beIN Sports* in 2021. "I remember the first day [he arrived] without a precise role, the coach [Fabio Capello] said: 'What do we do with him? Full-back, central?' We told him to play him in front of the defence and there he showed a sort of 'driving,' an incredible ability to cover [spaces] and a simplicity we needed at the time."

Desailly quickly made himself indispensable to Capello, leaving fellow international luminaries Zvonimir Boban, Dejan Savićević, Jean-Pierre Papin, and Brian Laudrup to vie for the two remaining foreigner slots on a matchday. Milan marched back to the Champions League final to face Johan Cruyff's vaunted Barcelona "Dream Team."

In the buildup, Cruyff cited Milan signing Desailly for the same fee Barcelona had paid for Romário as "telling" evidence of the superiority of the Catalan giants' philosophy. Desailly emphatically rebuked the Dutch great's Olympian hubris in Athens, dominating Pep Guardiola with elegant physicality in midfield and even surging forward to curl a shot above and around Andoni Zubizarreta for the fourth Milan goal in an immortal 4–0 victory.

Yet despite producing one of the most decisive big-game midfield performances of the modern era, Desailly had no illusions about the true nature of his game. "Over the years, I knew I could not last in that position because I was a heavyweight in the midfield," he said later. At his core, he was a dominating central defender, equipped to win any battle in the air or on the ground.

This was the version of Desailly that helped propel France to glory at the World Cup on home turf in 1998 and at the European Championship in the Netherlands and Belgium two years later. It was also the version he insisted on reviving at club level when the time came to leave Milan—a club in decline since giving Desailly his only taste of Champions League final defeat, against Ajax, in 1995—for Chelsea's ambitious international project under Ken Bates in 1998.

Six years at Stamford Bridge did not sate Desailly's desire for winning, but he left an indelible mark. His veteran mentorship primed talented young defenders John Terry and William Gallas for future success. "He was like a father for both of us," Terry told Chelsea's official website in 2016. "He used to tell us off and tell us what to do. He was the best and learning from him made us better players."

His equalizing header against Liverpool in May 2003 also helped Chelsea secure Champions League qualification on the final day of the Premier League season, paving the way for Roman Abramovich's momentous takeover and a golden era of trophies.

Those moments belonged to others, but Desailly has plenty of his own—chief among them that extraordinary, exasperating, exultant World Cup final.

Player name: Marcel Desailly
Born: September 7, 1968
Position: Center-back, defensive midfielder
Debut: 1986
Main teams: Nantes (1986–92), Marseille (1992–93), AC Milan (1993–98), Chelsea (1998–2004), Al Gharafa (2004–05), Qatar SC (2005); France (1993–2004)
Career highlights: Won the World Cup on home soil in 1998 and the European Championship in 2000. He claimed the Champions League in 1992–93 with Marseille and in 1993–94 with AC Milan, scoring in the final in the latter. Won Serie A twice.

88.

Gigi Riva

Riva's record of 35 goals for Italy has never been seriously challenged since he won the last of his 42 caps.

The adopted son of Sardinia

By Oliver Kay

On a cold January day, they came in their thousands. Not just thousands, but tens of thousands. Not just from across the city of Cagliari, but from all over the island. Not just football fans, but men and women of all ages, boys and girls, all eager to pay their respects to the outsider who had made Sardinia his home.

Thousands queued up at the Sardegna Arena, where Gigi Riva was lying in state. Thousands more lined the mile-and-a-half route from there to the Basilica of Our Lady of Bonaria. The crowd waiting outside the basilica was estimated at around 30,000, spilling over into Piazza dei Centomila, applauding as the cortège arrived and then standing in somber silence, many of them holding *rossoblu* scarves aloft, as they watched the live transmission of the funeral service taking place inside.

They were still there almost two hours later when Riva's coffin was carried out of the basilica—World Cup winners Gianluigi Buffon and Fabio Cannavaro among the pallbearers—to the heartfelt strains of "Quando Gigi Riva Tornerà" ("When Gigi Riva Will Return"), described by folk singer Piero Marras as a love song to "a legend of world football, a man and a champion who gave the dream to Sardinia and the Sardinians."

The legends of world football are those who leave an indelible impression not just on the game, but on the communities they represent.

In that respect, there are few whose legacy at a single club surpasses that of Riva at Cagliari. He arrived in 1963 as an 18-year-old, unsure of his place in the world. He stayed there for the rest of his career, helping Cagliari win promotion to Serie A for the first time in their history and then—by now a prolific, inspirational, talismanic center-forward—leading them to the league title in 1970, the first time a club south of Rome, let alone from beyond the mainland, had been champions of Italy. When he died there in January 2024, aged 79, Sardinia was plunged into mourning.

It might not match the quasi-religious fervor the people of football-mad Naples retain for Diego Maradona, who inspired their first Serie A title success in 1987, but it is not far off.

As John Foot wrote in *Calcio: A History of Italian Football*, Riva transformed Cagliari from "a provincial team who had won nothing" to one that "terrorized all those around them . . . reversing a centuries-old tradition of subjugation to occupying forces. It was a rare moment of triumph, a symbolic retribution for hundreds of years as the pawn of continental expansionism."

Or, as Gianfranco Zola, the wonderfully gifted Italian (and Sardinian) forward of the 1990s, put it in an interview with *Gazzetta dello*

Sport after Riva's death: "For me, he was God, the center of the universe, the man who represented a people—our people. He was not born in Sardinia, but he chose my land and he cultivated it."

The relationship went both ways. Sardinia proved to be a haven for Riva, whose upbringing in Leggiuno, on the banks of Lake Maggiore in the northern Italian province of Lombardy, was in direct contrast to the beauty of the surroundings. After his father was killed in an accident while working at a foundry, the young Riva spent his formative years in an institution that housed the most deprived children in the region.

Years later, when asked how he dealt with the physical treatment from opposition center-backs (in an era when "physical treatment" really meant something—especially in Italy), he would say that knocks from defenders were "like caresses compared to the beatings of mourning, loneliness, and deprivation."

Riva lived with depression for decades and did not, in terms of personality, appear an obvious candidate to carry the hopes of a region on his shoulders. He had the looks and aura of a movie star but didn't always welcome the attention his status brought. "I am not an actor, writer, salesman, singer, or anything," he said. "I live only for football."

But the adulation he felt in Sardinia—and at a far more basic level, the warmth and acceptance of the locals who opened their doors to him—was an inspiration from the moment he arrived as a teenager, having attracted Cagliari's attention while playing for Legnano in the third tier.

He initially played on the left wing for Cagliari, but he evolved into a center-forward of the highest quality: intelligent, athletic, instinctive, brave, and blessed not just with excellent close control, but with prodigious shooting power in his left foot. His explosive shooting led the eminent Italian sportswriter Gianni Brera (who loved an extravagant moniker) to give him the nickname *Rombo di Tuono* ("Rumble of Thunder" or "Thunderclap"). It stuck.

In an era when the ultradefensive philosophy of *catenaccio* saw scoring rates plummet in Serie A, Riva was the league's outstanding goalscorer by far, winning the *Capocannoniere* award in 1966–67, 1968–69, and 1969–70.

He opened the scoring as Italy beat Yugoslavia to win the European Championship in 1968 and scored three times in the knockout stage of the 1970 World Cup (twice in the quarterfinal defeat of hosts Mexico and once in the epic semifinal victory over West Germany, cutting back onto that fearsome left foot and lashing a low shot past Sepp Maier) before he and his teammates were overwhelmed by Brazil in the final in the heat of Mexico City.

Take a look at the list of record international goalscorers by team and you will see it is dominated by players from the past two decades, reflecting the proliferation of games against low-quality opposition in Europe in particular. But Riva's record of 35 goals for Italy has never been seriously challenged in more than half a century since he won the last of his 42 caps. It is a curiosity that a nation with such a rich football heritage has produced so few top-class goalscorers, but Riva's claims to greatness are beyond dispute.

Had he played for a more glamorous club, his name might be more widely known, but the beauty of Riva's story and legacy lies in the loyalty he showed to Cagliari—and Sardinia—by turning down lucrative offers to join Juventus and Inter Milan in particular.

That song, "Quando Gigi Riva Tornerà," is a lament not just for a glorious period in Cagliari's history, but for who Riva was and what he stood for: excellence, passion, glory, and love.

Player name: Luigi Riva

Born: November 7, 1944

Died: January 22, 2024 (aged 79)

Position: Striker

Debut: 1962

Main teams: Legnano (1962–63), Cagliari (1963–76); Italy (1965–74)

Career highlights: Won Euro 1968, scoring in the final. Scored three times as Italy finished as runners-up at the 1970 World Cup. Italy's all-time top goalscorer. Won Serie A in 1969–70 with Cagliari.

87.

Oleg Blokhin

Blokhin was a man born at the wrong time. He would have been a world superstar today.

The striker who sprinted to prominence from behind the Iron Curtain

By Nick Miller

The list of Ballon d'Or winners in the early and mid-1970s throws up something of a curveball in its midst.

Johan Cruyff and Franz Beckenbauer dominate. Cruyff won in 1971, 1973, and 1974. Beckenbauer was the top dog in 1972 and 1976. These were two gold-plated greats of the game, transformational figures for club and country who were both instrumental in teams winning the European Cup three times in a row and who had captained the opposing sides in the 1974 World Cup final.

Cruyff and Beckenbauer were in the top three in 1975, too. But neither won. The man elected as the best player in Europe (the award was not global then) that year is not a name that echoes down the generations quite as much, to the point that the most common response from people after telling them I was writing this section of the book was "Who?"

Indeed, who is Oleg Blokhin?

Blokhin was a man born at the wrong time. He would have been a world superstar today. One reason he is relatively undercelebrated, in the West at least, is that his talent was largely hidden behind the Iron Curtain. He spent almost all of his career at Dynamo Kyiv, from 1969 to 1988, with whom he won eight Soviet titles and was the league's all-time top scorer and appearance maker. He played at two World Cups and stood out for Dynamo as they became the first Soviet club to win a UEFA trophy, the 1975 European Cup Winners' Cup.

Other than that, it was incredibly difficult to watch him.

Back then, Soviet players weren't allowed to move abroad until they were 29 and many never bothered even then. There was an innate suspicion of Soviet athletes from the West, partly informed by Cold War politics, partly by the number of athletes from the Communist Bloc whose performances at Olympic Games were fueled by performance-enhancing drugs, or at least were heavily suspected of doing so. The celebrated London *Times* football correspondent Geoffrey Green once rather sniffily referred to Blokhin as "a poor man's Tom Finney."

But he was undoubtedly brilliant and ahead of his time, a visceral player whom you could comfortably drop into the modern game without any problems, blessed as he was with the combination of physicality and skill that you can't really get anywhere without now.

It was possibly for this reason that he managed to endure so long playing under Valeriy Lobanovskyi, the Dynamo Kyiv coach who was notorious for running his players into the ground. Many only lasted a few years and emerged from his tutelage battered and exhausted.

Blokhin endured the better part of two decades under Lobanovskyi, for both Dynamo and the Soviet Union.

Because Blokhin was fast. Not fast for a footballer, or fast for the 1970s, just fast.

His best time for the 100 meters was 10.80 seconds, apparently. To offer some context, the Soviet 100 meter record was 10.07 seconds. Speed was in his genes. His mother, Kateryna Adamenko, was a hurdler and pentathlete who ran for the Soviet Union at the 1952 Helsinki Olympics. His father, Volodymyr Blokhin, was a police officer but also an amateur sprinter.

If you watch highlights of most games from the 1970s, you'll see a lot of footballers. But if you watch highlights of Blokhin, you'll see an athlete, someone you'd probably guess was a 400-meter runner rather than a footballer.

Blokhin would catch, overtake, and outpace opponents like those videos you see from news helicopters of police chases, weaving in and out of sluggish traffic at a seemingly uncontrollable speed. The difference was that he was very much in control.

He was a player that would stop you in your tracks. *Who is that?* Which explains the 1975 Ballon d'Or victory. Aside from the Messi-Ronaldo duopoly era, domestic brilliance tended not to be enough to earn individual awards. You usually needed to be the standout player in either a European trophy or an international tournament victory. Blokhin came to the attention of the France Football jury of football correspondents, the solemn judges who decided which players were worthy of the Ballon d'Or, through the former when Dynamo became the first team from the Soviet Union to win a European trophy.

Under Lobanovskyi, Dynamo cut swaths through the competition. Blokhin was their standout player throughout, particularly in the final against Hungarian side Ferencváros, despite the forward playing the game while hampered by injury.

But perhaps equally as influential was a single goal, scored again on the European stage, this time in the UEFA Super Cup against Bayern Munich, who were there after winning the second of their three European Cups in a row. It started deep in the Dynamo half as Bayern right-back Rainer Zobel tried to take a quick free kick, which was intercepted and found Blokhin about 35 yards from his own goal.

He looked up and all he saw were the red shirts of Bayern ahead of him. "I look around. All of our guys are far away," he told Ukrainian newspaper *Molod Ukraini* afterward. "This is bad. The four Bavarians see this, they are calm, confident that I will not go forward."

But forward he went at warp speed. He outstripped Bayern center-back Hans-Georg Schwarzenbeck like a cheetah outrunning a sloth. He reached the left side of the Bayern area, stopped, looked up, and realized that his teammates were still nowhere to be seen. He'd have to do this on his own. So he did.

Schwarzenbeck eventually caught up but rapidly regretted doing so. Blokhin sent him one way then the other, causing the German to stumble backward like a man trying to escape from a runaway boulder. He flicked the ball past another defender and dropped his shoulder away from one more, meaning he only had goalkeeper Sepp Maier to beat.

"Maier, as it seemed to me, was so confident in his defenders that he did not have time to prepare," Blokhin said. He slammed the ball into the corner. Even the usually impassive Lobanovskyi was overjoyed.

If ever a goal encapsulated a player, it was this. Skill, grace, speed, power, and ruthlessness. It caught the eye of the Ballon d'Or voters because, well, how could it not? But also because this was, according to France Football, "a time when people fear for football the hardening of defences and the 'de-poeticization' of the game." When people were worrying about the game becoming drab, in swept this Ukrainian hurricane, blowing back the hair of the football cognoscenti.

Not only did he win the vote, but he won it by an extraordinary margin. He gained 122 points, the most anyone had ever been awarded at that stage and a figure that wouldn't be eclipsed until Michel Platini amassed 128 in 1984.

Maybe we would remember him more if he had played for Bayern, or Liverpool, or Barcelona, but the name Oleg Blokhin belongs alongside Cruyff and Beckenbauer. If you didn't know it before, hopefully you do now.

Player name: Oleg Blokhin
Born: November 5, 1952
Position: Forward
Debut: 1969
Main teams: Dynamo Kyiv (1969–88), Vorwärts Steyr (1988–89), Aris Limassol (1989–90); Soviet Union (1972–88)
Career highlights: Won the European Cup Winners' Cup in 1974–75 and 1985–86, scoring in both finals. Won the Soviet Top League eight times and the Soviet Cup five times. Claimed the Ballon d'Or in 1975.

86.

Paolo Rossi

The Italian's hat trick in 1982 confirmed a second-round exit for surely the greatest side never to lift the World Cup.

The man who made Brazil cry

By Richard Sutcliffe

Paolo Rossi's crowning moment changed the destiny of two great footballing nations.

The striker's hat trick in what many regard as the greatest World Cup game of all time set Italy on their way to glory in 1982. It also left an indelible mark on Brazilian football.

That 3–2 defeat for Brazil confirmed a second-round exit for one of the greatest sides never to lift either the famous 18-carat gold trophy or its Jules Rimet predecessor and prompted a marked shift away from the free-flowing, flamboyant football that had seen the likes of Zico and Sócrates light up the initial stages of the tournament in Spain.

Instead, a more defensive, European style was adopted. Brazil, for all the success since then, including two World Cups and six Copa Américas, have never again been quite as joyful or carefree.

That glorious summer proved a cathartic moment both for the Italian striker with matinée-idol looks and a nation who had not lifted the World Cup since 1938. For Rossi, it was the high point of a colorful career littered with peaks and troughs.

He won two Serie A titles with Juventus as well as a European Cup, the latter success coming in 1985 at Heysel on an occasion utterly overshadowed after 39 fans died when a wall collapsed as they tried to escape clashes between Liverpool and Juventus supporters.

Rossi also won Serie A's Golden Boot after netting 24 times for newly promoted Vicenza in the 1977–78 season—a tally made all the more remarkable by the smothering defensive mindset of the competition during that era.

The flip side to those honors was the three-year ban, later reduced on appeal, imposed for his part in the Totonero match-fixing scandal that rocked Italian football when first revealed in 1980.

Rossi always denied the allegations, insisting he'd made his excuses and left after a couple of minutes' conversation with those planning a sting. The fallout would eventually see AC Milan and Lazio punished with relegation and another five clubs hit with point deductions. Twenty players from 11 different clubs were also handed bans of varying lengths. Rossi lost two years of his career along with the chance to lead the Italian attack on home soil in the 1980 European Championship.

Few believed his protestations of innocence, but national team manager Enzo Bearzot stuck by the striker following his return to action with Juventus just weeks before the 1982 World Cup, a stance that drew fierce criticism from an Italian media pushing for Roma's Roberto Pruzzo to lead the attack instead, having finished as Serie A's top scorer for two consecutive seasons.

Bearzot's faith seemed terribly misplaced during the first group stage in Spain as Italy bumbled their way to three draws, with Rossi's rustiness in front of goal all too evident as he failed to score in their games against Poland, Peru, and Cameroon.

Having scraped through in second place by scoring one goal more than Cameroon, next came the daunting task of facing defending champions Argentina and free-scoring Brazil in a second group stage, from which only the winners would progress to the semifinals.

Diego Maradona and Argentina were surprisingly dispatched 2–1 but, heading into the final group game, Brazil required only a draw to go through. Cue a quite remarkable contest inside Espanyol's Estadi de Sarrià, now demolished but back then a much more intimate venue than its neighbor, the Camp Nou.

"That's the greatest game I've ever seen in what must be more than 3,000 games as a commentator," says John Helm, handed microphone duties by British channel ITV for that group decider.

"Everything about that day just felt perfect, right down to the vivid team colors and, of course, the players. Names that just tripped off the tongue. You're not often blown away in this job, but I was that day in Spain."

Rossi's hat trick on a sweltering hot July 5 was as clinical as it was unexpected. Previously goalless in the tournament, he opened the scoring with a fifth-minute header after arriving unmarked at the back post to meet Antonio Cabrini's floated left-wing cross.

Brazil quickly leveled through Sócrates, but Rossi, his goalscoring mojo now restored, fired in ruthlessly from the edge of the area after pouncing on a loose pass from Toninho Cerezo.

Italy's advantage was again canceled out, this time midway through the second half after a ferocious drive from Falcão. But neither Rossi nor the Azzurri would be denied a place in the last four, the 25-year-old turning instinctively to capitalize on a knockdown inside the six-yard box and finish with just 16 minutes remaining.

"Rossi was fantastic that day," adds Helm, who has commentated on 10 World Cups and five Olympic Games during a career spanning 60 years. "[Former Manchester United and Scotland striker] Denis

Law was my co-commentator and he recognized straightaway we were watching a striker at the very top of his game.

"The second goal is the one that really stands out, even today. The way he strode onto the ball, there was never a doubt he'd score after taking that first touch."

Rossi's switch from fallen idol to national hero was sealed by netting both goals in Italy's semifinal victory over Poland and then breaking the deadlock against West Germany in the final in Madrid with a stooping header.

Marco Tardelli's manic, eye-bulging celebration after scoring the second in that night's 3–1 victory perhaps best epitomizes just what victory meant to Italy, who, after winning two of the first three World Cups, had been forced to wait another 44 years to complete the hat trick.

Rossi, meanwhile, had his redemption. He left Spain with the Golden Boot and Golden Ball awards for top scorer and best player, plus a place in the tournament's best XI. Later that year, he picked up the prestigious Ballon d'Or.

Further success followed at club level, but it was the golden summer of 1982—and, in particular, the hat trick that inspired the title of his memoir, *I Made Brazil Cry*—for which Rossi was most fondly remembered. He passed away at the age of 64 from lung cancer in December 2020.

"This will sound terribly unprofessional, but I could have cried that day in the commentary box when Brazil lost," adds Helm. "They were such a wonderful team and I do believe football, as a sport, would have benefited from Brazil winning the World Cup in 1982 because others around the world would have copied their style.

"Instead, Paolo Rossi became the hero, propelling Italy to a World Cup success that no one saw coming. Only a few of the true greats can claim to have done that."

Player name: Paolo Rossi

Born: September 23, 1956

Died: December 9, 2020 (aged 64)

Position: Striker

Debut: 1974

Main teams: Juventus (1973–76, 1981–85), Vicenza (1976–80), AC Milan (1985–86), Hellas Verona (1986–87); Italy (1977–86)

Career highlights: Won the Golden Ball and the Golden Boot as Italy won the World Cup in 1982, as well as that year's Ballon d'Or. Claimed two Serie A titles, a Coppa Italia, and the 1984 European Cup Winners' Cup and 1985 European Cup with Juventus.

85.

Philipp Lahm

Lahm won 21 major trophies at Bayern and the World Cup with Germany.

The World Cup–winning captain who revolutionized full-back play

By Greg O'Keeffe

It is perhaps not your average footballer's way to unwind.

Renowned for being difficult to master, the German card game Schafkopf demands quick thinking and shrewd reading of opponents. Philipp Lahm would play it after hard training sessions with Bayern Munich.

Lahm, of course, was very far from average, so it is not altogether surprising that Schafkopf would be the Munich-born defender's way to relax. His intelligence was one of the key qualities that helped him etch his name into football's wider history by helping to evolve an entire position.

Perhaps another Bayern Munich hero, Mehmet Scholl, put it best. When attempting to describe the meticulous standards that made Lahm one of the greatest full-backs of all time, he could only load one compliment on another. "In 75 percent of all the games you played in, you were outstanding," said Scholl at Lahm's retirement ceremony in 2017. "And in the other 25, you were world-class."

It would be wrong to suggest full-backs were not attacking threats before the 2000s when Lahm's career began, but his emergence in the noughts as a new kind of wide defensive player, capable of inverting into midfield at different moments from either full-back role, set a new standard.

The tactic is relatively common these days and is showcased in elite divisions around the world, but it was Lahm, particularly under the tutelage of Pep Guardiola at Bayern Munich from 2013, who showed the benefits that a cerebral and tactically astute full-back in a hybrid role could offer.

In fact, Lahm, who won 21 major trophies at Bayern—including the Champions League—and the World Cup with Germany, could "play in 10 positions" such was his talent, according to Guardiola. "An exceptional person, an exceptional player," added the Catalan in a heartfelt tribute delivered to a room of journalists hanging from his every word around the time Lahm hung up his boots.

Claudio Pizarro collected four Bundesliga winners' medals with Lahm in that formidable Bayern team and fondly recalls the unassuming youngster who joined first-team training in 2002. "He came through from the under-23s with Bastian Schweinsteiger," says the Peruvian striker, who scored 125 goals during his time at the club.

"You could see immediately that Philipp was a very intelligent player. He was not the biggest or strongest, but he was clever: He would look, he would learn, and he'd do it. That was the key. You could tell even then that he was going to be a very special player in the future."

Pizarro noted how quickly Lahm absorbed instruction. "He was not that loud or talkative," he says. "He was a quiet guy, respectful, but he was observant and he would learn fast. Then, in training, you saw the quality he had with his feet and the quiet confidence he had."

It would be more than 10 years before Guardiola oversaw the pair in training, but, when he arrived in Bavaria, the former Barcelona coach quickly identified Lahm's potential to play a far greater role in his team's attacking impetus. He tasked him with moving infield, harnessing his calmness on the ball in tight spaces and ability to spot a pass under pressure. As a result, Bayern were able to create Guardiola's trademark overloads to devastating effect.

"At the beginning of the 2000s, this position was interpreted much differently, in some cases much more defensively," said Lahm in 2023. "In forward play, it was all about orientating yourself on the touchline and crossing. Gradually, the position changed due to the influence of coaches such as Guardiola. Now the role of the full-back is more variable and also more impactful for the team. It has taken on a new meaning.

"When defending, it's about making as little space as possible for the opponent; taking up a lot of space and occupying it. When attacking, it's about utilizing the space, creating as much space and as many opportunities for others as possible."

The man nicknamed *Zauberzwerg* (Magic Dwarf) for belying his 5'7" stature was perfect for Guardiola's vision for the full-back role. "He [Lahm] knew how to use his positional sense very well as a defender, even if he wasn't the strongest or fastest," recalls Pizarro. "And then he had that offensive quality. He would help out the players around him on the field. It made him a very important player in every team he played in.

"I scored many goals from his crosses. I knew where he would put it. We'd do our video analysis before games and then break off and talk about it some more. We'd see where the opponent was vulnerable and he would put it at the front or back post."

Moving into midfield positions allowed Lahm to dictate games. During the 2012–13 season, he was not just an inverted full-back; he actually filled a defensive midfield brief for entire games, returning to a position he frequented in his youth with Bayern's junior and second team.

"For Philipp, that was an easy transition," says Pizarro. "Pep liked players to get on the ball and play, then get it back really fast if we lost it so we could tire the other team out playing football. He wanted players comfortable playing that way and Philipp could do that in any position.

"He could do so much with the ball. It was helpful for games when strikers weren't scoring because he could step up. He deserves his place in the list of the best players. He could do things other footballers just couldn't."

Lahm became a hugely important player for his country, too. He won his first senior cap aged 20 in 2004 and was a regular in the side by that summer's European Championship. In the opening group game of the 2006 World Cup, in his home city of Munich, he scored a powerful goal to give Germany the lead over Costa Rica—a moment Lahm always cherished.

"I grew up near the stadium, my whole family was in the stands, but before the game, it wasn't clear whether I would be allowed to play because I had a cast on my arm," he told *The Guardian* in a column ahead of Euro 2024. "My shot flew in the top corner of the goal—a moment for the ages. I experienced the symbolism of that goal a year later in a township in South Africa.

"I set up a foundation there and the children couldn't believe that I was standing on the pitch with them. For them, I was the boy who scored *that* goal."

For Lahm, the pinnacle came eight years later, in 2014, as he led Germany to victory over Argentina in Rio de Janeiro and claimed his country's first World Cup since 1990. Just days later, still basking in the afterglow, he announced his retirement from international football.

His club career, spent at Bayern barring two seasons on loan at VfB Stuttgart as a youngster, was prolonged for a few more years. He had already won a Champions League final—at the third time of asking—in 2013, but there were three more Bundesliga titles to savor even after Rio.

He retired as one of the greatest full-backs to have ever played the game, a trailblazer to be cherished.

Player name: Philipp Lahm
Born: November 11, 1983
Position: Full-back, defensive midfielder
Debut: 2002
Main teams: Bayern Munich (2002–17), VfB Stuttgart (loan, 2003–05); Germany (2004–14)
Career highlights: Captained Germany to victory at the 2014 World Cup. Won the Champions League as part of the treble in 2012–13 and claimed the Bundesliga eight times.

84.

Raúl

Raúl was skillful, a sharp finisher, and blessed with a silky first touch.

Real Madrid's quiet leader

By Daniel Sheldon

It is February 15, 2009, in Gijón's Estadio El Molinón and, as the play develops down Real Madrid's right flank, Raúl González Blanco is loitering with menace near the penalty spot. The ball is fizzed across by a rampaging Sergio Ramos to be met emphatically by the striker's left foot. In that moment, Raúl etches his name into the record books.

The newly established most prolific goalscorer in Real Madrid's history wheeled away in celebration but was quickly engulfed by jubilant teammates. The goal was his 308th for the club—number 309 would follow later in the afternoon as Real won 4–0—to eclipse the tally rattled up by the mighty Alfredo Di Stéfano over an 11-year stint in the Spanish capital.

That record had stood for 45 years. Now it was Raúl's, the Madrid-born striker who had joined the club in his early teens and, from 1994, went on to secure his reputation as one of the great center-forwards in world football.

He was skillful, a sharp finisher, blessed with a silky first touch, and prolific for club and country over his distinguished career. But that moment in Gijón, for a while at least, set him apart.

Juande Ramos, Real Madrid's manager as Raúl's shot flew past Iñaki Lafuente to see him edge ahead of Di Stéfano, remembers that moment and recalls what it was like coaching a player of such quality and class.

"Breaking the record was a result of having a very long and successful career, a longevity, but it was rightly celebrated as something special," says Ramos. "He was already captain of the team, an honor that carried huge responsibility within the club and the team, but people respected him because of the influence he carried. He transmitted a lot to the group.

"He had played with [David] Beckham, [Zinédine] Zidane, and Ronaldo [Nazário], but they were no longer there and the only one who had stayed—the only player whose reputation was established at the time—was him, so he was very important to the team. His teammates looked to him for inspiration.

"He was a player with a lot of experience and intelligence, a fantastic temperament and fiercely competitive, and he set an example with the way he worked. He was a magnificent professional. That's what caught my eye. What made him a good captain was that he cared so much about what was going on in the dressing room.

"Perhaps what is most remarkable is that he reached those numbers without being a naturally gifted player in the same way as Lionel Messi or Cristiano Ronaldo, which gives you an idea of how professional he was and what he worked for. He worked at his game and made himself the player he was."

Both Cristiano Ronaldo (450 goals) and Karim Benzema (354) have overtaken Rául in the scoring stakes in the years since, but for a while, the Spaniard was simultaneously the leading scorer for Real, the national team, and in the revamped Champions League. He scored three for Real against Hungarian club Ferencváros in October 1995 at the age of 18 years, 114 days, making him the youngest scorer of a hat trick in UEFA's elite competition. He remains Real's leading appearance-maker, with 741 games to his name.

"Despite having played and shared a dressing room with lots of stars, he made a place for himself," Ramos adds. "I would say he was a quiet leader. More than giving orders, he was the example to follow among the other teammates.

"With his work and daily effort, he stood out. Maybe those gifted players didn't need to work at 100 percent and he, being more normal and through hard work, managed to make up for those shortcomings."

Raúl had actually been schooled across the Spanish capital at Atlético Madrid, only to be released at age 13 when the club disbanded its youth system. He made his professional debut for Real in 1994—briefly becoming the youngest-ever player, 17 years and 124 days old, to make a senior appearance for the Spanish club before that record was broken by Alberto Rivera in the same season—under Jorge Valdano, who turned to him with Emilio Butragueño approaching the end of his career.

The youngster actually endured a difficult debut, his performance a mess of missed opportunities, but he had the self-belief to persevere. He scored, assisted, and won a penalty on his second appearance a week later and went on to play his part in Real winning La Liga for the first time since 1989–90.

He ended up spending 16 years at the Bernabéu, captaining the team, winning six La Liga titles, three Champions Leagues, one UEFA Super Cup, and four Supercopas de España along the way. He first appeared in European competition at 18 and went on to become the first player to score in two finals—2000 and 2002—since the competition was revamped in 1992, as well as the first to 50 goals and 100 appearances in the new Champions League.

"Raúl is synonymous with Madrid; the face of the club for the last 25 years," Jorge Valdano told *The Guardian* in 2015. "If you wrote a list of Raúl's qualities, it would be a list of the values of Real Madrid. He is the Di Stéfano of our time. He is the people, the incarnation of *Madridismo*."

The closest the striker ever came to winning the Ballon d'Or was in 2001 when he finished second to Michael Owen, the Liverpool forward and England international. Some in Spain never forgave the Englishman for denying Raúl his moment, even after Owen moved to the Bernabéu himself.

Raúl had just enjoyed his second-most-prolific La Liga campaign in 2000–2001, scoring 24 goals, one fewer than he had managed in 1998–99. He would take the armband two years after finishing runner-up to Owen and retain the captaincy until he left the club at the end of the 2009–10 campaign, 16 years after scoring his first goal against Atlético Madrid in 1994. He boasted 323 goals in all competitions.

His subsequent career path took him to the Bundesliga with Schalke, then a stint with Al Sadd in Qatar, and, briefly, a spell with the New York Cosmos. When he retired at 38, he had scored more than 400 club goals, 71 of which were scored in the Champions League, and appeared 102 times for the Spain national team, featuring at three World Cups and two European Championships.

His influence in a Real Madrid shirt will stand the test of time and he'll forever be an icon at the Santiago Bernabéu. Indeed, when Cristiano Ronaldo eclipsed Raúl's club scoring record, he sent the Spaniard a message. "For me, you were the No. 1 at Real Madrid," he said in a video message, "as a player and as a professional."

Player name: Raúl González Blanco
Born: June 27, 1977
Position: Striker
Debut: 1994
Main teams: Real Madrid (1994–2010), Schalke (2010–12), Al Sadd (2012–14), New York Cosmos (2014–15); Spain (1996–2006)
Career highlights: Won the Champions League three times and La Liga six times. Scored a then-record 323 goals for Real Madrid.

83.

Dixie Dean

Dean's tally in 1927–28 was rattled up across 39 league appearances.

The man who scored 60 goals in an English top-flight season

By Michael Walker

On the way to becoming champions of England in 1927–28, Everton defeated Manchester United 5–2 at Goodison Park. Dixie Dean scored all five Everton goals. Asked about it decades later, Dean replied: "Well, that was before half-time."

Four of them were, and Dean said he was in a hurry because he wanted a cup of tea at the interval. Only 20, he was already used to going places fast.

William Ralph "Dixie" Dean was more than a free-scoring center-forward. To Everton, he was a talisman, a character—on and off the pitch. He was the most important player in the storied club's history, as evidenced by his statue outside Goodison Park, the ground they have just left after 133 years.

Precocious, there are elements of his life that could have appeared in a twentieth-century comic; it is almost an aside that he played 16 times for England and scored 18 goals.

Above all the other details of a fascinating life and career, to Evertonians and to the wider football world, Dixie Dean was the man who scored 60 goals in a season, a feat unmatched before or since.

His 60 goals in 39 league games came three seasons after the alteration of the offside law allowed strikers more freedom, which coincided with Dean's arrival from Tranmere Rovers, ferried across the River Mersey from Birkenhead, where Dean was born in 1907.

His age was just one of the many remarkable aspects of Dean's 1927–28 achievement. He turned 21 during its course and, just over three months later, sealed the 60-goal record on the last day of the season with a hat trick against Arsenal, a comic book detail in itself.

There were 50,000 inside Goodison and an estimated 20,000 outside that afternoon. Dean's mother was seated in the press box praying. The previous season, Middlesbrough forward George Camsell had scored 59 goals and, while that was in the Second Division, Camsell's record stood and was viewed across the UK with awe.

With nine games left of Everton's season, Dean was on 43 goals. He missed one of those matches through international duty, but scored 14 in the next seven.

That meant three goals were required on the last day against an Arsenal team shaped by the man considered to be the first great football manager, Herbert Chapman. Moreover, Chapman's captain, the celebrated Charles Buchan, was bowing out at the age of 36 and, with Everton confirmed as champions the week before, the trophy was present for a postmatch celebration. Goodison Park was in a blue frenzy.

Dean got off the tram he took to games and, cool as can be, walked through the hordes down Goodison Road and into the heaving stadium.

When Arsenal scored early, the occasion was in jeopardy. But then Dean equalized. Goal number 58. Soon after, Everton were awarded a penalty and Dean converted it. Goal 59, equal with Camsell.

And then nothing. Arsenal equalized, the hour mark came and went, so did 70 minutes, 80 minutes. Then, with just eight minutes left of the game and the season, Everton had a corner. Dean met it with his head and there it was in the back of the net. Goal 60. History.

One fan ran on and kissed Dean. He was stunned and never forgot it. In its small way, it was a symbol of what every Evertonian then and in subsequent generations felt about Dixie Dean. "It was a scene beyond description," said Buchan.

Everton were champions for the third time and would be again in 1931–32. In Dean, they possessed the most dynamic young player in the country, if not Europe, where his fame had spread.

"Dixie Dean was Everton, make no mistake about that," said eventual captain TG Jones. Even at an early age, Dean was alleged to pick the team and it was he who ordered Everton not to perform a Nazi salute when on tour in Germany in 1932. Nor was Dean fond of the "Dixie" nickname, with its American South connotations—his skin was dark compared to most on Merseyside.

Although 5'10", Dean was intimidating in the air and scored 20 of his 60 goals with his head. Many were deft flicks, but there were some so powerful it was said Dean could head a ball harder than some players could kick it. A legend arose that this was because Dean had a metal plate in his head, which had been inserted following a bad motorbike accident.

The accident part of the story was true and, with Dean in and out of hospital for treatment, Everton, unthinkably, were relegated two years after the title win of 1928.

With Dean back to fitness, Everton won the Second Division, with Dean scoring 39 times in 37 appearances. They immediately reclaimed their league title, with Dean scoring 45 goals in 38 games. He was still only 25.

In 1933, he then led Everton to their second FA Cup triumph and their first for 27 years. It was the first time in a cup final that players wore numbers on their shirts, Everton numbers 1 to 11, Manchester City 12 to 22. Dean wore 9; he was an original No. 9 and, of course, he scored.

He continued to do so despite injuries, until 1938 when a new Everton club secretary controversially sold him to Notts County. Dean moved on quickly to Sligo Rovers in Ireland and, on retirement, ran a bar in Chester.

In 1980, aged 73, he was a guest for the Everton–Liverpool derby at Goodison. Bill Shankly, the celebrated former Liverpool manager, stood up at lunch and declared Dean to be "in the company of the supremely great—like Beethoven, Rembrandt, and Shakespeare."

Dean, a tough man, cried and then, during the game, collapsed. Dean died having, as the journalist John Keith said, "heard his own obituary."

Goodison Park was where Dean had lived his sporting life, where he had thrilled and made his name, and it was where his ashes were scattered. As *The Everton Encyclopedia* put it, "It was somehow fitting that Dean spent his final moments at Goodison, for being an Evertonian was elemental to his existence."

Most Goals Scored in an English Top-Flight Season

Player	Club	Season	Goals Scored
Dixie Dean	Everton	1927-28	60
Tom Waring	Aston Villa	1930-31	49
Dixie Dean	Everton	1931-32	44
Ted Harper	Blackburn Rovers	1925-26	43
Dave Halliday	Sunderland	1928-29	43
Ted Drake	Arsenal	1934-35	42
Vic Watson	West Ham United	1929-30	41
Jimmy Dunne	Sheffield United	1930-31	41
Jimmy Greaves	Chelsea	1960-61	41

Player name: William Ralph "Dixie" Dean
Born: January 22, 1907
Died: March 1, 1980 (aged 73)
Position: Forward
Debut: 1924
Main teams: Tranmere Rovers (1924–25), Everton (1925–38), Notts County (1938–39), Sligo Rovers (1939); England (1927–32)
Career highlights: Scored 60 goals in the 1927–28 English First Division, 11 more than anyone else has ever managed in an English top-flight season. Won the league title twice with Everton.

82.

Gheorghe Hagi

Hagi was an archetypal No. 10, a player who wore the burden of creativity on his sleeve.

The Maradona of the Carpathians

By James McNicholas

Gheorghe Hagi was an artist. His goal against Colombia, during the 1994 World Cup, was his masterpiece.

Thirty-four minutes into Romania's opening match, Hagi picked up the ball wide on the left touchline. Two light touches, a quick glance up. The watching world, including Colombia goalkeeper Óscar Córdoba, expected him to cross. Instead, Hagi sent a powerfully struck shot arcing into the far top corner.

With any other player, one would question whether it was a fluke, a cross gone wrong, a mis-hit.

But Hagi had prepared for this. Romania had spotted Córdoba's tendency to tiptoe off his line in anticipation of the cross. During their final training session, Hagi persuaded Romania's goalkeeper, Bogdan Stelea, to emulate Córdoba's positioning while he practiced taking pot-shots. He even had a sighter or two in the opening minute of the match.

Córdoba was barely a few yards off his line, with one eye on Romania center-forward Florin Răducioiu, when Hagi's shot soared beyond him and into the net.

"It was the most difficult goal to score," Hagi recalled in 2023. "It takes talent, personality, inspiration, power, decision, and risk—all of those things."

Personality: perhaps that word, above all others, sums Hagi up. It was in every touch, every shimmy, every flick of his left boot. It was in every shrug, every snarl, and every glare.

In modern football, it can feel as if the long-range goal is a disappearing phenomenon. With so much focus on patterns of play and retaining possession, the individualists looking to go it alone from distance are a dying breed.

"I always tell my own players: Believe in what you're doing and have courage," added Hagi, the maverick player turned manager. "If there's no courage, you can't risk.

"My first coach told me to shoot as much as I could, so I opted to shoot rather than lose the ball many times in my career. I scored incredible goals thanks to that sense I had."

Hagi scored more than 300 goals in his career. He has claimed that more than 70 percent of them were converted from outside the box. There may be some exaggeration there, but it only adds to the myth.

And this player warranted a myth. He was an archetypal No. 10, a player who wore the burden of creativity on his sleeve. He was a crotchety, combustible character—when he wasn't dribbling away from defenders, he was squaring up to them. Yes, he had personality, but his reserves of talent were deeper still.

The 1994 World Cup in the United States saw his creative powers at their peak. "Everyone in Romania wanted to conquer America," Hagi told *FourFourTwo* magazine. "After the fall of communism, we wanted to go to the free world. You can go a long way with sport, just as Romania did in gymnastics and tennis. It was football's turn to go and conquer."

Hagi's performances earned him the nickname "The Maradona of the Carpathians." It was apt. Not since the diminutive Argentinian's emergence more than a decade earlier had an international team been so galvanized by one individual's brilliance.

The win over Argentina in the last 16 was the high point of Romania's tournament. Coach Anghel Iordănescu called the victory "the greatest event celebrated by our people since the revolution."

It remains one of Hagi's great regrets that El Diego did not feature, having been expelled from the competition for failing a drugs test. The duel between the two No. 10s might have been a crowning moment for Hagi.

Romania were drawn against Sweden in the quarterfinals. Inspired by Hagi, the squad were beginning to believe they could go on and win the tournament. When they were eliminated on penalties, Hagi was heartbroken.

"I am convinced that with our style of play, we could have beaten Brazil and taken them on without any fear," he said in 2014. "I'm also sad for myself as I might have won the best player of the tournament."

Hagi was born on February 5, 1965, in the small Romanian town of Săcele. Football is the family trade: His father, Niculae, was also a professional. By the age of 11, young Gheorghe was already playing matches against adults.

He joined Steaua Bucharest at the age of 22 and, at Romania's most famous club, his talent exploded. Hagi scored 76 goals in 97 league games—an absurd tally for someone who was ostensibly a playmaker rather than a goalscorer.

In 1989, Steaua achieved the extraordinary feat of reaching the European Cup final, where they were beaten by the might of AC Milan. Hagi's performances en route to that showpiece attracted a host of admirers, including the *Rossoneri*. But it was Real Madrid who ultimately pried him away from Romania in the summer of 1990.

It appeared a perfect match: this mercurial jester lured to perform on one of Europe's grandest stages. In the end, the usually extroverted Hagi succumbed to stage fright. In a squad packed with renowned names such as Hugo Sánchez and Emilio Butragueño, he struggled to find his place. "I failed," he later admitted. "Faced with all those superstars, I nearly shat my pants."

Hagi spent two underwhelming years at the Bernabéu before moving to Brescia in Italy. That move saw him reunited with former Romania manager Mircea Lucescu, but it turned into another disappointment. At the end of Hagi's first season, Brescia were relegated to Serie B.

In the second tier of Italian football, however, Hagi rediscovered his mojo. He carried that form into the tournament in 1994 and his performances at international level saw him take center stage once again.

Although he departed without a medal, he did earn a place in the team of the tournament and a move back to La Liga, becoming one of the select few to play for both Real Madrid and Barcelona.

"The best thing was that Johan Cruyff signed me," Hagi told *Marca* in 2022. "I became a footballer thanks to him and watching Ajax in the 1970s. That was already incredible. I learned the philosophy of Barcelona."

After two years with Barcelona, Hagi joined Galatasaray and, in Turkey, his career flourished again. He scored 43 minutes into his debut and went from strength to strength. From 1996–97 and 1999–2000, he led Galatasaray to four consecutive league titles, culminating in a remarkable treble of Super Lig, Turkish Cup, and the UEFA Cup.

In just four years, Hagi achieved hero status in Istanbul. Some regard him as Galatasaray's finest-ever player.

But it is his performances for Romania in that summer of 1994 for which he'll be most remembered—for his personality, for his talent, and for that extraordinary goal.

Player name: Gheorghe Hagi

Born: February 5, 1965

Position: Attacking midfielder

Debut: 1982

Main teams: FC Constanța (1982–83), Sportul Studențesc (1983–87), Steaua Bucharest (1987–90), Real Madrid (1990–92), Brescia (1992–94), Barcelona (1994–96), Galatasaray (1996–2001); Romania (1983–2000)

Career highlights: Romania's best player as they reached the 1994 World Cup quarterfinals and the country's joint all-time top scorer. Won the UEFA Cup with Galatasaray in 1999–2000.

81.

Denis Law

Law joined George Best and Bobby Charlton in Manchester United's Holy Trinity.

The King of Old Trafford

By Michael Walker

In October 1963, when England's Football Association sought to mark its centenary with an occasion of scale, it invited FIFA to create a "Rest of the World XI." It was to face England at Wembley Stadium in London.

In front of a crowd of 87,000, FIFA named a five-man forward line. Although Santos in Brazil would not release Pelé, the team included global greats Alfredo Di Stéfano, Eusébio, Raymond Kopa, and Paco Gento. The fifth forward was Denis Law.

It is an indication of the esteem in which Law was held by his contemporaries. Di Stéfano was 37, Law 23, but Law was already a football phenomenon, a Manchester United player of great courage, dash, and unpredictability. His style of play endeared him to supporters as much as the many goals he belted in. For that at Old Trafford, they christened him "The King."

One year after that Wembley game, in which Law scored the Rest of the World's only goal, he joined Di Stéfano and Kopa on a then very short list of winners of the Ballon d'Or. Law became only the second Briton after Stanley Matthews to win the award. Law was the first and, to date, the only Scot to collect it.

Law was in his pomp, a visceral eruption of a striker, a scorer of what United's fabled manager Sir Matt Busby called "miracle goals." Bobby Charlton, Law's teammate, once said of Law, "All some of his most brilliant interventions lacked were puffs of smoke."

It is an indication of how Law dazzled spectators and teammates alike. On scoring, his right arm shot up straight in celebration when that was something new. He was funny with it. He oozed charisma.

Law had joined Charlton and Busby at United in 1962 for a British record fee of £115,000. Busby was reconstructing United after the devastating 1958 Munich air crash. Law was 17 at the time of the disaster; he had made his debut for Huddersfield Town in England's Second Division at 16.

The seventh child of an Aberdeen North Sea fisherman, Law had arrived in Huddersfield at age 15, so small and frail, with a pronounced squint, that the club thought they had signed the wrong boy.

His childhood was one of poverty, though that was not extraordinary in his area of Aberdeen. "When my father went to sea on Monday, his suit would go straight to the pawnbroker," Law recalled in *The King: My Autobiography*. He was 14 when he got his first pair of proper shoes.

But when Huddersfield saw Law play, the club knew no mistake had been made. He was sent for corrective surgery on his squint, was beefed up physically, and, at 18, was capped by Scotland under the temporary management of Busby.

The scrawny boy from Aberdeen was a young man in demand. Bill Shankly wanted to take Law to Liverpool. Busby wanted him at United. Arsenal also pursued him. Yet when Law left Huddersfield in 1960, it was for Manchester City. It was the first time he broke the British transfer record. He was 20.

He stayed in a struggling City team for just over a year, famously scoring six goals in an FA Cup tie against Luton Town only for the game to be abandoned with 20 minutes to go.

Law then joined the exodus from English football to Italy, where there was no salary cap. He was signed by Torino, a club still in recovery from its Superga air crash in 1949, where 18 players had died.

On the pitch, he found Italian defensive football culture frustrating—"Not only was it difficult, it was boring." Law was still voted "best foreign player" by the Italian newspapers and, unknown to him, was "transferred" across Turin to Juventus in 1962. He refused to go, flew home to Scotland, and awaited a call from Busby.

United signed Law that summer and he stayed at Old Trafford for 11 often glorious seasons. He won the league title twice, the FA Cup, and the European Cup.

In September 1963, a 17-year-old from Belfast, George Best, made his United debut, and over the next five years, culminating in the European Cup victory at Wembley, "Law, Best, and Charlton" became known as the most exciting, talented, and watchable trio anywhere in football. All three won the Ballon d'Or.

In 1964–65, when United were champions for the first time since Munich, Law scored 28 goals in 36 appearances in the league. The previous season he had scored 46 in all competitions. In United's history, only Charlton and Wayne Rooney have scored more than Law's 237 goals.

That he did this in 404 appearances, and despite a persistent knee injury requiring surgery in 1968 at the moment United were winning the European Cup—10 years after Munich—spoke of Law's physical bravery. Missing that night at Wembley was his "greatest disappointment" and, as he reminded people later, he was United captain then.

Law stayed another five seasons at United and continued to score regularly, but he was in a team that had peaked. To his annoyance, he was released by the club in 1973 and accepted a surprise offer to rejoin Manchester City. He was 33, had five children, and needed employment.

The dramatic upshot of United's decision came near the end of the 1973–74 season. United faced City at Old Trafford knowing they could not lose as relegation beckoned.

With eight minutes left and the score 0–0, the ball broke to Law six yards out. Wearing City's sky blue, he instinctively backheeled the ball. It went in. There was no trademark celebration this time.

A pitch invasion followed and the game was called off, but the result stood. United went down. It turned out to be Law's final kick in domestic football. He retired at the start of the following season.

Before then, he appeared for Scotland at the 1974 World Cup, 16 years after his international debut. In 55 games for Scotland, he scored 30 goals.

After playing, Law worked as a co-commentator for the BBC, but no one forgot Denis Law the footballer. There are three statues in his honor: one inside Old Trafford, one in the middle of his native Aberdeen—unveiled by Sir Alex Ferguson in 2021—and then the "Holy Trinity" outside Manchester United: Law, Best, and Charlton.

Denis Law kept good company.

Player name: Denis Law
Born: February 24, 1940
Died: January 17, 2025 (aged 84)
Position: Forward
Debut: 1956
Main teams: Huddersfield Town (1956–60), Manchester City (1960–61), Torino (1961–62), Manchester United (1962–73), Manchester City (1973–74); Scotland (1958–74)
Career highlights: Won the European Cup in 1968 and the English league title twice with Manchester United. Scotland's joint all-time record goalscorer with 30 goals in 55 appearances. Won the Ballon d'Or in 1964.

80. John Charles

Charles was a prolific scorer at Leeds and Juventus.

Il Gigante Buono from the backstreets of Swansea

By Phil Hay

Off a roundabout and up a steep incline is the humble stretch of Alice Street, deep in the belly of inner-city Swansea. Terraced houses line it on either side, built of blackened Welsh stone. It is deserted and quiet, save for the melodic hum of traffic from the main road nearby.

Close your eyes and you can hear the sound of feet thundering up the pavements, of children spilling out of their front doors, footballs under their arms. A few hundred yards away is Cwmbwrla Park, a large expanse of grass with goalposts wedged in the turf. Swansea has seen a million days like this; watery skies leaving puddles on the pitch and patches of mud in both six-yard boxes. The unremarkable scene keeps the field's rich history hidden.

When childhood matches were played out here in the 1930s and '40s, the sound of kids arriving en masse was not accompanied by the rattle of football studs, or not from 19 Alice Street, anyway. The man of that house, Edward Charles, drew a wage from the local steelworks, but industry in Wales was in decline and Swansea sagged under high levels of unemployment. The neighborhood was impoverished. Few people had money for luxuries like football boots. The sporting icon born here would pull himself up by his bootstraps. Pull himself up and then some.

Number 19 Alice Street was the first home of John Charles—to many, the finest Welsh footballer who ever lived.

Growing up, the world beyond Cwmbwrla was the great unknown and in 1948, when he left Wales to sign for Leeds United more than 200 miles away in the north of England, his mother was said to have asked if he needed his passport to cross the border. Charles made a habit of traveling blindly, but travel he did, geographically and professionally. By his 26th birthday, home for him was the warm, tree-lined boulevards of Turin, where football treated him like a king.

Certain things in life got the better of Charles. School bored him, so he left when he was 14. Managing money was a perennial battle, leading him briefly to prison in his retirement years. It was a tragedy of the sport that a player so complete and revered was rendered virtually penniless. His son, Mel, described him as "an accidental hero, an introvert who had a hard time expressing himself. The fame? He found it awkward. I don't think he understood it."

The fame of Charles, the legend and the aura, was built on the very fact he was complete.

Charles the athlete could do everything. He was imposing at 6'2", thickset with chiseled cheekbones, and only his shy eyes betrayed the teddy bear in him. His touch was nimble and he moved like the wind with the impact of a hurricane, towering in the air and deadly with both feet. His seamless switch from defense to attack in the 1950s made him a world-class center-back and a world-class center-forward rolled into one. Scouts from Leeds spotted all of that in him at 17 and plucked him quickly out of Swansea City's youth training system.

Charles's style, and his record of never being booked or red-carded, was a contradiction. His uber-sporting nature spawned the nickname "The Gentle Giant" (*Il Gigante Buono* in Italian), but people reflected on his honorable streak while he was trampling opponents underfoot. Mel always remembered a quote from Jack Charlton, Charles's former teammate at Leeds. "It went along the lines of 'Gentle Giant, my arse!'" Mel said. "I guess Dad must have been a nightmare to play against. It's what everyone who saw him at his best tells me."

Mel died in 2024, 20 years after his father. We had previously met in 2020 to reminisce about Charles's achievements prior to Leeds's centenary. The stories were endless and they swung between happiness and sadness, sometimes in the same breath. Charles brought Pelé's shirt home after Wales played Brazil in the quarterfinals of the 1958 World Cup. Mel took it to school to show his friends and lost it. Charles was highly decorated, but the only memento Mel had left was an Italian championship medal from Juventus. The rest was gone; sold or donated to charity.

"That stuff just didn't bother him," Mel said. The Pelé shirt never showed up.

Juventus, and Charles's five years there, were a particularly intriguing part of his history. The world is smaller these days, but in 1957, a leap from England to the Italian leagues was intrepid beyond belief. No wonder at all that Juve fancied him. He scored 154 goals in his first spell at Leeds at a rate of almost one every two games. His haul of 43 in the 1953–54 Division Two season is an existing club record and probably will not be surpassed; 38 in the top division in 1956–57 was Juve's cue to dispatch transfer negotiators to England.

The deal was done at the Queens Hotel in Leeds. Juve coughed up £65,000, a new British record, and Leeds were only too pleased to pocket the cash. A fire had destroyed the West Stand at their Elland Road stadium and the money helped to pay for a replacement—a replacement that still stands today.

Charles was told of rival interest from Real and Lazio. It had to be explained to him that "Real" were Real Madrid and that Lazio played in Rome, frontiers about which he knew next to nothing. Juventus were a mystery, too. "My mum was apprehensive about going," Mel said. "She was a Leeds girl. She met my dad in the ballrooms of Roundhay. Italy was a million miles away."

Arriving there underlined the point. Turin was warm, exotic, and salubrious, so far removed from 19 Alice Street. In his book, *The Gigante*, Robert Endeacott explained how the Charles family were given an apartment by Juve on Via Susa, in central Turin and a little way south of Juve's Stadio Delle Alpi. It had polished, parquet floors, a huge television, a bidet, and iron gates outside the property. Fans and reporters took to congregating outside as Charles's exploits in Italy made him royalty.

Mel was two when the family moved to Italy, but Charles's lengthy stint with Juve gave him clear memories of their lifestyle there. "We were spoiled," he said. "We had maids to look after us, which wasn't what we were used to. The whole house was beautiful. People would stand by the gates hoping for autographs. You'd get lots of journalists there, too. They were there to see or speak to this fella who had come from the backstreets of Swansea but was now in the realms of a lord.

"Even then, I don't think he realized how popular he was. All he knew was football and he didn't think much outside of the fact he was playing it. He didn't get the other stuff. My mum was the boss out there. She put us, my brothers and me, into Catholic school and we had to wear smocks. She called the shots. That's why, when she wanted to come home [to England in 1962], we did."

There was a suspicion—completely unfounded, as it turned out—that Charles might sink in Italian football. Italy's top league, Serie A, was tactically defensive and extremely combative. In no way was it England's top division by another name or under a different flag.

By then, Charles was not the central defender he had been at the outset. His first manager at Leeds, Major Frank Buckley, uncovered the goalscorer in him around 1952 and let that talent run wild. On top of the tactical questions, there were grumblings in the British press about the loss of a top domestic name to foreign climes. The Italians, in contrast, were intrigued by the transfer and by Charles's reputation. That curiosity rapidly turned into outright worship of him.

Charles was the perfect foil for Omar Sívori, Juve's Argentinian winger who, at 5'4", cut an amusing figure alongside the well-built Welshman. Sívori was himself exceptional, a hyperactive runner and dribbler whose creative touch dovetailed perfectly with Charles's strengths in front of goal. They would be spoken about as a pair long after their careers were done. They would die within 12 months of each other, Charles aged 72 in 2004 and Sívori aged 69 in 2005.

Shortly before his passing, Charles—after what would be his last public appearance at Stadio Delle Alpi—had been due for a reunion with Sívori on an Italian television broadcast. Instead, he was taken ill and rushed to hospital for a heart bypass. A few weeks later, news of his death arrived.

"You go to Italy and there are kids who know about my dad," Mel said. "His name has been passed down through the generations." As it should be. Charles was a phenomenon in Turin.

His 155 appearances for Juve yielded 108 goals, three *Scudetti,* and the Coppa Italia twice, but, owing to homesickness on the part of his first wife, Peggy, the adventure ended in 1962. On his return to England, Charles was hit by an unexpected turn. He rejoined Leeds but found the English game beyond him. Tactically, physically, whatever it was; changes in the meantime and half a decade in Turin conspired to leave him floundering at the club where his name was so spectacularly built.

"He should have retired a lot earlier," Mel said. "People often remember players as they finish, not how they were at their best. He should have packed in after he came back from Italy. That's my take on it."

Charles, however, was not condemned to be remembered for his time on the downward slope. His place in Juventus's history is secure and the club led the tributes to him after he died, mourning "a great champion and a great man." His place in Leeds's history is equally solid and the stand he helped to fund at Elland Road was duly named after him.

There are specially commissioned busts of him at both Leeds and Swansea City. No evidence of him is obvious at Cwmbwrla Park, save for those who know the genius that was nurtured there, but, dank and dreary on this September afternoon, it represents the first pin on the route of his journey.

I once heard Jack Charlton, the World Cup–winning England defender, speak in awe about Charles. I heard him joke about the day when he, a fresh-faced Charlton, learned he was to make his Leeds debut. The first-team list was pinned to a wall and Charlton was transfixed by it. Charles came up behind him, pointed to Charlton's name, and—in complete seriousness—asked: "Who the fuck's that?"

So much about Charles could be unintentional: the humor, the adventures, the celebrity. Sure, he strove for a career in football, but it rarely seemed to dawn on him that he was special.

Mel long regretted the loss of Pelé's shirt. Where it is now, who knows? He incurred Charles's wrath for that but, he believed, more because of the act of him mislaying somebody else's property than Charles resenting the loss of an iconic strip. Many years later, and after his father's death, Mel sought to redeem himself at an auction by stumping up for a different Pelé top, signed by the great man himself. "I looked up and asked my dad: 'Should I buy this?'" Mel said. "I could hear him say: 'I think you better had, son.'"

The deal was done for £600 and an itch was finally scratched.

That itch was largely Mel's, though. Charles was not the sentimental type; an accidental hero, as his son put it. *Il Gigante Buono* and fame were awkward bedfellows, and you wonder what he would have made of Great Western Railway, the service that runs in and out of south Wales, naming a train after him in 2018.

It's an appropriate tribute to the backstreet boy who put aside trepidation, took the path out of Alice Street, stepped into the big wide world, and kept on going.

Player name: John Charles
Born: December 27, 1931
Died: February 21, 2004 (aged 72)
Position: Center-forward, center-back
Debut: 1949
Main teams: Leeds United (1949–57), Juventus (1957–62), Leeds United (1962), Roma (1962–63), Cardiff City (1963–66), Hereford United (1966–71); Wales (1950–65)
Career highlights: Helped Wales reach the 1958 World Cup quarterfinals. Won Serie A three times and twice claimed the Coppa Italia.

79.

Paul Gascoigne

For a while, Gascoigne was “the most famous and probably the most popular person in Britain.”

The man. Not the moniker.

By George Caulkin

Here begins Paul Gascoigne’s story.

This is less a statement of the bleedin’ obvious than it first might appear, if only because the existence of one of England’s most talented and charismatic footballers can be split into halves—the sporting equivalent of Robert Louis Stevenson’s *Dr Jekyll and Mr. Hyde*. On the one hand, there was Gascoigne; gifted, exquisite, deft, sharp elbowed. And then along comes Gazza, with carnage in his slipstream.

Gascoigne was the pudgy midfielder with a love of Mars bars who grew up in Gateshead and sent a spasm through Newcastle United in the mid-1980s. When his young Newcastle side beat Watford to win the FA Youth Cup, Gascoigne scored twice. After one of the goals, Jack Charlton, the first-team manager, turned to Maurice Setters, his chief scout, and said (as told in his autobiography), "If you live to be a hundred, Maurice, you'll never see a better goal than that."

Gazza was a phenomenon; larger-than-life (which is putting it mildly) and fodder for the tabloids, a bastardized King Midas who brought chaos to everything he touched, including his own career. He was a back-page, front-page wrecking ball who wore fake plastic breasts to get a laugh, who caused consternation when he belched into television microphones, a sucker for controversy who drank himself to addiction and whose mania drifted toward tragedy.

One could not exist without the other, and between the pair of them, Gascoigne and Gazza, the perception of football in Britain was wholly transformed.

This separation is not a journalistic conceit. In his lowest moments, when alcohol gripped him tightly, he "lived a plonky life, being a plonky person, being Gazza instead of being Paul Gascoigne." This was a sentence Gascoigne wrote in his autobiography, which, naturally, was called *Gazza, My Story*.

Others recognize it, too. Like Gascoigne, Alan Shearer was a native of Tyneside and a boyhood Newcastle fan. They played together for England, most notably in the 1996 European Championship, when, in a group game against Scotland, Gascoigne scored one of the most iconic goals in tournament history.

Gazza then produced one of its most memorable celebrations, mimicking a drinking game that had earned the squad infamy.

What kind of thoughts leap into Shearer's brain when he hears the word *Gazza*? "Crazy," he says. "Infectious. Mad behavior. A lovable rogue. The roughest of rough diamonds."

And what about *Paul Gascoigne*? "A great footballer who was just totally in love with the game," says Shearer, who has never been loose-lipped with descriptions like "great." "In terms of our country, we should be talking about one of the very greatest. It was incredible what he could do. But there's Gazza and there's Paul. There's both of those things."

Arguably, Gascoigne's zenith—and the foothills of what became known as Gazzamania—came early. In 1988, he had left Newcastle for Tottenham Hotspur and then made a late dash for England's World Cup squad two years later. By 1990, he was integral to Sir Bobby Robson's side and when he was shown a yellow card in the semifinal against West Germany, which would rule him out of the final (if England got there), the 23-year-old wept on the pitch. Those tears were fertilizer for the Turin turf and something grew.

As it happened, England lost on penalties—they always lost on penalties—but suddenly romance and beauty were attached to our national sport, which, over the previous two decades, had been castigated and shunned for its grime and rudimentary tactics and for hooliganism. Within a couple of years, the Premier League was born.

In that World Cup year, Gascoigne came home from Italy and appeared on a prime-time chat show on BBC television. Terry Wogan, the host, introduced him as "literally the most famous and probably the most popular person in Britain today," and it was not an exaggeration. Everybody was talking about him. From Sir Bobby's dignity and class, from the dramatic agony of England's near miss to Gascoigne's relatable humanity, Italia '90 made football acceptable, chic, fun.

The sadness of it is this: Gazza rather than Gascoigne controls the public discourse. There was innocence at the start, a relentless, cheeky personality that was adorable and exhausting. "He's still lovable, even when he does something diabolical," Gary Lineker, a teammate for Tottenham and England, said in 1991.

By the end of his career and then into the awful void of what came next, there had been so many acts of wanton stupidity, so much daftness and self-sabotage, that Gascoigne's ability was almost an afterthought. Less lovable, more diabolical.

Everybody has heard of Gazza, the mishaps, and worse, but Paul Gascoigne deserves to be remembered, too.

His story is worth telling because it is also no exaggeration to say that he was as good as we have seen, or might have been if Gazza had not been around to trip him up, point, and laugh. In this era of Jude Bellingham and Phil Foden, we take English quality for granted, but back then he was unrivaled.

Our game was tough and frenetic; it was hard and furious. We played with a big man up top, our center-halves would rather launch it toward Row Z than dally in possession, we didn't encourage slow buildup play, and if there is a bit of stereotype at work here, then it isn't a lot. Football grounds were often ramshackle. It was not a family environment. To be a fan took commitment.

Gascoigne was not alien to that. It was his background, too, and he was built for it. He was bulky, pink, and muscular. He had big hair and chunky thighs, a strong upper body. He glistened as if dipped in chip fat. There was no filter. A personal memory from a moribund day at St. James' Park is when someone close by yelled: "Gazza man, pull ya finger oot."

He swiveled on his boots, held his fingers up in a wide V, and yelled back at full volume: "FUCK OFF."

Yet, with the football at his feet, there was delicacy. There was alchemy. He had astonishing close control. When he ran, the ball ran with him, as if connected. Because of his power, he could go through people as well as around them. He also had the vision to pick out players and then deliver the ball on a sixpence to unlock other teams. He was always looking to attack and his delivery from set pieces was marvelous. He scored goals.

By the time of Gascoigne's emergence at Newcastle, Shearer had moved to Southampton at the other end of the country. "Like me, he was brought up in a football-mad area where you have no choice but to love football and love Newcastle," Shearer says. "We were starting to hear all these rumors about this young kid who was incredibly gifted and making a noise, who was as raw as they come but pure as well, you know?"

To watch him in the flesh was something else. You knew he was special and, even better, one of ours. "What sums him up more than anything is that he loved the football," Shearer says. "He loved having the ball. He caressed it, he looked after it, he didn't want to give it away, and he was prepared to take a risk. He yearned to be the star of the show. It's not often you see somebody with that level of talent."

As his fame and personal situation altered beyond recognition and often spun out of control, this part never did. "For me, the life I had, the lifestyle, the press, and being followed, pictures being taken, people writing lies about me and stuff like that, or getting stitched up left, right and center . . . my life was 90 minutes on that pitch," Gascoigne said in an interview with Shearer for *The Athletic* about Euro '96.

"Once I got on the pitch, everything went away until the game was finished, when obviously it all came back again. I made sure I loved every second of that 90 minutes. I always wanted the ball. For England, I used to look at you or Lineker and see where you were and I knew, once I got the ball, where I would put it first time.

"For 90 minutes, I knew it was my time and to just enjoy it because I also knew what I was going to get afterwards."

But Gazza and Gascoigne were engaged in a constant wrestling match and, on occasions, the pitch was not a haven. In 1991, he scored an astonishing long-range free kick against Arsenal, Tottenham Hotspur's great rivals, to propel his club toward the FA Cup final, but when Spurs won the trophy, Gascoigne was pictured holding it in a hospital ward. Fifteen minutes into the match, he had launched himself—ludicrously high, haywire high, batshit high—at Nottingham Forest's Gary Charles, rupturing his own cruciate ligament.

Injury ruled him out for the entirety of the following season, delaying a transfer to Lazio in Serie A. He proved a hit with Italian fans, but he broke his cheekbone and broke a leg and there were issues with his fluctuating weight. By the time he moved to Rangers in 1995, he was diminished, although still capable of making an impact. The same applied to Gazza, too. Gazza relished the madness and rivalries and mayhem of Glasgow.

Another high point came in 1996, clambering sharply from a low. The Euros effectively began for England with a pretournament booze-up during their preparations in Hong Kong. Shirts were ripped and players sprawled on a dentist's chair had drink poured down their throats. When the papers found out, *The Sun* ran with a picture of a sozzled Gascoigne and the headline "DISGRACEFOOL" and wrote: "Look at Gazza . . . a drunk oaf with no pride."

A few weeks later, after Gascoigne had flipped the ball he loved above Colin Hendry's head and connected brilliantly as it fell to score against Scotland, he hared to the touchline where his teammates used a plastic bottle to ape that dentist-chair drinking session. This time, the headlines were different. "Mr. Paul Gascoigne: An Apology," read an editorial in the *Daily Mirror*. "Gazza is no longer a fat, drunken imbecile. He is, in fact, a football genius."

Next up, England demolished the Netherlands, a match Shearer described in *The Athletic* as "the greatest performance of my lifetime."

"That was the biggest moment for me playing for England," Gascoigne told Shearer. "Terry [Venables, the manager] said, 'All we've got to do is play them at their own game,' and we did. To beat them 4–1 . . . David Platt came on as a substitute, I gave him the ball, he gave it back and said, 'Go on, it's your game.' To have a whole stadium singing your name . . . I went back to my hotel room and cried my eyes out . . . I was so proud."

England again got to the last four. Again, they were knocked out on penalties. By Germany. Again.

From Rangers, Gascoigne moved to Middlesbrough, then to Everton, and then Burnley, his fitness and body undermined by the turmoil of Gazza's unquenchable lifestyle. He was omitted from Glenn Hoddle's England squad for the 1998 World Cup at the last moment, leaving him on 57 caps and 10 goals. It could easily have been double.

In his final book, *Newcastle, My Kind of Toon*, Sir Bobby Robson wrote of Gascoigne: "God knows what he would have gone on to achieve if he hadn't flung himself so recklessly at Gary Charles, but I think people would have talked about him in the same breath as George Best, Bobby Charlton, Denis Law, Kenny Dalglish. He would have been one of those.

"But that sour May afternoon was the beginning of the end for him in many ways. He was never quite the same. Paul was now Gazza, a publicity magnet from whose pull he struggled to escape."

On the grass, he escaped. On the field, he felt peace, at least some of the time. So let us allow him to escape here, too, just for a moment, as we remember Paul Gascoigne. Not as Gazza, but as the tubby Gateshead kid with the ball at his feet, doing things that did not compute, making poetry from mud and dirt and mess and flailing tackles.

How we gasped and smiled and spoke with wonder about this shiny, gurning lad. Our lad. How his future shimmered in front of him.

Player name: Paul Gascoigne
Born: May 27, 1967
Position: Attacking midfielder
Debut: 1985
Main teams: Newcastle United (1985–88), Tottenham Hotspur (1988–92), Lazio (1992–95), Rangers (1995–98), Middlesbrough (1998–2000), Everton (2000–2002), Burnley (2002); England (1988–98)
Career highlights: Instrumental in England's run to the 1990 World Cup semifinals. One of the key players as England reached the semifinals of Euro '96. Won the FA Cup in 1991 and two Scottish Premiership titles.

78.
Gordon Banks

The England goalkeeper's save against Brazil in 1970 is one of football's truly immortal moments.

The save that defined the best goalkeeper of his generation

By Jack Pitt-Brooke

In the dying seconds of Austria's last-16 game against Turkey at Euro 2024, Alexander Prass desperately looped a high cross into the box. Christoph Baumgartner, his side striving for an equalizer, leapt above Ferdi Kadıoğlu and thumped his header into the ground.

As the ball bounced back up, it looked certain to fly high into the net, securing Austria a draw and extra time. But Turkey goalkeeper Mert Günok changed direction, dived to his right and somehow had enough strength in his right hand to divert the ball away from his net and out for a corner. Günok was congratulated by his teammates while Baumgartner turned away, hands on head in disbelief.

Austria coach Ralf Rangnick was asked in his postmatch press conference whether Günok's brilliant save, a stop that had barred Austria's passage into the quarterfinals, could be compared to the most famous save of all, that mustered by Gordon Banks to deny Pelé at the 1970 World Cup. Rangnick was initially in no mood to compare the two at length, but later in his briefing, he warmed to the idea.

"It's difficult," he said, smiling, "with Gordon Banks in the goal."

That wet chaotic night in Leipzig was 54 years and 25 days after Banks saved from Pelé in Guadalajara and the similarities between the two saves were striking: the leap before the header, the downward trajectory of the ball, the goalkeeper throwing himself to his right and propelling the ball upward to safety. Above all, the shock of the man who was convinced he had scored a goal, scarcely believing what had happened before his eyes.

But it is also testament to the remarkable power of that one moment that it is still held up as the gold standard for saves, the save against which all others are measured.

Banks passed away in 2019, Pelé in 2022, but that one moment in which they combined will live on for as long as football involves a contest between striker and goalkeeper, which is to say for as long as the game is played.

It is one of football's truly immortal moments.

The meeting of England and Brazil in Guadalajara had an epic feel even before a ball was kicked.

It was unquestionably the most prestigious tie of the whole group stage. Many expected it to be the eventual final at the Estadio Azteca in Mexico City. Alf Ramsey's England were the holders, having won the trophy on home soil in 1966. They retained the spine of that team; not just Banks, but Bobby Moore, Bobby Charlton, Martin Peters, and Geoff Hurst, as well as new additions such as Alan Mullery, Francis

Lee, and Brian Labone. Banks had just been made an OBE, a sign of how highly he was regarded even before his most famous moment.

Up against them were Brazil, winners of the World Cup in 1958 and 1962. They had more individual quality than any other team at the tournament: Jairzinho, Rivellino, Tostão, Gérson, and, most famous of all, Pelé. He was past his peak at this point: This was to be his fourth and final World Cup. He had scored his famous 1,000th goal just seven months before. His last game for Brazil was just one year away. But he still had an aura unlike anyone else in the game.

The day after England's opening game—a 1–0 win over Romania—the whole England team went to watch Brazil thump Czechoslovakia 4–1. Pelé was brilliant, scoring an emphatic volley, looking just as powerful and precise as he ever did. In the buildup to the game, the England players were asked about how they would try to handle him. He remained a clear and obvious threat.

England did not have a smooth preparation for their own meeting with Brazil. It was no secret where in Guadalajara the team were staying, in the Hilton hotel, and the night beforehand, hundreds of local fans decided to try to deprive them of any sleep, causing as much of a racket as possible throughout the hotel; banging on doors, playing drums, anything to keep the English players awake. Banks barely slept at all.

It was a baking-hot day in Guadalajara, with temperatures on the pitch reported by Banks himself to be 102 degrees Fahrenheit (almost 39 degrees Celsius). The crowd was vocal in its support for Brazil from the outset. These England players had been through a lot together, but they knew this was one of the biggest tests they would ever face, up against a team that could dominate them physically as well as technically.

So England, all in white, would need to be at their sharpest to live with Brazil. It was ferociously competitive out there in the heat, a game of supremely high quality between the two best teams in the world. It felt as if it would take one moment of magic to break the deadlock. In fact, it took a moment of magic to keep the score at 0–0.

The move, 10 minutes into the game, started with Brazil goalkeeper Félix passing the ball to his right-back, Carlos Alberto. He drove forward into space and struck a perfect through-ball with the laces of his right boot.

The ball curled inside the England left-back, Terry Cooper, right into the path of Jairzinho. The winger's first touch was perfect, knocking the ball forward beyond Cooper, who considered fouling him but then thought better of it. Jairzinho lengthened his stride, pursuing the bobbling ball before it went out of play, stretching to meet it at the byline. Off balance and running at full pelt, Jairzinho still managed to deliver a cross to the far post that was just asking to be attacked.

At this point, Banks was still at his near post, wondering if Jairzinho would pull the ball back along the ground to Tostão. Brazil's No. 9 was free in space, with Moore having abandoned him to run toward Jairzinho seeking to cut out the cross.

But in the split second between Jairzinho's first touch and his second, Banks had time to glance over his right shoulder and assess what threats there were beyond Tostão. That is when he realized the gravity of the situation: Pelé racing into the box, nowhere near his marker, Mullery. Behind Pelé, Banks spotted the lurking figure of Rivellino, capable of anything if he could get the ball onto his left foot.

"Ladies and gentlemen," Banks told an audience at a Football Association event at Wembley almost 50 years on, "this is when I knew the true color of adrenaline."

As the ball flew over toward Pelé, Banks also moved to his right, making sure not to drop too far back and too close to his line. He knew that if he was too close to his line and had to dive backward, then the ball would already be in. All Banks could do as he reset himself on the far side of his goal was wait for the contact.

Pelé leapt higher than anyone could have expected, far higher than England right-back Tommy Wright. The forward's timing was perfect and he generated enough power to head the ball hard back down into the ground to Banks's right. As Pelé landed back on earth, the England players heard him shouting: "Gol!"

What Banks did next was more than just throw himself to his right.

The genius of this save was mental as much as physical. If Banks had merely dived down to his right, the ball would have bounced up over him and into the net. So he had to calculate, almost as he moved, how high the ball would rear from the rock-hard ground that had been baking in the sun all day.

He dived slightly backward, taking advantage of the room he had given himself by staying in front of his line. As Banks stuck out his hands, they met the ball just inside the right-hand post and, just as Banks predicted, used the momentum of the bouncing ball to propel it high up away from the goal and out for a corner kick.

It took a while for everyone to process what had happened.

Moore held his hands up in shock at the fact England had not conceded, before joking with Banks that he should have considered catching the ball instead. Pelé, who had already extended his arms in celebration, had to withdraw them sheepishly. Tostão put his head in his hands in shock. Mullery gave Banks a pat on the head. Then Brazil took the corner and the game continued.

Eventually, Jairzinho managed to beat Banks and Brazil won 1–0.

The fascinating question all these years on is whether people understood in 1970 that they had just witnessed one of the greatest moments in football history.

The newspaper reports from the time showed that people recognized how good it was. Geoffrey Green in the London *Times* wrote that it was "one of the world-class saves of [Banks's] life." Albert Barham in *The Guardian* referred to it as "acrobatics by Banks," but left it at that. It was Ralph L. Finn, who came back from Mexico and swiftly wrote a book about it, who seemed to grasp where things might be heading. He described the save in his book *World Cup, 1970* as "one of the most remarkable feats of goalkeeping ever" and, astutely, "a save that will be talked about for many years."

But when England were knocked out one week later, it was not Banks's brilliance that everyone was talking about. It was his stomach.

Banks took ill just before England's quarterfinal against West Germany with a stomach bug that left him too weak to play. He was replaced by Chelsea's Peter Bonetti. England were 2–0 up with a little over 20 minutes left but contrived to lose 3–2. If Banks had stayed fit, England would likely have been into the semifinals to face Italy.

When England flew back, the main questions were over the international futures of Charlton, who never played for England again, and Ramsey, who managed the team for another four years. When England landed, Banks was presented with a silver disc at the airport. Not because of his save, but because England's World Cup song, "Back Home," had already sold 250,000 copies.

Over the years, the circumstances of Banks's illness and England's elimination faded out of the popular memory. It was just a minor detail, a small, unfortunate accident that ultimately told us nothing. But the save lived on. Only two years after the World Cup, Green published a book, *Great Moments in Sport: Soccer*, which referred to the growing legacy of that one moment: "Shown a score of times again on television since then, it remains one of the 1970 World Cup high-water marks."

Even now, that save remains one of the high-water marks not just of that World Cup, but of all modern professional football. Only the famous Carlos Alberto goal for Brazil in the final against Italy can compete as a popular memory from that tournament. Banks played his last game for England in 1972 and his last in club football in 1978, but as that save grew and grew in the public mind, he found himself talking about it more and more.

Take a look on YouTube and you will find countless clips of Banks talking about his pride in that save, always with the same generosity and enthusiasm. There is a video with FIFA, one at an FA event at Wembley, and one at a Football Writers' Association dinner that was given in honor of Pelé in London in 2018. Banks spoke with gratitude and pride about the bond that save created between the two and how when Pelé would come to the United Kingdom, he was always asked about the one goal he did not score rather than the thousand he did.

Banks never tired of talking about it. "He didn't mind talking about it again and again," says director Martin Pickering, who made a short film with Banks about the save in 2010. "He said it was great that it sticks in people's minds and every time people ask about it, it brings the memory back to me."

Some might argue that Banks's career was so great that it would be wrong to reduce it to one single moment. He won the World Cup four years before Mexico and yet almost no one could name a save he made in that tournament. And if Banks had not saved Pelé's header in Guadalajara, he would have been just as great; still a World Cup winner, still an OBE, just without that one signature moment. Just in the same way Johan Cruyff would have been equally great if he had never completed a Cruyff Turn.

But like the Cruyff Turn, the power of the Banks save is in encapsulating one brilliant career within one perfect moment.

All the things that defined Banks—the awareness, athleticism, and speed—were there in that one moment. It summed up not just what made Banks great, but what makes goalkeeping great and what makes football great. What more can you ask from one moment than that?

Player name: Gordon Banks
Born: December 30, 1937
Died: February 12, 2019 (aged 81)
Position: Goalkeeper
Debut: 1958
Main teams: Chesterfield (1958–59), Leicester City (1959–67), Stoke City (1967–1973), Fort Lauderdale Strikers (1977–78); England (1963–72)
Career highlights: Won the World Cup with England in 1966 and the League Cup with Leicester in 1972. He was voted FIFA's Goalkeeper of the Year six years running from 1966.

77.

Roberto Carlos

Roberto Carlos was a violent striker of the ball with perhaps the most accurate instep we have ever seen.

The Brazilian free-kick specialist who even built bridges with Argentina

By Felipe Cárdenas

Roberto Carlos's free kicks have come to define the Brazilian great. A three-time winner of the Champions League with Real Madrid and a member of Brazil's 2002 World Cup–winning side, he is a beloved star adored by football lovers around the world.

Considered one of the best full-backs ever, Roberto Carlos was a creative force on the left flank for Brazilian powerhouse Palmeiras, Spanish giants Real Madrid, and Brazil's five-time World Cup champion national team during one of the most joyous times in their recent history. He was also a peacemaker who viewed the opposition as peers rather than foes.

"I don't have enemies in football," he told reporters in 2022 before a celebrity match in Florida.

While representing Brazil, Roberto Carlos played in several heated matches against archenemy Argentina. Brazil versus Argentina is among the most contentious rivalries in sport. There is no love lost when the countries meet on a football pitch, but Roberto Carlos viewed that reality differently. In a land that produced Pelé and where football is tribal, the left-back bucked all trends when he revealed the identity of his football hero.

"It may seem odd because I'm Brazilian, but my biggest idol has always been [Diego] Maradona, the greatest ever," he told *La Gazzetta dello Sport*'s weekly periodical, *Sports Week*, in 2003. "Yes, it's true. In Brazil Pelé, The King, is the idol of Brazilians, but I saw Maradona play and I was always impressed. He's a true phenomenon."

It borders on sacrilege for a Brazilian to say such a thing, but Roberto Carlos was intentional with his admission. Two years later, in Buenos Aires, Brazil and Argentina met for a crucial World Cup qualifier. By then, Maradona and Roberto Carlos had become close friends.

Before the match, Maradona requested Roberto Carlos's match-worn jersey and asked his friend to help him secure the game jerseys of Ronaldinho, Kaká, and Brazil's captain, Cafu.

Argentina stormed to a 3–0 first-half lead, eventually defeating the defending World Cup champions 3–1, with Roberto Carlos scoring Brazil's solitary goal that day—a vintage free kick from distance that pierced the Argentine net with venomous power.

The victory, however, sealed Argentina's passage to the 2006 World Cup in Germany. After the match, Maradona walked into the visitors' dressing room. An Argentine reporter for ESPN who accompanied Maradona that day was surprised to see the four jerseys laid out waiting for him, even after such a humbling defeat.

"It wasn't just for Diego," Roberto Carlos said in 2022. "It was to end or try to end so much conflict between Brazil and Argentina. [To Brazilians] Diego was one of us. Nationality doesn't matter. We wanted to show the world that rivalries exist inside a dressing room and on the pitch, but, when the match is over, everything goes back to normal. Diego was a great friend.

"Yes, I had idols like Júnior and Branco and other great full-backs, but the player who I believe is the best ever? For me, that's Diego."

Roberto Carlos was a violent striker of the ball with perhaps the most accurate instep we have ever seen. Sure, the Netherlands' defender Ronald Koeman could hammer a laces-first strike past a wall, but Roberto Carlos's free kicks from distance are the stuff of legend. His physics-defying set piece against France in the opening fixture of the four-team Le Tournoi in 1997 cemented him in football lore.

Quite casually, he told *Omnisport* in 2014 that he simply chose a corner of the goal that was not defended by France goalkeeper Fabien Barthez and struck the ball with as much force as he could summon.

"A lot of people ask me how I was able to score that famous goal against France in 1997, but there's no secret," he said. "I didn't have any doubts. I looked where I needed to shoot and I didn't change my mind."

The distance to Barthez's goal was roughly 40 yards. Everyone inside Lyon's Stade de Gerland that day knew what was coming. Roberto Carlos was a specialist, whose mastery of a dead-ball situation first emerged when he was an up-and-coming full-back at Palmeiras, well before he became an international star.

The crowd grew quiet in anticipation as he backpedaled toward the center circle. After a 20-yard run-up, he struck the ball with so much power that the thud from the strike reverberated around the stadium.

"I think God helped me, too," he added. "The wind pushed the ball. I had time to see how it was unfolding. That day everything happened the way I wanted it to."

The free kick against France lives on online. Nearly 30 years later, it's still so impressive. Everything had to be perfect: how he angled his left foot toward the ball, the power needed to manipulate the ball's spin, and, most importantly, his follow-through and body positioning. Clearly, Roberto Carlos had done this before, as he revealed in 2022.

"I trained a lot," he said. "Think about all of those goals I scored. Every day, I practiced those free kicks for 30 or 40 minutes, focusing on the goal and how I was going to score. I was never scared of getting things wrong. Many times my play came out well, many times it didn't. But I always played without fear."

This was a player also defined by his competitive mentality and a mean streak that he would channel toward the hundreds of leather-stitched balls that he encountered throughout his storied 21-year professional career. Even today, one could debate whether he was a full-back, a winger, or, perhaps more appropriately, a wing-back with dual responsibilities.

And even though fellow Brazilian Carlos Alberto first revolutionized the full-back position, Roberto Carlos perfected it. In retrospect, his ability to shut down his flank with aggressive defending and attack with purpose would perfectly suit today's tactical trend.

He was a once-in-a-generation player who shunned football's traditions to become a timeless talent. The full-back position was hardly sexy. It was never cool until Roberto Carlos showed the world that skill and flair could be part of a defender's repertoire. He stood alongside Brazilian greats Romário, Ronaldo Nazário, Rivaldo, and Ronaldinho to epitomize the national team's adapted concept of *Jogo Bonito* (the Beautiful Game), the samba-inspired style of play that so enamored the football world.

"I attacked well and defended even better," he told *The Athletic*. "People always focus on my offensive techniques, but if they looked closely, they would see that my defensive techniques are even better still. I could attack with the same speed as I could defend."

In the 1990s, Italy's Serie A was crammed with *galácticos*. The best

South America could offer flooded the league, creating a pathway to Europe for many of today's most cherished players. To learn the art of defending was one of Serie A's main selling points and Roberto Carlos lapped up the chance to learn from *catenaccio*, Italy's famed defensive tactical system.

He moved from Palmeiras to Inter Milan in 1995, but was never on the same page as Inter manager Roy Hodgson. The Englishman insisted on playing the Brazilian higher up the pitch as a winger. He scored one goal for Inter on his debut in 1995. Unsurprisingly, it was a free kick from distance.

"My problem at Inter was Hodgson—Roy Hodgson," Roberto Carlos told *FourFourTwo* magazine in 2005. "He wanted me to play as a forward when I'm a defender—I prefer to have space ahead of me to run into rather than be a winger already up there. For me, it's better to have 80 meters to play in than 20 meters.

"I didn't like the system or where Hodgson wanted me to play in it. I had to leave because I didn't want to jeopardize my chances with the national team. If I couldn't play the way I do, I wouldn't be able to play for Brazil."

Real Madrid's Italian manager, Fabio Capello, jumped at the chance to sign the Brazilian. He understood that a talent like Roberto Carlos could change the direction of a team, even at a superclub like Real Madrid. The left-back became a mainstay of the starting XI during his 11-year stint in the Spanish capital, starring for some of Real's greatest teams.

"I moved to Real Madrid because I didn't like being a forward player and that was it," Roberto Carlos told *The Athletic*. It appears, though, that any frustration with Hodgson has mellowed. He holds no grudges.

"He was a coach that lived football. An excellent coach. And he wasn't guilty of anything. Hodgson taught me to put pressure on myself more, to score goals. A lot of the press coverage claimed that I was constantly arguing with him, but we weren't having any arguments at all.

"I don't speak much about Roy Hodgson because I don't believe in answering things that aren't true, but he was extremely important in my career."

Roberto Carlos won 25 senior-level trophies with Palmeiras, Real Madrid, Turkish club Fenerbahçe, and his national side. In 2002, he finished runner-up to Brazil teammate Ronaldo for the Ballon d'Or award.

He would later win back-to-back UEFA Defender of the Year awards in 2002 and 2003, with Brazil winning their record fifth World Cup in 2002. He earned 125 caps for Brazil and played 120 Champions League matches across his glittering career.

He was also a member of Brazil's 1996 Olympic squad, a star-studded team that featured 1994 World Cup hero Bebeto, Rivaldo, a 19-year-old Ronaldo, and goalkeeper Dida. That side won the bronze medal following a 5–0 win over Portugal in the third-place match.

"But in Brazil, finishing second or third is like finishing last," he told *Kaiser Futbol* in 2021. "Brazil is accustomed to winning. Brazil always has to win."

"Everything I dreamed of—winning all those trophies, being a team captain, winning all those titles—it all came true," he said during his interview with *The Athletic*. "I just enjoyed playing, nothing more than that. I had a wonderful career."

Like many former professionals, he has since tried his hand in football management. There were coaching stints in Russia and Turkey, which were largely forgettable, certainly never rising to the achievements he fulfilled as a player.

But what a player he was.

He certainly wasn't flawless, but the Brazilian combined speed and strength with audacious skill and elite positional awareness to transform and modernize a position that had become one-dimensional. He was also well-known for his competitive spirit and hardened mentality. Roberto Carlos had an illustrious career that included the honor of wearing the captain's armband for both Real Madrid and Brazil.

He told UEFA in 2022 that the keys to his success and to the countless moments of brilliance he shared with the world were rather simple.

"To be a great footballer, you have to be strong mentally," he said. "Your head must be strong and both your professional and personal life must be extremely positive in every aspect. Be an example. Be a leader.

"Those are my essential pieces of advice."

Player name: Roberto Carlos da Silva Rocha
Born: April 10, 1973
Position: Left-back
Debut: 1991
Main teams: União São João (1991–93), Palmeiras (1993–95), Inter Milan (1995–96), Real Madrid (1996–2007), Fenerbahçe (2007–09), Corinthians (2010–11), Anzhi Makhachkala (2011–12); Brazil (1992–2006)
Career highlights: Won the World Cup in 2002 and the Copa América in 1997 and 1999. He was a Champions League winner three times with Real Madrid and won La Liga four times. Scored world-famous "banana" free kick for Brazil at Le Tournoi in 1997.

76.

Gabriel Batistuta

The Batistuta brand was about swagger and goals.

The striker who took particular delight in clobbering a football

By Felipe Cárdenas

Gabriel Omar Batistuta was feared.

He had the pace to outsprint defenders and a ruthless appetite for scoring that garnered him the nickname *Batigol*. In many respects, Batistuta was the perfect striker. The ideal profile. The ideal build. He was violence in the form of a center-forward. His goals were often emphatic finishes and ferocious strikes that epitomized his relentless nature.

In South America, it is a sign of respect when a player is referred to by his first, middle, and last names. It symbolizes his journey from youth football to international stardom. Batistuta was a prized young talent who grew up under the critical eyes of the Argentine public. A player who excelled for the national team and then exported his talents to Italy, where his reputation continued to soar. But his journey toward iconic status was initially challenging.

He was first mentored by Marcelo Bielsa at Newell's Old Boys in 1988. Having initially struggled to adjust to life away from home, Batistuta thrived under the coach and Newell's appeared to be the ideal springboard for the teenage striker. When his career was long over, having taken in stints at seven clubs on three continents, Batistuta still credited Bielsa—who later coached him at international level—as his most influential manager.

Yet while Newell's had given Batistuta that initial platform upon which to make his mark, it was River Plate that set upon speeding up his development. The Argentine giants, alerted to his talents, lured the youngster to Buenos Aires. At first glance, they offered the perfect stage. As it transpired, his stint there would be his first disappointment as a professional.

The newspapers at the time suggested the River Plate manager and former Argentina international Daniel Passarella—the captain of the side that lifted the 1978 World Cup—discarded Batistuta too readily and never came close to maximizing his potential. "The times I did play, Passarella would use me for 10 minutes because other players were missing," Batistuta told reporters in 1990 after he had terminated his contract with River. "It was like I was there to make up the numbers. I'm not going to do that at 21 years of age."

His inability to make an impact was surprising given the incredible promise Batistuta had shown back in Rosario at Newell's. That team had been veteran-led and won the title a year before the teenager's arrival. He was unnerved by that spotlight and quickly showcased his ability to score important goals in Argentina's top division, a skill that prompted River's interest. Indeed, before Passarella was appointed head coach, Batistuta threatened to flourish in River's famous red-sashed kit.

But it all petered out. A clash of stubborn personalities was blamed for the fallout. The player retreated, his progress checked. Even so, Passarella hoped Batistuta would return to Newell's rather than land at a rival club. He was conscious there was a talent there.

Instead, it was Boca Juniors, River's eternal nemeses, who swooped in and signed the young striker, pairing him with Uruguayan manager Óscar Tabárez, *El Maestro*, a fatherlike figure who harnessed the player's energetic style of play in a way Passarella had not been able to. Batistuta excelled at La Bombonera, tapping into the heart and passion that is at the core of the club. His presence there was seismic. The goals poured in. The emotion he displayed every time he scored endeared him further to Boca's ultras. His movie-star smile captivated the country.

This all coincided with Batistuta's introduction to the Argentina national team. In 1991, just five years removed from winning the World Cup in Mexico, the *Albiceleste* won the Copa América in Chile. Batistuta was the tournament's top scorer and a force of nature throughout the competition.

He would cement himself as Argentina's first-choice No. 9 through the 1990s and eventually become the country's all-time leading goalscorer. That record was broken in 2016 by Lionel Messi, who went on to surpass Batistuta as Argentina's top goalscorer in World Cup history, too, in 2022. The deposed forward told Argentina outlet *Clarín* shortly after that he wasn't "hurt" by being overtaken by Messi. There was no disgrace in being eclipsed by him.

"I enjoyed it while I had it," Batistuta said. "Leo deserves this. If there's one person who has to be up there, it's him. Messi is not an alien, he is a human being who plays better football than anyone else. When that person exceeds you, you can't suffer. He just gives you pleasure."

Batistuta still has his own unique legacy. It is not one replete with Ballon d'Or trophies or millions of social media followers. His brand was about swagger and goals. In his era, a center-forward had one job: to score goals. They were not charged with dropping into midfield to rack up touches. There were no false nines. The directive was to shoot and score and, in Batistuta's case, destroy the ball if you can along the way.

From Boca, he moved to Italy to join upstarts Fiorentina, and it was in Serie A where Batistuta's legend grew. Fiorentina's Nintendo-sponsored purple-and-white kits became synonymous with the Argentinian's heavy-metal-band hair and perfectly shaped goatee. He would later regularly refer to his hair as his registered trademark.

Some athletes are said to run like a gazelle, but Batistuta ran like a Hollywood action star. He was unmissable on matchday. There were 183 goals in Serie A with Fiorentina and, later, Roma and Inter Milan; textbook headers, penalties that rattled the net and direct free kicks were among his specialties. The occasional deft chip over a goalkeeper was also part of his repertoire.

Two goals scored for Fiorentina best described his prowess as a player.

In a match against AC Milan in San Siro in 1998, Fiorentina were awarded an indirect free kick inside the opponents' six-yard box. Seven Milan players and goalkeeper Jens Lehmann stood on their own line, clogging up the goalmouth, as Batistuta and teammate Rui Costa deliberated by the ball.

"I remember Rui Costa asked me, 'How do we shoot this?' 'Let me aim for their heads,'" Batistuta recalled on social media in 2023. "I knew that [Milan's players] were afraid. If I aimed at their heads, no one would try to get in the way of the ball."

So Rui Costa tapped the ball to Batistuta, whose thunderbolt of a shot ripped through the clutch of bodies and almost punctured Lehmann's net. "I kicked it . . . hard. Very hard," Batistuta added.

That goal completed his hat trick; a 3–1 win for Fiorentina and a dominant performance for their star man. It was vintage Batistuta.

That Fiorentina side, led by the esteemed Italian manager Giovanni Trapattoni, also made inroads in Europe. They advanced to the second group stage of the 1999–2000 Champions League—a major feat for the modest club from Florence—and the highlight of that run was a 1–0 win over Arsenal at their temporary home at Wembley Stadium in October 1999.

Batistuta scored the only goal in the 75th minute that night, a crushing blow that jettisoned much-fancied Arsenal from the competition.

In a video he posted on his social media platforms in 2022, Batistuta looked back at the goal, and the win, that sent the Premier League club packing. "We had to win and the odds were not good," he admitted.

The hosts swarmed all over Fiorentina. They hit the post, missed gilt-edged chances, and were denied consistently by the massive frame and reflex saves of goalkeeper Francesco Toldo. Yet the wave of attacks kept coming, Arsenal pinning the visitors back, and there was no respite in sight. "Until this ball came out to [Jörg] Heinrich just in our half," said Batistuta. "He brought the ball forward and I already understood the situation. I was on the right. Rui Costa was to [Heinrich's] left and I thought: 'Please give it to me. I'm going to smash the goal.'"

Batistuta, unmarked on the touchline, waved his hands above his head to attract Heinrich's attention, knowing that if he received the pass, he had an open run toward goal. The German probably held the ball slightly longer than was necessary but did eventually pick out his teammate. Now on the edge of the box, the Argentinian collected the ball with his right foot and quickly nudged it forward with his left. That touch did for the Arsenal left-back, Nigel Winterburn, who had closed in to block but quickly discovered he had been bypassed.

The angle was horribly narrow. Batistuta was beyond the level of the six-yard box and still out wide when he struck his shot. There seemed little prospect of him conjuring an effort that would beat David Seaman, who had advanced and was in position to make a save and block anything fired toward his near post. Surely a pass across the face of goal, where Rui Costa lurked in anticipation of a cross, was the safer option.

But Seaman should have known what was coming. The probability Batistuta would pass from inside the penalty area was extremely slight. He had one objective in mind.

"I'm going to smash the goal."

The shot he summoned with his third touch defied belief. It was leathered over Seaman, whose knees were only marginally bent, and careered into the far top corner. Arsenal's players could not comprehend what they had just witnessed. Fiorentina had shocked Arsenal at Wembley courtesy of a trademark bludgeoned goal from their talismanic striker.

Batistuta's taste for punishing the ball invariably bullied the opposition into submission. There is, however, another side to the Argentine great, one that is rooted in three core pillars that guided him throughout his spectacular career.

Onstage at a TED Conference in 2019, Batistuta detailed how humility, discipline, and having a clear objective defined his rise as an elite player. "That mentality allowed me to keep my ego where it belonged," he said.

To illustrate his point, he revisited his reunion with Passarella at the national-team level ahead of the 1998 World Cup in France.

Passarella, who had won the trophy twice in his playing days (he was an unused squad member in 1986), had one rule as a manager. Long hair was not allowed. "A player with long hair loses focus during the match," Passarella told reporters ahead of the tournament. Argentina's stalwarts Claudio Caniggia and Fernando Redondo refused to comply and were duly left out of the World Cup squad.

It sounds trivial but, back then, Batistuta's flowing shoulder-length hair contributed to his aura. It was part of his makeup. "I was an established player. I thought it was a joke. I was surprised," Batistuta told his audience 21 years later. "But my humility allowed me to control my ego and I decided to cut my hair because my objective was to make history with the Argentina national team."

The striker, shorn of his locks, scored five times at the tournament, though Argentina were knocked out in the quarterfinals by a late Dennis Bergkamp winner in Marseille.

There is also a shyness about Batistuta. The on-field bravado may have suggested otherwise, but he is actually soft-spoken and reserved. The fury and intensity he displayed on matchday is detached from his personality away from the game.

"Even at 50, I'm surprised when I come across people on the street who can't believe that these are my hands . . . who can't believe that this is me in the flesh," he said in 2019. "As if the person they're talking to isn't really me. That's the myth of success. It makes you appear to be something strange. Like you're not human."

In 2021, he confessed to Fox Argentina that he never enjoyed himself on the pitch. He felt indebted to the fans who paid to watch him play. Every pass had to be perfect. Every shot precise. It was his job, and the effort he gave was open to criticism or adulation.

"Maybe it was because of that excess of responsibility," Batistuta said. "But that's what also drove my success. I never relaxed. It was a beautiful job—but it was a job."

Batistuta is an icon. He was feared and respected by his opponents and idolized by his fans. That was deserved praise for one of the best center-forwards of all time, someone who in Argentina was known to millions simply as *Bati*.

Player name: Gabriel Batistuta

Born: February 1, 1969

Position: Striker

Debut: 1988

Main teams: Newell's Old Boys (1988–89), River Plate (1989–90), Boca Juniors (1990–91), Fiorentina (1991–2000), Roma (2000–2003), Inter Milan (loan, 2003), Al Arabi (2003–04); Argentina (1991–2002)

Career highlights: He scored 10 goals at World Cups and is the only man to score a hat trick at two different editions of the tournament, doing so in 1994 and 1998. Won Copa América twice, scoring a double in the final in 1993. Won the Italian top flight in 2000–2001 with Roma.

75.

Günter Netzer

Netzer made 358 appearances for Borussia Mönchengladbach, scoring 137 goals.

From Lovers' Lane to Bökelberg—how Mönchengladbach still celebrates its favorite son

By Richard Sutcliffe

Reminders of what Günter Netzer means to Mönchengladbach are everywhere.

There's the giant 30-foot mural staring out across the city's bustling Alter Markt from the front of BrauHaus MaNaMaNa, a pub popular with Borussia fans on a matchday. With trademark flowing locks, Netzer is shown holding aloft the DFB-Pokal, won on his final appearance before moving to Real Madrid.

Just a raking midfield pass away can be found the recently restored building that once housed Lovers' Lane, the early-1970s discotheque owned by Netzer that, for a couple of years, turned this previously sleepy corner of northwest Germany into one of the hippest places around.

Happily, the 2021 refurbishment by the local authority included a return of the old club sign that, along with Netzer's Ferrari parked outside, let a celebrity clientele ranging from Franz Beckenbauer to the latest pop singing sensation know they had arrived.

These modern-day homages to Mönchengladbach's favorite son continue a mile or so away in the Eicken district, Borussia's birthplace and, until 2004, their home at the atmospheric Bökelberg.

First, there is a bronze statue depicting Netzer in action alongside teammates Herbert Wimmer and Berti Vogts. Then, farther down the same pedestrianized street, a giant ornamental stone football is decorated with a list of the trophies that turned this onetime provincial club into a genuine powerhouse of German football, including the back-to-back Bundesliga titles of 1969–70 and 1970–71 that owed everything to Netzer's guile and creativity.

Those wanting to visit where football history was made can also take a short stroll to the club's former home, Bökelberg's natural bowl having been preserved on three sides along with small sections of terracing and even crush barriers. Stand here on a winter's afternoon and it is still possible to picture Netzer, Jupp Heynckes, et al. weaving their magic where an upmarket housing estate now sits.

Borussia Park, the club's 55,000-capacity stadium these past two decades on the southern fringes of the city, may have been built long after the heyday of a team dubbed *Die Fohlen* (The Foals) due to their youth and energetic spirit, but Netzer is everywhere here, too, with his giant image adorning the northwest entrance, plus dozens of tributes in the club museum.

Such reverence, more than half a century after he last kicked a football competitively in the Rhineland, feels justified. He was a one-off, both in ability and character, with even Netzer's shoulder-length hair—the first German footballer to adopt such a style—marking him out as someone who refused to conform.

He also loved fast cars, but it was as the driving force of the national football team that Netzer's famously large boots—he wore a size 13 (a European 47, UK 12) despite being just 5'10" tall—would make their biggest mark.

Down the years, German football has been renowned for its methodical efficiency. This was particularly the case in the 1980s, when a wall still divided the country into east and west, and in the 1990s when opposing international teams would be regularly ground into submission by what felt like a relentless, trophy-mining machine.

Things did improve with the emergence of Mesut Özil, Toni Kroos, and Manuel Neuer as Germany landed a fourth World Cup in 2014. But really, there is still nothing to compare to the early-1970s side that danced to the beat of Netzer's brilliance.

Ramba-Zamba-Fußall is how tabloid newspaper *Bild* described West Germany's footballing philosophy back then. There's no literal translation into English. "Fairground Football" is perhaps the best attempt at capturing the fun element of their approach.

Even this description, though, does not quite do justice to the free-flowing nature of the 1972 European Championship winners. That team remains one of a kind in Germany; just as Netzer does.

His 75th birthday in 2019 was marked by a special exhibition at Borussia's club museum. It covered everything from his humble beginnings in the family home on Gasthausstraße—where his mother, Barbara, ran a grocery shop on the ground floor and his father, Christian, was a flower seed salesman—to those glory days as the heartbeat of a successful team.

There was even a re-creation of Lovers' Lane, which he opened with girlfriend Hannelore Girrulat in a former hairdresser's salon just around the corner from where he had spent those formative years as a child.

"The door is pitch black, just like the entire facade at Waldhausener Straße, 55, and initially locked," read the accompanying information panel. "There are no windows. And if you want to get in, you have to ring the bell and let the doorman examine you through a viewing slit."

Lovers' Lane proved a roaring success after opening in 1971, drawing footballers from far and wide along with celebrities such as actress Elke Sommer and singer Udo Jürgens. No one was surprised that the nightclub took off, given that Netzer's sharp business acumen had already been established long before then.

Borussia's maiden season in the Bundesliga (1965–66) under head coach Hennes Weisweiler saw the star midfielder take on the editor's role of the newly launched matchday program, *Fohlen Echo.*

Netzer was just 21 at the time, having scored the decisive promotion-clinching goal in the final playoff round against Wormatia Worms just a few months previously. He used the wage for the program to supplement what were then still modest football earnings. He would later open a restaurant called La Lacque and run a taxi business along with Lovers' Lane.

As much as Netzer did for the city's nightlife, however, it is his football that left the biggest legacy.

He made 358 appearances for Borussia after joining as a teenager from FC Mönchengladbach, scoring 137 goals. He was named German footballer of the year in 1972 and 1973, the second of those awards capping a final season in Germany before moving to Real Madrid for 1.6 million deutsche mark. His farewell game has gone down in Borussia folklore.

Weisweiler, an authoritarian coach who had often clashed with the team's free-spirited playmaker, dropped Netzer to the bench after news of his impending transfer had broken days before the cup final against Cologne.

Netzer, who had to be talked out of going home by Vogts before the game, could only watch from the sidelines as the two teams reached the end of 90 minutes level at 1–1. He then glimpsed his chance during the break before extra time, sidling up to a clearly exhausted Christian Kulik and asking if the youngster could continue.

The next moment, Netzer was bringing himself on without consulting the head coach.

Just three minutes later, the reward for such incredible chutzpah came when the substitute exchanged passes with Rainer Bonhof before rifling in what proved to be the winner. With that, he was off to the Bernabéu in a transfer that prompted regional daily newspaper *Rheinische Post* to declare: "The great Borussia era is over."

He won two La Liga titles with Real, pipping Johan Cruyff's Barcelona in the process, but his contract was not renewed after three years and he moved to Switzerland for one final season at Grasshopper Zürich.

Even after retiring as a player, the trophies kept coming as Hamburg's general manager. Netzer led the club into a golden age that yielded three Bundesligas and, having been beaten by Nottingham Forest in the final three years earlier, the 1983 European Cup.

Wembley Stadium, Saturday, April 29, 1972.

The European Championship, then a very modest affair compared to today's 24-team tournament, had reached the two-legged quarterfinal stage. Only once the identity of the last four was known would the country staging the semifinals and final be named.

Belgium eventually got the nod as hosts, but it was West Germany who were destined to lift the trophy after producing what is still regarded as one of their greatest displays to beat England 3–1 at Wembley in the first leg of an epic quarterfinal.

"You didn't get any bigger games than England–West Germany back then," recalls Rodney Marsh, who played in both legs of the 1972 quarterfinal for England, the second game of which finished goalless in Berlin. "Both teams had so many world-class players.

"The funny thing considering how that game went at Wembley is that Netzer wasn't one of them. Not when you looked at the lineups and there's Franz Beckenbauer, Bobby Moore, and so on. Great, great footballers.

"On the night, though, Netzer dominated the game with those

great big feet of his, displaying this tremendous balance and passing the ball so well."

Netzer was, indeed, the star of the show on a damp London evening as he and Beckenbauer constantly swapped positions in what was effectively a 3-3-3-1 setup.

Whether dropping deep to cover his captain's surging runs forward or spraying the ball around from midfield, Netzer, with his blond, flowing hair, made a sodden Wembley pitch his own. Gerd Müller was the chief beneficiary, the forward provided with such stellar service he was able to cause the home defense all manner of problems.

Then there was Netzer's ability to accelerate past an opponent, with one explosive first-half gallop leaving Colin Bell, Francis Lee, Martin Peters, and even the great Moore horribly flat-footed.

It helped that Sir Alf Ramsey chose not to tightly mark the midfielder. Yet, with Uli Hoeneß's early strike canceled out by Lee, it would be Netzer's 84th-minute penalty that restored the visitors' advantage and was a fitting reward for his masterful endeavors. Müller rounded off the scoring just before the end to seal a first German victory against England on English soil.

Judging by the crude challenges England meted out in an attempt to stop Netzer during the goalless return leg in Berlin two weeks later, Ramsey had belatedly realized his error. Even then, though, the target of this damage-limitation strategy still came close to breaking the deadlock when his 40-yard free kick flew just inches over Gordon Banks's crossbar.

"What was different about Netzer is he had the haircut that a lot of British players had at the time," adds Marsh. "We'd been influenced by the Beatles and the Rolling Stones, so a lot of footballers had long hair. But here was this German lad with the same; probably the first one over there. He was a very confident lad and that particular game at Wembley rocketed him to the peak.

"West Germany had always been a very functional team. Only when Netzer came along did everyone start asking, 'What the fuck's he doing?' He was, basically, trying the things you expected to see from other world-class players from, say, Brazil.

"I'd suggest he only really had that one great game for West Germany. In Berlin, Alf Ramsey brought in Peter Storey to man-mark him and he hardly got a kick. But he was sensational at Wembley and became a world superstar on the back of it."

Netzer did go on to create both goals for Müller in the semifinal triumph over hosts Belgium with delightfully floated passes. He then had a role in all three goals as the Soviet Union were well beaten in the final.

Having previously labeled West Germany's performance at Wembley as "football from the year 2000," respected French newspaper *L'Équipe* named Netzer the best player of the tournament.

That 1972 success proved to be the high point of his international career. By the time the next World Cup came around on home soil two years later, Cologne's Wolfgang Overath had replaced him as the playmaker. He did pick up a winners' medal as West Germany won back-to-back tournaments, but he barely figured as the team adopted a more functional style, setting the tone for much of what would follow over the next two decades.

In a way, this only added to the legend surrounding Netzer, whose tendency to move in different social circles than the average footballers of that era was perhaps best illustrated by how he once shared a table with Dean Martin, Sammy Davis Jr., and Neil Diamond at Tina Sinatra's wedding in Las Vegas.

Frank Sinatra, the father of the bride, even helped score him tickets to watch Elvis before flying back to Madrid, where a blissfully unaware Real held his passport. Netzer being able to secure a temporary document from the German embassy to make the unsanctioned trip to Sin City during the La Liga season again points toward someone who had friends in high places. His determination to enjoy life can only be admired.

Put that together with the exquisite beauty that Netzer brought to the football pitch and it's no wonder his home city still honors one of its own with such reverence.

Player name: Günter Netzer

Born: September 14, 1944

Position: Attacking midfielder

Debut: 1963

Main teams: Borussia Mönchengladbach (1963–73), Real Madrid (1973–76), Grasshopper Zürich (1976–77); West Germany (1965–75)

Career highlights: Inspired West Germany to win Euro 1972 and was a member of their squad as they won the World Cup in 1974. Won La Liga and the German title twice each, with Borussia becoming the first side to successfully defend the title in the Bundesliga era.

74.

Michael Laudrup

Laudrup's nomadic career took him to Italy, Spain, the Netherlands, and Japan.

"If I didn't have a good game, Cruyff would kill me"

By Greg O'Keeffe

It should not come as a surprise that the sublime piece of footballing artistry that Michael Laudrup pioneered was born of pragmatism, not showboating.

Watching the Dane in his heyday, it looked so simple. He never gave a name for what later became known as *La Croqueta*, after Spain's Andrés Iniesta adopted it in the age of social media and YouTube skill clips. But for Laudrup, the move—quickly switching the ball from one foot to another to evade an opponent before surging away—was just something he had done since childhood kickabouts with his younger brother, Brian.

Most importantly, it worked. So a player considered one of the greatest attacking midfielders of his generation, who won trophies at Juventus, Barcelona, and Real Madrid, prioritized the functional. He may have glided across the pitch like an artist, but his mind was fixed upon the end product. If he entertained along the way, then great.

The difference between the midfielder and most other players was that his tool kit of "functional" skills at his disposal seemed limitless. "I was using that bit of skill because it was effective," he explains, "especially when you don't have much space but you have the ball on one foot and need to move it on and then run.

"We did it for years then, in the new era, players like Iniesta and Ronaldinho were doing it. It's about forcing defenders to commit themselves."

Another trick Laudrup popularized was to look away before making a pass; a split-second deception that bamboozled defenders. "I had never seen anyone do that before," he says. "It began in training at Barcelona when we played smaller five-versus-five games. Football is about doing the thing most people don't do. My teammates learned to know to be prepared for anything when I got the ball. They would laugh: 'Give us a little clue.'"

Laudrup stood out as special when he burst onto the scene at his local club, Brøndby IF, where he was named Denmark's player of the year aged just 18, before Europe's leading clubs began to covet him. In 1983 he agreed to join Juventus, only to be loaned immediately to Lazio because of rules restricting the number of foreign players who could feature in matchday squads to two. Juventus already had the acclaimed midfielders Michel Platini and Zbigniew Boniek on the books, so the teenager had to bide his time.

But the culture shock of being thrust into Italian football helped his already formidable talent evolve. "You are born with a talent, but you are not born with everything in that talent—at least, I wasn't," he says. "I always had that individual skill, one against one, the dribble and such things, since I was 10. But the vision took time. I got to Italy and although it was a very tough league, I was fast and had individual quality. I did not have great vision then, though."

Laudrup had two difficult seasons at relegation-fighting Lazio, but he also learned some eye-opening lessons. "I was protected in the Danish league, but Italy was totally different," he says. "Especially in the away games, so much was allowed. No cameras filming every moment. Really bad fouls. Sometimes a yellow card and sometimes no, just get up. That's one of the good things that has changed over the years—more protection for the offensive players.

"Then there are the pitches, of course. People sometimes ask me to imagine if I was playing now instead of then. They talk about the hundreds of millions in wages I could have earned. No, the one thing I am envious of is the pitches. I remember the surfaces in the 1970s when they looked like there was no grass on them and now you go in January and 95 percent of the pitches in England or Germany are like carpets. You can never miss a touch on those."

Laudrup's cultural education entailed some other lessons before he returned to Turin. "I remember one game at Lazio, we were playing against one of the bottom teams and we were winning at home. It was 3–0 with 20 minutes left and one of the central defenders on the other team said to me: 'Hey, Laudrup, you have won the game. Don't be smart.'

"I didn't understand, but he carried on: 'In six months, you'll visit us, so don't be smart.' He was saying there was no need to embarrass them and make it five or six. You would never hear that in Denmark, but that was the mentality in Italy. Don't take the piss. It was just cultural, you don't do that.

"I asked my teammates what was going on and they said the game was finished. Sure, if they give up a chance in front of goal then you score, but you don't go all out to score more. But that was then, with 90 percent Italians and two foreigners. I don't know if it'd be the same mentality now. A lot has changed."

In the summer of 1985, Laudrup replaced Boniek at Juventus and, alongside Platini, helped the team win the *Scudetto* in his first season. The learning went on. "I think Platini was the best player in Europe at the time," he recalls. "He was another with vision. So clever. It was great to play with him, but also just to watch him in training. That taught me about timing: when to play a short pass or play a bit more. He had a big impact on developing that part of my game."

Four years later came another huge move, this time to Spain where his childhood hero Johan Cruyff was building a Barcelona team to topple their rivals Real Madrid.

During his remarkable time at the Camp Nou, he helped Barcelona do just that. Cruyff's "Dream Team"—with Laudrup excelling alongside Ronald Koeman, Hristo Stoichkov, Pep Guardiola, Romário, and José Mari Bakero—claimed La Liga four times in a row and lifted the 1992 European Cup.

"That's when my 'vision' made a big step forward and I began to make the passes," he says. "If I knew a player, when I got the ball, even if I don't look at him, I know he would run and *he knew* I knew. I don't need to look up. It's automatic. It's a mix of skills and knowing your companion.

"I remember we were playing against Osasuna and I had the ball. There was no space, so I just made a pass over all of them to Romário and he put it over the goalkeeper. After the game, journalists asked me if we trained that. Why did I think to do that? For me, it was because there was no space on the ground, with four or five defenders, but there is always space over the top and I could make that pass. It just made sense and I knew he would run.

"Sometimes when we played, I was the false nine, another thing Cruyff invented all those years ago, and I would drop into the midfield to get the ball. The two central defenders weren't used to following me, so they'd look at their coach and he'd tell them to stay. I'd get in between the lines, receive the ball, and [his teammate] Txiki Begiristain would run to collect my pass.

"He'd either finish the move himself or give it to Bakero, who came from the second line. We scored so many goals like that. Defenses didn't know what to do."

• • •

Laudrup respects creativity on the field above everything else. "It has always been more difficult to create than defend and it always will be," he insists. "It is easier to stop an attack than *actually* attack.

"Until I was about 32, I was fast, so opponents never knew if I was going to pass or go myself. If you're a defender and you know someone is fantastic with the passing but can't go past you one-on-one, then you just get very close when they get the ball. But if they did that and I took them on, then they had a problem because I went past them, so somebody else needed to leave their marker and go to me.

"My teammates were always laughing at me because Cruyff would say: 'Okay, we take one on one and then we leave Michael alone, so just give the ball to Michael.' If you can be the one who does the 'thing,' then you don't have to work so much when the team doesn't have the ball.

"But if I didn't have a good game, Cruyff would kill me. I think today about how some of those managers acted or spoke and if they did that now, I don't know what would happen."

He later learned Cruyff's tough love was honed by his own experiences as a singular talent and the responsibilities that went with that status. "My first year in Barcelona was a little difficult because we were second and not winning and he was talking to me about being the best," he says. "Cruyff said: 'It's about winning. Look at me—I won the penalty from which we took the lead in the 1974 World Cup final, but then we lost and I was criticized for not being a world champion.'

"He was trying to tell me that you need to win, otherwise the best will always get criticism."

Although he won 104 caps for Denmark, Laudrup was not around to make that difference at his own national team's biggest moment. Denmark failed to qualify for the 1992 European Championship but were granted last-minute entry after Yugoslavia, a country in the grip of civil war, were barred from competing.

Laudrup had already withdrawn himself from selection for various reasons, chiefly citing a need to focus on leading Barcelona back to glory and a disagreement with Denmark manager Richard Møller Nielsen over what he perceived to be overly defensive tactics. The younger Laudrup, Brian, had initially also withdrawn but changed his mind and was back in the fold ahead of the tournament in Sweden. Michael did not.

Against all the odds, Denmark won—securing their only major trophy while their greatest player kicked his heels at home.

"Could I have said: 'I want to go now?' Yes, I could," he says. "They probably would have taken me because people wanted me there, but once you make a decision, you have to stand with it. I did not discuss it with Brian. He went back some time before he knew we had qualified, before UEFA's decision.

"But I felt it would not have been fair on the guys who had been playing. When I did come back, in 1993, it was because I was at a different stage in my life. I had established myself at Barcelona.

"Do I wish I had been there lifting the trophy? Yes, that would have been nice, but I took the decision I did. When you make a decision based on rational thoughts, things you have considered, then there is no problem. If I had made a rash decision in a moment and missed out, *then* I would have regretted it."

Laudrup is no stranger to brave choices. He left Barcelona after five successful years to join their fierce rivals Real Madrid. He had found himself out of favor in the latter stages of his time at the Camp Nou and was dropped by Cruyff for the 1994 European Cup final, which the Catalans went on to lose 4–0 to AC Milan. Unlike others who made that switch to Madrid, he managed to remain broadly popular with both sets of supporters in the long term—a remarkable feat given he played in 5–0 *Clásico* wins for both clubs, assisting for Barcelona in January 1994 and doing the same for Madrid a year later.

"I did not join Madrid on a whim or to get back at anyone," he says. "Even Cruyff thought it was [out of a desire to exact revenge] because he did that himself when he left Ajax and joined Feyenoord. I had been in Barcelona for five great years, but the last six months were not so good. I had Cruyff for five years and I still say he's the best manager I ever worked with, but it felt the moment to go. My contract was running out and the club wanted me to renew, but I felt it was better to go while I was only 30.

"We had won four titles in a row with Barcelona and Madrid had been number two, but I knew they wanted to be back up there. Not all the supporters were okay with it. Some really let me know about it the first time I returned with Madrid. It was not as bad as with [Luís] Figo because they knew I hadn't left for money. But the first year at the Camp Nou it was still 100,000 people going crazy every time I touched the ball.

"Four games from the end of the first season, we went to Camp Nou and, if we won, we were champions. It was strange going into the away dressing room there because the club had been such a big part of my life. We ended up losing 1–0 but won the game after and had the title.

"You have to enjoy the good moments because the story of football is filled with teams who thought they would always be on top. You never know what's coming. Football is always moving on."

No team, even those featuring Laudrup, can win forever. He had time for one more league title, in the Netherlands with Ajax, after his successful spell at the Bernabéu before he retired in 1998.

Yet the memories of him ghosting imperiously past defenders remain. But as with *La Croqueta*, Laudrup maintains his skills were never about showboating and always born of a desire to create for his team. "For me, respect on the pitch has always been the most important thing," he says. "I would never put the ball through the legs of an opponent just for the sake of doing it. I would do it because I could get an advantage."

Among his many magical moments was a solo goal for Denmark against Uruguay in the 1986 World Cup, gliding past defenders like they were not there. "Honestly, it wasn't so difficult. It was special because it was a World Cup and the Danish commentary was memorable: 'Michael, now he shoots, no, he waits,' etc. But if we're talking about difficult goals, there were harder ones. I am just as proud of some of the passes I made at speed or under pressure.

"There was one for Raúl at Madrid that was hard. I had my back to goal and he ran past me. I made a half-step, turned, and then passed the ball to him and he scored on the half-volley. The pass cut out four defenders.

"Sometimes the pass before the assist can be the most important thing. I remember I also made some fantastic passes and the player didn't score. Some of those could have been the goal of the year. There was a pass through eight players at Barcelona for Stoichkov and, instead of just using his right foot, he wanted to use his left and the goalkeeper saved. It was the best pass ever but no goal, so no one remembers."

Fortunately, plenty of memories of Laudrup's brilliance linger on.

Player name: Michael Laudrup
Born: June 15, 1964
Position: Attacking midfielder
Debut: 1981
Main teams: KB (1981), Brøndby IF (1982–83), Juventus (1983–89), Lazio (loan, 1983–85), Barcelona (1989–94), Real Madrid (1994–96), Vissel Kobe (1996–97), Ajax (1997–98); Denmark (1982–98)
Career highlights: Won Serie A with Juventus, La Liga four times with Barcelona, and once with Real Madrid. He was a European Cup winner in 1992 and won the Eredivisie in his last season as a player, with Ajax.

73.

Karl-Heinz Rummenigge

Rummenigge was the Bundesliga's top scorer three times and Germany's player of the year once.

The bank clerk from Lippstadt and the step into the unknown

By Phil Hay

It reads like a rite of passage or a watershed moment of acceptance, the day in 1974 when Gerd Müller told a timid Karl-Heinz Rummenigge: "Call me Gerd."

Until then, Rummenigge had quivered in the presence of greatness, new to Bayern Munich and surrounded by royalty. The arrival of players for his first training session was a who's who of West German excellence. Müller first, Franz Beckenbauer last, and [illegible] like Sepp Maier's in between; World Cup winners newly crowned, all of them walking on water.

Rummenigge retold that story in an interview with Bayern's in-house magazine, *51*, in 2019. "I hid away in a corner at first," he said. "I had massive respect for them and for the first two weeks, I was extremely polite."

Then Müller insisted on first-name terms and the penny dropped. "It was clear to me, the only thing that counts here is winning. That's the school of FC Bayern," Rummenigge said. "If you don't internalize that, you'll never make it here."

Müller had helped create that culture.

Gerd Müller. Bayern's greatest goalscorer and Germany's greatest goalscorer, across east and west. Even now, maybe the world's greatest goalscorer. There was the benchmark for Rummenigge, an 18-year-old bank clerk who knew no more than the simplicity of the amateur game. Intimidated or not, he had to be a winner in Munich. And Rummenigge would be.

But who was this winner, the son of a toolmaker and master craftsman who people nicknamed "Kalle"? The boy who became Bayern Munich royalty and a European Championship winner with West Germany, embracing the headlights in which he was caught in 1974? How much did he owe to "street-kicker" battles back in his hometown of Lippstadt?

And, in those scary early days with Bayern, how close did he come to throwing it all away?

Lippstadt sits in the northwest of Germany, within driving distance of the old West German capital, Bonn. It produced one Rummenigge for Bayern Munich in Karl-Heinz. Then, eight years later, it produced a second, his younger brother, Michael. Sporting genes spilt out of that household.

In the 1960s and '70s, the town was industrial and, as Michael describes it, "a large development area with a lot of high-rise buildings."

A nearby military barracks housed British soldiers and, as a result, British kids were itching to take part in kickabouts with the natives. Immigration soon brought Italians and Turks to Lippstadt. It was a melting pot and a healthy one for football-mad kids like the Rummenigges.

"It was Germany, England, Scotland," Michael says. "Three against three, four against four, five against five, all of us street kickers or street footballers. That was our training."

The brothers turned out for their local team, Borussia Lippstadt, too (not together, owing to the differences in ages), but part of the appeal of that was the chance to wear a proper shirt. "The actual footballers we learned from, it was on the street," Michael says. "That's where we learned most and the fastest, in a small space. It was my game. It was Karl-Heinz's."

There were three Rummenigge siblings: Wolfgang, the eldest; Karl-Heinz in the middle; and Michael, the baby, born in 1964, 12 years after Wolfgang. Because their father, Heinrich, was a blue-collar worker, the boys attended a *Realschule*, intended to set pupils up for a trade rather than the more academic *Gymnasium*. Rummenigge would secure his first job in a bank, the Volksbank in Lippstadt.

Michael also entered banking before his playing career took off. "It was right that we did it," he says. "Knowing finances is always very good, a very good basis. Everything was wonderful for us, a lovely childhood."

Michael is talking from his office in Dortmund. He retired in 1995 and now runs a soccer school. He tells the youngsters there that Karl-Heinz Rummenigge in his prime was a twentieth-century version of Cristiano Ronaldo. As a teenager, the middle brother had a distinctive look and Michael glows with pride as he paints a picture of the striker with "his socks always down, always around his ankles, with this speed, this dribbling ability, this natural talent."

Wolfgang accepted that Karl-Heinz was the most gifted of the siblings. Michael, who was 10 when Rummenigge signed for Bayern, felt no jealousy either. "Oh, he was the best," Michael says. "It's clear. I don't know how many goals he scored, too many to count, but he was the best of us brothers. But then he became the best in the world, which is actually incredible because that's what we would ask ourselves. Can he do this right up to the Bundesliga? To the national team? Does he have all of that?"

Rummenigge had it. His list of honors proves it.

Once Müller had left Bayern in 1979, Rummenigge took the mantle on. He was the Bundesliga's top scorer three times and West Germany's player of the year once. With Bayern, he won two Bundesliga titles, two DFB-Pokals, and two European Cups. West Germany dominated the European Championship in 1980 and the World Cup was the only thing that got away, twice rendering Rummenigge a losing finalist in 1982 and 1986.

Look back at the 1986 final—the Diego Maradona final—and it's Rummenigge you see shaking hands with Argentina's No. 10 before kickoff, his guarded smile that of a fierce competitor ready to go.

Rummenigge and Bayern were meant to be. It was nature taking its course for a forward with his talent and a man who, in 2016, told German newspaper *Westfälischer Anzeiger* that football in his hometown was "the meaning of life." But he and Bayern were not meant to be without first experiencing a momentary wobble in the summer after he left Lippstadt and took the road south.

Within weeks, a message reached the Rummenigges with words to this effect: Karl-Heinz is struggling. He wants to come home.

The fight to sign 18-year-old Rummenigge was ferocious, and it is ironic, given the scale of the interest in him, that Bayern paid Borussia Lippstadt a pittance—around 17,500 deutsche mark (roughly $4,000 as the exchange rate had it in 1974). Michael would cost them fractionally more at 18,000 DM in 1982.

He laughs as he repeats those fees but then points out that, in 1974, the sport was waiting to boom commercially. Wolfgang had talent and a wicked left foot, but he sought out training as a wholesale merchant and, unlike the other Rummenigge boys, reckoned that life as a footballer had limited earning potential. Rummenigge's initial Bayern wage of about $600 a month did not exactly contradict him.

"It was a different time, a different world," Michael says. "But because West Germany won the World Cup in 1974, it was like the dawn of modern football, even for me as a 10-year-old. It was the dawn of how football was marketed." As a measure of his trajectory in Munich, Rummenigge's subsequent transfer from Bayern to Inter Milan for more than $6.4 million in 1984 went close to breaking the world record.

But, back when the striker was a player of potential at Lippstadt, Hamburg wanted Rummenigge, as did 1860 Munich, Schalke, and Borussia Dortmund. An amateur or not, word of his finishing and trickery had spread and Bayern were alerted to him on the advice of a scout from the city of Rheine. "He said to them, 'There's a great player here in the Westphalian province,'" Michael says. "He said they had to go look at him."

When an offer arrived from Bayern and their general manager, Robert Schwan (also the personal manager of Beckenbauer), the decision was made. Rummenigge's father, who was handling negotiations, signed the contract on the grounds that Rummenigge was too young to do so himself. Schwan succeeded in banging the same drum over and over again: We want your son and this transfer will be the making of him. Neither side had long-term cause for regret.

Rummenigge's family were heavily present. Heinrich was registered as a referee and that status gave him access to Bundesliga matches for free, a perk he made the most of. From 1974 until he joined Bayern himself, Michael went everywhere to watch his brother. Eventually, in 1983, they would appear in the same lineup for Bayern, Rummenigge up front, and Michael—a technically proficient operator who would later be capped by Germany—in midfield. "The hype was huge," Michael says.

Despite the moral support, Rummenigge did not settle easily. I ask Michael if he and his parents were anxious about Rummenigge joining Bayern and stepping into the domain of Müller and Beckenbauer, German icons without comparison. The change in standards seems unfathomable.

"Oh, yes, we were already worried," he says. "And after three weeks, they were in a training camp and the call came that he was homesick. He actually wanted to come home, back to Lippstadt.

"So what we did was this: My mother packed up all her cooking pots. His girlfriend, Martina [now Rummenigge's wife], came with us. We put everything in the car, we went to Munich, and we had a six-week vacation there. My mother cooked in this small apartment, cooked all the time. She was resolute when he called, saying, 'No, no, no. You stay there. We're coming.'

"And after that? Everything was fine. His career took off."

The West Germany teams Rummenigge went on to captain in the 1982 and 1986 World Cup finals were fated to be extras in somebody else's show.

Italy ran away with the 1982 final, and the abiding memory of it—well, the only memory of it—is Marco Tardelli's emotional reaction to scoring their second goal. In 1986, the entire narrative revolved around Maradona, the sport's new superstar, whose hands on the trophy were all the planet wanted to see.

West Germany went close in Mexico City. From 2–0 down, Rummenigge sparked a comeback by sliding in a flick-on from a corner before Jorge Burruchaga got Argentina over the line six minutes from time, his goal sealing a 3–2 victory. The assist for the winner? Maradona, naturally.

Despite coming up narrowly short, I say to Michael that his brother must have been a hero in Lippstadt. Michael must have held celebrity status, too. "No," he insists. "It was my father who was the hero."

It figures. Heinrich was well respected and renowned as a parent of two Bayern footballers, one of them the national skipper. The night before the 1982 final, the fire brigade in Lippstadt hung a West Germany shirt on the back of a monument in the town, with Rummenigge's No. 11 on the back.

"My father was there," Michael says. "You have to imagine what it was like. We knew Karl-Heinz was good, but we didn't expect all that.

He went from Lippstadt to being one of the best players in the world in six years. Who would have believed it?"

Stepping into Bayern, Rummenigge was genuinely unknown to a wider German audience, let alone a worldwide one, but his ascent vindicated Bayern's appraisal of his potential. In little over a year, he was a regular in the first team. In marginally over two, he made his debut for West Germany.

Rummenigge had a poacher's nose and an unerring finish, but he was also highly adaptable, capable of playing through the middle, as a secondary striker or in wider attacking areas of the pitch. He is sixth in the all-time list of goalscorers for Germany and he sits in Bayern's top five, with 217 to his name. Müller going over the hill was not the nightmare it might have been for club or country.

In 1979, by which point Rummenigge and Bayern were perfect bedfellows, the club signed another forward, Dieter Hoeneß, and challenged him to thrive in the winners' enclosure. Hoeneß, the brother of Rummenigge's Germany teammate Uli, joined from VfB Stuttgart and had cut his teeth to a far greater extent than Rummenigge in Lippstadt. He would go on to score in spades for Bayern.

But still, you can imagine him at his first training session, looking around, feeling Rummenigge's aura and waiting for his teammate to pass on that same reassuring invitation Rummenigge received in 1974: "Call me Karl-Heinz."

Player name: Karl-Heinz Rummenigge
Born: September 25, 1955
Position: Forward
Debut: 1974
Main teams: Bayern Munich (1974–84), Inter Milan (1984–87), Servette (1987–89); West Germany (1976–86)
Career highlights: Captained West Germany to two World Cup finals and won the European Championship in 1980. At Bayern Munich, he won the European Cup in 1974–75 and 1975–76 and was twice the recipient of the Ballon d'Or.

72.
Alessandro Del Piero

Del Piero was a stalwart over 19 years with Juventus.

A love affair born of loyalty

By Greg O'Keeffe

But for the vagaries of life, Alessandro Del Piero might have been a truck driver.

As a youngster with itchy feet from a working-class family in the rural commune of Conegliano, he considered it a practical way to see the world. Imagine how many masterpieces would have been missing from the game's gallery if he had chosen the open road ahead of his local dusty football fields, where, for a while as a slight youngster, he was forced to go in goal by his mother. She was afraid he might get injured.

Instead, the player later nicknamed *Pinturicchio*—little painter, after a famous Renaissance artist—chose to etch his name in football's rich tapestry in the famous black and white of Juventus and Italy's *Azzurri* blue.

As a stalwart over 19 years with Juventus, the attacker helped the Turin giants win six Serie A titles and the Champions League, while also firing Italy to World Cup victory in 2006.

Yet he is adored as much for his loyalty as for those successes. Del Piero was one of the few major stars who decided to stay with Juventus after the *Calciopoli* scandal. In the same year the national team triumphed in the World Cup in Germany, Juve were stripped of their titles from the previous two seasons and relegated to the second tier, Serie B, with a points penalty.

"A true gentleman never leaves his lady," he told *Corriere della Sera* at the time.

Thankfully, Del Piero's mother, Bruna, eventually let him play out of goal and his talent did not go unnoticed for long. He had started to play regularly for his local amateur side, San Vendemiano—Del Piero's family lived a stone's throw from their stadium—when scouts from professional outfit Calcio Padova spotted him before his 13th birthday.

He joined Padova's youth ranks, which meant leaving home at such a tender age to live in the city, but continued his education while playing with the club's academy. Despite concerns over his early physical development, Padova remained patient and did not regret keeping hold of the teenager. By 17 he was filling out and ready for a senior team bow during the 1991–92 season. That same campaign, Del Piero was a standout performer for Italy in the Under-17 World Cup and he excelled for Italy's under-18s the following year.

It put him firmly on the radar of Serie A's big guns and, in 1993, Juventus made their move.

Their sporting director, Giampiero Boniperti, ensured they outbid other suitors and Del Piero was on his way to Stadio delle Alpi. He did not walk straight into the first team, even if he was one of the nation's most exciting young players. There was a formidable list of stars ahead of him, with Roberto Baggio, Gianluca Vialli, Fabrizio Ravanelli, and Andreas Möller all at the club.

But a glut of injuries in the second half of that first season offered him a route into the side and, in March 1994, he scored an explosive hat trick against Parma and ended his breakthrough season with five goals from just 11 appearances in Serie A.

The genie was out of the bottle and Del Piero went on to become a hero for almost two decades at the club. Such was his talent that Juventus manager Marcello Lippi, along with owner Umberto Agnelli, decided to sell the great Baggio in 1995. Del Piero was handed his No. 10 shirt. "The No. 10 shirt is the most desired of all," he said in 2023. "Everyone wants it. It's the number the most talented players wear, the ones able to bring together imagination and strokes of genius, dribbling, and vision. The No. 10 is a way of seeing the game."

He quickly proved to be deserving of it.

In December 1994, Del Piero scored a goal against Fiorentina that ranks among his finest and exemplified the stroke of genius he listed as a prerequisite for a No. 10. Left-back Alessandro Orlando sent a long ball forward and Del Piero slipped between two Fiorentina defenders as he watched it arc into the area. He quickly scanned the ball's velocity as it dropped and then, instead of taking the shot on his left foot, he flicked it with his right on the volley and beyond the dive of opposing goalkeeper Francesco Toldo. It was the 87th minute and the goal sealed a 3–2 win for Juventus.

The following season, he helped the club win the Champions League, finishing as the joint-second top scorer in the competition, and did not look back. He was in sensational form for the next four years before a serious knee cruciate ligament injury, suffered in November 1998, left him sidelined for the last six months of that season.

Del Piero worked hard to build extra strength and power while he was sidelined and returned a different player. If he had lost some pace, he compensated with even greater guile and was Serie A's top creator the following season with 14 assists. The injury took nothing away from his other formidable asset—dead-ball mastery. Del Piero could score free kicks from any angle with sumptuous accuracy and often saved his best for the Champions League.

On the *Bianconeri*'s return to that competition after their *Calciopoli* downfall, he scored the only goal of a 1–0 group-stage win against Zenit Saint Petersburg—and *what* a goal. Lining the ball up from long range, he struck it perfectly with his right foot into the top corner. Del Piero celebrated with a somersault as everyone in the Juventus dugout rose to their feet in applause.

It was during that most turbulent of times with his club that Del Piero enjoyed his greatest moment in an Italy shirt. As the grim ramifications of the *Calciopoli* scandal were emerging in the summer of 2006, the forward was helping to propel the *Azzurri* to their first World Cup success in 24 years in Germany.

It was his finish from a stunning counterattack that sealed a 2–0 semifinal victory over the hosts. He scored the penultimate Italy penalty in the shootout in the final, too, as his country prevailed at France's expense. For Del Piero, this was redemption six years in the making.

He had suffered against the same opponents in the final of Euro 2000. As a second-half substitute, he had missed two presentable opportunities in extra time at Rotterdam's De Kuip stadium with the game still level. David Trezeguet's golden goal ended up securing the trophy for *Les Bleus*, with photographers capturing Del Piero's agonized reaction in the immediate aftermath. He lay flat on the turf, covering his eyes in despair. Back in Italy, he became the scapegoat for the narrow, heartbreaking defeat.

But he made amends in Germany six years later. "I never forgive myself for making a mistake," he later admitted. "Those errors weigh on you a lot. I was in pieces at the end of that game. Luckily, a few years later, I earned forgiveness. But did you notice how strange and irrational football is? Trezeguet scored a golden goal in that final. Six years later, he missed the crucial penalty [in the shootout in 2006]. Destiny is cruel, but it can also smile on you."

• • •

Del Piero's love affair with Juventus quickly became a happy marriage, so when the unthinkable happened, he was not about to walk away.

For the 2006–07 season, Juventus were demoted to Serie B as a result of the fixing scandal. Many of their best players—Patrick Vieira, Zlatan Ibrahimović, Fabio Cannavaro, Emerson, Gianluca Zambrotta, and Lilian Thuram—left and there were suitors for Del Piero, too.

He had been regularly courted by Manchester United and their manager, Sir Alex Ferguson, having previously been knocked back, sounded the forward out once again in the wake of Juventus's demotion. "I called him directly, avoiding talking to Juventus: 'Alessandro, I'd like you at United,' I said. 'You'll be the star of the squad and together we'll win everything. Don't listen to Real Madrid and come here,'" said Ferguson when interviewed by Gary Neville in 2021. "He laughed and replied: 'Sir, you know that nothing has changed from all those years ago. Juve are facing difficult times and I have to help them. I can't be a coward.'"

"I was club captain, a fan, and Juve had given me so much," Del Piero later explained. "John Elkann [the heir of the Agnelli family] called me and I told him he could count on me. I never thought twice about it and I've no regrets about not going somewhere else to play. Getting back into Serie A and winning the league again were the biggest joys of the final part of my career."

He made 35 appearances in the second tier, scoring 20 goals and supplying 14 assists as Juventus were crowned Serie B champions.

Perhaps no title was greater than his last with the club—even if there was also something bittersweet about the 2011–12 *Scudetto*. It was Juventus's first since their return to the top division and the completion of their renaissance, but it was secured in the knowledge that Del Piero, the figurehead who had stayed during such a traumatic period, would be leaving at the end of the campaign, with the club having decided not to renew his contract.

"The unique link between the old Juventus and the new Juve is our captain, Alessandro Del Piero," the club's president, Andrea Agnelli, announced at a shareholders' meeting. "He is the link between the Stadio Comunale, Stadio delle Alpi, and the Juventus Stadium where we are now. He wanted to stay with us for one more year, but this will be his last season wearing the black-and-white jersey."

The decision not to hand him a new contract came as a surprise, even with the forward turning 37 years old that season. He would probably have accepted any deal proposed to him, but nothing ever was. The club had decided to move on.

At the time, he admitted to being "a little upset," telling a reporter from the Italian television show *Striscia la Notizia* that such situations are "usually handled differently." But he did not let it affect his form. He even scored in the club's final league game of the season, a 3–1 win against Atalanta that meant they were unbeaten throughout the entire Serie A campaign.

Asked which of his many match shirts he would favor above all, he admitted that one could be the most precious. "I played for Juventus for so many years, there were so many successes, so many things I went through," he said in 2023. "The one that comes to mind is from Serie A given the fall, the rise. The last league title I won meant my adventure with Juventus came full circle in the best way possible."

For all the disappointment that his time at the club was up, his was a typically understated response from a classy player. Juventus's decision may have hinged on cost-cutting and other nuances, but for him, things were always black and white. He bowed out, reluctantly, conducting business as usual: with a crucial goal and, ultimately, a trophy in his hands.

Player name: Alessandro Del Piero
Born: November 9, 1974
Position: Forward
Debut: 1992
Main teams: Padova (1991–93), Juventus (1993–2012), Sydney FC (2012–14); Italy (1995–2008)
Career highlights: Won the 2006 World Cup with Italy. His time at Juventus yielded the Champions League in 1995–96 and six Serie A titles. He scored a record 290 goals for the club.

71.

Didier Drogba

Drogba's status as a Chelsea icon was sealed at the Champions League final in Munich in 2012.

Divinity, destiny, and the path to hero status

By Liam Twomey

July 12, 1998. In Stade de France, a 20-year-old Thierry Henry sprints wide-eyed onto the pitch in celebration of a final whistle that signals his country's first World Cup triumph. Approximately 125 miles southwest of the capital, in Le Mans, another 20-year-old, named Didier Drogba, watches on the television in his apartment while eating takeout pizza, his leg in plaster.

Drogba already considered Henry a contemporary football benchmark, though their paths to that point could hardly have been more different. One had been marked for future greatness from his teenage years at Clairefontaine and Monaco. The other had been scrapping in French amateur football with Levallois until Ligue 2 club Le Mans were convinced enough to offer him a place in their academy team at the age of 19.

The game is in his blood. His paternal uncle, Michel Goba, was a striker on the books at Brest in 1983 when he accepted guardianship of a five-year-old Drogba from his parents, who did not follow him from Côte d'Ivoire to France for another 10 years. Goba could not offer Drogba a fixed abode as he pursued a nomadic career in the French lower leagues, but he did show him how to use his body against a defender and time his jump for a header—two skills that would later serve him particularly well.

In the insecure moments of those formative years, Drogba could not help wondering if playing in the junior teams of the clubs for whom Goba signed rather than joining an academy had left him at an insurmountable disadvantage relative to his most talented contemporaries. Would his technique ever be as polished as the effortless, gliding Henry?

Now, even as an unused substitute in France's 3–0 victory over Brazil, Henry is a world champion. Earlier in the summer, Drogba had endured a nervous wait before finding out that Le Mans had decided to renew his trainee contract, having broken his ankle and fibula toward the end of his first season with the club. It will be another 10 months before he makes his Ligue 2 debut and a full year before he signs his first professional deal.

A measure of resentment at witnessing Henry's historic moment of euphoria would be understandable, even natural, but Drogba's instinctive reaction is rather different.

"Not 'you bastard,' as some might imagine," he recounts in his 2015 autobiography, *Commitment*. "No, my main thought was: 'I would love to be there. And one day I will be there.'"

October 22, 2003, and Olympique de Marseille are taking on Porto in the Champions League group stage. In the Stade Velodrome tunnel, a 25-year-old Drogba is approached by the visiting manager and addressed in French. "I don't have the money to buy you, but do you have any cousins in Côte d'Ivoire who can play like you?" José Mourinho asks.

"Actually, there are lots in Africa who are better," Drogba jokes back.

The sight of him bursting between two Porto defenders and poking the ball past Vítor Baía to open the scoring for Marseille in the 24th minute makes that hard to believe. Drogba is in the early stages of a breakout season that will see him score 19 goals in only his second Ligue 1 campaign and 11 more in Europe, powering a run to the UEFA Cup final that will enshrine him as an eternal hero in the city.

Mourinho ends the brief, banterous exchange by pledging to sign Drogba, who replies that one day he will manage a club rich enough to afford him.

It all seems frivolous, but it begets a bond that changes everything.

A bond that emboldens Mourinho, he will tell *beIN Sports* in 2019, to urge Chelsea owner Roman Abramovich to "pay and don't speak" when it comes to signing Drogba for £24 million in the summer of 2004. A bond that sustains Drogba through a storm of media criticism and abuse from his own supporters in his first two seasons in England and allows Mourinho to convince him to accept being one of his "22 kings" at Stamford Bridge rather than return to his comfort zone in Marseille.

A bond that makes Drogba honest enough to tell Mourinho he is cramping in extra time of the 2007 FA Cup final against Manchester United and makes Mourinho clear-eyed enough to tell him to stay near the penalty area and wait for his chance to score the winner. A bond that compels Drogba to run back to the Wembley dressing room before the trophy presentation and tell Mourinho, on the phone to his wife, that Chelsea's players will not celebrate without him.

A bond that leaves Drogba openly sobbing when Mourinho is sacked in September 2007 and elated to reunite with him for a glorious second act at Chelsea seven years later. A bond that yields seven major trophies, including three Premier League titles, across two spells at Stamford Bridge.

A bond that puts Drogba on a path toward legend.

October 8, 2005. In Al-Merrikh Stadium, Drogba and his Côte d'Ivoire teammates huddle anxiously around a phone. At the other end of the line is a team physio who, having been forced to return to France after forgetting his passport, is now their only source of information about the World Cup qualifier between Egypt and Cameroon in Yaoundé.

Côte d'Ivoire have beaten Sudan 3–1, but it will mean nothing if Cameroon win. This qualification campaign, played out against the backdrop of violent clashes between government and rebel forces back home, is on the line. The score is 1–1 in Cameroon, and Drogba has a horrible premonition that a penalty is coming for the visitors. In the 95th minute, it happens.

Prayers break the radio silence as Cameroon's Pierre Womé lines up the kick. Then shouting, incomprehensible at first, morphs into news of salvation: Womé has missed.

Wild celebrations spill into the dressing room, followed by Radio Télévision Ivoirienne cameras. Seeing an opportunity, Drogba requests a microphone, gathers his teammates around him, and speaks from the heart.

"Men and women of Côte d'Ivoire," he says. "From the north, south, center, and west. We proved today that all Ivorians can coexist and play together with a shared aim: to qualify for the World Cup. We promised you that the celebration would unite the people."

He drops to his knees. "Today, we beg you, on our knees. Forgive! Forgive! Forgive! The one country in Africa with so many riches must not descend into war. Please lay down your weapons. Hold elections. All will be better."

The plea ends with a smile and a song. "We want to have fun, so stop firing your guns," he beams tunefully, rising again as those around him join in.

Drogba has only been Côte d'Ivoire captain for a matter of months, but the moment expands his leadership well beyond the band on his arm. Less than a month after peace terms are signed in March 2007, he will present his African Player of the Year award in the rebel stronghold of Bouaké and advocate for it to host an Africa Cup of Nations qualifier.

Three appearances at World Cup finals will prove the admirable limit of his attempts to match Henry, with two AFCON finals ending in penalty heartache. Yet, through all the triumphs and disappointments to follow with Côte d'Ivoire, that day will ensure he remains forever theirs.

May 9, 2010. Martin Atkinson has just shown Wigan Athletic defender Gary Caldwell a red card for hauling down Frank Lampard in the penalty area. Carlo Ancelotti's Chelsea are already 1–0 up in a game they need to win to edge out Manchester United and win their first Premier League title since Mourinho's sacking. Another goal in the 32nd minute will start the party at Stamford Bridge.

Lampard picks himself up to take the spot kick, but Drogba wants the honor. The Ivorian is level with Wayne Rooney on 26 goals and desperate to win his second Premier League Golden Boot. "It's 1–0," Lampard mouths at him before drilling the ball into the bottom corner. Drogba does not join in the goal celebrations and his personal gloom lasts until halftime.

A little selfishness is understandable. Drogba, 32, is in the form of his life. For the last nine months, he has been confident, injury-free, and every attribute that makes him feared—his overwhelming physicality, his silky touch, his sharp movement, his explosive finishing with his head or either foot—has coalesced into a perfect storm that has laid waste to the Premier League.

The journey to this final day has seen him score four of his 13 career goals against his favorite victims, Arsenal, a critical winner against United at Old Trafford in April, and the opener against Liverpool at Anfield on the Premier League's penultimate weekend. He is level with Rooney despite missing all of January for AFCON. A league title is no small reward, but such individual excellence demands greater recognition.

Drogba's chemistry with Lampard is too deep, born of endless extra combinations after training at Cobham, for disagreements to linger. Chelsea push beyond 3–0, then 4–0, until in the 63rd minute it happens: Drogba's bicycle kick is parried by Mike Pollitt, Lampard gathers and floats it to the back post, where Drogba's flying header connects with the force of a volley.

Five minutes later, Lampard grants Drogba his penalty, which he kisses in off the post. His hat trick goal falls onto his left foot in front of the Matthew Harding Stand. He jogs to the corner flag and strums it like a guitar with Florent Malouda, his old friend from Guingamp, miming the drums behind him.

Twenty-nine goals, 10 assists. No player has been directly involved in more goals in a Premier League season since Henry five years earlier, and no player is more beloved at Stamford Bridge.

May 19, 2012. At no point during his walk from the Allianz Arena halfway line to the penalty spot does Drogba consider that he might miss the most important kick of his life.

Drogba is a believer. He has spent many of the biggest moments of his career talking to God on the pitch, pleading to be shown the way to score, to have the ball delivered to him in the right place at the right time. His prayers are not always answered, but he would be the first to admit he has done well out of his bargain with the Almighty: nine goals in cup finals, the ninth of which—a towering near-post header powered through the giant left hand of Bayern Munich goalkeeper Manuel Neuer—has brought him and Chelsea to this moment.

His faith is further bolstered by an unshakable sense of destiny. Drogba has been on a four-year mission to win the Champions League, spurred by the shame of being sent off for slapping Manchester United defender Nemanja Vidić in the 2008 final in Moscow minutes before a penalty shootout he could only watch Chelsea lose. Every year since has seen the dream recede further from view. Until now.

Chelsea's ludicrous path to Munich has provided plenty of validation for someone inclined to believe in divine intervention. Drogba has himself been saved twice by forces outside his control as this Champions League run crescendoed to its conclusion, conceding penalties taken by Barcelona genius Lionel Messi in the second leg of the semifinal and Bayern star Arjen Robben in the final itself.

Both failed to find Petr Čech's net.

This does not feel like Moscow, into which Drogba went under the shadow of the news that his grandmother was gravely ill in Côte d'Ivoire. It feels like the moment he has been waiting for. One kick to make Chelsea kings of Europe, to write his name forever into the first page of the club's history. "You love that responsibility," he tells himself.

Drogba shortens his run-up to two steps to make it harder for Neuer to read his body language and waits for the referee's whistle. His stride is sure, his strike is firm, and as soon as he sees the ball going one way and Neuer the other, he wheels around, his face contorted with emotion, making the sign of the cross as he goes.

Divinity and destiny are in the eye of the beholder, but Drogba's legend is undeniable.

Player name: Didier Drogba
Born: March 11, 1978
Position: Striker
Debut: 1999
Main teams: Le Mans (1998–2002), Guingamp (2002–03), Olympique de Marseille (2003–04), Chelsea (2004–12), Shanghai Shenhua (2012–13), Galatasaray (2013–14), Chelsea (2014–15), Montreal Impact (2015–16), Phoenix Rising (2017–18); Côte d'Ivoire (2002–14)
Career highlights: Won the Champions League in 2012, scoring the winning penalty in the shootout in the final. Won the Premier League four times. Scored 65 goals for Côte d'Ivoire and reached two Africa Cup of Nations finals.

70.

Matthias Sindelar

Sindelar would become one of the sport's first commercial stars, advertising everything from wristwatches to yogurt.

National hero and martyr? Or an extraordinary player who died an ordinary death?

By Mark Critchley

In Carol Reed's seminal 1949 film, *The Third Man*, an American author of pulp westerns travels to postwar Vienna to meet a friend on the promise of a job, only to discover that his friend has been hit by a car and killed. At least, that is the official account of Harry Lime's death.

Spoiler alert, if there can be such a thing for a film that came out three-quarters of a century ago: It transpires that Lime is very much alive. He is in hiding, wanted for maiming and killing hundreds by selling diluted penicillin on Vienna's black market. Hilarity does not ensue.

But at least the mystery is wrapped up in a running time of a little over an hour and a half, a good deal faster than the case of another death in the same city a decade before *The Third Man*'s release—that of Austria's greatest-ever footballer.

Matthias Sindelar was found dead on the morning of January 23, 1939, lying naked next to his unconscious girlfriend, Camilla Castagnola, at her apartment in Annagasse in central Vienna. Castagnola later died in hospital. The cause of their deaths was carbon monoxide poisoning.

Those are the facts. Practically everything else about Sindelar's death is disputed, as is much about his life. To many he was the sporting embodiment of Vienna's thriving cultural sphere before the Anschluß. He is also remembered as a symbol of resistance against Nazi Germany's annexation of his country.

What is certain is that he was one of the most heralded European players of the prewar era and the central genius of Austria's Wunderteam of the 1930s.

Sindelar was born in 1903 in Kozlov—a village in modern-day Czechia, then part of Austria-Hungary—but his family emigrated when he was still a toddler. His father, Johann, was one of many immigrant bricklayers to leave Moravia and build a new life in Vienna's working-class district of Favoriten.

When Johann was killed fighting at the Isonzo Front during World War I, the 14-year-old Sindelar was forced to take up an apprenticeship to help support his mother, Marie, and his three sisters.

But he still spent much of his time kicking a ball around Favoriten's workers' quarters, where he was spotted by an official at ASV Hertha, a club that had recently started developing a new stadium on land near the family's home.

Sindelar spent the next six years at Hertha, making his debut as an 18-year-old in 1921, although he suffered several misfortunes along the way. Besides being laid off from his day job, he struggled with injury, tearing the meniscus in his knee after tripping over a railing at a local swimming pool.

Surgery was required to prevent the injury from repeatedly disrupting Sindelar's playing career, but it was only carried out once he left a cash-strapped Hertha in 1924 to join Austria Vienna, a club closely associated with the city's Jewish bourgeoisie. Football was beginning to capture the imaginations of Vienna's cultural and intellectual classes at the time and was the subject of lively debate in the city's coffeehouses.

From his breakthrough season in 1926–27, when he scored 18 goals in 23 league games, Sindelar became the darling not only of the Café Parsifal, which was frequented by Vienna supporters, but also the Café Ring, where artists, novelists, poets, and playwrights pored over his performances.

"Sindelar's shot hit the back of the net like the perfect punchline," wrote the theater critic Alfred Polgar, "the ending that made it possible to understand and appreciate the perfect composition of the story, the crowning of which it represented."

As his popularity grew, Sindelar earned the nickname *Der Papierene*—"The Paper-Man"—because of his slender frame and graceful, almost weightless movement. In time he would become one of the sport's first commercial stars, advertising products as varied as wristwatches and yogurt. His reputation transcended Austria through one of the early forerunners to the European Cup.

Sindelar twice won the Mitropa Cup, in 1933 and 1936, and finished as joint top scorer in the first of those triumphs. As he helped Vienna overcome the likes of Juventus and Inter Milan, vying with Giuseppe Meazza for recognition as Europe's best player, Italian newspaper *La Stampa* honored Sindelar as "an artist."

But Hugo Meisl, founder of the Mitropa Cup and Austria's manager, was not initially sold on Sindelar. Despite giving him his international debut in 1926, Meisl came to prefer a more brutish, physically dominant brand of center-forward over the following years.

Meisl eventually caved to public pressure for Sindelar to play before a friendly against Scotland in 1931, slapping a team sheet that included his name down on a table at the Café Ring in front of a group of journalists.

The 5–0 victory a few days later, over opponents whose style had greatly influenced central European football, was the beginning of Meisl's Wunderteam and Sindelar was the key component. Victories over Germany—6–0 in Berlin, then 5–0 in Vienna—followed and, a year later, the Wunderteam triumphed over their fellow central European nations by winning the Central European International Cup.

In December 1932, a trip to play England at Stamford Bridge was billed as a meeting of Europe's best. Despite falling to a 4–3 defeat, even the British press hailed Austria as the superior team and Sindelar as the best player on the pitch. John Langenus, the Belgian referee that day, described Sindelar's goal as "a masterpiece." It started at the halfway line, with him dribbling around several players in his "inimitably elegant" manner, then "finishing with a backheel into the net."

Austria were among the favorites for the 1934 World Cup, although financial difficulties affected preparations and the Wunderteam lost to Italy in the semifinals. That, ultimately, was the extent of their success.

Meisl died in 1937 and Sindelar's international career effectively ended once Nazi troops crossed the Austrian border a year later. The Austrian Football Federation quickly disbanded and withdrew from the 1938 World Cup.

Sindelar would represent his country one last time, however. A week before the Anschluß referendum in April 1938, an *Anschlußspiel* was played between German and Austrian XIs—or Altreich and Ostmark respectively, the regions' names under the Reich.

Widespread claims that the result was fixed as a draw or that the Austrians were told not to score, perhaps stemming from a string of chances that Sindelar and his teammates uncharacteristically missed in the first half, have never been substantiated. And if that was the agreement, they did not stick to it.

Two second-half goals handed Ostmark victory, with Sindelar opening the scoring. When his close friend Karl Sesta doubled the lead, Sindelar supposedly joined him dancing in celebration near the swastika-draped rostrum holding several Nazi officials.

Much has been made of that moment since. In some retellings, Sindelar danced a waltz. In others, it was ballet. Whatever exact footwork was involved, Sindelar's dance entered posterity as an act of courageous defiance.

Except, it is not entirely clear whether there was any dancing at all. Contemporary reports only reference ordinary celebrations—which may well have passed through the German censors—between Sindelar and Sesta, which, if directed at any part of the crowd, may have been for Austrian supporters sitting above the section holding the Nazi representatives.

And if any offense was taken, that did not stop Germany from trying to persuade Sindelar to join some of his international teammates playing at the forthcoming World Cup. He declined, citing his age and his damaged knee. Sepp Herberger, Germany's manager, suspected an ulterior motive.

"I almost had the impression it was down to feelings of uneasiness and rejections to do with the political developments that weighed on his mind," he said.

Sindelar's politics and sentiments toward the Nazis are difficult to parse from the idealized memory of him propagated by the Viennese intelligentsia following his death, although it is not unreasonable to suspect he held broadly left-wing sympathies.

A child of the workers' quarters, his formative years of adolescence and young adulthood coincided with those of "Red Vienna"—a period when the left-wing Social Democratic Workers' Party of Austria enjoyed widespread support and held power across the city's institutions.

And, surely, he would not have taken kindly to the Nazis forcing out Jewish officials within Austria Vienna's hierarchy, including

Emanuel Schwarz, the club president and a close friend who had helped arrange the knee surgery that prolonged Sindelar's career.

Sindelar was not one to publicly profess any antiestablishment beliefs, though. Nor did he avoid being used as a propaganda tool for the Anschluß. On the day of the referendum itself, his image was published in *Volkischer Beobachter* under a handwritten message: "We players thank our Führer from the bottom of our hearts and will vote YES!"

Also, the memory of him as a principled antifascist—or at least anti-Nazi—is complicated by his purchase of the Annahof, a coffeehouse in Favoriten.

Its previous owner, Leopold Drill, was dispossessed of the café because he was Jewish. In 1938, Sindelar paid 20,000 Reichsmarks—15,000 up front—to take over the business. Some argue that was a fair price, even generous. Others, including Drill's descendants, claim it was rapacious expropriation and that the price was well below the café's true valuation of around 50,000 marks.

Either way, Sindelar materially benefited from the Nazi policy of "aryanizing" Jewish businesses, and it is hard to argue with several Austrian journalists and academics who have questioned the mythologization of Austria's greatest player as a symbol of Viennese resistance on that basis.

Drill, it is believed, did not receive the 20,000 marks. He was deported to Theresienstadt, a Jewish concentration camp in Nazi-occupied Czechoslovakia, where he died.

If you send an email to the helpful international press office at the city of Vienna, you can acquire a copy of the coroner's report into Sindelar's death for yourself.

The digital scan is of such a low resolution that even native German speakers may struggle to make out the small print. The handwriting is not the neatest, either. Fortunately, the most legible entry on the form is typed under "cause of death."

"Kohlenoxydgasvergiftung, Unfall," it reads—"carbon monoxide poisoning, accident."

Yet according to Sindelar's friend Egon Ulbrich, that is not the whole story. In a 2003 BBC documentary, *Fascism and Football*, Ulbrich recalled a night of gambling and drinking with Sindelar before he retired to Castagnola's apartment.

After Sindelar's body was discovered the next morning, Ulrich was informed that those who had either been murdered or had committed suicide could not receive a state funeral, so he enlisted a local official—described as "a Nazi but a nice guy"—to register Sindelar's death as an accident.

The notion that Sindelar was murdered by the Nazis, possibly as retribution for his performance and that supposed dance in the *Anschluß-spiel*, has captured imaginations. It has been fueled by suggestions he was of Jewish heritage himself—plainly false. Sindelar was Catholic.

In the coffeehouses, meanwhile, the suicide theory took hold, with many in Vienna's literary circles believing Sindelar's death was a self-inflicted protest against totalitarianism extinguishing the culture that he came to represent.

"The good Sindelar followed the city, whose child and pride he was, to its death," Polgar wrote in his obituary. "He was so inextricably entwined with it that he had to die when it did. All the evidence points to suicide prompted by loyalty to his homeland." Only, it does not.

There is no suicide note and no smoking gun, either; only the knowledge that Castagnola's neighbors had complained of a defective chimney in the days leading up to her and Sindelar's tragic end.

To conclude a story that has sparked spin-off novels and true-crime podcasts by citing Occam's razor might be unsatisfactory—*The Third Man* it ain't—but in the absence of anything concrete, the simplest explanation remains the likeliest: that this was all an unfortunate accident.

To the public who wondered at his talents, the intellectuals who romanticized him, and in a country eager to distance itself from a dark chapter of its history, Sindelar is remembered as a hero, even a martyr.

It may be that he was simply an ordinary man, blessed with extraordinary gifts, living at an extraordinary time, who died an ordinary death.

Player name: Matthias Sindelar
Born: February 10, 1903
Died: January 23, 1939 (aged 35)
Position: Striker
Debut: 1921
Main teams: Hertha Vienna (1921–24), Austria Vienna (1924–39); Austria (1926–37)
Career highlights: Reached the semifinals of the 1934 World Cup with Austria. Won the Austrian top flight in 1925–26 and the Austrian Cup five times. Claimed the Mitropa Cup twice.

69.

Francesco Totti

Totti's career feels like something from a comic book.

The Italian playmaker who combined glitz and glamour with consistency

By Michael Cox

There are essentially two completely different considerations to take into account when assessing historically great No. 10s.

The first element, which tends to dominate our memories, is about the style, the feel, and the aura of a footballer. It's about their grace on the ball, their physical appearance, their ability to produce brilliant individual moments. Essentially, it's just about how cool they were.

The second is something completely different. It's simpler yet more difficult to convey. It's purely about how consistently well they played over the course of their career.

The danger with Francesco Totti is getting too swept away by the former. Everything about Totti was unbelievably cool.

Totti is a brilliant name for a footballer. Totti was born in Rome, the city that would dominate his life. Totti was briefly set to sign for Lazio but spent his entire career playing for Roma, creating two decades of, *What if?* Totti was handed the captaincy at the age of 22, becoming the youngest captain in Serie A history. Totti almost exclusively wore the No. 10 shirt. Totti is often considered the pioneer of the modern false nine role, the position Lionel Messi perfected. Totti could be referred to as both a *fantasista* and a *trequartista*, the monikers bestowed on creative playmakers in Italian football. Totti had a reputation for scoring spectacular goals, particularly long-range chips. Totti was renowned for his elegance but also had a petulant streak. Totti had fantastic hair. Totti wore a snood before they were fashionable. Totti was married to Ilary Blasi, one of the most famous models in Italy. Totti spent his entire career with the same club.

It all feels like something from a comic book.

But the thing that gets missed about Totti is that in addition to all that—perhaps, you could say, *in spite* of all that—Totti was unbelievably consistent.

In many other nations, newspaper player ratings are considered the lowest form of football coverage, halfheartedly thrown together by journalists more concerned by their match report. But they're taken very seriously in Italy, with dedicated reporters compiling the *pagelle*. And, in 2013, *La Gazzetta dello Sport* announced it had compiled all the player ratings it had recorded, for every game in Serie A going back 40 years, and ranked all the players by their average score. Throughout that period, which included the era when Serie A was unquestionably the greatest league in the world, the highest-ranked player was Totti. His average score was 6.45, just ahead of Swedish striker Zlatan Ibrahimović and goalkeeper Gianluca Pagliuca.

Totti was a superstar renowned for moments of magic, but he also offered almost unprecedented consistency.

It's worth pointing out that by that stage, Totti had already played for two decades. He carried on for another four years, too. And to achieve this consistency during that period was highly improbable. He was chiefly a No. 10, and No. 10s often have moments when they lose their magic. It can be forgotten that Alessandro Del Piero had a hugely difficult injury-affected period, or that Zinédine Zidane's form suffered dreadfully between his successes at World Cup 1998 and Euro 2000, that Juan Sebastián Verón lost his way badly at Lazio amid a fake passport scandal, Rui Costa took two and a half years to score his first Serie A goal for Milan after leaving Fiorentina, and Roberto Baggio was bombed out of Italy's three major clubs—Juventus, AC Milan, and Inter Milan—and probably enjoyed his best spells at the more modest Fiorentina, Bologna, and Brescia.

This was a period when there was a serious debate about whether teams could afford the luxury of a proper No. 10, with some believing that the ultracompact 4-4-2 favored by Arrigo Sacchi's Milan was the future of football. Not only did teams like that have no place for a No. 10, but they crushed the life out of opposition No. 10s, too.

But Totti rose above all of this to become the most consistent footballer Serie A has seen. On three occasions—2000–2001, 2005–06, and 2012–13—he received the highest average rating in a season, which is also a record. These ratings are, of course, entirely subjective. Cognitive biases cannot be entirely ruled out. But then, these ratings *did* take into account hundreds of games and were awarded by dozens of different reporters.

Totti always found the right balance between playing his own game and evolving to suit the demands of his managers. He first became established as a top-class player when drifting inside from the left of the 4-3-3 system favoured by Zdeněk Zeman, a period in which he was first handed the No. 10 shirt.

His best years, though, came in central positions. He fired Roma to the title in 2000–2001—their first since 1982–83 and the only one he would win—from a classic No. 10 position as part of Fabio Capello's 3-4-1-2. That in itself was interesting. Capello had succeeded Sacchi at Milan and had initially been considered part of the new generation of Italian managers who wanted a solid 4-4-2 system with no space for a No. 10. He continued with that approach in his year at Real Madrid, but at Roma, he was so convinced of Totti's quality that he changed his approach to accommodate Totti in his most obvious position, behind two strikers—generally Gabriel Batistuta and Vincenzo Montella. In that role, Totti found space between the lines, provided incisive through-balls for the two strikers, and increasingly scored himself, too.

The most surprising development of Totti's game came in 2006–07. With Montella past his best and Roma lacking another top-quality center-forward, he was asked to lead the line. He inevitably dropped deep into familiar positions and linked play effectively, although he didn't score in his first six league matches that season. But an hour into the seventh, a home game against Chievo, a blocked shot bounced into his path, right in front of goal. A seasoned striker would have tucked it away quickly, but Totti, as you expected him to shoot, paused. The goalkeeper went to ground and Totti calmly rolled the ball home. Suddenly it felt like that ability to stop time, which had previously served him so well between the lines, was now an asset in front of goal.

Totti kept scoring that season. He notched close-range poacher's goals and converted after hopeful long balls were hit in his direction. He deflected one home with his backside and scored four headers.

At the same time, he still scored spectacular goals. There was a wonderful 35-yard free kick away at Palermo, where he struck across the ball, fading it away from the goalkeeper and into the top corner. There was also a dipping left-footed volley from an incredibly tight angle away against Sampdoria—perhaps his most famous goal of all, which drew a round of applause from the home supporters.

By the end of the season, despite the slow start, Totti had scored more goals, 26, than anyone else in Serie A. Moreover, he'd scored more goals than anyone else in Europe and was awarded the European Golden Shoe, an award that had never previously been won by a player of Totti's profile, more No. 10 than No. 9.

By the end of his career, Totti had notched 250 goals in Serie A, second on the all-time list to Silvio Piola. He was inevitably less prolific in his latter years but remained majestic in terms of through-balls and particularly the swept-around-the-corner pass toward the right flank, having come short to link play. In a way, he almost reverted to the young Totti. He twice topped Serie A's assist table: in 1998–99 and 2013–14, at the age of 22 and 37.

There are only two possible criticisms of Totti.

The first is that he didn't win more: One World Cup, one Serie A, and two Coppa Italias represented the extent of his haul. But that can easily be explained by his loyalty; he always used to say that winning a single *Scudetto* in Rome was worth 10 in Turin. He won his only title at 24 and, therefore, even if he never triumphed again, his career could never be considered a failure.

The second is that he dominated the side too much and that Roma became reliant on him. Indeed, at times there was almost a comedic inevitability that Totti would somehow hog the spotlight when he didn't truly deserve it. In 2002, for example, when Roma were thrashing Lazio 4–1 in the derby, with Montella having scored all four Roma goals, Totti crashed the party by dribbling forward and scoring one of his classic chips from 25 yards. Suddenly Totti was the man on the front pages of the Italian daily sports newspapers.

In 2010, Roma hosted Bayern Munich in the Champions League and found themselves down 2–0 at the break. Claudio Ranieri reshaped dramatically, switching from 4-3-1-2 to 4-2-3-1, and Roma produced a brilliant second-half performance to bring it back to 2–2, with Marco Borriello particularly impressive. Totti didn't even come on until the 75th minute and yet inevitably was the star once again, smashing home a late penalty for the winner in a famous 3–2 victory. That was classic Totti.

Whenever Roma appointed a new manager during the latter years of his career, there was always a *what will he do with Totti?* question, as if everyone reluctantly acknowledged that it was time to move on. The slight problem with that, though, was that Totti was always playing too well and he can't be faulted for his club's reliance on him.

For all the glamour of Roma, they are not a historically successful club. Totti helped to win one of only three *Scudetti* in their history. He was also part of a side that finished second on nine occasions—they've only finished second five other times. Before and after Totti's era, Roma have been accustomed to finishing around sixth. Totti's presence ensured they were regularly part of the top three.

He also played a crucial role in Italy's World Cup 2006 campaign, playing just off the man he would succeed as the European Golden Shoe winner, Luca Toni. He started six of Italy's seven games, the only exception being the 1–0 victory over Australia in the last 16. In that game, Italy were seriously struggling after the dismissal of Marco Materazzi, but typically defended their box well. Totti was introduced 15 minutes from time as Italy's final substitute and, in typical Totti fashion, slammed home a stoppage-time penalty to make himself the hero.

But that wasn't actually typical of Totti's tournament. Although credited with four assists, two of them were simple passes for long-range blasts from Andrea Pirlo and Gianluca Zambrotta and the others were standard deliveries for Materazzi and Toni. Totti and Toni—who both only scored in one game—were credited primarily for their work rate and for sacrificing themselves for others. Those in deeper positions were Italy's best performers.

The World Cup final, when he was 29, was Totti's final game in international football. He only played at four international tournaments: He was excellent at Euro 2000 as Italy lost in the final to France, but he was sent off in Italy's World Cup 2002 last-16 loss to South Korea, while his Euro 2004 ended early when he was banned for spitting at Denmark midfielder Christian Poulsen. Despite that memorable World Cup success, you instinctively picture Totti wearing the jersey of Roma rather than Italy. He was a club player rather than a national team player—and a club player who never enjoyed great success in European competition.

But week in, week out, in league football, Totti was the most consistent attacker of his generation. The headline figures are that he played in 25 straight Serie A seasons and scored in 23 straight Serie

A seasons, but the crucial detail—backed up by the *pagelle*—is that Totti was genuinely outstanding for 20 straight seasons.

Player name: Francesco Totti
Born: September 27, 1976
Position: Attacking midfielder, forward
Debut: 1993
Main teams: Roma (1993–2017); Italy (1998–2006)
Career highlights: Won the 2006 World Cup with Italy and Serie A in 2000–2001 with Roma. Scored 250 goals in the Italian top flight.

68.

Gianni Rivera

Rivera won the league and European Cup with AC Milan while still a teenager.

The Golden Boy of Italian football

By James Horncastle

When AC Milan became the first Italian team to win the European Cup in 1963, the players were considered like precious stones on a jeweller's velvet presentation tray. There were gems, rupees, and sapphires; Cesare Maldini, José Altafini, and Dino Sani. But the brightest light of all scintillated from the crown facets of a diamond so well cut it was football's Cullinan—Gianni Rivera.

Rivera did not feel like "Signor 125 milioni," his price tag in Italian lire, and which became one of the monikers bestowed upon him by the media of the day, when he walked up the Wembley steps that May afternoon. He had swapped shirts with Eusébio, Benfica's greatest-ever player, only for someone to pull the coral jersey out of his hands and make off with it. Moments away from meeting Queen Elizabeth II, Rivera, the epitome of elegance on the pitch, found himself in an undignified state of undress.

He recovered his style by borrowing a mackintosh and lifted the trophy after Maldini, his skipper, as if opening an umbrella under the London rain.

Rivera didn't win the Ballon d'Or that season. He finished second behind Lev Yashin, the only goalkeeper to ever receive the award. But Rivera was already known to everyone in Italy as the Golden Boy. It was both a blessing and a curse for him; a name tag and a price tag with which he was burdened his entire career.

Rivera grew up in Alessandria. His old man, Teresio, was a farmer. He worked the land in the nearby paddy fields of Piedmont. His mother, Edera, kept an inn. They moved from the Piedmontese countryside when Teresio got a job in the railway yard. Alessandria was a transport hub at the time between Turin and the port of Genoa, which is why it was bombed by the Allies during World War II.

Teresio used to take Rivera to play in the parklands of Piazza d'Armi. A frustrated footballer himself, Teresio had been discouraged from using his feet for a living by his father. He set no such limit on his own boy, who came to believe the speed with which he went professional was in some way owed to the transference of Teresio's pent-up potential.

Rivera began playing for the Don Bosco parish team. Over the years, reporters descended on the churchyard to discover the secrets of his emergence. Three priests (Don Piero, Ceschia, and Carlo) squabbled over who found Rivera first. It was all part of his legend, along with the story that the second word he uttered as a baby was *palla*—ball.

One day, an ad in the local paper, *Il Piccolo*, notified its readers that Alessandria were holding trials for their academy. Rivera went along in his Sunday best. He was asked to play one-touch passes with both feet, to head the ball, trap the ball. Then he was sent on his way. Rivera hopped on his bike without knowing the outcome and pedaled out to the village of Valle San Bartolomeo in the countryside where his grandparents lived.

Two years later, in 1959, Rivera made his Serie A debut for Alessandria. He was still a couple of months shy of his 16th birthday when he played against Inter Milan, the team that became the great rival of his career.

The hype escalated when Rivera played for Italy at the Rome Olympics at the end of the following season. He scored twice on his debut against Taiwan and started the comeback against Brazil in the final group-stage game. Although Italy lost the bronze-medal match to Hungary, the narrative that followed him set the tone for his life in football.

It revolved around money. Weren't the Olympics supposed to be amateur? Rivera had already turned professional and AC Milan were well on the way to signing him.

Alessandria's assistant coach, Franco Pedroni, played under Gipo Viani at Milan in the early 1950s. Viani had since moved upstairs into a technical director role. One day after Rivera scored a hat trick to turn a 3–0 defeat to Torino into an improbable 3–3 draw at under-18 level, Pedroni told Viani to organize a trial for Rivera. It happened in Linate, the area now synonymous with Milan's inner-city airport.

Rivera showed up for a *partitella*, a classic mini-game. He was instructed to try out for the first team against a third-division outfit. All of a sudden, Rivera was exchanging passes with greats like Maldini, Nils Liedholm, and World Cup winner Juan Alberto Schiaffino. He was characteristically unfazed. The only thing that bothered him was the need to break in a new pair of boots. Rivera feared the pain might be irritating enough to put him off his game. Then it rained, the leather softened, and Rivera shone.

Days later, Viani struck a deal to buy half of Rivera's rights in exchange for an option and half of those in Giancarlo Migliavacca. It also allowed Alessandria to keep Rivera for another season. They beat Milan on the opening day but, in the end, went down to Serie B. Rivera wore No. 9 and scored six goals in 25 games.

The papers heralded him as the "Meazza di Domani"—the heir to double World Cup winner Giuseppe Meazza.

Endorsements came from the man who surpassed Meazza as Serie A's all-time top goalscorer, too. Silvio Piola said: "At his age, I didn't even dream of the things he does." Like lifting the ball across his body with his right foot and then volleying a shot past the Napoli goalkeeper with his left in what was his best goal that season.

Rivera, however, wasn't a striker. Italy's love affair with No. 10s arguably began with him and his contemporary, Inter's Sandro Mazzola.

The game seemed to come so easy to them, yet in Rivera's case, it was not as linearly genetic. Mazzola's father, Valentino, was the captain of the Grande Torino side that had been wiped out in the Superga air disaster. Reductively, he was portrayed as destined for greatness. Rivera, on the other hand, came out of nowhere, like Superman turning up as a baby in the Kent barn in Smallville.

Whereas there was relatively little question about Mazzola being a world-class player on account of his heritage, Rivera became a lightning rod for scrutiny. He used to joke that if he wasn't the best player in Italy, he was definitely the most talked about.

When the great interviewer of the age, Oriana Fallaci, visited Rivera, she was struck by the dissonance between his public image and reality. Upon moving to Milan, the Golden Boy still lived with his parents. He shared a room with his little brother. He was serious, studious, and self-aware. Fallaci kept repeating his price tag. "Mez-zo Mi-li-ar-do." Half a billion lire. Rivera accepted that a nuclear physicist probably wouldn't fetch the same money on the open market.

Then again, football is more entertaining than physics and people pay to watch Pelé, not Albert Einstein.

What stood out about Rivera was his coolness, not only in his aesthetic but his approach to life. Nothing seemed to ruffle his feathers. When he walked onto the pitch, it didn't matter if 10 people were watching him or 100,000. Rivera didn't see them. "If you worry about people," he told the Italian weekly *L'Europeo*, "then you become emotional. And when you become emotional, you're finished. I think part of my good fortune came from learning how to control myself very early."

It was easier said than done.

Rivera won the league and European Cup with Milan while still a teenager. He was the reason fans bought a ticket. Italian football has always idolized the No. 10 role more than any other on the football pitch. In the age of *catenaccio*, impregnable chain-linked deep defenses, the No. 10 was often the only player capable of picking the lock with a stroke of inimitable genius. Rivera got into double figures for goals in both of his first silverware-winning seasons with Milan.

But nobody polarized opinion on the sports pages quite like him. Gianni Brera, the disproportionately influential columnist who, in many respects, defined Italian football for decades to come by endorsing *catenaccio* on weird ethnographic grounds as reflective of the Italian spirit, did not believe Rivera incarnated it. He was too *leggerino*, lightweight, and morally scrupulous like an *abatino*—a little priest wandering around the pitch.

Brera, on the other hand, thought Italians could only win through sneakiness and cunning rather than skill and technical supremacy. He affixed this sobriquet on other players like Giacomo Bulgarelli and Mazzola, but it stuck with Rivera because he hit back. Beyond the philosophical basis for his argument, Brera claimed all he was doing was pushing back against the fanaticism of the Rivera-ites. The player, to his credit, did not allow it to change him. He continued to take that "extra touch," as he titled his 1966 autobiography.

However, no one's word carried more weight than Brera's and he used to grow angry if anyone else criticized the target of his intellectual ire. It did not matter when Rivera won his second European Cup in 1969 against Johan Cruyff's Ajax, a feat that persuaded journalists to vote him the winner of that year's Ballon d'Or. Nor did it change things when he claimed the last of his three *Scudetti* 17 years after his first. Rivera rarely caught a break.

On international duty, he was in the squad for the 1962 World Cup and the infamous Battle of Santiago against hosts Chile when two teammates were sent off, punches were thrown, and police needed to intervene. Then, as a more established player, Rivera was on the pitch at Ayresome Park in Middlesbrough when Italy suffered the defeat by which all humiliating defeats are judged: a 1–0 defeat by North Korea, which precipitated their elimination from the 1966 World Cup.

The *Azzurri* bounced back by winning the Euros two years later. Then, at the 1970 World Cup, Rivera scored the extra-time winner in the "Game of the Century" against West Germany, a 4–3 epic played out at the Azteca Stadium in Mexico City. The goal booked Italy a place in the final for the first time in more than three decades.

But Rivera played only six minutes against Brazil.

It was the tournament of the *staffetta*, or relay, when the Italy coach Ferruccio Valcareggi succumbed to pressure from the suits upstairs in the press box and the executive suites to alternate between Mazzola and Rivera rather than play both together.

"If there was a game I should have played in, it was the one against Brazil," Rivera told *La Repubblica* years later. "For my way of playing, they were ideal opponents; skillful rather than physical. Instead, I had to sit on the bench and watch my team lose. They collapsed."

Having forthright opinions, at times, distinguished Rivera. Written off as physically fragile, he had to be mentally tough. Strength of character was shown not only in how he resisted Brera's barbs.

In 1979, he took the microphone before Milan's title decider and warned the fans that if they did not behave, the police would postpone the game. One ran onto the pitch and confronted him. "I've come all the way from Calabria!" he shouted at Rivera in a panic at having to leave a section of San Siro and the prospect of missing the game in which Milan won their tenth league title, a feat entitling the club to stitch a prestigious star over their crest.

Go back further to 1972 and Rivera called out perceived corruption, which led to a two-and-a-half-month ban.

Upon his retirement, Milan rightly offered him the role of vice president. But Rivera did not enjoy the same success off the pitch as he did on it. Milan suffered relegation twice and nearly went bust. But politics suited him. He had a center-left code and he stuck to it. This meant his views did not align with those of Silvio Berlusconi.

Shortly after Milan's takeover by the media mogul in 1986, Rivera left the club and ran for parliament as a Christian Democrat. However, unlike in British politics, there was no No. 10 for Rivera to move into. Wearing that jersey at San Siro was the highest office he ever held and the greatest influence he ever wielded.

Player name: Giovanni Rivera
Born: August 18, 1943
Position: Attacking midfielder
Debut: 1959
Main teams: Alessandria (1959–60), AC Milan (1960–79); Italy (1962–74)
Career highlights: Scored the winning goal in the "Game of the Century," the 1970 World Cup semifinal, before Italy finished runners-up at the tournament. Won the 1968 European Championship and the European Cup twice.

67.

Mohamed Salah

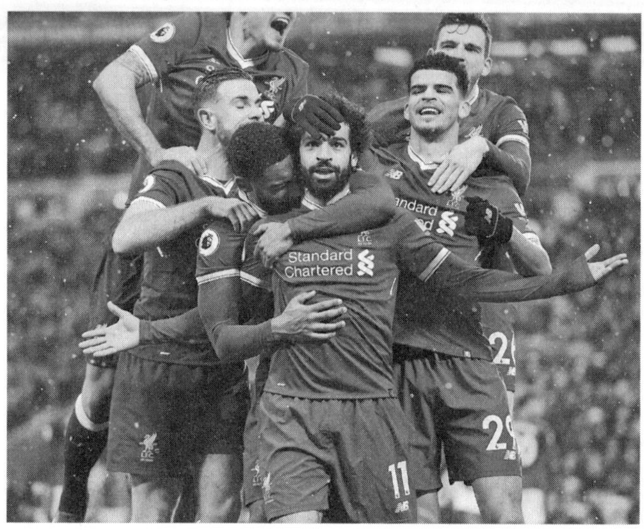

Salah had been branded a Premier League flop after an unsuccessful spell at Chelsea, but Liverpool's scouting reports were glowing.

How a 44-goal season proved Liverpool right and all the doubters wrong

By James Pearce

Jürgen Klopp needed some convincing that Mohamed Salah would flourish at Anfield.

The Liverpool manager had initially preferred the idea of signing Bayer Leverkusen's Julian Brandt as he looked to add a dynamic wide attacker to his squad in the summer of 2017. But the Germany international had doubts about making the move to England, fearing that a reduction in his game time might dent his national-team aspirations ahead of the 2018 World Cup.

As it happened, Liverpool's sporting director, Michael Edwards; chief scout, Barry Hunter; director of scouting and recruitment, Dave Fallows; and director of research, Ian Graham, were all on the same page regarding the perfect alternative.

Salah had been branded a Premier League flop after an unsuccessful spell at Chelsea, but Liverpool's scouting reports and data analysis of his performances in Italy, first for Fiorentina and then Roma, were glowing. Having previously missed out on the Egyptian's signature in January 2014, with José Mourinho convincing him to move to Stamford Bridge when he left Swiss side Basel, the club's senior recruitment figures were determined to ensure lightning did not strike twice.

"They were really in my ear: 'Come on, come on, Mo Salah, he's the solution,'" Klopp told reporters in November 2017. "They wanted to do it even earlier so that nobody could jump in."

Despite Salah scoring 15 goals and providing 13 assists in 31 Serie A matches in 2016–17, Liverpool faced little serious competition for his signature. Roma urgently needed to raise funds to satisfy UEFA's Financial Fair Play rules, and Edwards, who flew to Italy to negotiate with his opposite number, Monchi, agreed to a club-record transfer fee of £43.9 million, including performance-related add-ons.

It proved to be one of the most significant deals in Premier League history as Salah rewrote the record books and inspired Klopp's side to Champions League, Premier League, and Club World Cup success.

"We couldn't believe we were able to sign him," Graham told *The Athletic* in August 2024. "Why aren't Manchester City and Arsenal putting bids in for this player? We didn't understand it.

"Mo came with the baggage of having failed in the Premier League, but our data analysis helped us understand that we could ignore that failure. He's a multifunctional forward and, from a complicated data point of view, he ticked all the boxes. He had scored and assisted at a ridiculous rate in Italy for someone who isn't a center-forward.

"Doing something different is an easy way to be made to look stupid. Signing Mo because he had failed at Chelsea *was* doing something different, but all we cared about was making the right decision.

Jürgen was convinced to go for Mo and was gracious enough to speak publicly about the part others played in that. We were so excited we could get him."

When Salah arrived on Merseyside in the summer of 2017, Klopp told the club's media channels that Liverpool had signed "the perfect mix of experience and potential." His tactical understanding and stamina had improved markedly during his time in Italy. His new teammates were immediately struck by his blistering pace and clinical finishing in training. He also possessed a burning desire to silence the doubters, who questioned whether he could handle the physical demands of English football after being cast aside by Chelsea.

Sadio Mané had impressed in the right-sided attacking role for Liverpool since joining from Southampton a year earlier, but Klopp switched the Senegal attacker to the left to accommodate the new arrival. Salah's impact at Liverpool was extraordinary from the outset. His first season yielded a staggering 44 goals and 14 assists in 52 appearances in all competitions. His longest barren run spanned just three matches.

Only Ian Rush (47 goals in 1983–84) had ever enjoyed a more prolific campaign in the club's illustrious history. Salah not only won the Golden Boot but broke the Premier League record for most goals in a 38-game season, scoring 32 times, eclipsing the previous best, 31, mustered by Alan Shearer, Cristiano Ronaldo, and Luis Suárez.

Salah scored on his debut against Watford and never looked back. He truly announced himself to Anfield against Arsenal in late August when he got the better of Héctor Bellerín and dribbled from inside his own half before calmly slotting home in front of a jubilant Kop. His work ethic out of possession was as eye-catching as his quality on the ball, with supporters taking him to their hearts. They crowned him the "Egyptian King," the chant growing louder with every passing week.

The bigger the game, the better he seemed to perform.

He marked his first Merseyside derby against Everton on a bitterly cold December afternoon with a piece of stunning individual brilliance. After shrugging off Cuco Martina, he skipped past Idrissa Gueye and curled an unstoppable shot beyond Jordan Pickford and into the far corner. It won him FIFA's 2018 Puskás Award for the most aesthetically pleasing goal in world football over the previous 12 months.

"This one is so special," Salah told *Sky Sports* after the match. "I can see power, I can see skill, I can see finishing. I can say that I am using everything, protecting the ball, to do one skill and a good finish."

Among those watching on with pride that day was former Basel sporting director Georg Heitz, who helped launch Salah's career in Europe in 2012. It was in the city of Barranquilla in the north of Colombia that the teenage winger from Cairo club El Mokawloon first caught the eye of Basel's scouts while playing for Egypt at the Under-20 World Cup in 2011.

"Our scouting department was very impressed," Heitz told the *Liverpool Echo* in 2017. "But then you think: 'Well, he's Egyptian and we don't know many success stories of Egyptian players coming to Europe.' We thought it was a risk to sign him at that point."

Those doubts evaporated in March 2012 when the Swiss club organized a friendly against Egypt's Olympic team. The Egyptian League had been suspended following the Port Said stadium riot, in which 74 people were killed. "Mo played the second half and he scored twice—that was when we decided we had to sign him," said Heitz, who agreed a €2 million deal.

"You could see the talent after five minutes on the pitch. Not only was he quick, but he always had his head up. What I loved about this player then, and it's still true today, is, for him, football is still a game. Some people forget that. But he's out there with a smile on his face. It was clear from the beginning that he wouldn't stay for long, but that wasn't a problem for us. This was always the business model of Basel. We pick unknown players, develop them, and then give them to the big clubs in the big leagues."

Salah was only 21 when he moved to Chelsea and had Eden Hazard blocking his path into the first team. He started just six Premier League matches for the London club before being loaned to Fiorentina in February 2015. He made the switch to Roma initially on a temporary basis six months later, before—having been crowned the club's player of the year—the transfer was made permanent for €15 million in August 2016. Chelsea proved an outlier in a glittering, prolific career.

"The Premier League is the most fascinating league in the world, but it's also the most difficult, especially for young players," Heitz explained. "Mo was very young, very ambitious, and very sensitive. He needed a lot of confidence. He was a bit unlucky at Chelsea. What impressed me so much is how he came back from that disappointment. It was so good what he went and did in Italy. He was ready to go to another country, another language. He was outstanding there. And it's easier to go back to England from Roma than from Basel."

The winter transfer window in 2017–18 proved eventful for Liverpool as they broke their transfer record to sign defender Virgil van Dijk from Southampton for £75 million. They also sanctioned the £142 million sale of Philippe Coutinho to Barcelona, with the Brazilian playmaker having tried and failed to force through the move the previous summer.

His exit placed even more responsibility on Salah's shoulders, but he embraced it, forming a lethal three-pronged attack with Mané and Roberto Firmino. He produced a dazzling display in the 5–0 home rout of Watford, scoring four and creating the other for Firmino amid a snowstorm, but it was not just the Premier League that witnessed this ruthless edge. He lit up the Champions League, too, with 11 goals (including one in qualifying) in Liverpool's thrilling and unexpected run to the 2018 final against Real Madrid.

He scored in both legs of the quarterfinal triumph over rivals Manchester City. Two days before the first leg of the semifinal, against his former club Roma, he was named PFA Players' Player of the Year. In a video message broadcast to Salah and the audience present, Klopp said: "Please grab the trophy and come home. We play on Tuesday!"

The Liverpool manager need not have worried. Back at Anfield,

Salah took center stage. Italian newspaper *Corriere della Sera* described his two goals as "works of art." Salah, who did not celebrate, out of respect for his previous employer, created two more as Roma were routed 5–2. "The first goal is just a genius strike," Klopp told reporters postmatch. "What a player. He is in outstandingly good shape."

By the time Liverpool headed to the final in Kyiv, having survived a scare in the return leg in Rome, Salah had rattled up his 32-goal haul in the top flight, securing the team their top-four finish. He had also added the Football Writers' Association Footballer of the Year and the Premier League's Player of the Season awards to his growing collection.

"It's amazing what he's done for us and what he's done for himself," Liverpool goalkeeper Simon Mignolet told the *Liverpool Echo* before the Champions League final. "Nobody spoke about Mo before the season started. What's impressed me most is how he's stayed normal and humble. True to himself. He is a superstar, but he doesn't act like one. He's a winger but, in this team, he has to defend, too.

"If we had a passenger superstar, then it wouldn't work because we defend with 11 and we attack with 11. He's such a special player. To score 44 goals is remarkable."

Salah's record-breaking season ended in heartache. He left the field in tears just half an hour into the final against Real Madrid after being cynically dumped to the turf by Sergio Ramos and damaging his shoulder in the fall. The agony was compounded by the sight of goalkeeper Loris Karius's blunders consigning Klopp's side to a 3–1 defeat.

After intensive treatment, Salah rushed back from injury to play for Egypt at the 2018 World Cup in Russia, but he was not fully fit as they bowed out at the group stage. He carried the hopes of a nation, but given the dearth of talent around him, success on the international stage was always likely to elude him. That undoubtedly hampered his chances of winning global individual accolades. He finished sixth in the 2018 Ballon d'Or and was fifth 12 months later.

Yet his value to Liverpool was clear. The years since may not quite have scaled the heights of that 44-goal campaign, but his all-around game evolved and his levels of consistency were astonishing. There were 27 goals in 2018–19, the last of which was the penalty hammered home against Tottenham Hotspur in Madrid as Liverpool secured redemption by claiming the Champions League. There were 23 goals in all competitions in 2019–20 as Liverpool won the Club World Cup and ended their 30-year wait for the English league title.

The following season he scored 31—a tally he equaled in 2021–22 when he reached a century of top-flight goals in fewer games, 151, than any player in Liverpool's history. In October that season, he became the first Liverpool player to score a hat trick at Old Trafford since Fred Howe in 1936 as bitter rivals Manchester United were humiliated 5–0. That was a club record tenth game in succession in which he had scored and also established him as the highest-scoring African player in Premier League history, eclipsing Didier Drogba. The goals have continued to flow in the years since.

His durability proved as astonishing as his clinical edge as he continued to average 50 club games per season. All those concerns over his physicality that had accompanied his arrival at Anfield had long since been forgotten. He turned 32 as Klopp's successor, Arne Slot, took control at Liverpool, but he still left his teammates trailing in the preseason fitness tests. He ended the 2024–25 campaign having claimed the Premier League's Golden Boot, his tally of 29 comfortably clear of the pack, to inspire Liverpool to the title.

The doubts proved laughable with the benefit of hindsight. The winger who had failed to make an impression at Chelsea is now established in the pantheon of greats to have graced the revamped Premier League. That prolific first Liverpool season set the tone. Salah really was the solution.

Player name: Mohamed Salah Hamed Mahrous Ghaly

Born: June 15, 1992

Position: Winger, forward

Debut: 2010

Main teams: Al Mokawloon (2010–12), Basel (2012–14), Chelsea (2014–16), Fiorentina (loan, 2015), Roma (loan 2015–16, 2016–17), Liverpool (2017–); Egypt (2011–)

Career highlights: Won the Champions League in 2018–19 and the Premier League in 2019–20 and 2024–25 with Liverpool and is the Premier League's highest-scoring African player.

66.

Kevin De Bruyne

De Bruyne's genius is not quantified through raw numbers. Rather, it is about perspectives and angles.

Analyzing the game that marks the Belgian out as the Premier League's pass master

By Mark Critchley

It is a broad, sweeping statement, but hardly a controversial one as far as broad and sweeping statements go: Kevin De Bruyne should be considered the singular, most ingenious creative player of the Premier League era.

Except, he isn't. Judging solely by the numbers, at least. That's Ryan Giggs, who, post-1992 revamp, leads in assists with 162, comfortably more than the Belgian.

Look at it another way, though, and De Bruyne is Giggs's closest challenger despite a substantially shorter spell in the English top flight, playing not even half as many games across half as many seasons. Or approach it from a different angle entirely: De Bruyne is the only player to finish as the league's leading assist-maker four times, more than Cesc Fàbregas, Frank Lampard, and David Beckham's three. Giggs did not manage that once.

And, from another perspective still, De Bruyne has set up more goals per game than any other player in this era of the English top division by a distance. For players with over 50 Premier League appearances to their name, nobody else has been as close to assisting a teammate almost every other game they take to the pitch, which is what De Bruyne does.

Because that's the thing. De Bruyne's genius is not quantified through raw numbers, as impressive as his are. It is about perspectives. It is about angles. It is about looking at a problem in an entirely different way from the rest of us.

As a couple of celebrated City-supporting brothers almost once said, he sees things they'll never see. There was no finer example of that than early in the 2017–18 campaign, a season that was arguably De Bruyne's best.

Christian Vater, an assistant professor in sports science at the University of Bern, is watching a clip of a De Bruyne pass in the first half of a 7–2 win over Stoke City in October 2017. Of the tens of thousands of passes he has played during his City career, it is the one that most defies explanation.

De Bruyne initially receives the ball from Leroy Sané just outside the penalty area, then turns to stand side-on from goal and shapes as if to shoot. Instead he plays a square pass that splits Stoke's defense like a neutron shot through the nucleus of an atom.

The ball glides along the ground, through the gap between Darren Fletcher and Kurt Zouma, past an almost-entranced David Silva, and somehow finds its way back to Sané, who has made a diagonal run into the box. Sané's cutback-across goal allows Raheem Sterling to convert at the far post.

De Bruyne's passes are often immaculate. This one was incomprehensible. As Jonathan Liew noted, writing in *The Independent*: "De Bruyne turns away from Sané before Sané begins his run and does not lift his head again until after the pass is played.

"There's no way he could have seen Sané running. And so, the crux: how did De Bruyne know to do that?"

Vater has spent years researching the role of peripheral vision in football and is quick to stress how difficult it is to know exactly what De Bruyne can or cannot see at that moment, especially when using TV replays from only a couple of different angles and in 480 pixels. More sophisticated eye-tracking technology would be required.

De Bruyne might simply have expected Sané's run based on their familiarity with each other's games or hours of work on the training ground. That, surely, was at least part of the secret.

But even if De Bruyne knew Sané's run *might* be coming, he also knew when, where, and how to find a player who was behind him; by weaving a pass through opponents to the side of him, all while keeping his eyes fixed on the ball in front of him.

"It's about pattern recognition," says Vater. "You can see in the pattern of the defenders and the attackers, they're running in opposite directions, and this difference probably helps De Bruyne to perceive that Sané is now doing the run.

"Peripheral vision is not accurate in perceiving detailed information, but if we just have to detect the motion change in the environment, then it's really good."

De Bruyne does not *need* to see Sané's run itself, then, and probably didn't at the time. The movement of those closer to him provided a trigger to play the pass. And, perhaps counterintuitively, Vater says focusing on the ball helped De Bruyne interpret where spaces were opening up.

"If you're moving your eyes a lot, you always need to update the visual environment during each fixation," he explains. "But if you keep looking at the constant position, the environment is changing constantly and you don't have to update it after every eye movement."

There is another advantage to De Bruyne keeping his eyes on the ball, too. "You're hiding your own intentions," says Vater. "The defenders all think he will shoot on goal because that's what you mainly do when you're just looking at the ball. They're not expecting that pass to happen. Nor do we as spectators."

Nor did Pep Guardiola. "I am a manager, but I'm a spectator, too, like you," he said in his postmatch press conference that day. "In that moment with Kevin De Bruyne, you expect to shoot, you expect something, but you don't expect him to play again in the same position where the ball came from."

For a player who has won multiple Premier League titles, the Champions League, and two PFA Player of the Year awards, De Bruyne's performance against Stoke is not one that jumps off the page in the black and white of the record books. He did not score that day. He only set up two of City's seven. He only played a little more than an hour before being replaced by İlkay Gündoğan midway through the second half.

Ask City supporters, though, and many will cite it as arguably his best. When he left the pitch to a standing ovation from every corner of the Etihad, including the away end, the consensus was that this was the most naturally gifted player in the country. That consensus has held ever since.

De Bruyne was hardly an unknown or even unappreciated talent at the time. It was already his third season at City. His second ended with him as the Premier League's leading assist-maker.

It was also his 100th City appearance. In his 99th a couple of weeks earlier, he had scored the only goal in a victory at Stamford Bridge against the reigning champions, Chelsea: his first against the club who had discarded him three years earlier.

In the meeting that sealed his fate, Chelsea manager José Mourinho opened by listing a handful of statistics. "'One assist. Zero goals. 10 recoveries,'" De Bruyne later recalled. "It took me a minute to understand what he was doing."

Mourinho was making three mistakes at once: he was judging De Bruyne purely by numbers; he was committing the double sin of doing so when having barely played him; and worst of all, he was letting De Bruyne go.

Upon returning to the Premier League from VfL Wolfsburg, where De Bruyne had registered an assist at a rate of more than one every other game, much was made of his rejection by Chelsea and Mourinho. But De Bruyne has always been reluctant to look back when asked about that episode of his career. And in fairness, why should he?

After his surge and drive through midfield to score at Stamford Bridge in 2017, Mourinho's successor, Antonio Conte, admitted Chelsea had willingly relinquished "the complete player." Yet a fortnight later, De Bruyne played as if he had added a whole new dimension to his game.

City's official website produced a video of De Bruyne's every touch against Stoke. The first, a speculative, overhit ball down the right wing sent in search of Kyle Walker, only to run out of play, is just as representative of De Bruyne's style as any other. In an age when midfielders are judged by their passing accuracy, De Bruyne has been a throwback to an age when what you did with the ball mattered more than if you kept it.

In his first eight Premier League seasons working under the high priest of possession football from 2016–17 to 2023–24, he never completed more than 85 per cent of his passes in a campaign. In a team of metronomic midfielders, he has always had the license to take risks and make things happen.

And so, remarkably, De Bruyne's pass to Sané in the first half against Stoke is not even remembered as his best pass that day. Many argue it was not even his best to Sané.

Not long after setting up Gabriel Jesus's second and only a few minutes before being substituted, he stretched to win a loose ball just inside Stoke's half, lifted his head up, then threaded a low, crossfield pass with enough speed to beat four defenders, yet weighted to come to a stop in front of Sané.

All that was left for the winger to do was to beat Geoff Cameron to the ball and fire past goalkeeper Jack Butland at his near post. "It was so cool," the Germany international later said. "I'd just screamed like: 'Hey! I'm here!' And then suddenly the ball's at my feet."

Many City supporters rank it as the best of all De Bruyne's assists. It is one of his personal favorites, too. "I see Leroy running and I think there's an open space," he told *Sky Sports* when asked to talk through his thinking a few weeks later. "Sometimes it's about making choices. I like to see it like NBA. I'm a big NBA fan."

LeBron James is one of De Bruyne's idols. "He can do whatever he wants, but he always tries to make the best play for the team," the Belgian said.

As a pass, it is not quite as mind-bending as the pre-assist, but it is more difficult to pull off from a technical perspective. "This is probably more about his unique skills," says Vater, as opposed to the player's vision. "In this situation, he has the majority of players in front of him." His attention is on picking out Sané.

Still, he has to find the path through to him, which is where his peripheral vision comes in again.

"He has to play the pass across so many players that, if one would stand in the line to block the pass, he probably wouldn't have played it or he would have played a different pass instead," says Vater. "He has to be aware of all the players in his environment that could potentially impact if he's playing the pass or not."

Is he able to spot not only Sané but the path to him simply because he has a wider field of vision than his peers? Because he sees things the rest of us cannot? Not quite.

"If we are talking about the visual field—the general ability to see something in the periphery—there's no difference because that's mainly driven by anatomical differences," Vater says. So it is not about how much he can see, but how much of what he sees he can understand and act upon in an instant.

"Having the task-relevant information in the visual field is important, but being able to process this information separates experts from novices. This ability is affected, among other factors, by stress and fatigue. The higher the stress or fatigue level, the more it leads to tunnel vision."

And Vater might know why. "De Bruyne is such a calm player. Since he never seems stressed, he might have a better ability to use his peripheral vision."

When you can understand and interpret space like De Bruyne, the only limiting factor is time. He will not have Giggs's longevity, but then, he does not need another half century of assists to demonstrate that he sees the game like no other player in English football's modern era.

He already did that in the space of one game and two passes.

Player name: Kevin De Bruyne
Born: June 28, 1991
Position: Midfielder
Debut: 2009
Main teams: Genk (2009–12), Chelsea (2012–14), Werder Bremen (loan, 2012–13), VfL Wolfsburg (2014–15), Manchester City (2015–25); Belgium (2010–)
Career highlights: Has won the Premier League six times at the time of writing and claimed the Champions League as part of the treble in 2022–23. Reached the semifinals of the 2018 World Cup with Belgium, whom he captained at Euro 2024.

65.

Zlatan Ibrahimović

An interview with Zlatan feels more like an audience.

"I am not like the others"

By Adam Crafton

Could Zlatan Ibrahimović *be* any more Zlatan Ibrahimović?

We met in the lobby of a spa hotel in New Jersey during AC Milan's preseason tour in the summer of 2024 and, immediately, Zlatan was in character. He began by joking that any journalist who wishes to interview him must first put on the costume of the Milan mascot, which lay on the table beside us. Then he suggested we get on with things "because time with Zlatan is precious and expensive."

There are not many footballers who would be immediately identifiable by solely their first name, but Zlatan is one. The name, of Slavic origin, means "Golden" and you sense the man himself would be rather pleased with that.

An interview with Zlatan feels more like an audience, exuding all the same preening surety that he exhibited during a stunning playing career that began at the Swedish side Malmö before passing through Ajax, Juventus, Inter Milan, Barcelona, AC Milan, Paris Saint-Germain, Manchester United, and LA Galaxy. He scored more than 550 goals for his clubs and his country, Sweden, winning a dozen domestic league titles. By the time we met, he was 42, a year out of the game and lending his personality and expertise to Milan, where he was an advisor to the club's board and majority owner RedBird Capital, the private equity fund that manages over $10 billion across the sport, media, and entertainment sectors.

He also had a hand in coaching hires, while regularly observing training sessions for the first team, which meant helping guide star names, including the United States captain, Christian Pulisic. In typical Zlatan fashion, however, he quickly pointed out that he is "not a babysitter."

In our interview, first published in *The Athletic* in August 2024, the Zlatan character was on full display, including self-deification ("I am not like the others," he said) and comparisons to apex predators. The performance can be wearisome, but all the self-aggrandizing statements are greeted with just enough of a knowing grin or a side-eye wink that you get the sense Ibrahimović the person is very deliberately playing on Zlatan the brand. If this was boxing, he would be both the fighter and the promoter. I briefly considered asking Milan for a second interview for the sole purpose of this book, but it seemed impossible to compel some poor Italian press officer to explain to Ibrahimović that he had been placed 65th in the rankings.

As a journalist, you go into a meeting with Zlatan hoping you might uncover the real Ibrahimović, wondering if you may unmask hidden vulnerabilities that lie behind the persona, but you quickly realize that the showmanship is mutually beneficial. He gives you headlines and one-liners, creating content that suits both your publication and the performer himself.

He told me his home is not filled with photographs from his playing career, except for a photograph of his feet in the family's gym. "That is for my family to know where everything comes from."

Even as he veered between bravado and sincerity, he does give the impression of believing much of what he says. So, at this point, maybe this simply is who he really is.

There were moments when the mask slipped a little and a human being threatened to break out. He is clearly proud of the manner in which he returned to Milan in early 2020. He was by then a 38-year-old, but he inspired a group of players with an average age of little more than 25 to their first Serie A title in 11 years in 2021–22.

"When I came the second time, it was more about giving than taking. I wanted to open the way for a new generation. You're the example, saying, 'Listen, this is how it works.' When you're in Milan, it's the elite of the elite: pressure, demands, obligations. You have to take responsibility, become a man, because a player is not only about the field, but also the person outside. I was the reference point. I didn't have an ego about it."

Was this a humble hero exposed? Almost. He paused, searching for the right word. "Guardian angel," he said when asked to describe his role in the dressing room. Just like that, we were back into the realm of the supernatural.

Ibrahimović is open about his childhood, a challenging upbringing in Rosengård, an immigrant neighbourhood in Malmö. He is the son of a Croatian Catholic mother, who worked as a cleaner, and a Bosnian Muslim father, who was a caretaker. They split when he was only two years old and, revisiting a theme he had raised in his autobiography, he spoke about "aggression" in the home.

"My parents gave me discipline," he told me. "I was raised with my father, but I went to my mother every day. The first thing he taught me was discipline. And I followed this discipline until today. I give it to my children and to the team. When you have discipline, you are right.

"An easy example: if my father said to me, 'Get home at night,

8 p.m.' then I didn't go over one minute because I know if I came one minute later, I would get punished.

"In my world, it is aggression. Everybody has their different way of educating. In my family, it is the hard way. They came from difficult backgrounds. And that is because I was born in Sweden and my parents met 10 years before the [Yugoslav] war and then the war came into the picture. So the surroundings were very, very hard."

To delve further beyond the surface, I attempted a clichéd journalistic trick, asking about the many tattoos that adorn his body. When I told him I had read up on his body art, he appeared perplexed. And then decided to test me. I did not fare well.

"I don't know if you learn a lot from my tattoos. But okay. Tell me my tattoos. Tell me the position and why."

So on your chest, I said, you have written, *Only God can judge me.*

"I don't have anything on my chest. So you didn't study well."

He lifted up his shirt. It turned out the tattoo is on his rib cage. Oh dear.

But okay, back to the tattoo. You are the son of a Catholic and a Muslim—are you religious?

"No. I believe in respect. So if I tell you, 'Only God can judge me,' who am I aiming at?"

The critics? "No."

Yourself? He nods. "I'll give you a perfect example. When my brother passed away, he had leukemia. Where was God to help him? You thank God every day, you pray to God. But where was God now? In my world, you are your own God. That's what I believe. And that's my mindset."

The conversation felt sincere. His motivation did come from within. His self-belief *was* on a scale unintelligible to many of us.

He says he does not feel any insecurity, which is simultaneously admirable and unattractive. How can he never feel those anxieties? "It is because if I'm objective, I go all in, and then either you succeed or you fail. Is it a 50–50 chance? No, in my case, it's 99–1. I will do everything to succeed. It's all mental. I know how good I am. Even higher, actually, 99.9 percent.

"It depends on you. I am sure about myself. The 0.1 percent chance or 1 percent chance [of failure] depends on them. Either they follow or they go against, but whoever goes against, they fail."

The 0.1 or one percent chance of failure did emerge at Barcelona, where a $72.7 million transfer in 2009 and a move to Pep Guardiola's dream team rapidly went wrong. He has written plenty and said much more about Guardiola, under whom he won La Liga at Barcelona but has also since described as a "spineless coward." The problem, Ibrahimović maintained in this interview, is that he simply felt Guardiola never explained to him what, exactly, his issue was with him.

His reflections on other coaches were more positive. "At Juventus, I had Fabio Capello. He was destroying me, but at the same time building me."

How? "Easy. Today you were shit. Tomorrow you're the best. And it would go like that. So when you think you're the best, he would destroy you. Then it becomes confusion and you don't know: 'Fuck, am I really the best or am I shit?' So when you were down, he was building you up."

Did it work? "I became the best. So, yes."

Did he enjoy it? "I didn't understand it. He made my head . . . like there was no balance. But it made me always give 200 percent. He shaped me. But you also need an identity, culture, and a tradition from the club, as well as a coach. A winner creates winners. Losers don't create winners. That's a culture. So when you come into the club, as a young talent or a player with potential, the club will shape you because you grow to understand the way a club works and the surroundings."

During his period at Manchester United between 2016 and 2018, he was individually successful—scoring 29 goals in 53 games—but the team did not come close to winning the Premier League as their decline in the post–Sir Alex Ferguson era continued.

"They were different from what I was used to. You're just a number there, I felt. Then, in my mindset, I want to make my own history. I was not interested in what happened before, with all respect. Yes, that brings pressure to live up to what they were used to, but I was not interested in listening to the Class of '92. That doesn't help me because it's not my team [that I support] and I wanted to do my own history. I wanted people to say, 'You won and United won this together.'"

Ibrahimović's career is a rich tapestry, traversing many of the most famous clubs and cities in Europe. "Changing clubs is to test myself. I take my backpack and I come to your garden. Different culture, different language, away from home. In your own garden, your mother cooks for you, cleans your clothes, you have everything you want."

Milan, however, appeared to be his true love. Ibrahimović said they gave him "happiness the first time" when rescuing him from Guardiola's Barcelona, "and the second time, they gave me love."

In this interview, I sensed he was searching for a true purpose beyond his playing career. He told Piers Morgan, the British YouTube interviewer, that he would make a fine James Bond villain and said again to me he was "curious about entertainment." He ruled out coaching, laughing about his hair turning gray and the exhausting workload placed upon managers. At Milan, his role appeared to be more than ceremonial, leveraging the club's growth in the United States, where he appeared alongside the club's USMNT forward Christian Pulisic on *CBS Mornings* during their preseason tour and then took part in a spicy-chicken-wing eating contest.

And there may be another legacy, through his children. His son, Maximilian, is a winger and is signed to the club's youth team. When speaking about his children, the bombast gave way.

"It's not easy for him because, obviously, his father is who he is. So he carries a heavy last name. Wherever he goes, he will always be compared. He has to learn, he has to work, and he has to earn. Then what happens, happens. He's strong mentally. People think football is easy and that everybody arrives. But it is not the case."

Player name: Zlatan Ibrahimović
Born: October 3, 1981
Position: Striker
Debut: 1999
Main teams: Malmö (1999–2001), Ajax (2001–04), Juventus (2004–06), Inter Milan (2006–09), Barcelona (2009–11), AC Milan (loan 2010–11, 2011–12, 2020–23), Paris Saint-Germain (2012–16), Manchester United (2016–18), LA Galaxy (2018–19); Sweden (2001–23)
Career highlights: Won the league in the Netherlands, Italy, Spain, and France and scored more than 550 goals in his career, many of them outstanding.

64.

Frank Rijkaard

For all his excellence and the silverware gathered en route, Rijkaard's path to greatness was far from smooth.

The calm yet reluctant leader who stood up to Cruyff

By Simon Hughes

Frank Rijkaard was approaching his 33rd birthday when, in the penultimate game of his professional career, he won Europe's greatest club prize for the third time.

Only a few footballers can claim to have left the sport on such a high. Maybe Rijkaard's was the highest of them all.

One of his former coaches was Johan Cruyff and he, for example, claimed the Dutch Eredivisie in a Feyenoord shirt immediately before retirement, having made the controversial decision to move to Rotterdam from Ajax, the club with whom he is still so identified.

Yet not even Cruyff, a figure who would play such a significant role in Rijkaard's career, can claim to have gone out lifting the European Cup. More about Cruyff later.

In 1995, Rijkaard was one of two elder statesmen in an Ajax team to whom he had returned after five years with AC Milan, their opponents in the final in Vienna. It had been Rijkaard's goal against Benfica in 1990 that had clinched the *Rossoneri* their second European Cup in successive seasons. Now, five years on and at the very same end of the Ernst-Happel Stadium, here he was making a similar hard-charging run from midfield.

On this occasion, rather than finishing the move off himself, he supplied a teenage Patrick Kluivert with the chance to etch his name into history.

The 18-year-old's scuffed shot was enough to beat Sebastiano Rossi. It was an appropriate way to win a scruffy match with few goalscoring opportunities, a showpiece that is more remembered for its subplots, with perhaps the most intriguing of them relating to the presence of Rijkaard.

The average age of that Ajax team was just 23, but it would have been much younger had it not been for the involvement of the veteran midfielder and the team's 33-year-old captain, Danny Blind. Seven of the players who featured in the final had emerged through the club's youth system, including Rijkaard.

This was an era that saw 16 teams compete in the group stages. Ajax had already defeated Milan twice in their section, with 2–0 victories at home and in Italy. In the semifinal, Ajax swept aside a Bayern Munich team managed by the celebrated Italian coach Giovanni Trapattoni, winning 5–2 in Amsterdam following a goalless draw in Germany.

Milan's coach, Fabio Capello, thought he had learned from Trapattoni's mistakes and decided to try to close the final down, reducing Ajax's creative threats by curbing his own team's instincts. This left space in Ajax's defensive third. Rijkaard duly touched the ball more than any other player as he created space for himself by switching positions between defense and midfield.

With neither team looking like scoring, Rijkaard would speak first in the Ajax dressing room at halftime, telling his young teammates to raise their tempo.

For Milan, this was their third straight final. Rijkaard's last European game for the Italians had been in the first of those, a 1–0 loss to Marseille in Munich's Olympic Stadium; a game that also turned out to be the last for his compatriot, Marco van Basten, before he was forced into retirement by injury. The Italians had since beaten Barcelona 4–0 in Athens, a resounding result achieved, according to some of the Milan players, because they had gone into the game feeling inferior to their opponents. That had served as motivation.

Ajax, in contrast, were considered talented but, despite their results earlier in the competition, did not carry the same level of threat. Few in Milan's ranks considered their opponents *better* than them this time around.

But, for all that Capello's team had experience, they struggled to live with Ajax's energy as the game wore on. Louis van Gaal, the Dutch side's manager, made brave substitutions. Before Kluivert was introduced in the second half, on came Nigerian Nwankwo Kanu—another 18-year-old.

Kluivert would later tell *The Guardian* that he was able to get up to speed quickly because of the Ajax production line that allowed players to "plug straight into the system and play like I had for years." Milan striker Daniele Massaro told the same newspaper that he had "never seen such intense rhythm and concentration from young players."

Rijkaard's former Milan teammates tended to point to his leadership as decisive in helping Ajax secure the title at their expense. Despite being right at the end of his career, Rijkaard still had something to prove.

Though Milan had wanted to keep him two years earlier, he was never absolutely convinced of their commitment. He could be a difficult person and a difficult player to keep down—as even someone as formidable as Cruyff had found out.

• • •

In 1987, Rijkaard told Cruyff, then Ajax's head coach, that he was giving up his role as captain and walking out of the club.

After selling Van Basten to AC Milan, Rijkaard had assumed a senior role in the dressing room at the age of only 24. Except he just wanted to play football. With Cruyff's expectations of him enormous, the midfielder quickly found the experience of being a leader under his stewardship draining.

Overnight, he had become embroiled in politics: discussions over wages, transfers, and the welfare of other players. And Cruyff continued to peck away at him. After one dispute during a training session, according to Jonathan Wilson in his book, *The Barcelona Legacy*, Rijkaard turned to Cruyff and shouted, "Fuck you and your eternal whining," before walking out of the session.

Cruyff was shocked, later telling *Voetbal International* that his initial comment to have provoked that reaction had been "the sort you make a hundred or so times a day."

Perhaps that was the problem. Cruyff had a distinctive way of addressing people. When Pep Guardiola was interviewed by *Marca* in 2016, he revealed that, following his Barcelona debut, the Dutch master had told him he was "slower than my grandmother."

Some put up with such talk. But Rijkaard had a threshold.

As a young player at Ajax at the start of the 1980s, Jan Molby, a future Liverpool midfielder, had witnessed Rijkaard's physical capabilities during preseason training in the forests outside Amsterdam. "We used to do 150-meter runs on a slight incline," Molby said in 2015. "Our coach had trained the Dutch Olympic athletics team. Frank was my partner. I was absolutely flat out just to be 10 meters behind him and he wasn't trying. . . ."

According to Molby, Rijkaard was "laid-back," but he had a tendency to let things build up. And then, at some point, it would all come pouring out.

So, having endured everything the captaincy brought with it and having been riled by what he perceived to be Cruyff's constant sniping, Rijkaard opened up to a journalist who had doorstepped his home. He calmly said he would not be returning to Ajax until either he was sold or Cruyff was sacked.

Something had to give. And it was not Cruyff.

Rijkaard ended up signing for Portugal's Sporting Lisbon, only to leave the club without playing a game after an issue with his registration. There was a loan spell in Spain with Real Zaragoza before he joined Van Basten and fellow compatriot Ruud Gullit in Milan, where the trio contributed significantly to the club's subsequent domination of Serie A and European football.

A player who had won three Eredivisie titles, three KNVB Cups, and a European Cup Winners' Cup in his first spell at Ajax claimed two European Cups and a pair of Serie A titles with the *Rossoneri*. He was a key member of the Dutch squad that won the European Championship in 1988, still their only major international honor, and would return to Ajax to enjoy two more Dutch title successes as well as that Champions League in 1995.

Yet, for all his excellence and the silverware gathered en route, Rijkaard's path to greatness was far from smooth.

The enduring image of the Dutchman is from the 1990 World Cup in Italy, where he spat at the German striker Rudi Völler in a game where both players were sent off. Rijkaard tended to glide across the pitch with a distinctive scowl, but he and his friends in football have always suggested his reaction to the confrontation between the pair was completely out of character.

Inside dressing rooms, he tended to bring calm to chaos. Yet when pushed, he could snap. He made his professional debut at age 17 but was soon dropped from the team. However, his confidence returned and he became an Ajax regular.

Given the power and influence wielded by Cruyff, Rijkaard did well to reestablish himself elsewhere after that messy divorce and gradually repair their relationship to the extent that when Barcelona needed a manager, Cruyff vouched for him.

Reflecting on their relationship as player and coach, Rijkaard told *Voetbal International* that he had a "great time at Ajax and a great time with Johan Cruyff," but their separation in 1987 was inevitable because they "just didn't click anymore."

According to Rijkaard, their approaches to football were "diametrically opposed." Cruyff seemed to feed off tension, wanting training sessions where groups of players were "set against each other." By the time he left, Rijkaard was simply tired of the environment in which he had been working, though Cruyff ultimately forgave him.

In Barcelona, where Cruyff is also revered, it seems unfair that Rijkaard's achievements as coach are largely overlooked because of what followed under Guardiola, whose team arguably changed the way the game was played.

Barcelona claimed two Champions League titles under Guardiola and another while Luis Enrique was in charge, but it is easy to forget that, until 2006, they had won the European Cup only once. In Paris against Arsenal, Rijkaard helped improve that record with a squad that was arguably just as talented as the one overseen by Guardiola.

That he lasted five years at the Camp Nou is a testament to his staying power, yet Rijkaard is rarely commemorated for his work as a manager. His achievement in taking the Netherlands to the semifinals of the European Championship in 2000 tends to be forgotten. He later took charge of Galatasaray before an 18-month spell with Saudi Arabia that ended in 2013.

Since then, he has disappeared from view, occasionally appearing publicly in his role as an ambassador for the Johan Cruyff Foundation.

Those who have followed his career closely in the Netherlands are not surprised. He never relished the attention that came with football, just as someone as revered as Cruyff discovered.

Player name: Franklin Rijkaard
Born: September 30, 1962
Position: Midfielder, center-back
Debut: 1980
Main teams: Ajax (1980–87, 1993–95), Real Zaragoza (loan, 1988), AC Milan (1988–93); Netherlands (1981–94)
Career highlights: Won Euro 1988 and the European Cup three times. Claimed five Dutch titles with Ajax and the *Scudetto* twice with Milan.

63.

Mario Kempes

Kempes was the driving force behind Argentina's first World Cup triumph in 1978.

El Matador, Argentina's original No. 10

By Felipe Cárdenas

When it comes to Argentina's best No. 10s of all time, Diego Maradona and Lionel Messi represent the pinnacle, players known around the world as the country's very best exports. They are considered the finest the sport has ever seen. And there has only been one other compatriot worthy of sitting at the same table.

Mario Kempes was actually Argentina's first great No. 10. At the

1978 World Cup, a finals played on home soil, Kempes was the driving force behind Argentina's first World Cup triumph. The reward was the *Albiceleste*'s first star above one of the heaviest badges in international football, with Kempes ending the tournament as the top scorer.

Maradona himself was awestruck by the lanky, long-haired Kempes, a prolific goalscorer whose style was ahead of its time. He was one of the younger man's role models, a left-footed playmaker who could thrive in any position in the attacking third and a European-based star at a time when few from Argentina plied their trade abroad. Indeed, Kempes was the only player on the World Cup–winning squad who did not play professionally in his homeland. His success served to raise the Argentina flag internationally during the military dictatorship that gripped the country back home.

For the young Maradona, who did not make the 1978 squad but would go on to speak out against the regime's atrocities through his own stellar career, Kempes symbolized everything a national team hero should be.

Etched in the memory was the brace Kempes scored in the World Cup final to defeat a Netherlands side boasting their own wealth of talent. "Thank you, Mario, for what you did at the World Cup," Maradona, then only 19, said in 1979 after a friendly between Argentina's under-20s and Valencia, the Spanish club where Kempes excelled across two stints. "Today, the Argentine people applauded him and understood what Mario is. He is the best player in the world."

Three years later, Kempes would cede the No. 10 shirt to Maradona at the World Cup in Spain, yet the legacy he had established was already deeply rooted. The number on the back of his jersey was almost incidental.

"When you hear what Diego said, you have to be grateful. You would expect my chest to puff out, but I was never one of those people," says Kempes. "I had the great honour of wearing the No. 10 shirt for Argentina and maybe I was the 'first' to make his mark in it, but you can't win a war by yourself. *We* were world champions in 1978.

"At the World Cup, I just wanted to play. I didn't care about the number I wore. In fact, I was only given the 10 because of where my name was on the squad list alphabetically. Had I been given the 11 shirt or any other number, maybe my story would have been different."

The notion of destiny in sport is a popular narrative and Kempes believes his moment of glory in 1978 was almost too perfect.

He had cemented his name among the country's best players by featuring for Rosario Central and playing in every game for Argentina as a teenager at the 1974 World Cup, before his move to Valencia in 1976. Kempes was La Liga's top scorer in consecutive seasons as the World Cup in his homeland approached. But out of sight, out of mind. Despite his resounding success in Spain, Kempes was not really on national manager César Luis Menotti's radar before the competition began.

Argentina's head coach had been determined to build a squad made up of domestic-based players. To this day, Kempes does not know who convinced Menotti to add an outsider to a group that had become tight-knit over their World Cup preparations, yet even now he refers to himself as "the only foreigner" in the 1978 squad. He was also the difference-maker.

Daniel Passarella may have lifted the World Cup in Buenos Aires on June 25, having been carried off the pitch on the shoulders of the rabid Argentina fans, but it was Kempes who had been a class apart. His six goals over the tournament—braces against Poland, Peru, and the Dutch in the final—told the story of a player at his peak. In the bright lights of River Plate's Estadio Monumental and under the critical eye of the Argentine public, the Valencia forward became a hero.

Journalists who attended the finals voted him the player of the tournament, an honor eventually echoed by FIFA, who retrospectively selected him for the Golden Ball despite that award only officially being adopted in 1982. "I thought everything was predetermined for me, as if everything had been calculated," he adds. "In addition to wearing the No. 10, I was the top goalscorer and I was voted the best player in the world. It was the perfect combination."

• • •

It is important to acknowledge that Kempes hardly caught anyone by surprise in 1978. Surely Menotti remembered the forward's tenacity as a young professional for modest club Instituto Atlético Central Córdoba. He would have confronted an eager-to-please Kempes as the manager of Huracán in the early 1970s. At that time, the player was a budding center-forward enduring something of an identity crisis.

When he first arrived at Instituto for a trial, Kempes was an attacking midfielder with the physical attributes of a striker. When Instituto's staff asked him if he had ever played as a No. 9, he answered in the affirmative. But that was not entirely truthful. "I had just traveled 200 kilometers from home for the tryout," Kempes says. "I had never played as a No. 9 before—I was a midfielder, a No. 10—but I did have the instincts of a goalscorer."

Kempes also had rockstar hair. He kept his socks at shin level, his left foot was silky and powerful, and he was a relentless runner who always wanted to be on the ball. He was far from a prototypical center-forward who fed off service into the penalty area, but he would give everything. And, even if he craved a deeper role, his movement when thrust farther forward and the spaces he occupied unsettled opposition back lines.

"I liked to be involved all over the pitch. I didn't like to stay still. That must have been an advantage for me. I didn't mind defending and I had no issues joining the attack. I wanted the ball at all times. A lot of my goals came after I started a run from a deep-lying position. I was always moving, moving."

He was always scoring, too. While playing for Rosario Central, whom he joined in 1973, renowned Argentine commentator José Maria Muñoz challenged Kempes to score more goals away from Central's Estadio Gigante de Arroyito. Muñoz felt the youngster saved his best performances for the home crowd and had not been as dominant against the Buenos Aires–based clubs.

"Muñoz told me after a match: 'I'll give you a nickname if you score two goals in your next game in Buenos Aires,'" Kempes recalls. "I scored three against Banfield and [Muñoz] was there. That day, he gave me the nickname *El Matador*. The Killer. He challenged me and the nickname stuck. There have been many others who have taken that nickname on, too . . . but after me."

Kempes was special. He was no box-dwelling killer, as most clinical center-forwards tend to be. His late-arriving runs and coolness in front of goal were his trademarks and both attributes were on display against the Netherlands in the 1978 World Cup final. His second goal was vintage Kempes. A burst behind his midfield marker left him running at full tilt at the Dutch defense, hurdling one defender before sidestepping another. His shot was saved initially by Jan Jongbloed, but Kempes, always active, beat two more Dutch defenders to the rebound to poke the ball into the net.

Argentina's third goal was born from another line-breaking run by Kempes. He was involved in all three scored by the hosts that day in what is still considered one of the greatest World Cup final performances of all time.

All these years on, he prefers to deflect praise for that display and points to the efforts of his teammates, who he says deserve all the credit for Argentina's success in 1978. He concedes, however, that every championship-winning team benefits from a dash of good fortune.

"As they say, the first one is always the most difficult," says Kempes through a laugh. "Football isn't always about having the best players. Sometimes you need a little bit of good luck, too. Argentina didn't have that luck in Brazil [in 2014] when they got to the final and Germany did that day. Back in 1974, the Dutch took the lead against West Germany and still lost.

"Against us, they equalized and could have won the game late on, but Rob Rensenbrink's shot hit the post. They didn't have the luck that we had."

Luck is like destiny. There is no way to quantify it. But Kempes's legacy *can* be measured. He was a high-scoring elite player during a transformational time for football. He briefly stood alongside Johan Cruyff and Gerd Müller, greats of that era, as an equal. And a World Cup winner.

And yet Kempes's impact has been overshadowed in the years since, first by the force of nature that was Maradona, and then, again, by the prolonged brilliance of Messi. Maybe he suffered for being at the very top for a relatively short span of time in comparison to his compatriots. Although he featured in three World Cups and gained the last of his 43 caps in 1982, his goals in the 1978 final were his last for his country.

Regardless, the people of Córdoba have never forgotten, with the Estadio Mario Alberto Kempes named after their favorite son. So does he think he should be mentioned in the same breath as the great No. 10s, both World Cup winners in their own right, who followed in his footsteps?

"If we're talking about the No. 10 role, then yes," he adds. "But I can't even say that I was the best player on that [1978] team. What I would say is we were obligated to win that tournament. We were playing at home and we knew the fans—the people—would be all over us if we made any mistakes. All the work we had done would go to the trash if we lost. So there was real pressure on us.

"It was a difficult era for Argentina. Everything was militarized, but we were just footballers who wore the Argentina shirt without any military insignia on the jersey. We were there to play football for every Argentine."

Player name: Mario Alberto Kempes Chiodi
Born: July 15, 1954
Position: Striker, attacking midfielder
Debut: 1970
Main teams: Instituto (1970–73), Rosario Central (1973–76), Valencia (1976–81, 1982–84), River Plate (1981–82), Hércules (1984–86), First Vienna (1986–87), St. Pölten (1987–90), Kremser SC (1990–92), Pelita Jaya (1993–94); Argentina (1973–82)
Career highlights: Won the 1978 World Cup on home soil and won the Golden Boot at the tournament, scoring twice in the final.

62.

Ryan Giggs

Slight of build but fearless, Giggs broke into the Manchester United team as a 17-year-old.

The evolution of an icon told through three of his finest goals

By Stuart James

A Manchester United icon. There is no other way to describe a man who made 963 appearances for the club across 23 years, becoming the most decorated player in the history of English football along the way. By the time he retired in 2014 at the age of 40, Ryan Giggs had won 35 trophies, including 13 Premier League titles, and scored 168 goals.

To tell the story of Giggs's talent, his evolution as a footballer, and his extraordinary longevity at the highest level, let us reflect upon three of his finest goals for United.

Goal one: Tottenham Hotspur 1–1 Manchester United Premier League, White Hart Lane, September 1992

"I remember the first time I saw him. He was 13 and he floated across the ground like a cocker spaniel chasing a piece of silver paper in the wind."

That wonderful Sir Alex Ferguson quote perfectly encapsulated what it was like watching Ryan Giggs playing for Manchester United in the early 1990s, when he glided past defenders with such élan, tormenting them with his pace, beautiful balance, and superb dribbling ability.

Slight of build but fearless, Giggs broke into the United team as a 17-year-old in March 1991, a time when Ferguson was still chasing his first league title at Old Trafford. An early graduate from the "Class of '92"—the exceptional group of United apprentices that also included David Beckham, Gary Neville, Phil Neville, Paul Scholes, and Nicky Butt—Giggs was transformed into a star overnight.

He was named the PFA Young Player of the Year in 1991–92, at the age of 18, and was immediately compared to George Best. Fittingly, the former United superstar was at White Hart Lane in September 1992 to see Giggs score the second of his 109 Premier League goals—a goal that showcased everything so special about him as a teenager.

The game was approaching halftime when Dean Austin, the Spurs right-back, slipped as he attempted to control a long pass on his chest. Like a cat after a mouse, Giggs was on the loose ball in a flash, his first touch nicking it away from Austin, who ended up face down on the floor, eating the grass.

Jason Cundy's humiliation was greater. The Spurs defender was caught square-on, flat-footed and with his legs wide open as Giggs ran toward him. In short, Cundy was a nutmeg waiting to happen and

Giggs wasn't going to turn down the invitation. He pushed the ball through Cundy's legs and scampered around him. By the time Cundy had regained his bearings, Giggs was through on goal.

Giggs's directness when dribbling was astonishing. Two touches of the ball had taken two Spurs defenders out of the game and a third touch was about to eliminate the goalkeeper, Ian Walker, who made the fatal mistake of underestimating Giggs's pace as he dashed from his line.

Remarkably, Giggs said in 2005 that he hadn't sprinted "flat out" for a decade because he was so worried about suffering a recurrence of his hamstring problems. But the 1992 version had no such concerns. There was no speed limiter fitted, and good luck to anyone who tried to keep up with him.

Giggs pushed the ball beyond Walker with the outside of his left foot and, despite the angle narrowing significantly, finished emphatically, sweeping the ball into the far corner with a mixture of power and precision. Barry Davies, the BBC commentator, was so impressed that he said a word that was a mixture of brilliant and beautiful, which summed the goal up.

"I think that was one of the goals that probably really announced Ryan," Gary Pallister, the former United defender who was playing that day, says. "His balance was fantastic—he could just dip his shoulder and send someone the wrong way—and there was the speed, which was quite a force of nature. But then, at the end of it all, there was the cool finish, too."

It was a goal that was reminiscent of one that Best scored for United against Sheffield United in 1971, albeit from the right-hand side of the penalty area. Not that anyone had to look hard for the similarities. "Ryan's going to be a great, great player," Best told *Sky Sports* after the game. "He's going to have to suffer, if that's the word, with the comparison. But he's got so much confidence in his own ability."

Goal two: Arsenal 1–2 Manchester United (AET) FA Cup semifinal, Villa Park, April 1999

Giggs, by his own admission, had been "having a nightmare" before scoring what he considered to be the greatest goal of his career. Introduced as a second-half substitute on a night when Ferguson picked a curious starting lineup, the Welshman gave the ball away repeatedly, which was the last thing United needed when they went down to 10 men following the dismissal of Roy Keane.

Ironically, though, it was an Arsenal player passing the ball to Giggs that provided the "assist" for a classic FA Cup moment.

A little bit of context first. Arsenal were going for a second successive double. United were trying to win the treble. The rivalry between the two clubs was intense. They both had great managers—Ferguson and Arsène Wenger—and brilliant teams. There was mutual respect for one another, but mutual dislike, too, and all of that made for a compelling spectacle whenever they met.

Three days earlier, Arsenal and United had drawn 0–0 at the same venue. The replay—the last FA Cup semifinal replay—was an epic that was decided by a combination of a Peter Schmeichel penalty save to deny Dennis Bergkamp a late winner in normal time and a moment of individual brilliance from Giggs.

But the backdrop to the replay was interesting, to say the least. As well as omitting Giggs from the starting XI (Jesper Blomqvist took his place), Ferguson started with Dwight Yorke on the bench and left out Andrew Cole. Yorke and Cole were United's first-choice strike pairing and ended up scoring 53 goals between them that season. Ferguson's rationale was that he needed to freshen things up, especially after playing 120 minutes against Arsenal a little more than 72 hours earlier, although he did later acknowledge that the team he picked had surprised the club's directors.

In between the two FA Cup ties against Arsenal, Ferguson called Giggs into his office to remind him that his pace and direct running—"his capacity to terrorize defenders," as the United manager put it—were his biggest assets.

Twenty-five at the time, Giggs had started to adapt his game. In his autobiography, Giggs wrote about how he thought he looked like "a headless chicken running with no real purpose" when he watched his younger self, prompting a shift toward becoming more of a "pass-and-move midfielder."

Ferguson clearly felt the pendulum had swung too far the other way and wanted to see more of the Giggs of old. That said, the United manager admitted he was urging Giggs to take the ball toward the corner flag when he ran onto Patrick Vieira's wayward pass in the second period of extra time, believing that a penalty shootout was the best chance of victory.

Giggs had other ideas.

What followed was a mesmerizing solo run that started from inside the United half and saw him skip away from the retreating Vieira, tear outside Lee Dixon, past Martin Keown, and beyond Dixon again. As Tony Adams came across to make a desperate attempt to block, the Arsenal goalkeeper, David Seaman, stooped low at his near post and Giggs unleashed a powerful shot over his head and into the roof of the net. It was a sensational goal. "He's cut Arsenal to ribbons," Sky commentator Martin Tyler said.

"It would be nice to say that I had it all in my head, what I was going to do, but it doesn't happen like that. It unfolds too quickly to think. Instead, instinct and feel take over," Giggs said. "Dixon and Adams tried to get to me, but I got away from them and then I'm up against David Seaman. Now, I did pause for a millisecond and thought, 'Just hit it.' And I did."

Cue bedlam as Giggs, with considerably more hair on his chest than United's Dutch center-back Jaap Stam had on his head, sprinted back down the touchline swinging his shirt above his head. It was Giggs's 10th goal of the season, his 76th in a United shirt and, in his own words, "the one I'd like to be remembered by." The following month, United completed the treble.

Goal three: West Ham United 0–1 Manchester United Premier League, Upton Park, February 2009

In many ways, this felt like a collector's item. "I am searching my memory bank for the last time Ryan scored with his right foot," Ferguson said after a narrow victory at West Ham in 2009. "I think it was against Coventry 12 years ago."

Giggs was never really encouraged to develop his weaker foot when he was younger. Indeed, he saw that as one of the few negatives about being promoted to the United first team so early—in his mind, he missed out on some of the basic technical work that the apprentices were doing to address weaknesses in their game. In fairness, it didn't exactly hold him back.

In February 2009, at the age of 35, Giggs was approaching 800 first-team appearances for United. He was still producing match-defining moments, too, and making Premier League players look silly. Is Carlton Cole still sliding somewhere in east London?

The West Ham forward came running across at breakneck speed to block Giggs's "cross" from the left wing, throwing himself to the floor. Giggs, who had received possession from a trademark Scholes diagonal pass, saw Cole coming a mile off, faked to deliver a center, and coolly chopped back inside. Cole carried on down the water chute.

Next up was Scott Parker, who made the same mistake of assuming Giggs would swing a ball over with his left foot. Giggs ducked inside Parker, too, the West Ham midfielder skipping by like Dick Van Dyke.

Michael Carrick, positioned about 25 yards out, was screaming for the ball now, but Giggs only had eyes for goal and swept a low, crisp shot into the far corner with his weaker foot, before being mobbed by Dimitar Berbatov, Cristiano Ronaldo, Carlos Tevez, and Scholes. Giggs was in good company in that respect and his United teammates knew they were, too.

It was the only goal of the game, and at the time maintained Giggs's record of scoring in every Premier League season since its formation in 1992. It also provided a timely reminder of his enduring quality at a point in the season when votes were being gathered for the PFA awards.

Two months later, at the end of April, Giggs was named the PFA Player of the Year for the first time in his career, pipping four of his United teammates—Ronaldo, Rio Ferdinand, Nemanja Vidić, and Edwin van der Sar—as well as Liverpool's Steven Gerrard, to the award.

At the time of the announcement, Giggs had started just 12 Premier League games for United that season and his only goal was his winner at Upton Park. Some felt sentiment and nostalgia had clouded the judgment of those who voted for him.

Others pointed to Giggs's adaptation as a player, from a winger to a creative central midfielder, and the fact he was still influencing matches at the highest level, whether as an impact substitute or a starter, as justification for the accolade. Either way, nobody could dispute that Giggs's class was permanent.

Incredibly, he would go on to play for United for another five years, leaving an indelible mark on the game in England and beyond. "You get players who come along and you say, 'They are once-in-a-lifetime players'; I would say Ryan Giggs is that," Ferguson told UEFA in 2009.

Player name: Ryan Giggs
Born: November 29, 1973
Position: Winger
Debut: 1991
Main teams: Manchester United (1991–2014); Wales (1991–2007)
Career highlights: Won the Premier League 13 times, the Champions League twice, and overall, 35 trophies at Manchester United. That included the treble in 1998–99. He played a record 963 games for the club.

61.

Sócrates

Sócrates had the skill, intelligence, and technical ability to excel despite his lack of commitment to training.

The medically trained, chain-smoking midfielder at the heart of Corinthians Democracy

By Sarah Shephard

Footballer. Doctor. Social activist. Drinker. Smoker. Leader.

Sócrates Brasileiro Sampaio de Souza Vieira de Oliveira was all these things, but as captain of the Brazil squad that headed to the 1982 World Cup in Spain expected (and expecting) to return home with the trophy, he was acutely aware that some of those roles would have to take a back seat, at least for the duration of the tournament.

At the start of the year, he decided he would give up the half pack of Minister cigarettes that had been a daily pleasure for so long, down from the two packs a day he had consumed up until mid-1980, and dedicate himself to training in a way he never had before.

It paid off. The player who once described himself as an "anti-athlete," based on his penchant for cigarettes and copious amounts of beer, outperformed his teammates in pretournament fitness tests. And when Brazil found themselves trailing in their opening game against the Soviet Union, it was Sócrates who scored the goal that put the favorites back on track. When a poor clearance fell kindly into his path in the 75th minute, around 35 yards from goal, the mercurial midfielder glanced up, skipped over one tackle, swerved right to avoid another, and unleashed a beautiful right-foot shot from 25 yards out that flew into the top left-hand corner.

"No, not a goal," he later recounted. "An endless orgasm."

It's a description that perfectly encapsulates a man for whom life was about experiences. Connections. Freedom. Winning was nice and it was important to him at certain times (not least at that World Cup in 1982, when he was crushed by Brazil's defeat against Italy in the second-round group stage), but more important for Sócrates was being able to live a life of true freedom—and enabling others to do the same.

The firstborn child of Guiomar Sampaio de Souza and Raimundo Vieira de Oliveira, Sócrates was born in 1954 and so named thanks to the fascination of his self-educated father with Greek philosophers. His first three sons were all named after them, but by the time the fourth arrived, Guiomar put her foot down. Raimundo Jr. was born five years after Sócrates.

Their eldest son was a gangly child—later in life, friends called him *Magrao*, or "Big Skinny"—who spent his formative years in Belém, on the banks of the Amazon, where he spent his days watching his father devour books and study hard to earn the qualifications needed to become a tax inspector. Shortly before Sócrates's sixth birthday, Raimundo secured a job in Ribeirão Preto, a city in São Paulo state, and the entire family relocated south.

It was there that Sócrates became increasingly preoccupied with the sport that would ultimately change his life.

He was introduced to a scintillating Santos side featuring the sublime skills of Pelé, Coutinho, and Pepe via his father's radio and got up close to the game by going to watch local side Botafogo-SP with his dad every weekend. But playing the game brought Sócrates even more joy than watching it and joining local amateur side Raio de Ouro at the age of 11 gave him a first glimpse of the true power that football possessed. He traveled to games on the back of a flatbed truck, alongside teammates from a vast array of backgrounds, some far less privileged than his own.

"Football gives you a contact with reality that other professions don't," recounts Sócrates in Andrew Downie's 2017 biography, *Doctor Sócrates*. "Football is so democratic. I was always around people with different social situations from my own, with different levels of education. So you see reality up close."

As much as he loved football, for many years it came second to another of his passions: medicine.

Sócrates dreamed of being a doctor and, during his teenage years, prioritized his studies over training. By 16, his talents on the pitch had got him noticed by Botafogo, who wanted to sign him for their junior side. But when he discovered their training sessions clashed with his night classes, Sócrates told the club he would only sign on the understanding that he would be available for weekend matches, but his presence at the twice-weekly training sessions was not guaranteed.

He never missed a match, but there were some close calls. On one occasion, Sócrates arrived so late for Botafogo's game away at Corinthians that he had to buy a match ticket to get into the stadium and sprint around the terraces to find the dressing rooms while dressed in a white coat and carrying a medical bag.

Sócrates had the skill, intelligence, and technical ability to excel despite his lack of commitment to training (and growing love of drinking, smoking, and socializing). In 1976, his goals and ability to control a game from midfield helped Botafogo win the Torneio Vicente Feola, putting them—and him—on the map.

A year later, 23-year-old Sócrates became a qualified physician, putting him at a crossroads. In one direction, the career in medicine he'd worked toward for so long. In the other, life as a professional footballer.

Two days before he was due to take on a resident's position in a hospital, Sócrates swerved the other way and signed a new contract with Botafogo. His father's constant reminders that he could always practice medicine *after* football were one reason. The money on offer from the club was another—Sócrates was guaranteed to earn at least 10 times more as a footballer than a young doctor.

There was only one problem with Botafogo. As big a name as Sócrates had become at the club, and even with those on the outside who had noticed the tall, skinny player whose vision and technique set him apart from his peers, it was not enough to convince those in charge of the national team that he was deserving of a place in Brazil's 1978 World Cup squad.

Sócrates dreamed of wearing the famous yellow shirt at a World Cup and believed the way to make it happen was to move to a bigger club. In 1978, he joined one of Brazil's biggest, Corinthians, marking the start of what would become a beautiful, eternal love story between player and club—though it took some time for that love to develop.

"I've never been a Corinthians supporter," Sócrates told reporters in his first interview after joining the club (he was rarely anything other than brutally honest). "Quite the contrary, I was a very big Santos fan."

Not only were fans' suspicions immediately aroused, but his teammates were initially uncertain, too. This guy was different. He spoke differently. Dressed differently. Behaved differently.

In time, they would realize just how different Sócrates was.

When Sócrates was 10, he watched as his father burned those of his books that could be considered supportive of left-wing politics.

It came in the wake of a military coup in Brazil that marked the beginning of an increasingly restrictive, authoritarian regime. Sócrates was too young to fully comprehend what was happening at the time, and even as he got older, he was too consumed with playing football, studying medicine, and chasing women to devote too much thought to political matters.

Gradually, that changed.

At Botafogo, Sócrates noticed how some players, especially those not blessed with his middle-class, educated background, were treated like children. If they dared to speak out, they risked losing their careers. Sócrates saw it as a situation designed to keep players in a position of powerlessness, something he resolved to change.

A few years later, when he'd been a Corinthians player for about a year, Sócrates took issue with the team's shirt sponsor, Topper, who gave players just two shirts a month. If they wanted any extras to auction or give to a friend, they had to pay for them. Sócrates told his teammates they had the power to change this situation, suggesting they turn their training gear inside out so the Topper logo wouldn't be visible in newspaper articles or on television.

They all agreed and, soon after, Topper started supplying each player with 10 shirts a month for their own use.

Around the same time, in 1979, Sócrates was called up to the *Seleção* for a series of friendlies in which he showed the nation just how special a player he was; an intelligent midfielder with a creative vision and technical ability that sometimes left even his own teammates stunned.

"When he got the ball, we didn't know what was going to happen," said Walter Casagrande, a center-forward who played with Sócrates for both club and country. "If you didn't accompany his thought process even a little bit, you'd get lost and end up looking like a fool."

So adept did Sócrates become at deploying a perfectly weighted backheeled pass from any part of the pitch that Pelé once joked that he played better with his back to goal than most players did facing forward.

When new Brazil manager Telê Santana made Sócrates captain

the following year, it solidified his position as one of the most famous faces, and names, in Brazil.

Sócrates's newfound sense of responsibility had an impact on his role at Corinthians, too. In 1981, the team were struggling and he believed the only way to change things was to create a sense of solidarity around the club. In an interview with *Placar* magazine, he talked about the need to close the gap between boss and employee; to create an environment where players felt they were cared about as people as well as employees. "What I want," said Sócrates, "is that Corinthians becomes an extension of each of our families."

His words became the basis of Corinthians Democracy, a radical movement that transformed the club into a place where no individual was more important than another. Where those working behind the scenes, washing kit, massaging players' tired limbs, and cleaning the changing rooms received a percentage of the team's win bonuses and where players would get to vote on all important decisions affecting the club, including signings.

By the mid-1980s, one of the country's biggest football clubs was being run as a democracy, operating in stark contrast to the brutal military dictatorship that had ruled Brazil since 1964. Corinthians Democracy would go down in history, writes Downie, as "the most transformative movement ever to rock a major football club." And Sócrates was at the heart of it.

The World Cup side Sócrates led in 1982 dazzled fans across the world with its attacking flair and fast, one-touch football. He dubbed their style "organized chaos," signaling both the freedom the players felt on the pitch and the solid foundations the squad had put in place over two years of working together.

"That Brazil side was extraordinary," says Pep Guardiola, who describes their football as "the most beautiful I've ever seen from a national side."

Sócrates never got his hands on the trophy, though, missing out in 1982 and 1986 when Brazil were knocked out by France in the quar-

terminals. But it was the *Seleção*'s shock 3–2 defeat by Italy in 1982—a team whose more pragmatic style was in direct contrast to the free-flowing Brazil—that left its deepest scar.

"Football as we know it died on that day," Sócrates said in an interview with Brazilian journalist Fernando Duarte in 2004, some 22 years after the event, believing their defeat led the Brazil teams that followed to eschew creative freedom for a more pragmatic style of play.

In the wake of 1982, Sócrates's political influence strengthened.

Earlier that year, he and his teammates at Corinthians had taken to the field wearing shirts bearing the words *Dia 15 Vote* (Vote on the 15th) ahead of Brazil's first multiparty elections under military rule. And in 1983, the team carried a huge banner reading "Win or Lose, But Always with Democracy" as they took to the field for a title-deciding match against São Paulo.

Over the two-legged tie, Sócrates scored twice, each time raising a clenched fist in celebration, a salute that became something of a trademark and tallied perfectly with the Corinthians Democracy movement that carried so much momentum.

His finest political hour came in 1984 when he played a leading role in a rally of more than a million people who gathered in São Paulo to show their support for the *Diretas Já* (Direct Elections Now) campaign, putting pressure on the flailing military dictatorship to announce a general election. It was a cause Sócrates felt passionate about and, with the rally coinciding with a period of huge uncertainty over his future at Corinthians (talk of interest from Italian clubs was rife), he knew exactly what he had to do.

Taking to the stage alongside some of his teammates, Sócrates made a promise to the people: If the parliamentary amendment allowing direct elections for president were to succeed, he would reject an offer to play in Italy.

"He's staying here! He's staying here! He's staying here!" chanted the masses.

"He was one of the few players who put principles and life ahead of money," explained Sócrates's biographer Downie in a recent interview with *El País*. "He was willing to give up millions for playing in Italy to take part in the transition to democracy."

Later that month, the amendment failed by just 22 votes, sealing Sócrates's move to Europe, where he spent a season with Fiorentina before returning to Brazil until his retirement in 1989 barring a brief cameo for nonleague side Garforth Town in England in 2004, at the age of 50. Seven years after that 12-minute reprise, Sócrates was gone, suffering from septic shock after an intestinal infection.

An icon of world football, immediately recognizable by his long, lean physique, curly dark hair, and Che Guevara-esque beard, Sócrates's hero status in his home country and beyond remains, secured in respect for a player who led his country both on and off the pitch and remained unapologetically, unashamedly himself.

Footballer. Doctor. Social activist. Drinker. Smoker. Leader. He was all of them and so much more.

Player name: Sócrates Brasileiro Sampaio de Souza Vieira de Oliveira
Born: February 19, 1954
Died: December 4, 2011 (aged 57)
Position: Midfielder
Debut: 1974
Main teams: Botafogo-SP (1974–78, 1989), Corinthians (1978–84), Fiorentina (1984–85), Flamengo (1986–87), Santos (1988–89); Brazil (1979–86)
Career highlights: Captain of brilliant, if underachieving, Brazil team at the 1982 World Cup.

60.

Just Fontaine

Fontaine scored 13 goals at the 1958 World Cup.

The striker whose World Cup record may never be beaten

By Liam Twomey

In the first act of Jean-Pierre Jeunet's classic 2001 film, *Amélie,* Audrey Tautou's titular hero lures the former occupant of her apartment, Dominique Bretodeau, into a phone booth so she can anonymously reunite him with an old metal box he hid as a boy. It is filled with decades-old childhood memorabilia that will reduce him to a sobbing wreck and quickly convince him to reconnect with his estranged daughter.

The first thing he—and the viewer—sees when he opens the box is a black-and-white photograph of Just Fontaine, the white-rimmed Gallic cockerel badge visible against the dark stain on his France shirt, with a match ball clamped tightly between his right palm and hip as he walks off the pitch.

It is an image that conjures more than just one man's nostalgia. Fontaine will forever be synonymous with 1958, the first golden summer of French football, when one of the deadliest strikers the sport has ever seen scored 13 goals in six matches to set the one World Cup record that may never be broken.

Fontaine wasn't even supposed to start for France. That honor belonged to RC Paris striker Thadée Cisowski until the French league's top scorer in 1955–56 and 1956–57 broke his leg in the run-up to the tournament. Fontaine had dealt with an injury of his own, undergoing knee surgery in December 1957, but the timing effectively gave his body a winter break.

His blistering form after returning to action in February 1958 propelled Stade de Reims—the club he had joined from Nice in 1956 to fill the void left by the great Raymond Kopa's move to Real Madrid—to a league and cup double and he finished the 1957–58 campaign with 34 goals in 26 league games. "I did what I needed [to do] to come back and so, by the time June came around, I was walking on water," he said later. "Like Jesus."

Fontaine and his Reims teammate René Bliard were in contention for Cisowski's spot, but Bliard flew home injured shortly after the team's arrival in Sweden. Fontaine's final obstacle was his footwear; his only pair of boots ripped during the last training session before the tournament and neither Adidas nor Puma could supply immediate replacements. He ended up borrowing the pair belonging to substitute striker Stéphane Bruey, who fortunately wore the same size.

None of France's group-stage opponents gave Fontaine as much trouble. He opened his World Cup with a hat trick in a 7–3 victory over Paraguay, added two more in a 3–2 defeat against Yugoslavia, and then scored and assisted Kopa in the 2–1 win over Scotland that ensured his team's passage to the quarterfinals.

Watching the grainy footage of those goals, it is impossible to ignore the suspect nature of some of the opposition defending and the vast expanses of space left for Fontaine to exploit. But just as obvious in the clips is the perfect timing of his runs in behind, the sureness of his touch at top speed, and his clear-eyed composure when the moment arrived to finish with either foot.

Those skills were honed during a childhood spent playing football and basketball in Marrakech, the city of his birth in 1933 in what was then French Morocco. Fontaine always specifically credited basketball for the unpredictability of his movement, which gave defenders such problems. “The sport taught me to pretend to look one way and then go the other,” he explained.

Fontaine’s innate mutual understanding with Kopa, an inspired No. 10 who won the Ballon d’Or in 1958, was the foundation of France’s attacking success in Sweden.

“We shared a room, but we kept very different hours: Kopa went to bed late like the Spanish, whereas I got up early,” he said. “We were very different, but on the pitch, we clicked instantly. I learnt quickly that I had to wait for the end of his dribbles before making my runs. We began finding each other straight away.”

France swept aside Northern Ireland in the World Cup quarterfinals. Fontaine raised his tournament tally to eight with two goals in a 4–0 win: his first and only headed goal in Sweden, glanced in at the near post from a right-wing cross, and his third left-footed strike in four matches after cleverly faking to shoot with his right.

Their reward? A semifinal showdown with favorites Brazil.

One of the many amusing stories Fontaine liked to tell was the moment when, after a match in the 1990 World Cup, he decided to try to say hello to his old friend Pelé.

As he stood in the adoring crowd that always surrounded Brazil’s greatest player, Pelé spotted him and waved him over. Many in the impatient throng did not recognize the slightly short, stocky man being summoned to jump the vast queue to meet their idol and did not hide their displeasure. Pelé, according to Fontaine, quickly silenced the complaints.

"He told them: 'The day you score 13 goals in a World Cup, you can shout,'" Fontaine later recalled. "'In the meantime, let him pass!'"

Pelé recognized Fontaine as the other hero of the 1958 World Cup in Sweden, the stage for his own sporting apotheosis as a cherubic 17-year-old possessed by genius. He also saw in the Frenchman a kindred spirit, an insatiable goalscorer with a speed and sharpness of movement that would have distinguished him in any era, and a footballer who played and lived with joy.

Their first meeting on June 24, 1958, in the semifinal of that tournament at Rasunda Stadium in Solna, linked them for life.

Pelé was the prodigious teenager who, having missed the first two group games with a knee injury, had firmly established himself in a formidably talented Brazil team with an assist against the Soviet Union and the only goal in their quarterfinal win over Wales. Fontaine was the sensation who had fired an unfancied France side to the last four with a ridiculous eight goals in four matches.

He scored his ninth in the ninth minute of the semifinal, darting behind the Brazil defense after some brilliant interplay with Kopa and beating goalkeeper Gilmar to the ball before lashing a left-footed shot high into the net to cancel out Vavá's early opener. A France upset win was suddenly conceivable—until the 36th minute when an unintentional kick from Vavá broke the leg of their captain, Robert Jonquet, in two places.

Reduced to 10 men (incredibly, substitutes were not allowed), France and Fontaine had no hope of containing Brazil or their teenage phenomenon. Pelé became the youngest player in World Cup history to score a hat trick in a 5–2 victory that set up a final showdown with hosts Sweden and condemned France to the third-place playoff against West Germany.

Fontaine was magnanimous in defeat and never felt inclined to use Jonquet's injury as an excuse. "We would have scored more goals [with 11 players], but we would still have lost [to Brazil]," he admitted later. "Garrincha, Pelé, Didi, Vavá, Zagallo, and Zito were as quick as us and they were better technicians."

France's defeat left Fontaine needing three more goals against West Germany to surpass the scoring record for a single World Cup, set at 11 by Hungary's Sándor Kocsis in 1954. Fontaine got four in a wild 6–3 victory, netting twice from close range in the first half and finding the bottom corner with right-footed shots from an angle twice in the second.

Asked after the match if he had anything to say about finishing the tournament with 13 goals, Fontaine replied with a mischievous look, "I hope to do better next time."

It ended up being 13 and it could have been even more. Fontaine hit the crossbar twice at the 1958 World Cup, in the group stage against Scotland and in the quarterfinal against Northern Ireland. He also did not request to take a penalty off Kopa in the third-place playoff against West Germany despite being on 10 goals, only one shy of tying Kocsis's record, when it was awarded.

"I know that today it would be different," Fontaine said later. "But, at the time, it would never have occurred to me to ask [Kopa] to let me take it."

Asking for more would probably have constituted something far beyond greed; by his own count, Fontaine scored with 13 of his 18 shots at the tournament, putting him in strong contention to be considered the proud owner of the greatest, most high-profile hot streak in the history of football.

His only tangible individual reward before going home was a hunting rifle, presented by Swedish newspaper *Expressen*, with his signature on the stock. It was not until 1997 that Fontaine received a Golden Boot courtesy of Gary Lineker, who interviewed him for a BBC program on the history of the award. FIFA formally acknowledged his unique achievement with a platinum boot, presented by former Brazil striker Ronaldo, in 2014.

Fontaine was 24 in the summer of 1958, at the peak of his physical powers and with every reason to believe he had many more prime years ahead. The following season he scored 10 goals as Reims reached the European Cup final, losing 2–0 to Kopa and Real Madrid in Stuttgart.

But, on March 20, 1960, a heavy tackle from Sochaux attacker Sékou Touré in a French league game broke his left leg in two places. He broke it again in January 1961 against Limoges and was forced to retire in July 1962, aged just 28. "Afterwards, he came to see me, in hospital, at home. . . . He put his head between my arms and I had to cheer him up!" Fontaine said of Touré.

He did much more than simply forgive and raise the spirits of the man who had effectively ended his career: Touré became godfather to his son.

Fontaine hung up his boots having scored 259 goals in 283 club matches and went on to pursue a mixed coaching career, lasting two matches in charge of the French national team in 1967, securing Paris Saint-Germain's promotion to Ligue 1 in 1974, and leading Morocco to a third-place finish in the 1980 Africa Cup of Nations. He also co-founded the French players' union.

But his legacy is the 1958 World Cup and those 13 goals. Fontaine's final numbers for France highlight both his brilliance and his brevity: 30 goals in 21 international appearances overall and 21 goals in 10 competitive games for his country, of which six were in Sweden.

Fontaine said on numerous occasions that he would have traded his World Cup scoring record for a longer playing career, but he also took immense pride in just how insurmountable it has proven; in the 16 subsequent editions of the competition, no one has come closer than West Germany great Gerd Müller, who managed 10 goals in six games in 1970. The best attempts this century, by Ronaldo in 2002 and Kylian Mbappé in 2022, fell five goals short.

When he was asked how long his record might last, Fontaine often cited a joke told by Mario Zatelli, the man who brought him from his first club, USM Casablanca, to Nice in 1953.

"One day, in 3050, an archaeologist discovered a sarcophagus.

He opened it and discovered a mummy inside. He removed the bandages, including those around her face. The mummy asked him: 'Does Fontaine's record still stand?'"

The expansion of the World Cup to 48 teams from 2026 makes a genuine challenge to Fontaine's record slightly more achievable; from now on, the four teams who reach the final or third-place playoff will play eight games rather than the seven of the 32-team era.

But it is and will remain a daunting task, a fittingly towering monument to a striker whose peak was as fleeting and spectacular as a bolt of lightning. "My record? It's like a fine wine," Fontaine said. "The older it gets, the more it's worth."

Most Goals Scored at One World Cup

Player	Country	World Cup	Goals scored
Just Fontaine	France	1958	13
Sándor Kocsis	Hungary	1954	11
Gerd Müller	West Germany	1970	10
Ademir	Brazil	1950	9
Eusébio	Portugal	1966	9
Guillermo Stábile	Argentina	1930	8
Ronaldo	Brazil	2002	8
Kylian Mbappé	France	2022	8

Player name: Just Fontaine
Born: August 18, 1933
Died: February 28, 2023 (aged 89)
Position: Striker
Debut: 1950
Main teams: USM Casablanca (1950–53), Nice (1953–56), Stade de Reims (1956–62); France (1953–60)
Career highlights: Scored 13 goals to win the Golden Boot at the 1958 World Cup, a record for a single edition of the tournament. He is one of three players to score two hat tricks at one World Cup. Overall, he scored 30 goals in 21 games for France and won the French top flight four times.

59.

Stanley Matthews

Matthews was never booked, never sent off, never retaliated at a time when defenders were allowed to chop down wingers with brutal force.

The Wizard of Dribble

By Michael Walker

If searching for a way to encapsulate English football in the twentieth century, Wembley Stadium, the FA Cup, and Stanley Matthews could be offered as exhibit A. That is how significant Matthews was.

Born in 1915, Matthews stretched his considerable talents across the century and died two months into the year 2000. Having started his professional career in Stoke City's reserves in 1930, aged 15, Matthews was still playing, back at Stoke, in 1965. Five days after his 50th birthday, he retired after a 3–1 win over Fulham.

To many, Stanley Matthews became English football and in his lean, dashing frame and restrained personality, English football saw reflected virtue. He was never booked, never sent off, never retaliated at a time when defenders were allowed to chop down wingers with brutal force.

Matthews had received news of a knighthood on January 1 of the year he retired. He was football's first active player to be a "Sir." It was one of many firsts: the first man to be named England's Footballer of the Year (1948); the first man to be named European Footballer of the Year (1956). Fifteen years after that 1948 award, Matthews won it for a second time.

He was 48, a sporting phenomenon.

Matthews won 54 caps for England, his first in 1934 aged 19 and his last in 1957 when he was 42. He scored on his debut and his second cap was the notorious affair against Italy known as the "Battle of Highbury." Giuseppe Meazza scored Italy's two goals that night; in Matthews's last appearance, Tommy Taylor, killed in the Munich air crash nine months later, scored two. Matthews's unprecedented longevity made these different-era connections possible.

Gabriel Hanot, the *L'Équipe* journalist and former France international, once made the comparison: "In his own way, Stanley Matthews is a brilliant clown, the Charlie Chaplin of football." His career was a long list of individual achievements, but it was so much more. Reducing it to statistics is like naming Chaplin's films and leaving it at that. Like Chaplin, Matthews transcended his profession; like Chaplin, his was a quintessentially black-and-white career. And like Chaplin, Matthews was adored for his footwork, artistry, and integrity.

Matthews's fame, which arrived in his teens, grew season upon season before and after World War II so that he was the global game's first superstar. Reverence and respect came from everywhere, not just from the supporters of the two comparatively small English clubs he played for, Stoke City and Blackpool.

"I hear some modern players being described as 'great,'" said Alfredo Di Stéfano. "They are not. They are good, some very good, but none are great in the way Stan was great."

When Matthews died, Franz Beckenbauer said "football has lost its greatest player . . . Wherever you went in the world, they knew the name Stanley Matthews."

Matthews was never short of recognition from officialdom or from such peers, who were mesmerized by both his ability and durability. In September 1947, for example, he starred for England in a 5–2 victory against Belgium in front of a massive crowd in Brussels. It was one of Matthews's greatest performances as he created all five England goals. After the fifth goal, the Belgian players applauded him back into position.

The Belgian press hailed Matthews as *Le Sorcier*—the Wizard. It was the tag Matthews had been given—"The Wizard of Dribble"—as he reinvented the art of the winger.

"The newspapers were generous . . . too generous, I would say," Matthews said.

Tucked away in his 600-page autobiography, *The Way It Was*, Matthews wrote of the post–World War II surge in attendance at English matches and what feels like the approval he cherished most.

In the 1947–48 season, he noted proudly that Arsenal, Aston Villa, Bolton, Burnley, Liverpool, Manchester United, and Sunderland all recorded their biggest attendances of the season against a club that had never won the league title or the FA Cup: Blackpool.

Matthews had joined the provincial club on England's northwest coast toward the end of the previous season. His £11,500 transfer was a sensation. He was 32 and some at Stoke thought they could see the end of his career, even though Matthews was still playing for England.

By then, he had long been a national and international figure. Blackpool may not have won much silverware, but now, in the shape of Matthews, they had a trophy shining on their right wing every Saturday. And everyone wanted to see him.

He was aware of this, and while Matthews was not an openly

boastful character, no one does what he did without being sure of their gift. He also knew his economic importance to the game. Players were then tied to a meager maximum wage, but Matthews, like others, found a way around the system. He had a ghosted newspaper column; he took sponsorship from Craven A cigarettes, even though he never smoked; and when it came to testimonial appearances, payment came in cash. Sometimes in gold sovereigns. Matthews was able to open a hotel in Blackpool.

There were occasional critics: Some decried his lack of assistance to his defense and some saw selfishness in his self-assurance. Less known was that from the 1930s until he finished, before big games, Matthews would vomit through nerves. A Stoke player, Eddie Clamp, even gave it a name: "Stan's Technicolor yawn."

Matthews was born into a working-class family in Hanley, Stoke, in the seventh month of World War I. He was one of four sons. His father, Jack, mixed running a local barbershop with being a jobbing 20-round boxer—"The Fighting Barber."

Jack Matthews knew the value of fitness and instilled in Stan a lifelong obsession. Before club training, the young Matthews would rise at 7 a.m., start deep breathing and stretching exercises, and begin a series of sprints. Then, as he said, "I'd make for home and breakfast at a very brisk walking pace." After training with Stoke, he would also practice dribbling.

Later, Matthews would fast on Mondays to detoxify his body, although he was not a drinker of alcohol like most in football; his daughter, Jean, talking to the *Daily Mail* in 2015, remembered him having carrot juice every day. In the 1950s, it was rare for a sportsman to pay close attention to diet.

At 15, he had joined Stoke City, then in the Second Division. Boys were not allowed to turn professional until 17 and, despite offers from clubs placed higher, Matthews chose Stoke. He was paid £5 per week during the season and £3 per week in the summer months. It meant he could live at home; it also meant he could see Betty, the daughter of the Stoke trainer, Jimmy Vallance. The two were married when Matthews was 19.

Stoke City were promoted in Matthews's first full season, 1932–33. He scored 11 goals in his debut campaign in the top flight, then 10 and 10 again as, in the 1935–36 season, Stoke finished fourth in the First Division, which remains the club's joint highest-ever finish. But after that, Matthews never made double figures again. He said it was because he changed the nature of his game.

Matthews gave what he did a lot of thought as well as physical practice. In his embryonic professional days, he realized that the game was much tougher athletically than he expected, but also that full-backs were attuned to playing only one way—aggressively closing down the opposing winger. It was an accepted piece of the game that the defender was always the protagonist.

It sounds odd now and it was Matthews who changed it. He decided a winger should be a supplier rather than a scorer of goals.

"In those days, you waited until the defender came right on top of you and then tried to jink your way around him," Matthews explained in his autobiography. "In a game against Manchester City reserves, I bucked the trend. I decided instead of waiting for their left-back to approach me, I would make a beeline for him. . . . Once on top of him, I'd put into operation the body swerve I was cultivating."

Matthews's plan worked. "He looked absolutely dumbfounded," he said of the defender.

Although this was a teenager in a reserve match, the local press picked up on Matthews's maneuvers, and soon, so did the nationals. He was young, new, and excitingly different.

As Hanot was to say of Matthews's tactical innovation: "It's not the defender chasing the attacker; the defender, in an extraordinary paradox, is suddenly the one who is being chased." Pure, thoughtful players like Di Stéfano were impressed.

Arguably the most famous FA Cup final of them all—in 1953—illustrated this. It was called "The Matthews Final" and it was more than a football match. It was a national event, one of the sporting moments of the English century.

At that time, the FA Cup final was the only game many people saw broadcast, with highlights shown in cinemas by Pathé News in the days before widespread television ownership. But television rental soared in May 1953.

Matthews was the story—he was 38, the most famous footballer in the world, and, with Blackpool, he had lost the finals of 1948 and 1951. This seemed like the hero's last chance. Yet, with 25 minutes left, Blackpool were losing 3–1 to Bolton Wanderers.

Matthews, who had been pressed by his father on his deathbed to one day win the FA Cup, sprang into action, crossing for Stan Mortensen to make it 3–2. Mortensen then scored his third to make it 3–3, and in the last pulsating seconds, with the crowd roaring "On Stanley, on," Matthews jinked down the right wing once again and crossed for Bill Perry. Suddenly it was 4–3 to Blackpool.

An epic match with a suitable story line, it was, as Matthews called it, "the final of finals."

It was an emotional occasion; the first time the cup winners staged a lap of honor. Despite Mortensen's hat trick, Matthews was the headline act, hence "The Matthews Final." Matthews disagreed strongly. In his book, he titled the chapter on the game "The Mortensen Final."

Arsenal had tried to buy Matthews on at least two occasions and tried again, but he stayed at Blackpool until October 1961, when Stoke City brought him home. They were back in the Second Division; in Matthews's second season, they won promotion, with him scoring in the decisive game at home to Luton Town.

The renowned British television documentary program *World in Action* accompanied Matthews to the game, filming from the back seat as he drove from Blackpool, where he continued to live.

"I believe in enthusiasm," Matthews told them, explaining his endurance, and he quoted an old saying: "The years may wrinkle the skin but, without enthusiasm, it wrinkles the soul."

He had begun a long relationship with Africa, coaching in Ghana, Nigeria, and forming a club called Stan's Men in Soweto, South Africa. "I never had any truck with it," he said of apartheid and the "misguided people who inflicted it."

After he stopped playing, he became the unpaid general manager of Port Vale in Stoke, but it was a difficult job. He lasted three years.

Before then, in April 1965, Matthews had an unforgettable testimonial at Stoke's Victoria Ground, when the guests included Di Stéfano, Eusébio, Raymond Kopa, and Uwe Seeler among a glittering cast. At its end, the players gathered in the center circle as 40,000 spectators sang "Auld Lang Syne." "I was moved to tears," Matthews said.

Lev Yashin and Ferenc Puskás then hoisted Matthews onto their shoulders and carried him to the dressing room one last time. He left his boots hanging on the peg.

Player name: Stanley Matthews
Born: February 1, 1915
Died: February 23, 2000 (aged 85)
Position: Outside right
Debut: 1932
Main teams: Stoke City (1932–47, 1961–65), Blackpool (1947–61); England (1934–57)
Career highlights: Won the FA Cup in 1953 with a performance in the final so outstanding that the match was nicknamed after him.

58.

Sergio Busquets

Over 15 seasons in the Barcelona first team, Busquets won 32 trophies.

The ultimate unsung hero

By Dermot Corrigan

Sometimes the extent of a player's influence can best be reflected by the sheer weight of numbers.

During 15 seasons in the Barcelona first team, Sergio Busquets won 32 trophies, a haul that included three Champions Leagues and nine La Liga titles. With Spain he claimed the 2010 World Cup and followed up with the European Championship two years later as a key member of a dominant national side. His 143 caps and seven major tournaments reflect as much.

Even since joining Inter Miami in the summer of 2023, he has thrived in the twilight of a glittering career. The Leagues Cup and Supporters' Shield followed. That mountain of team silverware has never been matched by individual prizes—La Liga's Young Player of the Season in 2008–09 and a Player of the Tournament in the 2021 Nations League finals represent relatively meager reward—and few, if any, of the players on this list can point to a starker distinction between collective trophies and individual recognition from fans and media.

That may partly be down to Busquets forever being flanked by supertalented teammates with club and country; players ranked ahead of him in this list.

If the prolific Lionel Messi did not draw the focus, then Xavi Hernández's penetrative passes or Andrés Iniesta's mesmeric dribbling skills eclipsed the man at the base of Barcelona's midfield. From there, his contribution could go unnoticed. Or, possibly, taken for granted. A tally of 18 goals and 46 assists in 722 games for the Catalan club is hardly likely to make waves, and there were just two goals and nine assists in more than 13 years playing for Spain. Busquets rarely conducted media interviews, had few sponsor contracts, and was not a regular poster on social media.

But for those closest to the action—the players and coaches who counted on him, or the opponents desperately attempting to negate his influence on games—Busquets was integral.

"You might think that 'Busi' is nothing special," says Jordi Roura, a former Barcelona player turned coach who headed the club's La Masia academy between 2014 and 2021. "He's not especially fast or strong, not especially skillful, not great in the air, doesn't arrive in the penalty area to score goals. Yet he's the best player in the world in his position. Why? Very few players can predict the play, anticipate the danger, and be there before it happens. *That* has been Busi's great quality."

Busquets knew elite football from a very early age. His father, Carles, was a goalkeeper for Barcelona in the 1990s, playing over 100 times for the club and winning nine trophies there.

It was not obvious that young Sergio would enjoy similar success, or even become a professional footballer. He was not recruited by La Masia's scouts, instead playing for various lower-profile Catalan youth teams. He was 17 before he wore a *Blaugrana* jersey and, even when inside Barcelona, he still struggled to nail down a role. Roura recalls he was tried in different positions, including as a winger, in the academy.

"People only really realized his potential when Pep Guardiola took over at Barca's B team [in the summer of 2007] and put Busi as a '*mediocentro*,'" Roura says. "As the games passed, people realized they had an extraordinary player on their hands."

The following summer, Guardiola took charge of Barcelona's senior side and brought the then 20-year-old midfielder up with him. Pep had been the *mediocentro*, a pivot or holding midfielder, in Johan Cruyff's Barcelona side that won the 1992 European Cup. Now he and assistant Tito Vilanova realized that Busquets was ideal to sit between Xavi and Iniesta in their team's 4-3-3 tactical setup.

Many around the Camp Nou needed convincing at first.

"When you start something new in football, it's always difficult, like everywhere in life," says Roura, who became a part of Guardiola's backroom staff. "There are always people who don't understand. We began that first season with a defeat and a draw at home. Fans were asking 'Why not use other players?' but Pep and Tito were absolutely convinced of Busi's quality. They stuck to their idea and were proved correct."

In Busquets's first senior season, Barcelona won La Liga, the Copa del Rey, and the Champions League, all while playing a spectacular style of attacking football, dominating possession and controlling the pace of games. In 2010–11, Guardiola's side won the Champions League again and were widely acclaimed as the best club team of all time.

At the center of it all was the unassuming No. 16, a player who may rarely have stood out but whose vigilance and intelligence served to protect the team. It was Busquets who would quickly regain possession whenever it was lost and it was Busquets who would then cleverly initiate the next wave of attacks.

"There is obviously a part which is innate," Roura adds. "He understands football perfectly. He is always in the right place at the right time, arriving and stealing the ball. He allowed us to organize again and begin another move. When Busi was on his game, Barca were on their game. The things he does are maybe not the most visible or attractive to the fan but, for our way of playing, they were absolutely essential."

The transition to key player at international level was almost as rapid.

Spain coach Vicente del Bosque—also a *mediocentro* during his playing days with Real Madrid—gave Busquets a senior debut after less than 12 months in Barca's first team. There had been opposition among some Spanish pundits, especially those centered around Madrid, to his selection ahead of the 2010 World Cup. Plenty were doubtful he should make the first XI, but del Bosque knew better.

Busquets started every game as Spain claimed their first World Cup in South Africa. At Euro 2012, he played every minute as *La Roja* won a third consecutive senior international tournament.

"As a player, he had immense quality," says Jesús Navas, a teammate at both the 2010 and 2012 tournaments. "The way he saw football was so impressive. He always saw the move two or three seconds before anyone else and that is really huge. He gave us a lot of joy."

If that level of appreciation was not always shared by those on the outside looking in, it was perhaps because no one had ever played the *mediocentro* role quite this way before.

Quique Setién confronted Busquets's Barcelona regularly through the 2010s in his capacity as coach of Las Palmas and Real Betis. He, too, asked his team to play a Cruyff-influenced, possession-based style of football. "It was impossible for other teams to limit Busquets's influence," Setién says. "Nobody could be quicker than him as he was the quickest. No player had his understanding of the role. He would be reading the game two or three passes ahead. He could see the situations which would develop, where the space would be, and when to take advantage."

Teammates and opponents also grew familiar with Busquets's ability to control games from a position near the center circle. Denis Suárez played 47 games with him for Barcelona from 2016 to 2019 and faced him regularly while representing Sevilla, Villarreal, Celta Vigo, and Espanyol.

"When Busi received the ball, he already knew what he was going to do," says Suárez. "He was always well positioned to be able to cover for his deficiencies. The difference in today's football, when everything is so evenly matched, is the first touch and the reading of the game. Thinking before the rival. For me, he is one of the best holding midfielders ever, if not the best."

By 2019 and the start of the 2020s, with Xavi and Iniesta having departed, it was down to the tall, skinny *mediocentro* to spear quick, vertical passes through the opposition's defensive lines for Messi to collect. "Busquets always knew what was happening around him," adds Setién, who by then was coaching at Barcelona. "Before he received the ball, he was ready. He has that awesome perception and field of vision, so he does not even have to look at the ball.

"He just plays a simple pass. Or maybe the opponent is closing in, so he plays it first touch. And 'bam,' his team is on the attack."

There were still those who found reason to pour scorn on Busquets. Rival managers, players, and supporters worked themselves into a frenzy over his perceived gamesmanship; those tactical fouls to check rival attacks or the feigning of injury to deceive referees and break up the play. "Busquets has all the moral weaknesses that help in football," the then–Arsenal manager Arsène Wenger told Eurosport in 2012.

This idea of Busquets as the "bad" Barcelona player followed him through his career, but his presence and his approach were also a virtue in a team packed with smaller, less physical players.

While most of them had been more cosseted within the La Masia academy, he had learned as a teenager playing in neighborhood leagues how to get down in the dirt and battle when required. Later, he was always there to back up Messi or Iniesta when other sides tried to physically intimidate them. Catalan author Martí Perarnau called him their "invisible friend" in his 2011 book, *The Path of Champions: From La Masia to the Camp Nou*. It was a shrewd assessment.

That need to stop an opponent in his tracks is part of any *medio-centro*'s job; even the most technically brilliant and positionally intelligent. But Busquets never went out to hurt a rival player or lost his cool in personal feuds. His uncanny ability to tread the line meant that while he received more than 200 bookings in almost 1,000 senior games, he had received just one straight red card at the time of writing—for a poor challenge against Benfica in a 2012 Champions League group game.

"Busi is a normal guy, one of our own," says Roura. "He also had that 'street' gene, that strong character. You could see that on the pitch and it helped the team a lot. Sometimes opponents did not end up too happy with him. But for us, for the team, that personality and character were absolutely essential."

It made Busquets a natural choice for team captain for both club and country. He led Spain to the Euro 2020 semifinals, with national coach Luis Enrique saying during the tournament that "his game is a manual of how to play *pivote*, in both attack and defence." When he won La Liga in 2022–23, Xavi, by then Barca's coach, said, "With Busi, there is a before and after in his position."

Never entirely comfortable when called upon as a public spokesperson in media or commercial appearances, behind the scenes Busquets would raise his voice to demand the behavior required for success. "Off the pitch, Busi is like a policeman," Suárez adds. "He's a very good guy, but he likes to control everything with the other players—who arrives late, who is messing around."

In recent years, emerging Barca and Spain midfielders Pedri and Gavi benefited from Busquets guiding them on and off the pitch. The ability to influence and organize a team and squad was why Inter Miami identified him as a vital associate for Messi in Major League Soccer.

"Busi can set the rhythm of the play and make the team work like few other players," Roura says. "He was always talking to his teammates, putting them in the right positions. I was not surprised that Leo and Miami wanted him."

Busquets retired from international football after the disappointment of Spain's 2022 World Cup campaign. His successor as *mediocentro* as they claimed the European Championship in 2024 was Manchester City's Rodri, whose outstanding performances won him that year's Ballon d'Or. Yet, while the Catalan never received such personal recognition, those who played with and against him recognized his worth.

"Rodri has reached such a high level of understanding of the game, but Busquets was there first," Setién adds. "Football, fortunately, is not about strength or power. It's about intelligence. Sometimes doing things simply is the most difficult. And Busquets, without great physical attributes, developed how his position is played with an awesome intelligence."

Player name: Sergio Busquets Burgos
Born: July 16, 1988
Position: Defensive midfielder
Debut: 2008
Main teams: Barcelona (2008–23), Inter Miami (2023–); Spain (2009–22)
Career highlights: Won the World Cup in 2010 and Euro 2012 as a key member of Spain's squad, as well as the Champions League three times at Barcelona. Overall, he claimed 32 trophies while at the Catalan club.

57.

Giuseppe Meazza

Meazza was idolized on and off the pitch.

El Fòlber, the national icon who was football personified

By James Horncastle

Does a name loom larger in Italian football than that of Giuseppe Meazza? A year after his death in 1979, representatives from Milan's city hall held a ceremony outside San Siro. Amid solemn applause and the gray concrete surroundings, curtains were drawn to show a plaque renaming the ground after the first player who made football a box-office event.

Considering San Siro's significance as a temple to the game, this tribute was equivalent to naming the basilica of the Vatican after St. Peter. It reflected Meazza's standing in *calcio*. They called him, in the local Lombard dialect, *El Fòlber* (effectively, "he is football"). Meazza was football personified.

He dribbled and scored like another future Inter Milan great, the original Ronaldo. A *gol alla Meazza* involved deftly weaving through defense—imagine a moped bobbing in and out of traffic at rush hour in Milan. He'd then elude the flailing goalkeeper and walk the ball nonchalantly into the back of the net. Meazza scored plenty of them—216 in the league, which made him Serie A's all-time top scorer until his protégé, Silvio Piola, eclipsed him in 1949.

As the centenary of Meazza's debut for Inter nears, he remains fourth on that list. The association with San Siro has ensured his name has had a recurring resonance as a truly mythical figure. Only Gigi Riva, who in 1973 broke his record to become the national team's leading scorer, holds a place as revered in the collective consciousness as the greatest Italian striker ever.

Meazza grew up in the Porta Romana neighborhood of Milan. Tourists visit it today for the Fondazione Prada art and culture institute. Italy's best university, Bocconi, is nearby. But when Meazza was born in 1910, it was on the edge of town. There was countryside all around and he used to play in the ditches and furrowed building sites of new housing estates. "Peppino! Peppino!" Ersilia, his mother, used to call out.

Ersilia was widowed relatively soon after Meazza's birth. His father lost his life on the front in World War I when their boy was just seven years old. It made Ersilia protective. She didn't want her boy playing football. She wanted him by her side. "Peppino! Peppino!"

But keeping Meazza next to her at the fruit and veg stall she ran was futile. He bound his bare feet with rags and made a ball out of other bits and bobs. Disheveled and gangly, Meazza hung out at a dairy in Via Arconti. The milkmen had a team, AS Costanza, which he turned out for as he entered his early teens.

The city's best side, AC Milan, didn't rate him.

When Meazza went to Trotter, the pitches near the horse track, to try out for them, they saw a malnourished kid with drooping shoulders. He must have weighed less than 90 pounds. Milan thought Meazza would never make it. How wrong they were . . .

Inter took a chance on him instead.

There is another plaque at San Siro in tribute to the coach who gave Meazza his first start. Árpád Weisz was a Hungarian Jew who had a tremendous impact on Italian football in the interwar years. He won the league three times with Inter and Bologna before Benito Mussolini's racial laws forced him to leave the country for the Netherlands. Weisz and his family were later rounded up by the Gestapo and put on a train to Auschwitz, where they were killed in the Holocaust.

Meazza, in many respects, owed his career to him. He made his debut at 17 in the Coppa Volta, a preseason tournament in Como named after the town's most famous son and pioneer of electricity. Meazza sent shock waves through the Italian game. He scored twice as Inter put six past Unione Sportiva Milanese.

One of the team's senior players, the great Fulvio Bernardini, who would later become the only coach to win the league with two different teams outside of Italy's traditional big three, continued to push Weisz to play Meazza even at his own expense. Bernardini was a striker who reinvented himself as a midfielder to create space for such a prodigious and precocious talent. A fellow veteran, Leopoldo Conti, couldn't quite believe it. "We're even letting kids play now, are we?" he said.

But Meazza was no ordinary *bagaj*, Lombard dialect for "kid." He scored 11 goals in his first season, including one in his first Derby della Madonnina. The numbers don't seem anything out of the ordinary. In the following season, Gino Rossetti netted 36 times, a record Gonzalo Higuaín and Ciro Immobile only equaled in 2015–16 and 2019–20.

Meazza was still schoolboy age when he became as prolific. In his second year in the league, he graduated to 33 goals in 29 appearances. At 19, he won the first of three *Capocannoniere* crowns. The 31 goals Meazza racked up were the difference when Inter won the league in

1929–30. It was their first *Scudetto* in a decade and Meazza mania was by then in full effect.

When Meazza made his debut for the national team in the spring of that year, Neapolitans caught the train up to Rome, where Italy were due to play Switzerland at the old Stadio del Partito Nazionale Fascista, a ground later demolished to make way for the Stadio Flaminio. They did not buy tickets to support the team. They instead wished to protest Meazza's call-up over Napoli's Paraguayan-born striker Attila Sallustro.

Every time Meazza touched the ball, insults rained down from the stands. Ersilia, who had rushed down from Milan to see her beloved Peppino, was so offended she broke down in tears and left with Italy down 2–1.

Meazza stayed and scored twice in a 4–2 win. The abuse transformed into applause.

Some 20,000 fans gathered on the platform at Milan's Stazione Centrale to welcome Meazza back from an away day in Hungary in May. A hat trick in a 5–0 win against the Magyars, one of the great teams of the era, made Meazza a national icon.

Fans of Inter's opponents crushed through the turnstiles to catch a glimpse of him. In June, as Inter prepared to play Genoa, a wooden stand buckled and collapsed at the Goldoni ground. "If you score, I'll be all right," a stricken supporter called over to Meazza. Another hat trick followed.

Another nickname, too.

Meazza became known as *il Balila*. On the one hand, it was a variation of "The Kid." On the other, it referenced the folkloric story of Giovan Battista Perasso, a Genovese boy who led a popular uprising against the Habsburg occupation of his city in the eighteenth century and liberated Genoa. This myth was coopted by the Fascist regime, as was Meazza's rise to fame. Mussolini's organization for the "physical and moral education of the youth," a forerunner and equivalent of the Hitler Youth, was known as the ONB, or *Opera Nazionale Balilla*.

If the heavyweight boxing champion Primo Carnera, who won more fights by knockout than anyone in the sport's history, became the poster boy of the strength Mussolini's Italy wished to project, Meazza was another beacon of the prowess of the nation. He wasn't Bruno Neri, the Fiorentina midfielder who courageously refused to perform the Roman salute at the inauguration of the Stadio Giovanni Berta (now Artemio Franchi) in 1931. Nor was he Eraldo Monzeglio, the Bologna full-back and teammate of Meazza with Italy who doubled as a tennis teacher to Mussolini's children at his residence in Villa Torlonia.

Sport was not only bound up in the ideology of fascism; it was used to make the regime credible and legitimate on the global stage. By hosting the second World Cup in 1934, Mussolini's ambition went beyond winning the competition. The rail network and ability to host multiple games on the same day in stadia that are still in use today were all part of a plan to showcase the capabilities of a one-party state built on his ideals.

Italy's coach, Vittorio Pozzo, naturally came under pressure to deliver. He coached his country for free because it was a privilege. That way he could also walk away at any time. A former member of the Alpini, the specialist mountain infantry of the Italian army, Pozzo served three years in World War I. Old habits die hard. He summoned the team to training camps up in the hills above Florence and set the tone for generations of Italian coaches by secluding the players from society and its distractions until game day.

Meazza scored the last of seven goals in Italy's opener against the USA, then got the decider in the quarterfinal replay against Spain. The great Ricardo Zamora frustrated him in the first meeting between the sides. The goalkeeper by whom all goalkeepers are still judged in Spain did not play when they resumed action just 24 hours later and Meazza capitalized on his absence through injury.

Peppino did not score again in the tournament. The winner in the final against Czechoslovakia came from Monzeglio's colleague from Bologna, Angelo Schiavio, in extra time.

To some it mattered that holders Uruguay did not attend to defend their trophy and that England, the reputed best team in the world, refused an invitation to play, as they would until 1950, on the arrogant grounds that the tournament was beneath them. It is why a friendly in north London that same winter assumed great importance to Italy.

It was a test to see whether they deserved their title—and it could not have started worse.

Almost immediately, goalkeeper Carlo Ceresoli gave away a penalty that England, luckily, failed to convert. The *Azzurri* then, effectively, went down to 10 men as Luis Monti broke his foot. There were no substitutions in this day and age, and although Monti valiantly tried to play on, Pozzo had no choice but to withdraw him without replacement. England soon took advantage and went 3–0 up inside the first 15 minutes. It risked becoming a humiliation.

Italy's captain, Attilio Ferraris, issued a rallying cry at the interval in the bellic tones of the era—there would be no deserting the cause—and his team came roaring back. And so the Lions of Highbury entered into legend.

Meazza scored twice and hit the bar. Broadcasting as the English supporters applauded the visitors off the pitch, the radio commentator Nicolo Carosio called it a "victorious defeat." The performance, if not the result, demonstrated that Italy were not world champions by default. They proved that again by retaining the Jules Rimet trophy in France in 1938.

Meazza came full circle at that tournament. He reinvented himself à la Bernardini in order to free up a place in the team for Piola who is still, to this day, Serie A's all-time top scorer. Meazza found the net only once but, as was the case against Spain four years earlier, his goal weighed heavier than many others.

The penalty he put away decided the semifinal against Brazil. As Meazza ran up to take it, the elastic in his shorts snapped and they began to fall down. Brazil's goalkeeper, Walter, was given more than the eyes. Ultimately, however, the indignity was his own. Meazza caught his shorts and in the same movement buried his spot kick and the tie.

The moment perfectly captured Meazza's aura.

One of only three Italy players to win the World Cup twice, he was idolized on and off the pitch. The great columnist Gianni Brera once told an anecdote about Meazza waking up in a bed that wasn't his own one Sunday, a girlfriend either side, when he checked his watch, rubbed his eyes, checked it again, and realized he had a game in less than an hour. Meazza hurriedly pulled on his clothes, hailed a cab to the Arena Civica, which now holds Brera's name, arrived just after kickoff, came on, and scored twice to redeem himself.

Piola would perhaps never have caught and overtaken him in the all-time scoring charts if Meazza hadn't suffered an embolus in his left foot at 30. The bad circulation meant he lost feeling in it. Inter then let him go in 1940 after he made a single appearance in their title-winning campaign. They sold him, in tears, to rival Milan.

Meazza even played for Juventus, but his association remained forever with Inter, where he returned in various roles, not to mention the early exploits of his country.

As Brera outlined in his obituary of the player, "It was Meazza who lifted our game to its current status. . . . The triumphant Peppino avenged the anxieties of his humble ancestors and all of us poor peers, passing for a genius to whom any extravagance was permitted."

Player name: Giuseppe Meazza
Born: August 23, 1910
Died: August 21, 1979 (aged 68)
Position: Forward
Debut: 1927
Main teams: Inter Milan (1927–40, 1946–47), AC Milan (1940–42), Juventus (1942–43), Varese (1944), Atalanta (1945–46); Italy (1930–39)
Career highlights: Won the World Cup in 1934 and 1938, the latter as captain. Won Serie A three times. Inter Milan's all-time top scorer with 287 goals. He is still Serie A's fourth-highest scorer with 216 goals.

56.

George Weah

There are goals that put people on the map, and then there is what George Weah did against Hellas Verona in September 1996.

An icon of Africa

By Carl Anka

We'll start with the goal.

There are goals that put people on the map and then there's what George Weah did against Hellas Verona in September 1996.

It's a goal that takes less than 25 seconds to watch, but don't put this book down to find it on YouTube just yet. This chapter has a specific moment when we want you to do that. For now, just take in our description.

It is the opening weekend of the 1996–97 Serie A season and Verona have a corner kick in the 85th minute. AC Milan are at home and clinging to a 2–1 lead. They need to start the season strongly—Juventus finished as runners-up last season and are out for blood this time around. Christian Vieri joined the Turin club over the summer to bolster an attack already featuring Alessandro Del Piero, as did a talented attacking midfielder from Bordeaux—a man called Zinédine Zidane.

Milan had won the previous season's title with 73 points, scoring 60 goals in 34 matches. They drew 10 games on their way to their 15th *Scudetto*. At the time, one didn't tune in to Serie A in the hope of witnessing high-scoring games. The appeal of the league was to watch the most skilled attackers in the world compete against tactically astute, well-organized defenses.

Even a match between the reigning champions and a newly promoted side from Serie B carried a degree of intrigue. Goals came at a premium at this juncture. Strikers were akin to professional lockpicks, layering subtle movements inside the penalty area before opening up gaps in defense.

This is why Weah's solo goal against Verona is important. This is why it is more than an incredible solo dribble from one penalty box to another. In an age of safecrackers and lockpicks, Weah's goal is a long fuse to a stick of dynamite, blowing Verona's game plan to smithereens.

It starts with the first touch. Verona's corner is struck off target, and rather than a visiting player, it finds Weah alone in space at the far post. His first touch is a delicate sweep of his right foot that sees him go from facing the corner flag to opening up his body and facing the distant opposition goal.

If you want to look the goal up on YouTube, now is the time to do it, but focus on that first caress of the ball for now. The surrounding players have not realized it yet, but Weah's touch has transformed a tactical retreat for Milan into an ambush on Verona.

Then there's the run. Five touches take him from the penalty area to the halfway line. Milan manager Óscar Tabárez hauled every player back to defend the corner, so it is only once Weah reaches the halfway line that he has passing options ahead. Still, three defenders close him down as he ventures into enemy territory. One on his rear and two coming from his right. No problem. The striker cuts inside to protect the ball from the man behind him, hops over the slide tackle of the closest defender, and does a little roulette to restore some lost momentum.

A deliberately heavy touch takes the ball past his next marker and Weah is into the Verona box with opposition players scrambling. They don't understand what has happened. Weah's finish is drilled low past goalkeeper Attilio Gregori into the bottom corner. San Siro goes wild.

Weah scored that goal nine months after winning the 1995 Ballon d'Or, the first edition of the prize when players active at European clubs but not from a European country were allowed to receive votes. The accolade made him simultaneously the world, African, and European Footballer of the Year, a feat no player has matched since.

There are goals that put people on the map and there is what George Weah did against Hellas Verona in September 1996.

A goal that reminded football how big the map actually was. For a short period of time in the 1990s, the best footballer on the planet was a striker from Liberia, an unheralded nation in Africa; a player who helped transform what we expected of strikers. A forward who would never feature in a World Cup, but still had the world at his feet.

Weah is a stunning example of the adage, "Talent is distributed evenly, but opportunity is not."

It should not have taken so many strokes of fortune for a player of his skill to be recognized by the world at large, but we must be eternally grateful that Weah found the right people at the right time to help his growth.

His emergence in the late 1980s and early 1990s came at a time when FIFA allowed World Cup qualification places to only two African nations. The FIFA presidency of Stanley Rous (1961–74) was so damaging for the continent that CAF (Confederation of African Football) members threatened to withdraw en masse from FIFA in 1966 after the Englishman attempted to establish a new confederation to allow apartheid South Africa and Rhodesia to compete. João Havelange's subsequent tenure (1974–98) was an improvement, but he mostly used African nations as a lobbying instrument whenever he needed to secure additional votes on contentious issues.

African football went without the same attention, institutional apparatus, and financial growth that other parts of the world experienced in the middle of the twentieth century. As a result, it was a challenge for talented people across the African diaspora to reach their full potential.

Weah helped change that.

The multitalented and multifaceted forward shattered preconceptions of African footballers and helped redefine the role of the striker in the 1990s.

Born in Liberia's capital of Monrovia, Weah would have become a telephone technician had he not been spotted playing football in the Clara Town district. He entered professional football in 1981, joining Young Survivors in the fourth tier and having a shot so powerful it dented goalposts. By age 18 he had helped Young Survivors reach Liberia's second division.

A short stint at first-division side Bong Range United in 1984 was followed by spells at the country's two top clubs: Mighty Barrolle and Invincible Eleven. At the end of the 1986–87 season, Weah was the Liberian football league's top scorer (24 goals in 23 games for Invincible Eleven) and won the season's best-player award. But civil war in Liberia made it hard for Weah to continue with football in his homeland and left him looking set to continue his career in neighboring Côte d'Ivoire.

But a performance against the Cameroonian side Tonnerre Yaoundé started the next step of his journey. The club president, Pierre Semengue, was wowed by Weah and made moves to sign him. He scored twice on debut for his new club and powered them to a

Challenge Cup victory in 1988. In the space of six months, he had become a household name in the nation.

That, too, could have been the pinnacle for Weah—as one of sub-Saharan Africa's most feared strikers.

Enter Arsène Wenger.

Claude Le Roy, head coach of the Cameroon national team at the time, believed Weah's future lay in Western Europe. He contacted Wenger, then manager of Monaco, who notified him about the prodigious talent he had witnessed firsthand. Wenger flew to Cameroon to watch Weah play and signed him to Monaco for $15,000. It was a transfer that changed the lives of both men, along with perceptions of African football as a whole.

"Weah was a real surprise," Wenger later said of the player's four-year spell at the club. "For me, it was like a child discovering a chocolate bunny in his garden at Easter. I have never seen any player explode onto the scene like he did."

Wenger became a father figure, nurturing his talent and helping him adjust to life in Europe. The 21-year-old was raw but thrilling. His new teammates were confused by his African robes on his first day at the club, only to be dazzled by him as soon as the session started. Weah became a brilliant trainer, staying on to further refine his technique and work with the likes of Glenn Hoddle and Mark Hateley. It was at Monaco that Weah became a forward of maximum efficiency, capable of all manner of flicks and tricks but preferring croquetas or roulette spins to beat defenders.

His one-touch finishing was superb, providing the final flourish to many a team move. He would often start those moves himself. He scored 47 goals in 103 league matches from 1988 to 1992, but the Liberian was more than a penalty-box operator. Watch George Weah highlights now and it is possible to spy aspects of his game play from which other greats have since drawn inspiration.

Eric Cantona does not find his groove at Manchester United without Weah providing the blueprint for how to thrive in the liminal space between midfield and attack.

Thierry Henry's runs down the left-half space? And that trademark finish where the Frenchman opens his body up and curls a shot inside the far post? Those were a favored goalscoring path for Weah, too.

Yaya Touré does not make waves without Weah paving the way. The Ivorian's buccaneering runs from midfield, such a feature of his style, drew inspiration from Weah.

Didier Drogba and Victor Osimhen's peeling runs from the penalty area to deliver thumping headers at the back post against a smaller full-back? Those can be sourced from Weah.

Although he was not the first African footballer to thrive in France during this time—Marseille fans, for example, speak fondly of Abedi Pelé's time at the club from 1987 to 1993—it is noteworthy how unapologetic Weah was about his brilliance. In 1992 he moved from Monaco to Paris Saint-Germain and took his game to another level following the introduction of the backpass rule. Though he was not as politically outspoken to the degree of Ruud Gullit, who notably spoke out against the apartheid regime of South Africa, his play was a stunning rebuke to claims that African footballers were greedy or less intelligent than their European counterparts.

Weah's form did not dip in the winter months, as has been claimed too often of Black footballers, and he did not wilt in the face of more physical defenders. There is a trap that writers and commentators often fall into when describing African players, focusing too much on their physical traits while overlooking their technical skills or football intelligence. Weah was a strong, mercurial player, but also one of phenomenal technical skills and stunning tactical awareness. His time at PSG saw him nicknamed "Paris Saint George" after their league title win in 1993–94 and he became one of the most feared strikers on the continent.

He scored 16 goals in 25 European excursions for the club, including a memorable thumping finish against Bayern Munich in November 1994. He would win 1995's European Footballer of the Year for his performances in the French capital before decamping for AC Milan that summer.

At Milan, Weah was undeniable. He was the best player in the world, working in a team finely tuned to tap into his strengths. It was fitting the Italian club sought Weah out to compensate for the injury-related absence and downturn of Marco van Basten. Both men were phenomenal, skeleton-key style forwards. Innovators and game-breakers able to provide myriad attacking solutions to all manner of problems.

Solo goals such as the one scored against Verona live long in the memory, but there was also Weah's ability to create for others. In March 1996, Weah sensed weakness in Vicenza's full-back Gabriele Grossi early in the second half and began to drift toward the right wing. He quickly dismantled the visiting side's defense, providing three assists in the space of 12 minutes. Milan eventually won the game 4–0, with Weah assisting every goal.

There was an 18-month spell in Italy when a defender's best approach to "stopping" Weah was to hope his many through-balls merely found less talented teammates who might waste the opportunities provided. Weah the goalscorer was an off-the-scale talent. Weah the goal creator was more of a hostage to fortune.

League titles in 1996 and 1999 further reaffirmed his talent. Yet, as the decade neared its end and the twenty-first century approached, Milan looked to move away from Weah, with coach Alberto Zaccheroni shifting him to the wing to make space for Andriy Shevchenko. Weah would leave Milan in January 2000 on loan to Chelsea, where he won the FA Cup. Spells at Manchester City, Marseille, and Al Jazira followed before he retired in August 2003.

Not that his involvement with football was quite done yet. In the years that followed, he set about helping his national team: personally paying for players' travel, supplying sports equipment, and helping Liberian talent to gain proper agent representation as they looked for moves across Africa and Europe. He ventured into politics, founding the Congress for Democratic Change, with his humanitarian work including collaborations with UNICEF and the United Nations. In January 2018, having tried and failed to be elected in 2005 and 2011, he became the president of Liberia.

He was the ultimate African groundbreaking forward, spending his post-playing career ensuring the next generation's journeys would be much smoother than his own.

Compare the way strikers did their work when Weah began his career to how they did in 2003, and you realize just how influential he was. He is one of the greatest footballers never to have played in a World Cup, yet world football owes a huge debt to him for how he changed the cultural consciousness. Both on and off the pitch, Weah remains an icon of Africa.

Player name: George Weah
Born: October 1, 1966
Position: Striker
Debut: 1981
Main teams: Young Survivors (1981–84), Bong Range United (1984–85), Mighty Barrolle (1985–86), Invincible Eleven (1986–87), Tonnerre Yaoundé (1987–88), Monaco (1988–92), Paris Saint-Germain (1992–95), AC Milan (1995–2000), Chelsea (loan 2000), Manchester City (2000), Marseille (2000–2001), Al Jazira (2001–03); Liberia (1986–2018)
Career highlights: Won the French top flight once, Serie A twice, and claimed the Ballon d'Or in 1995.

55.

Johan Neeskens

Neeskens: "If someone passes me, he's basically walking away with a chunk of my salary."

The *other* Johan who made Total Football tick

By Jacob Whitehead

The 1974 Dutch team. Total Football. The greatest team not to win the World Cup. But, for many, totally Johan Cruyff, the No. 14 around whom 10 other orange-clad automatons pirouetted.

That is not strictly accurate, of course. This was a side laced with talent. There was the midfielder Willem van Hanegem, who was slow but blessed with one of the century's outstanding passing ranges.

The rebellious Johnny Rep, the side's baby-faced speedster. Recall, too, Jan Jongbloed, a pioneering ball-playing goalkeeper picked for his technical ability and key to the team's approach.

There was also Johan Neeskens. The *other* Johan. The man Barcelona fans called Johan *Segundo,* but who was so much more than that.

"I didn't mind being the second-greatest player in the world," he said of the constant comparisons with Cruyff many years later.

His own man, then and after, he allied technical ability, strength, and versatility in a way that made him arguably the most modern player in the side. If Cruyff was Total Football's inventor, Neeskens was its epitome.

Take a career that was always roaming, from Ajax to Barcelona, to New York and back. Making his debut as a center-back, he settled as a right-back early in his career before Ajax coach Ștefan Kovács moved him into midfield because of his physicality. At points in 1974, he played as a prototype of the false nine, pushing forward from midfield to allow Cruyff and Rep to exploit the space between the lines.

Neeskens, who won 49 caps for his country, always boasted that versatility. As a child, he was a gymnast and an outstanding baseball player, representing the Dutch junior team and competing for them in the 1967 Baseball World Championship. He was named best hitter and developed a reputation for his ability to slide into the bases—a skill he later transformed into brutal tackling.

But all that was ahead.

Born in 1951, Neeskens grew up in the Amsterdam satellite town of Heemstede, enduring a difficult childhood on the edge of poverty. His mother was extremely ill throughout his upbringing, while his father, a worker at the local steel mill, was unathletic. Somehow they would produce one of the best physical players of the century.

The family supplemented his father's salary with a smallholding where they kept chickens, cows, pigs, and goats. From time to time,

Neeskens would be expected to drive their horse and cart through town, calling for their neighbors to bring out peelings and trash to feed the animals. Later, when he made the first team at Racing Club Heemstede (RCH), the teenager would still be expected to do the same.

"Every now and then, I was embarrassed to ask for peelings and old bread," he said later. That, combined with academic struggles at school, left him with an inferiority complex, which he spent much of his life trying to shake. "I was not good enough. You could tell when I was hanging out with the other boys, they thought: 'He is just a fool.'

"But during the gym lessons, I hit back. Then I was the best. Whether it was running, long jumping, or high jumping, I won the prizes."

In the Netherlands, he was nicknamed "The Silent One" by teammates due to his lack of communication on the field. "I didn't dare to give interviews," he explained. "I was afraid that people would say: 'He plays football well, but can't open his mouth.'"

Yet the reality was that for the first years of his career, he simply needed to focus on survival, both on and off the pitch. Needing to supplement his scholar's wage, he worked as a cleaner in local apartment buildings, while as a 17-year-old center-back in a particularly physical era of the Dutch domestic game, he was targeted by opposing center-forwards. They soon learned.

"I never act softly," said Neeskens, in what amounted to a manifesto. "That's because I have a bit too little technique. My dedication and toughness have to compensate for that."

It was these characteristics—centered on his "fight"—that later piqued the fascination of Ronald Koeman, who pretended to be Neeskens when playing on the street as a child while his playmates cosplayed as the more fashionable Cruyff and Van Hanegem. They drew other monikers, too.

After shutting down Benfica's Eusébio in the European Cup in 1972, his Ajax assistant manager, Bobby Haarms, called him a "kamikaze pilot." At Barcelona he was given a better nickname than Johan

Segundo—*El Torero*, the bullfighter—though that summons the image of a player who would wrestle the creature to the floor rather than step to the side.

"If someone passes me, he's basically walking away with a chunk of my salary," Neeskens later explained.

But Neeskens did himself down in his own descriptions. He would not have made the national side in 1974 if he was a one-dimensional midfield bruiser.

"It's just *different* technique," says defender Wim Rijsbergen, who played alongside Neeskens for the Netherlands at the 1974 and 1978 World Cups. "If you can juggle the ball 50 times, that is one thing, but if you can control the ball in one step, pass it in the second step, and do that among the best, that is also technique. Neeskens wasn't dribbling past three or four guys, but his passes were always under control and he had the intelligence to get into a gap without the ball. That's more important than running there with the ball."

Yet in a World Cup qualifying match against Belgium, just three weeks after scoring a hat trick against Norway, Neeskens found himself criticized for overly physical play in a game in which he committed 13 fouls. In his mind, he was battling for a place in the squad, but the press mauled him.

"I was completely devastated by it," he said soon after, revealing the sensitivity he always carried with him. "I cried terribly. I had fits of crying, I felt depressed, and I thought: 'I'll never play for the *Oranje* again.' That's how far I was gone."

But then 1974 became his starring moment. Playing alongside Feyenoord duo Van Hanegem and Wim Jansen in midfield, he was tasked with bursting forward to occupy the opposition defense, distorting their shape, and allowing Cruyff and fellow forward Rep to drop into midfield to exploit the chaos.

Though they are remembered as Cruyff's team, Neeskens and Van Hanegem were arguably the side's most consistent performers across the tournament. Neeskens scored five goals, the joint-second-most at the finals, including a sliding lob against Brazil that became the finals' most memorable goal.

He also scored in the final against West Germany after Cruyff won a penalty in the second minute with a mazy run. He smashed his spot kick centrally after correctly gambling that goalkeeper Sepp Maier would feel compelled to dive.

The Netherlands overplayed though, with several of the Dutch squad, bereaved in World War II, saying later that they had wished to humiliate West Germany. Their opponents fought back to lead 2–1 until, with minutes left, Maier somehow conjured a save to deny Neeskens's volley as it threatened an equalizer. With that went Dutch hopes. They had lost.

Four years later, without Cruyff this time, Neeskens was the key player in a side that once again reached the World Cup final. Having suffered a serious rib injury against Scotland in the first group stage, he missed two games before undergoing five injections to return for the final match of the second group stage. The Netherlands got through but they were beaten 3–1 by hosts Argentina in the final.

At that time, Neeskens was at Barcelona, having followed Cruyff there in 1974. He soon began to have issues with the club, falling out with Cruyff after he discovered his teammate had insisted on a contract clause ensuring he was paid more than his compatriot. Bizarrely, he also allegedly offended club president José Luís Núñez by refusing to pass him toilet roll in the executive's moment of need—and was sold to the New York Cosmos soon after.

Neeskens found life in the United States challenging.

"I don't want to talk about that time," says Rijsbergen, who played alongside him for the Cosmos. "But I tried to help him."

A combination of fame, money, insecurity, and New York's environment combined to swallow Neeskens. He began to use cocaine and quickly became mired in both alcohol and gambling addictions. At one point, he was unavailable for selection for 10 months.

"He was still a great player," remembers Rijsbergen, who lived in the same apartment building as his teammate in New York. "We played on the most difficult pitch in the NASL, a terrible artificial turf, but it made no difference to him. He was still making so many sliding tackles."

When he left, in 1984, Arsenal and West Ham United had still seen enough to try to sign him. In the midst of his addictions in New York, Brian Clough's Nottingham Forest were also reportedly interested. But Neeskens instead went back to the Netherlands, to FC Groningen, and with the help of his second wife, Marlis, turned his life around.

The remainder of his playing career was itinerant, but he became a respected coach, working as an assistant for the Dutch national team for five years, including at the 1998 World Cup, with three of those under Guus Hiddink, before taking relatively tiny NEC Nijmegen to their first European appearance for 20 years in 2003. He also launched his own charitable foundation in 2001 at a time when that was still unusual for footballers.

Later, Hiddink appointed him assistant head coach of Australia, where the duo led the side to their first World Cup since 1974—the tournament that had been Neeskens's crowning moment.

"One of the biggest memories I had as a player was that we used to do rondos and Johan always used to join in," remembers former Australia midfielder Tim Cahill of working under the Dutchmen around the 2006 World Cup. "He was very fit and physical and he liked to be aggressive with his challenges. He was always 100 percent committed and throwing himself about.

"He was one of the most humble people I've ever met within an organization and I think he really softened that [Australia coaching] staff, from a Dutch mentality side, and just had the experience that meant we looked up to him."

He was still coaching when he died in October 2024, aged 73, in Algeria while working for the Dutch FA in outreach programs. Just weeks before, he, Rijsbergen, and Van Hanegem had been playing golf with other former teammates from the national setup.

"We were playing in 40 degrees and Johan, we all said, was so fit," adds Rijsbergen. "But we cannot look inside. Of course, he will be remembered. But it would be better for me, for you, for Johan, if he was still alive."

Player name: Johannes Neeskens
Born: September 15, 1951
Died: October 6, 2024 (aged 73)
Position: Midfielder, right-back
Debut: 1968
Main teams: RCH (1968–70), Ajax (1970–74), Barcelona (1974–79), New York Cosmos (1979–84), Groningen (1985); Netherlands (1970–81)
Career highlights: One of the Netherlands' best players as they reached the World Cup final in 1974 and 1978. He won the European Cup in three consecutive seasons with Ajax as well as two Dutch titles at the club. Claimed the European Cup Winners' Cup with Barcelona.

54.

Hristo Stoichkov

The tournament in the US was the stage upon which Stoichkov established himself as a mainstream star.

When Bulgaria gate-crashed the party at USA 1994

By Felipe Cárdenas

Hristo Stoichkov's delivery was terse and deliberate. The Bulgaria and Barcelona great did not mince words as he recalled what he believes led to Bulgaria's elimination from the 1994 World Cup.

"We had a referee who was a son of a bitch," Stoichkov told *The Athletic* in 2020. "He was French. He was an idiot."

Bulgaria lost 2–1 in a heated and controversial semifinal to Italy at that World Cup in the United States, but Stoichkov still returned home a hero. His six goals had nearly taken the underdogs to the final against eventual champions Brazil. The 28-year-old ended the tournament level with Russia's Oleg Salenko in the scoring stakes. He was awarded the Bronze Ball, with Brazil's Romário, his strike partner at Barcelona, and Roberto Baggio of Italy winning the Golden and Silver Balls, respectively.

Stoichkov was already an elite player in Europe, his reputation forged at CSKA Sofia and Barcelona, but the 1994 World Cup was the stage upon which the fiery forward established himself as a mainstream star. His performances at football's biggest showcase event were recognized when he claimed that year's Ballon d'Or ahead of Baggio. Not that he basked in an individual award.

"Winning that may change other players, but I remained unchanged," he said, his voice betraying his adopted Spanish dialect. "The Ballon d'Or is not Hristo Stoichkov's award. It belongs to my wife, my kids, my parents, teammates, coaches, and my fans. It belongs to the team masseuse and physios. It's everyone's award. You can't win it without them. What are you going to do? Buy a Ballon d'Or at a supermarket?

"Behind every individual award is a team of many people. So it never changed me and it never will."

Stoichkov was football's bad boy, a scowling and powerful forward who became soccer royalty during a golden age for attackers. He rose to prominence under the Dutch master tactician Johan Cruyff as a prolific member of the great Barcelona sides of the early 1990s. He went to the 1994 World Cup backed up by four years of excellence at club level. Indeed, before winning the Ballon d'Or, he had finished as runner-up in 1992.

Under Cruyff, Stoichkov formed a short-lived but formidable partnership with Romário. The two spearheaded a Barcelona juggernaut that poured in goals and hoarded trophies. But it was about more than just their pairing. "Everyone talked about the attacking duo of Stoichkov and Romário, Romário-Stoichkov," he said. "But we had a great team behind us.

"We were extraordinary in possession. It allowed us to attack at will when Romário and I were strike partners."

Stoichkov won five La Liga titles, a European Cup, and a European Cup Winners' Cup in his two stints with Barcelona, but his first major headline as a Barca player would establish his controversial reputation.

During the first leg of the 1990 Spanish Super Cup, the man nicknamed "The Dagger" stamped on the foot of referee Ildefonso Urizar Azpitarte after being sent off. He would receive a six-month suspension, later reduced to a two-month ban.

"There were always one or two referees who were arrogant sons of bitches," Stoichkov said. "Back then you'd get carded for raising your arms before even saying anything."

Unpredictable. Intimidating. Ruthless.

Stoichkov was all three at any given moment. He had a cannon for a left foot, a relentless mentality, and the tactical awareness to play as both a creator and a goalscorer. He was also the heart and soul of a Bulgaria team considered the country's golden generation—a moniker that does not always glitter in international football.

Before USA '94, Bulgaria had experienced few moments of grandeur at senior international level. A round-of-16 exit at the 1986 World Cup in Mexico was their lone highlight and, despite boasting a talented group of players, Stoichkov's generation failed to qualify for the 1988 European Championship, the 1990 World Cup in Italy, and Euro '92.

Those disappointments hardened Stoichkov and his teammates. A nation's hopes had been pinned on this group, but now they were on the verge of being branded as underachievers. Nothing came easy for them and Bulgaria qualified for the 1994 finals courtesy of an unexpected, last-minute win over France. From the outside, they arrived in the US with low expectations, but in Bulgaria, there was hope that Stoichkov, a player at the peak of his powers, could inspire them to achieve something remarkable.

Bulgaria were certainly expected to advance out of their group. Stoichkov remembered the confidence that was pulsating through the squad. The win over favored France had emboldened them. Success on the international stage may have been elusive, but the majority of Bulgaria's starting XI were in solid form at their respective clubs. There was quality in their ranks.

"That was a mature team with a lot of important players from that era," said Stoichkov. "Krasimir Balakov, for example, was at Sporting Lisbon and would go on to be an undeniable starter for Stuttgart. Yordan Letchkov was starring in Germany [at Hamburg]. Emil Kostadinov was starting for Porto. Trifon Ivanov, rest in peace, had played at Real Betis and in Switzerland, and Nasko Sirakov was an important player for us. He had played in France. And I had been a starter at Barcelona for many years.

"That team started its path in 1982 when we were 14 and 15 years old. We knew that our winning mentality was a plus. We knew how to manage a game. We knew how to read and control the tempo of the match. That team was made to compete at that World Cup and we had a very clear objective: Win one game."

That might sound like limited ambition, but for all that Bulgaria feared no one at the tournament, they had never even won a World Cup match in their five previous appearances at the finals. Even progress into the round of 16 in 1986 had been achieved via two draws in the group.

Yet the long runway toward USA '94 and the failures Stoichkov and Bulgaria had endured in Europe would end up standing them in good stead when the World Cup campaign proper started against Nigeria on June 21 in Dallas. "We lost 3–0 and I thought: 'Damn, we're going to lose every game,'" Stoichkov said.

That defeat stunned the veteran Bulgarians. Was this tournament to be another letdown for the Balkan nation?

It took a collision with a hapless Greek side in their second group match for Stoichkov and his teammates to find their groove. These were ideal opponents to help erase the embarrassment of five days prior. Bulgaria's magical summer ride duly began.

Stoichkov scored twice against Greece from the penalty spot to lead Bulgaria to a 4–0 success, their first-ever World Cup win. He added another goal against a star-studded Argentina. His cunning finish from outside the penalty area left Argentina goalkeeper Luis Islas helpless. It was a vintage, lung-busting run and finish from Bulgaria's star performer and a goal he would replicate against Mexico in the round of 16.

The Mexicans had initially looked the more fluid side in possession, but six minutes in and from Bulgaria's first counterattack, Stoichkov latched on to an exquisite pass from Ivaylo Yordanov that split Mexico's defense.

The forward had started his run inside his own half. He maintained a full sprint until he reached Mexico's penalty area before unleashing a strike high into the net past flamboyant goalkeeper Jorge Campos. There was a stunned gasp from the partisan Mexican crowd in New Jersey. It had taken two touches from Stoichkov to pry their team apart, even if Bulgaria eventually only advanced after a tense penalty shootout.

Defending world champions Germany were next.

The quarterfinal against the Germans is etched into Bulgarian football lore. It was supposed to be Bulgaria's final stop on a whirlwind tour of the US, not least because Germany had top names in nearly every position: Lothar Matthäus, Jürgen Klinsmann, Matthias Sammer, Jürgen Kohler, Rudi Völler, Andreas Brehme, Thomas Häßler . . . the names tripped off the tongue.

Still, the Germans *had* looked beatable throughout the tournament and, at this point, Bulgaria's self-belief was unwavering. "Man for man, we were a better team," said Stoichkov. "Inside the dressing room, we knew we could beat Germany."

It was a tight contest, with both teams striking the woodwork. Matthäus's penalty thrust the champions ahead, only for Stoichkov's wonderful free kick to draw Bulgaria level 15 minutes from the end. Instead of using power to beat Germany goalkeeper Bodo Illgner, Stoichkov finessed a dipping shot over the German wall. Illgner never stood a chance.

Three minutes later, Letchkov's diving header secured Bulgaria an incredible victory—their most storied win of all time.

For Stoichkov, that free-kick equalizer was his most cherished goal from a glittering summer. "Obviously, [my favorite] was against Germany because my eldest daughter was born that same day. I'll never forget that goal. The 'Berlin Wall' was toppled on that day. During the pregame team talk, we believed that it was the German team that would be the easiest to defeat. They scored on a nonexistent penalty. We should have scored more.

"Then we went on to play Italy. . . ."

His voice tailed off as thoughts turned to that semifinal in New Jersey. The dream ended that day. Stoichkov scored his sixth goal of the tournament from the spot, halving a deficit after Baggio's brace midway through the first half, but it was not enough. Even years on, the simmering frustration boiled over into conspiracy theories and anger.

"One has to understand that Italy and Brazil hadn't met in a final in 24 years," he said. "That's part of the game."

Then came a deep breath.

"Look at Italy versus Spain [in the quarterfinal]. Mauro Tassotti hits Luis Enrique with an elbow and doesn't get ejected from the game. There are things in football that are unforgivable. Against Italy, there were two penalties in our favor that weren't called. Why? Because if they call those penalties, I'm not going to miss from the spot. I don't miss. Italy were dead in that second half."

The way it ended at USA '94 did not tarnish Stoichkov's impression of the US.

In 2000, after stints in Saudi Arabia and Japan, he moved to the Chicago Fire in Major League Soccer. "I fell in love with the city of Chicago," he said. "There were more than 250,000 Bulgarians there."

He stayed stateside after his playing days were over, too, moving to Miami and joining Spanish-language broadcaster Univision as a Champions League pundit. Before ending the interview in 2020,

Stoichkov reflected briefly on his biggest disappointment. "Losing the Champions League final to Milan in 1994," he said. "From a sporting perspective, they were better than us. 4–0 . . . we have to accept that."

By contrast, the 1992 European Cup that Barcelona won remains etched in his heart. "It was special for all *barcelonistas* and my teammates. We'll never forget May 20, 1992." Despite that, the birth of his granddaughter, rather than anything achieved on a football field, was the happiest day of his life.

For someone with such a combative personality, Stoichkov struck an amicable tone in describing what football truly meant to him.

"Relationships cannot be bought," he added. "You can have strong relationships outside of the game. I experienced many highs but, for 90 minutes, it's just a game."

Player name: Hristo Stoichkov
Born: February 8, 1966
Position: Forward
Debut: 1981
Main teams: FC Yuriy Gagarin (1981–82), Hebros Harmanli (1982–83), CSKA Sofia (1984–90), Barcelona (1990–95, 1996–98), Parma (1995–96), Al Nassr (1998), Kashiwa Reysol (1998–99), Chicago Fire (2000–2002), D.C. United (2003); Bulgaria (1987–99)
Career highlights: Bulgaria's best player as they reached the semifinals of the 1994 World Cup. He was the joint winner of the Golden Boot at the tournament. Won the European Cup in 1992 and the European Cup Winners' Cup in 1997 with Barcelona and five La Liga titles. Won the Ballon d'Or in 1994.

53.

Wayne Rooney

Rooney was a force of nature.

The last of the street footballers

By Daniel Taylor

Take a walk past the redbrick terraced houses bordering Old Trafford and you will see the statues that take prominent positions outside Manchester United's stadium.

On your right, there is the Holy Trinity of Denis Law, George Best, and Bobby Charlton. Law is in goal-celebration mode, a single hand raised in the air. Charlton and Best are on either side of him, both with an arm around their teammate. All three are looking toward the stadium that, in the distant past, a 21-year-old Charlton described as "the theatre of dreams."

Sir Matt Busby's statue peers down from one of the vertiginous stands, as the manager who rebuilt a grief-stricken club after the 1958 Munich air disaster and led United to the European Cup a decade later.

Sir Alex Ferguson, winner of 13 league championships, is immortalized in bronze at the front of a stand that has been named in his honor. In time, other statues will inevitably follow. And here's a suggestion that will polarize opinion among United's supporters: How about one to commemorate the leading goalscorer in the club's history?

A statue for Wayne Rooney? Well, yes, why not? No other player in United's entire existence can beat Rooney's 253-goal haul for the 20-time league champions. Rooney won 16 trophies at Old Trafford and, while there are others with more, his time in Manchester was also synonymous with him catching and overhauling Charlton's record as England's all-time leading goalscorer. Rooney, in short, is a history-maker for club and country.

It is complicated, though. Rooney's relationship with United was never quite the same after handing in a transfer request in 2010 while fluttering his eyelashes in Manchester City's direction. City had been taken over by Abu Dhabi's billionaires two years earlier and were intent on transforming the landscape of English football. Rooney's mutinous thoughts led to spiteful banners at Old Trafford and a balaclava-wearing mob turning up outside his house.

He abandoned the idea of a cross-city switch, apologized, and knuckled down to hear his name being chanted enthusiastically again. Yet his greatness—because it was, undoubtedly, greatness—was not quite so easy to discern in his final years at Old Trafford. At times the crowds no longer seemed quite so willing to place their trust in him.

Louis van Gaal once made the point that, when he took over from David Moyes in the list of managers from the post-Ferguson era, Rooney was no longer capable of troubling defenses in the way that had once come so naturally to him. Van Gaal felt he had inherited a player on the wane. Yet the most shocking part of that statement was that Rooney was only 28 at the time. It seemed awfully young to be describing him, in football, as over the hill.

As for Ferguson, in private moments, he would refer to genetics and confide that he had misgivings of his own. Rooney's mother, Jeanette, was a dinner lady at De La Salle Academy, the school in Croxteth, Liverpool, that her son had attended. His father, Wayne Sr., was a thickset man who worked as a laborer and, as a younger man, had been pretty handy in the boxing ring. "Look at his dad," Ferguson would say, without meaning to sound uncharitable. Rooney was built the same way, and as the years passed, it started to feel like a trick of the mind that he regularly used to outperform Cristiano Ronaldo during their days together in Manchester.

Ronaldo was the older man by eight months, yet while the Portuguese superstar flexed his abs and continued to flourish at the highest level, Rooney never recovered the jet-heeled speed and running power that had helped to make him such a formidable opponent in his earlier years. Van Gaal was right and so was Ferguson. "With the kind of physique Wayne had, it was always hard to imagine him playing into his mid-30s," said the most successful manager in United's history.

Before then, however, Rooney was a force of nature.

He was often described as the last of the street footballers and that was very apt during his peak years in particular. Rooney played with a spark. It was competitive anger smoldering behind those pale blue eyes. "I like to play with a little bit of temper," he said at Euro 2004. And, boy, Ferguson was a fierce protector of his own.

In one media conference, away from the television cameras, United's manager was asked about an incident when Rooney had pushed his hand into the face of a Bolton Wanderers player, Tal Ben Haim, with enough aggression for the Football Association to open disciplinary proceedings. Ferguson's reaction to this question was an explosion of rage, machine-gunning 22 F-words toward the journalists in his presence in roughly 45 seconds and finishing with him swiping his hand at the tape recorders on his desk, sending them flying into a wall 10 feet away.

One was smashed beyond repair. "You've got me to lose my temper, wonderful" was Ferguson's parting shot, pointing to the door to make it clear he had finished answering questions.

Rooney's first game in United's colors was a Champions League tie against Turkish team Fenerbahçe and, still only 18, he marked the occasion with a hat trick. Yet he had already introduced himself to the Old Trafford crowd, aged 16, in a game for Everton, his first club, when he came on during the second half of one match and had the nerve to accelerate past three players in a surging run through the home defense.

In another visit to Old Trafford, the young tyro clattered into Ronaldo with a scything challenge not too far from where Ferguson was standing on the touchline. That was another form of introduction. Rooney might have been young, but he came from a tough family, raised in one of the most unpretentious areas of Merseyside, and he would take that streetwise edge onto the football field.

Just consider the moments before and after one of his more memorable goals, when Newcastle United visited Old Trafford in April 2005.

Something had got under Rooney's skin. He was angry that the referee kept allowing Alan Shearer to get away with perceived fouls. As the television cameras zoomed in, Rooney was raging at the official. The ball, meanwhile, had been headed clear and was dropping from the sky. And that was the precise moment when all of Rooney's pent-up anger and frustration attached itself to a volley, 30 yards out, that was still picking up speed as it flew into the top corner of Newcastle's net.

It was one of the greatest goals ever witnessed at Old Trafford and the man responsible for it—because Rooney was very much a man at the age of 19—still could not rid himself of the fury that had been coursing through his veins. "Even when it went in, he kept running to hit the rebound in," Shay Given, Newcastle's goalkeeper, told *The Athletic* 15 years on. "You could see he was still angry."

The saddest thing, perhaps, is that Rooney's relationship with Ferguson had broken down in the weeks and months before the manager's retirement in 2013. Ferguson was unhappy with various aspects of the player's lifestyle. Rooney had been removed from the team and there was only a cursory handshake, with barely any eye contact, when Ferguson went on the pitch after his final match at Old Trafford to give his farewell speeches.

It would be unfair, however, to dwell too much on that when, overall, Rooney's achievements for the club are as solid as the foundations of Old Trafford itself.

Rooney was not just a great goalscorer, but a scorer of great goals. His overhead kick against Manchester City in 2011 was voted the following year as the best goal of the Premier League era, going back to 1992. Another beauty was looped in from near the halfway line in a game at West Ham United. Or there were times when Rooney would pick up the ball in deep positions and just surge past opponents in a blur of speed, competitive courage, and ball control.

Ferguson sometimes had to remind his striker to stay near the penalty area, the old-fashioned way, but Rooney just loved to be involved, to hunt the ball down and to dominate rather than merely decorate football matches.

He had, Ferguson wrote in his 2013 autobiography, a "natural instinct to play the game, an intuitive awareness of how football worked. A remarkable, raw talent. Plus natural courage and energy, which is a blessing for any footballer. The ability to run all day is not to be undervalued."

It brought Rooney five Premier League titles, one Champions League, one FA Cup, three League Cups, the Europa League, and the FIFA Club World Cup, as well as four Community Shield wins and enough individual awards to fill an aircraft hangar.

At Everton, the 16-year-old Rooney announced himself to the Premier League by scoring an 89th-minute winner in a 2–1 victory over Arsenal at Goodison Park. It did not seem to matter to him that the opposition were the league champions and unbeaten in 30 games. Yet the teenager almost froze when he had to face the media for the first time on the occasion of his first professional deal, aged 17.

Rooney was so unprepared for the barrage of flashing cameras that the words stuck in his throat and his audience could hardly hear him.

David Moyes, Everton's manager, told him off for chewing gum and there was another awkward moment when Rooney reached for the large bottle of water on their table. He was about to swig it straight from the bottle until Moyes intervened. "Pour it in the glass, Wayne," came the advice.

Bill Kenwright, the theater producer and future Everton chairman, summed it up neatly: "This whole thing's potty, like a Jim Carrey movie. There's too much fantasy in this lad's story for one of my theatre shows. A boy who sits muttering in his monosyllabic way when the microphones are there can go out and bring 50,000 men to their feet in joy."

Rooney became the youngest player to win a full England cap. His first goal for England also came before his 18th birthday. He went on to make 120 international appearances—a national record for an outfield player—before a new manager, Gareth Southgate, began the same kind of phasing-out process that José Mourinho had already undertaken as Van Gaal's successor in the Old Trafford dugout.

It ended, as it often does with England, with a collection of what-if moments. What if, for example, Rooney had not been injured in Euro 2004? He was 18 at the time and had been blitzing opposition defenses in a way that had never been seen before from any England player in any international tournament.

People tend to roll their eyes now when they remember Sven-Göran Eriksson describing Rooney in that tournament as England's Pelé. At the time, however, not everyone felt the Swede's eulogy bordered on recklessness. Rooney was 18, a sensation, a wonderkid with the world at his feet and a rare, thrilling collection of skills.

Just consider Eriksson's final words as England manager after the team had been eliminated from a World Cup quarterfinal against Portugal that will always be remembered for Rooney's red card—and Ronaldo's infamous wink toward the Portuguese dugout—for the flash of temper that involved him stamping on Ricardo Carvalho, the opposition center-half.

In different circumstances, Rooney might have returned to England to the same kind of vitriol and scapegoating that David Beckham experienced after being sent off for his kick at Argentina's Diego Simeone in the 1998 World Cup.

Eriksson, though, made the point that Rooney was too precious to be given the pitchfork-mob treatment. "You, more than me, need Wayne Rooney in the next few years. So, please, pay attention, don't kill him. I beg you: Take it easy with Rooney, for your own sake. You need him. He's the golden boy of English football. Please, make it easier for him to come back than it was for Beckham. I have no hard feelings with him, none at all, and nor should you."

Rooney's international career lasted more than 15 years total—the third longest of any England player, behind Peter Shilton and Stanley Matthews—and he would almost certainly have ranked higher in this list if his performances in three World Cups had not, for a variety of reasons, been shrouded in disappointment.

When he left United in the summer of 2017, it was to go back to Everton, linking up again with the club he had supported as a boy. He then had a spell with D.C. United in Major League Soccer before returning to England to play for Derby County in the Championship. He experimented with dropping back to operate as a central midfielder and, to some extent, it worked.

Ultimately, though, he will always be remembered for his uniqueness as an elite center-forward and the years, in particular, when *The Guardian* called him "the assassin-faced baby" (Michael Owen once having been known as English football's baby-faced assassin) and opposition players could have been forgiven for wanting to check his birth certificate.

"He's not just a footballer," Míchel Salgado, the Spain international defender, once said. "He's so damned strong he'd be just as good helping you move house as playing football."

Player name: Wayne Rooney
Born: October 24, 1985
Position: Forward
Debut: 2002
Main teams: Everton (2002–04, 2017–18), Manchester United (2004–17), D.C. United (2018–19), Derby County (2020–21); England (2003–18)
Career highlights: Won the Premier League five times and won the Champions League in 2007–08. Scored a club-record 253 goals for Manchester United.

52.

Toni Kroos

Kroos played at one speed because he never really needed a second.

A midfield talent who would have thrived in any era

By Seb Stafford-Bloor

There is a story about Toni Kroos that sums up just how unusual he is. It comes from the beginning of his career, in 2014. His Bayern Munich contract was dwindling away, with just a year left to run, and Kroos and the club were deadlocked in their attempts to extend it.

In the background, Bayern were balking at the wage demands. The figures have always been quite hazy, but the two sides were roughly €4 million per year apart. Kroos wanted €10 million, Bayern—who were not yet sold on his value—were only offering €6 million.

After a game against Eintracht Frankfurt, Kroos encountered an angry Uli Hoeneß, then the club president, in the players' tunnel. In his book, *My Moves: How I Became Germany's Most Successful Agent*, Kroos's agent Volker Struth writes: "Hoeneß marched towards Toni with his face bright red, yelling, 'You need to get your agent under control; you'll never get €10 million here.'"

It's worth acknowledging that, in many ways, Hoeneß *is* Bayern Munich. Among all those responsible for the club's position in the global hierarchy today, nobody sits above Hoeneß. His playing career was cut short by a knee injury that forced him to retire at 27, so he is no Gerd Müller, Franz Beckenbauer, or Sepp Maier. But in terms of vision and infrastructure and understanding the value of commercialism, Hoeneß is like no other.

He became the club's business manager after he finished playing and, in the 30 years between then and becoming Bayern president, he was the principal architect of what they became: a European superpower, capable of competing across the continent without the backing of an oligarch or sovereign wealth fund.

So, Hoeneß was a pretty big deal. Today Kroos is a celebrated player with a ton of silverware that places him among the modern greats. Then he was 24, yet to win the World Cup with Germany (which would happen a few months later) and still to prove that he was fundamental even to Bayern's future in the long term.

He recounted his recollection of that incident and what happened next on the *Einfach mal Luppen* podcast, which he records with his brother, Felix.

"We negotiated for a relatively long time. Then, Uli Hoeneß didn't know exactly what the relationship was like between me and Volker Struth. Hoeneß said I should call my agent back and told me that what he was demanding in terms of salary was impertinent. I replied: 'Yes, that's your opinion. But, to be clear, they are not his demands, but *ours*. Either we come to an agreement or we don't.'"

Few people are that forthright with Hoeneß. Struth's reputation is that of one of the fiercest and most successful agents in Germany. He is aggressive on his clients' behalf, and so, with an ally like that, Kroos must have felt emboldened, but it remains a striking portrayal of his self-confidence. Bayern is the endgame for many German players and the destination club beyond which there is nothing. Many would have been submissive in that situation.

"Ja, Herr Hoeneß. Entschuldigung! Entschuldigung!"

Germans are funny about money. In fact, materialism occupies quite a strange place in the national psyche and largesse is generally seen as brash or vulgar. Do not build your house too high. Do not shine your car too much. Some will tell you that wages and salary are entirely off-limits within their friendships, even with those they have known for decades and trust implicitly.

Throw in the fact Germany and the state of Bavaria are almost two different places and the trait might be more pronounced in the latter than anywhere else in the country. At Bayern, it shows in which players are celebrated for being true to the club's vision of itself. It would be a mistake to believe that winning is enough to ingratiate a player with fans. It's not. Winning a certain way is important.

The club motto is *Mia san Mia*. It means "we are who we are" and has become an umbrella term for the virtues that club members—and football players—are supposed to embody. There are 16 of them, golden rules, and most extol virtues like industry, humility, ambition, and loyalty.

The human form of *Mia san Mia* is Thomas Müller, the forward who has played more games than anyone else in Bayern's history. He is what the club sees when it looks in the mirror, and with good reason. Müller has been completely unaffected by his career, his fame, or the wealth he has racked up. He is humble and hardworking, playing and behaving without so much as a hint of ego. He is also Bavarian, was born just south of Munich, and was raised in the club's academy.

It is hard to imagine Müller ever telling Hoeneß that he was wrong. Or that he would cheerfully play for another team if Bayern Munich were not willing to pay him what he thought he was worth.

Kroos grew up in East Germany and did not arrive at Bayern until he was 16, but he is hardly Müller's opposite. Not at all. He has an everyday quirkiness that makes him tangible and is by no means aloof. Yet that story from 2014 remains representative of his take-it-or-leave-it attitude toward Bayern.

He left Germany for Real Madrid that summer and would never return. Ever since, there has remained a distance between Kroos and his former club, as if, despite over 200 appearances, three Bundesliga titles, and a Champions League win, he was never really there at all.

Kroos is different and that seems to show in so many other parts of his football life.

Another story concerns his choice of boots. In 2013, Adidas released the Adipure 11Pro. The rhythms of football's manufacturing industry mean players under endorsement could expect a new pair most years. But Kroos kept wearing his. And wearing them and wearing them. They were heavier. They absorbed far too much water when the pitches were wet. The studs were bladed rather than screwed in. They were a different era's technology, but he wore them for the rest of his career.

Adidas kept coming to him with something new, with a lighter leather or better-made sole. Each time he would send them away, until eventually they knew to stop asking. "We tried to get Toni into different boots and he's tested them," Björgvin Hreinsson, Adidas's global product manager, told *The Athletic* in 2024. "The feedback has never been negative, but it's always been more of 'This is what I'm comfortable with and this is why I'm playing very well.'

"But you can't really break a stable relationship like this one, can you? You talk about Disney love stories and stuff like that and that's kind of what this is: the perfect match."

When Kroos retired in 2024, he played his last pass with his 11Pros. By that time, the factory mold to make those boots only existed in his specific size. They were one-of-one, like their wearer. The boots have since been renamed the TKpro.

Greatness is a strange thing, especially in sport. Usually it is measured in trophies or in moments that can be set to music and played forever. Kroos might be different in that respect, too, because while his career earned him all manner of titles—almost everything worth winning in club and international football—and did have its individual highlights, it was really just a long, steady sequence of excellence.

Is there a signature moment? Perhaps the free kick that earned Germany a stoppage-time win over Sweden in 2018 and a temporary reprieve from likely World Cup elimination. Or maybe the 35-yard thunderbolt that crashed in off the Celta Vigo bar in 2019 while playing for Madrid.

Really, though, he is remembered for a narrow range of abilities honed to extraordinary levels. A player of 10,000 passes. One of the reasons Kroos was so loyal to his boots was that they gave him the right feel for the ball. His first touch always had to be perfect and he wanted just the right contact between his foot and the ball when he pushed his passes through the lines or drove a diagonal across the pitch and into space (with a gentle check of backspin).

He represented a mastery of the basics, and that tells you a lot—and explains much more. Kroos's time at the top of the game spanned 2007 to 2024; 17 years during which the sport was redefined by impossibly gifted players, each possessing previously unimaginable technical ability, incomprehensible power, or, in some cases, both.

Lionel Messi, Cristiano Ronaldo, Zlatan Ibrahimović, Kylian Mbappé, Neymar. Even just among midfielders, Kroos often seemed to lack the ethereal glint of Andrés Iniesta or Xavi, the thrusting yet elegant class of Kaká, or the dimensions of Yaya Touré or Rodri.

Instead he received the ball and passed it. He played at one speed because he never really needed a second.

In that sense, perhaps Toni Kroos could have played forever. The irony, though, is that a player who was so often different—so often slightly apart from the game—would likely have been a great at any point in history.

Player name: Toni Kroos
Born: January 4, 1990
Position: Midfielder
Debut: 2007
Main teams: Bayern Munich (2007–14), Bayer Leverkusen (loan 2009–10), Real Madrid (2014–24); Germany (2010–24)
Career highlights: Won the 2014 World Cup with Germany and the Champions League six times. Overall, he claimed 32 trophies in his club career.

51.

Sándor Kocsis

Kocsis's story is one of sadness and tragedy, but he was a prolific scorer and one of Barcelona's first foreign stars.

How a footballing miracle, a revolution, and a quagmire held back the Golden Head

By Tim Spiers

It would be quite annoying if you were one of the true great players of your generation and yet your career was effectively defined by two defeats at a stadium with a silly name in Switzerland's fifth-largest city.

"Defined" might be a bit harsh given the great things he achieved, but Sándor Kocsis would have been a World Cup and European Cup winner were it not for two fateful dates at the Wankdorf Stadium in Bern. Both ended in 3–2 defeats, a scoreline that popped up at three inopportune moments in Kocsis's career.

In terms of name recognition, Hungarian striker Kocsis is probably one of the least celebrated players on our list, and ultimately his tale, like that of his national team, would end in sadness and tragedy. But having been the prolific arrow at the tip of the Magical Magyars' bow in the 1950s, as well as a devastating goalscorer for two of Europe's most prominent club teams of the era in Budapest Honvéd and Barcelona, Kocsis is more than worthy of his place.

Were it not for a footballing miracle, the Hungarian revolution, and a pitch reduced to a bog by Ron Atkinson, his star would have shone even brighter.

First, the numbers, which are quite something.

Kocsis scored 177 goals in 160 league matches for Honvéd from 1950 to 1956, becoming one of the most celebrated players in Hungary's history, arguably second only to Ferenc Puskás. He scored 82 goals in 126 games in all competitions for Barcelona, where he played from 1958 to 1965 and is renowned as one of the club's first foreign stars. Barcelona recognize his status in the club's museum, noting that he netted a further 84 goals in 116 "unofficial" matches.

With Hungary, Kocsis scored 75 goals in just 68 internationals. That is an insanely good record.

Among postwar men's footballers who have scored at least 50 international goals, Kocsis has the best scoring rate. Only Gerd Müller, with 68 in 62 for West Germany, can rival Kocsis in terms of scoring more than a goal per game, but go an extra decimal place (yes, we're pernickety and that's exactly what we're doing) and Kocsis pips him with 1.10 goals per game to Müller's 1.09.

Cristiano Ronaldo, Lionel Messi, and even Romelu Lukaku may have scored more than Kocsis's 75, but none of the world's great goalscorers has netted at a faster rate than the Hungarian. None of them also saw their international career cut short in their prime aged 27 by a political uprising against a pro-Soviet government.

What made him so prolific? It helped that he had one of the most creative, innovative, and groundbreaking sides in the history of international football behind and around him in Hungary's Golden Team, led by innovative manager Gusztáv Sebes, who introduced a stringent fitness regime and utilized an early form of Total Football.

But Kocsis's ruthless ability in front of goal, particularly via an endless armory of headers, which earned him the nickname the "Golden Head," made him stand out. Or, more to the point, leap out over panicked defenders.

"As an exponent of heading a football, there is probably none better than Kocsis," David Bailey wrote in his 2019 book, *Magical Magyars*, on that celebrated Hungarian side. "He was only of average height but had an abnormally long and powerful neck, a high forehead, and a lithe upper body coupled with powerful squat legs, enabling him to jump head and shoulders above other players. His emergence into the national team sparked not a little jealousy in Puskás."

If there was an underlying dislike between the pair, said to stem from jealousy on Puskás's part, it did not negatively impact Honvéd or Hungary's performances. Indeed, the inside forwards were not averse to passing to each other. Perhaps more importantly, they constantly wanted to outdo each other.

"They both wanted things their own way—they were huge rivals," teammate László Budai said. "They were both so hungry for the ball that they were crazy. Sometimes I'd make it to the byline and look up and I'd see Puskás pointing to his left foot and Kocsis pointing to his head. I'd say to them, 'You two need a ball each.'"

Kocsis's goalscoring exploits for Hungary included seven hat tricks. His first came against Sweden in November 1949 during a 5–0 rout. So one-sided was the match that Hungary goalkeeper Géza Henni was substituted because he was so cold and had nothing to do to warm him up.

This would become a theme—one-sided games, not players being subbed because they had lost feeling in their extremities—of Hungary's matches over the coming years. They scored in a record 73 consecutive international matches from 1949. Between 1950 and 1954, they enjoyed an unbeaten streak of 31 games, sweeping all before them, including England, twice, via two humiliating shellackings. Then, from 1954 to 1956, they went on another run, this time untouchable across 18 matches.

The problem was that in between those mind-boggling sequences, they lost the game that mattered most.

The World Cup of 1954 was meant to be Hungary's. It was meant to be Kocsis's, too. The team had started in Switzerland by beating South Korea 9–0 (Kocsis scoring a hat trick), then, in the second and final group game, he scored four as West Germany were annihilated 8–3. Those hat tricks made him the first player to score two trebles in one World Cup, a feat emulated by Just Fontaine in 1958 and Müller in 1970.

"There has never been anybody better with his head," Sebes said of Kocsis. "But he was also a very complete striker who held the ball up and could finish with both feet."

Kocsis scored two more in a tempestuous 4–2 quarterfinal win over Brazil, also known as "The Battle of Bern" as three players were sent off. The striker then rescued a tiring Hungary in the semifinal as he scored twice against Uruguay in another 4–2 success. So that's 11 goals in just four games for Kocsis, 25 goals for the team, a goal difference of +18 in only four matches and a rematch with West Germany in the final, a side they had already beaten 8–3.

And yet, dear reader, and yet . . .

It started going wrong the night before when, outside the Hungary team hotel, the annual Swiss boys' orchestra festival took place until dawn. Typical.

Sebes, who had booked the hotel, was livid and his mood hardly improved when he spotted Kocsis and Budai, among others, sneaking back into the hotel in the early hours, having clearly disobeyed orders to stay in their rooms and rest. The players insisted they had gone out for some fresh air as they couldn't sleep, probably not helped by the whole orchestral-festival thing, but Sebes was not having it.

Kocsis was indispensable and thus avoided anything other than a stern talking-to, but his good friend Budai, who had grown up with him at Ferencváros and provided him with a conveyor belt of assists from the flank, was dropped. Kocsis was devastated.

All of which left the squad fractured—with Puskás literally fractured, having suffered an ankle hairline break that forced him to miss the quarter- and semifinals and left him unfit for the final. To top it off, West Germany blocked the parking lot at the stadium, meaning the players had to walk through the crowd to get in.

Not that this impacted Hungary's start to the game—Kocsis may not have scored, but Puskás, playing through the pain barrier, did and they were 2–0 up after eight minutes. However, West Germany, who had watched Hungary's 6–3 win over England the night before the match to focus on Hungary's defensive weaknesses, knew the early lead flattered the favorites and, just 18 minutes in, it was 2–2.

Hungary bombarded the West German goal in the second half but, after that bruising win over Brazil and extra time in the semifinal, they were running on fumes. West Germany withstood it all. Then Helmut Rahn scored a late winner.

Kocsis, the most prolific scorer the World Cup had ever seen, could not save his team. He was denied by a ridiculous save from goalkeeper Toni Turek, who was immediately proclaimed a "football god" on West German television. Puskás thought he had equalized late on, only to be flagged offside. Hungary, unbeaten for four years, had lost the World Cup despite mustering 27 goals in five games and 26 shots to West Germany's seven in the final. And despite Kocsis scoring for fun.

It was an absolute disaster. Hungary remain, with the Dutch side of the 1970s, one of the greatest teams never to have lifted the trophy.

Kocsis wasn't used to losing, for neither club nor country, but there were two more very notable 3–2 defeats to endure in his career.

One was admittedly in a friendly, but Honvéd's trip to play Wolverhampton Wanderers in December 1954 was an unofficial title contest between two of Europe's best teams. This was in the pre–European Cup era, so the only way to pit your wits against clubs from across the continent and beyond was in exhibition matches. Wolves, the dominant force in England at the time, hosted a series of floodlit friendlies at Molineux in the 1950s, also taking on Real Madrid and Dynamo Moscow.

Honvéd, with national-team players up the spine of the side, were the big draw. Coming in the wake of Hungary's demolition of England, the fixture was billed locally as a revenge mission of sorts, with Wolves the reigning English champions and Honvéd carrying all before them in Hungarian domestic football at the time.

This time Kocsis did score, with a trademark header having soared to reach a cross. He helped make it 2–0 to the visitors when splitting the Wolves defense with a through-ball. Atkinson cooed at the best football he had ever seen.

What has this got to do with Atkinson, a future Manchester United and Aston Villa manager? Well, he was a young apprentice at Wolves at the time and helped influence the result that night without even kicking a ball.

Wolves manager Stan Cullis, an advocate of direct football, ordered the pitch to be soaked at halftime, so Atkinson joined the ground staff to help transform the playing surface into a bog. Wolves used the quagmire to their advantage in the second half, coming from 2–0 down to win 3–2.

Cullis proclaimed Wolves world champions and "Cullis' Kings of the World" was the headline in the *Daily Mail* the following day, which led the influential French newspaper *L'Équipe* to retort that it was time to create a European tournament to back up the wild claims. The European Cup was launched a year later.

Cullis, Atkinson, and Kocsis may have helped—indirectly—to push the formation of Europe's premier club competition, but neither Wolves nor Honvéd were in the inaugural competition, with many clubs declining invites.

By the time Kocsis did regularly play in the European Cup with Barcelona, life had become very different for the Hungarian forward. He'd first moved to Swiss club Young Fellows Zürich, with his homeland gripped in revolution. That uprising against Soviet control in 1956 provoked the breakup of not only Honvéd's celebrated team but also that of Hungary.

The national federation placed a one-year ban on Kocsis, later reduced by FIFA to three months, due to his refusal to return home, so he missed out on qualifying for the 1958 World Cup. Indeed, his tournament record with his country ended up as 11 goals in five matches.

He moved to Barcelona after a year in Switzerland, joining his gifted compatriot Zoltán Czibor, with Puskás now at Real Madrid. More than 60,000 turned up to watch Kocsis and Czibor in a preseason friendly. For all that the striker was homesick, he maintained his prolific form and both he and Czibor scored in the 1961 European Cup final against Benfica. They also both hit the woodwork as Barcelona wasted a host of chances and lost 3–2 . . . back at Bern's Wankdorf Stadium.

It was an irony not lost on Kocsis, Czibor, or their fellow Hungarian László Kubala that the scoreline was the same as it had been in 1954.

Kocsis retired in his late thirties, but little more than 10 years later he would be dead. A fragile, sensitive soul, Kocsis suffered a freak accident in 1974 when a bathroom cabinet fell on his right foot. He had an aversion to doctors, and when he belatedly sought medical help, the wound had become infected and gangrene had set in, leading to the amputation of his foot.

He turned to drink in the aftermath and suffered from depression. While undergoing treatment for stomach cancer in a Barcelona hospital in 1979, he fell to his death out of a second-floor window. He was only 49.

Player name: Sándor Kocsis

Born: September 21, 1929

Died: July 22, 1979 (aged 49)

Position: Striker

Debut: 1946

Main teams: Ferencváros (1946–50), Honvéd (1950–56), Young Fellows Zürich (1957–58), Barcelona (1958–65); Hungary (1948–56)

Career highlights: One of the key players in the Hungarian team that reached the 1954 World Cup final and beat England 6–3 and 7–1 in consecutive years. The striker won the Golden Boot at the 1954 World Cup and is one of only three players to score two hat tricks at one tournament. He scored 75 goals in 68 games for Hungary, and won the Hungarian top flight four times and La Liga twice.

50.

Kenny Dalglish

Dalglish scored more than 350 goals in over 900 appearances in all competitions, but he was recognized more as a pure footballer than a goalscorer.

"I was happy just to get along. Nobody at Liverpool got above his station."

By Oliver Kay

Kenny Dalglish played among the shadows. He made sure of that. Turning out for Celtic and Liverpool in the 1970s and 1980s, when a heavy challenge from behind was an occupational hazard, he used to take a second to look on the floor to see if the shadows could tell him which way to turn as the ball came in.

As manager of Blackburn Rovers years later, he told Alan Shearer, arguably the greatest center-forward of the Premier League era, that he was missing a trick. "Use the shadows," Dalglish told him.

Shearer thought his manager was joking. "What if we're playing at night?" the England forward asked.

"Well the floodlights will be on, won't they?" Dalglish replied, as if it were the most obvious thing in the world.

Shearer had never heard anything like it but put his skepticism aside and decided to give it a try. He would later reflect that this simple piece of advice, which he has never heard from any other player or manager since, had been "life-changing."

To Dalglish, a celebrated figure at both Celtic and Liverpool and the joint-record goalscorer for the Scotland men's team, these were just tricks of the trade. "It's common sense, isn't it?" he asks. "It depends if it's raining or the sun's shining, but it has to help. Well, it helped me, anyway."

Numerous teammates have described Dalglish as a "genius." He snorts at the suggestion, saying he would have done better at school if that were the case. But he was one of those players blessed with what seemed like a sixth sense on the football pitch: an instinctive understanding of space and time and how he could use it to his team's advantage. He always appeared to be one or two moves ahead of everyone else.

There is a goal I'd always wanted to ask him about. You can find it on YouTube. It was a Liverpool game against Watford in December 1982 and, unlike some of the most celebrated goals from that era, it looks as stunning now as it did at the time.

It wasn't Dalglish's goal, but in essence, it was. It was his pass—a pass I vividly recall seeing on the BBC's highlights program *Match of the Day* and thinking I had never seen anything like it before, not even when watching Zico and the rest of the marvelous Brazilians at the World Cup earlier that year. To quote the BBC commentary from the time: "Ian Rush celebrates the goal, but Kenny Dalglish the creator supreme."

Dalglish has his back to goal, about 45 yards out, when a header comes his way. With one touch, he brings the ball down with the outside of his right foot, turns, and throws his marker, Ian Bolton, totally off-balance.

I wanted to ask about the thought process. At what point did he know he was going to play that pass? He didn't even look up until the last moment, so was it instinct or something preconceived?

"The boy [Bolton] was tight on me—and that wasn't the first time," he says. "If you watch it, he takes a step to the left. I didn't see him do that, but I knew he would be tight, so if I played it anywhere I would get away from him. And then I put it behind the other guy and Rushy finished it."

Slow down, Kenny. What of the pass itself? It is obscene, hit with geometric precision, a perfect arc just beyond the reach of Watford defender Steve Sims and into the path of Rush. How do you develop the vision and the ability to play a pass like that?

"How does anybody know, in any sport? How do they get the feel for it?" Dalglish asks. "It could be golf, tennis, football, whatever. How do you get the feel for the right distance and the right pace on the ball? I don't know. If someone knew how to develop that in a player, they would have a hell of a product there. But if you can see it, you've got to try it."

He was an extraordinary player. He scored more than 350 goals in over 900 appearances in all competitions for club and country, but he was recognized more as a pure footballer than a goalscorer. He was more an old-fashioned inside forward than a striker, but the way he dropped deep, dragging defenders with him, seemed to be ahead of its time. He somehow combined the competitive instincts of a street footballer with the guile and cleverness of a chess player.

Anyone watching a Dalglish highlights reel for the first time would struggle to guess whether he favored his right foot or his left. (He confirms he was happiest on his right foot but felt comfortable on his left in any situation.) Most players have a signature move, but his repertoire was vast, as was his knowledge of the right move in any situation. With either foot, he could dink it, chip it, curl it, blast it, or pick out a teammate whose run no one else on the pitch had spotted.

Dalglish grew up during a golden era for Scottish football, watching players such as Jim Baxter at Rangers, Jimmy Johnstone at Celtic, and Denis Law at Manchester United. Television coverage was scarce in those days, but he talks of studying those players as much as he could, looking to learn from them.

But the player he singles out as his teenage inspiration is less heralded. "Very few people nowadays would have heard of him, but it was a wee guy called Ian McMillan, who played for Airdrie and moved to Rangers," he says. "They used to call him 'the wee prime minister' and I used to watch him and pick up a few things that I would try if I was playing in the street or in the park."

Or in Celtic's youth teams, having been rejected by Rangers, the club he supported. And indeed, by Liverpool after going on trial as a 15-year-old. He was part of an exciting Celtic reserve team known as the "Quality Street Gang," along with future Scotland teammates such as Danny McGrain, David Hay, and Lou Macari. The challenge they faced was to displace the "Lisbon Lions," who had won the European Cup in 1967. "We're talking about one of the strongest teams in history," he says, "so it wasn't going to be easy to break in as a young player."

Dalglish made his first-team debut at 17, but it was another three years before he truly began to establish himself at senior level. It is telling that when asked to pick out a goal from all those he scored in his professional career, he opts for the first: a penalty to clinch victory for Celtic in a League Cup tie at the home of their bitter rivals Rangers in August 1971. That took nerves as a 20-year-old (and as a boyhood Rangers fan). As he suggests, "You don't know what might have happened in my career if I'd missed that."

What happened was that Dalglish went on to achieve greatness with Celtic as the star of a team that continued to dominate Scottish football, winning the title and the Scottish Cup four times each during his time as a regular at the club. Dalglish became a mainstay of the Scotland national team, winning 102 international caps in an era when such a milestone was a rarity in Europe. That remains a record at the time of writing, as does his all-time goalscoring record, held jointly with Law.

Dalglish speaks very fondly of his time at Celtic and of his debt to their manager, Jock Stein, but after two European Cup semifinal defeats, he craved a new challenge. When the opportunity came to join newly crowned European champions Liverpool in the summer of 1977, he could not resist.

At Liverpool, he replaced crowd favorite Kevin Keegan, who had left for Hamburg after helping Liverpool win the European Cup. Far from daunted by that challenge, Dalglish helped Liverpool scale even greater heights, winning the European Cup in 1978, 1981, and 1984 and the English league championship five times over the same period before taking over as player-manager in 1985 and leading the club to three more league titles.

Perhaps the most celebrated of his goals is the European Cup winner he scored against Club Bruges in 1978: a typically deft chip over the advancing goalkeeper Birger Jensen.

For 64 minutes, Jensen had kept Liverpool at bay, but the way he denied Terry McDermott (twice) and David Fairclough planted a seed in Dalglish's mind. "You've got to study how the opposition is playing and I had seen earlier in the game the way [Jensen] dropped himself down low in those situations," he says. "I knew what I was going to do if I was one-on-one with him. That goal was an important one not because it was my goal, but because it meant we won the European Cup. It wouldn't have bothered me one iota if Davie Fairclough had got the final touch and put it over the line—as long as we won."

It is for his time at Liverpool that he is best known, not only as a player and manager but for the role he played in supporting so many grieving families in the aftermath of the Hillsborough disaster in 1989, in which 97 people lost their lives. No matter what heroes like Steven Gerrard and Mohamed Salah have contributed to the club's illustrious history in the modern era, Dalglish's status is, in the eyes of many supporters, unsurpassed—perhaps even unsurpassable.

Just how good was Dalglish? His former Liverpool and Scotland teammate Graeme Souness believes that at the peak of his powers in the late 1970s and early 1980s, there was no better player on the planet—"better than Maradona, better than Rummenigge, better than Platini"—and certainly none more complete. "In his best days at Liverpool, I would say he was the best player in the world without a shadow of a doubt," Souness said.

Did he ever feel that was the case? "Me? No," Dalglish says. "I was happy just to get along. One thing I loved about playing for Liverpool was the modesty. There was nobody at Liverpool who got above their station—and if they got above their station, they got knocked down again very quickly.

"Some players might have got a better press than others or got spoken about more than others, but that wasn't important to us. What was important was what the score was at the end of the game. Unless everyone's doing their job, you won't win anything. It's a team sport. People forget that sometimes."

It is true, but Dalglish was one of those rare individuals who can transform a team, elevating all around them to another level. His talent attracted the spotlight, but with that came the opportunity to bring others out of the shadows.

Player name: Kenny Dalglish
Born: March 4, 1951
Position: Forward
Debut: 1968
Main teams: Celtic (1968–77), Liverpool (1977–90); Scotland (1971–86)
Career highlights: Won three European Cups and the English league title six times with Liverpool. At Celtic, he claimed the Scottish championship four times. Scotland's joint all-time top scorer.

49.

Dennis Bergkamp

Arsenal had never recruited a comparable player to Bergkamp—he was a game-changer in every way.

The imperfect perfectionist

By Amy Lawrence

The art of the casual bombshell is in its timing.

Arsenal were at the pivotal point of one of the most stunning transfers in their history, and the man responsible for the negotiations, Vice Chairman David Dein, was in his element as the contracts were being readied. Dein plucked something out of his inside blazer pocket, his "contract pen," a Montblanc, and he would offer it to all new signings—a ceremonial touch to make them feel they were being passed a baton, which would be passed on as part of the club's lineage of great players.

It is more than 30 years later now and the context is important. This was 1995 and international transfers were still relatively rare in the newly formed Premier League. There was so much reticence about the value in importing talent that Alan Sugar, the entrepreneur who was, back then, the chairman down the road at Tottenham Hotspur, tutted about a generic, overpaid, over-here foreigner he nicknamed "Carlos Kickaball."

Arsenal signing a player with the stature of Dennis Bergkamp was monumental. They had never recruited a comparable player. He was a game-changer in every way.

Bergkamp was a combination of excited and relieved to make this move. Excited to relaunch himself in a football environment he hoped would make him feel liberated and loved. Relieved to be leaving Inter Milan after what had turned out to be an unhappy and pressurized period of his career. Arsenal were overjoyed to make a transfer so sensational it would make shock waves.

The $9.5 million fee obliterated their transfer record. Bergkamp was widely regarded as world-class, a product of the Dutch school at Ajax, who epitomized refined technique. He had been a prodigy at the age of 17 when he was tutored by the master, Johan Cruyff.

Upstairs at Highbury, in one of the wood-paneled rooms, Bergkamp, his entourage led by the agent Rob Jansen, and Arsenal's officials were completing the deal with signatures and warm handshakes. The ink from the contract pen was barely dry when Jansen turned to Dein and mentioned that his client had a severe fear of flying. To put it bluntly, Bergkamp would not countenance getting on a plane. Naturally, that brought into question any matches Arsenal participated in overseas, particularly in European competition. Dein was taken aback. How could such a significant matter only come up now?

Dein was never shy about thinking creatively about problems, so he bought some time, not wanting to disrupt the welcome he wished to give to a new recruit. Later that day, he began researching solutions for aviophobia. British Airways ran a course with a high success rate in helping people who suffered the level of anxiety that afflicted Bergkamp ever since he experienced an emergency on a flight during the 1994 World Cup.

A couple of days later, Dein invited Bergkamp into his office for a chat. How was he settling in? Did he need anything? Once the pleasantries were over, it was time to tackle the travel issue. "I started to tell him about the fear-of-flying course," Dein recalls in his autobiography, *Calling the Shots*. "He put his hand up to interrupt me. I could see beads of sweat on his brow and he went pale. 'Mr. Dein,' he said. 'I don't want to fly. I won't fly.'

"I had to make an instant decision. Do I stop talking about it? Do I try to persuade him? Do I provoke a confrontation when I could see it meant so much to him? I wanted to get the relationship off to a good start."

Dein decided not to push it but instead to offer him an open door—if Bergkamp ever wanted to give it a try, he just needed to ask. Otherwise, he promised, it would be the last time he would mention this subject.

"That was it," Dein recalls. "We never spoke about it again."

Bergkamp always was an unusually precise thinker. If he had an idea, he was all in.

As a child growing up in the Amsterdam suburbs, he developed his own personal method for the technical accuracy that would go on to define his sporting style. On the wall outside the apartment block where he lived, young Dennis would take a ball and spend endless hours kicking it, flicking it, controlling it, rebounding it, again and again. That in itself doesn't make him remarkable, but the way his mind worked as he practiced does.

He might choose one particular corner of one particular brick and then repeat different kicks at it—left foot, right foot, instep, outside of the foot, spin, dink, power, all the while analyzing why the ball moved in a certain way and how it returned to him. His individual football training involved geometry, physics, and the biology of feel and brain reaction, all at once. Not a bad education for a kid on his own in his neighborhood.

"It interested me. Maybe other people wouldn't bother. Maybe they wouldn't find it interesting. But I was fascinated," Bergkamp said in his autobiography, *Stillness and Speed*. It explains a lot about the roots of this player's relationship with the ball; how it moves and how to control it. He developed such a deep appreciation of it that he could write a thesis on the art of the first touch.

There is a clear connection between that and the goal he scored at the 1998 World Cup against Argentina. That is his favorite goal. None of it was left to chance. Each of the three touches to manipulate the hoisted pass from Frank de Boer was measured. The first tames the ball with a cushioned touch, the next deceives his marker to create the clear sight of goal, the final action curves his shot with the perfect mix of élan and efficiency to beat the goalkeeper.

It was the match-winner in the last moments of a game played in the full heat of a Mediterranean afternoon. In a split second, Bergkamp had the clarity to calculate exactly what he needed to compose to distill the space around him and the position of his opponents into a masterpiece of a goal.

Arsène Wenger described him as having "super, super intelligence" ahead of his testimonial in 2006, and sometimes when talking to him, as he pondered the right expression for what he was thinking, it was as if you could detect his brain whirring away in there. That intellect is why any discussion about Bergkamp is just as valid when assessing his passing and the magnificence of his assists.

He was prolific enough to actually break the Netherlands's all-time top goalscorer record with that goal against Argentina in Marseille, so for a while was their supreme marksman. But, goodness, he loved to execute a brilliant pass just as much. Perhaps even more. It was in these moments that Bergkamp's teammates marveled at how he would see their runs ahead of time and weight a pass to ensure it fell to their superior foot without them having to break stride.

Bergkamp's perfectionist streak was a hallmark. He amused his effervescent Arsenal teammate Ian Wright when they shared a room on away days by turning up with neatly pressed silk pajamas in his suitcase. He was invariably first to training and last to leave. In that way, his example changed the philosophy of the players he met when he came to England, who were more used to a looser training regime. He looked after himself and did not cut corners. If relentlessly high standards of dedication were good enough for Dennis, it had to be good enough for everybody else. Just by being Bergkamp, he lifted those around him.

His teammates loved him. Not only because he was so talented, but also because he showed other sides of his personality, which chipped away at this concept of pure excellence. He had his flaws, not least an edgy determination on the pitch that sometimes invited trouble (and red cards). He was also a famed practical joker, arguably making that into an art form, too.

While on the bench for a preseason friendly in which Igors Stepanovs, a plodding Latvian center-back, was on trial, he spent the entire game talking about how impressive the trialist was, purely to wind up Martin Keown, who was always ferociously competitive about anyone who might want his place. The more Bergkamp enthused, the more Keown steamed.

Perfectionism is a trait that is not unusual in people with exceptional gifts. The artist Claude Monet ruined a series of his own paintings on the eve of an exhibition because he was not happy with them. During the filming of *The Shining*, filmmaker Stanley Kubrick insisted a typist tap out the sentence 'All work and no play makes Jack a dull boy' again and again to ensure the sound recording accurately captured the note of each letter.

Is there an innate eccentricity allied to high art? Is that part of the genius package? Maybe that goes some way to explaining why such an exceptional footballer would take a choice as complicated and pressure-inviting as refusing to fly. After all, it is part of the job of a top player to attend games wherever they may be.

The chapter of his book titled "Turbulence" begins thus: "Annoyingly often I was told I should *do something* about it. People would say, 'You can take a course to cure it, you know?' That really pissed me off."

It is not as if he took that choice lightly. He knew exactly what the consequences were and had to live with the fact he was not always there to help his team. To this day it is not his favorite topic of conversation. It is, and always was, a personal choice and if the level of anxiety and physical stress he experienced toward the end of his time forcing himself on planes is one end of the spectrum, the relief he felt when he decided he would no longer do it is far away at the other extreme.

During his time with Inter, he and the team took flights regularly to and from away matches. At times he felt unwell, claustrophobic, exhausted, in a cold panic, not just during but before and after these ordeals. It was debilitating. "It got so bad I would look up at the sky during away games to see what the weather was like. Were there clouds coming? Sometimes I was preoccupied by the flight home while I was playing football."

At Arsenal, and with the Netherlands, the club and country that supported him during his peak years, there was a general understanding of his position. Arsenal did try to work out if they could get Bergkamp to their away matches in the Champions League—he was, after all, one of the team's leading players, but on the occasions when he was driven a long distance for an important game, he seldom performed at his best. Maybe it was not ideal preparation for such a finely tuned athlete. Perhaps there was an extra pressure to deliver that came from his unique circumstances.

Does this make him the imperfect perfectionist? This brainy, brilliant footballer has his foibles just like anybody else and nobody admires him any less for it.

To this day, visitors to the Emirates Stadium pass by his statue, which gives a carved impression of that exquisite first touch. It is balletic and elegant. It was quite a challenge for the sculptor to capture him finely balanced in midair, eyes on the ball, leg positioned to greet it in the ideal way. A golden talent immortalized in bronze.

Player name: Dennis Bergkamp
Born: May 10, 1969
Position: Forward
Debut: 1986
Main teams: Ajax (1986–93), Inter Milan (1993–95), Arsenal (1995–2006); Netherlands (1990–2000)
Career highlights: Won the Premier League three times and the UEFA Cup twice. Won the FA Cup three times. Scored one of the greatest goals in World Cup history in 1998.

48.

Rivaldo

The three goals Rivaldo scored against Valencia in June 2001 defied belief.

From fighting for airtime with *EastEnders* to the greatest hat trick ever scored

By Adam Hurrey

April 5, 2001. Barcelona and Liverpool, two of European football's grandest institutions, were about to meet for just the third time in history. It was the first leg of the UEFA Cup semifinal at Camp Nou, where Michael Owen, soon to be winner of the Ballon d'Or, was up against the best player in the world over the previous couple of years.

Rivaldo was in the most prolific form of his career. He had a Ballon d'Or of his own, from 1999, the same year he'd been player of the tournament and joint top scorer as Brazil won the Copa América. He was a towering, magnificent presence; a true spectacle.

But none of those things could compete with the British Soap Awards' Villain of the Year. That same night, 20 million people were watching *EastEnders* to find out who had shot Phil Mitchell. A special extended episode was broadcast and, in an astonishing flex of media muscle, the BBC had somehow persuaded UEFA to delay the kickoff in Barcelona by 15 minutes to accommodate the big reveal.

"We asked both sides nicely and they agreed to start later because of *EastEnders*," a BBC spokesman said at the time. "It is a well-known programme, so the Spanish realize it was important for the BBC."

Duly overshadowed, the two sides played out a benign, cagey 0–0 draw. Rivaldo's own climactic scene would come 73 days later.

Rivaldo Vítor Borba Ferreira sits 48th in this book's ranking, a suitable hiding place for a player whose footprint on world football around the turn of the millennium remains surprisingly unexamined. The decades in which he rose and peaked were awash with international superstars, but what was Rivaldo's true standing among them?

He has his Ballon d'Or. So does Jean-Pierre Papin. He has won a World Cup. So has Kléberson. He scored the goals that made his nation the champions of South America. So did former Queens Park Rangers loanee Eduardo Vargas. He was named the best foreign player in La Liga one season. So was Nihat Kahveci. He has been the top scorer in a single Champions League campaign. So has Fernando Morientes.

The point here is that reeling off a player's CV can only do so much to illuminate their true worth for the undecided. For anyone who cares about football, actions should always speak louder than an honors list.

But there is little need for hyperbole when it comes to Rivaldo's definitive action: He scored the greatest hat trick of all time.

• • •

June 17, 2001. Valencia arrived at Camp Nou for the final game of the Spanish league season fresh from falling short in the Champions League final for the second year running. There was a whiff of a La Liga power shift in the air as, crucially, they held a three-point advantage over Barcelona for the fourth and final Champions League qualifying place. Barcelona had to win to steal that place by virtue of their head-to-head record that season.

That sets the scene sufficiently because framed by that hour of need, Rivaldo produced not just the greatest hat trick of all time and not just, as *The Observer* declared it, "the most gloriously implausible hat-trick anyone has ever scored in a top-class game." It was (narratively, at least, given Rivaldo found no use for his head or his right boot in the process) the most *perfectly formed* hat trick ever seen. Its goals came in the third, 45th, and 88th minutes, a sequence punctuated by potentially world-collapsing Valencia equalizers.

In full flow, Rivaldo belied his gangly frame, but at walking pace, he was a fascinatingly awkward sight. He looked taller than his 6'1" but was almost geriatric in his gait, significantly bowlegged from his formative years raised in poverty in Recife. This was not a musculoskeletal system ideally designed for the elite-level manipulation of a football.

But Rivaldo mastered his own flawed body, no more so than with his free kicks. While his set-piece contemporary David Beckham (runner-up for the Ballon d'Or in 1999) came to a dead ball at pace and from an angle, swinging his arms for pendulous, power-generating effect, Rivaldo was entirely different. He would take five methodical steps back, two giant, purposeful paces forward, and—while Beckham would spread himself for whip—contract his praying mantis of a body into itself to dig the ball *upward*.

His opener against Valencia—a free kick almost dead center, just over 30 yards from Santiago Cañizares's goal—was the perfect showcase of the counterintuitive Rivaldo routine.

As he struck the ball, he was leaning back—breaking one of the first golden rules of shooting for "any youngsters watching"—but the controlled, waist-high follow-through of his left foot took over, ushering the ball to its destination like an Olympic curler finally letting go of a stone. Five of the six-man Valencia wall jumped in hopeful unison, leaving just the 6'5" John Carew, on tiptoes, understandably thinking he might be enough.

He wasn't. The ball whistled and spun past his right temple before dipping into the bottom-right corner via the post.

If Rivaldo's first goal was artful geometry and his third goal an astonishing act of initiative, his second, to make it 2–1 just before half-time, captured his uniqueness. Nineteen different players won the Ballon d'Or from 1990 to 2009, but none of them was anything like Rivaldo.

At 22, then a dribbling winger with Palmeiras, Rivaldo was left out of Carlos Alberto Parreira's Brazil squad for the 1994 World Cup because he was deemed "too selfish" and "unreliable." Two years later, at the 1996 Olympics, he was made the scapegoat for a semi-final collapse from 3–1 up against Nigeria. By his late 20s, though, he was muscular, assertive, and a devastating dagger through the middle: still slaloming on occasion, but now consistently lethal from 25 yards.

"One day in training, I saw Rivaldo shooting the ball, turning three-quarters of his body," recalled Carles Rexach, the coach drafted in to rescue Barcelona's season in April 2001. "I tried to tell him that it was easier if he used a more natural movement and didn't turn so much on himself. The next day he scored a goal giving a whole turn, so I decided to let him do as he wished."

Rivaldo received a square pass, in a pocket of space 30 yards from the Valencia goal. Winger Kily González raced back to try to pick his pocket just as that left foot was cocked, only for Rivaldo to produce two dummies blended into one: The shot became a feint, which in turn pretended to become a Cruyff Turn. By the time the Brazilian had prodded the ball back on its original infield course, González had rotated 360 befuddled degrees to see him now three yards away, with the ball on almost the exact patch of Camp Nou turf from which the free kick had been taken.

The rest was beautifully unsophisticated. Rivaldo threw his entire body into a brutal, low, daisy-annihilating torpedo that he caught so flush that the ball had no rotation, looking like the face of a boxer knocked out before they had even hit the canvas. First it scudded straight toward goal, then swerved left and slammed into the back of Cañizares's net. Rivaldo, through his own sheer torque, left the ground and landed on his backside.

The setup, the shot, and the furious, badge-kissing, shirt-yanking celebration that followed felt like a silencing of every doubter who had said Rivaldo could not be trusted.

Valencia equalized just moments into the second half. Rivaldo proceeded to probe, charge, stumble, lunge, and dive at the Valencia defense in the hunt to restore Barcelona's crucial lead. He almost scored from a corner, forcing Cañizares to pluck an absurd in-swinger from underneath his crossbar. Then, in the 88th minute, Frank de Boer chipped the ball to Rivaldo on the edge of the Valencia box, Barcelona's Cruyffian approximation of putting it in the mixer.

Rivaldo had rehearsed for this moment.

In 1998, he left Peter Schmeichel statuesque with a bicycle kick against Manchester United. In 2000, against Real Valladolid, he flicked the ball up twice before sending another acrobatic effort into the corner. His third version would make those look like backyard kickabout stuff.

Rivaldo's hat trick–completing, Champions League qualification–sealing, legacy-confirming bicycle kick against Valencia that night is surely, in its hold-your-breath context, the greatest ever scored.

De Boer's pass was exquisite, arcing tantalizingly over the head of Rubén Baraja to the chest of Rivaldo, 18 yards from goal. This was no split-second adjustment to a wayward cross: Rivaldo knew exactly what he wanted to do. His chested first touch sent the ball 12 feet into the air, the perfect hang time in which to set himself and launch into a cinematic masterpiece of this particular goalscoring subgenre—no suspicion of contact with the shin, no panicked hitch kick, no cartoonish loop to the trajectory, no danger of the referee calling it dangerous play.

There isn't a single camera angle of that goal that fails to capture its majesty. One view, of the crowd behind the goal as Rivaldo scores, shows a single fan with his hand to his head, resigned to Barcelona's fifth-place fate. The gradual dawning of what he is witnessing is well worth looking up.

Rivaldo couldn't have placed it better with his own hands. The ball arrowed into the bottom corner, the first ever truly clinical bicycle kick, with Cañizares at futile full stretch. Rivaldo galloped away, shirt off. Barcelona president Joan Gaspart pumped his fists to the skies. An emotionally spent Rexach searched for somebody to confirm it had actually happened.

"If my time was today," Rivaldo told *Globo Esporte* in 2015, "I'd bet with anyone that I would be the best player in the world two or three times. I'm sure I would score 50 goals per season."

This rare public declaration of his self-regard is not wide of the mark. Perhaps the closest postmillennial equivalent of Rivaldo's stature and skill set is Cristiano Ronaldo, who was at the 2010s vanguard of stratospheric goal tallies, a winger turned central La Liga totem, a match winner in the most gripping moments. Rivaldo had both the range and the delivery to put him, for a few seasons at least, at that level.

A few months after that night at the Camp Nou, *EastEnders*' "Who Shot Phil?" saga was named Most Dramatic Storyline at the Inside Soap Awards. By now, though, Rivaldo was no afterthought.

Player name: Rivaldo Vitor Borba Ferreira
Born: April 19, 1972
Position: Forward, attacking midfielder
Debut: 1991
Main teams: Santa Cruz (1991–92), Palmeiras (1994–96), Deportivo La Coruña (1996–97), Barcelona (1997–2002), AC Milan (2002–03), Cruzeiro (2004), Olympiacos (2004–07), AEK Athens (2007–08), Bunyodkor (2008–11), São Paulo (loan, 2011), Kabuscorp (2012), São Caetano (2013); Brazil (1993–2003)
Career highlights: Won the 2002 World Cup, scoring five goals in the tournament, and the Copa América in 1999, the year that he also claimed the Ballon d'Or. Won the Champions League in 2002–03 with AC Milan.

47.

Raymond Kopa

Kopa was a short, irrepressibly skillful outside-right or withdrawn center-forward.

France's first footballing star and his devotion to Stade de Reims

By Tom Williams

Raymond Kopa was a few months shy of his 33rd birthday and approaching the twilight years of his glorious career, but in René Masclaux's recollection, he had lost none of his fabled ability.

"He still had the same way of playing, the same enthusiasm," recalls Masclaux, who was a green, 18-year-old full-back when he first lined up alongside Kopa with Reims in 1964. "You just had to give him the ball and you knew he'd look after it and pick out a teammate. He had exceptional qualities, with his dribbles, his gear changes, his sudden bursts of pace and his crosses, and he brought them to bear for us.

"He played on the right wing and he was constantly in motion. That was Raymond Kopa."

In tandem with visionary coach Albert Batteux, Kopa had helped lay the foundations for Stade de Reims (pronounced "rhanse") to become the preeminent French club side of the 1950s. His departure for Real Madrid in 1956 brought him international stardom, Ballon d'Or glory, and three European Cup winners' medals, but after only three seasons in Spain, he returned to the club where he had made his name.

Although further success followed, including French league title triumphs in 1960 and 1962, Reims were relegated in 1964. Yet Kopa stayed, helping the club from the Champagne region east of Paris to return to the French elite two years later before finally hanging up his boots, at the age of 35, in June 1967.

"He came back to Reims to share his know-how with us," says Masclaux, who would go on to make a record 553 appearances for the club. "Reims was his club—he wanted to help us and try to turn us into a team again. He'd moan a lot in training because he was a winner. Like every person who is a winner, he had a personality that could be a little bit difficult. But that's normal. Those years he spent in the second division, it was for the love of the club. There's no doubt about that."

A short (at 5'6"), irrepressibly skillful outside-right or withdrawn center-forward, Kopa was French football's first true superstar and the player who sparked France's long love affair with the dashing playmaker.

He was also a pioneer. These days, French football fans can cite several examples of players from modest immigrant backgrounds who have shone for *Les Bleus* on the international stage, conquered Europe in the colors of the continent's most glamorous clubs, and won the Ballon d'Or. But before there was Karim Benzema, before there was Zinédine Zidane, and before there was Michel Platini, there was Kopa.

"He's the one who showed us the path," Zidane said after Kopa died aged 85 in March 2017. "He's the one who paved the way."

• • •

Kopa's paternal grandparents came to France by train from Poland in 1919 and settled in an industrial town called Noeux-les-Mines in the northern Pas-de-Calais region. Kopa, whose surname at birth was Kopaszewski, spoke Polish at home with his parents, François and Hélène, and older brother Henri.

The family lived at 5 rue du Chemin-Perdu (Lost Way Road) in a house whose red bricks were blackened by soot from the nearby coal mines. In a nod to the destiny that awaited little Raymond, their garden backed onto the local football stadium. His childhood friends, struggling to pronounce his slightly cumbersome surname, rechristened him "Kopa." It was the name by which he would become known around the world.

The mines horrified Kopa, but after failing to find work as an apprentice electrician, he was left with no choice but to follow his grandfather, his father, and his brother down the pit.

Between the ages of 14 and 16, he worked 2,000 feet belowground from 5 a.m. until 1 p.m. every day, lugging around heavy wagons piled high with coal. "Eight hours a day in the depths of the earth, sweating, breathing in coal dust, working like a dog for a few francs," he wrote in his autobiography. "For nearly three years. And with each day the agonizing fear of an accident, of not being able to return to the surface alive."

He narrowly escaped tragedy one day when his left hand was crushed beneath a rock following a landslide. It cost him the top half of his left index finger.

If his toil in the mines cast a dark shadow across the young Kopa's life, football was a light amid the gloom. He formed his first team with a group of friends at the age of eight and was soon showing off his dazzling repertoire of feints and dribbles for local club US Noeux-les-Mines. The professional game came knocking in 1949 when, after impressing in France's annual Young Footballer Competition—which ran as a curtain raiser to the Coupe de France final between 1930 and 1979—he was picked up by second-tier Angers.

The club from western France finished 13th and 14th in Kopa's two seasons there, but he performed consistently on the right wing and, in April 1951, his display in a 4–4 friendly draw with Reims opened the doors to the footballing stratosphere. Just 10 days later, he found himself lining up as a trialist for Reims in a friendly match against the Spanish national team at Estadio Nuevo Chamartín in Madrid. Renamed the Santiago Bernabéu four years later, it was a stadium that he would come to know rather well.

Reims had won their first French league title in 1949 and followed it up by winning the Coupe de France the following season. Over the ensuing decade or so, their red shirts with white sleeves became synonymous across Europe with stylish, winning football as Reims amassed five more league titles and a further Coupe de France crown and reached two of the first four European Cup finals, losing on both occasions to Real Madrid.

Batteux, a former Reims midfielder, took over as coach in 1950 and introduced a swashbuckling style of football based around quick, short passes, attacking ambition and creative freedom that was christened the *jeu à la rémoise*. Kopa would later describe Batteux as "the man of my life."

"He was an extraordinary teacher who spoke about football with great talent," Kopa said. "He prioritized a player's intelligence above all and didn't box him into a system that was too rigid. With him, we were free. When I joined Reims, the press and the fans criticized me for holding on to the ball too much, but he threatened to drop me if I stopped dribbling. That said everything!"

Kopa hit the headlines with Reims for the first time in November 1951 by netting a superb individual goal against Racing Club, cutting in from wide on the right and arrowing a right-foot shot into the top corner from 20 yards.

Deployed on the right wing in his debut campaign, he was moved by Batteux to a deep-lying center-forward role the following season, which enabled him to strike up a fruitful attacking partnership with new inside-forward Léon Glovacki. Alongside Glovacki, who also had Polish roots, and hulking Dutch forward Bram Appel, Kopa helped

Reims to glory in both the league and the Latin Cup, a precursor to the European Cup.

More championship success arrived two years later in 1955, which was the year of another trip to Madrid that would have a significant bearing on Kopa's fate.

"England, take heed. This afternoon I saw one of the great one-man football threats of all time—a sturdy French outside-right named Kopa—who shocked the highly rated Spaniards into a shattering 2–1 defeat."

So began the report filed by celebrated *Daily Express* journalist Desmond Hackett on France's 2–1 friendly win over Spain in March 1955. Kopa played a starring role in the match, canceling out the hosts' opener and helping tee up a 73rd-minute winner for left-winger Jean Vincent.

Hackett dubbed Kopa France's "Napoleon" and the nickname stayed with him for the rest of his career. The journalist's warning to England would also turn out to be prescient: Kopa scored the only goal, from the penalty spot, in a 1–0 friendly win over the Three Lions two months later.

The victory in Madrid was Batteux's first as France coach—a role he juggled with his responsibilities at Reims—and proved to be the first staging post on a journey that would lead to a rousing third-place finish at the 1958 World Cup in Sweden, where Kopa's sparkling performances and Just Fontaine's record-breaking 13-goal haul created a sensation.

The game would also have significant consequences for Kopa's club career. Watching on among the crowd of 125,000 were Real Madrid president Santiago Bernabéu and secretary general Raimundo Saporta, who quickly determined to see the diminutive Frenchman wearing their famous all-white kit as swiftly as possible.

After playing for Reims in a 4–3 defeat by Madrid in the inaugural European Cup final at the Parc des Princes in June 1956, Kopa swapped the stately vineyards of the Marne countryside for the shimmering plazas of the Spanish capital. Playing alongside Alfredo Di Stéfano, Paco Gento, and, for one season, Ferenc Puskás, the man known as "Kopita" won two Spanish league titles and three European Cups with Madrid and was awarded France's first Ballon d'Or in 1958. No French footballer had ever known such glory or fame.

Kopa turned down the offer of a five-year contract from Madrid to return to Reims in 1959. He was eager to be reunited with Batteux and excited by the prospect of linking up again with his international teammates Fontaine, Vincent, Robert Jonquet, and Roger Piantoni. He was also beginning to think about what he might do in retirement—Kopa would go on to found a successful sportswear brand—and felt it would be easier to enter the world of business on home turf.

Yet, despite initial on-pitch success, Kopa's second Reims spell would coincide with a profoundly challenging period in his life. He lost his infant son, Denis, to cancer in February 1963, having also recently lost his father and brother-in-law. The same year yielded Batteux's dismissal by Reims and the end of Kopa's international career after a falling-out with selector Georges Verriest.

He was dogged by a bothersome ankle and became increasingly outspoken about footballers' lack of control over their careers, earning himself a six-month ban for describing players as "slaves." Shorn of Batteux and with illustrious players either bowing out or moving on, Reims gradually lost their luster, but Kopa rejected multiple opportunities to leave. "Leaving Reims during such a difficult period would have been a real act of desertion in my eyes," he said. "How could I leave a club that had given me everything?"

The year after his death, Reims unveiled a bronze statue of Kopa outside Stade Auguste-Delaune. The first statue dedicated to a footballer in France, it shows Kopa in trademark pose—head down, mid-dribble, a ball between his feet—and was joined six years later by a sculpture of Fontaine, who passed away in 2023.

"There's huge respect for Raymond Kopa in Reims—that's why they made the statue," says Patrice Buisset, a former Reims defender and president of the club's association of former players.

"Everyone knows who Raymond Kopa is here. He's part of the people's history."

The passage of time has seen Kopa somewhat eclipsed by Platini and Zidane in debates about France's greatest footballer, but for those who saw him play, there is no doubt. "Raymond Kopa was the best," adds Masclaux. "It's difficult to compare, but there are no more players like Kopa. There was only one."

Player name: Raymond Kopa
Born: October 13, 1931
Died: March 3, 2017 (aged 85)
Position: Forward
Debut: 1949
Main teams: Angers (1949–51), Stade de Reims (1951–56, 1959–67), Real Madrid (1956–59); France (1952–62)
Career highlights: Won the European Cup three seasons in a row. Won the French top flight four times and La Liga twice. Claimed the Ballon d'Or in 1958.

46.

Neymar Júnior

Neymar's entire career has been about expectation.

The Kid, *that* goal, and a weight of expectation

By Nick Miller

It starts rather unpromisingly, with a long punt upfield by Santos goalkeeper Rafael Cabral. The setting is a match between Santos and Flamengo in the 2011 Campeonato Brasileiro and the player who, six years later, will become the most expensive footballer in the history of the game is about to score a goal that will win him the Puskás Award and change his life forever.

The loose ball is knocked down and eventually makes its way to Santos midfielder Ibson on the left flank. His only real passing option is The Kid, who is only 19 but already a marked man; a double-marked man because there are a pair of Flamengo defenders in close attendance, even though The Kid is probably 50 yards from goal. But it's already 2–0 to Santos and they can't afford any further damage.

Ibson's pass is awful. It's only about four yards, but The Kid has to really fight to keep it in play. He manages it, but doing so throws him off balance, which is less than ideal when you have a couple of defenders camped on your toes.

The Kid has options: Left-back Leo has made an underlapping run and a smart pass would give him a good crossing opportunity. But he has something else in mind, something more befitting his status as the chosen one, the great hope of Brazilian football earmarked to deliver them a home World Cup in three years' time.

Neymar Júnior arrived on the scene at a sticky moment for Brazilian football.

His senior debut was in 2009, and while the national team had won the Copa América a couple of years earlier, there were some lean years ahead. They barely made an impression on the 2010 World Cup, and with the careers of Kaká and Robinho beginning to wane, they lacked a star, the icon that most of the best Brazil sides boasted.

Neymar's domestic brilliance for Santos in 2010 had inspired Pelé and Romário to lobby for his inclusion in that year's squad for the tournament in South Africa, despite him being only 18. In retrospect, it was a good thing Dunga was too conservative to call him up because the opprobrium directed at the team after their limp quarterfinal exit might have engulfed this young star, too.

Instead, he made his international debut just after that tournament, which began the lead-up to 2014: Brazil's home World Cup, the chance for them to exorcise the national trauma of 1950 when glory was assumed to be theirs only to be surrendered to Uruguay.

From that point, Neymar became their hope, their icon, the man—The Kid—who was expected to carry the team on his back. The pressure was unfathomable. Not that you would guess it from listening to him at the time. "There is no pressure," he said as he collected his man-of-the-match award after scoring twice in Brazil's 4–1 group-stage win against Cameroon. "I've always said that there is no pressure when you are making a dream come true, something that you sought since you were a kid."

Perhaps he genuinely did not worry about pressure and expectation because he had never known anything else. From his earliest games, expectation followed Neymar around like a rain cloud over a depressed cartoon character. His talent combined with the paucity of other options meant he was predestined to be the next great.

The trouble was that even Brazil's greatest had a supporting cast. Pelé had Vavá, Garrincha, Rivellino, Jairzinho, and Carlos Alberto. Romário had Bebeto. Ronaldo had Rivaldo and Ronaldinho. In 2014, Neymar had—bless him—Fred, the perfectly decent but much-maligned center-forward. Neymar *was* the Brazil team, which would have been a big enough burden had it been a friendly against Paraguay, never mind a home World Cup with 64 years of emotion piled on top of it.

It was absolutely unfair. Neymar was 22. He had moved to Barcelona by that time but should have been perfecting his game and learning from others. He should have been the supporting cast, not the *whole* cast.

When Colombia's Juan Zúñiga kneed him in the back during the quarterfinal and broke his vertebrae, the national grief was as if a beloved member of the royal family had died. Before the semifinal against Germany, Júlio César and David Luiz stood in line for the national anthem while tightly holding a Neymar No. 10 shirt in tribute to their fallen comrade. It may have been intended as a tribute, but it came across as a sort of mourning, an admission that their only real proper star was absent.

Maybe it's too much to blame their subsequent 7–1 humiliation on Neymar's absence entirely, but his teammates' reaction was undoubtedly a factor. Their voices might have said, "Let's do this for Neymar," but their eyes said, "Without him, we're fucked."

• • •

The Kid rolls the ball back slightly with his studs and sways into a half Cruyff Turn, which leaves one of his markers—a scrappy midfielder named Willians—stabbing at where the ball was a second ago with his foot like an unskilled huntsman trying to spear a salmon with a blunt twig.

Then The Kid pauses, almost imperceptibly but for long enough that the other defender, full-back Léo Moura, stops and chooses not to commit himself, which affords a half yard of space through which to wriggle. The Kid takes that opportunity, as both defenders resort to grappling in their attempts to thwart this skinny teenager with dyed blond, semi-mohawk hair that would look more at home on the head of a keytar player in an early 2000s nu-rave band.

The Kid lays the ball off to journeyman striker Borges, but there is an understanding that this is a loan; it's in everyone's best interests that it is passed back at the earliest opportunity. Borges is aware and promptly returns the ball to its rightful custodian.

Flamengo midfielder Renato Abreu, like his predecessors, can only think of foul means to stop The Kid. He drags his arm back in the hope of at least distracting The Kid from his run and it almost works. By now The Kid is central, about 25 yards from goal, but with his pulls and tugs, Abreu has managed to almost turn him away from goal.

With central defender Ronaldo Angelim approaching from the edge of the box, this attack should be snuffed out.

Three years after Neymar was expected to perform a miracle at that World Cup, he actually did produce one in the Champions League.

His Barcelona team had lost the first leg of their round-of-16 tie against Paris Saint-Germain 4–0 at Parc des Princes. They went 3–0 up in the return at the Camp Nou, but then Edinson Cavani scored, making it 5–3 on aggregate and giving PSG an away goal. Barca had surely lost.

Then Neymar won it. In the 88th minute, he whipped an astonishing free kick into the top corner. In the 91st minute, he nervelessly scored a penalty. Then, after 94 minutes and 40 seconds, he curled a brilliant ball over the top of the PSG defense for Sergi Roberto to complete an unfathomable comeback.

Neymar was expecting to receive the glory. As it was, the pundits gave more acclaim to Lionel Messi. The Spanish papers the following morning had essentially everyone but Neymar on their covers. His agent, André Cury, confirmed to AS a few years later that was the night Neymar realized he was never going to be "the man" at Barca. It was always going to be Messi.

Maybe that would not have been such a problem if Neymar had not been told he needed to be the man, from such an early age. He was the man at Santos while he was still a boy. He was the man for Brazil when he wasn't much older than that. He joined Barcelona to be the man, eventually, because that was what he was expected to be.

So when it became clear that wasn't going to happen, he left to become the man at PSG and all it took was for them to pay his €222 million release clause.

The Kid was now the most expensive footballer in the history of the game.

This is when things really get extraordinary.

At the same time as shrugging Abreu off, and facing toward the right touchline rather than goal, The Kid performs a skill that's quite difficult to understand, never mind explain. Again, he rolls the ball with his studs in such a way that it puts his body between Abreu and the ball, while also tilting himself back toward goal. Abreu is defeated by this simple shimmy and has to assume Angelim will deal with the threat instead.

The Kid's touch puts it within grabbing distance of defender Angelim, who, with a semi-well-timed tackle, should retrieve the ball. But that's exactly what The Kid wanted him to think. This is part football, part playing with a stupid kitten, putting a ribbon on the floor only to whip it away when the cat tries to pounce.

Angelim moves in, but suddenly the ball isn't there anymore. The Kid's left foot has nipped it around him. He stops, so flummoxed that he throws his arms up in the air in the classic "I didn't touch him" pose of defenders who have committed a foul. Of course you didn't touch him, you didn't get close enough to touch him.

Now The Kid is through on goal.

Flamengo's only hope is left-back Júnior César, who has charged across from his berth armed with a set of studs that he launches at The Kid's ankles. But, like his colleagues, he is too late. Only a fraction too late, but a fraction may as well be a mile. The Kid flicks the ball over the goalkeeper with the outside of his right foot. Goal. *Gol. Golazo.* One of the most astonishing you're likely to see. Skill, speed, the maximum use of what physicality his skinny frame had, imagination, poise.

If you didn't think he was a star before, you are sure of it now. And from that point, everything is different.

Neymar's entire career has been about expectation.

Sure, most top-level players could say the same, but few have been as heavily weighed down by it and from such a young age. When he first came through at Santos, there was some debate about whether he or the midfielder Ganso would be the bigger star and, at the time, there wasn't really a wrong answer to that question.

But his breakout season in 2010 put him on a higher level at home, and that goal, which went viral in 2011, made him an international star. People could put the talent to the name that was vaguely familiar: "Oh, the kid who all the big European teams wanted." Chelsea, Real Madrid, Barcelona . . . West Ham United. "That's him? He looks amazing."

There is a school of thought that Neymar's career since has been a disappointment. That he never quite lived up to his talent. That he never quite achieved as much as that game against Flamengo promised he might. That the goal, somehow, was his individual peak.

This is also informed by the fact that plenty of people just don't like him. The hair, the cocky attitude, the diving, the individualism, the slightly bratty pretty-boy face, the series of controversial transfers: Santos to Barcelona, Barcelona to PSG, PSG to Al Hilal. People seem desperate to be offended by the notion of Neymar.

But if you strip all of that away, you're left with one of the most astonishing talents of his generation. No, he did not score another goal like the Puskás winner, but then again, Stevie Nicks only wrote "Landslide" once and Fleetwood Mac had plenty of other great songs.

Neymar won the Copa Libertadores, the Champions League, domestic titles in four countries, the Club World Cup, the Olympics, and, with Messi and Luis Suárez, was one-third of one of the greatest forward lines in one of the greatest teams ever. He is also Brazil's all-time top goalscorer. Basically, the only thing he's never won is the Ballon d'Or, which, considering he played in the era of Messi and Cristiano Ronaldo, is not the diss that some seem to think it is.

Then there's his talent. If you have a soft spot for Brazilian brilliance—and most of us do—then what you want is someone who combines speed and skill, someone with imagination and impudence, someone whom, if the concept of winning and losing didn't exist in football, you'd still want to watch. That's Neymar.

The only way you could consider Neymar a disappointment, in terms of his on-pitch feats at least, is when he is set against the unrealistic expectations of others, particularly from his early years, summed up by that goal. They wanted a deity but merely got a genius. From that perspective, maybe it would have been better for Neymar if he hadn't scored that goal when he was just 19.

But just watch it a few times and you'll be glad that he did.

Player name: Neymar Júnior
Born: February 5, 1992
Position: Forward
Debut: 2009
Main teams: Santos (2009–13), Barcelona (2013–17), Paris Saint-Germain (2017–23), Al Hilal (2023–); Brazil (2010–)
Career highlights: Won Copa Libertadores in 2011 and the 2015 Champions League as part of Barcelona's treble. Brazil's record goal scorer and Olympic gold medalist in 2016 on home soil.

45.

Fabio Cannavaro

Cannavaro led a defense that, aside from an own goal against the United States, did not concede from open play while winning the 2006 World Cup.

The ball boy who tackled Maradona and ended Italy's 24-year wait for the World Cup

By Simon Hughes

Only three defenders in the history of the game have won the Ballon d'Or. The most recent is Fabio Cannavaro.

The Italian received the award in 2006 after captaining his country to its last successful World Cup, earning his 100th cap in the final in Berlin. Before him, the only players in his position to take the same accolade were German: Franz Beckenbauer (1972 and 1976) and Matthias Sammer (1996). Cannavaro mingles in exalted company.

When he took over the captaincy of the *Azzurri* from Paolo Maldini in 2002, the chances of him accomplishing more than his decorated predecessor seemed unlikely. Maldini, alongside his teammate at AC Milan, Franco Baresi, had come to define defensive greatness. Yet unlike Cannavaro, neither Maldini nor Baresi was able to win a World Cup (the latter was an unused squad member when Italy triumphed in 1982) or collect the game's most prestigious individual award.

Like Baresi, Cannavaro was not tall. While the former stood at 5'9", Cannavaro came in an inch shorter. Yet height was never a weakness because of each player's positional awareness and jumping reach. They could dominate far bigger opponents while instructing and inspiring teammates from the heart of the back line. They were utterly reliable, the foundations upon which success was built.

Nothing illustrated that better than Italy's World Cup campaign in Germany in 2006. Cannavaro led a defense that, aside from an own goal shipped against the United States in the group stage, did not concede from open play at a tournament that culminated in penalty shootout glory against France at the Olympiastadion.

That match is remembered for Zinédine Zidane's infamous red card in the last game of an otherwise glittering career, France's talismanic attacking midfielder having headbutted Marco Materazzi, Cannavaro's partner in the center of Italy's defense. Few could comprehend Zidane's rush of blood. It was a misdemeanor that handed the Italians the initiative, but it was seized upon by a national team desperately attempting to deliver some positivity. Back home, storm clouds were gathering.

There may have been confidence in Italy's quality and a belief they were capable of winning a first title since 1982 given their blend of natural talent and rugged experience, but their campaign was played out against an unsettling backdrop of acrimony and infamy as the true extent of *Calciopoli*—a match-fixing scandal that involved the clubs of several members of the Italian squad, as well as coach Marcello Lippi, formerly in charge of Juventus—emerged into the public domain.

Cannavaro was a key player for Juventus, the team at the center of the controversy that allegedly involved favorable decisions from referees. The careers of many of the players, including Cannavaro's, as well as the clubs they represented, were in serious doubt.

Ahead of Italy's opening game with Ghana, there were questions about whether Cannavaro should remain captain and whether Lippi should be removed as coach. The buildup to the semifinal against hosts Germany was overshadowed by news that prosecutors were calling for Juventus, Inter Milan, Lazio, and Fiorentina to be relegated. The reputation of the domestic game was in tatters, with public faith eroded.

Yet, amid the maelstrom, the national team steeled themselves and found a way to progress.

The route to the final was not without other, albeit more conventional challenges. Inspirational midfielder Daniele De Rossi was suspended for four games for violent conduct after being sent off for flinging an elbow at Brian McBride in that disappointing draw with the US. The striker was left bloodied by the offense and De Rossi saw red. Then Cannavaro's established partner in the center of Italy's defense, Alessandro Nesta, aggravated a long-standing groin issue in the team's last group game against the Czech Republic. He did not play again at the tournament.

His replacement, Materazzi, was sent off in a round-of-16 tie with Australia in Kaiserslautern, meaning Italy played most of the second half of that match with 10 men, only sealing a place in the quarterfinal with a fortunate stoppage-time penalty that Francesco Totti converted.

Yet it was Cannavaro, the 32-year-old captain who would play every minute of Italy's tournament, whose excellence inspired the *Azzurri*'s progress. Against Germany in Dortmund, he helped check the host nation's momentum with a performance even he considered to be flawless. It was his tackle on Lukas Podolski in the closing moments of extra time that sparked the counterattack from which Alessandro Del Piero scored the Italians' second goal.

"It was perfect," offered Cannavaro when reflecting on that defensive display against Germany in a conversation for FIFA's website in 2022. "To do it again exactly as it happened would be impossible."

His performance in the final against the much-fancied French earned him the moniker *Muro di Berlino* (Berlin Wall), even if the Italy captain thought his team's approach that afternoon was "too tense, both before and during the game—tired even, to be honest—and we didn't play that well." Yet with Zidane dismissed and the Italians holding their nerve in the shootout, Cannavaro was able to return to his room at the squad's base in Duisburg early the next morning with his eldest son, Christian, and the "little girl," as Italians called the World Cup trophy.

Over two million people took to the streets in Rome to welcome the team home in the celebrations that followed. "At the time, there was the euphoria and craziness of getting over the finish line," he said. "You can't take it all in straightaway. Only now, many years later, can you appreciate that history was being written. That event transformed us from regular players into legends.

"When you win a World Cup, everyone will always recognize you for what you have done, wherever you go. It's gratifying to know that you have brought joy to a whole nation. You remain etched into the history of this sport and the history of an entire country."

Fuorigrotta is the working-class area on the western edge of Naples where Cannavaro learned to play football "between cars, everywhere." There he honed the athleticism and leap that would make up for his diminutive stature and establish him, one day, as a giant of the game.

The neighborhood includes the Stadio San Paolo—since renamed the Stadio Diego Armando Maradona after Napoli's most celebrated player—and in the shadow of the stadium is a watering hole called the Monnalisa. The bar is owned by Antonio Arenoso, whose daughter, Daniela, was Cannavaro's girlfriend and later became his wife.

Arenoso saw Cannavaro scouted by Napoli and incorporated into their youth structure, but he always imagined the youngster was likelier to become a bartender. His height would surely rule him out of making an impact at senior level. The boy's parents, Pasquale and

Gelsomina, wanted him to pursue his studies and were dismayed when his grades dipped. Pasquale, a bank clerk, had played further down the football pyramid. Perhaps he shared Arenoso's skepticism.

But the young Cannavaro would not be dissuaded.

At least his timing was in. Fabio was 10 when Maradona signed for Napoli and, in an instant, everything changed. Over the next five seasons, the club won the Serie A title for the first time in their 61-year history, then secured it again three seasons later. They were a force.

Maradona was at his peak, inspiring Argentina to win the World Cup in 1986 and consistently decorating San Paolo with his brilliance. On the side of the pitch, Cannavaro acted as a ball boy, witnessing genius at close quarters. Soaking it all in.

He was a midfielder at the time, too, idolizing Marco Tardelli, whose goal in the 1982 World Cup final he had watched on television at home as an eight-year-old. Then one of the youth coaches suggested a change of position. "And that was it," Cannavaro told *The Players' Tribune* in 2017. "No explanation, no reasons. I was shorter than most of the other guys on the pitch, so I didn't look like a defender and certainly not a centre-back. But from that moment on, that was my position.

"Lucky for me, I loved playing defence and I was pretty good at it, too."

Cannavaro was also fortunate to be breaking into a team marshaled in defense by another local boy, Ciro Ferrara, a stalwart who played over 300 games for the club and the ideal figure from whom to learn the new position. "Like many Italians, [he] didn't mince words," added Cannavaro. "He would tell you where you needed to be, what you needed to do, and whether or not you had any chance against your opponent."

Ferrara once playfully handed him a ball before training one day and advised him that he should cherish having it in his possession because, once they were out on the practice pitch, Maradona would take it and he would never see it again. The Argentinian tended to spend the sessions with the ball glued to his instep, with his Napoli teammates incapable of robbing him of it.

Cannavaro had other ideas, and as Maradona bore down on him that day, he spied his opportunity. He tracked the run, his eyes fixed on the ball, and then dived into the tackle.

As soon as Cannavaro emerged from their duel with the ball, he felt the eyes of his more experienced teammates on him. They feared how the volatile Maradona might react to someone so much younger getting the better of him.

Yet at the end of the training session, a smiling Maradona, impressed at such impudence, handed over his muddied boots as a keepsake. Cannavaro still had posters of the Argentinian on his bedroom wall. Now he had something better to cherish.

In those early years, the defender was underestimated because of the way he looked. He would come to realize that central defenders can be all shapes and sizes.

"You can be short and fast or you can be tall and jump high; it doesn't matter," he said. "The only necessity is that you are confident when you take the pitch because every week there is a new challenge."

Maradona had departed by the time Cannavaro established himself in the Napoli first team under the manager who later delivered the World Cup. Lippi had previously done well with Atalanta and, despite the squad lacking the sparkle of the title-winning teams, guided them into the UEFA Cup, finishing sixth in the Serie A table. That earned Lippi a move to Juventus.

Cannavaro featured in 27 Serie A games that season. A second campaign as a regular culminated in Napoli selling their bright young talent to Parma, easing the financial crisis that had gripped the club.

This was a player of obvious potential. He had helped inspire Italy's under-21s to victory at the 1994 and 1996 European Championship, forging a blossoming partnership with Nesta at the heart of defense. A senior debut followed in January 1997. A few weeks later, he marked Alan Shearer out of the game as Italy beat England 1–0 in a World Cup qualifier at Wembley. He ended up playing 12 times for his country that year alone, his role established.

At Parma, Cannavaro won the Coppa Italia twice, as well as the UEFA Cup. After a disappointing two-year spell at Inter, there were two Serie A titles with Juventus. Yet those were the honors subsequently tainted and revoked following rulings in the aftermath of *Calciopoli*, a scandal where much of the evidence derived from tapped telephone conversations between club executives and referee organizations between 2004 and 2006.

Juventus's relegation to Serie B was confirmed just five days after Cannavaro helped steer Italy to a fourth World Cup triumph.

His own club career would not include slipping into the second tier. Chelsea and Real Madrid vied for his signature that summer. The lure of La Liga was strongest and he claimed two league titles over his three-year stint in Spain. The presence of his compatriot, Fabio Capello, helped him adjust to life in new surroundings but, even so, he found that transition "difficult."

"I had a lot to learn, but when I got to Madrid, I wasn't 21," he said. "I had just won a World Cup. I had my confidence. I don't know if I could have made that move as a young man. But after what Italy accomplished in 2006, I knew my game. And at Real Madrid, we went on to win La Liga two years in a row."

He would succeed Maldini as Italy's most-capped player, eventually pulling away from the international stage with 136 appearances, a record for an outfield player. He put his consistent availability down to three things, telling reporters at a press conference in 2009 about the benefits of "eating well, getting plenty of sleep, and having sex."

Throughout his career, he had taken room 202 of Coverciano, Italy's training base on the outskirts of Florence. One of the subsequent tenants of that room was his successor in the team, Giorgio Chiellini, who called him out of respect before taking residence in it.

Such was the reverence in which Cannavaro was held.

Player name: Fabio Cannavaro
Born: September 13, 1973
Position: Center-back
Debut: 1993
Main teams: Napoli (1993–95), Parma (1995–2002), Inter Milan (2002–04), Juventus (2004–06, 2009–10), Real Madrid (2006–09), Shabab Al Ahli (2010–11); Italy (1997–2010)
Career highlights: Captained Italy to victory at the 2006 World Cup. Won La Liga twice. Claimed the Ballon d'Or in 2006.

44.

Kaká

Kaká was the last winner of the Ballon d'Or before the age of Lionel Messi and Cristiano Ronaldo.

"The last CD you purchased from your local store before digital distribution and next-day delivery took over"

By Carl Anka

Kaká was the last of his kind. A balletic cavalier who orchestrated his team's attack, with few responsibilities centering on what to do in defense. A Brazilian who traveled to Western Europe and became the best footballer in the world. The last AC Milan great from their era of European dominance.

He was the last football icon from an era when the sport was broadcast in standard definition. The artistic flourishes to his game quickly became overly luxurious defects as the twenty-first century moved to a sharper, more angular version of the game. His career high—winning the 2007 Ballon d'Or—serves as a unique turning point. It was the very first year in which all professional footballers worldwide, even from clubs outside Europe, were eligible to win the competition.

It was also the last win before the age of Lionel Messi and Cristiano Ronaldo.

Kaká's victory saw him win 445 votes from the assembled nomination pool. In second place came a 22-year-old Cristiano Ronaldo (with 277 votes) and a 20-year-old Messi (255). No player wishes to acknowledge their career high point when it arrives—to recognize you have peaked is also to recognize that you are set upon a downward trajectory—but when Kaká took to the stage at the Zurich Opera House in December 2007, he knew a shift was occurring.

"It shows that this is a new era in football, a new cycle is starting," said the then 25-year-old about the three podium finishers at the ceremony. "There were great players before, but now the new players are starting to make history."

Many expected the Brazilian to go on to define the next decade of football, but Kaká could not keep pace with the two all-conquering attackers he bested in 2007. Messi and Ronaldo enjoyed a 10-year duopoly when it came to the Ballon d'Or award, transforming its importance and reshaping the sport as we know it.

To be the best footballer in the world no longer reflected a good season. Rather, it gained you entry to the GOAT (greatest of all time) conversation. These days, footballers are no longer sporting heroes but cultural superheroes; divine figures of athletic and creative excellence, impervious to the waxing and waning seen in regular civilians; athletes capable of bending things to their will on the biggest occasions. Again and again and again.

Kaká was some of those things, but also not.

He was brilliant in bursts. He could dominate games but generally served as a creative garnish. He succumbed to injury, not to a concerning amount, but enough to remind you that he was, in fact, human. During Kaká's six-year spell at Milan, Carlo Ancelotti often deployed him as a second striker and other figures behind him compensated for his insouciant approach to defending.

In 2024, he was still one of only nine players to have won the World Cup, Champions League, and the Ballon d'Or, but his contribution to Brazil's triumph on the world stage was limited to a substitute appearance in a group-stage game against Costa Rica in 2002. It was hoped Kaká would grow to lead Brazil in subsequent World Cups, but he struggled to show his best as part of the "magic quartet" in 2006 and his powers were on the wane by the tournament in South Africa in 2010. Present-day discussions of Kaká are often prefaced with the word *only*.

How did a player of his talent *only* win one Serie A title with Milan?

Why did he *only* win one Champions League?

If *only* he hadn't picked up those knee and groin injuries that robbed him of his pace.

Yet here he stands, 44th on our list. A genuine great who made other greats swoon. When we refer to the figures who compensated for Kaká's timid defensive work rate, we are talking about tigerish tacklers like Gennaro Gattuso, but also virtuosos such as Andrea Pirlo and Clarence Seedorf. All were willing to take on extra dirty work to enable Kaká to play better. Why? Because, at his best, the Brazilian played with a watchmaker's precision.

Standing at 6'1", Kaká was one of the most potent dribbling threats the game has ever seen, able to maneuver through tight spaces with tricks and feints but also capable of outsprinting defenders when the time came. His hidden strength was born of a phenomenal sense of balance and well-practiced gait. Each touch and every step fed into the next seamlessly.

He did not run with the ball so much as *glide*, rarely having to alter pace to regain control of the ball. Kaká is one reason fans often (incorrectly) say dribbling cannot be taught. He made the act of running with a ball mesmerizing to the point people assumed it was a gift bestowed from above. His two-footedness meant he could go both ways, be it shooting, running, or passing. Indeed, his shooting repertoire boasted long-range sledgehammer strikes—a goal against Empoli in 2003 is a particular highlight—and scalpel-like strikes of pure precision.

If you ever stumble upon a picture of the Brazilian shooting in a Milan shirt, pay attention to where his standing leg is planted. His form was impeccable. Time after time.

Then came his passing, a scintillating mix of imagination, instinct, and technical craft. A passing range that could hit 30- to 40-yard switches to teammates in space, but a passing intelligence that recognized when a five-yard reverse pass would be of greater benefit. Put it all together and you have one of the more unique combinations of technical skill and physical drive the twenty-first century has seen to date.

Given the increased emphasis on out-of-possession attributes these days, we might not see another Kaká again. He was a joy to watch at his peak. He also—and forgive the clumsy description—felt *expensive* to watch.

His goalscoring output was too high and too consistent during his initial six-season stint at Milan to call him a "luxury" player, but there was something about how Kaká shaped a ball in the red-and-black shirt that felt beyond the reach of the common man. Watching him felt like a rare treat if you could not access coverage of Serie A in the 2000s. He was an elegant, exotic wonder who occasionally appeared on free-to-air television to deliver master classes in the Champions League.

Manchester United fans still talk about his goal in April 2007 at Old Trafford, when he first took a long pass down the left flank and burned beyond Darren Fletcher before hooking the ball over Gabriel Heinze. Patrice Evra tried his best to nullify the danger, only for Kaká to head the ball past him and into the penalty box. Evra and Heinze collided with each other as if it were a Three Stooges sketch. Kaká latched on to the ball again and calmly finished past goalkeeper Edwin van der Sar.

The Brazilian regards it as one of the best goals of his career, along with a thrilling solo dribble-and-strike against Argentina in a 2006 friendly for Brazil. He was a footballing artist, a player with an Impressionist's eye and a grand pianist's timing.

Remarkably, his career could have been over before it even started. His route to professional football was colored by his middle-class background in an age when many top Brazilian footballers grew up in relative poverty. Kaká's early years were marked by rivals and members of the Brazilian press wondering if he had the necessary grit to succeed at the highest level. He was an artist, yes, but was he willing to *suffer* for it? The answer, of course, was yes.

He did not play with a noticeable chip on his shoulder, but he was a brilliant competitor. The son of a civil engineer, the man born Ricardo Izecson dos Santos Leite started life in Brasília. His footballing pen name was given to him by his younger brother, Rodrigo (best known as Digão), as a young Ricardo struggled to pronounce his own name when they were children. The "ca" noise repeated itself, but Caca was mercifully changed to Kaká to avoid comparisons with a certain Spanish expletive.

The playmaker we know today was a product of São Paulo's academy. His family moved to the city when he was six and he started to use the leisure facilities at the football club when he was eight. This was unusual for Brazilian footballers of the era. Kaká got an early start playing football in controlled settings because his father could afford club memberships.

"For me, it became football in the morning [at school], afternoon, and evening [at São Paulo]," he would write in a 2024 essay for *The Players' Tribune*. "The ball was the air I breathed. I went to compete in the championship for club members and the coaches soon pulled me to train with the youth team."

Starting with the club at 12, a later-than-expected growth spurt meant Kaká did not shine in their youth ranks until his mid-teens. Then, in 2000, a freak accident jeopardized everything.

"Innocently playing at the water park, I went down a slide and hit my head on the bottom of the pool—fracturing the sixth cervical vertebra," he said. "I ended that year without playing, wearing a neck brace, fearing for my future. It was hard. Apart from my relationship with God, everything else was uncertain. I started thinking about what I would study at university, if that was to be my path. But the recovery was surprising and I was allowed back to train as early as January."

Kaká's return to football saw the start of a beautiful journey: a World Cup winner's medal in 2002 and an €8.5 million move to Milan in the summer of 2003. The Italian club was the perfect landing place. Club owner Silvio Berlusconi gushed over the new signing's skills, and under Ancelotti's tutelage, Kaká steadily improved his off-ball movement. Pirlo helped him add deception and disguises to his passing, while Gattuso served as his bodyguard when opposition players tried to kick him out of matches.

He became a luminous talent, compared to the likes of Johan Cruyff, Zico, and Michel Platini. A disappointing 2004–05 season, with the team finishing second in Serie A and falling to Liverpool's Miracle of Istanbul, dented things, but the 2006–07 Champions League final victory over the same opponents reminded the world of his brilliance.

Unfortunately, he was never quite the same after that.

Knee and groin problems sapped the strength from his powerful midfield dribbles. Belatedly, the football world at large got wise to leaving so much space in central areas, making it harder for him to thrive. Real Madrid cared little and still forked out €67 million to sign him in 2009 to kick-start a new *galáticos*-esque era. Yet Cristiano Ronaldo's arrival at the Spanish club later that summer was the beginning and the end of the next stage of Kaká's career. He was an admirable team player for *Los Blancos* but far from the best player in the side, let alone the world, when compared to his Portuguese teammate.

When he returned to Milan in 2013, his time at football's top table had finished. A final transfer to Orlando City in Major League Soccer (with a brief loan to São Paulo) followed before his eventual retirement in December 2017.

When we look back at Kaká, we do not view his shortcomings as demerits, but as reminders of a bygone age. Kaká is the last CD you purchased from your local store before digital distribution and next-day delivery took over. Yes, the playmakers today come with less friction, but they don't quite bring the same experience for you to luxuriate in. Going to watch Kaká was an event you could relax into for several days, rather than a two-hour sugar rush to get out of the way before the next match in 72 hours.

He was beautiful, brief, and brilliant, but he still burns long in memory.

Player name: Ricardo Izecson dos Santos Leite (Kaká)
Born: April 22, 1982
Position: Attacking midfielder
Debut: 2001
Main teams: São Paulo (2001–03, loan 2014), AC Milan (2003–09, 2013–14), Real Madrid (2009–13), Orlando City (2014–17); Brazil (2002–16)
Career highlights: Won the Champions League in 2006–07 and Serie A in 2003–04 with AC Milan. Won La Liga in 2011–12 with Real Madrid. Won the 2002 World Cup, albeit only playing one match. A Ballon d'Or winner in 2007.

43.
Cafu

Cafu is the only man to play in three World Cup finals.

Brazil's Mr. Dependable

By Michael Cox

Past greats are remembered chiefly through moments, and the reality is that Cafu—the most-capped player for the most successful nation in World Cup history and the only man to play in three World Cup finals—probably never had a single outstanding memorable moment. That he is considered among the top 50 players in history is a testament to his longevity, consistency, and sheer popularity.

The two players he is often compared to very much did have moments. The first is Carlos Alberto, the only right-back ahead of Cafu on this list, who rounded off perhaps the most celebrated goal in history, Brazil's fourth in the final of World Cup 1970. The other is Cafu's longtime teammate Roberto Carlos, who played on the opposite flank and performed in a more spectacular manner. His swerving free kick against France in 1997 provided a concise summary of his primary quality: his thunderous left foot.

Cafu, on the other hand, merely got on with business. He was solid, dependable, workmanlike.

When asked for his favorite moment from his hugely successful career, Cafu mentioned the time when, midway through the Rome derby, he knocked the ball over the head of Pavel Nedvěd, collected it, and did the same in the reverse direction, then did the same once again. A triple *sombrero* is perhaps unique on a football pitch, but it still ultimately only led to a free kick inside Cafu's own half—Diego Simeone was in danger of becoming the victim of the fourth *sombrero*, so he knocked the full-back to the ground. It was a brilliant piece of football, but it was a minor part of the match. Even if there's an argument for showmanship for the sake of it, you wouldn't put Cafu down as a natural-born entertainer in comparison to other Brazilian greats.

Cafu was born two weeks before Carlos Alberto's famous goal in World Cup 1970 and continued the tradition, probably started by Djalma Santos, of Brazil producing very attack-minded right-backs. Like most full-backs, he was initially a more attacking player and the man named Marcos Evangelista de Morais (his five siblings were named Mara, Margaeth, Marcelo, Mauricio, and Mauro) took the name Cafu because of comparisons to Cafuringa, a flying right-winger at Fluminense.

But when Cafu's São Paulo teammate, right-back Zé Teodoro, sustained a minor injury, he was asked to deputize for three weeks. Of course, he looked so comfortable there that he never again played as a true winger.

Cafu disliked playing right-back at first and wasn't an entirely perfect fit. He had become renowned for driven crosses from the byline, but at right-back, he was forced to become more refined. While he adjusted by practicing 150 crosses after training every day and became a competent deliverer from wide, he wasn't necessarily associ ated with crossing throughout his career. He was more about energy, work rate, positional sense, and tackling ability. Sir Alex Ferguson once marveled at his performance for AC Milan against his Manchester United side, telling reporters in 2005 that Cafu "must have two hearts." That summed him up.

Indeed, Cafu often says his brother was a more talented footballer and boasted a magical left foot. Cafu made it, and his brother did not, simply because Cafu had more drive to succeed.

He was finally signed by São Paulo after missing the cut in four separate trials and having been rejected by several other clubs. But he eventually enjoyed a truly remarkable career, which included winning both the Copa Libertadores and the Champions League.

His was a long journey—he won the first of his two Copas in 1992 and the European equivalent 15 years later. In the intervening period, Cafu moved from São Paulo to Spain, where he had an injury-hit half-year at Real Zaragoza before returning to Brazil with Juventude. If this seemed a surprise move—they were relegation scrappers—it was really because Cafu had lined up a move to Palmeiras, but joining one of São Paulo's rivals after such a short time in Spain would have caused problems. Juventude was essentially just a holding club.

His second move to Europe after a two-year stint with Palmeiras was more successful. He spent six years with Roma, playing a crucial role in their title victory in 2000–2001, forming a wonderful wingback partnership with Vincent Candela in Fabio Capello's 3-4-1-2 system. He was nicknamed *Il Pendolino* after the express train that most famously charges between Rome and Milan. That proved prescient.

He had signed a contract to move to Japan's J1 League in 2003, at the age of 33. But a surprise call from AC Milan convinced him to remain in Italy. Initially, manager Carlo Ancelotti wanted him as a short-term backup, but Cafu ended up being a regular for five years, often playing in a defensive quartet featuring Jaap Stam, Alessandro Nesta, and Paolo Maldini. Defending isn't about individualism, and Milan's most celebrated back four will forever be Mauro Tassotti, Franco Baresi, Alessandro Costacurta, and Maldini from 15 years earlier, but that is still possibly the highest-caliber quartet of defenders ever assembled in football.

Alongside the other three, Cafu became a better defender than ever. "At Roma, I was playing in midfield and sometimes almost in attack," he said of his adjustment. "At Milan, I am a right-back and have had to improve my defending. Only if I defend well can I think about attacking."

The ultimately successful 2006–07 Champions League campaign was a particularly long one for Cafu. Because of the knock-on effects from the *Calciopoli* scandal that overshadowed Italy's World Cup–winning year of 2006, Milan were placed in the qualifiers for the competition at short notice. Ancelotti had to phone up the players who had reached the latter stages of the World Cup, scattered around the world on holiday, and tell them they were suddenly needed—over a month before the Serie A campaign was due to start.

Cafu flew back from Brazil and arrived in Italy less than 24 hours before their qualifier against Red Star Belgrade. He was their chief attacking threat in a 1–0 victory. That, as much as anything else, was him all over.

For all Cafu's club achievements, it is clearly his international career that makes him so revered. If you were a very casual football fan and only watched the World Cup final once every four years, you would have come across the full-back in 1994, 1998, and 2002.

In 1994, he was a mere backup, introduced as a second-half substitute in Brazil's knockout stage wins over the United States and the Netherlands. Then, in the final against Italy, an early injury to right-back Jorginho meant Cafu played the majority of a dour contest. He was, as ever, entirely solid as Brazil won on penalties.

Four years later, he was a regular, playing the entirety of every game with the exception of the semifinal against the Netherlands, when he was suspended. In the final, a Brazil side still reeling from Ronaldo's seizure was easily defeated by France in Paris. In a very narrow game between two sides lacking proper wingers, Cafu offered more drive and width than anyone, but his overlaps down the right were constantly ignored by Leonardo, who drifted infield from that flank without looking to feed his full-back. It summed up Brazil's disconnect.

In 2002, Brazil won all seven games, Cafu didn't miss a minute, and he lifted the World Cup as captain. That had not always been on the cards.

Brazil endured a hugely difficult qualification campaign and, as one of the older players who was receiving criticism from fans, new manager Luiz Felipe Scolari took the captaincy away from Cafu and handed it to Emerson, a trusted midfielder from his Grêmio days. But on the eve of the tournament, Emerson injured his shoulder while playing in goal during training. Cafu tried to convince Scolari to keep Emerson with the squad, but it was judged he would not be fit enough to play in Japan and South Korea. The captaincy returned to Cafu.

With Scolari favoring a system featuring wing-backs, Cafu and Roberto Carlos pushed forward more aggressively than ever, launching long crossfield passes to one another. They were the fourth and fifth attackers, either side of Ronaldo, Rivaldo, and Ronaldinho. Cafu, the man who came from the family of the six M's, would benefit from the genius of the three R's.

He assisted a goal for Ronaldo in the 4–0 group-stage victory over China in a manner typical of his style—briefly positioned as Brazil's most advanced player, he collected a long Rivaldo diagonal on his chest, broke past two defenders with speed and determination rather than with any real trickery, and fired the ball across the six-yard box for Ronaldo to turn into an empty net.

In a team composed of slightly error-prone defenders, inexperienced central midfielders, and flair players up front, Cafu was unquestionably the side's leader.

"I need to talk about a very special player," Scolari said on the eve of Cafu's third World Cup final. "If there is one man who has made sacrifices and lent himself to the cause of the Brazil team, this man is Cafu. He has been my commander on the field. He is a great example of dedication and humility."

He was faultless throughout the final as Germany were defeated 2–0 and afterward decided to clamber up on the narrow, wobbly plinth that held the trophy. The most-viewed scene in world football was also very personal. Having scribbled "100% Jardim Irene" on his shirt—a reference to his poor hometown on the outskirts of São Paulo—Cafu also mouthed "I love you" to his wife as he hoisted the trophy into the air.

With Brazil struggling to produce another generation of full-backs, he and Roberto Carlos were badly past their best by 2006. In a quarterfinal elimination by France, Cafu looked desperately short of pace when up against Thierry Henry, while Roberto Carlos was busy fiddling with his socks and allowed Henry to volley home a Zinédine Zidane free kick for the only goal. Both had received heavy criticism throughout the tournament and, in a postmatch interview, Cafu declared that as the most-capped player in Brazil's history, he deserved a little more respect.

In those 142 caps, it is notable that he very rarely scored goals—just five, all in friendlies. When he did, they were often excellent hits, and Cafu had a manner of arriving at the far post and striking across the ball that brought to mind, yes, Carlos Alberto. But those situations were rare. Even at club level, across 19 league seasons, all with top clubs and some of them as a wing-back rather than a full-back, he scored only 18 times.

It was only 17 times until the final game of Cafu's professional career, for Milan at home to Udinese. Ten minutes from time, he received the ball out on the right flank and spotted his compatriot Kaká free on the edge of the box. He knocked the ball inside and made a run in behind the defense. Kaká responded by cushioning a pass first-time in behind for Cafu, who received the ball in precisely the situation he'd received it hundreds of times before.

In the six-yard box, Filippo Inzaghi screamed for a low cross that would allow him to score his trademark tap-in. Udinese goalkeeper Samir Handanović was expecting a cross, too. But Cafu, uncharacteristically, took the selfish option.

He put his head down and drove the ball home at the near post, catching Handanović out. His Milan teammates initially looked surprised, but were then even more jubilant than the goalscorer himself, who raised both hands to the air and, as he'd done for much of the previous two decades, simply smiled. It was the perfect ending to a perfect career.

At last, Cafu had his own moment.

Player name: Marcos Evangelista de Morais (Cafu)
Born: June 7, 1970
Position: Right-back
Debut: 1989
Main teams: São Paulo (1989–95), Real Zaragoza (1995), Juventude (1995), Palmeiras (1995–97), Roma (1997–2003), AC Milan (2003–08); Brazil (1990–2006)
Career highlights: The full-back won the World Cup in 1994 and as captain in 2002, and is the only man to play in three World Cup finals. Won the Copa América in 1997 and 1999 and the Champions League with AC Milan in 2007. He also won Serie A once each with Roma and Milan.

42.

Luís Figo

Figo, a former Barcelona player, braves the bear pit that was Camp Nou.

The man who crossed Spanish football's great divide

By Rory Smith

That night, the missiles came so thick and fast that Luís Figo did not see the one that would hurt most of all until the next morning. He had seen the coins, the cigarette lighters, the golf balls raining down from the stands at Camp Nou. He could hardly have avoided them. Every time he drifted close to the edge of the field, every time he came within range, the bombardment had started again.

He had known the reception would be hostile. Two years previously, he had left Barcelona for Real Madrid. The transfer had been, when seen in one light, deeply strategic, almost surgical. In another it was kind of accidental. In both it was bitter, acrimonious, hostile. It turned both the *Clásico* and Figo himself toxic.

He had been back once before, a few months after the transfer had been completed. Figo had told *Marca* before the game that he felt like he was being "treated like a murderer." One of his teammates, Steve McManaman, had elected not to sit next to him on the bus that carried Madrid's players to the stadium. It was a wise choice: The bus was pelted with missiles as it wound through the streets of Les Corts, the double-glazed windows splintering under the barrage.

Inside the stadium, fans had showered Figo with fake 10,000-peseta notes. The jeers had been so great when he first stepped onto what used to be his pitch that he covered his ears. Madrid removed him from corner-taking duty, essentially for his own protection.

Two years on, no one was naïve enough to think time had healed the wounds, but still, the fury in the stands was striking. This time, Barcelona's fans had brought more than counterfeit notes. Instead, the ordnance included pocket change, rocks, bike chains, even a couple of mobile phones. Every time Figo strode over to take a corner, as *El Periódico de Catalunya* put it, Camp Nou had turned into "Vietnam."

Somehow he kept his cool. At one point, he noticed an empty bottle of Coca-Cola among the shrapnel. He picked it up and posed with it as if shooting an ad for one of his sponsors. Others were not quite as calm. The referee suspended the game for 16 minutes, hoping that a break in play might preserve the players' safety. It did not work. Míchel Salgado, Madrid's right-back, would later add a knife and an empty bottle of whisky to the list of matériel. "Johnnie Walker, I think, or J&B," he said.

It was not until he picked up the newspapers the next day, though, that Figo saw one projectile in particular, the one that would come to define far more than just that game. It appears in the background of one of the many photos of that night. In the foreground, Figo is taking a corner, the ground at his feet littered with debris. But just behind him, not quite in focus, is the unmistakable shape of a head: a *cochinillo*, a roast suckling pig, its snout jutting into the air. Figo had not seen it at the time. From that moment on, he would be unable to escape it.

Almost instantly, it entered the iconography of the *Clásico*. Over time, it would come to symbolize not just the game, but the rivalry and the era to which it belonged, too. For years it would cast a shadow so long that it felt like it swallowed up the rest of Figo's career; that it shrouded all of his achievements, all of the shimmering brilliance of his peak, in darkness.

More than two decades later, Figo himself would be sufficiently at ease with the image that he took part in an ad reveling in its notoriety: In 2024, he filmed an ad for Uber Eats in which he extolled the virtue of having *cochinillo* delivered straight to your home. "Now it is OK to play with food," ran the social media slogan. It even came with a serving suggestion: roast suckling pig is best eaten with baked potatoes.

His relationship with the image—with the dish itself, in fact—has not always been so easy. He has often seemed, understandably, to resent the outsize prominence given to that game, that controversy, that period of his life.

He would, he told *The Guardian* in 2022, prefer it if the *cochinillo*, and the betrayal it came to represent, was not the first thing people thought of when they considered what he was. "I would," he said, "like more value given to my whole career than one episode that marks an age."

The transfer that shaped Luís Figo's career should not be confused with the one that came to define it. In the summer of 1995, Figo was 23 and one of the most coveted players in Europe. In his early years at Sporting Lisbon, he did not particularly see himself as a winger. He was, instead, used more as a creative midfielder, a No. 10, in the mold of his hero, Paulo Futre.

He did, though, have all the requisite skills. If he was not blisteringly quick, he did not need to be. He boasted a keen eye, a vivid imagination, and a craftsman's technique, both with his favored right foot and his left. "You could put Figo in a phone booth along with 11 opponents," Carlos Queiroz, who coached him at Sporting, would later tell the London *Times*, "and he would find his way to the door."

He played for the club's first team at 17, eventually taking permanent possession of the No. 7 shirt. Among his devotees in those early years was Cristiano Ronaldo. Even among the glittering stars of Portugal's nascent "golden generation"—Rui Costa, Jorge Costa, and João Pinto—he gleamed, turning the country into Europe's under-16 champions in 1989 and helping retain the FIFA World Youth Championship two years later.

After five years in Sporting's first team, Figo had come to believe that his rich promise was not being reflected in his contract. He felt he deserved improved terms, ones that better suited his blossoming status. The club, though, appeared to have other ideas. Sporting, it seemed, had decided the time was right to cash in and had not thought to say anything to Figo about it.

The precise order of what happened next is, even this far removed, subject to some dispute. In an interview with *FourFourTwo* magazine some years after the event, Figo suggested Sporting had "reached a deal with Juventus" for his transfer that summer and that he had been so "angry when I found out about it" that he had signed a contract with another Italian side, Parma, simply to have some agency over his career.

It is perhaps not quite so clear-cut as that. Figo admitted signing some sort of agreement with Juventus, though he would later state he did not believe it to be a valid contract. Reports in Italy at the time, meanwhile, suggested Parma reached an agreement with the winger first, before Juventus attempted to gazump their Serie A rival.

The consequences, though, were plain. Luciano Moggi, the Juventus chief executive who acted as Italian football's great Svengali, petitioned to have both contracts declared illegal. It worked. As a bonus, Figo was banned from playing in Serie A for two years. It left him in limbo: out of contract at Sporting, suddenly devoid of suitors.

His career might have stalled then. It did not. "Maybe it was my lucky moment," he said. "Because in the end, I went to Barcelona instead." Five years later he was the most expensive and, as officially as it is possible to be, the best player in the world.

In hindsight, those years around the turn of the millennium feel like a sort of no-man's-land. European football had been owned by Serie A for much of the 1990s but as the decade drew to a close, its power had started to wane; 1999 brought the first Champions League final not to feature an Italian team (since the competition's revamp in 1992–93).

Also, in the course of the 2000s, football's individual awards would come to be the private property of two players in particular. Yet in the late 1990s and early 2000s, several Ballon d'Or winners picked up the honor for the first time. Matthias Sammer got one. So did Pavel Nedvěd, Rivaldo, and Michael Owen.

It would be easy to treat Figo as just another name on that list, a player whose greatness burned brightly but briefly. He won his prize in 2000, the acrid taste of his move to Real Madrid still stinging Barcelona. He would lead Madrid to a Spanish title in his first season at the club. Within a couple of years, he would help deliver the Champions League, too.

He had done exactly what Florentino Pérez, the construction tycoon who had engineered his signing, hoped he would. Pérez had unilaterally promised Madrid's members that he would sign Figo during his insurgent campaign to become the club's president in 2000. His bid was not, initially, seen as a strong one: The incumbent, Lorenzo Sanz, had delivered the Champions League in 1998 and 2000, after all.

The idea that he might be able to lure Figo seemed far-fetched, too. He had celebrated Barcelona's title victory the previous year by singing a derogatory chant about Madrid. He was settled in Catalonia. Jupp Heynckes, the former Madrid head coach, had declared him one of the best three players in the world. The other two were his teammates: Rivaldo and Pep Guardiola.

Just as he had at Sporting, though, he was starting to feel as though the club had been slow to offer him the sort of contract he deserved. Pérez had spotted the impasse and inserted himself—and Real Madrid—directly into it. He reached a deal with Figo's agent: if he won the election, he would pay the $71.5 million buyout clause written into Figo's contract.

Figo would sign for Real Madrid.

The player himself did not seem to be aware of any of this. At first, he has since admitted that he used the threat of Madrid as something of a "bluff."

"And then things took the direction they took," he said.

Madrid's members clearly wanted to see how it played out. Pérez won the election. Figo, ultimately, felt compelled to move. When he was presented at the Bernabéu, handed a white shirt by Alfredo Di Stéfano, he was ashen-faced. Somber.

The transfer made him the first of Pérez's *galácticos*, the superstars brought in to great fanfare in every summer of his presidency. Zinédine Zidane followed in 2001. Ronaldo Nazário arrived in 2002. David Beckham came a year later.

Slowly, though, the club started to buckle under the weight of their cumulative fame. Less celebrated, but no less important, players were sold to accommodate them. Others felt ostracized. Pérez could not settle on a manager. He interfered in team affairs. The Champions League victory in 2002 could not be repeated. In 2006, he announced he was standing down.

Figo had left by that stage, joining Inter Milan on a free transfer when his contract expired in 2005, but the stain of the failure of the *galáctico* project—its pride, its pomposity, its colossal hubris—clung to him, just a little, nonetheless. It tarnished his status, diminishing his luster. It is possible now to see in him a player trapped by his decisions, by his era; a great in that period between what football was and what it became.

That interpretation, though, deprives Figo of the one thing he sought throughout his career: agency. He was, in his own words, a "guinea pig," the first iteration of Pérez's experiment in harnessing the raw power—sporting, commercial—of a star.

Figo's initial success was enough to justify the rest of the *galáctico* model, the one that would eventually bring Zidane to the Bernabéu and, in time, turn Real Madrid into Pérez's plaything; it would provide the blueprint for everything from Roman Abramovich's takeover of Chelsea to Neymar's move from Barcelona to Paris Saint-Germain. Much of modern football owes no small debt to Pérez's playbook.

His impact on Barcelona was no less significant. Joan Gaspart, the Barcelona president whose first act was to ratify Figo's departure, would later claim that the move "destroyed" the club: not just the loss of a player of his rare gifts, not just the blow to its prestige, but the revenue it generated.

Barcelona spent years squandering its unwanted windfall, desperately trying to throw good money after bad. By 2008, the situation would be so desperate that it handed control of the team to one of Figo's closest friends, tasking him with rebuilding the club around players from the youth academy. Pep Guardiola's ascendance has its roots in Figo's betrayal. Figo does not just straddle the border between what football was and what it became; he is the border.

He was, in many ways, the first player from the future.

Player name: Luís Filipe Madeira Caeiro Figo
Born: November 4, 1972
Position: Winger, forward
Debut: 1990
Main teams: Sporting Lisbon (1990–95), Barcelona (1995–2000), Real Madrid (2000–2005), Inter Milan (2005–09); Portugal (1991–2006)
Career highlights: Won the Champions League in 2002 and La Liga four times. Won Serie A four times with Inter. Claimed the Ballon d'Or in 2000.

41.
Karim Benzema

Benzema is arguably the best player of his generation who is least associated with international football.

France's brilliant mass of contradictions

By Nick Miller

When Karim Benzema moved to the Saudi Arabian club Al Ittihad in 2023, he was the reigning Ballon d'Or winner.

The Saudi Pro League was supposed to be a retirement league, the sort of place that an aging superstar might go for a late payday. That has been happening for generations. In the 1970s, it was the United States. For a while in the 2000s, it was Qatar. China took the mantle in the 2010s. It wasn't new.

But for a player who had just been voted the best in the world, the implication being that they are at or at least near to the peak of their powers, to go there was . . . unusual. Not unique—Franz Beckenbauer held the title when he signed for the New York Cosmos in 1977—but surprising and certainly uncommon.

At the same time, it was oddly appropriate for Benzema, whose career has not followed the usual path of a generational great.

Here was the superstar who submitted himself to someone more super for years. The hyped youngster who didn't really blossom as a standout individual talent until his late 20s. The idol whose career was pockmarked by off-the-field scandal.

Perhaps most of all, he is arguably the best player of his generation—maybe among the best players of all time—who is least associated with international football. Most of his contemporaries have been defined in some way by their performances for their national team, even if much of their notable work was domestic.

The first three-quarters of Lionel Messi's career came with the asterisk of perceived "failure" with Argentina until he won the 2021 and 2024 Copa Américas and the 2022 World Cup. Cristiano Ronaldo dragged Portugal to the 2016 European Championship final and turned himself into their coach when he went off injured. Luka Modrić took Croatia to one of the more unlikely World Cup final appearances. Gareth Bale's preference for playing for Wales became a punch line. Even Neymar, for whom the crushing disappointment of the 2014 home World Cup was mitigated slightly by redemption in the 2016 home Olympics.

Benzema, though? It is difficult even to conjure up an image of him in a France shirt, even though he is in the top five French forwards of all time—perhaps even the greatest pure center-forward.

It is not even as if he never played for France. He won 97 caps and scored 37 goals, making him, at the time of writing, their joint 10th-highest appearance maker and their sixth-highest goalscorer. It is just that the undulations of Benzema's international career—up and down for a variety of reasons both self-inflicted and otherwise—have meant he was around for some of their high-profile disasters but missed their greatest successes.

• • •

Benzema signed for Real Madrid in 2009 from Lyon. He was probably the highest-rated young striker in the world at the time, his style in his early days at the French club evoking memories of the Brazilian Ronaldo—an astonishing combination of physicality and skill, imagination and finishing.

If someone made you God for a day and for some reason limited your powers to constructing a perfect No. 9, he is what you would come up with.

A transfer to the biggest club in the world seemed like a natural move for a 21-year-old superstar. He cost an initial $37 million, which these days feels quite quaint but at the time was a decent amount of money. Around 20,000 people attended his unveiling at the Santiago Bernabéu—one of Real's more absurd traditions where genuflecting masses show up to watch someone wave, speak broken Spanish into a microphone, and, if you're lucky, juggle a football. The kind of thing that *would* happen to a superstar, a singular idol whose star shines brighter than everyone else.

The difference was that Benzema moved to Real in the same summer they bought Cristiano Ronaldo and Kaká, who cost $100 million and $72.7 million and whose unveilings attracted crowds of 80,000 and 57,000, respectively. In relative terms, the Frenchman was eclipsed.

That proved an appropriate summary of his early career in Spain, which at least initially was a failure.

He only scored eight league goals in his first season, with Gonzalo Higuaín generally preferred as the team's No. 9. In Benzema's second season, José Mourinho sniffily commented during a minor injury crisis that Real only had "one attacker and that's Benzema," as if he were talking about some no-mark, skinny 17-year-old. When the Frenchman failed to find the net in a 0–0 draw against Murcia of the third tier in the Copa del Rey in October 2010, the front page of *Marca* the next morning declared him "dead."

Eventually, though, he became a fixture in the Real first team, but not in the role that someone of his individual talents might expect.

Benzema essentially supplicated himself to the team, recognizing that, even in those relatively early days in Madrid, he had by his side one of the top five players of all time. He did not quite turn himself into a water carrier, but he was definitely the bass player to Cristiano Ronaldo's lead singer. To extend that last analogy, Gareth Bale, when he signed a couple of years later, was the keyboard player who specialized in occasional, spectacular solos.

"The finisher was Cristiano," Benzema told *RMC Sport* in 2019. "With him, I played another role. More in the build-up, in movement, to create space. A No. 9 doesn't necessarily have to be a goalscorer. For me, Cristiano was the goalscorer. With Bale, all three of us scored goals, but Cristiano scored 30 more than the rest."

By the time Ronaldo left Madrid in 2018, Benzema had won two league titles, four Champions Leagues, and three Club World Cups, and had quietly amassed 192 goals for Real. Had he never played another game, his career would have been in the top one percent of the top one percent. But it was arguably only after the Portuguese's departure that Benzema truly started to flourish.

Most players hyped to the extent Benzema was as a teenager tend to burn out, physically and mentally exhausted by the time they should be at their peak in their late 20s. But Benzema continued to climb. It was as if he spent that first two-thirds of his career biding his time, waiting for the moment he could truly be the best version of himself.

"When you play with a guy who scores 50 or 60 goals a season, of course you're at the service of the team," he told ESPN in 2021, "but you're at the service of the player, too. I had to adapt. I had a very good connection with Cristiano. Once he left, it was down to me to take a step forward and show that I could make the difference, too."

And he did, winning that Ballon d'Or in 2022, bringing his club career full circle, becoming the individual hero that his young promise suggested he should be.

But if his club career was unusual, his time in the international game was even more so.

• • •

Benzema was first called up to the France squad in late 2006 by Raymond Domenech. Over the next few years, he was in and out of the team, playing in two games of France's calamitous Euro 2008 first-round exit, but was left out of the 2010 World Cup squad. When Laurent Blanc took over from Domenech and Didier Deschamps succeeded Blanc, Benzema became more of a mainstay, the French attack built around him despite the striker at one point going over a year without scoring.

He was part of the team at Euro 2012 and the 2014 World Cup. Even though he scored three goals at the latter, France's performances at both were forgettable.

But at least he was allowed to play. His international career ended (or so we thought) in December 2015 when the French Football Federation announced that Benzema would not be eligible for selection for the following summer's home European Championship because of his role in what would unimaginatively be known as *L'affaire de la Sextape*.

Benzema had already been involved in one scandal when he was one of four France players—the others being Franck Ribéry, Sidney Govou, and Hatem Ben Arfa—investigated over their role in an alleged prostitution ring, specifically the allegation that he had solicited a woman called Zahia Dehar when she was 16. Benzema always denied being involved and charges were eventually dropped due to a lack of evidence.

But in November 2015, Benzema was arrested by French police as they investigated the extraordinary claim that he had been involved in an attempt to blackmail his France teammate Mathieu Valbuena. Benzema was essentially accused of being a go-between after a childhood friend claimed to have obtained a sex tape involving Valbuena, the intention being to extort money from the midfielder.

"He would say: 'I can introduce you to my friend . . .' It kept coming back to that," Valbuena told *Le Monde* in 2015. "Then when he was about to leave, Karim said: 'What shall I do? Shall I give him your number? Should I give you his number?' He was inciting me. He was saying, indirectly: 'You will have to pay.'"

Benzema always denied being involved in the blackmail plot but, this time, he was found guilty, given a one-year suspended prison sentence, and fined $80,000. But the greater punishment was being denied involvement in probably the greatest sustained period of success in the French national team's history.

He missed France reaching the final of the 2016 European Championship when they were beaten 1–0 by Portugal and then the 2018 World Cup in Russia, when Deschamps's side went all the way and defeated Croatia 4–2 in the final. In his place at both of those tournaments was Olivier Giroud, an undeniably more limited player in an individual sense, whom Benzema would later stoke controversy by comparing to a go-kart.

Then, unexpectedly, Benzema was recalled for Euro 2020. While he scored four goals in that tournament, *Les Bleus* were eliminated in the round of 16 by Switzerland. And to cap off a truly strange international career, Benzema was selected for the 2022 World Cup only to be left on the sidelines watching his teammates once again reach the final after he suffered a thigh injury.

With Benzema there was always a sense that he was never truly accepted by his country, despite being arguably their greatest-ever center-forward. He is proud of his Algerian roots and, even in a roundabout way, once admitted that he chose to play for France for professional reasons rather than emotional ones. He is also a Muslim in a country that has, to say the least, a tricky relationship with Islam.

When he was left out of the 2016 squad, he suggested Deschamps had bowed to "the racist part of France," comments that outraged the French coach and made his recall for Euro 2020 even more of a surprise. The suggestion that his treatment could be down to race didn't go down well with some. Former France rugby union player Vincent Moscato asked on his RMC radio show: "Are we going to give the national team jersey to a guy who said that half of France is racist?"

And so here we have a sensational player, one of his generation's greats, whose narrative arc was never straightforward.

He was the young superstar who willingly became a supporting act. He was the Ballon d'Or winner who chose to move to a footballing backwater. He was his country's finest striker who missed their greatest moments.

If there is a quote that epitomizes Benzema, it is the one he gave to the Spanish newspaper *Marca* in 2019. "People ask a striker to score goals," he said, "but I think I am a No. 9 who has the soul of a No. 10."

And that rather sums him up.

A brilliant mass of contradictions. There are players who have won more, there are players who have been more talented, there are players who are more famous, but there can be few who are as fascinating as Karim Benzema.

Player name: Karim Benzema
Born: December 19, 1987
Position: Forward
Debut: 2005
Main teams: Lyon (2005–09), Real Madrid (2009–23), Al Ittihad (2023–); France (2007–22)
Career highlights: Won the Champions League five times and, overall, claimed 25 trophies at Real Madrid. Won the Ballon d'Or in 2022.

40.

Paco Gento

Gento was a reserved but determined character in a dressing room crammed with world superstars.

La Galerna del Cantábrico and a sporting family for the ages

By Dermot Corrigan

The most decorated player in Spanish football history was a force of nature whose reputation endures.

Known as *La Galerna del Cantábrico* after the gale that whips off the sea in his home province in the north of Spain, Paco Gento won 24 major trophies playing for Real Madrid across three decades, the last piece of silverware coming in the summer of 1970. This total included a record 12 Spanish league titles and a joint-record six European Cups.

Gento was a left-winger known for his powerful running down the flank, as well as the quality of his crossing and the force of his shooting. A reserved but determined character in a dressing room crammed with world superstars, he became one of the most respected and loved figures in Madrid's history.

His influence on Spanish sport did not end with retirement. Among Gento's descendants are world and European champions in football and basketball, as well as Spanish league and cup champions in both sports, and an Olympic medalist.

The Athletic met with three members of arguably Spain's most famous sporting family at a bar in the shadow of Real Madrid's Santiago Bernabéu, to learn more about Gento, his times, and his legacy.

Francisco Gento López was born in October 1933 in the rural Cantabrian village of Guarnizo. His father, Antonio, drove a truck, while the family owned a small farm. Money was always tight and became even tighter during and after the Spanish Civil War, from 1936 to 1939.

"They were difficult years—there was not much trade or industry," says José Luis Llorente, whose biography of his uncle, *Gento Real*, was published in 2024. "After any civil war, the people with family members on the losing side suffer a lot. My grandfather's brother was jailed. Another brother went to France."

Sport had always been an escape for all the family. Both Gento's parents played organized football in Guarnizo and running fast was deep within his DNA. "Famously, when his mother, Prudencia, was a girl, she won races against the boys in the village," says José Luis. "His father, Antonio, was a starter in Cultural Deportiva Guarnizo's first regional championship game in 1922."

Brothers Paco, Antonio, and Julio played football with their cousins and neighbors on the streets and in the fields. After leaving school at 14, Paco tended the family's cattle, pigs, and hens, bringing along his makeshift ball made from bound-together rags. Any idea of becoming a professional player was very distant.

"They did not see football as a 'way out' or a chance to get rich," says José Luis. "There were six siblings. What Antonio really needed was help on the farm."

But young Paco had caught the football bug and his talents drew the eye of the area's biggest youth teams. Family lore has him at age 15 running 10 kilometers (about six miles) to play for SD Nueva Montaña. He scored nine goals, then ran back home afterward. On joining Unión Club de El Astillero, he was given his own boots and jersey, a relief for the family finances.

At 18, Gento scored twice in a 2–1 win for Astillero against the youth side of Racing Santander. Suitably impressed, the provincial capital's La Liga team offered him a professional contract. In February 1953, he made his Primera División debut for Racing, excelling against that season's champions, Barcelona, at El Sardinero. In April he dazzled away against Real Madrid. After just 10 senior games and two goals, he was already establishing a reputation.

"People began to talk about this really fast kid who was a really good footballer," José Luis adds. "At one game in El Sardinero, all the neighbors were there, congratulating his father. Antonio was a man of few words, but he cried with pride."

In August 1953, Real Madrid president Santiago Bernabéu sanctioned the signing of Gento for a fee of 1,750,000 pesetas (around $43,000 at the time). Two players joined Racing as part of the deal.

Gento's first season at Madrid saw the team win their first Spanish championship in 21 years. Fellow new arrival Alfredo Di Stéfano was the star, with Gento playing just 17 of 30 La Liga games and failing to muster a goal. Supporters and journalists scoffed that their skinny new winger could run fast but lacked technical ability. The shy northerner was just taking time to get used to the pace of life in the capital.

"Paco was already a very good player when he arrived at Madrid," José Luis says. "Madrid would not have paid so much money for a kid who could only run. Maybe there were some directors who wanted to sell Paco [after that underwhelming first campaign], but he had the vital support of Bernabéu and Di Stéfano."

The following summer, Madrid signed Argentine playmaker Héctor Rial, who specialized in threading passes behind the opposition defense onto which wingers could run. Gento duly reaped the rewards. In 1954–55, he scored six goals in 24 league games as Madrid retained La Liga and made his debut for the Spain senior side.

Now he was finding his feet in a side accumulating silverware with gusto. In June 1956, Madrid faced the French side Stade de Reims in the first-ever European Cup final, at Paris's Parc des Princes. Reims went 2–0 up, but the Spanish side roared back to win 4–3. Gento crossed for Rial to score the winning goal.

Madrid won the next two European Cups, too, and Gento scored in both finals against Italian sides Fiorentina and AC Milan. His winner in extra time in the 1958 final in Brussels, bursting clear of the defense and firing past the goalkeeper, was maybe his finest moment.

"Paco told me one day much later that during the break before extra time against Milan, Alfredo [Di Stéfano] said, 'Paco, we're all dead [on our feet]. Either you win us this or we'll lose,'" Gento's nephew Antonio "Toñin" Llorente says. "So Paco went out and scored the goal which won the third European Cup."

That summer, Madrid added Hungarian superstar Ferenc Puskás to complete their "famous five" front line alongside Gento, Rial, Di Stéfano, and Raymond Kopa.

"They were all very intelligent and respectful characters," José Luis says. "Alfredo was the boss. Kopa was an idol in France. Puskás was a global celebrity. Paco was the most 'normal' of the five. All the Gentos are the same: very reserved, especially at first."

In the 1960 European Cup final, Di Stéfano and Puskás scored the goals in a famous 7–3 victory over Eintracht Frankfurt. Yet it was Gento's name that Madrid's fans chanted in the aftermath. While most Spaniards were struggling under the grim dictatorship of General Francisco Franco, the successful Madrid team in their dazzling white jerseys was a source of pride.

"In those days, there was just one television channel," Toñin says. "Paco would have been one of the most famous people in Spain . . . well, maybe some bullfighters, [the flamenco singer] Lola Flores, and my uncle. I remember when we were small, on the beach, or in the village, and absolutely everyone knew him. He was more famous than today's footballers."

Later that year, Gento scored from 40 meters out as Madrid beat Uruguayan side Peñarol 5–1 to win the first-ever Intercontinental Cup. Most of the team's superstars then started to fade and retire, but Gento remained and became captain of a much younger all-Spanish side. During the 1966 European Cup final against Partizan Belgrade, he moved inside from the wing and used his experience and guile to direct another comeback victory.

"Nobody expected Real to win the European Cup in 1966," José Luis says. "Paco was the only superstar left, but he was one of those people who led by example, without having to say anything. Just showing what must be done."

Gento won 43 senior international caps, scoring five goals, but did not feature as Spain won the 1964 European Championship. He continued to play for Madrid until he was almost 38. *La Galerna* finished with 600 official games and 182 goals for the club.

Two younger Gentos joined Paco in making the journey from Guarnizo to Real Madrid.

Neither right-winger Julio nor creative midfielder Antonio could claim a first-team place. The only time all three wore the white shirt together was in a 1959 friendly against FC Zürich. "Julio was fast, skillful, but not as strong as Paco," José Luis says. "Toñin was very good, too, but Paco had the character."

The younger brothers went on to have decent professional careers at other clubs, including a spell as teammates back home at Racing Santander. Each summer, the whole family came together for sprawling games on the Cantabrian coast's wide sandy beaches.

"My dad and his brothers would play," Paco Gento Jr. says. "There'd also be lots of uncles, cousins, brothers. I went in goal as I was the worst. There'd be rows, for sure. It was competitive, but it was also such fun."

Antonio ended up opening a restaurant, which became a gathering point for Real Madrid supporters in the area. "Paco himself would come, play a game on the beach, then go to the bar to eat prawns, have a beer, and watch Madrid on the TV," says José Luis, who visited each summer as a boy.

The sporting prowess continued into the next generation. Gento's nephews, Paco Llorente and Julio Llorente, played for Real Madrid in the 1980s and early 1990s, winning five La Liga titles between them. Their brothers, José Luis and Toñin, preferred basketball to soccer and excelled. José Luis won a silver medal with Spain at the 1984 Olympic Games in Los Angeles and a European Cup with Real Madrid's basketball team. Toñin represented Spain's underage sides and played 16 seasons in Spain's ACB top division.

"Dad would watch all the family members' games, he really enjoyed that," Paco Jr. says. "During the Olympics, he got up in the middle of the night to watch José Luis play."

The family presence in both sports continues. José Luis's sons, Sergio and Juan, are professional basketballers. Their cousin, Marcos Llorente, came through Real Madrid's youth soccer system, scored as Madrid won the 2018 Club World Cup, represented Spain at the 2022 World Cup, and now plays for Atlético Madrid. Another Paco Gento—a cousin—has kept the link to CD Guarnizo alive in the twenty-first century.

"Each of us has had our particular qualities," says José Luis. "We've all been very fast, although not as fast as Paco. And we all worked for the team, even Paco, who was a world star. You can see it all now in Marcos."

After retirement, Gento oversaw Madrid's Castilla youth team for three seasons, then coached Spanish sides Castellon, Palencia, and Granada. He received gold medals of sporting merit from the Cantabrian regional government and Madrid's city council, but mostly shied away from the spotlight for decades.

"My dad never gave importance to what he had done," Paco Jr.

says. “He was always invited to the Bernabéu’s VIP zone but preferred to go with his own season ticket and not bother anyone. He would wear his hat, his glasses, and try to pass unnoticed.”

In December 2015, Gento succeeded his old friend and teammate Di Stéfano as Real Madrid’s honorary president, an ambassadorial role that involved attending games and club events.

“He did not really want to at first, as he did not want the attention,” Paco Jr. adds. “But it was the most beautiful thing—to be honorary president of Real Madrid at the end of his life. We were so proud. He had a special spark, a man of few words, but he knew the right phrase to get you to smile.”

When Gento died in January 2022, aged 88, he was remembered by many in Spain as the best left-winger of all time. That 2021–22 season saw a Madrid team featuring Vinícius Júnior, Thibaut Courtois, and Luka Modrić win yet another European Cup, albeit now revamped as the Champions League. Through the competition, they kept repeating the stunning *remontada* comebacks that were such a key part of the club’s identity back in the 1950s.

“What happens at Madrid is inexplicable,” Toñin says. “They’re the only team capable of winning European Cups during a bad season. They believe they can still win and they do win. And this winning spirit, this belief, for sure comes from Paco’s era. There is no doubt about that.”

Player name: Francisco Gento López
Born: October 21, 1933
Died: January 18, 2022 (aged 88)
Position: Winger/outside left
Debut: 1952
Main teams: Racing Santander (1953), Real Madrid (1953–71); Spain (1955–69)
Career highlights: Won the European Cup six times and La Liga a record 12 times.

39.

Roberto Baggio

Silverware was not required to justify or validate Baggio's angelic greatness.

Il Divin Codino

By Tim Spiers

He could never have been a center-back with *that* hair.

Not even a defensive midfielder either, really. If you're going to have the kind of ponytail that could be lobbed onto the back of a Renaissance poet and not look out of place, then you had better be the kind of creative genius that can make a football quiver with anticipation when you're about to curl it toward the net.

Fortunately for Roberto Baggio, he fit the bill. *Il Divin Codino,* The Divine Ponytail, was one of the more apt football nicknames.

The standing of some players on this list is undoubtedly embellished by the trophies they won with their teams; a World Cup or a Champions League can mythicize a player's career. Baggio did not win either of those trophies, but he did not need them to make himself whole in the eyes of his adoring public. Silverware was not required to justify or validate his angelic greatness.

Whether Baggio needed those trophies to make himself whole in *his* eyes is a very different question, but to the wider world, the Italian would always be a conjurer of magic, a creator of unimaginable beauty, the ultimate hipsters' choice, and to many, the undisputed greatest Italian footballer of all time. The best to ever kick a ball. There were harps playing in those calves; he had paintbrushes for feet.

Yet his career saw him move from club to club, forever struggling to find a home. He failed at AC Milan and Inter Milan and was cast out by Juventus. That contrasted with his exit at Fiorentina when fans were so angry at his departure that they lobbed Molotov cocktails and 50 people were injured. Discipline-focused managers would readily dispense with him. Even the national team abandoned him for a number of years.

Yep, it's complicated.

Speak to fans of all seven of his clubs—adding the relative lesser lights of Vicenza, Bologna, and Brescia to the list—and he is perhaps revered by so many like no other who has played the game. Certainly among players who have featured for Italy's "big three"—Inter, Milan, and Juventus. But he was always far more popular with supporters than with managers.

Why? Well, he could caress the ball with the delicacy of a father holding his firstborn child. He could dribble with the dexterity, trickery, and wonder of a Cirque du Soleil performer, and he could finish with the deadly accuracy of an Olympic archer. Off the pitch, he was endeared yet further because Baggio, for all his superstardom, did not chase fame. He was a Buddhist who shunned materialism and sponsorship deals. He was a throwback's throwback, even in the 1990s. And people loved him for it.

As Julie Cart wrote in the *Los Angeles Times* on the eve of the 1994

World Cup in the United States: "While Baggio is recognized as one of the world's best players, his reticence about embracing his celebrity and his ambivalence on the concept of fame have football fans puzzled. Baggio is so different from other stars that this difference creates more fans.

"The agony for the Italian public is to know that its love is spent on an icon that neither seeks adulation nor much acknowledges it. Baggio is an infuriating superstar. The three sponsors his IMG agent does allow into the endorsement fold want more out of the private man. The fans wish only that he dedicate every lovely goal to them by racing to the edge of the field and saluting them rather than jogging back to his place in midfield. Baggio allows no one that power."

But it was also the way he moved, the way he carried himself. Like all great artists, Baggio was nonchalant and laissez-faire. He was nimble and deft, his legs bent like rubber when he changed angle.

Did he track back a lot? Well, no. Did he press and harry opposition defenders in pursuit of winning the ball back? Nah, that wasn't exactly Baggio's thing. He was a team player, sure, but you don't stick Freddie Mercury in the choir, do you? If his talents are to be truly appreciated, he needs to be front and center.

In a regimented 4-4-2 system employed by Arrigo Sacchi, for example, Baggio was a poet working in a factory. When things went wrong, it was easy for managers like Sacchi, Fabio Capello, or Marcelo Lippi to blame Baggio, or at the very least drop him in favor of someone less talented but willing to run and adhere to instructions.

But if a team was on a losing run and Baggio was on the bench? Call for the Divine Ponytail.

This was reflected with the national team, too. It was no coincidence that his most fruitful years came at Bologna and Brescia, where teams were built around him.

All this maybe portrays Baggio as selfish or egotistical, but he was nothing of the sort. He was just an individual, a maverick, probably born in the wrong era. "I've often wondered why they really wouldn't consider me, but I never found the real answer," Baggio wrote in his 2002 autobiography, *Una Porta Nel Cielo* (A Goal in the Sky).

"Perhaps they were a bit jealous as everybody used to love me, even opposing fans. Was I stealing the show, denying them the role of protagonists they were desperately claiming for themselves? Modern football is increasingly dominated by the coaches and their narcissism."

There was a brief period when being at a big club under a big manager *did* work for Baggio. In the mid-1990s, whether judged by romantic hipsters or old-fashioned dinosaurs, Baggio could legitimately lay claim to being one of the best players in the world when at Juventus under Lippi.

While in 1993, he was unequivocally the greatest, winning the Ballon d'Or after finally ending an inexorably long wait to claim the first trophy of his career (the UEFA Cup) aged 26, in his 11th season as a professional.

He scored 30 goals in all competitions that season, 21 of them in Serie A, and was at his magical best. His teammate David Platt said of a game against Udinese: "We won 5–1, Baggio scored four goals. I don't think I've ever seen a better performance from any player in any game I've played in." Platt's playing career extended for 16 years.

More trophies followed a couple of years later when Juventus won Serie A and the Coppa Italia, but by then Baggio was becoming a peripheral figure—in part owing to what happened in 1994.

Baggio, more than any Italian player of his era and perhaps of all time, was intrinsically linked to the fortunes of the national team. Each of the four World Cups held over the course of his international career came with a story, starting with Italia 90, when he was one of the breakout stars, dribbling from halfway via a one-two with Giuseppe Giannini to score against Czechoslovakia.

Then, in 1994, the best player in the world headed to the United States, charged with bringing home Italy's first World Cup in 12 years. He gave virtuoso performances throughout that tournament, dragging Italy through three group games, then, in the knockout stage, supplying a late equalizer and an extra-time winner against Nigeria, a late winner against Spain, and both goals against Bulgaria in the semifinals.

It was his World Cup. The pressure on his shoulders was unimaginably great, but he made it look like feathers in a bag.

Those three knockout games had seen Italy score six goals, five of them supplied by Baggio, who was at his beguiling best. But then disaster struck; he suffered a hamstring strain in the semifinal and, despite the *Azzurri*'s progress, was clearly unfit for the final against Brazil.

He trundled through the match in Pasadena's Rose Bowl, making little impact. In truth, both teams did over 120 minutes.

As with Baggio's masterful performances before the dirge of that 0–0 against Brazil, it often goes forgotten that in the penalty shootout that ultimately defined his career, he was the third Italian to miss. Franco Baresi had skied Italy's first penalty, while the fourth, from Daniele Massaro, was saved by Brazil goalkeeper Cláudio Taffarel. So when Dunga then converted, Brazil were 3–2 up with one penalty left apiece. Had Baggio scored, it might not even have mattered.

Then again, it also might have mattered a lot. Either way, the image of this tortured genius, hands on hips, head down, ponytail limp and drooping, was too poignant to tone down as anything other than one of the World Cup's great tragedies.

"Unfortunately, and I don't know how, the ball went up three meters and flew over the crossbar," he recalled in his autobiography. "As for taking the penalty in the first place, I was knackered, but I was the team's penalty taker. I've never run away from my responsibilities.

"Only those who have the courage to take a penalty miss them. I failed that time. Period. And it affected me for years. It was the worst moment of my career. I still dream about it. If I could erase a moment from my career, it would be that one."

Baggio seemed to spend most of the rest of his career chasing redemption, or at least a chance to put right that wrong.

This is a man who dropped down the league to chase his gnawing ambition for World Cup glory. In 1997, having tanked at AC Milan under his 1994 World Cup boss Sacchi, Baggio shaved off his ponytail, eschewed offers from abroad—including interest from Manchester United—and moved to Bologna in the hope of staying in the national spotlight as a big fish in a smaller pond and hopefully winning a place in the 1998 World Cup squad.

"I want it so badly," he told *Gazzetta Football Italia*, a popular highlights show that brought Baggio to a UK audience in the 1990s. "We all know how things turned out in California and I still haven't accepted it. It's my last chance. That's my one regret, to have lost in that way. Having lost, it makes me return to my childhood [dreaming of winning a World Cup] and I get very angry about it. I almost realized my dream but saw it slip from my grasp."

After more than three years with only fleeting appearances in the side, Baggio was recalled for the World Cup in France in 1998 and did find redemption of sorts, scoring a penalty against Chile in the group stage, although he was confined to cameo appearances for most of the tournament. Post-1998, there was one last crack at a big club with Inter, but with the appointment of Lippi at San Siro the following year, his days were numbered once more.

Off he went again, this time to Brescia, where he twirled and chipped and lobbed and dribbled to his heart's content. He wrote a letter to Giovanni Trapattoni, the latest national-team coach, talking about his burning desire to play in the 2002 World Cup. This time the call and the public clamor went unanswered.

That many greeted that with disappointment reflected his undoubted status as one of the most popular Italian players of all time. As John Foot wrote in *Calcio: A History of Italian Football*: "A shy, reflective family man, he shunned the high living of stars like [Christian] Vieri and [Francesco] Totti, with their model-and-media girlfriends and expensive nightclub and yachting lifestyles. Baggio was a Buddhist in a Catholic country and rarely displayed the histrionics so common at all levels of Serie A.

"He knew what he wanted, but he could also express emotions that seemed to have no place in the modern, cash-dominated game. His decision to play out his final seasons with lowly Brescia allowed him the space and security that he had rarely had in the rest of his career, and he created yet another set of loyal, almost fanatical Baggio followers."

His last cap had come in 1999, but there was to be one more in 2004, a celebration in Genoa of his greatness in a final Italy friendly against Spain. He wore the captain's armband in the second half. A banner in the crowd summed things up succinctly: "Italy loved you, Baggino, but it also obscured and humiliated you."

No Italian has scored more goals for his country in the last 50 years, with Baggio a joint fourth on the all-time list alongside Alessandro Del Piero on 27 goals (from 56 caps). Had he played as many times as his talent dictated, he would certainly have broken Gigi Riva's all-time scoring record. "This game will be the most beautiful memory of my career," Baggio told reporters after taking his bow. "Over the course of a professional career, there are the goals and the victories, but nothing was as beautiful as the demonstration of affection that these people gave me today."

In 643 club career appearances, he scored 291 goals. For a man told at 18 that he would not be able to play anymore because of injury, who missed almost two years in the 1980s because of knee surgeries and by the end of his career needed help getting out of his car after matches, he did pretty well.

For a man castigated, shunned, and unfairly blamed by a succession of managers, he did pretty well.

Without the injuries, he could have been even more. With faith and freedom from certain managers, he could have been even more.

But he was *Il Divin Codino*—and that's all he ever needed to be.

Player name: Roberto Baggio
Born: February 18, 1967
Position: Forward, attacking midfielder
Debut: 1983
Main teams: Vicenza (1982–85), Fiorentina (1985–90), Juventus (1990–95), AC Milan (1995–97), Bologna (1997–98), Inter Milan (1998–2000), Brescia (2000–2004); Italy (1988–2004)
Career highlights: Italy's best player as they reached the 1994 World Cup final. He won Serie A twice and the UEFA Cup in 1993. Claimed the Ballon d'Or in 1993.

38.

Manuel Neuer

Neuer is languid and lithe, and his saves barely make a sound.

A goalkeeping protagonist in three episodes

By Seb Stafford-Bloor

Some believe it should have been a red card. They might have a point, too. It was violent and shocking and might have left one of the players involved seriously injured.

Had it been judged a foul—and a sending-off—then the decade of international football and the many story lines that followed would surely have been different.

But they were not. Germany won the 2014 World Cup final. Argentina lost it. And for Manuel Neuer, there was no red card. Instead, this was an incident that encapsulated so many of the intangible qualities that have made him one of the great goalkeepers of his generation and, unquestionably, one of the finest of all time.

It is the Gonzalo Higuaín moment and it occurred in the 56th minute of that final in Rio de Janeiro.

A long ball forward from inside the Argentinian half bounced toward the German box. It drew Neuer out of his goal, right to the edge of his area, and Higuaín forward to meet him. Nobody who watched the game at the time will need reminding of what happened next. Many will wince at the memory.

For those who did not see it, Neuer barrelled over the top of Higuaín, punching the ball fiercely into the stands and, with his momentum, leaving the Argentinian flat on his back. Broken on the pitch.

It is a difficult moment to recall because it might have left Higuaín seriously hurt. Neuer's knee caught him on the jaw and had the angles been different and the force been ever-so-slightly greater then . . . well, that does not bear thinking about. Higuaín got up and, thankfully, only his pride was irreparably harmed.

But in the abstract, removed from those potential consequences, it captured the sense of invulnerability that has allowed Neuer to remain at the top of the game for so long.

Goalkeepers, by definition, are destroyers. They are there to deny goals and rob football matches of their joy. The nature of their position also means they must remain unmoved by the emotional flows of a game—never too up, never too down. Minute to minute, great saves and terrible mistakes must never spike adrenaline or dent self-confidence.

And is that not Neuer? At least, was that not him in those seconds, with a facial expression that barely registered what had just happened. Watch him after any save. The modern trend is for defenders and goalkeepers to celebrate their critical interventions—and why not?—but there is rarely anything in Neuer's demeanor to describe what he feels minute to minute.

So, these are the anecdotes with which to describe him. Clearly, the binary record of his career is impressive: 124 caps for Germany;

one World Cup win; 12 Bundesliga championships at the time of writing; and two Champions League titles. But none of that explains just how different Neuer is to every German goalkeeper who came before him, who played against him, or who now has a hope of succeeding him.

Sepp Maier was a study of technical excellence. Strong down his right and left side, impossibly agile and with reflexes to die for. But he was orthodox. His techniques—when to use the right hand, when to use the left, and how to collapse into a save and to create a barrier with the body—are all still taught today, nearly half a century after Maier's career ended.

From one Bayern Munich great to another: Oliver Kahn.

Kahn belonged to an era when the bigger a goalkeeper was physically, the better he was presumed to be. Writing in *The Outsider*, his history of modern goalkeepers, the journalist Jonathan Wilson recalled that "so closely did Kahn fit the template of the hulking modern 'keeper that at one point he had to stop going to the gym because his muscle mass was so great it was restricting his movement. Not for nothing was he nicknamed *Der Titan*."

But where Kahn was bulky and imposing, Neuer is languid and lithe. When the former dived, every sinew of his body stretched and the ground would shake when he landed. Neuer's saves barely make a sound.

There is a sharp contrast in presence, too. Kahn was a barker and a bawler. At times it seemed like he chided the ball for coming near him and was intent on keeping it out through force of will. Conversely, Neuer's heart rate never seems to change.

Perhaps that's why, outstanding as they have often been, many of his saves are not easy to recall. Even the most dramatic among them have had a habit of fading into the background. It's why Neuer is best described through his body of work—and by three saves in particular.

In the autumn of 2015, Pep Guardiola's unbeaten Bayern traveled to north London to face Arsenal in the Champions League group stage. They would lose that night, but after an hour the score was 0–0 and Theo Walcott, the capricious forward, found himself alone on the penalty spot, unguarded by defenders and free to put the hosts into the lead.

Walcott's header was firm enough and steered away from Neuer—who had been drawn to his near post—and toward the yawning net. But out jutted a long, left arm within the blink of an eye to claw the ball off the goal line. It was lost to the drama of the night and to yet another false Arsenal dawn under Arsène Wenger, but it was a remarkable save and as good as any made in Europe that season.

It was a reminder, too, of Neuer's unusual physiology and how it perfectly suits his position—his arms with their slightly disproportionate length and his hands large enough to cup around the ball, almost like a baseball glove.

Eighteen months later, in April 2017, Bayern faced Real Madrid at Allianz Arena, again in the Champions League, and Neuer found himself in one of the loneliest positions a goalkeeper could hope to be: alone, with Cristiano Ronaldo shaping to shoot from 10 yards out.

A ball was played across Bayern's box where Ronaldo separated from his marker, shifted his feet in the way that he does, all a blur, and fired his shot fiercely back across Neuer's body, surely toward the net.

No. Neuer flicked out his wrist to slam the door shut and bat the ball away and out to safety.

On first viewing, it looked like he barely moved, as if Ronaldo had simply shot straight at him. On the second, it demonstrated a perfectly efficient movement, trained to produce the quickest reaction time possible. Watched one more time, though, it showed Neuer as the aggressor in the situation.

His response to Ronaldo's shot was disdainful, almost contemptuous, and the slow-motion replays showed how little impact its velocity had on him. There was no trauma on the body at all—as if Neuer were made of iron, not flesh and bone.

If the Walcott save was unusually dramatic, this was more typical—and more indicative of how throughout the course of his career, Neuer produced less a reel of highlights and more a long, drawn-out demonstration of his authority. It was more abstract goalkeeping. It looked a bit strange, it contravened the technical orthodoxy, and it did not seem all that impressive. Yet it was utterly dominant, leaving Ronaldo to trudge forlornly away.

Much of Neuer's greatness could be seen in the effect he had on his opponents. One instance might be more famous than any other.

Three years before that encounter with Madrid, Neuer and Bayern traveled to Old Trafford to face an ailing Manchester United, then under the control of David Moyes. United were adrift following the end of Sir Alex Ferguson's tenure and about to enter a decade of futility, but they were competitive and lively that night. In the first half, Danny Welbeck stumbled past the last Bayern defender and into a one-on-one against Neuer.

Welbeck could be an elegant, technical player, and as Neuer came out to meet him, he dropped a shoulder, feinted to shoot, and tried a delicate chip. It was feeble. Had Neuer not been there, the ball might not have even made it to the goal line. But he was and, springing up from a long-barrier position, he pawed Welbeck's shot away with ease.

In the aftermath, Welbeck would be pilloried. Ignoring that he was a player short of confidence who was never quite assured of a starting place at United, he was criticized for the perceived arrogance of his finish and for choosing style over substance. It was hardly fair, especially given who and what he was facing.

Because if Neuer had a hidden attribute, it was his aura. Across history, great goalkeepers have shared the ability to influence how an opponent behaves. What shot do they choose? How precise do they feel they need to be? How much power must they apply? In Welbeck's case, the other issues he was experiencing were multiplied by the need to be overly precise—to overthink his options. His thought process was altered by the reputation of the player in front of him.

And what a perfect way of approximating Neuer's impact and differentiating him from his peers.

Goalkeeper, by definition, is a reactionary position. They are a passive part of the game and can only respond to what happens around them. They are often bystanders. But Neuer was never that and never subservient in any way. What all the episodes described here share, the commonality between them, is the inversion of a 'keeper's typical role.

Neuer is invulnerable, dominant, and great, but he has also always been a protagonist, which is rarer still.

Player name: Manuel Neuer
Born: March 27, 1986
Position: Goalkeeper
Debut: 2006
Main teams: Schalke 04 (2006–11), Bayern Munich (2011–); Germany (2009–24)
Career highlights: Won the World Cup and the tournament's Golden Glove in 2014. Won the Champions League twice with Bayern Munich, doing the treble in both seasons, and has claimed the Bundesliga 12 times at the time of writing, the second most won by a player. He is credited with revolutionizing the goalkeeping position by playing as a sweeper-keeper.

37.

Andrea Pirlo

Pirlo was the conductor who, from any pitch anywhere, could effortlessly land a ball on a nine-inch circle of the moon.

An afternoon nap, some PlayStation, and a World Cup win

By Phil Hay

The problem as the video rolls is that you can't take your eyes off Roberto Baggio. His first touch is not so much a touch as the swish of a wand, the football melting into his boot and flowing from right to left in midair. Edwin van der Sar scrambles but falls on his face. Baggio jogs past the goalkeeper and slots a shot in, with no apologies given. *Bellissimo.*

But for that, Juventus versus Brescia in April 2001 would be tucked away in the list of games some people saw, very few remember, and nobody ever thinks to revisit. Baggio had been injured for much of the Serie A season to that point. It was the risk he carried. Upon being asked to sign the forward after his under-a-cloud exit from Inter Milan, Brescia owner Luigi Corioni said the most famous ponytail in football was like "cheese on spaghetti." Perhaps he meant Baggio was a luscious garnish. Perhaps he meant Baggio was liable to melt at any time, being 33 and brittle. Both points of view were fair.

Real though his history of injuries was, Baggio's knack of turning it on for posterity had not abandoned him and his equalizer in a 1–1 draw with Juventus is, arguably, the very best 13 seconds of his highlights reel. Baggio, for all his prowess, did not win many trophies. He was criminally underdecorated for one so blessed with skills that can't be taught, but he was singular and part of the birth of 1990s cool. The mesmerizing highlights are his badges of honor.

What happens before Baggio's finish in the April 2001 passage of play, however, resonates as strongly 24 years on.

On the halfway line, a young player has time to look up and scan the pitch in front of him. You can tell he is young because his hair is ruffled and unkempt, more punk-rock style than the sex-god look he will perfect later. He plays a pass forward to Baggio. It's long, it's lofted, and it's on the button, finding the equally intelligent run of an equally intelligent teammate. The connection is new and experimental and the die is cast.

Say hello to Andrea Pirlo, football's ultimate deep-lying midfielder.

This chapter is not about Baggio (you'll find him at number 39), but, intentionally or otherwise, his career and Pirlo's evolution were directly linked. Without one, world football might not have had the other—or not a peak Andrea Pirlo in his exact form, anyway.

Pirlo's loan move to Brescia at the midway stage of the 2000–2001 season was a return home. After turning professional, Brescia had been his first club. In 1998 they sold him to Inter Milan, where chances were very limited. He was 21 and, more relevant in the context of his development, he had grown up as an attacking midfielder, with an expectation of making his name in that guise or as a secondary striker.

It might be that a defining change of role for him was always on the cards—an inevitable product of Pirlo's true skill set—but the pecking order at Brescia left little room at the front end of their starting lineup. A healthy Baggio was an automatic pick as No. 10, all day, every day. The artistry of his goal against Juventus explains why. Brescia also had Dario Hübner, a rugged and fairly prolific striker who notched 17 league goals in 2000–2001. The club were not top-eight material despite them.

If Pirlo's loan wasn't to fritter away, he had to reinvent himself. Or, more accurately, he had to be reinvented by somebody else. His coach at Brescia, the wholehearted and charismatic Carlo Mazzone, is always spoken about by Pirlo as a shining light. "I consider him one of the most important people in my whole journey," Pirlo told *La Gazzetta dello Sport* after Mazzone died in 2023. He felt that way even though he and Mazzone worked together for only half a domestic campaign. "He showed me my new position on the field."

Who can say how much Mazzone's decision to try something different with Pirlo was motivated by the presence of Baggio? All that can be said is that trying Pirlo out in a withdrawn playmaking role—the *regista*, as Italian football has it—proved Pirlo's calling. Some in the squad at Brescia laughed and joked when Mazzone told them what he was planning. It wasn't that Pirlo was short on ability, just that very few people saw a deep position utilizing his strengths. That was, until his performances spoke for themselves.

"He made me understand right away how much he believed in me," Pirlo said in his 2023 interview. The job of holding and orchestrating, lodging him in front of Brescia's defense, was "the turning point of my career. I liked it, especially the way [Mazzone] was able to explain it to me. That's when the spark of a different idea of the game was ignited."

Pirlo the attacking midfielder was gone. It is largely forgotten that he tried to cut his teeth as one. People would instead come to know

Pirlo only as the conductor who, from any pitch anywhere, could land a ball effortlessly on a nine-inch circle of the moon.

Somewhat sadly, Pirlo was never a Ballon d'Or winner; not like Baggio, who claimed the prize in 1993. At no stage did Pirlo make the top three. As with Baggio missing out on European Cups and international trophies, retiring without a Ballon d'Or deprived Pirlo of an honor he would have worn with style.

There were obvious reasons for him falling short. From 2008 to 2017, the voting was a straight-up two-horse race between Lionel Messi and Cristiano Ronaldo. Pirlo also hit his zenith at a time when Spain were in their untouchable phase, dominating the club scene and internationally. Andrés Iniesta had the ball on a string. Xavi, too. They were midfield royalty to the same degree as Pirlo and they were on the winning side when Spain beat Italy in the final of Euro 2012. To derail the Spanish bandwagon that year, Italy boss Cesare Prandelli would have needed 10 Pirlos instead of one. Pirlo in his prime was not enough.

All of the three—Pirlo, Iniesta, and Xavi—comprised football intelligence. Their era was a golden period for midfielders who made manipulation of the ball an art form, orchestrating patterns of play, dictating the tempo of matches, and killing opponents with their passing ranges. Pirlo liked to have fun, to enjoy his craft, but showmanship was not prone to interfering with his productivity.

At 35, he casually pulled the strings in a World Cup win over England, amassing more passes than the opposition's entire midfield combined. Roy Hodgson, the England coach, admitted before that game in Manaus that it was Pirlo he feared; Pirlo he feared but could not negate.

Pirlo was press-resistant and infuriatingly economical with his errors; the textbook decision-maker. Only the very best could get to him and, even then, a battle royale was guaranteed. There is a famous quote attributed to the former Italy goalkeeper Gianluigi

Buffon, who, on seeing Pirlo join him at Juventus from AC Milan in 2011, said to himself, "God exists!" Baggio, his old foil, referred to him as a superstar.

As a result of crossing paths at Brescia, Baggio and Pirlo would be different footballers, but personality-wise, they were on the same plain: both wholly comfortable in the realms of fantasy.

Pirlo's autobiography, first published in English in 2014, was given the title *I Think Therefore I Play* and, as football memoirs go, his is highly atypical. It's short at 150 pages and there's no blow-by-blow account of his life and exploits, but more a stream of consciousness, much of it shunning classic structure, in which Pirlo thinks out loud. He is opinionated, forthright, and almost a little too dreamy, but not a raconteur or a self-publicist in the form of Zlatan Ibrahimović.

It was fitting that when he left Milan for Juventus (on a free transfer, for goodness' sake, after two *Scudetti* and two Champions Leagues), he received a Cartier pen as a parting gift. Call it a miserly present, but in keeping with Pirlo's character, it beat an expensive watch because simplicity was more his thing. "All I'm after is a few square metres to myself," he wrote in his memoir. "A space where I can profess my creed: take the ball, give it to a teammate, teammate scores. It's called an assist and it's my way of spreading happiness."

There is another paragraph, though, that gets much closer to the crux of Pirlo's persona.

In 2006, he and Italy won the World Cup for just the second time since 1938. The final was no gimme: a meeting with Zinédine Zidane and France, a country who had mastered the knack of bringing home the bacon from major tournaments. The tension was ramped up and the contest sat on a knife edge until Italy won it on penalties after Zidane's infamous red card, the bull-charge headbutt on Marco Materazzi. Zidane's rage showed what they mean about keeping your head when all around are losing theirs.

For Pirlo, the final was just another rodeo. *I Think Therefore I Play* could hardly have been more explicit. "I don't feel pressure," he said.

"I don't give a toss about it. I spent the afternoon of Sunday, July 9, 2006, in Berlin sleeping and playing the PlayStation. In the evening, I went out and won the World Cup." The funniest thing? You know it's true.

Fast-forward six years to a different night and a different city: June 24 and the Ukrainian capital of Kyiv. It's the quarterfinal of Euro 2012, the business end of the competition. Italy versus England has gone to a shootout. Italy find themselves in trouble after Riccardo Montolivo's sloppy attempt goes wide of the left-hand post. Pirlo is on penalty three for the Italians. If he does not convert, they are probably cooked.

Coolly and quietly, he has been studying England goalkeeper Joe Hart. Hart's body language is frenetic in the extreme, either an attempt to distract Italy's takers or a giveaway about the nerves jangling in his body. Pirlo deduces that Hart's high electric voltage will compel him to dive one way or the other. Hart is too fired up to stand still, too engaged to stop and think about any tricks Pirlo might play. It is a case of counting cards, of playing the odds, of minimizing risk.

Pirlo walks forward with the ball under his arm and gives it a little spin before placing it on the spot. A few steps back, a lick of the lips, a little sniff, and then showtime. Hart goes early, tumbling to his right. Pirlo all but walks through the ball, barely swinging his kicking leg and floating his penalty into the net, as though no goalkeeper is in front of him. There's no hint of a celebration or any release, just a quick glance at Hart, who is on the deck and avoids making eye contact.

It's the Panenka to beat all Panenkas and the mood swing is extraordinary. England miss their next two penalties. In the blink of an eye, Italy are through. A sleep, the PlayStation, and a world-class moment have become the Holy Trinity. Headlines in the days that follow record how Pirlo's chip swung it.

The audio on UEFA's YouTube highlights of his Panenka is amusing with hindsight. "This is a pressure penalty for Andrea Pirlo," the commentator says as the midfielder strolls up from the halfway line. Except, where Pirlo was concerned, there was no such thing.

Baggio retired three years after playing alongside him. In keeping alive the bloodline of Italian flair, it's safe to say now that the baton passed on. There was no point in asking how Baggio did it or how Pirlo did it. All you could do was sit back and marvel at the mystique, assured that they were born with it.

Player name: Andrea Pirlo
Born: May 19, 1979
Position: Midfielder
Debut: 1995
Main teams: Brescia (1995–98, loan in 2001), Inter Milan (1998–2001), Reggina (loan, 1999–2000), AC Milan (2001–11), Juventus (2011–15), New York City (2015–17); Italy (2002–15)
Career highlights: Won the 2006 World Cup, the Champions League twice, and Serie A six times.

36.

Luka Modrić

Modrić was voted player of the tournament at the 2018 World Cup.

A global Croat, a quiet superstar, a modern great

By Michael Walker

In the summer of 1998, the newly independent nation of Croatia enjoyed a magical sporting month in France. Just under five years after staging its first international fixture as a member of UEFA, a fabulously talented Croatian squad announced itself on the global stage at the World Cup.

Superb players such as Robert Prosinečki, Davor Šuker, and Zvonimir Boban led Croatia through the group stage, then past Romania and Germany, to meet the hosts, France, in the semifinal. Croatia lost narrowly in Paris but won the third-place playoff against the Netherlands.

There was no dispute: As a soccer force, as a country, Croatia had arrived.

Watching this unexpectedly enthralling story unfold back home in the coastal town of Zadar was a transfixed 12-year-old Luka Modrić. His father, Stipe, had been stationed at the nearby airport as part of the Croatian military during the war for independence, and the Modrić family were now housed in temporary accommodation in a hotel.

From there, the impressionable Modrić observed the events in France, game by marvelous game. The Croatian players' overachievement inspired him, and the teenager took note of the reaction around him on Zadar's streets.

"I was impressed by the atmosphere," Modrić said in his 2019 autobiography, "by the euphoria of the grown-ups as they watched our national team's sensational performances. Those emotions are held fast in my memory. Like every boy, I fantasized about experiencing all this as a player."

Twenty years later, Modrić led Croatia to the 2018 World Cup final in Russia as the country's captain and star performer. Ultimately, Croatia lost the final in Moscow 4–2 to France, but the scoreline was not a true reflection of a match in which Modrić was outstanding. He was named player of the tournament, even in defeat.

For a nation of four million people, Croatia's overperformance was again acknowledged by the global game, as it had been since France '98. At its heart was the boy-turned-man who had relished that tournament and never forgot it.

It was also felt deeply within Croatia itself, where football and Modrić have distinct status—he has been named Croatian player of the year no fewer than 12 times at the time of writing. As Andrej Kramarić, one of Modrić's national team colleagues, told *Sportske Novosti* in October 2024: "We will forever admire Luka. He is a gift to Croatia and I doubt that such a Croatian will be born again. We must thank him for everything. He will remain immortal and eternal."

In Russia in 2018, Modrić was approaching his 33rd birthday. He had been a renowned and respected player for 15 years and had a vault full of medals and honors won individually and collectively with Dinamo Zagreb, Tottenham Hotspur, and Real Madrid at club level, as well as with Croatia.

But he was not stopping. Just as his diminutive size as a child did not deter him, nor was age defining him. Plus, the awards kept coming—also in 2018, Modrić received the Ballon d'Or, to end the Cristiano Ronaldo–Lionel Messi duopoly that began in 2008.

Madrid had won the Champions League against Liverpool that May and then came the World Cup. Modrić was able to say, "I felt at peace—like a man who could say he had fulfilled his dreams."

That November came a phone call from *France Football*, originators and organizers of the Ballon d'Or, to say Modrić had won "by a wide margin." After the ceremony in Paris, he flew back to Madrid, where the club had altered training to accommodate him. Modrić walked into the treatment room and the players and physios there "went crazy," he recalled. Modrić was given a standing ovation. It went on and on and, as he said, "Is there bigger recognition than that?"

For all the silverware, the admiration of a player's peers matters just as much, if not more. Modrić has had plenty and deservedly so.

As Goran Vlaović, a member of the France '98 team, put it, "Modrić is still irreplaceable. He is to Croatia what Lionel Messi is to Argentina. One cannot believe that a football player of Luka's age is playing at such a high level. It is phenomenal."

Modrić was 33 by the end of his golden year of 2018. He then appeared at the COVID-delayed Euros of 2020—held in 2021—followed by the 2022 World Cup in Qatar and, although 38, at Euro 2024 in Germany—18 years after he first tasted World Cup football there.

When asked in press conferences if he was thinking of playing at the 2026 World Cup, which begins three months before his 41st birthday, Modrić would not rule it out.

Having celebrated his 39th birthday and moved into his 40th year, still playing for and captaining Madrid as well as Croatia, Modrić kept playing, motivated by his personal fitness and by national pride.

Before a Nations League game against Scotland in Zagreb in October 2024, Modrić discussed the opponents in nationalistic terms.

"You can see a certain patriotism," he said approvingly of the Scots, "and that's what I see, very similar to the Croatian team."

Three days later, Modrić won his 182nd Croatia cap in Poland. It meant that since independence, he had appeared in more than 50 percent of all Croatia's internationals, a startling statistic revealing the scale of his longevity, stamina, and talent. "An almost mystical dependability," as Boban said.

The explanation for this is Modrić's dedication to his profession. Almost every day, and certainly before every Madrid training session, Modrić will be doing lengthy stretching exercises with elastic bands around his legs. The repeated resistance training has brought remarkable resilience; Modrić has been injured rarely and, considering he has played so many games and is a midfielder, Boban's awe is not isolated.

Of all the Croat players Modrić cherished, Boban was, he said, "my idol." A midfielder of touch and presence—and political significance to the new nation—Boban played for AC Milan and was the reason, as a boy, Modrić had a tracksuit with the club's badge on it. Compliments from Boban carry extra meaning for Modrić.

In return, Boban called Modrić "a humble genius" and part of the widespread affection Modrić has generated in two decades at the top of world football has been down to his calm, undemonstrative demeanor. There is no unnecessary drama when Modrić plays. His humility is not an act. He simply passes, moves, and plays the game. After Croatia's elimination at Euro 2024, an Italian reporter at a press conference beseeched him not to retire.

Were Modrić ineffective, his personality would not matter, but he has been operating weekly at the highest levels since first making his name at Dinamo Zagreb.

Saluting the "richness of Modrić's footballing intuitions," Boban said, "Luka and his football: so simple yet so special, so unique and different. The ease and sophisticated geometry, the harmony, the dynamics, the calmness."

• • •

Luka Modrić was born in 1985 in what was then Yugoslavia. He was five when the country was torn apart by civil war and 10 when the conflict ended. The Modrić family experienced some of the worst of the fighting and were displaced to Zadar on the coast, around 30 miles away from their inland home in Obrovac. There, Stipe and Radojka, Modrić's parents, had worked in a clothes factory.

Modrić is named after his grandfather, Luka, a road maintenance worker in the Velebit mountains. In December 1991, Luka Sr. was murdered in the escalating violence. He was 66.

Modrić was six, but he had spent time with his grandfather and the memory lives with him—as he collected that award as player of the tournament at the 2018 World Cup, Modrić said he departed the stage in Moscow thinking of "Grandpa Luka."

"What kind of people can coldly take the life of an innocent old man?" he asked in his autobiography. It is an additional reason why playing for Croatia matters so much to Modrić.

For a while, after moving from Obrovac, the family lived in a refugee camp, before ending up in Zadar. Modrić grew up there. He was quickly immersed in football and wore shin pads with the Brazilian Ronaldo on them. He was rejected by his favorite team, Hajduk Split, for being "too small" but, despite some at Dinamo sharing similar sentiments about his size, Modrić became a professional there, played in Champions League qualifying against Arsenal, and began to be noticed by some of the biggest clubs in Europe.

In the summer of 2007, Modrić, 21, thought a transfer to Chelsea had been arranged for the January window in 2008, but it fell through. He was bitterly disappointed, but a move to London did happen—in April 2008, he was sold to Tottenham.

Juande Ramos was the Tottenham manager when Modrić arrived, but he was swiftly replaced by Harry Redknapp, and under him, Modrić thrived. There were no trophies won by Spurs in Modrić's time, but he developed season on season and was courted by Chelsea again—he was invited onto the yacht of Chelsea owner Roman Abramovich to discuss a move.

Manchester United were also interested. United manager Sir Alex

Ferguson later said of Modrić, "I made him my target in 2011, but Spurs wouldn't sell to us."

Ferguson put Modrić in the same company as three great recent midfielders—"Xavi, [Andrés] Iniesta, and [Paul] Scholes."

Another ambitious club trying to recruit Modrić was Paris Saint-Germain. Modrić made a furtive visit to their then manager, Carlo Ancelotti, at his home.

But it was Real Madrid who won the race for Modrić's signature. He signed for Madrid in August 2012 for $38 million under head coach José Mourinho. Mesut Özil wore their No. 10 shirt then, so Modrić chose No. 19—1 + 9 = 10. He wore that number for five years. The first one of those years was difficult at a club where the scrutiny is as great as it is constant. It was a rare season, 2012–13, for Real Madrid—there was no major trophy secured—and in a fan poll in Spanish sports newspaper *Marca*, Modrić was labeled the club's "worst foreign signing."

But in season two for Modrić, with Ancelotti having replaced Mourinho, Madrid won the Champions League for a historic 10th time, *La Decima*. Along with the Brazilian Casemiro and, later, Germany international Toni Kroos, Modrić became central to Madrid and this was the beginning of a torrent of trophies.

The success at Wembley in 2024 was Modrić's sixth Champions League title with Real—no one in the history of the competition has won more. He has won La Liga four times and the Copa del Rey twice. He has played for Real Madrid, the biggest club in world football, for 13 seasons at the time of writing. He has appeared in more than 500 matches in the famous white shirt and, even as he has aged, Modrić's level of performance has never dropped.

He has lit up major European games with his trademark pass using the outside of his right foot. He has scored wondrous goals the same way.

In October 2024, Modrić became the oldest player ever to represent Real Madrid, surpassing Ferenc Puskás. The club is over 120 years old and has contained some of the greatest players the game has seen. Puskás was one of them; a legendary player. In front of our twenty-first-century eyes, that is what Modrić has become. From *Marca* running a poll mocking him, he transformed their perception. Having gone past Puskás, they called Modrić "the eternal solution."

A global Croat, a quiet superstar, a small giant in midfield—Luka Modrić is a modern great.

Player name: Luka Modrić
Born: September 9, 1985
Position: Midfielder
Debut: 2003
Main teams: Dinamo Zagreb (2003–08), Tottenham Hotspur (2008–12), Real Madrid (2012–25); Croatia (2006–)
Career highlights: Captained Croatia to the 2018 World Cup final and won the Golden Ball at the tournament. Has won the Champions League six times and, to date, claimed 28 trophies at Real Madrid. Won the Ballon d'Or in 2018.

35.
Jimmy Greaves

Greaves was prolific with Chelsea, Tottenham Hotspur, and England.

England's most prolific striker who mastered the art of standing still

By Michael Walker

Goals, goals, goals. And more goals. If ever it is asked what Jimmy Greaves brought to a football pitch, the answer would present itself at the end of the latest dashing run from the sleek, 5'8" forward from east London who scored more goals than anyone in English football's top-tier history. Greaves would glide past the goalkeeper and the net would ripple.

The rest would stand and watch in admiration. It was not merely the number Jimmy Greaves scored; it was how he did it. Geoffrey Green, the renowned sports reporter from the London *Times*, once likened Greaves's smooth, technical goalscoring to "someone closing the door of a Rolls-Royce."

Soft, satisfying, and apparently simple, Greaves made goalscoring look an everyday matter, deceptively so.

Entering professional football in the mid-1950s when a traditional, burly center-forward like Nat Lofthouse was nicknamed the "Lion of Vienna," Greaves was different.

Greaves was both cat and mouse, apparently effortless even amid the rage of big-game action. His movements were economic and balletic. Then came the climax, the goal, often delivered as a pass.

No one in England, not even Dixie Dean or Alan Shearer, has scored more goals than Greaves's top-flight total of 357.

Spotted by Chelsea when playing for London schoolboys at 15, Greaves scored those 357 goals in 516 league games. Add his goals in other competitions and the 44 he scored in 57 England internationals—plus the nine in that all-too-brief episode in Italy with AC Milan—and his career tally was 491 in top-level football.

This was an era of limited protection for strikers and when surfaces were frequently barely fit for purpose. But Greaves, small and light, floated over the ground; that was when he was not standing still, loitering with an intent some misconstrued as disinterest.

"A good centre-forward will attack space," Greaves said of the striker's art and industry. Intuitively, Greaves also understood how to create space by freezing when defenders moved.

It was and remains a contradiction. There were a few of those attached to Jimmy Greaves.

He was the greatest English goalscorer of his generation, but he did not supply the hat trick that won England the World Cup in 1966. Geoff Hurst did that, Greaves having been badly injured in the group stage. He scored all those hundreds of goals but never won a league title. He was the glamorous young player signed by AC Milan who ended up an isolated alcoholic, divorced and alone in a north London bedsit.

Then came a third act, as a hugely popular television personality. It meant Greaves was as famous at 50 as he had been at 20.

"It's a funny old game" was his sardonic catchphrase, and at one time or another, Greaves probably said his was a career of three halves.

Greaves was born in east London in February 1940. His street in Manor Park was hit by a German bomb and the family were moved to Dagenham on the rural edge of the blitzed city. His father, Jim, worked on the London Underground.

In the youth system at Chelsea, Greaves found scoring as easy as he had done in the playground. He scored 122 goals in a single season (1956–57), seven of them coming in a game against Crystal Palace.

The Chelsea first-team manager then was Ted Drake, famous for scoring seven goals himself for Arsenal in a 7–1 win at Aston Villa two decades earlier. As manager, Drake was distant from the youth setup and had never spoken to Greaves, but he congratulated the teenager on his achievement and told Greaves to "cherish it forever. That day will never come again."

In his next game, Greaves scored eight against Fulham.

Even Drake, a difficult man to please, could not ignore what lay in front of him. At 17, Greaves was given his Chelsea debut.

It was against Tottenham Hotspur in 1957 and, naturally, Greaves scored. It was the first in a sequence: On his debut for England in 1959, Greaves scored; on his debut for AC Milan in 1961, he scored; on his debut for Tottenham, also in 1961, he scored a hat trick; and on Greaves's debut for West Ham in 1970, just after turning 30, he scored again.

Greaves was at Chelsea for four full senior seasons. He scored 22 times in 35 First Division appearances in that first season as a boy moving from 17 to 18. In the next season, still a teenager, he supplied 32 in 42, then 29 in 40. In what became Greaves's last season at Stamford Bridge, starting with him aged 20, he scored 41 goals in 40 league games. He was the first player to score more than 40 in a top-flight English league season since his manager, Drake, in 1934–35, and no one since has surpassed Greaves's total.

Yet Chelsea finished 12th in the table in 1960–61, having been 18th the season before. Chelsea could not defend, conceding 191 goals in those two league seasons combined.

Off the pitch, finances were equally troubling and, in 1961, Italy's Serie A ended its ban on recruiting foreign players. Greaves was immediately a target for Milan and an £80,000 transfer was agreed. Greaves, earning £20 a week at Chelsea, was to receive £130 per week plus bonuses in Milan, not to mention a £15,000 signing fee. "It was the stuff of my dreams," he said.

But he was only 21, recently married and he and his wife, Irene, lost their second child, Jimmy Jr., to pneumonia aged just four months. Private turmoil led to professional hesitation and Greaves tried to engineer a way out of the Milan deal. Chelsea even sent a barrister to Italy to negotiate. Greaves went with him but was not allowed in the room, an example of how footballers were treated at the time.

Milan were adamant, however, and Greaves was a player at San Siro. It lasted four months. In that time, he scored nine goals in 10 league games, playing alongside Italy's golden boy, Gianni Rivera.

But Greaves was unimpressed by the defensive football, by the restrictive club culture, as he saw it, and by criticism in the Italian press. When Tottenham manager Bill Nicholson appeared at his apartment in person to orchestrate an exit, Greaves was thrilled. Eventually, a fee of £99,999 was agreed to—Nicholson did not want Greaves to bear the weight of the "first £100,000 player"—and nine sometimes-glorious years at Spurs were underway.

Greaves was adored at White Hart Lane. He was a witty, sharp, quintessential Londoner. As former teammate and later England manager Terry Venables said, "He was a sort of Dickensian type of character, like the Artful Dodger."

He scored 266 goals in 379 Tottenham appearances, but to Greaves it was not all about volume; it was about style and making a material difference. He put a premium on scoring decisive goals, for example, not the third or fourth in a 4–0 win. To an elite footballer—and

Greaves would be in the top 10 English players ever—the opening goal or an equalizer held far greater value.

At the end of his first Spurs season—1961–62 (as Chelsea were relegated)—he scored the opener in the FA Cup final, which Tottenham won.

One year later, in May 1963 in Rotterdam, he scored the opener in the European Cup Winners' Cup final. That was against the holders, Atlético Madrid. Tottenham won that, too, becoming the first English club to win a European trophy.

That was the end of Greaves's first full season at Spurs. He scored 37 goals in 41 league games as the club finished second and they made that European breakthrough. In 1963, Greaves was third in the Ballon d'Or voting, behind Lev Yashin and Rivera.

That season was the third of six when Greaves was the leading scorer in England's top division. As colleagues noted, he would celebrate rarely, just shake a few hands and trot back to the center circle. Sometimes those goals were late in games when up to then Greaves had been peripheral. Suddenly he would become the decisive actor with a velvet intervention that left opponents motionless.

The great Manchester United goalkeeper Harry Gregg once asked the German striker Gerd Müller: "Can you at least try to make it look hard?" Gregg's up-close experience led him to add: "The only one who could compare with him [Müller] was Jimmy Greaves."

The supposed nonchalance was an interpretation Greaves went along with during the bulk of his career.

But a few saw it differently. The perceptive Manchester City manager, Joe Mercer, who had been a fine player for Everton and Arsenal, was assembling a title-winning team at City in the 1960s. Mercer analyzed Greaves like this: "Jimmy is the greatest finisher I have ever seen.

"You can't mark him. The reason: he is prepared to stand still. It takes great courage as a footballer to appear lazy, to look as if you're doing nothing. But then all of a sudden, when the chance arises, Jimmy is gone."

In retirement, Greaves came around to Mercer's view. In a 1984 interview in *The Observer*, British sportswriter Hugh McIlvanney spoke of Greaves's "charming resentment" at being seen purely as a goal-scorer.

"I feel robbed in a way by that reputation," Greaves said. "I feel I was a better player than some people gave me credit for. A lot of them, including other players, thought I was idling about for 80-odd minutes and somehow managing to make myself a hero by scoring an exceptional goal. It was a crazy version of what I was doing.

"To be a goalscorer, you have to work very hard. . . . You need a lot of conviction, moral and physical, to do that job."

Greaves won a second FA Cup with Spurs in 1967—against his former club Chelsea in the first all-London final—which in part made up for his Wembley World Cup disappointment the previous summer.

Greaves's England career had begun in a rush of goals. In his first 20 internationals, he scored 20. He made defenders gulp. There was a hat trick against Scotland in a 9–3 rout in 1961 and four in a friendly in Norway shortly before England's first game at the 1966 finals.

Greaves was selected by manager Alf Ramsey for the first three group games, but in the third, against France, he was cut by a tackle and required 14 stitches. Earlier in the year, Greaves had suffered a bout of hepatitis. He thought he lost some speed and worked hard to get it back.

After France, and though it was not stated publicly, deep down Greaves felt his tournament was effectively over. His instincts were correct. At Wembley for the final, he wore a suit—1966 was the last World Cup without substitutes.

Greaves did later receive a winner's medal, but the morning after the final, as English football basked in its supreme moment, he flew out of the country for vacation.

His absence from that seminal English afternoon was never forgotten. Greaves was 26, an established star and in his prime, yet to onlookers it was as if the first half of his career had ended.

• • •

Now came the second, which featured highs as well as decline and bad decisions in football and his private life. He played only three more times for England, and in 1970, with Spurs fading, he was dropped, then sold to West Ham a month after turning 30.

The 1970–71 season was his last. He kept scoring goals, if at a reduced rate, and West Ham finished third bottom. He retired at 31, which he later realized was premature. He made some small-time comebacks, but his drinking, which had previously been social, upped in tempo. He lost his marriage and spent periods in a nursing home.

Greaves recovered and successfully fought alcoholism and he and Irene reunited. He worked in television for decades.

When he died in 2021, there was an outpouring of affection. He was a national figure. Greaves said ruefully once that the public "only remember the goals," but he was wrong. People recalled his happy smile as well as his happy feet.

Player name: James Greaves
Born: February 20, 1940
Died: September 19, 2021 (aged 81)
Position: Striker
Debut: 1957
Main teams: Chelsea (1957–61), AC Milan (1961), Tottenham Hotspur (1961–70), West Ham United (1970–71); England (1959–67)
Career highlights: Scored a record 357 goals in the English top flight. Won the FA Cup twice as well as the European Cup Winners' Cup in 1962–63.

34.

Dino Zoff

Zoff won the World Cup with Italy in 1982.

Celebratory stamps and card games with the president

By James Horncastle

When Italy won the World Cup in 1982, the Post Office commissioned Renato Guttuso, one of the great neo-realist artists of his era, to commemorate the triumph in the form of a stamp. Guttuso, a Sicilian painter not to be confused with the brutalist expressionism of Gennaro Gattuso, a midfielder and World Cup winner himself in 2006, settled on an image of outstretched arms lifting the golden trophy aloft.

No profile was depicted, but the facelessness of his design did not matter. Everyone knew whom he had chosen as his muse.

The sky in Madrid, where the final in 1982 was held, was not flecked with clouds. Instead it featured the net of one of the goals at the Santiago Bernabéu. The sleeves of the jersey were gray with savoy blue cuffs. They belonged unmistakably to Italy's captain and goalkeeper, Dino Zoff, who at 40 became the oldest player ever to win the World Cup.

A man of few words—"Don't talk for the sake of opening your mouth, don't fool life with adjectives," Zoff wrote in his autobiography—it is easy to imagine him preferring Guttuso's portrait to be incomplete. Zoff thought of goalkeeping as a way of life rather than a position on the pitch. You were part of a team but at a distance. He likened his approach to a farmer watching the field in solitary, concentrated stillness as his crops began to grow.

Zoff grew up on Italy's borderlands. Udine, a barrack town on the Slovenian border, risked being incorporated into Tito's Yugoslavia when he was born in 1942. Zoff's father, Mario, tilled the land. Captured during World War II, he spent time in a German labor camp fixing railway lines and building fortifications against the Russians. When VE Day came, his old man walked home from Austria.

For him, talking was tough. One word was one too many.

When Mario did speak, however, his words carried more weight than a cart at harvest time. Zoff, for instance, recalled a formative experience from his childhood when a flight of swallows were nesting in the eaves of the family barn. Young Dino wanted to knock it down to prevent mites from crawling into the homestead, so one day he went up to the loft and impulsively hung out the window, waving a stick at the nest.

Mario passed below, observed his boy's perilous ill-thought-out position, and taught him a lesson. Zoff needed to straddle the windowsill to be safer and better able to reach the nest. If he had paused and assessed the situation before rushing into it, he would have made a better decision. Zoff lived his life by that simple suggestion.

That he became a goalkeeper, however, was down to someone else on the farm. Zoff's grandmother, Adelaide, looked after him while his father was out in the fields. One of the games she came up with to keep Dino entertained involved collecting prunes. Adelaide used to throw them at Dino for him to catch. Watching him dive to the ground, reaching for the fruit, persuaded his mother, Anna, to unspool a yarn of cotton and knit a goalkeeper jersey with No. 1 on the back.

It wasn't long before Zoff began looking for a club. He cycled about 12 miles to nearby Mariano and started out with Marianese. They called him *il Portierino*—"the little 'keeper." It alluded less to Zoff's age and more to his size. The eggs Adelaide made him for breakfast weren't having an effect. Zoff wasn't growing at the same rate as his peer group. It did not impact his performances at that level—Zoff stood out and scouts quickly got word of his talent—but when they came to watch him, his lack of height was a concern.

Inter Milan's World Cup–winning striker Giuseppe Meazza, who became a recruiter upon retirement, disregarded Zoff, as did Cesare Nay, a former Juventus player.

"You've got what it takes," Zoff recalled Nay telling him. "But we need to see how you develop. You don't have the centimeters."

Fearing his career might be over before it started, Zoff made sure he was not dependent on football. He worked as an engineer in a factory making vehicles for the military. In the meantime, Udinese took a chance on him and Zoff shot up. He made his Serie A debut on an away day in Florence in September 1961. It did not go as well as that of his successor as Italy's greatest-ever goalkeeper, Gigi Buffon, who kept a clean sheet against an AC Milan team featuring a couple of Ballon d'Or winners, George Weah and Roberto Baggio.

By contrast, Zoff let in five goals. There was no social media in those days, so Zoff, then 19, could escape the scrutiny such a bad performance might bring today. He went to the cinema to take his mind off it.

Unfortunately, during the interval, a segment called *Settimana Incom* was projected on the big screen. It showed highlights of the week's events in Italy, including all the goals from Sunday's games in

Serie A. All of a sudden, Udinese's defeat appeared on the big screen. "In the darkness, I sank into my seat, hoping no one would recognize me," Zoff wrote in his memoir. "Then, like a thief, I slipped out of the theatre before the film ended."

Fans cruelly chanted *zuf, zuf, zuf* when he collected the ball, associating him with the poor man's soup of flour and milk Italians ate during the war. But Zoff didn't allow it to affect him for long. He recognized he had not played all that badly in the thrashing by Fiorentina. Instead, he was playing on a poor Udinese team that was struggling against relegation. Serie B ultimately claimed them in 1962.

Mantova plucked Zoff out of the second division and then Napoli came calling. Zoff expected to move to AC Milan, but Achille Lauro, the shipping magnate and politician who backed Napoli, got in the way. Mantova agreed to break their word with Milan, thinking it was too late for Napoli to complete a deal. The transfer deadline passed, but Lauro managed to get someone, presumably a Napoli fan, in the Post Office to backdate the paperwork and the next thing Zoff knew he was on his way south.

Napoli were due to play Independiente in a friendly shortly after the conclusion of the deal. Zoff, on the other hand, was still in Bologna finishing his military service. He jumped in his Alfa Romeo Giulietta Sprint, put the pedal to the metal, and raced down the motorway in order to make his debut. He got to the Stadio San Paolo an hour before kickoff and, with the adrenaline still pumping hard, managed to put in a great display. "Superman is here," the local papers declared in their morning editions.

Naples as a bustling metropolis and Zoff as a reserved farmer's lad did not seem a marriage made in heaven. "Like Rome, it's a liquid city," he observed. "It carries you away in a torrent of overwhelming passion. It distracts you." But personally and professionally, Zoff loved it.

Paradoxically, it brought him out of his shell off the pitch and made him more introspective on it. He was self-aware enough to know that to be a footballer in Naples, you have to show even more focus. It was an exercise in heightened concentration.

Zoff earned the first of his 112 caps for Italy as a Napoli player. It came on the eve of the European Championship in 1968, which he unexpectedly started and won. Zoff remains the only Italy player to claim the two biggest prizes in international football: the Euros *and* the World Cup.

Incredibly, 14 years elapsed between both victories and a lot happened in between. Zoff was bitterly disappointed to be overlooked for the No. 1 shirt at the World Cup in 1970. Enrico Albertosi, a *Scudetto* winner with Cagliari, reclaimed it, and when Zoff controversially left Napoli for Juventus a couple of years later, many suspected the motivation related to the national team.

Juventus were the most successful popular (and unpopular) club in the country. Association with their winning brand made it almost impossible for whoever was the coach of Italy at the time to disregard a Juventus player.

Squads became dominated by *il blocco Juve*. In 1978, for instance, nine of the 22 players sent to the World Cup in Argentina were *Juventini*. Zoff's sale got the Napoli fans on the back of Lauro's successor as owner, Corrado Ferlaino. He was unable to shake them off until he broke the world transfer record to sign Diego Maradona a decade later.

In Zoff's first season in Turin, he won the first of six league titles and reached the European Cup final. Had Juventus beaten Ajax in Belgrade, many think he would have followed Lev Yashin and become the second goalkeeper ever to be awarded the Ballon d'Or. Instead, Zoff finished runner-up to Johan Cruyff. As was the case with Buffon, the European Cup eluded Zoff.

He had to wait a decade to play another final, against Hamburg in Athens in 1983. Juventus, to great incredulity, lost 1–0 again. The core of that team had been part of Italy's World Cup–winning squad only a year earlier. Andrea Agnelli, the scion of Italy's equivalent of the Kennedys and patron of Fiat and Juventus, had added Michel Platini and Zbigniew Boniek to it, too.

Blame was laid at Zoff's door after he was beaten by a Felix Magath shot of improbable trajectory. The columnist Gianni Brera scathingly surmised that Juventus's defeat had been a "question of diopters" (a metric used in an eye test).

Zoff never played again, which was unusual in itself for a generation of Italians who had seen him feature in every single league game for Juventus for 11 straight years (that's 330 consecutive games). A stage play was even made about his backup, Massimo Piloni, on the theme of hopeful and perhaps futile existentialism. It was called *Perseverare Humanum Est*. To persevere is human.

Zoff later coached Juventus, winning the UEFA Cup and Coppa Italia. It was a bittersweet time. His old roommate, friend, and fellow World Cup winner Gaetano Scirea died in a car crash in 1989 in Poland while scouting an opponent. Zoff carried on, but Juventus were changing. The rise of Silvio Berlusconi and the Milan of the Three Dutchmen led Agnelli to restructure the club and find his own Arrigo Sacchi, a former champagne salesman named Luigi Maifredi.

The experiment fell flat and it led Juventus to lose identity. They went nine years without winning the *Scudetto*.

Zoff instead coached and became honorary president at Lazio before becoming the coach of Italy, whom he led to the final of Euro 2000 only to be beaten by David Trezeguet's golden goal for France.

Acidic in his criticism, Berlusconi, by then a former prime minister who would soon return to office, so offended Zoff that he quit. It left a bad taste. Zoff, after all, was and remains a national icon, immortalized in the photo of him playing cards with Italy's president Sandro Pertini, coach Enzo Bearzot, and winger Franco Causio, the World Cup on the table, as they flew back from Madrid in 1982.

Pertini felt he had caused him and Zoff to lose against Causio and Bearzot and wished he'd played his hand as well as his partner had done when using it to stop Oscar in the epic 3–2 win against Brazil.

Years later, correspondence was found in Pertini's personal archive. He had sent Zoff a letter of apology. "Dear Zoff," he wrote. "I will never forget your prowess in the World Cup and your good-naturedness when I, your teammate in a game of scopone on the plane taking us back to Rome, made you lose. . . . Come and see me, we will play scopone and I will try not to make the mistakes you rightly reproached me for. Best wishes my dear Zoff!"

In the end, the Post Office needn't have commissioned Guttuso a piece of artwork, as Zoff's exploits were already stamped on the nation's collective memory forever.

Player name: Dino Zoff
Born: February 28, 1942
Position: Goalkeeper
Debut: 1961
Main teams: Udinese (1961–63), Mantova (1963–67), Napoli (1967–72), Juventus (1972–83); Italy (1968–83)
Career highlights: Won the 1968 European Championship and the 1982 World Cup, as well as Serie A six times, the Coppa Italia twice, and the UEFA Cup with Juventus.

33.
Gianluigi Buffon

Buffon played 176 times for Italy and was a source of reassurance at Juventus.

The goalkeeper who bridged generations

By Will Jeanes

Gianluigi Buffon's footballing journey began and ended at Parma. In the two decades between his sale and eventual return to his boyhood club, the Italian established himself as indisputably the best goalkeeper on the planet and a Serie A and World Cup winner in whose presence forwards were invariably diminished. His was a fairy tale culminating in a homecoming, the kind of wholesome footballing story that stands out almost as too perfect in its conception.

Yet take a step back to survey a glittering career and what truly stands out is his astonishing longevity and all the records and mind-boggling statistics that went with it. Buffon did not revolutionize his position in the way Lev Yashin or Manuel Neuer undoubtedly did, but he remained at the top for so long. That felt exceptional and marks him out as a great.

The raw numbers tell part of the story.

His career lasted almost 28 years—nearly three decades spent at the pinnacle of European football playing in a position given frighteningly little on-field support and where every mistake carries the threat of calamity.

Buffon appeared for Italy 176 times, winning more international caps than any other goalkeeper for any country. His time in the national team spanned more than 20 years—comfortably the longest in the history of the *Azzurri*—beginning in the snow in Moscow in 1997 when a gangly 19-year-old was thrust into the unforgiving glare of a playoff to reach the World Cup and ending in 2018 with a 40-year-old, his beard now streaked with gray, playing in a friendly in Manchester following his country's failure to qualify for that summer's tournament in Russia.

His last appearance in the Champions League came more than 23 years after his first. For context, Vinícius Júnior, who made his debut in the competition at a roughly similar age, will have to be playing in the tournament in 2042 to surpass the Italian. Unsurprisingly, no one can eclipse that time spent in Europe's elite club competition. Only one other man—the Ukrainian Oleksandr Shovkovskyi, a goalkeeper for Dynamo Kyiv—can point to a similar gap of more than 20 years between a first and last appearance. And he was never considered elite in the way the Italian was.

Buffon has played the most games in the history of Serie A (657), won that competition the most times (10), and also enjoyed the longest period without conceding a goal in it—974 minutes in 2015–16, or longer than it takes to drive from Turin to Reggio Calabria on the toe of the Italian boot. Oh, and nobody has ever kept more clean sheets in a single World Cup than the then 28-year-old did (five) when

Italy were crowned world champions for a fourth time in Germany in 2006.

He saved his first penalty in December 1996 and his last in November 2021. The man thwarted that last time was Como's Ettore Gliozzi, born less than two months before Buffon made his first-team debut.

Italy was still using the lire as its currency when Buffon started as a professional, DVDs were yet to be released, and Diego Maradona was still playing football. When he finally retired, the euro had been legal tender for more than two decades, DVDs had come and gone, and Maradona's heir—Lionel Messi—was in the twilight of his own career.

We could go on, but you get the point.

Buffon's staggering consistency, which allowed him to operate at the highest echelons of the world's biggest sport in a unique position for so long, is as much a testament to his brilliance as any highlights reel.

Italy has produced some exceptional goalkeepers over the years, and Buffon, according to our rankings, is the best of the lot, just edging out fellow World Cup winner Dino Zoff. Only Yashin of the Soviet Union stands above him in the pantheon of goalkeepers, and he played his last game in 1970. Buffon has had no equal between the sticks over the last half century.

It all started in 1995 at Parma, then a star-studded team that had already won the Coppa Italia, European Cup Winners' Cup, and UEFA Cup in the 1990s by the time a 17-year-old Buffon made his senior debut. That first appearance for Nevio Scala's side came in November against AC Milan, a team fresh from reaching the Champions League final in each of the previous three seasons and spearheaded by the fearsome front line of Roberto Baggio, George Weah, and Dejan Savićević.

"I was doing my usual round of knocking on the players' doors and when I got to Gigi's room, I asked: 'You're playing tomorrow, what do you think?' He just said: 'What's the problem, boss? That's what I'm here for,'" Scala told *La Gazzetta dello Sport* in 2015. "It was a risk giving him his debut, but Gigi became the best around."

Naturally, the rookie saved from Baggio and Weah on the way to keeping a clean sheet.

His six-year stint in the first team at Parma, incorporating the first 168 Serie A appearances of his career, established his reputation. He returned at the age of 43—after over 700 appearances in the interim for Juventus and, briefly, Paris Saint-Germain—when most footballers are several years into comfortable retirement.

He found the *Gialloblù* a club reborn, albeit competing in Serie B. Declared bankrupt in 2015 and relegated directly to the fourth division, they had rebranded and fought their way back into the elite before dropping down to the second tier at the end of the 2020–21 season. Buffon rejoined that summer and played 26 of the team's 38 games in Serie B, keeping his 500th clean sheet along the way.

That was not his first taste of life at that level. Juventus had been relegated in 2006 as a result of the *Calciopoli* scandal and whereas plenty of his teammates jumped ship, the goalkeeper stuck with them at the lower level. Buffon's loyalty was every bit as impressive as his longevity.

Yet the appearances for Parma are bookends to his brilliance. It is what went on between those stints that saw him heralded as one of the best goalkeepers to have graced the game.

He joined Juventus in 2001 for 100 billion lire, around €52 million, a record fee for a goalkeeper that stood for 16 years. "Juventus went to see me play, thought 'Fuck, this Buffon really is a phenomenon,' and paid a lot of money for me," he said in 2014. "The market determines the price. A good goalkeeper is vital for a good team. Just as valuable as a good striker and sometimes just as expensive."

In Turin, he was a commanding presence, coupling superb shot-stopping ability with an agility that belied his 6'4" frame. He was first choice for 17 years, from age 23 to 40; a period spanning the tail end of the club's time at the Stadio delle Alpi and the move into the new, sparkling Juventus Stadium. He was a stalwart before the scandal brought Juventus crashing down and a mainstay as they clambered back to the top.

Buffon won 22 trophies during his time with *La Vecchia Signora*, including those 10 *Scudetti*. He spanned eras, his concentration unwavering, his imposing presence a source of reassurance.

"Everyone, whether they are a teammate or an opponent, says he makes the difficult things look easy," said Giorgio Chiellini, who played alongside Buffon 428 times for Juventus and Italy, in 2017. "Gigi is an extrovert. He is always smiling and there are no airs and graces about him. He is always a role model for his teammates, both young and old. He is a leader during the big moments in any season, on the pitch and off it. The happy times and the tense moments we've shared before big games are the things that will stay with me the most."

It was not always easy. There was a period in his midtwenties when he suffered from depression, struggling to fill what he called a "black hole of the soul" despite the success he was enjoying on the pitch. He has spoken since of how a visit to an art exhibition, where he lost himself in a painting by Marc Chagall called *The Walk*, helped him find a way out of the darkness. That willingness to embrace vulnerability felt significant.

Yet his performances rarely dipped. His excellence at Juventus was reflected at the international level with Italy. Having watched Gianluca Pagliuca and Francesco Toldo selected as first choice at the 1998 World Cup and Euro 2000 respectively—Buffon was injured just before the latter tournament—he established himself as No. 1 shortly after moving to Turin as a 23-year-old. The next tournament for which Italy qualified and Buffon was not his country's go-to No. 1 was Euro 2020, played in 2021.

He only conceded twice as the *Azzurri* triumphed in Germany in 2006, the first of those a Cristian Zaccardo own goal in a group-stage draw against the United States, the second Zinédine Zidane's chipped penalty in the final. He ranked his save to deny Zidane's header in extra time, shortly before the Frenchman's infamous dismissal for a headbutt, as "one of the most important of my career," if not necessarily the best.

Captaincy for both club and country squeezed even more from him and that desire to maintain standards was reinforced yet further. Every error he made along the way ate at him, even in his years as a veteran. "When I mess up in a game, I feel totally distraught," he told *The Guardian* in 2021. "I am used to expecting the maximum from myself, so if I can't do things perfectly, I feel this huge embarrassment.

"But I need to have my own experiences. I need to mess up. If a person never messes up and never pays the price for it, in my opinion, they will never really understand. It's important to get things wrong in life and it's even more important to pay for your mistakes. If you don't pay the duty, that duty will still be owed to the end. Feeling embarrassment is an essential part of growth. It makes you feel bad, it makes you reflect, it makes you look at the nuances of a situation."

That desire to learn and improve fueled his longevity. "I've admired him since he first emerged as a young, charismatic goalkeeper for Parma in the mid-1990s," said UEFA president Alexander Čeferin when presenting Buffon with a lifetime achievement award in 2024. "Beyond his commanding presence between the posts, his longevity and determination make him an inspiration to football fans worldwide.

"His remarkable consistency across generations might lead many to believe that staying at the top is easy. The fact he chose to follow his club to Serie B during his prime, despite being sought after by top clubs around the world, speaks volumes. Buffon is also one of the first athletes to openly discuss mental health and depression, helping to raise crucial awareness of this issue in professional sports."

Many of Buffon's records seem destined to stand the test of time. So much so that even Cristiano Ronaldo, who seems determined to go on forever, will still have to be playing in 2030 if he is to surpass the length of the Italian's career.

The goalkeeper shared training pitches with a player born in 1958 (Giovanni Galli) and another born in 2005 (Francesco Borriello). He appeared for Italy alongside both Enrico Chiesa and then his son, Federico. Players were born and then retired during the time he stood guard between the posts in professional football.

Through almost all of it, he was playing at the very top of the sport—regularly picking up trophies that in no small part had been won thanks to his match-defining saves, remarkable composure, and ceaseless dependability.

Player name: Gianluigi Buffon
Born: January 28, 1978
Position: Goalkeeper
Debut: 1995
Main teams: Parma (1995–2001, 2021–23), Juventus (2001–18, 2019–21), Paris Saint-Germain (2018–19); Italy (1997–2018)
Career highlights: Won the World Cup in 2006 and conceded just twice in the tournament. Won Serie A 10 times and the UEFA Cup in 1999. Won the French top flight in his only season at PSG.

32.

Romário

"Trying to knock Romário off the ball was like trying to tip over a safe."

The barrel-chested brilliance of a World Cup–winning goal machine

By Adam Hurrey

It is an exclusive club, incorporating Craig Bellamy, Faustino Asprilla, perhaps even Cole Palmer in his own semi-oblivious way. But what unifies the list of footballers with a default facial expression of "not giving a single shit" is the ability to back up their nonchalance.

"I have scored against *every* team, *every* country, *every* defender in the world."

Romário, famously, is not one for forensic statistical proof. The irresistible but futile task of deciding just how many goals he scored in his career—from Eindhoven to Adelaide—has been gamely taken on by FIFA, the supremely diligent Rec.Sport.Soccer Statistics Foundation, and, naturally, the man himself. None of those totals match up, of course, with the confusion crowned in 2008 by Romário releasing a DVD about his life's work of a thousand goals. It featured, he said, "about 900 goals."

Did he really care? Well, enough to be making phone calls to Dutch journalists, 15 years after the event, to ask them if they remembered how many he had scored in PSV's preseason friendlies of the early 1990s.

What there is plenty of evidence for is that between the relentless goalscoring, demolition-job one-liners, and globally renowned refusal to do what he was told, Romário represents a historical line in the sand when it comes to anglophone appreciation of world football. He was, and remains, one of the last great *mystical* Brazilian footballers.

Jorge Valdano, somehow modern football's philosopher laureate but, at the time, Real Madrid's head coach, described Romário back in 1994 as "like a player from a cartoon."

At a slightly top-heavy 5'6", he was a rare physical spectacle. Perhaps it was no coincidence that, alongside the equally barrel-shaped Hristo Stoichkov, Tomas Brolin, and Gheorghe Hagi, it was at the 1994 World Cup that Romário hit his peak. A couple of inches shorter than Gerd Müller, his generational predecessor in many senses, Romário's nickname of *Baixinho*, "Shorty," only added to the caricature. "Trying to knock him off the ball," a curious *Washington Post* reporter observed during that tournament, "is like trying to tip over a safe."

Romário's road to that World Cup was not easy. His final international tally of 55 goals in 70 games disguises an astonishing stretch of nearly four prime years, an entire World Cup cycle, without scoring for Brazil. After the goal that crowned his nation as South American champions in 1989, Romário watched the majority of Italia '90 from the bench, was left out of squads for the Copa América in 1991 and 1993, and then missed the first seven games of Brazil's stuttering qualification campaign for USA '94.

This was not because of his form. Between scoring for the *Seleção* against Venezuela in 1989 and Uruguay in 1993, Romário amassed 102 goals in 115 games for Dutch club PSV Eindhoven and a hat trick on his debut for Barcelona. Those few electric seasons, during a transformative time for a game about to embrace the back-pass law and the Champions League, framed him as an *inter*generational talent. Squeezed in between the reigns of Marco van Basten and Ronaldo, Romário was the best striker in the world.

Plenty of players have treated the Dutch top flight like a playground, but Romário—despite taking an instant dislike for the cold weather and, curiously, the applesauce—was toying with Eredivisie defenders from the very start. In 2024, PSV's YouTube channel ranked his 40 best goals. Down at No. 38, in a 6–0 win over NEC Nijmegen in February 1990, was Romário flicking up a cross with his thigh, popping the ball over the flailing torso of the goalkeeper and then volleying into an empty net. Impudence met sheer economy. Those three touches were made within 1.8 seconds.

Romário was big on economy. "There were days when he was pathetically lazy," Bobby Robson, his manager for two seasons at PSV, told *The Observer* in 1994, "but you had to pick him because, if you left him out, you might miss a hat-trick! Romário, to be frank, is just on another planet . . . he's a quite extraordinary finisher. He could get the ball past a goalkeeper from angles which would make you say, 'How did he do that?'"

Even if PSV wouldn't come close to matching their treble-winning European champions of 1987–88, Romário took intermittent advantage of the continental shop window, joint top-scoring in the European Cup in 1989–90 and the Champions League in 1992–93.

A perfect hat trick against Steaua Bucharest in 1989 was sealed with a 50-yard run and an emphatic feint to put goalkeeper and defender on their simultaneous backsides. Another hat trick against AEK Athens in 1992 was pure Romário: two first-time toe-pokes and then a showboating third after lobbing the ball over a defender's head and yet another goalkeeper's despairing body. His final Champions League goal for PSV—flicking the ball up twice with his back to goal before swiveling to volley into the far top corner against AC Milan—was not the sort being scored by anybody else in Europe.

"Let no one be surprised," wrote Catalan novelist Manuel Vázquez Montalbán in *El País* in 1993, "if Spanish football goalkeepers carry a notebook and a pen with them and, once Romário has scored a goal, they ask for his autograph and blessing."

Like Diego Maradona a decade before him, Romário in Barcelona's No. 10 shirt just looked intensely perfect, the number dominating his back and shoulders. But Romário could not be dominated. Not by the competition for places among foreign players at the Camp Nou, enforced by La Liga and UEFA's quotas; not by the explosive ego of new teammate Stoichkov; and certainly not a home debut in front of 100,000 expectant fans.

Against Real Sociedad, Romário scored an immaculate hat trick, the third goal of which was a majestic, luxurious, casual, obnoxious, side-footed, volleyed lob after taking a Pep Guardiola pass on the chest without breaking stride. In the Eredivisie, his goals looked like training exercises; at the cavernous Camp Nou, they now had scale.

In 1993–94, Romário scored five La Liga hat tricks, finishing six goals ahead of Davor Šuker. But there is one Barcelona goal from that season—perhaps even the one goal above any other of his entire career—that encapsulated everything about him, physical and emotional.

The *cola de vaca*, the "cow's tail," was pure Romário: straightforward, simple even, but irresistible and devastating. History should remember what Romário did to Real Madrid's Rafael Alkorta that night in the same way it has enshrined Ferenc Puskás's drag-back against Billy Wright at Wembley in 1953 and Johan Cruyff's eponymous twisting of Jan Olsson's blood in Dortmund in 1974.

Less than half an hour into that season's first La Liga *Clásico* against Real Madrid, Guardiola found himself 35 yards from goal but without a white shirt near him, the entire Madrid defense and midfield sitting, timid and narrow, on the edge of their own penalty area. Options presented themselves left and right, but Romário was poised in the eye of the needle, arms stretched down in front of him in that universal gesture of wanting the ball to feet.

Alkorta had already glanced over his shoulder twice to check Romário was there, before feeling compelled to jump out in an aborted attempt to close Guardiola down, then visibly panicking—one more desperate glance—and backpedaling toward his man again.

That palpable anxiety was because Alkorta had done his homework. If Romário wasn't running in behind, he'd want the ball to feet to go one-on-one with his marker. Guardiola knew it, too: He'd provided the passes for all three of Romário's goals on debut. Alkorta stood off, about three yards. That was his head start.

Romário cushioned the ball with his right instep, broadened his stance in anticipation of a challenge . . . but Alkorta stayed where he was. What happened next was less stunning than the Cruyff Turn of 20 years earlier but smoother and deadlier. Within 0.95 seconds of his first touch, Romário had used that same instep to whip the ball round his body, 180 degrees, employing the physics of an egg-and-spoon race but, crucially, with a $4 million spoon. By the time Romário took his third touch, a clinically stabbed toe poke into the far corner, he had taken six yards out of Alkorta with a puff of the cheeks and the squat acceleration of a 60-meter sprinter.

Romário's other two goals that night—of a hat trick in a *Clásico*—remain a mere footnote.

September 1993. Having been cast aside by Brazil's coach, Carlos Alberto Parreira, who was now facing an injury crisis, Romário was back. His last goal for Brazil at the Maracanã had been the winner in the deciding match of the 1989 Copa América against Uruguay. This time his job was to dig Brazil out of their World Cup qualification hole. Defeat to Uruguay would mean elimination.

"I already know what's going to happen: I'm going to finish Uruguay."

Brazil bombarded the Uruguayans for 72 minutes, until Romário met a cross at the back post with a downward header. Ten minutes later he raced through, poked the ball past the goalkeeper, and rolled it home. "They call me the saviour of the nation," he said afterward. "Well, I saved it."

From unfavorable to undroppable. By the time Brazil had reached the World Cup final in 1994, Parreira had fully relented. While the rest of the squad trained, Romário relaxed in the pool. "Let him do what he wants," Parreira said. "He can win the title."

Was this Parreira in sudden awe of the weapon he had at his disposal or a weary acceptance of Romário's immovable ego? Perhaps it was a bit of both. "I want a window seat on the plane," Romário told national television as Brazil prepared to embark for the USA. "And I'll sit next to whomever I want to."

Some patience was in order: Romário's father, Edevair, had been kidnapped just weeks earlier, with a $7 million ransom demand, prompting police in Rio de Janeiro to deploy 1,200 officers in the search before he was freed.

"Romário's weakness is that he seldom will go searching for the ball," wrote the *Los Angeles Times* in 1994, "but when it comes to him, he can be devastating. 'I stand there,' he says, 'pretending I am dead.'"

As USA '94 kicked off with Diana Ross's infamous profligacy in front of goal, Romário was in his full minimalistic mode in the group stages: a toe poke from a corner against Russia, a toe poke after racing through against Cameroon, a toe poke from the edge of the box against Sweden. His five goals were enough to win the Golden Ball—if not match Stoichkov and Oleg Salenko for the Golden Boot—and propel Brazil to a goalless final with Italy.

In the shootout, after trying to place the ball in front of the spot, Romário trotted up and clipped his penalty in off the post. Three and a half minutes later, Roberto Baggio's world collapsed and Brazil were world champions.

Baggio somehow regathered himself to enter a jubilant dressing room afterward to ask for Romário's shirt. "It was a matter of admiration and respect I had for him," Baggio explained. "The fact that I lost the World Cup didn't change my perception of him. Until today, I still feel the same respect and admiration."

As the focal point of Brazil's World Cup, Romário was an inevitable choice for FIFA's World Player of the Year award in 1994 and would likely have taken Stoichkov's Ballon d'Or, for which non-Europeans finally became eligible the following year. Such awards in World Cup years take on a symbolic feel, but this was no afterthought. Romário was the finest goalscorer in the world. And he knew it.

"This is my World Cup. Nobody is closer to the yearning of the Brazilian people. Nobody is more likely to fulfil their dreams."

Arrogance was simply in Romário's DNA.

Cruyff's Barcelona embarked on their 1994 preseason without him while he took in daily sessions of beach foot-volley back in Rio. "I'm sure they'll understand," he said. Cruyff did, briefly, but Romário was on his way out of Barcelona by January 1995.

And so, at 29, began the long tail of Romário's warped career path: 14 more years, eight clubs (including four flounces between Valencia and Flamengo in as many seasons), five continents (the glaring singular in the "Romário Adelaide—Skills & Goal" YouTube compilation says it all about his four A-League appearances), an intermittent and unstable strike partnership with the infamously volatile Edmundo . . . and around 450 more goals, depending on the generosity of the source of your data.

Football's fabled "yard of pace" has done for many a striker in their later years, but the way Romário's game parachuted into early-forties pedestrianism felt entirely on his terms. He was still standing, still pretending to be dead. One goal, toe-poked into the far top corner from an acute angle for Flamengo against Corinthians in 1999, seemed to take place in slow motion, save for a near-subliminal *elastico* against defender and former gravedigger Amaral. "He's still looking for the ball today," Romário deadpanned 17 years later in a commemorative post on Facebook, where he continues to upload grainy videos of his most impudent penalty-area conquests.

Romário was no mere goalscoring robot. One notable show of emotion was a tearful press conference after Mário Zagallo left him out of Brazil's 1998 World Cup squad. But that "so what?" look on his face persisted until he finally scored his "1,000th" goal, a penalty for Vasco da Gama in 2007. Romário was unapologetic about his methodology, counting goals from when he was 13 years old, in charity games and training-ground friendlies.

If there is a definitive image of Romário, it is not the sight of him kissing the World Cup trophy or wheeling away in celebration with arms outstretched. It is a photo from January 1994 on the beach at Barra da Tijuca in Rio, not long after he had been sent off for punching Diego Simeone in the face 5,000 miles away, standing defiantly for the camera. And wearing a tiny yellow Speedo.

Player name: Romário de Souza Faria
Born: January 29, 1966
Position: Striker
Debut: 1985
Main teams: Vasco da Gama (1985–88, 2000–2002, 2005–06, 2007), PSV Eindhoven (1988–93), Barcelona (1993–95), Flamengo (1995–96, 1997 on loan, 1998–99), Valencia (1996–97), Fluminense (2002–04), Miami FC (2006); Brazil (1987–2005)
Career highlights: Won the World Cup in 1994, winning the Golden Ball at the tournament. Won Copa América in 1989 and 1997. Won the Dutch top flight three times and La Liga once.

31.

Ruud Gullit

Gullit was a key performer as AC Milan became the best team in Europe.

A Haarlem globetrotter who reveled in being different

By Michael Walker

There was a day early in 1977 when a man called Barry Hughes knocked on the door of the Amsterdam home of George Gullit. Hughes was a charismatic Welshman who had arrived in the Netherlands as a player in the 1960s and stayed on to become a manager. He was standing there at Gullit's door—unannounced—on behalf of the small Dutch club Hughes coached, HFC Haarlem. He asked if he might be able to sign Gullit's teenage son.

George Gullit looked Hughes up and down and said no. There were other clubs interested in his son, Ruud, including, across the city, Ajax, who had been champions of Europe three times that decade.

But it was not an outright rejection: Hughes was told that if he returned at the same time on the same day the following year, Gullit would think again.

Hughes left disappointed, but he was not put off by the unusual challenge. He decided to wait.

One year later, on the same date at the same time, Hughes was back outside the same door. He knocked again.

This time, the answer was yes.

And so it came to pass that Ruud Gullit, one of the greatest Dutch footballers of all time, a standout player of his generation and a future Ballon d'Or winner, started his glorious career at little HFC Haarlem, around twelve miles from Gullit's home in Amsterdam and several other measurements away from that club on his doorstep, Ajax. He was 15.

"The story is real, not a myth," says Edwin Struis.

On what remains of HFC Haarlem's old pitch, in front of the lone disheveled stand at the dismantled stadium, Struis declares the truth of Gullit's unlikely Haarlem origin story. He was a young local fan who saw Gullit make his Haarlem debut aged 16 in August 1979. Struis later became a sports journalist in the Netherlands, reporting often on Gullit as he progressed from athletic teenager into one of the most revered footballers in Europe.

"It was typical of Barry Hughes," Struis says of the door-knocking story. "Barry was a man of imagination. Exactly one year later at the same time! Ruud was in the Dutch youth team, so not only Barry saw him. But he lured Ruud to Haarlem. Ruud's father thought it was fantastic.

"Ruud's debut was against MVV of Maastricht. He was at centerback. He was 16, so it was an attraction for us fans to see him play. He did well in that first game against MVV, but there were only about 5,000 here—the capacity was 18,000, but it never reached that number. Of course everyone today says they knew he'd be a star, but we didn't really. Yes, it was exceptional to see a 16-year-old play and he was a talent; physically big at 16, a presence.

"But the team were relegated in that first season and he went down with them. So he had to develop himself the next season, at 17, and he did."

Haarlem were promoted back to the Eredivisie and in 1981–82 finished fourth, qualifying for Europe. Gullit would soon be gone, but he had left indelible memories on the small club, which sadly folded in 2010.

"In Ruud's third season here," Struis says, "well, that was *his* season. He was growing. He was very strong. We saw we had the beginning of a diamond. He played everywhere. The whole pitch was his."

The ability to consume yardage was a strength that came naturally to Gullit, who could already feel his power was more suited to big-pitch professionalism than the street football of his youth in the Jordaan—the "garden" of Amsterdam. "In those tiny playgrounds in Amsterdam, I wasn't the star," Gullit wrote in his 2016 book, *How to Watch Football*. "On a real pitch, I found playing much easier. I was big for my age and there was plenty of space to spring past everyone with my long legs.

"I ran my way into all kinds of teams, from Amsterdam's juniors to the Dutch youth team, I just kept on running past everyone. The Netherlands were known in those days for technically refined combination football. I was different."

Being different. It was not only Ruud Gullit's Haarlem provenance that contrasted him with peers such as Frank Rijkaard, who came from the same Amsterdam area as Gullit. Whereas Rijkaard joined Ajax, Gullit went to Haarlem by scooter, train, and bus and moved on to Feyenoord and PSV Eindhoven, Ajax's—and Amsterdam's—Dutch rivals.

Then there was the uncommon sight of a poster of Austrian striker Hans Krankl on Gullit's bedroom wall and, rather more significantly,

Gullit's "winning mentality." It went with his big, winning smile but did not fit Dutch football culture with its prioritizing of style.

Plus, of course, there was Gullit's color and his dreadlocks. He became Holland's "Black Tulip," itself a reference to difference.

Gullit was painfully aware of racism from the moment, aged 14, an Amsterdam police officer used the n-word toward him. It was not the last time he would encounter racism.

Gullit was an only child. His Dutch mother, Ria Dil, who worked as a cleaner at the Rijksmuseum, was white and his father, George, had come from Suriname, a Dutch colony in South America. He was an economics teacher. Gullit was initially Rudi Dil until around 14, when he changed to his father's surname since he thought "Ruud Gullit" sounded more like a footballer.

In the 1980s, Gullit was a prominent anti-apartheid campaigner and supporter of Nelson Mandela, then incarcerated by the oppressive South African government. When Gullit was awarded the Ballon d'Or in 1987, he dedicated the trophy to the imprisoned Mandela, a gesture that made headlines worldwide and which, when free, Mandela recognized.

Simultaneously, as Gullit has said, he also found acceptance within football and the Netherlands. When the country won its one and only major trophy—the 1988 European Championship—Gullit was captain.

He may have looked different, taken a different path, played differently, and approached the game differently, but Gullit was definitely Dutch—he recalled that in 2004 when he was managing Feyenoord and things were going wrong, the criticism from fans in Rotterdam did not mention his race. To them, Gullit was "that Amsterdammer."

By then he was approaching his mid-40s, but at Feyenoord, he was still remembered as the player who arrived from Haarlem in 1982, not yet 20.

In Gullit's first season, he helped shift Feyenoord from sixth place to second and in his second season at the De Kuip stadium, 1983–84,

Feyenoord were champions of the Netherlands for the first time in a decade. The Dutch Players' Player of the Year award was not started until 1984. Gullit was its first winner.

That was all the more remarkable because in his second season at Feyenoord, Gullit was joined by Johan Cruyff. Cruyff was the ultimate Ajax man, but, angered by their refusal to give him a contract at 36, Cruyff moved to Amsterdam's greatest opponent. Amid the Eredivisie angst, the two gelled.

Having started at Haarlem as a central defender under Hughes, Gullit was moved to center-forward by their next manager, Hans van Doorneveld. At Feyenoord, Gullit was played wide on the right in a 4-3-3 formation and was told by Cruyff to "keep the game wide." As "Cruyff's will was law," Gullit did as instructed and, as well as the Eredivisie, Feyenoord won the Dutch Cup. Ajax, and Haarlem, were beaten along the way.

Gullit scored 25 goals in 45 appearances for Feyenoord that season, but 1984–85 was injury affected and the team slipped to third.

Quietly, another transfer was in motion. When Eindhoven took the Amsterdam man from Rotterdam, there was outrage. Gullit was called a "wolf," which in Dutch football means greedy, and he was pelted with bananas when he returned to play at De Kuip. Cruyff, Gullit said, had warned him it would be this way because Gullit was now considered "someone special, the great footballer with a huge personality." He was not yet 23.

But he was a major Dutch player, a Netherlands international since a debut on his 19th birthday, alongside Rijkaard, and on his way to 66 caps. And in Eindhoven, again, Gullit's impact was quick.

PSV had been pushed into the shadows by Ajax and Feyenoord, but with Gullit, they won the Eredivisie in his first season.

It was the first of four consecutive Dutch titles and Gullit scored 22 league goals the next season. His influence went beyond matches. He argued PSV's red shirts, black shorts, and red socks were drab. At Gullit's suggestion, the club changed to red shirts, white shorts, and white socks, with Gullit saying "we felt bigger and stronger." He later accepted his behavior was "a little overzealous." It illustrates the influence of his personality at that time.

His authority stemmed from performance. In his first PSV season, Gullit began in defense, from where he scored 15 goals, then moved forward and delivered another nine to clinch the title as PSV lost just one game. "Adaptation," he said, "is a theme that runs through my career."

Theoretically, a move out of Dutch football to Italy would have seemed problematic given the tight, defensive football of Serie A, but Milan paid 16.5 million guilders (€7.5 million) for Gullit in 1987. It was a world-record fee, beating the previous sum paid out by Napoli for Diego Maradona.

Milan signed Gullit's international colleague Marco van Basten that same summer, but Van Basten was injured early in 1987–88. It meant Gullit was placed beside Pietro Virdis by coach Arrigo Sacchi in a 4-4-2 formation. Milan started winning and took their first Serie A title in nine seasons.

"Once again I had to adapt," Gullit said. For his play at PSV and Milan, he was voted the Ballon d'Or winner in 1987.

It was a period of immense personal and collective achievement. In Gullit's second season, Milan won the European Cup for the first time in 20 years and they retained the trophy in 1990. There were two more league titles as Milan became the best team in Europe. Over the course of Gullit's seven seasons at San Siro, he also took pleasure in changing how Milan played. "In the end, we managed to shake off Italian orthodoxy. Chasing goals became our new tactic."

There was the odd criticism, Cruyff comparing Gullit unfavorably to Rijkaard in a 1987 interview. "Because Gullit is an extrovert, instinct is a large part of his game, whereas Frankie, how shall I put it, always wants to play thoughtfully."

A year later, Gullit and Van Basten were joined in Milan by Rijkaard and an indication of their success was seen in the Ballon d'Or voting for 1988—Van Basten won it, Gullit was second, and Rijkaard third.

The Milan trio were the new emblems of Dutch football and cemented their place in the country's football history by winning Euro

'88, held in West Germany. Gullit scored the opening goal in the final against the Soviet Union. Van Basten volleyed the unforgettable second and was the tournament's star. Gullit, not shy of his own ability, saluted Van Basten, saying, "My own role was modest, despite being the captain. I was exhausted, broken after that intense first season at Milan. I put my ego on hold."

Dutch fans celebrated in their millions in Amsterdam and many wore Gullit dreadlocks wigs. He was delighted.

Gullit played in the Netherlands' comparatively underwhelming efforts at the 1990 World Cup and Euro '92. He retired from international football in 1993, but agreed to return for the 1994 World Cup. Then, in the camp before the squad's departure, Gullit made public his disagreement with new national coach Dick Advocaat's tactics and walked out. He was 31.

Teammates such as Wim Jonk did not feel as if Gullit had put his ego on hold.

"It's never nice when a player leaves the national team," Jonk told reporters at the tournament. "All the less so when he walks out the way Gullit did. He just said, '*Ciao*, goodbye, everybody.' If Ruud had behaved like the great star we all knew he was, he wouldn't have gone like that." It is perhaps why, in the Netherlands, despite Gullit's list of achievements, a certain ambivalence remains. Or maybe it was his running football or club history. Or being different.

There was a spell at Sampdoria after Milan and yet another trophy, the Coppa Italia (won when on loan at Sampdoria ahead of moving to the club permanently), before Gullit joined the foreign-player surge into English football's new, lucrative Premier League by signing for Chelsea, where he later became manager. He was a hugely popular figure in England, where his style and smile were admired, just as they had been all those years before at HFC Haarlem, once Barry Hughes had knocked on the door, waited, and knocked again.

Player name: Ruud Gullit
Born: September 1, 1962
Position: Forward, midfielder, defender
Debut: 1979
Main teams: HFC Haarlem (1979–82), Feyenoord (1982–85), PSV Eindhoven (1985–87), AC Milan (1987–94), Sampdoria (loan 1993–94, 1994–95), Chelsea (1995–98); Netherlands (1981–94)
Career highlights: Won Euro 1988 with the Netherlands and claimed two European Cups while at AC Milan. Won the Dutch top flight three times and Serie A three times and was awarded the Ballon d'Or in 1987.

30.

Carlos Alberto

Carlos Alberto slides in to dispossess Italy's Sandro Mazzola in the 1970 World Cup final.

The greatest World Cup goal of all time

By Tim Spiers

Some World Cup goals define a specific tournament, like Pelé's chest, flick, and volley for Brazil against Sweden in 1958.

Some World Cup goals might define a tournament and that player's entire career, à la Marco Tardelli's strike and celebration in the 1982 final for Italy versus West Germany, or Diego Maradona against England in 1986 (either goal, to be fair).

Only one goal in the history of the game, though, can lay claim to defining not just a solitary World Cup, but perhaps even the World Cup, full stop.

You could also make a case for this goal defining a team, a footballing nation, maybe the entire sport itself.

"Tostão . . . Piazza . . . Clodoaldo . . . Pelé . . . Gérson . . . oh this is great stuff. They seem to take it in turns to give an exhibition. Jairzinho, No. 7 . . . Pelé . . . up comes Carlos Alberto on the right . . . and it's four! Oh, that was sheer delightful football!"

No commentary can do true justice to Brazil's enchanting fourth goal against Italy in the 1970 World Cup final in Mexico, but Kenneth Wolstenholme's comes close.

Ask your average football fan, particularly of a certain age, for a goal that characterizes the meaning of the beautiful game and there's a decent chance they'll say that Brazil goal. Carlos Alberto would be asked about it for the rest of his life and it seemed he never tired of reliving that golden moment, the finishing touch on the most famous Brazilian carnival of all.

"If I had to choose one moment to encapsulate my career, that would be it," he once told FIFA.

Not only did he score that most perfect of goals, the last of the 1970 tournament that has long been considered a high-water mark for the international game in terms of flair, quality, and entertainment (mostly provided by Brazil), but Carlos Alberto also captained the side. In a team heaving with so much lavish talent, he lifted the trophy. He was 25.

Born in 1944 with a twin brother, Carlos Roberto Torres, Carlos Alberto grew up in Vila da Penha, a northern suburb of Rio de Janeiro, and was a rising football star from a young age. He breezed through junior levels and was already cemented as Fluminense's first-choice right-back aged just 19. At the same age, he was already in the Brazil squad, making his debut marking Bobby Charlton at the Maracanã in 1964. Brazil beat England 5–1 and Carlos Alberto soon became a regular.

Two years later, his reputation as one of the best attacking right-backs in Brazilian football was reflected in his move from Fluminense to Santos, in the process becoming the most expensive player in the country's history. At his new club he became a teammate of Pelé. The fee was 200,000 cruzeiros and confirmed Carlos Alberto's status as not just one of the next big things in Brazilian football, but already one of its best players.

He was a competent if not perfect defender, but the vision of him gallivanting up and down the right wing to pierce opposition defenses was one of the most familiar and exciting in the domestic game at a time when full-backs whose principal aim was to attack were still a rarity, even in Brazil.

On the global stage, he would go on to become one of the world's first attacking, overlapping full-backs. Many expected that breakthrough to come in 1966 at the World Cup in England. In that context, there was considerable surprise when the man who had broken the national transfer record was not selected in Vicente Feola's 22-man squad. The head coach essentially struggled to whittle down from 44 players and played it safe, going with experience. A 32-year-old Garrincha was one of six over-30s in the squad, which included 37-year-old right-back Djalma Santos. The latter effectively took Carlos Alberto's place.

However, with Brazil and Pelé (literally) kicked out of the group stage in England, the discarded defender was soon restored to the side as Brazil looked to rebuild ahead of 1970.

In fact, in a remarkable about-turn, he was also handed the captain's armband. He had just been made captain at Santos, which at one point had seven players in the Brazil side and were considered one of the best teams on the planet. Their status undoubtedly helped Carlos Alberto's cause, as did his close friendship with Pelé—something that remained true throughout his life.

He was a calm captain who eschewed rabble-rousing pre-match rants in favor of prayers. He would encourage his teammates with almost incessant positivity, offering reminders of their duties along the way.

Carlos Alberto and Brazil's preparations for the 1970 World Cup in Mexico were meticulous. While they had the flair, the brilliance, and the magic, they had fallen behind the Europeans physically. But under the guidance of new boss Mario Zagallo, they trained hard, ate well, moved to Mexican time weeks before heading out, and even cut down on their smoking. Carlos Alberto himself went down to two a day; one at the start of the day, one at the end.

However, in their warm-up matches for the tournament, things weren't quite gelling and it was the right-back who in part was responsible for instigating a chain of events that would lead to him capping the most famous World Cup victory of all time.

He, Pelé, and Gérson—the squad's three senior players—held a meeting after a distinctly underwhelming 3–1 warm-up win over Atlético Mineiro, with Brazil booed off. They relayed their ideas to Zagallo: that the team should play without a proper center-forward and have Pelé adopt a slightly deeper role, interlinking with Tostão, with Jairzinho and Rivellino attacking down the flanks. Crucially, Clodoaldo would add protection in midfield alongside Gérson, leaving Carlos Alberto free to overlap the floating Jairzinho in a very loose 4-4-2. *Loose* being the operative word.

It worked. Brazil won all three of their group games, beating Czechoslovakia 4–1, a very good and stubborn England side 1–0, and Romania 3–2, before two-goal victories over Peru (4–2) and Uruguay (3–1) in the quarters and semis.

The final against Italy was a perfect contrast of creativity versus pragmatism, summed up by the Italians' decision to leave playmaker Gianni Rivera out in favor of an extra defensive player.

Carlos Alberto was confident he would lead his team to victory, not least because Italy's semifinal against West Germany had gone to extra time. But also because he was a key part of their attacking game plan, which involved dragging the Italian defense to the right side of the pitch, especially left-back and captain Giacinto Facchetti, who was tasked with marking Jairzinho, leaving space for Carlos Alberto to exploit. That sounds vaguely familiar.

Brazil's hope that Italy would tire rang true. The game was finely poised at 1–1 on 65 minutes, but 20 minutes later it was 3–1 and effectively over. Italy's players were walking. Brazil's were dancing.

Enter Carlos Alberto, in his words.

"I remember everything about that goal," he told the BBC in 2006. "We knew before the game it could happen because we knew how the Italian team played. They played man-to-man on the central line. They followed our forwards. And our coach, Mario Zagallo, said to Jairzinho: 'Always, if it's possible, make a movement to the left side to bring Facchetti with you to make space for Carlos Alberto to go forward.'"

When defensive midfielder Clodoaldo did his completely out-of-character dribble past four knackered, helpless Italians, in the manner of a father toying with his kids in the garden, Carlos Alberto, himself heavy-legged, started to creak forward. Jairzinho had drifted from the right flank to the left and brought left-back Facchetti with him like a faithful dog trundling after its owner.

"It was the only time [it happened] in the whole 90 minutes," Carlos Alberto said. "When Jairzinho received the ball from Rivellino and gave the ball to Pelé, my stride was totally open and Pelé waited a few seconds for me to be there and then gave a beautiful pass for me to score. Pelé knew I was coming because we had spoken about that kind of chance before the game, if Jairzinho made the movement to the left side.

"The emotion, of course, when I scored that goal was incredible, but after the game, and still today, I realize how beautiful and how important that goal was because everybody is still talking about it. Nobody talks about Pelé's goal, the first goal, the second goal . . . it is always about the fourth goal. I think it was the best goal ever scored in a World Cup."

Back home, 100 million Brazilians were starting a humungous party, but the whole world was in on it, too.

For Carlos Alberto, it was the most poignant moment of his life. As Garry Jenkins writes in *The Beautiful Team: In Search of Pelé and the 1970s Brazilians*: "In the eye of the euphoria, Carlos Alberto recalls finding a moment of tranquillity and composing himself for the presentation to come. In the cool of the dressing room, his mind was alive with images of the parties that would be going on back in Vila da Penha and beyond: 'That's where everything comes to your mind. A World Cup for Brazilians is like winning a war, so we knew there would be the biggest party.

"'We were conscious that Brazil was passing through a difficult moment, with the dictatorship. We knew that people would have forgotten the difficulties to celebrate. In Brazil, people suffer and when we are in the World Cup, we set ourselves free.'"

It is a goal, a win, and a tournament that left an indelible mark on an entire generation of football fans and changed people's perceptions of the entire sport. "It was exuberant, it was brilliant, and it wasn't just Brazil that reacted with euphoria, but it marked the end of the age of football's innocence," Jonathan Wilson wrote in his tactical history, *Inverting the Pyramid*. "In club football, in Europe at least, that era had ended much earlier, but in Mexico, the heat and the altitude combined to make pressing or any kind of systematic closing down of opponents impossible.

"For the last time in a major competition, there was space and Brazil had a team perfectly equipped to make the best use of it. What had appeared, as satellites beamed it in vibrant technicolor around the globe, as the beginning of a brave new world, actually sounded the last post for the old one. Even Brazil seem to have accepted that 1970 was a zenith never to be repeated."

Twinkling yellow shirts on color TV for the first time, sunshine, freedom, happiness, playing football not just to win, but for the fun of it . . . there was a purity about that team, perfectly encapsulated in that goal and by Carlos Alberto kissing the gleaming Jules Rimet trophy before lifting it aloft, something that would become commonplace but was not really done at the time.

If football didn't get any better, any purer, than that, then Carlos Alberto's career would certainly never reach those heights again.

Remarkably, it was pretty much his last notable act in a Brazil shirt; he played just seven more matches after the 1970 final, missing the 1974 World Cup through injury and, while he was selected in 1978 as a veteran center-back aged 33, he elected to retire shortly before the tournament.

Overall, he would play just short of 1,000 matches, most of them with Santos and then New York Cosmos with, yes, his good friend Pelé as part of the soccer boom in the United States in the late 1970s.

Then, after retirement, he moved into management, taking charge of numerous clubs in Brazil, Mexico, and Colombia as well as national jobs in Oman and Azerbaijan. Wherever he went, they would always ask him about one goal.

Player name: Carlos Alberto Torres
Born: July 17, 1944
Died: October 25, 2016 (aged 72)
Position: Right-back, center-back
Debut: 1963
Main teams: Fluminense (1963–66, 1974–76), Santos (1966–74), Flamengo (1976–77), New York Cosmos (1977–80, 1982), California Surf (1981); Brazil (1964–77)
Career highlights: Won the 1970 World Cup and scored one of the best goals of all time in the final. Also won the NASL Soccer Bowl four times.

29.
Kylian Mbappé

Mbappé's hat trick proved in vain at the 2022 World Cup final, but he is a previous winner.

The old-school charm of a career charted in World Cups

By Tom Williams

For the first 79 minutes of the 2022 World Cup final, Kylian Mbappé did next to nothing.

By the time Ángel Di María put Argentina 2–0 up in the 36th minute, Mbappé had only touched the ball seven times. He produced the occasional forward dart thereafter, a couple of neat one-twos with Théo Hernandez on the left flank, a shot that flew over the Argentine crossbar. But, like the rest of his teammates in France's gold-embossed, dark blue kit, he seemed off the pace.

Then, in the blink of an eye, and with a little over 10 minutes remaining in normal time, he came to life.

Over the course of the next hour at a rapt, airless Lusail Stadium near Doha, as a meandering contest suddenly sparked into one of the most pulsating matches the game has ever seen, he would cement his legacy as one of the greatest players in World Cup history. He was two days short of his 24th birthday.

Argentina's fans had just begun to greet their team's passes with goading cries of "Olé!" when Mbappé instinctively prodded a pass from Eduardo Camavinga toward goal, allowing Randal Kolo Muani to race into the box and draw a foul from Nicolás Otamendi. Ignoring Emiliano Martínez's attempts to put him off, Mbappé took a confident four-step run-up and swept his spot kick into the bottom-left corner. France had looked dead and buried, but here, from nowhere, was a lifeline.

A mere 97 seconds later, their talisman drew them level. Picked out by Adrien Rabiot, Mbappé alertly nodded the ball inside to Marcus Thuram and then stole in behind right-back Nahuel Molina to meet his teammate's lobbed return with an acrobatic side-on volley that skidded past Martínez's outstretched left hand and into the net. As the French fans in the stadium exulted, their No. 10 tore toward the corner flag with his arms spread wide in jubilation.

Four years earlier, in the Russian city of Kazan, France's madcap 4–3 win over Argentina in the last 16 had seemed to represent a symbolic passing of the torch from Lionel Messi to Mbappé—but in Lusail, the roles were reversed. Messi, by now Mbappé's clubmate at Paris Saint-Germain, had earlier put Argentina 1–0 up and he restored his side's lead in extra time. Mbappé sent the game to penalties with another nerveless spot kick in the 118th minute, but despite first he and then Messi keeping their cool in the shootout (Mbappé beating Martínez for the fourth time in the game), it was Argentina who prevailed.

Mbappé looked disconsolate as he collected the Golden Boot for being the tournament's top scorer—the first Frenchman to win the award since Just Fontaine in 1958—and he seemed unmoved by the podium-side pep talk that followed from French President Emmanuel Macron. But for all the disappointment, his place in the record books was now secure.

The first player to score a hat trick in a men's World Cup final since England's Geoff Hurst in 1966. Only the second player, after Brazil's Vavá, to have scored in consecutive World Cup finals. And with four goals across the deciding games of the 2018 and 2022 tournaments, the outright leading scorer in football's ultimate match. He was, *L'Équipe* said in its edition the following morning, a "king without a crown."

Mbappé is something of a throwback for a modern footballer in the sense that his most enduring accomplishments have been achieved on the international stage rather than in club football.

His prodigious exploits as a 19-year-old newcomer at the 2018 World Cup sparked comparisons with the great Pelé, who once tipped Mbappé to become his "heir." In much the same way the Brazilian is most commonly remembered in the canary-yellow shirt of the *Seleção*, when the young Frenchman has captured imaginations in his career to date, it has chiefly been with *Les Bleus*. In that respect, the native of Bondy in the northeastern Paris suburbs is the perfect poster boy for the French Football Federation, particularly having spent two years at the renowned Clairefontaine academy before embarking upon his professional career at Monaco.

Mbappé had his first taste of international success as part of the French team that prevailed at the Under-19 European Championship in 2016. "We lost the first game against England and Kylian produced a very average performance," recalls Ludovic Batelli, who coached France to glory at the tournament in Germany. "I had individual meetings with the players afterwards and he came to see me. He told me: 'Coach, I didn't play well. You would be perfectly justified in not picking me for the next match. But if you pick me, I promise you two things: One, we'll win the match and I'll produce a great performance; and two, the team will go on to the final and we'll win it.'"

True to his word, Mbappé scored in subsequent wins over Croatia, the Netherlands, and Portugal and although he failed to find the net in France's 4–0 defeat of Italy in the final, the game produced the first viral moment of his fledgling career when he nonchalantly scooped the ball over a defender's head in the buildup to his side's fourth goal. "An extraordinary piece of skill," says Batelli. "People were starting to talk about him."

Mbappé enjoyed his breakthrough season in the 2016–17 campaign, bursting into a spectacular Monaco team that would go on to blow Paris Saint-Germain out of the water in the Ligue 1 title race and reach the Champions League semifinals. He received his first senior call-up from France coach Didier Deschamps in March 2017, having just served notice of his exceptional qualities by scoring in both legs of a storming victory over Pep Guardiola's Manchester City in the Champions League last 16.

"Right from his first training session, you saw that even in small-sided games he had extraordinary powers of acceleration," says former France right-back Christophe Jallet. "The second thing that struck me—and I remember talking about it with Laurent Koscielny and Benoît Costil that evening—was his vision. He already had the ability to make the right choice at the right moment with the correct technical skill.

"Sometimes when you first join up with France, you're a bit worried about getting things wrong and you don't make the right choices. But although he arrived with lots of respect and humility, he seemed totally relaxed. I remember thinking: '*Oh la la* Kylian, go and play on the other side from me, please! My place in the France squad is important to me and I don't want to be humiliated.'"

By the time the 2018 World Cup in Russia came around, Mbappé was firmly on the fast track to superstar status, having just claimed a second successive Ligue 1 title following a €180 million transfer from Monaco to PSG that made him the world's most expensive teenage footballer. In a pretournament documentary interview, he spoke with characteristic expressiveness about his dream of propelling France to glory. "It must be something extraordinary to be able to say to yourself that the happiness of every French person is in your hands," he beamed.

There were precious few proclamations of happiness after France's opening game, however, with Mbappé singled out for criticism by Deschamps during a blunt team briefing following an unconvincing 2–1 win over Australia.

The coach's words did not go unheeded. Mbappé notched the only goal of a 1–0 victory over Peru that secured France's place in the knockout phase and then exploded across the international consciousness with a scintillating 70-yard sprint to win a penalty against Argentina in the round of 16. "That was 100 percent pure Kylian: making a difference all on his own, accelerating, causing havoc for the opposition defense, being decisive," says Batelli. "He was only 19 and he was already the leader of the attack."

A second-half brace, which made him the first teenager to score twice in a World Cup knockout game since Pelé in the 1958 final, earned him the man-of-the-match award and confirmed his status as the most exciting young talent in the sport. His postmatch embrace with a crestfallen Messi, meanwhile, became one of the images of the tournament; a Bobby Moore/Pelé shirt swap for the Instagram generation.

After years of handwringing headlines about morally bankrupt footballers from the *banlieues* (France's stigmatized urban suburbs), here was one who kept his nose clean, smiled for the cameras, and spoke with disarming maturity—in addition to tearing opposition defenses to shreds all on his own.

In the final, two weeks later, Mbappé rubber-stamped France's 4–2 victory over Croatia by bludgeoning a low shot past his former Monaco teammate Danijel Subašić from 25 yards. When he blew out the candles on his 20th birthday cake later that year, it was in the knowledge that he was already a footballing immortal.

Four years later, Mbappé arrived at the 2022 World Cup as the uncontested *patron* of the French attack.

Now playing in his preferred position on the left flank, having operated from the right in 2018, he netted once against Australia and twice against Denmark in the group phase before putting paid to Poland in the last 16 with an assist for Olivier Giroud and a customarily smooth brace.

In an echo of how his tournament had played out in 2018, he failed to score against either England in the quarterfinals or Morocco in the semifinals, but he saved his best for the final. Though he was ultimately eclipsed by Messi, his tally of eight goals was the highest at the competition since Ronaldo's triumphant eight-goal haul for Brazil in 2002; another all-time great's achievements duly matched.

"In 2018, it was like: 'If he plays well, great. He has the right to make mistakes,'" says Jallet. "In 2022, he no longer had the right to make mistakes. He was the star player in the team, he was the guy who was there to make a difference, so the pressure was much greater. He *had* to show up. And he did."

Mbappé's love affair with the sport's supreme competition has been rendered all the more precious by the misfortune that has befallen him at other major international tournaments. He was unable to find the net at the 2020 European Championship (played in 2021) and became France's fall guy when he missed the decisive spot kick in a penalty-shootout defeat by Switzerland in the last 16, later revealing that he had considered suspending his international career after receiving racist abuse in the aftermath of the team's elimination.

Although France's victory in the UEFA Nations League later the same year provided a measure of consolation, Euro 2024 proved every bit as disappointing. By now captain, Mbappé was unsettled by a broken nose sustained in France's opening game against Austria and drifted through the tournament in Germany like a ghost, scoring only one goal—from the penalty spot—en route to defeat by Spain in the last four. "My ambition was to become European champion and to have a good Euros," he said. "I did neither one nor the other."

Recent years have introduced further ripples of turbulence—a contentious exit from PSG and an underwhelming start to life at Real Madrid before form kicked in and the goals started to flow—to a career trajectory that had previously appeared to resemble a straight and inexorably rising line. But if there is one thing certain to fire Mbappé's imagination, it is the prospect of another rendezvous with World Cup history in 2026.

Player name: Kylian Mbappé Lottin
Born: December 20, 1998
Position: Forward
Debut: 2015
Main teams: Monaco (2015–18), Paris Saint-Germain (loan 2017–18, 2018–24), Real Madrid (2024–); France (2017–)
Career highlights: Won the 2018 World Cup. Four years later, in 2022, he claimed the Golden Boot at the World Cup and scored a hat trick in the final. He has claimed the French top flight seven times.

28.

Bobby Moore

Moore is chaired from the field by England's victorious players at Wembley in 1966.

The man of the people who lifted the World Cup

By Richard Sutcliffe

That Bobby Moore's final resting place is in the heart of London's East End feels entirely appropriate.

The site of the Boleyn Ground, the former home of West Ham United where Moore was so revered, sits a little under three miles away from where the former England captain's ashes are interred alongside those of his parents at the City of London Cemetery and Crematorium. But this sprawling 200-acre burial ground on the fringe of Epping Forest has also been open to everyone, regardless of class or creed, for nearly 170 years.

A good fit, therefore, for someone famously regarded as a man of the people despite being on first-name terms with royalty and prime ministers.

Moore's modest and humble nature is also reflected in the plaque indicating where he was laid to rest. There is no mention of his crowning glory as a footballer, a moment freeze-framed in the nation's conscience forever: Moore as the inspirational leader with a handsome smile, hoisted on the shoulders of his England teammates and holding the Jules Rimet trophy aloft.

Nor is there even a hint of his 16 years' service at West Ham or the 108 international caps, once a record tally for English football. Instead, above details of his father, Robert, and mother Doris's own passing 14 years apart, the inscription simply reads: "Bobby Moore OBE 1941–1993."

All around are similar memorials to loved ones from ordinary London families, making it easy to walk unnoticed past the Moore plot that shelters under a tree in this peaceful corner of the capital, the only accompaniment the distant hum of traffic on the North Circular Road.

Yet Moore's standing as a true giant of English football cannot be underestimated. The very epitome of graceful composure on the ball, he read the game beautifully. What he may have lacked in pace, he more than made up for with an ability to anticipate an opponent's next move. There was simply no better tackler around.

Teammates would joke about how meticulously tidy Moore was off the pitch, even folding his muddy shirt and shorts after a match before handing them over to the equipment man. He brought the same orderly manner to dispossessing forwards, whipping the ball away cleanly with inch-perfect precision.

"I still see that tackle by Moore . . ." chorused David Baddiel and Frank Skinner ahead of Euro 1996 on the Three Lions song that has since become an anthem for England supporters at every major tournament.

That the comedy duo should reference a mere tackle—even one as expertly timed as Moore's dispossession of Brazil's Jairzinho in the penalty area during the 1970 World Cup in Mexico—amid homages to iconic England goals by Gary Lineker and Bobby Charlton speaks volumes.

Moore's game, however, was about much more than just stopping the opposition. After leaving Jairzinho on the ground in Guadalajara, he calmly brought the ball out of defense before finding a teammate with trademark precision.

That calmness under even the most intense pressure also explains one of the greatest passes in English football history at Wembley four years earlier. With England leading West Germany 3–2 and just seconds remaining in the World Cup final, his defensive partner, Jack Charlton, implored Moore to boot the ball as far away as possible from the home goal. Anywhere upfield would do.

Instead, the unruffled captain took a couple of touches to assess his options before hitting a quite extraordinary, raking pass that was so perfectly weighted that Geoff Hurst was able to collect and bear down on goal without breaking stride.

One thunderous shot later into the roof of Hans Tilkowski's net and Hurst had what for 56 years remained the only hat trick in a World Cup final until Kylian Mbappé emulated Hurst's feat in vain for France in the 2022 final in Qatar.

England's World Cup triumph capped a remarkable Wembley hat trick of successes for Moore. In 1964, he lifted the FA Cup as West Ham captain following a 3–2 victory over Preston North End. A year later, he did the same with the European Cup Winners' Cup after seeing off 1860 Munich.

Moore was just 25 on English football's greatest day. He never won another major trophy. That, though, did nothing to dent his popularity in the eyes of the public, who if anything seemed to lionize the Londoner even more following the odd misstep he endured in the years that followed.

He was suspended early in 1971 by West Ham for breaking a drinking curfew on the eve of an FA Cup match in Blackpool, the club captain having mistakenly believed the tie would be postponed due to the arctic weather that had hit the Lancashire coast. His furious manager, Ron Greenwood, wanted to sack Moore and the others involved, only to be talked down by the directors.

Sir Alf Ramsey also disapproved of his captain's drinking, pointedly leaving Moore's passport on his pillow after an unauthorized drinking session on England duty two years before the World Cup triumph. It was later made very clear in a meeting with fellow miscreants, including Jimmy Greaves and Bobby Charlton, that a repeat would not be tolerated.

A notorious insomniac, Moore was subsequently caught by Ramsey sneaking out of the team hotel in New York City to watch a concert by Ella Fitzgerald. He was not due to play the following day in what proved to be an easy 10–0 win over the United States, but again, the manager was not best pleased.

Moore was still England captain when the biggest scandal of his career broke during the buildup to the 1970 World Cup.

An emerald and diamond bracelet had gone missing from a high-end jeweler located in England's team hotel in Bogotá, Colombia. The captain was arrested and detained for four days after a shopworker accused him of slipping the bracelet into his tracksuit pocket. The case eventually collapsed after it had been pointed out to the judge that no such pocket existed in England's training gear.

All manner of theories were later put forward by way of an explanation, including it being either a scam or a prank that went horribly wrong.

Either way, Moore's response to an unseemly saga that would have broken lesser men was to play some of his best football once the tournament got underway in Mexico, his stellar displays earning the respect of even the very best.

Moments after England's 1–0 group-stage defeat by Brazil, Moore and Pelé were captured by British photographer John Varley embracing warmly after swapping shirts, the mutual respect between two of the game's greats clear for all to see. It remains one of sport's most iconic images, encapsulating the spirit of fair play.

• • •

"My captain, my leader, my right-hand man. He was the spirit and the heartbeat of the team. A cool, calculating footballer I could trust with my life. He was the supreme professional, the best I ever worked with. Without him, England would never have won the World Cup."

No higher compliment can be paid to Moore than these words spoken by the manager who masterminded what remains England's solitary World Cup triumph, shortly after his captain's death in 1993.

Plenty of other heartfelt tributes were made in the hours and days following Moore's passing at the age of only 51, particularly from old foes from the international stage such as Pelé and Franz Beckenbauer. All articulated the profound sense of loss felt across world football.

None, though, quite summed up the man whose statue proudly sits outside Wembley as well as Ramsey's own words, which today decorate his profile in the Hall of Fame at the National Football Museum in Manchester.

First handed the captaincy after only 12 international appearances, becoming the youngest player to lead England in the process, Moore was everything Ramsey wanted from an onfield leader. Not least an ability to remain calm in pressure-cooker situations, a trait that undoubtedly helped England navigate occasions such as the stormy quarterfinal clash with Argentina in 1966.

That 1–0 victory for the hosts ended with Ramsey physically preventing George Cohen from swapping shirts with Alberto González, one of several Argentinian players the manager later labeled "animals."

Moore's response to the hair-pulling and spitting that afternoon was to urge his teammates to rise above the Argentine gamesmanship, something they did when Hurst fired in the only goal 12 minutes from time.

This ability to remain calm when others were in danger of losing their heads saw Moore remain the coolest man inside Wembley, even as the postfinal celebrations were underway and he led the rest of the team up to the Royal Box for the presentation of the Jules Rimet trophy.

Once at the top of the 39 steps that led from pitchside, he turned toward Queen Elizabeth II and spotted her white gloves. Not wanting to smear such a pristine garment and totally in control of his emotions as the rest of the country started a party that would last for days, Moore calmly wiped his hands on the parapet before continuing his walk toward Her Majesty.

Handsome, talented, and chivalrous, it's no wonder England bestowed national treasure status on Moore. What is less clear is why, after his playing career was over, the game did not afford him the same respect.

Unlike fellow greats such as Beckenbauer and Michel Platini, he never had the opportunity to wield influence on the world stage. Nor did the Football Association seek to tap into his considerable knowledge and expertise, a snub that should shame the governing body as much as the failure even to reply when Moore wrote to express an interest in the vacant England manager's job in 1977.

Around the same time, a path into club management appeared to open up when he was offered the Watford job, but chairman Elton John then reneged, instead turning to Graham Taylor. As one of football's most unlikely couples steered the unfashionable Hertfordshire club from the fourth tier to runners-up in the top flight and a Wembley appearance in the FA Cup final, Moore's own managerial career went nowhere.

He spent two and a half years in charge of Southend United before standing down in 1986, the fourth-tier club's financial struggles having made the job particularly onerous.

There had previously been a spell managing in Hong Kong with Eastern Athletic and in nonleague with Oxford City, the latter alongside a young Harry Redknapp. But neither job worked out. After leaving Southend, his professional involvement with the sport was done.

He moved into the media after several business interests had failed, initially covering games for the *Sunday Sport* newspaper.

Then came a switch to radio and a partnership with commentator Jonathan Pearce on Capital Radio that proved a big hit with listeners.

By now, though, cancer had returned to Moore's life.

He had first been diagnosed with testicular cancer as a player even before lifting the World Cup and made a successful recovery. But in 1991 he was found to be suffering from bowel cancer. This time it was terminal. Moore continued to work and his final public outing came at Wembley, with microphone in hand, as England beat San Marino. He died a week later, on February 24, 1993.

Losing the first member of England's only World Cup–winning team prompted an outpouring of grief across the country. Far too late, football realized the huge debt it owed Moore.

West Ham's South Stand was belatedly renamed in his honor, as was the main underpass taking fans from the nearest underground station to the old Wembley. His No. 6 shirt was also retired by West Ham 15 years after his death.

Other modern-day tributes include the *Champions* statue near the Boleyn Ground, which depicts West Ham's World Cup winners, and another unveiled outside the club's new London Stadium home in 2021, featuring Moore lifting the European Cup Winners' Cup in 1965 alongside Hurst and Martin Peters.

A third statue, this time solely dedicated to Moore, can be found in the entrance to the rebuilt Wembley. The 20-foot bronze depiction of England's greatest skipper looking north along Wembley Way remains a popular stop-off for supporters today.

Many of those reading the plinth will never have seen Moore play other than in video clips, but the inscription explains beautifully just some of the qualities that helped this humble son of the East End grow into the nation's ultimate sporting hero: immaculate footballer, imperial defender, hero of 1966 . . . gentleman of all time.

Player name: Bobby Moore
Born: April 12, 1941
Died: February 24, 1993 (aged 51)
Position: Center-back
Debut: 1958
Main teams: West Ham United (1958–74), Fulham (1974–77); England (1962–73)
Career highlights: Captained England to victory at the 1966 World Cup. Won the FA Cup in 1964 and the European Cup Winners' Cup in 1965 with West Ham.

27.

Zico

Zico in full flight during Brazil's game against Northern Ireland at the 1986 World Cup.

A portrait of simplicity, but a free-kick genius

By Jack Lang

Plink. Plink. Plink.

Some of them travel through the air like rockets. They rise slowly but defiantly, an inch at a time, up, up, forever up. They fizz with kinetic energy and menace. When they reach the net, they do so with a big old slap. "Hello, old friend; eat this, you bastard."

Some of them are lessons in applied physics. The ball traces a perfect arc, starting out right and then swooping left, spin and gravity momentary but willing coconspirators as it plunges into the goal. It's called the Magnus effect. Goalkeepers call it a real pain.

Some of them are games within the game. Everything else—all the other moving pieces, the sound and the fury—fades away for a second or two, leaving just the two duelists. Except, no, that makes it sound like they are on an even footing. What we really have here is a cat and a mouse. One is fighting for his life. The other is just playing with his food.

The best ones, though? The best ones are the ones that don't fizz, don't swoop, and require no recourse to misdirection.

You can watch the originals, but you can watch them in more recent videos, too. There he is, Arthur Antunes Coimbra, code name Zico, aged 46 or 55 or 68, flanked by starstruck presenters, patiently giving another master class on Brazilian or Turkish or Japanese television.

He's taking free kicks. Not blasting them or bending them; just delicately clipping them—just passing them, really—over metallic walls and into one top corner or the other.

There is no real run-up; he just takes a couple of leisurely steps, as if he is setting off to buy a newspaper from the local shop. And then, with a quick swish of his right leg, it's off, another little slice of geometric perfection, another knowing smile, another round of high fives and hugs.

You could never get bored of watching it. The real joy, though, comes through the speakers. The casual beauty of Zico's technique is best captured by the noise the ball makes coming off his foot.

Plink. Plink. Plink.

He doesn't need to thrash it or knock the leather off it. That's for the brutes. All it needs is a little encouragement, a little nudge in the right direction. The ball is Zico's friend. The sound is one of compliance.

The temptation is to think that this is just a factor of circumstance, a low-key noise for a low-key setting. Surely he was hitting it harder than this back in the day, goes the thought. Full stadiums want fire, brimstone, effort, not a dainty little golfer with a sand wedge.

Go back into the archives, however, and you will see an amazing number of these among Zico's greatest hits. The ball is on the floor 20 yards from goal; the ball is floating through the night sky; the ball is dropping just under the crossbar, right in the corner—where the owl sleeps, to use the charming Brazilian idiom.

People often say that for the very best takers, a free kick is as good as a penalty. It's a nice enough line. You can apply it to many of Zico's other free kicks. But not to this subset. A penalty is a battle of wits with a goalkeeper, but when Zico placed the ball on the edge of the area, the goalkeeper was an irrelevance.

These weren't free kicks. They weren't penalties, either. They were free throws. It was just him and the net and the air between them.

Oh, and somewhere beneath the decibel storm of the Maracanã or wherever else, the sound.

Plink. Plink. Plink.

For some young players, stardom is an inevitability. It was not like that with Zico. His technique, honed during endless street matches with his four older brothers, was eye-catching, but his body did not seem to have been briefed on the plan.

At 17, some of his teammates in the Flamengo youth team were 6' and rising. You could have stuffed Zico into your back pocket.

"I was seen as a good prospect, but the fact that I was very skinny made people doubt me," he later explained.

Flamengo might easily have cut him loose. Instead they bet the house on his potential, creating a bespoke training plan to bulk him up. Supervised by a team of doctors, fitness experts, physios, and nutritionists, Zico got down to work.

The routine was grueling. He would leave home at 5 a.m., train at Flamengo's Gávea complex in the morning, traipse to the center of Rio de Janeiro to study in the afternoon, then do an individual gym session in the evening. It was often 10 p.m. before he returned home to Quintino, his neighborhood in the north of the city.

"I barely saw him," his wife, Sandra, explained years later. "It was training, training, training, a bit of studying, more training. He was always very determined."

Already there is a point of departure here. Brazil has always valued natural ability—that lightning-in-a-bottle *something*, ungoverned by the usual rules of logic. Zico had talent and plenty of it, but he also had to work at it, an artist paying his dues on the factory floor.

That may endear him to you. In Brazil, it created a level of apprehension, at least at the outset. He was described as a "laboratory superstar," an image hardly undermined by Flamengo's clear desperation to take their share of the credit for his development. Publicity photos of Zico in the gym, pumping iron, abounded.

The work paid off. Zico, now a taut little pillar of muscle mass beneath his surfer's mop, took Rio by storm in his early twenties. There were the free kicks, obviously, but so much more: He could dribble, pass, and shoot. There was also a talismanic quality to his play. Like the very best No. 10s, he did not just decorate games, he decided them.

In 1978, he scored 19 times as Flamengo won the Rio state championship. It was the start of a golden era: In the five years that followed, the *Rubro-Negro* won their first three national championships, the Copa Libertadores and the Intercontinental Cup playing a brand of football that fundamentally altered the club's self-image. Flamengo had always been scrappers—popular scrappers, but scrappers nonetheless. With Zico pulling the strings, they became painters, romantics, rebels.

Zico's two spells at the club—he had a brief sabbatical in Italy with Udinese—yielded more than 500 goals in all matches. He is the top scorer in Flamengo's history, despite not being an out-and-out striker. No player has scored more than his 333 goals at the Maracanã.

Flamengo are the best-supported team in Brazil. Their fans number in the hundreds of thousands. You would struggle to find a single one who does not view Zico as the best player the club has ever had.

• • •

Zico does not command quite the same admiration outside Brazil. In part, that is a question of familiarity: He did much of his best work in domestic competitions and only briefly played in Europe.

That fact, though, did not work against other Brazilians on this list. The real difference is international football.

Make no mistake: Zico was superb for Brazil. He scored 48 international goals and filled the personality vacuum left by Pelé's retirement. You could convincingly argue that he is among the top three players to wear the canary-yellow jersey. But the World Cup was cruel to him.

In 1978, Brazil finished third—nothing to get too excited about, but a better result than had been expected. Zico, though, was poor, struggling with the pressure and losing his place in the starting lineup during the course of the campaign. "I made a pig's ear of that World Cup," he later said.

In 1986, he was older and wiser but not fully fit. He made a heroic effort to get to Mexico, just about recovering from a nasty injury sustained a year earlier, but was rewarded only with heartache: Zico missed a penalty as Brazil were eliminated by France at the quarter-final stage.

Between those two disappointments came something more complicated. The 1982 tournament was glorious and doomed, ecstatic and agonizing, beautiful and wretched.

Brazil played some of the best football ever witnessed. Zico, in his imperial phase, was central to all of it, the conductor of the orchestral maneuvers. If Brazil had won, it would have been a consecration. But they did not win.

It is testament to Zico's placid personality that the failure did not obliterate him. It hurt, sure, but he did not go in for melodrama. "I've come to terms with it," was one typical assessment, six years after the fact. "I did what I could."

Here again, it is tempting to wonder whether a different response might have embellished his legend. Zico, the stricken star, haunted by the ghosts of the Estadio de Sarrià: This thing almost writes itself. A phlegmatic shrug, on the other hand? That's not very dramatic. It's also not very Brazilian.

This, really, is the crux of what makes Zico interesting. He was—still is—a rare Brazilian icon unencumbered by existential matters. With Garrincha, Romário, even Pelé and Ronaldo, there was always some psychodrama bubbling away, explicit or otherwise. Each man cohabited with his own myth.

Zico has always been a portrait of simplicity. He was talented, then worked hard to hone the gift. He never struggled with drink or drugs. He had no nasty streak. He dealt with injuries and disappointments with the same equanimity. He was not prone to making explosive statements to the press. He has been happily married since 1975.

He is known in Brazilian football circles as a charming, generous, affable man. He is, perhaps more than any other living footballer, almost universally loved in his homeland. The lack of a World Cup medal might count against him when lists like this one are compiled, but there are bigger things in this life.

"I'd like to be remembered as someone who loved what he did," Zico once said, "as well as someone who always played fair and dedicated himself, body and soul, to football."

In 2016, journalists at *GloboEsporte*, Brazil's most prominent sports website, conducted a poll. They wanted respondents to name—in order—the three best Brazilian free-kick takers of all time. Three points would be awarded for each first-place vote, two for second, one for third.

So far, so standard. Except the people polled were not members of the public but . . . some of the best Brazilian free-kick takers of all time. There were 29 of them, including Ronaldinho, Rivaldo, Juninho Pernambucano, and Rivellino.

Nelinho, the scorer of a beautiful free kick for Brazil against Poland at the 1978 World Cup, finished in third position. Second was Marcelinho Carioca, little known outside his homeland but so proficient a taker that Corinthians fans used to call him Angel Foot.

First place? Zico. By an enormous margin.

Plink. Plink. Plink.

Player name: Arthur Antunes Coimbra (Zico)
Born: March 3, 1953
Position: Attacking midfielder
Debut: 1971
Main teams: Flamengo (1971–83, 1985–89), Udinese (1983–85), Kashima Antlers (1991–94); Brazil (1976–86)
Career highlights: Won the Brazilian top flight three times and the Copa Libertadores in 1981. Part of the great (though underachieving) Brazil team at the 1982 World Cup.

26.

Lothar Matthäus

Matthäus salutes the crowd after his goal against Yugoslavia at the 1990 World Cup.

Germany's unstoppable force

By Simon Hughes

Fun fact: Lothar Matthäus was the first outfield player in the history of the game to feature at five World Cups.

At the third of those, in Italy in the summer of 1990 (he also went to the 1982, 1986, 1994, and 1998 editions), his achievements as West Germany's captain led to him becoming the World, European, and German footballer of the year.

If a goal of the tournament award existed, Matthäus's effort against Yugoslavia in the opening group fixture would have been among the most persuasive contenders: Receiving possession in his own half, his antenna for an opportunity from his position in midfield flickered. He hurdled a challenge as he slalomed forward before larruping in a shot from 25 yards that went skidding past the goalkeeper, Tomislav Ivković.

That was his second goal of the game. His first had been struck just as forcefully, only with his left foot rather than his right and on the turn, having received the ball with his back to goal. Thanks to encouragement from his club manager at Inter Milan, Giovanni Trapattoni, Matthäus had worked so hard that he became two-footed.

Yugoslavia were among the dark horses to win the tournament—their leading club side, Red Star Belgrade, won the European Cup a year later—but this 4–1 filleting, inspired by Matthäus, gave warning of West Germany's intentions.

Matthäus's responsibilities included penalties. In a quarterfinal with Czechoslovakia, his composure from 12 yards proved to be the difference. In the semis, Matthäus also converted in a shootout against England. Yet in the final, Matthäus made the impromptu decision to hand the ball to Andreas Brehme when West Germany were awarded a penalty with just five minutes to go.

Matthäus knew that a goal would almost surely be the winner—teammate Rudi Völler, somewhat humorously, whispered into Brehme's ear before he stepped up just to remind him that if he scored, West Germany would win the World Cup.

Völler's confidence stemmed from the fact that Argentina, captained by Diego Maradona, were already down to 10 men following a red card (and would finish the game with nine men following another dismissal two minutes later). Yet, as Matthäus explained, he had identified a problem with his boots, having landed in Italy with four pairs: two for hard ground and another two for soft.

"We didn't have tons of gear with us and, to be honest, I was playing that tournament with one pair of boots," he later said. "The sole broke and, at halftime, I had to change into a brand-new pair which someone passed to me. They were half a size bigger than my real size, so I didn't feel comfortable enough and I was a hundred percent sure Andi would score."

In the immediacy of victory, the decision by Matthäus was viewed as the ultimate act of selflessness—the truest form of leadership, allowing someone else to write their name into history as the person whose goal won a World Cup final at his own expense.

His critics would later argue otherwise: This was another example of him disappearing when it really mattered, as he had allegedly done in the 1987 European Cup final with Bayern Munich in their defeat to FC Porto, and would do on the same stage in 1999 when back at Bayern. He left the field 10 minutes before the end that night with his team winning 1–0, only for Manchester United famously to score twice in stoppage time to snatch an unlikely victory at the Germans' expense.

Yet, for all the doubters, Matthäus was the best player on the planet at a moment considered pivotal in the evolution of the sport.

The advent of the Premier League and Champions League was just around the corner. "Italia '90 happened in a time before the Bosman ruling (allowing players to move under freedom of contract at the expiry of their deals) and super clubs. A time before satellite television and the internet made the football world a small place . . . ," wrote Simon Hart in his book, *World in Motion*.

The Cold War was coming to an end and never again would the names West Germany, Czechoslovakia, and the Soviet Union feature at a World Cup. Eleven days after the final, the German Football Association (DFB) announced plans to combine the leagues of West and East Germany and a unified German team, captained by Matthäus, would face Switzerland in December 1990, the same month a FIFA general secretary's report was published hinting at the change coming football's way.

"Not unexpectedly, the World Cup in Italy set off an as yet unequalled echo which continued to vibrate around the world long after the tournament had ended," it read.

Matthäus is one of the last players from a lost era to confirm his greatness. For Germany, it was thought the good times would roll on and on. Franz Beckenbauer, the World Cup–winning defender turned World Cup–winning coach, told reporters after the final in Rome,

"With players from the East joining, the German team will be unbeatable. I am sorry for the rest of the world."

Yet a united Germany did not win the tournament again for another 24 years.

This alone acts as a reminder of the scale of the achievement of the team from 1990 with a narrower pool of players, albeit one that was driven forward on the pitch by the relentless force of nature that was Lothar Matthäus. His tally of 150 caps for his country remains a record.

Just outside Nuremberg is Herzogenaurach, a town that is home to the two major international sports brands, Adidas and Puma.

Matthäus began his career with 1. FC Herzogenaurach, a club nicknamed the Pumas because of its links to the company for whom his mother worked in the canteen.

By the time he became a World Cup winner, he had established himself as Germany's most important footballer. Or, as the editor of *Kicker* magazine, Jörg Jakob, describes him, "the best German footballer in the best years of Italian football."

In 1990, Italy seemed bigger and better than anywhere else. A month before the start of the World Cup, AC Milan, Juventus, and Sampdoria had completed a clean sweep of European trophies.

Meanwhile, Matthäus's club, Inter Milan, had emerged as Serie A champions in 1989, having not won a trophy for seven years. It was his debut season in Italy and Inter did not lose a league game until February.

It had felt inevitable that Matthäus would end up in Italy. At Bayern, he had reached superstar status, but Germany's biggest club could not compete with Serie A in terms of wages and fees.

It has since been claimed that Matthäus's move from Bavaria saved Bayern from financial meltdown. Yet he could have gone to Italy earlier after Napoli representatives, encouraged by Maradona, flew to Munich to try to secure his signature. After winning the 1986 World Cup with Argentina at the expense of West Germany and Matthäus in Mexico, Maradona—who suggested in his autobiography that Matthäus was his greatest opponent—was already a hugely influential figure at his club. Within a year, Napoli would emerge as Serie A champions for the first time.

At a Munich restaurant, Matthäus was shown a black bag crammed with one million deutsche marks as a signing fee. It was four times his salary at Bayern, but Matthäus backed himself to remain in Munich and, potentially, sign for one of Italy's bigger clubs at a later date.

At Inter, Matthäus scored the goal that claimed the Serie A title, beating Napoli—and Maradona—in the process. The Neapolitans traipsed in second. We will never know what a team combining their talents might have achieved, yet, as Matthäus later suggested, the pair had very different abilities that surely would have complemented one another. "What Maradona saw in a small space, I saw over long distances," he told the football writer Simon Kuper.

The German was the first player to win the Ballon d'Or while playing for Inter. Within a year of becoming a World Cup winner, he also secured a first European trophy as Inter won the UEFA Cup—this at the end of a campaign that was his best statistically, yielding 23 goals in all competitions.

For a midfielder in Italy, during an era when defenses dominated and even some of the best strikers the game has seen struggled to reach the 20-goal mark (from 1978–79 to 1990–91, Serie A's leading scorer did this only twice), these were astonishing numbers for a midfielder, especially one who could perform two or three positions at once, whether that meant starting off deep, playing as a No. 8, or emerging higher up the pitch as a playmaker.

"What made me strong was that I could do all sorts of things," Matthäus told Kuper. Trying to pin him down is a challenge: Think of a cross between Graeme Souness, Roy Keane, and Steven Gerrard, an aggressive and dynamic presence whose determination and athleticism was so great that despite not being the tallest at 5'9", he was also a threat in the air.

His tactical understanding of the game meant that as he got older, Matthäus was able to move back through the team and remain as influential as he always was. His last World Cup in 1998 was spent as a *libero*, the position from where he led Bayern, upon his return to Germany, to three of his seven Bundesliga titles.

Jakob described Matthäus as "one of the most important players in German football history," yet he has never managed in the Bundesliga despite a coaching career that started almost as soon as he retired as a player at the age of 39 and lasted a decade.

Instead, Matthäus took jobs in Austria, Serbia, Hungary, Brazil, Israel, and Bulgaria. Despite his importance to Germany, he had many enemies and, over the course of his career, was accused of being too close to reporters at some of the country's tabloid newspapers. It also did not help that he seemed too close to Bayern, which is simultaneously Germany's most popular and by extension unpopular club.

When he seemed set to take over at Bavarian rivals Nuremberg, the club's board decided to choose someone else after pushback from the supporter base. A similar thing happened at Eintracht Frankfurt, where fans blamed Matthäus for a tackle that allegedly ended the career of local hero Jürgen Grabowski in 1980.

Matthäus, however, remains one of Germany's most famous pundits. Like Keane, formerly of Manchester United, he has struggled in management but has a way of swiftly arriving at a conclusion that engages a television audience.

Meanwhile, anyone who beats his 150 caps for Germany will be doing well. In 2024, Thomas Müller was closing in before he retired from international football in third place, still 19 appearances behind Matthäus: an unstoppable force as a player and seemingly an immovable object, even in retirement.

Player name: Lothar Matthäus

Born: March 21, 1961

Position: Midfielder, *libero*

Debut: 1978

Main teams: 1. FC Herzogenaurach (1978–79), Borussia Mönchengladbach (1979–84), Bayern Munich (1984–88, 1992–2000), Inter Milan (1988–92), MetroStars (2000); West Germany/Germany (1980–2000)

Career highlights: Captained West Germany to victory at the 1990 World Cup. Won Euro 1980 with the national team and 14 trophies over two stints at Bayern Munich, including the Bundesliga seven times. Won Serie A in 1988–89 at Inter Milan and the Ballon d'Or in 1990.

25.

Andrés Iniesta

Iniesta, sporting his T-shirt in tribute to Dani Jarque, celebrates his World Cup–winning goal in 2010.

From "rock bottom" to World Cup winner

By Dermot Corrigan

October 2023. Andrés Iniesta, wearing a T-shirt from his own sportswear company and joining the call by video link from his home, is opening up in an interview with two members of Spain's General Council of Psychologists. The conversation centers on how he felt back in June 2009.

"It was the summer when we had just won a treble and my life had all the positive things you could imagine," says the former Barcelona and Spain midfielder. "But then you start to feel bad, to not be yourself, to not have your normal energy and vitality. It was a general feeling of emptiness.

"You don't know what is happening to you, but you know things are not right and you hit rock bottom."

Iniesta had turned 25 that spring and recently starred as Barcelona beat Manchester United in the Champions League final. That trophy was added to the season's La Liga and Copa del Rey titles. The glorious campaign had followed Spain's success at the 2008 European Championship, a tournament in which the midfielder had been integral.

Off the pitch, things also seemed to be going well. Iniesta was in a strong relationship with Anna Ortiz, who would become his wife and the mother of his children.

Yet he was suffering.

"It should have been the best summer of my life, but it ended up being the worst," Iniesta wrote in his 2016 autobiography, *The Artist: Being Iniesta*. "I felt like I was in freefall. Like everything had gone dark."

Iniesta hit rock bottom just at the time when, from the outside at least, everything suggested he was at his peak.

Barcelona's 2008–09 campaign was maybe the best of any football team ever. In Pep Guardiola's first year as head coach, a team that included Lionel Messi, Xavi Hernández, Gerard Piqué, and Thierry Henry won every competition they entered.

The critical moment of the campaign came in the second leg of the Champions League semifinal against Chelsea at Stamford Bridge when Barcelona were seconds away from being eliminated. Iniesta smashed in a dramatic late equalizer from just outside the box to force them through on the away-goals rule.

That was one of five he scored that season, along with 16 assists, across 43 matches. Those numbers defied the reality that Iniesta had been hampered by injuries all year.

In November, he tore the thigh muscle in his right leg. In February, he had an issue with a hamstring in his left leg. March brought a groin problem. Four days after the decisive draw at Chelsea, he tore another muscle in his right thigh. His body was at the breaking point. He missed the last three La Liga games of the season and the Copa del Rey final.

But there was huge pressure on him to return for the Champions League decider in Rome.

This was his chance to realize a dream he had harbored ever since entering Barcelona's La Masia academy at the age of 12. He already boasted one Champions League winner's medal, but his contribution to the 2006 final had been limited to that of a substitute (he came on at halftime). Now he was among the team's leaders. They needed him to be fit to play Manchester United. And he needed to be there.

His buildup to the showpiece was dominated by intensive work with Barcelona's physio, Emili Ricart, and his recovery progressed quicker than many thought possible. There he was lining up at the Stadio Olimpico and there he was, 10 minutes in, providing a trademark exquisite pass to assist Samuel Eto'o's opening goal. Barcelona prevailed 2–0. Their historic season was complete.

Iniesta enjoyed the celebrations, but while holidaying with his family in the weeks that followed, he was unable to rest properly. Back for Barcelona's preseason camp in July, he passed the routine medical tests, only to break down with another thigh injury in the very first training session.

Scans showed the problem was not serious, so he commenced rehab as usual. But Iniesta knew something was badly wrong.

He did not tell anyone how he was really feeling, just as he hadn't when suffering silently from loneliness in Barcelona's academy as a teenager living far from his family. Throughout his career, he had accepted personal pain while striving to perform professionally. This time it was too difficult to handle.

"The problem snowballs," Iniesta writes in his book. "You're not right, not well, but the people around you don't understand it because the Andrés they know isn't this Andrés; they can't see that somehow you're empty on the inside."

• • •

It was on August 8, 2009, while Iniesta was working at Barcelona's training ground, that captain Carles Puyol came to tell him that their friend Dani Jarque had suffered a heart attack and died.

Jarque was a player with Barcelona's city rivals, Espanyol. He and Iniesta had shared a dressing room when playing for Spain's age-group teams. Together they had won the Under-19 European Championship in 2002 and would be teammates again with the under-21s.

They were not exactly similar personalities. Jarque was a big, imposing central defender. Iniesta, a year younger, was a smaller creative presence in midfield. But they clicked on and off the pitch, becoming the firmest of friends. Now, at 26, Jarque was gone. "I froze. I couldn't understand it. I didn't know what to do, what to think. I couldn't believe it. Dani, my friend Dani, had died. How? Why? This couldn't be."

Iniesta attended Jarque's funeral in the Catalan capital three days later. He was still reporting to the training ground each morning, but he did not seem to be improving. He lost weight. He was taking pills to sleep at night.

Finally, he called Barcelona's club doctor, Ricard Pruna, and said he had a problem.

Iniesta was soon working with club psychologist Inma Puig and external psychiatrist Eugeni Bruguera. Anna, his parents, and a circle of close friends also provided support. Most of his teammates had no idea what he was going through. They thought—like the fans and the media—that rehabilitation from his thigh injury was just proving problematic.

"Andrés wanted a medical explanation," said Pruna. "And we did tests, analysis, everything we could. But it wasn't tests that he needed. What he needed was harmony, balance. And slowly he was able to be what he is now. And no, I don't mean the footballer. I mean the *person*."

Barcelona allowed him the space and time he needed.

It was late September before he started a game. While he slowly became a regular on the team sheet again, his performances were still not up to his usual standard. His only goal that season came in a routine 4–0 La Liga win at home to Racing Santander in February. This was a gradual process.

In late March, he missed the first leg of the Champions League quarterfinal at Arsenal with a hamstring problem. He quickly returned for a *Clásico* against Real Madrid, but disaster soon struck.

At training, he tore his right thigh muscle again. Everyone's minds immediately leapt to the World Cup, now less than two months away. Iniesta broke down in tears. Ricart helped him limp from the pitch. Puyol whispered in his ear that "everything will be fine." But Iniesta himself did not really believe it would be.

By the time Barcelona succumbed to José Mourinho's Inter Milan in the Champions League semifinal, Iniesta was back at work with Ricart, Pruna, and the rest of the medical team. Guardiola sent him on with four minutes remaining of the final La Liga game at home to Valladolid on May 16, just so he could feel part of the team as they clinched another title.

Again, Iniesta did not feel much like celebrating. The World Cup was less than a month away.

The Spain coach, Vicente del Bosque, was certain he wanted Iniesta at the tournament in South Africa.

Once the club season had concluded, the national federation's physio, Raúl Martinez, worked with the midfielder every day. Staff bought the same gym equipment, including an identical running machine, that Iniesta used for his rehab at Barcelona. Nothing was left to chance.

Iniesta started Spain's final pretournament friendly against Poland and initially looked sharp, but after 39 minutes he walked to the sideline and asked to come off. He was close to being ready but not quite convinced.

A week later, he was declared fit for the opening World Cup game against Switzerland. Then, after an hour of play, he was kicked by Swiss defender Stephan Lichtsteiner. He played on but kept bringing his hand to the back of his right thigh. "I don't like the look on Iniesta's face," said commentator Michael Robinson on Spanish TV. The Swiss won 1–0.

Spain's medical staff decided on an unorthodox approach when it came to Iniesta. Although they suspected a new injury, they did no more tests. They told Iniesta it was just a knock. Nothing to worry about. As a precaution, del Bosque rested him for Spain's second group game against Honduras, but the message was consistent: He had not suffered anything serious.

Martinez kept giving him daily massages, working the muscles. Ricart was on the phone from Barcelona every afternoon. Then came a breakthrough. During an evening massage session, Martinez found a previously undiscovered knot deep in the right thigh muscle and applied pressure to loosen it.

Iniesta felt immediate relief. That night he waited until everyone was asleep at the team hotel, then raced down the corridor, testing his leg, and finally felt good. He wanted to shout "The torment is over" out loud, such was his relief.

Two days later, Iniesta started Spain's final group game against Chile. He scored and was named man of the match. The mood had changed completely. He played all 90 minutes as Spain beat Portugal in the last 16, then Paraguay in the quarterfinals, and Germany in the last four.

On the day of the World Cup final, amid all the hustle and bustle of pregame in the dressing room, Iniesta asked physio Hugo Camarero to find him a white sleeveless T-shirt to wear during the game under his No. 6 Spain jersey.

The final was horribly tense. The Netherlands worked to shut down Iniesta and his skillful teammates, often using overly physical means. It was goalless after 90 minutes and stayed that way deep into the second half of extra time. With four minutes to go and a penalty shootout looking inevitable, Iniesta took possession just inside the Dutch half after Jesús Navas's dart infield had been checked.

His backheeled pass found Cesc Fàbregas. The ball was shifted on, via a deflection, to Navas again and then to Fernando Torres out on the left. The striker spotted Iniesta alone on the other side of the penalty area, and while his cross was cut out, Fàbregas gathered the loose ball and this time slid a pass successfully beyond Rafael van der Vaart for his teammate to collect.

Iniesta's first touch cushioned the ball up, inviting the volley. He pulled back his right leg—the limb that had caused him so much trouble for months—and swung through the line of the ball, meeting it true. Maarten Stekelenburg in the Dutch goal did not stand a chance.

As he raced off to celebrate scoring the most important goal in Spanish football history, Iniesta removed his jersey to reveal the sleeveless white T-shirt sourced by Camarero. Millions of TV viewers around the world read the handwritten message across his chest: "Dani Jarque, always with us."

"To win a World Cup, there are no words," Iniesta said on Spanish TV in the immediate aftermath of his winner, before welling up. "I remembered Dani Jarque . . . my family and all the fans. It's the work of such a long time, of difficult moments.

"But now, to enjoy it . . ."

That summer, Iniesta was able to rest, both mentally and physically.

The following season, he barely missed a game through injury. It ended with the third Champions League title of his career, assisting a goal for Messi in another victory over Manchester United in the final.

He played for Barcelona until 2018, adding to his trophy haul and claiming another treble in 2014–15. During his final season, he wore the captain's armband and scored a fine goal in a 5–0 Copa del Rey final win over Sevilla.

Even as the twilight of his career took him to Vissel Kobe in Japan and then Emirates in the UAE Pro League, he continued to speak to a therapist. Those dark times from the worst summer of his life did not return.

"My career has been like a fairy tale," he said when announcing his retirement after 22 years as a professional in October 2024. "I've lived the best you can live on a human and professional level.

"It seems like it all boils down to the World Cup final goal. But we all scored it—the fans, the players . . . and Dani Jarque, wherever he was, helped us, too."

Player name: Andrés Iniesta Luján
Born: May 11, 1984
Position: Midfielder
Debut: 2002
Main teams: Barcelona (2002–18), Vissel Kobe (2018–23), Emirates (2023–24); Spain (2006–18)
Career highlights: Won the World Cup in 2010, as well as Euro 2008 and Euro 2012, with Spain. Won 30 trophies at Barcelona, including the Champions League four times. Instrumental in Barcelona and Spain's *tiki-taka* style of play, which revolutionized football.

24.

Jairzinho

Jairzinho is carried from the pitch after Brazil's victory in the 1970 World Cup final against Italy.

The Hurricane wreaking havoc in Pelé's shadow

By Rory Smith

Jairzinho's final gift to Brazilian football was a precious one. A few years after his playing career had ambled to a close—but a couple of decades after the explosive heyday of the winger they called *O Furacão*, the Hurricane—he found himself in charge of São Cristóvão, an unremarkable club in a modest suburb of Rio de Janeiro.

One day, as he tells it, a downpour forced him to cancel his training session. Bored, he asked around to see if there was any other sport for him to watch. Someone recommended that he head to the club's gym, where he might be able to catch one of the youth teams playing *futsal*, the small-sided, indoor cousin to football that has helped polish so many of Brazil's jewels. With nothing better to do, he accepted the recommendation. It would, at least, keep him dry.

As he sat and watched, he noticed one particular player—a 14-year-old—who seemed to him "ready" to play the full-scale version of the game. He had "all that skill, the vision, the speed," he said. He was talking, in this instance, to the Brazilian magazine *Vermelho*, but he has recounted the anecdote so often that it could have been to almost anyone.

He was sufficiently intrigued by the teenager's virtuoso gifts that he wanted to watch him again, just to check it had not been a fluke. He told the staff that they should let him know the next time the team played at home. He did not mention to anyone why he was suddenly so keen to attend.

"A month later, there was another game," he told *Vermelho*. "He played even better." He asked the youngster if he played football, the outdoor kind, too. He said yes. Jairzinho was sold.

The player was called up to train with São Cristóvão's youth teams. He was playing for their under-20 side as a 15-year-old. His performances drew the magpie eyes of the major teams in Rio de Janeiro and São Paulo.

Jairzinho, though, had recommended him to one of his former clubs, Cruzeiro. Though they played in different positions, he always saw in his prodigy quite a lot of himself. "He is a player who has a lot of the skills I used to have," he would later tell the BBC. "He has this ability of running very fast in the direction of the goal and dribbling at his opponents."

Within three months of arriving at Cruzeiro as a 16-year-old, Jairzinho's prodigy would make his debut for the first team. A year after that, he was called up to the Brazil squad that went on to win the 1994 World Cup. Within a couple of seasons, he would be recognized as the best player of his generation.

Jairzinho had given Brazil, and the rest of the planet, Ronaldo.

That, certainly, is how he has always seen it. As is so often the case with players of such rare talent, there is no shortage of people who wish to brand Ronaldo as their discovery. Few, though, have been quite as vocal as Jairzinho. "I think I deserve all the blessings," he told the newspaper *O Tempo* in 2021. "It is because of me he is having this success, as a professional, as a player and [later] as an executive."

Given his status, there is something just a little jarring about Jairzinho's insistence on claiming credit. He is, after all, one of the most celebrated players in history. He turned Botafogo, the club to which he devoted the prime of his career, into Brazilian champions. In his twilight years, he helped Cruzeiro become just the second Brazilian team to win the Copa Libertadores.

In between, of course, he was part of quite possibly the most celebrated team of all time. More than that, in fact. In 1970, Jairzinho played all six games as Brazil lifted a third World Cup. He scored seven goals, finding the net in every match of the tournament. That month in Mexico, as his teammate Rivellino later told FIFA, he was "the force, the explosion, the hurricane."

None of that has been forgotten, of course. True, as time has passed, some of the fine detail has been lost. The compilations of his highlights tend to portray him as a "potent combination of skill, speed and finishing power," as *Placar* magazine once described him. They tend not to illustrate his tactical sophistication, his versatility, the way he seamlessly, almost subconsciously, switched position to knit his team together.

But he is still mentioned, in dispatches, as one of the finest players Brazil has ever produced, in that small, select cohort of a dozen or so single names lined up just behind Pelé. More than half a century on from the glory of the Azteca, his name echoes down the generations. Jairzinho himself has done what he can to ensure that. "I'm sure that everyone in Brazil and around the world recognizes that, after Garrincha, the greatest right-winger to emerge in world football was Jairzinho," Jairzinho wrote in the foreword to Sam Kunti's *Brazil 1970*.

And there is something about that tendency toward self-promotion, that need to verbalize his successes, that hunger for recognition, that suggests, for a player permanently etched into football's collective memory, that Jairzinho feels he is not remembered enough.

What stands out about most of the goals Jairzinho scored in that hazy, glorious month is the stillness.

In the first, a long ball sails over a stationary Czechoslovakian defense. Jairzinho has time to control it on his chest, juggle it past an onrushing goalkeeper, and fizz it into the corner of the goal with what can only really be described as completely unnecessary force.

In the second, he dances around various lumbering, halfhearted tackles as though they were made in slow motion. The third, probably the most famous, sees Tostão wriggle through an English defense that appears to be on a satellite delay. The ball arrives with Pelé. It is only when he lays it off, almost nonchalantly, to Jairzinho that proceedings come back to full speed.

For the fourth, he darts to the edge of the Romanian six-yard box while the player theoretically marking him is buffering. He goes past Peru's goalkeeper so fast for the fifth that he would not even have stopped his shadow. Against Uruguay, he breezes past a defender with a single stride, clipping the ball into the corner before the goalkeeper has even had a chance to fall down.

That team has been immortalized as the ultimate manifestation of *futebol arte*, the purest incarnation of the Brazilian style of football as defined in 1938 by the social scientist Gilberto Freyre. "Our passes, our tricks, that something that is related to dance . . . [serve to] round and sweeten the game the British invented, the game which they and the other Europeans play in such an acute and angular way."

It was, after all, the Team of the Five 10s, a bold experiment in cramming as many creative players onto the field as possible. Pelé, Jairzinho, Rivellino, and Gérson all wore the cherished No. 10 jersey, denoting the central creative force, for their club teams. Tostão, strictly speaking, did not—he wore the No. 8 for Cruzeiro—but he had the status conferred on him honorarily, as Pelé's designated understudy for the national team.

But at the root of Brazil's glory that year was not just its sinuous natural talent, but a highly regimented, military-grade fitness program designed to turn the country's finest players into elite athletes. Brazil's military dictatorship dispatched Cláudio Coutinho, a military captain, to NASA to learn the secrets of their astronaut training regimen.

Another army man, Commander Lamartine DaCosta, drew up a schedule that would see Brazil acclimatize to the high altitude of some of the Mexican host cities by traveling gradually from their homeland. They would stop off in Colombia, as England famously did, before moving to Guanajuato, more than 6,500 feet above sea level. They arrived in Mexico 32 days before the tournament began, just to make sure.

The planning worked. In *Brazil 1970*, Rivellino recalled feeling fitter than ever. "In that tournament," Jairzinho wrote in his foreword, "in the first half of the matches, our opponents matched us physically, but in the second half, Brazil completely overwhelmed them."

Jairzinho was, without question, unusually quick, even for a winger. He has previously claimed that in a training session at Botafogo, he ran the 100 meters in 10.01 seconds—clocked manually—a time good enough that he would have finished fourth in the men's 100-meter final at the 1968 Olympics. But it was not just his speed that made his opponents in Mexico that summer seem so slow. It was the fact that the most romantic team football has ever witnessed, the one the game remembers as the great ideal of beauty, was in truth a triumph of cold, hard science.

As far as Jairzinho is concerned, the 1970 World Cup belonged to him. He was the one who scored in every round. He was the one who scored the crucial goal in the final—the third, a poacher's goal, bundled home scruffily as defenders flailed around him. The one that, in the sweltering heat of Mexico City, broke Italian resistance and hearts.

"I say that the 1958 World Cup was Pelé's because Pelé exploded that year," he explained to *Vermelho*. "In 1962, Garrincha scored goals with his left foot, which he didn't do before, with his head, from free kicks. The player gets inspired and assumes the role of leader. That's what happened to me in 1970. I got inspired."

That is not, of course, how everyone else remembers it. That month, in hindsight, belonged to Pelé. It was his final act, his coup de grâce, his apotheosis. He provides the defining image of the tournament, being hoisted aloft, a beaming smile on his face. He created the goal that has endured, more than any other, from that final.

Jairzinho features in that move, too, of course—once again, it is his intervention that brings the game to life, that injects a pace the exhausted Italians just cannot match—but his is a cameo. He plays the ball to Pelé, a pass that he described to *Portal da Copa* as "a little kiss." Often, though, that part does not feature in the clips. The move, in popular memory, starts with Pelé, who plays the ball of the century.

What is true of that game is true to some extent of the team as a whole. If Brazil at the time were seen as the Team of the Five 10s, posterity only records one player wearing that number. The side that was supposed to be a symphony is remembered largely as a solo act. Jairzinho, like all the others, has been reduced to a supporting role.

Doubtless Tostão, Rivellino, and the others have at times found that status difficult to accept, but for Jairzinho it may be more of a challenge still. He had spent all his career until that point in the shadow of Garrincha, the player he was compelled to replace first for Botafogo and then for Brazil. It was in Mexico that he finally matched, if not surpassed, his idol.

It was at that tournament that he forged his legacy, when he became, in the words of the commentator Geraldo José de Almeida, the "World Cup Hurricane." He scored in every round but did not win the Golden Boot; that went to Gerd Müller. He has said that his achievements that month are the first thing he thinks of every morning. "I constantly have the Azteca in my mind," he told *Vermelho*.

He regards it, understandably, as the crowning glory of his life; he self-defines as a world champion. Yet that is not how it is remembered. In other people's telling, he finds himself relegated to the supporting cast of someone else's story.

It is no wonder, then, that at times he wants to claim some of the credit he is owed.

Player name: Jair Ventura Filho (Jairzinho)
Born: December 25, 1944
Position: Winger, striker
Debut: 1960
Main teams: Botafogo (1960–74, 1981–82), Marseille (1974–75), Kaizer Chiefs (1975), Cruzeiro (1976), Portuguesa (1977), Noroeste (1978), Fast Clube (1979), Jorge Wilstermann (1980–81); Brazil (1964–82)
Career highlights: A World Cup winner in 1970, scoring in every game. Won the Brazilian top flight in 1968 and the Copa Libertadores in 1976.

23.

Thierry Henry

Henry was transformed from inconsistent winger to goalscoring genius at Arsenal.

An artist, an innovator, and a winner for whom legacy mattered

By James McNicholas

Thierry Henry is often revered for his pace, but it was his speed of thought that truly separated him from the pack.

"On average, a player—if he's great—can touch the ball for no more than one minute in the game. So, the rest of the time, what do you do?" Henry asked *The Athletic* in 2020.

"You're thinking. Most of the time, yes, you're moving, but people forget one of the most important skills in the world—thinking. That's all you do in the game. You think."

Henry's astonishing athleticism was coupled with intellect. "That is something that not a lot of people try to develop: the brain. People will try to make you faster, bigger, whatever it is, but how do you make people smarter? How do you trigger their brain? How do you make them understand space? Understand when, where, how?

"This makes the difference between a great player and an average player."

It also transformed Henry from an inconsistent winger into the world's most dangerous striker.

The catalyst for the conversion was Arsène Wenger. Arsenal's manager recruited Henry to replace Nicolas Anelka in 1999 and persuaded him that he could thrive as an unconventional center-forward.

For Henry, the adaptation was an intellectual process. During an early session at Arsenal's London Colney training ground, Henry felt his runs were being ignored by the Arsenal midfield. "I remember I went to see Arsène one day and we were talking about the midfielders and I was like, 'Sometimes those guys, they don't see me,' you know?" Henry said.

"And I remember Arsène said to me, 'Do you think that Freddie Ljungberg can see you the same way that Dennis Bergkamp can see you?'"

Henry understood the implication: If he wanted to see more of the ball, he had to anticipate the behavior of his teammates; to recognize and play to their strengths. "I took it to heart, what Arsène said. Suddenly I started to think about how I can make it easier for my midfielders, instead of them making it easier for me."

So began the metamorphosis of Henry from flighty winger to fearsome forward, from flaky individualist to quintessential team player.

Henry is renowned as a goalscorer—the greatest in Arsenal's history and ahead of Michel Platini and Karim Benzema for France—but as he matured, other dimensions to his game emerged. His 258 Premier League appearances also included 74 assists. In 2002–03 he set a record for the most assists in an English top-flight campaign (20), a figure Kevin De Bruyne matched in 2019–20.

It wasn't enough for Henry to merely be great. In a game where everything had been seen before, he wanted to offer something new.

"I saw it as my duty to evolve the position of the striker," he said. "At one point in my career, I was like, 'What can I leave behind me? What impact can I have in my position?'"

It's unusual to hear a footballer talk in those terms—to consider a legacy that extends beyond goals, medals, or trophies. But Henry had himself been influenced by watching Marco van Basten, studying the Dutchman's selfless movement that opened up other opportunities for teammates. He too wanted to redefine what a center-forward could be and ensure his presence brought a holistic benefit to the team.

"I realized at one point that the striker will always finish the job of the team and he gets the credit, sometimes for the wrong reasons. I can miss 10 one-on-ones and score the winner at the end and I 'had a good game.' A goalkeeper makes 10 saves, but he makes a mistake in the ninety-first minute and we lose the game—he's 'not a good goalkeeper.' How is that fair?

"So, I said to myself, 'If those guys are working hard for me, whenever I can return the favor, I need to return the favor'—and I started to add assists to my game. And so that was my way to say to the guys that we are a team."

Henry is right to acknowledge his teammates. Any striker relies on service. Henry had remarkable individual talent but also played alongside some of the game's greatest creators: Zinédine Zidane, Bergkamp, Lionel Messi, and Andrés Iniesta.

It will be said of many people in this book that they "had everything." In Henry's case, it rang particularly true—particularly when you were playing against him.

"As a defender against Thierry, you felt helpless," says former Liverpool defender Jamie Carragher, who faced Henry many times in his Arsenal heyday. "He was tall, he was powerful, he was quick, he was skillful. There was no obvious weakness. What could you do?

You're never going to push up the pitch because he's too fast, but if you defend deep, he scored goals like the one against Manchester United when he flicked it up and volleyed it into the top corner from outside the box.

"You could never leave him one-on-one because you saw how devastating he was. You could try to get two or three defenders around him, but then you left other men free."

Traditionally, a center-back's solution to a dangerous forward is to "leave one on them" early in the game—effectively attempting to bully them out of the match with a crunching challenge. "But that didn't work against Thierry," says Carragher. "He was the perfect physical specimen.

"I watch so many games now and sometimes I see a defensive player challenge an attacker early on and just bounce off him. It's a small thing—nobody will mention it in commentary—but as someone who played the game, I'll know it will have planted a seed in the defender's head. From that moment, he knows he's in for a hard day. That's how it was with Thierry."

Henry had been hardened to the rigors of the English game by daily training sessions with the likes of Martin Keown and Lee Dixon. Sometimes roughing Henry up could have entirely the opposite effect—it sparked him into life.

"Sometimes I was there dreaming and someone kicked me and then that's it, I'm on," said Henry. "That's me, I react quicker to that. Sometimes I said to the opponents in a joking way because you talk trash on the pitch sometimes, 'You shouldn't have kicked me, man. You shouldn't have kicked me because I wasn't in the game and you just woke me up. Thank you.'"

Although universally acclaimed, Henry's interpretation of the center-forward role was far from conventional. He favored receiving the ball out on the left flank, the territory he had grown accustomed to as a winger. His idiosyncratic positioning led some pundits to accuse Arsenal of lacking a "fox in the box," all while Henry racked up the records.

"I remember at the beginning when I arrived at Arsenal, people were like, 'He's never in the box, how can he score goals?'" said Henry. "Now wingers score as many goals as the guy inside.

"But I wasn't a box player. I wasn't great with my head. I could hold the ball up, but I wasn't a box player, so why am I going to stay in a position where you're going to see my weakness? I'm going to have to bring you on *my* field, right? Making that run out on the wing was bringing you back to my 'garden.'

"If you don't want to come to my garden, that's on you—I'll be alone. If you want to come to my garden, it's also on you because now we're one-on-one. Either way, I win."

Carragher experienced the sensation of chasing Henry down the touchline more times than he would care to remember.

"Coming up against Thierry as a center-back wasn't actually the toughest thing, in that he wasn't always there," the former England international explains. "I think playing right-back against him, as I did in the early 2000s, was more difficult.

"Playing right-back against Arsenal in that period was one of the toughest jobs in world football. There was so much movement and quality with Ashley Cole, Robert Pires, and Henry. Sometimes the game was just too quick. I almost ended up having to say to myself, 'Stand still. Let them do all the movement, just hold your position.' But I've never felt more helpless on a pitch."

Henry's graceful style appeared effortless, but it was only achieved through countless hours spent on the training ground. Take the archetypal Henry goal: running through in the inside-left channel before curling his shot beyond the goalkeeper and into the far bottom corner.

"Do you know the number of hours I spent to be able to master that?" Henry asked. "When I started to do it, you would have laughed. Trust me, at the very beginning, maybe one out of 50 was on target. And even when I started to master it, still, it was 30, 35, 40 minutes of shooting after training. At Arsenal, I'd grab one of the reserve goalkeepers or even shoot into an empty net. The amount of work behind it was just crazy."

The Frenchman had a penchant for the spectacular but insists he was never motivated by aesthetics. His intention was always just to find the most efficient solution—even if it was unconventional. Consider that flick and volley against Manchester United: It was the only way to score from that position.

He also scored with an outrageous backheel against Charlton Athletic, insisting it was more about expedience than aesthetics. "What else do you want me to do?" he asked. "I tried to shield the ball, the defender's on my back, I couldn't turn. I saw a window. Now, do you have the quality to execute it? That's a different story."

It is fitting that Henry is No. 23 on our list. There is something Michael Jordan–esque about him; a true football icon who transcended the sport and had a wider cultural impact. In 2004, Henry even inspired the addition of the phrase "Va-Va-Voom" into the eleventh edition of the *Concise Oxford Dictionary.*

Former teammates have drawn comparisons between Henry and Jordan's infamous locker-room demeanor. In 2020, former Arsenal forward Carlos Vela compared Henry's "hard" exterior to that of the basketball legend. The only thing more frightening than lining up against Henry as a defender was being a teammate on the receiving end of a steely glare after a misplaced pass.

Henry is unapologetic. "Listen, I grew up with the Bulls," said Henry. "I grew up with, and still love, Michael Jordan. If a guy is going to be extremely demanding with himself—the guy is always showing great desire, great professionalism—obviously he's going to demand a lot from his teammates. And if you can't handle what I'm doing in training, what do you think is going to happen at the weekend?

"Sometimes his teammates didn't know whether to like him or not. 'Yeah, but we won'—and then suddenly they all agree and, at the end, he showed emotion. Yes, because the war is over. People do not understand how the fighter only shows his emotion at the end of the fight, not while he's fighting."

Henry was an artist, an innovator, but also a winner. He was simply holding others to his own extraordinarily high standards.

"Like Michael Jordan said, 'You don't want to come on the ride? Go home.' The Arsenal shirt was too heavy? Don't wear it. That was my view."

Player name: Thierry Henry
Born: August 17, 1977
Position: Forward
Debut: 1994
Main teams: Monaco (1994–99), Juventus (1999), Arsenal (1999–2007, loan 2012), Barcelona (2007–10), New York Red Bulls (2010–14); France (1997–2010)
Career highlights: Won the 1998 World Cup and Euro 2000 with France. Won the Champions League in 2008–09 with Barcelona. Claimed the Premier League twice and La Liga twice and is Arsenal's all-time record goalscorer, with 228 goals.

22.

Ronaldinho

Ronaldinho played his own game, rather than one planned out for him.

The last of the great mavericks

By Jack Pitt-Brooke

It was the end of an era. The end of a footballing century.

When Pep Guardiola took over as Barcelona manager in the summer of 2008, he was charged with revitalizing a team that had grown old, complacent, and stale. It was two years since Frank Rijkaard's side had won the Champions League in Paris, their victory over Arsenal crowning them as one of the great sides of their time. But since then it had all been decadence, decay, and drift.

Guardiola had been promoted from coaching Barcelona B at the age of 37. His job was to bring in new ideas, new standards, and new young players to the team. He would need to break with the past, the situation demanding a decisive act of ruthlessness to show that things had changed. And how better to do that than to get rid of Barcelona's best-known and most popular player?

Ronaldinho never kicked a ball for Guardiola's Barcelona. At the manager's first press conference, he announced he was planning on life without him, Deco, and Samuel Eto'o (who, in fact, ended up staying for one more season). "That is the way I think after analyzing questions of performance in the time they have been with the team, and also less tangible questions," Guardiola said. "It is also for the good of the team." Ronaldinho was sold to AC Milan a few weeks later.

So what were those "less tangible questions" to which Guardiola referred? It was no secret at all that Ronaldinho was fond of the party lifestyle and that he was often photographed in nightclubs. It was well known that he had struggled with fitness over the last few years and that he did not always look to be in perfect athletic shape. Rijkaard had eked the best out of him, but when the disciplinarian Henk ten Cate left, so did Rijkaard's ability to control Ronaldinho. He was given plenty of leeway and took advantage of it, moving further and further away from the player with whom the world had fallen in love just a few years before.

Guardiola knew the levels he had to reach, the football he wanted his Barcelona team to play, and the standards he had to set. Discipline had been hugely important to him during his season with Barcelona B. He set strict rules about timekeeping, curfews, and the use of mobile phones. On the advice of his mentor, Johan Cruyff, he had removed players he felt were not pulling in the same direction as him. And at the back of Guardiola's mind, he knew he had a new generation of young players to protect. Lionel Messi was just 21. Sergio Busquets and Pedro Rodríguez were emerging through his B team. The last thing Guardiola wanted was for them to be led astray.

Who could possibly say now that Guardiola was wrong? He turned Barcelona into one of the greatest teams of all time quicker than anyone could have imagined. Barcelona won three La Liga titles in his four years there and two Champions Leagues. They did so by playing football nobody thought was possible anymore: proactive, dominant, and intense. Guardiola then took that style of play to Bayern Munich and Manchester City, establishing himself as arguably the best and most important coach of all time. None of that would have been possible with a bored, declining Ronaldinho in his team.

And Ronaldinho? He did two and a half years at Milan and offered little to arrest the idea that his career was fizzling out. Then back to Brazil, to Mexico, to Brazil again, India, and then retirement.

Yet when Guardiola sold Ronaldinho, he was doing more than just signaling the decline of one particular player. He was marking the passing of an age. You can clearly—and fairly—divide modern football into distinct parts before and after that line. Everything after that was dominated by Guardiola, his disciples, and his style of play. Football became more intense, more coordinated, more disciplined, and more planned. There was less space than ever before for individual expression, imagination, and style. Less space, in fact, for players like Ronaldinho.

Because if Guardiola is the avatar of twenty-first-century football, Ronaldinho represents everything that was best about football before him. He was the ultimate twentieth-century footballer. His sidelining by Guardiola marked the end of one era and the start of the next.

Think back to everything that was good about twentieth-century football. The players you loved to watch. What was it that stood out? Their capacity for winning a game single-handedly, regardless of who else was on their side or who was on the opposition. That sense that they were not executing their manager's plans but rather reaching into the well of their own genius. Making it up as they went along, but doing so with character and personality that could only have come from within. And carrying with them a remarkable power—the power to surprise you—that is one of the most thrilling feelings in sport.

Ronaldinho had all of this in spades. The point was not just that he was good; that he had a first touch that could stop time, halting his opponents dead and opening up the pitch for himself; that he had a change of pace that no one could see coming; that he was a technical wizard, able to send the ball wherever he wanted, with any part of either of his boots; a master of bend, dip, spin, and previously unknown ball trajectories.

No, the real point about Ronaldinho was that he was playing his own game rather than one planned out for him by somebody else.

Just look back at some of his greatest moments, the ones that make him a true immortal of the game. None of these were scripted or planned, none of them learned from somebody else's comprehensive playbook. They were all purely and characteristically *his*.

Take the winner against England in the 2002 World Cup quarterfinal in Shizuoka, Japan. Brazil had a free kick in a deep and wide position early in the second half with the game tied at 1–1. Ronaldinho shaped to curl an out-swinger into the box, waiting for someone to attack it. The world was watching and the world expected a cross. But rather than wrapping his foot around it, Ronaldinho ran up to the ball and stabbed it with the instep of his right boot. The ball looped up and then came down hard, right into the small gap between David Seaman and his crossbar. Who else could have imagined that, never mind executed it?

Or when Barcelona went to Stamford Bridge in the last 16 of the Champions League in March 2005. Ronaldinho received the ball on the edge of the D, just outside the Chelsea box. He had Ricardo Carvalho immediately in front of him, Frank Lampard behind him, John Terry to his left, and William Gallas to his right. Eidur Gudjohnsen and Paulo Ferreira were heading his way, too. The Brazilian took one touch to control the ball, dummied to shoot, and then, before anyone realized what was going on, followed the dummy with a genuine shot. The blank followed by the instantaneous bullet.

The ball flew in the gap between Carvalho and Terry and into the net. The response of players from both sides, not least Petr Čech, was utter shock. Even now when you watch it back it feels like a conjuring trick.

Perhaps his greatest night of all came at the Bernabéu when Barcelona visited in November 2005 to play Real Madrid. Ronaldinho scored two brilliant goals, similar in outline but different in details. The first started with him running down the left, skipping past Sergio Ramos, shaping as if to take the ball outside Iván Helguera but then cutting inside, leaving Helguera rooted powerless to the spot. Bearing down on goal, Ronaldinho appeared to be readying his feet to shoot across Iker Casillas, but it was pure deceit. Before Casillas was even ready, Ronaldinho put the ball in at his near post instead.

Then, just under 20 minutes later, he burst down the left once again, liberated by a pass from Deco. He taunted Madrid by doing the exact opposite from last time. He shaped to cut inside Ramos but instead exploded down the outside. And instead of shooting for Casillas's near post, he went across him. Even the partisan Bernabéu crowd stood to applaud.

We do not need any more evidence to prove the case of Ronaldinho's genius, but why not consider one more moment from 2006, after his crowning achievement of winning the Champions League? Barcelona were hosting Villarreal. Xavi had the ball on the right and played it into the box. Ronaldinho peeled off away from Pascal Cygan, leaned back, and chested it upward. With the ball in the air, Ronaldinho jumped, spun away from goal, and hit a low-slung overhead kick with his right foot. It was not the natural foot with which to hit it, but then again none of this was conventional. The ball flew over the head of Villarreal goalkeeper Mariano Barbosa and in.

Barbosa was left with the same confused look as Seaman, Čech, Casillas (both times), and all the other great goalkeepers Ronaldinho beat over the years: slightly embarrassed but mainly baffled at having let in a goal of which they had never conceived.

These moments—and plenty of others like them—are why Ronaldinho is still so popular now. Even 20 years on, they still retain some of their surprise factor. You want to keep going back to them to figure out exactly how he did it, like watching a magic trick. And because of how football has changed since the fall of Ronaldinho and the rise of Guardiola, these moments all have extra power. A sense of something lost.

The fact that Ronaldinho declined so quickly after his peak only adds to that sentiment. Because it was not only Guardiola who changed football from the mid-2000s onward, but also Messi and Cristiano Ronaldo, the two greatest players of the modern era. Messi and Ronaldo have changed football in so many ways, but one of them is their startling longevity. Not just that they have been professional players for more than 20 years each now, but the fact that each could claim to be the best player in the world over a 15-year span.

Nothing like this had ever happened before in football. "Having been so intimately acquainted with genius on a weekly basis for more than a decade, soccer fans and executives took it almost for granted," write Joshua Robinson and Jonathan Clegg in their book *Messi vs. Ronaldo*. "No one had seen Pelé or Maradona play this much."

In that context, Ronaldinho's peak looks almost fleeting. He was 22 at the 2002 World Cup when he shocked Seaman having joined Paris Saint-Germain the previous year. He joined Barcelona at 23. He peaked when he won the Champions League at 26. His decline started soon after that and Guardiola sold him at 28. His greatness had lasted for four, maybe five years at most.

That never used to be unusual. Ronaldo Nazário, Thierry Henry, Zinédine Zidane, Kaká, Pavel Nedvěd, all stars of the pre–Ronaldo and Messi era, were defined by shorter spells at the top. Some critics of Ronaldinho might point to his own lack of discipline, his social life, his enjoyment of the fruits of his success. They might judge him by the standards of the era that followed him rather than his own.

But it feels petty, and besides the point, to criticize Ronaldinho for his human weaknesses. It is not his fault that he was merely the greatest player of his generation rather than part of the next one. Maybe that is why he matters so much to people even now because he was the ultimate realization. The end point. The climax of a different age.

Player name: Ronaldo de Assis Moreira (Ronaldinho)
Born: March 21, 1980
Position: Attacking midfielder
Debut: 1998
Main teams: Grêmio (1998–2001), Paris Saint-Germain (2001–03), Barcelona (2003–08), AC Milan (2008–11), Flamengo (2011–12), Atlético Mineiro (2012–14), Querétaro (2014–15), Fluminense (2015); Brazil (1999–2013)
Career highlights: Won the 2002 World Cup having already claimed the Copa América in 1999. Won the Champions League with Barcelona in 2005–06 and La Liga twice. Won Serie A once with AC Milan and the Copa Libertadores in 2013 while at Atlético Mineiro. A Ballon d'Or winner in 2005.

21.

Xavi Hernández

Xavi was a mainstay in midfield and a star for Barcelona and Spain.

Why the Spaniard was more than just a master of the sideways pass

By Michael Cox

In terms of raw talent, Xavi Hernández has no business being this high on the list.

Compared to Ronaldinho's wonderful trickery, Thierry Henry's spectacular goals, Jairzinho's dribbling, or Andrés Iniesta's quick slaloms past defenders, Xavi was an entirely ordinary player. His main skill was the simple square ball, the type that any ordinary footballer could play.

But football isn't solely about technical skill—or indeed physical power, something Xavi also lacked. It's also about tactical intelligence. About understanding the game. About control and patience. And in those categories, there has probably never been anyone better than Xavi.

Breaking down the history of the game into miniature eras can be a difficult task, but the easiest to define is the period from 2008 to 2012 and considering it the Spain era, or the Barcelona era, or the Xavi era. During that period, his Spain side won three major international tournaments—two European Championships and the World Cup. His Barcelona side won three La Liga titles and two Champions Leagues, too.

It wasn't all about Xavi, obviously. For club and country, Iniesta was more elegant and had the glory of scoring the World Cup–winning goal in 2010. At club level, they played behind Lionel Messi, the player ranked top of this list. But Xavi put his imprint on Spain and Barcelona, elevating the concept of the short, safe pass to a level that would have seemed strange 10 years previously and actually felt odd 10 years afterward, too. For a short period, every midfielder seemingly wanted to play like Xavi.

This was the four-year period that Pep Guardiola was in charge of Barcelona and therefore an era when the concept of possession play was popularized, but before the rise of aggressive pressing had become the logical response. Conveniently, it was also the first time in-depth statistics were available for everyone to pore over, to discover quite how reliable certain players were in possession. Beforehand, we merely had access to metrics like shots on target, corners, and cards. A few years later, the concept of "expected goals" made things more complex, but during Xavi's period, it was all about passing numbers.

The availability of these statistics genuinely changed football. During this period, French midfielder Yohan Cabaye read an interview with Iniesta in which he said that Xavi's goal was to complete 100 passes in every game. "That stuck with me," Cabaye told *L'Équipe* in 2012. "One hundred passes, I must hit that! Since that day, I try to be at the heart of every move. For me, Xavi is the best player in the world. Whenever there is a Barcelona match, I watch it to learn and try to get closer to his level, even though I know it's impossible. But I can try. He always keeps the ball."

And he did so in the biggest games in football.

Spain 1–0 Germany, Euro 2008 final. Most completed passes: Xavi, 70.

Going into this tournament, Spain were considered serial underachievers, bottlers on the big stage. And not only did they win their first major tournament in 44 years, but they did so in style. At a time when European club football was overwhelmingly defensive, and cautious Greece and Italy sides had won the previous two international tournaments, Luis Aragonés packed his side with playmakers and Spain passed their way to victory.

Xavi was named player of the tournament and at 28 was finally being recognized as a world-class midfielder.

Starting deep alongside Brazilian-born holding player Marcos Senna, he also had the freedom to move forward into advanced positions. And when Senna threaded the ball to him between the lines in the final, Xavi instinctively looked up and played a through-ball in behind for Fernando Torres, who outmuscled Philipp Lahm and dinked the ball home.

"Aragonés took a gamble on the little guys, putting players like Iniesta, Santi Cazorla, Cesc Fàbregas, David Silva, and David Villa in the team," remembered Xavi later. "The football we played to win in 2008 was beautiful; not just the attacking side of things, but how we were set up on the pitch."

Real Madrid 2–6 Barcelona, La Liga, 2008–09. Most completed passes: Xavi, 89.

This was the game when Barcelona demonstrated they were not merely a good side, but an all-time great side, and when Messi popularized the false nine role that would come to define him.

But arguably the star was, once again, Xavi. As Barcelona ran riot, he dominated the passing numbers as usual, but he also assisted four of the six goals.

There was a flighted free kick for Carles Puyol to crash home a header. There was, unusually, a tackle high up the pitch that sent the ball straight to Messi to poke home. There was a lofted ball in behind for Henry to slide past the advancing Iker Casillas. And there were three brilliant touches with his right foot, which allowed Xavi to receive a pass from Messi, protect the ball from two defenders, spin, and feed it back into the path of the Argentinian to finish.

Barcelona 2–0 Manchester United, Champions League final, 2009. Most completed passes: Xavi, 75.

After winning this game to complete the treble, Barcelona were immediately declared among the best club sides football had ever seen—at the end of Guardiola's first season in charge of a senior side.

Samuel Eto'o slid home from Iniesta's pass to give them the lead against the run of play but, from that point, the result was never in doubt. The second goal sealed it, with Xavi sweeping a cross to the far post for Messi to head home from his new central position. The talk beforehand—effectively for the first time—was all about Messi versus Cristiano Ronaldo. Most agreed that the area where the latter was strongest was in the air. But Messi could head, too, as Xavi knew when he crossed.

United tried to force a way back into the game by throwing on two extra forwards and shifting to 4-2-4, but that simply opened up the midfield and Barcelona passed sideways and saw the final out comfortably, showcasing the quality that had taken them to an almost unprecedented level.

• • •

Real Madrid 0–2 Barcelona, La Liga, 2009–10. Most completed passes: Xavi, 71.

This was not one of the most memorable *Clásicos* of the era, but it was arguably Xavi's most dominant performance in a contest that effectively sealed Barcelona's title.

With Real Madrid manager Manuel Pellegrini fielding a midfield diamond in an attempt to compete in the center of the pitch, Xavi still constantly found space, often by simply standing in the middle of the four Real Madrid players.

He recorded both assists. The first was a clever chip over the top to facilitate a one-two with Messi, who crashed home with his right foot. The second was a measured ball to find the run of Pedro Rodríguez, who curled home with his left. And it could have been more. Xavi again found Messi running in behind with a neat pass to his feet, but his shot was turned around the post by Casillas. Then the same thing happened again, with Xavi's chip over the top, Messi's quickly taken effort, and Casillas coming to the rescue once more.

It was 2–0 with two Xavi assists, but it could have been 4–0, which would have meant four Xavi assists for the second year running at the Bernabéu.

Spain 1–0 Germany, World Cup semifinal, 2010. Most completed passes: Xavi, 105.

With all due respect to the Netherlands, who forced Spain to extra time in the final, this always felt like the true final.

Germany were a revelation at the tournament, playing an exciting brand of counterattacking football, but Spain were able to control the game, playing patiently and denying their opponents any opportunity to transition quickly.

You would not generally associate Xavi with stamina, with covering every blade of grass, but the interesting thing about his performance here was that not merely did he complete the most passes, but he also covered the highest distance of any player on the pitch.

Under Vicente del Bosque, Xavi was moved to the top of Spain's midfield triangle ahead of Sergio Busquets and Xabi Alonso, essentially playing as a No. 10. He disliked this position, feeling he wasn't seeing as much of the ball as usual and often received it with his back to goal and unable to assess his forward options. Still, it didn't mean he was any less influential.

As well as dominating the passing numbers, Xavi also provided the assist for another Puyol header. At 1–0, Spain became more committed to possession than ever. Germany, at this stage unaccustomed to pressing, simply couldn't retrieve the ball.

Barcelona 5–0 Real Madrid, La Liga, 2010–11. Most completed passes: Xavi, 110.

The defining victory of Guardiola's time in charge of Barcelona came in his first *Clásico* meeting against José Mourinho, who the previous season had denied Barcelona the chance to become the first side to defend the European Cup in the Champions League era with Inter Milan.

Here Mourinho tried to nullify Xavi by asking his No. 10, Mesut Özil, to mark him. But Özil was never the most diligent defensive player and Xavi knew that the higher he played, the less the Germany international would want to follow him. So, playing a more advanced role than usual, Xavi found himself as Barcelona's highest player, running in behind the opposition.

He collected a through-ball from Iniesta, it bounced up nicely, and Xavi lofted it past his close friend Casillas to open the scoring—and the floodgates.

For a calm central midfielder, Xavi actually scored an impressive number of goals. Over the course of his La Liga career, he scored every 8.7 games, whereas Iniesta—who played much higher up the pitch, sometimes as part of a front three—scored once every 12.6 games.

• • •

Barcelona 3–1 Manchester United, Champions League final, 2011. Most completed passes: Xavi, 141.

As he later admitted in his autobiography, Sir Alex Ferguson knew the optimum approach against Barcelona was to be more cautious. But he also desperately wanted to record a momentous, era-defining victory in a Champions League final, having previously won the competition with a last-gasp comeback in 1999 and on penalties in 2008.

But the era-defining victory was Barcelona's, in part because Manchester United's midfield was composed of the aging Michael Carrick and Ryan Giggs, with Wayne Rooney only halfheartedly helping out.

Xavi assisted the opener, waltzing into space between the lines and collecting a line-breaking pass from Iniesta. He then slowed down, paused, waited for the run of Pedro, and slipped him in with an outside-of-the-boot pass. Pedro finished calmly. By the end of the game, Barca's three midfielders had all recorded an assist and their three forwards all scored. But, as so often, it was Xavi who unlocked the game.

Spain 4–0 Italy, Euro 2012 final. Most completed passes: Xavi, 81.

Even at the time, this tournament felt like the end of Spain's reign. They played with more caution than ever, to the point they received major criticism for turning their possession play into something defensive rather than adventurous. They were fortunate to get past Portugal on penalties in the semifinal after a dreadful goalless draw.

But their performance in the final was a stunning response. After Xavi's pass allowed the front three—Iniesta, Silva, and Fàbregas, all midfielders by trade—to combine for the opener, Spain scored a picture-book second.

Left-back Jordi Alba, the only Spain player who had provided speed and directness, had the ball on the left and played it inside to Xavi. He controlled, then took a second, a third, a fourth, and a fifth touch, purely waiting for the run of Alba past the Italian defense. With his sixth touch, Xavi played a neat through-ball that Alba controlled, before slamming home.

Xavi also assisted the third, for Torres—just like he'd assisted Torres for the only goal in the final four years earlier. Xavi was primarily about the safe sideways ball, but he could also play the killer pass better than almost anyone.

Player name: Xavier Hernández Creus
Born: January 25, 1980
Position: Midfielder
Debut: 1998
Main teams: Barcelona (1998–2015), Al Sadd (2015–19); Spain (2000–2014)
Career highlights: Won the World Cup in 2010 and the European Championship in 2008 and 2012. His Barcelona career encompassed 25 trophies, including the Champions League four times. Instrumental in Barcelona and Spain's *tiki-taka* style of play, which revolutionized football.

20.

Bobby Charlton

Bobby Charlton, the boy from England's northeast who became a Manchester United icon.

How England's greatest player was changed by the Munich air disaster

By Oliver Kay

In the moments before tragedy struck, as the plane hurtled down the runway, Bobby Charlton felt a deep sense of unease. Then came a loud crash. The last thing he remembered was ducking his head to try to protect himself from whatever was going to happen next.

The next thing he knew he was lying on the airfield, still strapped to his seat, which had been catapulted out of the aircraft and across the runway. He turned his head to one side and saw a teammate, one of his closest friends, looking lifeless. All around him was a scene of chaos, death, and devastation that would haunt him for the rest of his life.

He spent the next hours drifting in and out of consciousness: recalling the bitter chill of the air in Munich, the ice and slush on the ground, the smell of the smoke and the burning wreckage; the sound of distressed voices shouting instructions in German and English; the comforting arms of his teammate Harry Gregg, cradling him and leading him to safety; the blaring sirens of an ambulance, ferrying him and others to hospital; the horrifying suggestion that many lives had been lost.

It felt like a nightmare. Make it stop, make it stop.

Charlton woke up in a hospital bed. All was quiet now, but the nightmare had been real. A young German man in the next bed was sitting up and reading a newspaper. In broken English, he told Charlton, "I am sorry."

Panicked, he asked the man who had died. The man read out a list of names: Roger Byrne, David Pegg, Eddie Colman, Tommy Taylor, Billy Whelan, Mark Jones, Geoff Bent, players Charlton had been honored to play alongside in a brilliant Manchester United team. Young men he had been honored to call friends.

An eighth teammate and close friend, the formidably gifted Duncan Edwards, died from his injuries 15 days later. Two other teammates, Johnny Berry and Jackie Blanchflower, were so badly injured that they never played again. The team's manager, Matt Busby, suffered multiple injuries and was left fighting for his life before eventually returning and leading United to further glories in one of the most compelling of all sporting tales.

The tragic events of February 6, 1958, and their harrowing aftermath would never leave Charlton. He could never come to terms with the injustice that had allowed him to escape with an injury to his head while 23 of those aboard British European Airways flight 609, which had stopped at Munich to refuel on the way back from a European Cup quarterfinal second leg away to Red Star Belgrade, had lost their lives.

"Sometimes it engulfs me with a terrible regret and sadness," he wrote in *Sir Bobby Charlton: My Manchester United Years*, "and guilt that I walked away and found so much."

Decades later, Charlton would reflect that the Munich air disaster changed him profoundly. Every triumph and every accolade that followed in an extraordinary football career—winning another two league titles, an FA Cup and finally the European Cup with United, 106 appearances and 49 goals for England, winning the World Cup, being crowned European Footballer of the Year—was accompanied by feelings of regret.

The survivor's guilt. "Why me?"

The only way he could even begin to rationalize it was by making a silent pledge to shoulder that burden, to play on in his teammates' memory, to carry that torch and to ensure that the "Busby Babes" were never forgotten.

He was only 20 years old at the time, only 16 months and 32 games into a first-team career that would span almost two decades and see him become a byword not just for sporting longevity but for excellence, integrity, and fair play. When Charlton died in October 2023, at the age of 86, he was widely acclaimed as the greatest English footballer of them all.

Charlton didn't set out to be a standard-bearer. Even before Munich, he was a quiet, shy, self-effacing youngster. He was nothing like his friend Edwards, who, although only a year older, was so sure of himself both on and off the pitch. Charlton was the complete opposite of his brother Jack, who was only two years older but had a boisterous, gregarious, uncompromising manner in keeping with the way he played at center-half for Leeds United and England.

Bobby was an introvert who came to life on a football pitch. The venerable British football writer Geoffrey Green described him as a player whose talents had an "elemental quality." "Jinking, changing feet and direction, turning gracefully on the ball or accelerating through a gap surrendered by a confused enemy," Green wrote in the London *Times* in November 1969, "he can be gone like the wind."

It is an illuminating description because, watching the highlight reels of Charlton's playing days, of his most famous goals for United and England, you could be forgiven for imagining him otherwise.

Careers in that era are too easily distilled to a few brief highlights in grainy black-and-white footage—in Charlton's case to a handful of goals, struck with sledgehammer force with either foot, calling in mind a particular type of British comic-book hero.

Those who played alongside or against Charlton always recalled his talent in very different terms, citing, like Green, his vision, his intelligence, his poise, and a body swerve that would leave opponents bamboozled, whether he was playing at center-forward, on the left wing, or in an advanced midfield role in which he excelled in his later career in particular.

Jimmy Murphy, United's assistant manager from 1946 to 1971, called him a player "with the grace of a ballet dancer yet with dynamite in his boots. With the ball at his feet, has there ever been a more graceful mover, able to drift either to the left or right of an opponent with consummate ease?"

The numbers are immediately striking. Charlton made 758 appearances for United, scoring 249 goals. Both were records that stood for decades until they were broken by Ryan Giggs and Wayne Rooney, respectively. He remained England's top goalscorer until September 2015, with Rooney again the record breaker (though he has since been overtaken by Harry Kane).

But neither the numbers nor the footage can begin to reflect the essence of Charlton's story as the player who, having witnessed and suffered the most appalling tragedy, played such an integral role in restoring United to preeminence in England, leading them to glory in Europe and inspiring his national team to what remains their only World Cup success.

On his return from Munich, heartbroken, Charlton sought comfort at his family home in Ashington, the coal-mining town in the northeast of England where he had spent his early years.

It has sometimes been claimed that he planned to stay there for good, unable to contemplate a return to Manchester after losing so many of his close friends. "Pals you go to the dance hall with, lads you would have round for dinner at Christmas," he told reporters in 2008, reflecting ahead of the 50th anniversary of the tragedy.

But Charlton's return to United's colors was never in doubt, so heightened was his sense of purpose. He did not return to action as soon as goalkeeper Gregg and defender Bill Foulkes, who remarkably lined up for an FA Cup tie against Sheffield Wednesday at Old Trafford just 13 days after the tragedy, but he was back within weeks, forced, like Gregg and Foulkes, to live with a post-traumatic burden with no access in those austere postwar days to even the most basic counseling or therapy.

A patched-up United team swept to that season's FA Cup final on a wave of emotion, only to lose to Bolton Wanderers. With Charlton scoring 29 league goals, they almost won the First Division the following season, finishing runners-up to Wolverhampton Wanderers, but a period in the doldrums followed as the rebuilding mission faltered. United finished 15th in 1961–62 and 19th a year later, only three points above relegated Manchester City.

But FA Cup success in 1963 proved the catalyst to greater glories, along with the acquisition of Denis Law from Torino and the emergence of the precocious George Best, whose talents on the wing enabled Charlton to return to a central role. United were champions of England again in 1964–65 and 1966–67, which brought the opportunity to compete for the European Cup once more.

Charlton's status as one of the game's greats was confirmed at the 1966 World Cup. He and England had fallen short of expectations at the tournament in Chile four years earlier, but on home soil they were inspired under the quietly forceful management of Alf Ramsey. Charlton thrived in an advanced midfield role, scoring with one of those blockbuster shots against Mexico in the group stage and twice in the semifinal against Portugal as he edged his shootout with the great Eusébio.

He would describe the final against West Germany as one of his quieter matches; he and Franz Beckenbauer effectively marked each other out of the game, with Geoff Hurst the hero on the day as England ran out 4–2 winners. But there is a beautiful image of Charlton letting out a rare smile at the final whistle. His brother Jack later recalled him breathlessly saying their lives would never be the same again. Jack laughed and asked Charlton what was left for them to win.

But Bobby still had a personal odyssey to fulfill.

He was desperate to win the European Cup—not just for himself or the teammates he had lost along the way, but for Busby, who had been weighed down by a deep sense of guilt, having defied the English football authorities by leading United into European competition in the first place.

Busby was a football romantic. So too, less demonstrably, was Charlton, who had become the on-pitch embodiment of the manager's vision. Both men were fiercely competitive but they shared a feeling that football was something to be enjoyed—if not always for the players, then certainly for the spectators. Charlton always liked to quote Busby's line about United's players having a duty to entertain the factory workers who would show up at Old Trafford on a Saturday afternoon to cheer them on from the terraces at the end of a long, hard week.

The Busby ideal reached its apotheosis on May 29, 1968, the night that Charlton, as captain, finally got his hands on the European Cup after United thrashed Benfica 4–1 after extra time at Wembley.

When I interviewed Charlton more than four decades later, he played down his involvement, going into great detail about the goals scored by Best and Brian Kidd that night but glossing over the two he scored. "I got the last one," he said, not thinking to mention that he also scored the first. "I just kind of . . . helped it on its way."

Talk about modesty. It was a terrific goal, the third in a seven-minute blitz in extra time. Charlton darted toward the near post and produced an instinctive first-time finish to whip Kidd's low cutback beyond Benfica goalkeeper José Henrique and inside the far post. Only Charlton could describe a goal like that as "helping it on its way."

Amid jubilation at the final whistle, Charlton sought out Busby and embraced him. "Everybody was pleased for the Old Man," he told me. "It was the end of a story."

A great victory celebration had been arranged in the ballroom at the Russell Hotel in central London. But Charlton didn't make it. Back at the hotel, he broke down, fainting three times as he tried to find the energy to head downstairs to join the party.

He was certain it was nothing more than dehydration, but several of his teammates felt it was something more: a sense of emotional overload as the immediate euphoria wore off and he found himself consumed with thoughts of lost friends and of everything that he, Foulkes, and Busby had been through since that awful day in Munich a decade earlier.

"My life, truly, has been a miracle granted to me," he wrote in the prologue to his book. "But in Munich in 1958 I learnt that even miracles come at a price."

Player name: Sir Bobby Charlton
Born: October 11, 1937
Died: October 21, 2023 (aged 86)
Position: Attacking midfielder
Debut: 1956
Main teams: Manchester United (1956–73), Preston North End (1974–75); England (1958–70)
Career highlights: Won the World Cup in 1966, and the European Cup with Manchester United in 1968. Claimed three league championships, one FA Cup, and the Ballon d'Or in 1966. Scored 49 goals in 106 England caps.

19.

Franco Baresi

Baresi holds the European Cup aloft after AC Milan's victory over Steaua Bucharest in 1989.

AC Milan's visionary *capitano*

By James Horncastle

Franco Baresi stood in the Amazon Theatre in Manaus. The salmon-pink opera house with a dome the color of Brazil's flag was built in 1896, when this city in the middle of the jungle became one of the richest on the planet during the rubber boom.

Baresi has received many invites since his retirement to promote football in some of the world's most obscure places. But this was a vacation. He wanted to see the opera house in Manaus for himself out of the mutual respect that exists between him and the German director

Werner Herzog, who shot the opening scenes of his film *Fitzcarraldo* there.

Baresi had been struck and surprised by a tribute Herzog once paid him. "There has never been a player who understood space so well," he said at an event at a film festival in Pennabilli, near Rimini, in 2021. "He saw the game better than any player from any country, from any era."

When Herzog surveyed the Amazon, he wished to convey to the audience the same vision and deep understanding of what lay in front of him, just as Baresi did for football from the back of the great AC Milan sides of the 1980s and 1990s. Both grew up on farms in the middle of nowhere, the horizon outstretched before them. Both became *regista*—"directors," as deep-lying playmakers are known in Italy—one behind a camera, the other behind a football as a center-back in arguably the greatest club side of all time.

While in Manaus, Baresi met a member of the Karapãna tribe. Her passion for archery had taken her far. Graciela Santos had become the first indigenous woman to represent Brazil in the sport. Baresi visited her village and related on a small level. He never forgot where he came from.

The Baresi family were raised in a horseshoe-shaped farmhouse in the countryside outside Travagliato near Brescia. They were one of six families on the property and lived in an apartment next to the stalls housing a herd of cows. He milked them, took them out to pasture, and offered a hand when he could.

It was an isolating early life. Hard, too. When Baresi played football in the farmyard with his older siblings, Angelo and Beppe, they did so barefoot so as not to ruin their only pairs of shoes. The ball itself was heavy and made of thick leather, an example of traditional craftsmanship. Baresi looked after it as well as he did when he turned professional. It was the only one on the farm and as the ball became scuffed and worn-out, he took some dried pork rind—the stuff used for bar snacks like scratchings—and buffed it up to preserve it longer.

There was no television on the premises, only a radio the Baresis huddled around to listen to the football. It was the 1960s when, over the course of the decade, AC Milan and Inter Milan reached five European Cup finals. Little did Franco and Beppe know at the time how significantly those clubs would figure in their destiny.

Their lives changed, unbeknown to them, when a priest in Travagliato, Don Piero, decided to start a parish football club with the support of a local businessman, Mario Verzeletti: Unione Sportiva Oratorio, or USO. In no time at all, the team began to attract scouts from the teams the Baresis used to listen to on the radio.

Giovanni Lorini, a midfielder, became the first of the Travagliato boys to pass a trial with AC Milan. He went on to make his Serie A debut with them and even won the Coppa Italia in 1977. Lorini was a year younger than Baresi's eldest brother, Angelo, for whom USO perhaps came a little too late. Angelo was four years Franco's senior and by the time recruiters began standing on the sidelines of USO games, he was already considered too old to be molded by one of their academies.

That wasn't the case, however, with Beppe, who had caught the attention of Inter. He was the first of the band of brothers to make it and acted as a North Star for Franco. Continuing to play with him was the ambition. Instead Franco ended up playing against Beppe, with the Baresis captains of both Milan sides in the Derby della Madonnina.

Contrary to urban legend, Franco never tried out for Inter. The *Nerazzurri* did not even let it come to that. They did not think he was physically ready, even if the same scout that recommended Beppe, a certain Dr. Garoia, had promised: "Franchino, you'll come with me to Inter."

Fate intervened, though. Garoia suddenly passed away and in the vacuum he left, USO turned to the competition instead.

It wasn't as if Milan snapped him up. Baresi flunked a trial in Linate, near the airport where the academy players used to train. Don Piero and Verzeletti, however, were not prepared to take no for an answer.

They persuaded Milan to play a friendly with USO at Milanello, the bucolic training ground in the middle of the countryside. It reminded Baresi of home. He was put at ease by it and scored a goal that showcased all his talent. Baresi collected the ball on the edge of his own penalty area, buccaneered forward, combined with one teammate then another, and went through one-on-one with the goalkeeper.

He thought he'd done enough, but questions remained about Baresi's size. Milan rolled the dice, and when they settled, the faces showed the greatest captain in the history of the club.

For the ultras in San Siro's *Curva Sud*, there is only one *capitano* and it is not Gianni Rivera, nor is it Paolo Maldini. It's him.

Baresi went through everything with Milan in ways the aforementioned greats did not. The club remains indistinguishable from the Maldini dynasty, with Cesare and Paolo lifting the European Cup and, more recently, Daniel making his Serie A debut in red and black.

But Milan and Baresi were family in more ways than one. By the time he moved to Milanello, Franco and his siblings were orphans. The club took him in and allowed the shy, taciturn boy to develop into one of Italian football's most celebrated leaders.

Baresi first appeared for Milan in the spring of 1978. He was 17 and stepped in for Maurizio Turone, who was suspended for an away trip to the Bentegodi for a game against Hellas Verona. At the end of the season, Milan sold Turone and backed the kid to step into the breach.

He played every game the following year as Milan won the *Scudetto* for the first time in more than a decade. It wasn't just any *Scudetto*, either. It was the tenth in the club's history. Landmarks like these are commemorated in Italy with a star that ensures they twinkle in posterity.

Many associate Baresi with the glory to come, but Milan were sensationally relegated in 1980 for the first time in their history after their owner and a couple of players were implicated in the *Totonero* betting scandal. It wasn't the last time they suffered demotion, either. After bouncing straight back up, Milan scored only once in the opening seven league games of the season and struggled for four months without Baresi, whose entire career fell into jeopardy.

Rather than an ACL tear, unrelenting pain in Baresi's lower abdomen kept him on the sidelines. The club's doctors thought it might be a hernia, but within a couple of weeks, Baresi was traumatized by suddenly being confined to a wheelchair. Whether he would ever play again became secondary to his ability to walk. More tests revealed he was suffering from a blood infection. Once diagnosed, Baresi underwent a course of antibiotics and made a full recovery.

Unfortunately for Milan, by the time he came back, they were still in critical condition. On the final day of the season in 1982, Milan went 2–0 down to Cesena and looked doomed. Somehow they rallied and came back to win, but a result elsewhere—Napoli 2–2 Genoa—sealed their fate.

It didn't stop Italy coach Enzo Bearzot from calling Baresi up for the World Cup that summer. He didn't play a single minute, but a winners' medal was nevertheless placed around his neck at the Bernabéu as Italy defeated West Germany.

As was the case with some of Juventus's Italian players in 2006, notably Gianluigi Buffon and Alessandro Del Piero, Baresi flew home a world champion, paraded through Rome in triumph, and then prepared himself for the second division. He could have left Milan, but Baresi remembered how the club rallied around him when his parents passed away. Milan was his family now.

At 22, he strapped the captain's armband around his biceps for the first time. Baresi did not remove it until he turned 37. Once again he helped Milan regain their top-flight status and guided them from rock bottom to the top of the world.

Baresi played for three great Milan sides. First, the *Scudetto della Stella* team, then the Immortals and the Invincibles. He credited Nils Liedholm in particular with playing a transformative role in his career. The Swede had granted Baresi his debut in 1978, then, upon his return to the club in 1984, he introduced the zonal marking schemes he had used at Roma.

Everyone else in Italy played man-to-man with a *libero* sweeping up behind the rest of the defense. This change laid the groundwork for Liedholm's successor, Arrigo Sacchi, to take the world by storm. It also allowed Baresi to express his full potential.

"Physically, I was not a giant," he admitted in his memoir, "and that limited me when playing man-to-man. I made up for it by being aggressive, anticipating what my opponent was going to do and then moving into tight spaces at maximum speed. These were all trademarks of Liedholm's system in which I went from being an old-school *libero*—a player detached from the rest of the defensive line by a few metres, acting as cover—to a centre-back in line with the rest of the defence, participating more actively in our attacks."

The synchronicity of Milan's offside line and the intensity of their pressing under Sacchi changed the game forever. So did the ambitious vision of new owner Silvio Berlusconi, who cared as much about how Milan won as winning itself. They lifted the European Cup in 1989 and retained it the following year, a feat no one repeated until 2017, when Real Madrid went back-to-back.

When Sacchi left to take over the national team, a drop-off was expected. Instead Milan went a record 58 league games without defeat and won the European Cup again in 1994.

Italy were expected to win the World Cup in the United States that year. Sacchi's presence on the bench and a core of Milan players made them a formidable proposition. However, they lost the first game to Republic of Ireland, fell down to 10 men against Norway in the second, and thought Baresi's tournament was over. He had torn his meniscus.

Yet 24 days later, Baresi improbably started the final against Brazil and to his mind played the best game of his career, too. Bebeto later told him that Romário was fuming in the dressing room at halftime that Baresi had miraculously recovered. Nil-nil after 90 minutes, the game went to extra time and penalties. Baresi had cramped up in the latter stages but still led by example.

He put his hand up to take the first penalty, changed his mind last minute on where he wanted to place it, and tragically missed.

As a child, Baresi had been left with the impression that crying was a sign of weakness. He did so only once, holding his pillow tight the night he heard Italy lose the 1970 World Cup final against Brazil on the radio. Years later, in the Rose Bowl he broke down in front of millions. This time Baresi felt he could do it. He had nothing left to prove and wept from a position of strength.

Upon calling it quits after rupturing his Achilles tendon in 1997, Berlusconi retired the veteran's jersey number and handed him a replica of the Ballon d'Or. Baresi never won one, but if anyone ever deserved the award, it was the greatest center-back who ever played the game.

Someone should make a film about him. Maybe Werner Herzog.

Player name: Franchino Baresi
Born: May 8, 1960
Position: Center-back, *libero*
Debut: 1978
Main teams: AC Milan (1978–97); Italy (1982–94)
Career highlights: Captained Italy to the 1994 World Cup final. Won the European Cup three times and Serie A six times, overseeing an incredible AC Milan defense.

18.

Lev Yashin

Yashin, clad in black, stretches to turn away a shot during the Soviet Union's defeat to West Germany at the 1966 World Cup.

The Soviet Union's revolutionary Black Spider

By Tim Spiers

Not even Lev Yashin wanted to be a goalkeeper.

The man who is widely credited not just with being the best to have ever stood between the posts but also with revolutionizing the position and inspiring millions actually wanted to be a striker. Yep, the goalkeeper's goalkeeper actually loved scoring goals. As it turned out, his 6'2" frame and lofty leap dictated that he would end up spending his career stopping them.

And stop them he did. Yashin played 432 matches for club and country and kept 204 clean sheets along the way. In one season he conceded only six goals in 27 league games. Dynamo Moscow and the Soviet Union rejoiced in his reassuring presence.

He remains the first and last goalkeeper to win the Ballon d'Or, in 1963. He beat Gianni Rivera, who had inspired AC Milan to their first European Cup that year, and Jimmy Greaves to the award. The Englishman had scored 44 goals in 49 matches for Tottenham Hotspur in the 1962–63 season, but it was the Russian whose contribution was celebrated.

He was goalkeeper of the tournament at the 1960 and 1964 European Championships, and by the time he retired he had claimed five league titles and an Olympic gold medal and won the European Championship. These days, the award for best goalkeeper at the Ballon d'Or is called the Yashin Trophy. In Russia they have the Yashin Club, awarded to goalkeepers who earn more than 100 clean sheets in their career.

And in a sport where goalkeepers don't have the honor of wearing the colors of their team or country, he made his black equipment—it was actually very dark blue, but let's not split hairs right now—recognizable all over the world.

So, yeah, Yashin was good, we all know that. Most football fans are well aware of the name and reputation. But what actually made him better than his contemporaries?

Footage isn't plentiful and, this being Soviet Russia, the mind wanders. Could he jump 10 feet in the air? Could his arms extend beyond the limitations that medical science dictates? Did he have claws for hands? What on earth made him so exceptional that when Eladio Rojas scored Chile's winner against the Soviet Union in the 1962 World Cup quarterfinals, he hugged Yashin? "I was in disbelief that I'd scored past the great Lev Yashin," he said years later. "I still am. I was overcome with excitement that all I wanted to do was hug him. Scoring past Yashin was like a trophy."

Imagine someone scoring past Emiliano Martínez, Argentina's World Cup–winning goalkeeper in 2022, and then giving him a big hug because it was such an honor to beat him. He would probably knock their block off, but you get the idea; such an unusual incident offers a glimpse into the unbeatable reputation Yashin had garnered.

Yashin was not the first sweeper-keeper, but he was by far the most prominent postwar example of a goalkeeper using imaginative techniques to contribute more to the team than just saving shots and lumping the ball upfield, as was generally the modus operandi at the time.

At a time when it was extremely uncommon, Yashin was an extra defender. He was aggressive in and around his own penalty area and would form part of his team's attacks by starting counters with brisk throws and passes instead of kicking it long.

He would punch a cross rather than catch it. Sometimes he even took off his famous cap and headed it clear. He would marshal the defense by organizing them at set pieces. He was vocal, he was active, he was someone strikers feared because he instigated a save before they had even taken their shot. He was proactive in everything he did.

Again, these might sound like pretty basic characteristics to the goalkeepers of today, but back then, goalkeepers were simply not involved in outfield play. He was an innovator; he broke the mold.

And all this is before you actually acknowledge the nuts and bolts of Yashin's orthodox traits; his exceptional shot-stopping ability and agility that earned him the nickname "The Black Spider" because, well, how could he conjure saves that ludicrous without having extra limbs? Or his abnormal leap, enacted with poise and precision, for which he was called "The Black Panther."

His reading of the game and his anticipation of shots and crosses also stood out, yet Gordon Banks said it was Yashin's positional sense that was his key attribute.

"We were so calm and relaxed when he was in goal," said fellow goalkeeper and Soviet Union teammate Anzor Kavazashvili. "He had a presence that resonated. When the Soviet Union national team was being selected, people would ask: 'Who should be the first name on the list?' The answer was always the same: Lev Yashin. Why? Because when he was in goal, you knew the defense would be solid.

"Yashin owned his area. He occupied a range of positions in the box. He gathered high balls, both inside the six-yard box and around the penalty spot, which prevented his opponents from heading the ball. This wasn't common at the time. He was among the first goalkeepers to punch the ball and he used to look to throw the ball out as quickly as possible. This was to accelerate our team's attack."

Yashin's career had actually been at a crossroads just a couple of years before he came to global prominence.

He was a very talented ice hockey player and, at one point, was a goalkeeper for Dynamo Moscow's ice hockey and football teams. In 1953, he won the Soviet Cup in both sports, underlying the reality that Yashin was one of those annoying people who were good at everything. He also tried boxing, fencing, diving, wrestling, basketball, skiing, water polo, and even shot put; he was decent in all of them.

A year after his cup success in two sports, he was called up by the national team to the ice hockey World Championship but turned it down to concentrate on football. That same year, he earned his first call-up from the Soviet Union (in football, to be clear) and the rest is history.

Yashin had not been perfect in his apprenticeship with Dynamo Moscow, taking a few cracks to establish himself as their undisputed No 1. But by 1954, his innovations were being honed and success followed. He starred as the Soviet Union won Olympic gold in Melbourne in 1956, beating Yugoslavia in the final.

He helped his country reach the World Cup quarterfinals in Sweden two years later. His reputation from his performances with Dynamo and that Olympic side was already well traveled; in a group-stage fixture in Gothenburg, England's Tom Finney took a late penalty against Yashin with his weaker left foot in an attempt to confuse the goalkeeper. And it worked.

In 1960 came the most notable team honor of Yashin's career: winning the inaugural European Championship in France, again against

Yugoslavia in the final. He commanded his penalty area expertly in that tournament, reading the game and sprinting out of the box to cut out through-balls when required. His headed clearances became a feature of the Soviet Union's campaign. The courage he displayed when up against hefty center-forwards bearing down on goal was remarkable.

As Jonathan Wilson wrote in his book, *The Outsider*: "He had been inspired, he said, by seeing Apostol Sokolov, Bulgaria's goalkeeper when they toured the USSR in 1952. 'That blond devil played high up and blocked any forward who might get behind the defence,' he explained. 'It was something completely new to me, but I followed his example.'

"Properly harnessed, what in his first two games had been seen as reckless charges to the ball became accepted as a virtue and, as he grew in confidence and authority, he began to command his defence in a way that would seem natural to modern goalkeepers, but which was unusual at the time."

Yashin's career was on a seemingly continuous upward trajectory, but in 1962, the Soviet Union's exit from the World Cup against Chile in the quarterfinal was attributed to his mistake, having also conceded direct from a corner against Colombia in the group stage. "He wanted to quit," his wife, Valentina Timofeevna Yashina, later told the BBC. "When Lev came back to Moscow, they were whistling in the stadiums as soon as his name was announced. There was screaming and jeering.

"They thought it was all his fault—that it was only him who had lost the game, not the whole team. The journalist who reported from the match did not know about sports. His job was to write about South American politics."

Yashin was being written off aged 32. *L'Équipe* described him as "a fading force." Yet, a year later, he would rebound from the toughest moment of his career to reach his pinnacle—claiming *France Football*'s Ballon d'Or in 1963. That revival was achieved in great adversity, a resilience that characterized Yashin's life.

This, after all, was someone who had grown up without a mother—

she died of tuberculosis when Yashin was six—and who, five years later, had evacuated Moscow with his family as the invading Nazis approached the Soviet capital. Yashin wrote in his autobiography, *The Black Spider*, that his childhood ended at the age of 11. Two years later, he was working in a munitions factory making bullets.

He waited in line for bread. A lump of sugar was considered a treat and Yashin suffered health problems because of the lack of nutrition in his diet.

He started playing football more regularly in 1944 when life resumed some kind of normality back in Moscow, but he would soon suffer a nervous breakdown when playing for his metalwork factory team. "Was it depression? I don't know," he wrote. "The fatigue accumulated over the years began to make itself felt and something in me suddenly broke. At that time, I felt nothing except emptiness."

It was a spell in the military that rekindled Yashin's zest for life and football. He took training seriously and was spotted by a Dynamo Moscow youth coach.

In the context of the hardship endured in his youth, a few people booing him for conceding a goal or two at the 1962 World Cup would have felt relatively insignificant. Still, it took doggedness and determination for Yashin to overcome that and enjoy a fine end to his career, not just with the Ballon d'Or, but with a special performance against England for a Rest of the World XI at Wembley in 1963, keeping a clean sheet in his 45 minutes on the pitch and wowing the crowd with his dexterity and aggression.

There was another European Championship final in 1964 (hosts Spain beat the Soviet Union 2–1) and a World Cup semifinal in 1966. He even went to Mexico in 1970 as a third-choice keeper and coach, before retiring not long after aged 41. More than 100,000 people attended his testimonial in Moscow, with Pelé, Eusébio, and Franz Beckenbauer joining him on the pitch.

His reputation has stood the test of time. It is hard to imagine anyone will revolutionize the position in quite the same way ever again. "Maybe in a hundred years' time, people will still recall Lev Yashin and how good a player he was," Russian goalkeeper Igor Akinfeev told reporters on the eve of the 2018 World Cup in his homeland. "Maybe football back then was different and some will say there were better goalkeepers, but not in my opinion. I believe he was the greatest goalkeeper of all time."

Life wasn't kind to Yashin after retirement; he suffered two heart attacks and two strokes, had to have his leg amputated, and died at age 60 of stomach cancer. He was given a state funeral, no surprise in a country that had already given him the Order of Lenin, the highest honor with which a citizen can be awarded, as well as the gold star medal for the Hero of Socialist Labor in the days before his death.

It was tragic that Yashin's post-football life mirrored his pre-football days, characterized by pain and suffering. In between, football was his salvation. And in goal, no one did it better.

Player name: Lev Yashin
Born: October 22, 1929
Died: March 20, 1990 (aged 60)
Position: Goalkeeper
Debut: 1950
Main teams: Dynamo Moscow (1950–70); Soviet Union (1954–70)
Career highlights: Won the 1960 European Championship and played in three World Cups, reaching the semifinals in 1966. Won the Olympic Gold medal in 1956 and the Soviet top flight five times. Changed the role of goalkeeper with his proactive approach to the game and remains the only goalkeeper to win the Ballon d'Or, doing so in 1963.

17.

Paolo Maldini

Maldini brings the curtain down on his glittering career in May 2009.

Why "the biggest loser in football" was one of the game's greatest defenders

By James Horncastle

Enzo Ferrari liked to say that if you were to hand a child a piece of paper and a set of crayons and ask for a drawing of a car, they would instinctively sketch one out and color it red. It was his way of explaining the mythology around Ferrari and how ingrained the brand has become in the collective psyche.

Let's imagine another scenario. What if an AI bot was programmed to think like the great Renaissance artist Michelangelo? What if the same bot then downloaded the entire history of Italian football and was asked to sculpt a new David out of a piece of marble, only one representative of *calcio*?

Its chisel would no doubt carve the statuesque Paolo Maldini, his piercing visage and those glacial blue eyes being just some of the classical features of arguably Italy's greatest football icon.

Some will hold up other players as being more representative. The popularity of Roberto Baggio, for instance, endures and he still tops polls asking fans to name their favorite Italian footballer ever. But considering Italian football's place in football culture and its association, first and foremost, with the art of defending and style, Maldini's face perhaps fits best.

Nike made a series of great ads in the 1990s, the most memorable of which was the one with the Brazil team in the airport on the way to the World Cup in France. However, the best Italy-related one they produced was a billboard in the colors of the nation's flag. Beside a silhouette of Maldini, his straggling long hair blowing behind him, was the statement, "Italy's goalkeeper: Easiest job in Europe."

It was, on the one hand, a disservice to the likes of Dino Zoff before and Gianluigi Buffon after. Even the likes of Walter Zenga, Gianluca Pagliuca, Angelo Peruzzi, and Francesco Toldo had reason to take offense.

Then again, the defense Maldini played in for club and country was and continues to be recognized as the greatest of all time. Italians know it by heart: Franco Baresi, Mauro Tassotti, Maldini, and Alessandro Costacurta. The irony is that when Maldini started out in football, he could well have taken the easiest job in the world.

Before his first trials, Cesare, his father, wished to know which position he wanted to try out for. Paolo liked playing in goal and the temptation was to carry on. In the end, though, he chose to follow in his old man's footsteps.

Cesare was AC Milan's captain when they became the first Italian side to win the European Cup in 1963. An elegant center-half, he was the one who led the team up the Wembley steps to collect the trophy from Queen Elizabeth II after a 2–1 win against Benfica.

Born five years later, Paolo never got to see Cesare play. He was the fourth of six children and later in life reflected that his parents never set out to have such a big family. But his elder siblings were all girls. Fortunately for Italian football, the Maldinis kept trying for a boy.

Even then, Cesare didn't immediately see the talent his son possessed. There was a photo on a side table outside the marital bedroom of "Paolino" in a maroon jersey, like the one in which Cesare finished his career at Torino. In the picture, Paolo is striking a football. The aesthetics are so perfect it is inconceivable to anyone who sees it to think he would become anything other than a footballer.

But Cesare still didn't know for sure.

Footage has emerged of Paolo slaloming from one end of the pitch to another in an interschool game. However, talent is never enough on its own, and between the ages of 10 and 14, Paolo acknowledges he was not the best player on his youth teams. He was given the choice of trying out with Inter and AC Milan. Cesare wasn't picky and he had seen his boy develop an affinity for Juventus during the 1978 World Cup, when the Italy team that came fourth in Argentina was drawn from the Turin giants.

Again, Paolo subconsciously let his father be his North Star. He joined Milan and played in defense. Inevitably, Paolo was initially perceived as *raccomandato*—someone who obtains a position through privilege rather than merit. A nepo baby. "That's Cesare's boy," they used to say. But in no time at all, this was flip-reversed and Cesare, a four-time *Scudetto* winner and authentic Milan great, became known not for his own glittering career but for his status as "Paolo's dad."

A lot has been written about Milan in the 1980s, particularly Arrigo Sacchi's Milan, the team that revolutionized the game. Pep Guardiola and Jürgen Klopp drew inspiration from Sacchi's pressing concepts and overall philosophy. That Milan side went down in history as the Immortals not just for what they won—back-to-back European Cups—but *how* they won, too. They were also known as the

Milan degli Olandesi, the team of the three Dutchmen. Ruud Gullit was the first of them to be awarded the Ballon d'Or. Marco van Basten has three on his mantelpiece at home. Frank Rijkaard made the podium twice.

In Maldini's opinion, though, everything started with Sacchi's predecessor, Nils Liedholm, and the four Italians at the back. It was the Swede who, on a freezing day in Udine, granted the 16-year-old Maldini his Serie A debut. Cesare was not in Friuli to see it. He was at San Siro watching Inter play Atalanta in his role on the national team's staff, a radio clutched to his ear.

"Where do you want to play, son?" Liedholm asked Paolo as he prepared to come on.

"Wherever you want, Mister," he replied.

Paolo had spent his time on the bench that afternoon with his boots unlaced. He had trained over the course of the week with the wrong studs for hard, winter pitches and had had to borrow a pair from his teammate Ray Wilkins. Once he ran out on the pitch to become the youngest-ever player to represent Milan in Serie A, a record he held until Francesco Camarda recently proved even more precocious, the pain in his feet disappeared. Paolo played well. So well in a 1–1 draw (Mark Hateley scored Milan's only goal) that when he trudged off, he knew he already had what it took to play in Serie A.

It was the first of 647 appearances in Italy's top flight and more than 1,000 in all competitions.

Liedholm's calmness, a trait Carlo Ancelotti inherited, the introduction of zonal marking at a time when no one else was adopting it in Italy, and his decision to base his defense around four Italians laid the foundations for decades of dominance. Baresi, a man of few words, became Maldini's role model. He wanted to become a *bandiera* like him—a talismanic figure—and finish his career at the club where it all started. It meant he rebutted overtures from Manchester United, Chelsea, and Arsenal.

All of them came in for Maldini when Milan were fleetingly at a low ebb, but he never wavered. Even if he was tempted, he did not consider it right to leave when his club were, by their impeccable standards, down-and-out. At the launch of the International Champions Cup in New York in 2019, Sir Alex Ferguson stood next to Maldini and told an anecdote about his attempts to lure him to Old Trafford. "I did try, but when I met his father," Ferguson said, "he was quite formidable. I got a shake of the head. That's all I got. He did say: 'My father's Milan. I'm Milan. My sons are Milan. Forget it.'"

All seven of Milan's European Cup and Champions League–winning teams have seen a Maldini involved in some capacity. It's why the family and the club are indistinguishable. That Paolo won five across three decades is testament to his longevity, adaptability, and professionalism. A left-back for years before he moved into the middle, he still has to remind people he was predominantly right-footed. Blessed with impeccable timing and coordination, he often made tackles and stopped crosses with unorthodox techniques. Coaches training Italy's youth teams often tell their players that their body shape is wrong in certain situations "unless you are Paolo Maldini."

It has been the source of some embarrassment because everyone is different. How you play is intuitive and bespoke to you. Nevertheless, Paolo is one of one. The success he enjoyed with his club contrasted with the near misses he experienced with his country. Paolo played in the World Cup final in 1994 and European Championship final in 2000. "You know that I'm the biggest loser in football," he told Christian Vieri in an Instagram Live during the COVID-19 pandemic lockdowns of 2020. Vieri laughed at the suggestion and pointed out he could only think such a silly thing because he played into his 40s.

But Maldini was serious.

"Wait," he interjected. "I lost three Champions League finals. A European Super Cup, three Intercontinental Club World Cup finals. I lost them, right? I lost a World Cup final, a European Championship final, a World Cup semifinal. I can keep going. I was lucky enough to win a lot [seven *Scudetti* and five European Cups or Champions Leagues]. I saw all of these defeats as a part of the game. I accepted them."

Again, this mentality stemmed from Liedholm, who regularly reminded his players that losing is a part of sport as much as winning. It should be taken seriously. But no one should ever lose sight of football being exactly what it is: a game.

One of Brazilian Ronaldo's favorite photos shows him between the sliding tackles of Maldini and Fabio Cannavaro in a game between Italy and Brazil from 1997. All three are demanding the utmost of each other in that moment. It's what Maldini guaranteed every time he walked out onto the pitch. In a sporting sense, he was prepared to die out there for his team. Once the final whistle went—win, lose, or draw—he expected to be left alone under the assumption he had given his all. It meant Paolo had little patience for the ultras who, in tough times, demanded the players be "ashamed" of themselves, "go to work," and "show some balls."

He clashed with them in the airport on the way back from Istanbul where Milan, up 3–0, lost the 2005 Champions League to Liverpool. Beating the same opponent two years later in Athens did not close the wound. On the day of Paolo's retirement in 2009, he was booed and whistled by the *Curva Sud*, where the ultras stand. They let him know that, as far as they were concerned, there was only one captain they recognized—and it wasn't him. It was Baresi.

In Paolo's absence, Milan drifted and declined between changes of ownership and a shift in the football landscape as Serie A lost financial competitiveness and state wealth at Manchester City and Paris Saint-Germain filled the gap left by Milan and Inter. It was not until Paolo returned as technical director that nature began to heal again and all seemed right in the cosmos. Milan won the league for the first time in 11 years in 2021–22 and reached a Champions League semifinal the following year, only for new owner Gerry Cardinale to sack Maldini as he would a portfolio manager in a hedge fund when the return on his investments in the stock market did not meet expectation.

At the time of writing, he is out of the game, but the dynasty continues into a third generation. After making his debut for AC Milan, Daniel, one of Paolo's sons, earned his first cap for Italy in October 2024 in Udine, the same (refurbished) ground where his father started in 1985. Daniel has since moved to Monza, a club owned by the Berlusconi family and Adriano Galliani, who ran Milan during Paolo's time as a player.

Speaking to *The Athletic* in 2022, Paolo was glad to see a Maldini play in a different role to him and Cesare. Young Daniel is a No. 10 rather than a defender. "It was about time," Paolo said. "As a family, we've spent a lifetime running around after attacking players. Now we have someone who defenders need to run after and I can assure you that being the chaser is much harder than being the chased. When I was a full-back, I didn't feel anything going forward, but when I had to track back . . ."

Let us finish that sentence for you, Paolo. When you had to track back, some of the best strikers of all time thought you were the best defender they ever played against.

Player name: Paolo Maldini
Born: June 26, 1968
Position: Left-back, center-back
Debut: 1985
Main teams: AC Milan (1985–2009); Italy (1988–2002)
Career highlights: Won the European Cup/Champions League five times and overall claimed 26 trophies with AC Milan as part of their incredible defense.

16.

Marco van Basten

Van Basten in action against the Soviet Union in the final of Euro 1988.

The trauma that built and broke the Netherlands' finest striker

By Jacob Whitehead

Marco van Basten won a major trophy for his nation, the only silverware the Netherlands have ever claimed, and scored the greatest goal in European Championship history. He played for just two clubs, both giants, in Ajax and AC Milan and averaged not far off a goal per game. He claimed six league titles and two European Cups. Across one five-season spell, he won three Ballons d'Or.

Those are Van Basten's highs.

These are his lows. He had just three injury-free years at the top. He still endures chronic pain. In the weeks before his 30th birthday, trussed up with a pin-filled cage around his ankle, it took him 120 seconds to crawl about thirty feet across the floor to the toilet. He convinced himself that bone cancer was the cause of his injuries and his mental health spiralled.

"If I had the choice again with all the knowledge I have today, it's not worth it," he told the BBC in 2020. "All the pain I had, it was not worth it. My ankle created so many problems, it affected my day-to-day living, but at that time, football was my whole life. Today, I would make a different decision if I had the choice."

There is a photograph of Van Basten, the prospect, as a 15-year-old in his room at home in the Dutch city of Utrecht. In it, such feelings look far, far away. His face is pockmarked. He has been dressed up in a formal ribbed jumper and his grin illuminates the wall behind him, filled with graffiti. It is the sort of content that would never be released in the modern age—a mural nakedly baring his dreams.

Alongside logos of FC Utrecht, he has scribbled proposed nicknames: "The Bas," "BASTA-BOOMM," "Marcodonna." There's a roughly sketched logo, MB10; a clothing brand, "mar & co"; and no lack of self-confidence. The words "Ik ben de beste" (I am the best) are just above his pillow. That phrase is repeated on his desk, scratched into the surface.

One doodle shows two legs, disassociated, kicking the ball into a net. Given the years he would spend attempting to understand his left ankle, it feels strangely poignant. This version of Van Basten was filled with desperation rather than regret.

In time, he would be adorned with real nicknames. There was the "Swan of Utrecht" and, most famously, a banner on the eve of the 1988 European Championship final that bestowed him with hyperbole even a teenage brain would dismiss: "And on the eighth day, God created Marco."

His rise seemed easy, a notion furnished by the grace and precision with which he played. He was scouted for Ajax as a child and made the first team as a 17-year-old in 1982. On his debut, he replaced Johan Cruyff, a moment that in hindsight marked the generational shift between Dutch football's greatest-ever attackers.

Van Basten was close to Cruyff throughout his career, unsuccessfully pushing for his mentor to be appointed as the Netherlands' manager. Later, in retirement, they fell out over plans to rebuild Ajax and failed to reconnect before Cruyff died. His widow, Danny, called him over when the pair ran into each other after her husband's death. "Please, let's just be normal with each other," she said. "Johan had two apples of his eye: you and Pep [Guardiola, the former Barcelona midfielder who went on to enjoy mind-boggling success coaching the Catalan club, Bayern Munich, and Manchester City]."

But despite his natural talent, Van Basten worked on the more challenging aspects of the game, such as finishing and heading, with his father, Joop, a former defender for local sides DOS and HVC. Marco's elder brother was named Stanley after former Blackpool and England winger Stanley Matthews, but it became a source of rupture in the Van Basten household that, recognizing his youngest son's ability, Joop only had eyes for Marco.

That attention came with its issues.

The Swan of Utrecht was an appropriate name for Van Basten because if you go back to that boy in the bedroom, there was turmoil under the surface.

As a small child, he went out playing on a winter afternoon with a close friend, Jopie. Alone, the two ventured onto a frozen lake, Jopie holding a rope. As they approached the middle, the ice cracked. Jopie dropped the rope and disappeared. Marco sprinted for help but, by the time it came, Jopie had drowned.

Marco was left with nightmares throughout his childhood and kept a picture of Jopie in his wallet. After a few years, worried about the impact it would have on his son's football career, Joop tore it up.

"My father is traumatically dominant," Van Basten wrote in a diary from 1995. "My mother walked into that trap. My mother wasn't able to cope with it. She put her body under a lot of strain. On Herderplein [a square in Utrecht], my mother once took an overdose of pills, I remember."

In 1985, with Van Basten fresh into the team at Ajax, his mother, Leny, suffered a stroke, leaving her in a coma. Two weeks later, recovering in hospital, she had a heart attack. The result was that she lost her entire short-term memory. She would be in assisted living for the rest of her life.

When he played against Utrecht, his hometown team whose crest once adorned his walls, their fans chanted, "Marco, your mother is a nutter." His father never set foot inside the club's Stadion Galgenwaard again.

In his recent autobiography, Van Basten expressed the belief that his ability, his obsession, came from the trauma of his childhood.

"An attitude, a lifestyle like that comes from the drive to be the absolute best," he wrote. "And where does that drive, that ambition come from? I wanted to show my father what I could do with a ball. I received a lot of approval from him for my performances on the pitch. That can motivate a child. I was trying to escape the unhappy situation at home and found joy on a football pitch."

The joy was visible. As a goalscorer, Van Basten had the full range of finishes—pure ball striking, cute dinks, the ability to whip a ball into the far corner. One famous overhead kick for Ajax showed his ability to control his own body while others had frozen theirs.

He was a master of manipulating defenders, beating them with his first three steps or timing a shot through their legs. Football looked simple. Every touch was dismissive; every touch meant everything.

But part of the sadness of Van Basten is that he was only truly unfettered by injury for three years of his professional career.

He first hurt his ankle in a fair and routine challenge against Groningen in 1986 as he competed for a 50-50 ball. "He was meteoropathic, he could literally change with the weather—a difference in air pressure or temperature seemed to provoke an injury," wrote his former Milan manager Arrigo Sacchi in 2021, but that is unfair. The issues, in part, worsened because of management.

Later, it transpired he had torn his ligaments in that initial challenge but had been asked, or rather challenged, by Cruyff to continue playing. The impact would permanently damage his ankle bones.

"I'll make a bargain with you," said Cruyff, then coaching Ajax. "You can skip league games if you feel you need to. Have your rest and recovery. But in return, and I want to be clear about this, you must then win that Cup Winners' Cup for us. And if you don't win it, I'll kill you."

Ajax won the 1987 European Cup Winners' Cup. Van Basten never felt himself again.

Part of Van Basten's appeal was his style. He was a player who didn't turn but swayed, minimalist in his touches, gliding with an upright stance. Former Italian Prime Minister Silvio Berlusconi, the owner who brought him to Milan, called him another nickname—Nureyev, after the peerless Russian ballet dancer.

Seemingly, the only person who didn't appreciate his grace was the man himself.

"What they all found so wonderful was that my style was so upright, though I didn't quite see it that way," he wrote. "As a sportsman, I think you really have to be closer to the ground, with a low centre of gravity, like Messi, Cruyff, and Pelé for example. They all look far more elegant because they have a masterful way of moving. But I couldn't get as close to the ground. I couldn't bend my ankle so well after the operation in 1987, so I was always a little more upright in the years afterwards."

After having his ankle ligaments reattached that season, Van Basten went into the European Championship in 1988 feeling as if the tournament was "a glorified training camp." John Bosman, his former Ajax teammate, was expected to start up front.

Instead, Van Basten ended as top scorer. Recalled after a drab loss to the Soviet Union in the Netherlands' opening match, he scored a hat trick in a vital group game against England, a late winner against

West Germany in the semis, before scoring again in the final—a strike that by now is more myth than goal.

This is the simple description. After 54 minutes, with the Netherlands 1–0 up in a rematch with the Soviet Union, midfielder Arnold Mühren overhits a cross toward the far post. Level with the six-yard box but close to the edge of the area and with nothing on in the middle, Van Basten lashes the ball toward the goal. His volley dips and swerves and kisses the far post as it goes into the net.

It is widely considered the greatest goal in major tournament history. Van Basten considers it a by-product of a deformed ankle.

"The strange thing about that goal technically was that I no longer had a full range of movement in my right foot," he said. "Since my ankle ligaments had been fixed in the operation, I had reduced mobility there and could no longer take on such a ball at full power. With a good ankle, I would very probably never have scored that goal.

"Ultimately, maybe it was a kind of divine intervention because of what happened to my ankle. I really do believe that. A certain balance between unfairness and payback. In a way, that goal was a gift from God."

And on the eighth day . . .

Playing against the Soviet Union gave him his greatest moment, but it was an Ilizarov apparatus, a Russian-made frame intended to reshape damaged bones, that hastened his retirement.

Van Basten had been in pain since damaging his ligaments, but in 1994, after subsequent operations to clean out his ankle failed, doctors recommended a last-gasp effort—respacing his bones to give new cartilage the opportunity to grow.

The apparatus resembled a large cage around his ankle and was agony; 22 pins passed through his bones, leaving open wounds that bled pus. On four occasions, he was rushed to hospital due to infection. Defenders were no longer his opponents. Rather, he struggled to lift his leg over the sill beneath his bathroom door. After almost

100 days, the apparatus was removed. There had been no improvement.

Van Basten remembers the moment in 1995 when he realized he was finished. Without knowing it, he had played his final game two years earlier, at the age of just 28.

"I will never forget it, it was an August day in Milanello," he told Spanish newspaper *AS* almost 25 years later. "I was training alone and could not do the planned exercises. It had been a long time since I met my objectives and I was getting depressed. I decided there, alone, on the grass."

It was a haggard Van Basten who bade farewell to Milan fans on the pitch of San Siro that month. Wearing a brown suede jacket, his eyes sunken, he ignored his limp to jog a lap of the pitch. Both arms went up as if celebrating, but this was funereal. Fabio Capello, whom Van Basten rated above Sacchi as his most influential coach in Italy, wept.

The next year, Van Basten would have his ankle fused, permanently stopping it from flexing, to remove the pain. Of all the players in this book, none had their career more disrupted by injury.

"Can you imagine what I could have achieved with a decent ankle?" Van Basten asks near the end of his autobiography. "I think I could have won three more European Cup finals. I could have ended up with Cristiano Ronaldo–like stats. But that's not how things turned out."

Listen to Van Basten and he is clear he would not have been the player he was without the tribulations. He played with languid ease because life on the football pitch was more straightforward than anything off it during his childhood. His style, his volley? He says neither would have been the same without his wretched, wrecked ankle.

Most players present their life story as a coming-of-age arc, a tale of overcoming where the glory justified the pain. Not Van Basten, a mayfly in the elite, diffident to the end.

Was the pain worth it? No.

Player name: Marcel van Basten
Born: October 31, 1964
Position: Striker
Debut: 1982
Main teams: Ajax (1982–87), AC Milan (1987–95); Netherlands (1983–92)
Career highlights: Won the European Championship in 1988 and scored one of the greatest goals of all time in the final. Won the league in the Netherlands (three times) and Italy (three times) and the European Cup twice. Won the Ballon d'Or three times.

15.

George Best

Best parades the European Cup after Manchester United's victory over Benfica at Wembley in 1968.

One night in Lisbon

By Michael Walker

On a Wednesday night in early March 1966, Dickie Best walked through the gates of the Harland & Wolff shipyard in east Belfast, Northern Ireland, and readied himself for another late shift. Dickie had worked in the yard, where the Titanic was built, for many years.

On this occasion, he had a small transistor radio with him. At around eight o'clock, furtively, Dickie nipped into the inspection hut and turned it on. Decades later, this is how he recalled what he heard: "There was this voice saying: 'And George Best has two goals!' There was only about 10 minutes gone.

"That was one of the most important nights for George. Afterwards, the press and the locals went daft for him."

Dickie's memory of that evening in 1966 was sharp, even though this retelling was in 1996. The game forever lodged in his mind's eye was the second leg of the quarterfinal of the European Cup in Lisbon, Portugal. Benfica versus Manchester United.

Benfica, the team of Eusébio, had been in four of the previous five finals and had won two of them. Theirs was a team of talent and experience, and rather more pertinently, or so it was thought, Benfica scored a late goal in the first leg at Old Trafford. United had been leading 3–1; 3–2 was a considerably less secure advantage.

The team flew out two days before the game to prepare. On United's previous visit to Portugal's capital, they had lost catastrophically to Sporting Lisbon in the quarterfinal of the 1963–64 European Cup Winners' Cup. Having won the first leg 4–1 in Manchester, United lost the second 5–0. It was one of the rare occasions Best saw manager Matt Busby visibly angry.

With hindsight, what is almost as striking as the 5–0 result is that Best played both of these huge games. He was 17. There were no substitutes back then.

Two years later, with Best already spoken about in excitable language, he and United were back in Lisbon. In 19 European Cup games at their Estádio da Luz, Benfica had won 18. They drew the other. There were 75,000 fans inside the ground, officially, with enthusiasm heightened when Eusébio was presented with his 1965 Ballon d'Or trophy before kickoff.

In the away dressing room, there was tension. Denis Law called it "electric" and that was before Paddy Crerand hit a ball against a full-length mirror and smashed it. "I would like to be able to say that everyone burst out laughing, but that didn't happen," Law added.

The teenager in the corner, however, was unmoved. George Best was born for this. "Before the noisiest crowd I have ever experienced . . . ," he said, "I felt superb. The atmosphere sent the blood coursing through my veins, adding power to my muscles, imagination to my brain. We were in bewildering form."

Busby, along with the hushed 75,000, was one of those bewildered. Best scored with a deft header to put United one up after six minutes. He was 5'9" and weighed around 130 pounds then, but he was an aerial presence throughout his short career.

With the aggregate score now 4–2 to United and with the Estádio da Luz unexpectedly wary, Best scored again. Even in black-and-white, the footage is vivid: Best running onto the ball with a snap of controlled acceleration that displayed the balance and balletic power that captivated supporters worldwide—"gliding like a dark ghost past three men," as the London *Times*' match report said.

Best's speed and skill took him clear. He drilled a right-foot shot into the bottom corner.

"What a player this boy is, he's got another!" declares the television commentator in one of those crackling, atmospheric early broadcasts from Europe. "What a player!"

Best had another goal—onside—disallowed for offside as United went on to win 5–1 on the night. The result caused a sensation. Charlton and Law would later say it was their finest United hour together.

"A tremendous roar greeted the first whistle," Charlton said. "From that moment, it was George Best's game, football history will always be sure about that, but in fact, the whole team functioned beautifully."

Busby referred to "75,000 Portuguese screaming their Latin heads off," adding "George Best was so overawed by all this he shut them up."

Not for long. Suddenly a continent was talking about this supple, spontaneous teenager from Belfast who played lyrical football under a mop of raven-black hair. At the stadium, one local fan approached Best with what looked like a knife. It was a pair of scissors: He wanted a lock of Best's hair. Another fan presented him with a canary. Best did not know why and could not accept the gift, though he remembered it.

Media interest erupted like a mushroom cloud. In his first autobiography, *Best of Both Worlds*, published just two years later when Best was 21, he called this chapter "The Explosion." He wrote of Lisbon: "George Best, I really felt at last, had arrived."

United flew home the next day. It meant they saw the Portuguese newspapers and the headline "A 'Beatle' Called Best Tore Benfica to Pieces."

The legend of Best as the "Fifth Beatle" was launched. One week earlier, the BBC had shown the *Beatles at Shea Stadium* documentary, illustrating the full force of Beatlemania. Now Best was included in what felt like a color-filled step-change from the postwar era of austerity into the midst of a new time. There was "Georgie-mania." Football had its first celebrity player.

Over 15 million newspapers were sold every day in the United Kingdom. Best went from back page to front and the first example was Lisbon. At the airport, he bought a giant sombrero "for some reason." He wore it as United disembarked in Manchester and the reaction was like the photographers' flashbulbs. No one wore sombreros in 1960s Manchester.

"It was a strange experience," Best said. "It added to the surreal nature of the previous few days, though it was a reality I was going to have to live with. I became an icon, I suppose."

Within a couple of weeks, on the suggestion of Law, Best had an agent—"*Me?*" was his initial reply to Law.

Meanwhile, in Belfast's shipyard, Dickie Best could not contain himself. Having heard the radio commentary, Dickie needed to get to a television to witness this. But he had a night shift to fulfill. He could not just walk out saying his son was playing for Manchester United.

"He had to climb a gate," Best's sister, Carol, recalled.

Thirty years on, Dickie was standing in the small council house on the Cregagh estate he and the Best family had occupied since 1949. They never moved from number 16 Burren Way, not even when George offered to buy them somewhere grand, nor when United asked the family to relocate to Manchester to bring much-needed guidance to their increasingly wayward player. In 1972, Frank O'Farrell, one of

Busby's successors, even flew over to see Dickie and George's mother, Anne, in this room.

The parents had seen it all by then. Dickie was correct about the transformative nature of the night in Lisbon. His son's life was never the same again.

There had been other big moments: George left Burren Way in the summer of 1961 wearing long trousers for the first time, United's Belfast scout Bob Bishop having sent Busby the telegram: "I have found you a genius."

At Old Trafford, they wondered about that when they saw a 15-year-old waif come over for a two-week trial. Outside Belfast for the first time, Best had boarded the *Ulster Prince* ferry to Liverpool—Ulster being the Irish province in which Northern Ireland sits—with another young hopeful, Eric McMordie. They asked to leave Manchester after one day.

Dickie could not believe it when he heard George's voice the next day.

"Homesickness" was the boy's explanation.

"That's all right, son, grown men get homesick," was Dickie's reply. Then he waited for his son to change his mind.

Sure enough, Best did. A letter to United led to a flight to Manchester, and Best took off. He was in the first team four months after turning 17 and, at 18, played 59 games in all competitions in the 1964–65 season as United won the league title. That set up the trip to Lisbon.

After that, United faced Partizan Belgrade in the semifinal. Belgrade was where Busby's "Babes" had played their last match in 1958 before the Munich air crash. Eight players were killed. United, to Europe's consternation, lost to Partizan.

It meant they had to win the league again to reenter the European Cup—Busby's Holy Grail. They did in 1966–67. Best played in every game.

Returning to the European Cup, in May 1968 at Wembley, United won it. Best scored but did not think he played well. It was one week after his 22nd birthday. He was voted England's Footballer of the Year and then European Footballer of the Year—the Ballon d'Or. Best was, at the time, the youngest winner ever.

That year of 1968, aged 21 going on 22, was described as Best's "annus mirabilis" by Germaine Greer. As unlikely as it sounds, the world's most famous feminist frequented the same Manchester pub, the Brown Bull, as the world's most sought-after footballer. Best would leave Greer tickets for Old Trafford.

In terms of fame, the fifth-Beatle line was accurate. Best's elegance on the pitch combined with attitude and pop-star beauty—"those heartbreaking Irish eyes," said Greer. Millions swooned, men and women. Then there was his courage, Best's willingness to take the fight to defenders who kicked him relentlessly. At the bottom of Irish white legs, Dickie said George had "mahogany" ankles.

"George was a genuinely hard man," Greer said. "But hardness results in fragility."

By 1969, Best had three staff just to answer the mail. He opened fashion boutiques, dated actresses and Miss Worlds, endorsed boots, suits, and sausages. His appeal crossed borders—in 1970, German filmmaker Hellmuth Costard kept the camera solely on Best for 90 minutes, 35 years before Zinédine Zidane received the same treatment at Real Madrid. There were George Best "Annuals," part of a library of books on Best and by Best. The ghostwritten *The Good, the Bad, and the Bubbly* opens with the line "I punched Michael Caine to the floor in Tramp one night."

Best had thought 1968 was a start, but for Busby and Charlton, it was an end. They had survived Munich and they had honored those who died.

Once Best comprehended this, it fueled his off-field behavior. He slid from social drinking into serious drinking. He stopped listening to Busby, started missing training, and drifted from his teammates—a pattern of self-destruction.

The public fascination lost its novelty. John Updike's comment that "celebrity is the mask that eats the face" applied as Best was consumed by his fame. Only Pelé seemed to have more global attention, and he played for Brazil and won World Cups. Best played for Northern Ireland, with home games held at rickety old Windsor Park, three miles from Burren Way. That was until 1971, when Best's home city collapsed into sectarian violence, meaning there were no Northern Ireland home games until 1975.

In one of many external episodes to define his career as much as any tactical instruction, there was an IRA threat to shoot him during a match at Newcastle United in 1971. Best was determined to play and lay on the floor of the team bus. Newcastle's previous game attracted 21,000; there were 56,000 to see Best and United. They won 1–0. Best scored. The Newcastle manager, Joe Harvey, said: "I wish they had shot the little bugger."

Stories like these, some true, some apocryphal, multiplied. Old Trafford press box lore has it that after one early glimpse of Best magic, a junior reporter was noting down the incident when he was informed by a mature colleague, "Don't write down the time, write down the date."

Sadly, the dates rushed by. By 1972, just four years after the European Cup triumph, United were in decline and, as O'Farrell said, only Best was keeping them up. He had been voted third in the Ballon d'Or in 1971 due to another golden burst of brilliance, but 1973 brought further personal trouble and on January 1, 1974, Best played his last game for United, a 3–0 defeat at Queens Park Rangers. He had just opened a nightclub. He was 27.

Many blamed Best for his indiscipline and he was certainly at fault, but Greer, while recognizing Best's culpability, saw his age and immaturity and said, "If the men in charge at Old Trafford had taken their job seriously, they would have made sure George Best didn't become alienated from the team, but they didn't."

After the drama of the United departure came spells in Scotland, the United States, and in England with Fulham, among other paid-for escapades.

But the shooting star of Lisbon fell to earth. When Best died in November 2005, aged just 59, the funeral was televised live and an estimated 100,000 people walked the streets of Belfast to say farewell. The mourning was sincere. Best's football touched people. He was their music.

The funeral procession began on Burren Way. That day in 1996, two of us stood with Dickie in the front room as he held a letter. It had just arrived, bearing a German stamp and postmark. It was addressed to "George Best. Footballer. Belfast." It was more than 22 years after Best's last Manchester United game.

"I get them all the time," Dickie said.

Player name: George Best
Born: May 22, 1946
Died: November 25, 2005 (aged 59)
Position: Winger, attacking midfielder
Debut: 1963
Main teams: Manchester United (1963–74), Stockport County (1975), Los Angeles Aztecs (1976, 1977–78), Fulham (1976–77), Fort Lauderdale Strikers (1978–79), Hibernian (1979–80), San Jose Earthquakes (1980–81), Bournemouth (1983); Northern Ireland (1964–77)
Career highlights: Won the European Cup in 1968 and scored in the final. Won the Ballon d'Or in 1968.

14.

Garrincha

Garrincha's brilliance decorated the Brazil national team's performances for 11 years.

The king of the playground

By Jack Lang

Before the hard sell comes a pause. He stands there, briefly upright. It's as if he is rifling through his mental hard drive, looking for the right words for a lover or a child or a jury—although, given what we know about him, it's more than possible he's just looking at distant clouds.

It's a split second, over in the flap of a bird's wing, but it seems longer. It feels like just this side of forever.

Then he launches into it, story time, the beats of the plot lovingly sketched out by his eyes and by his wonky legs. We are heading to his right, the defender's left. His shoulders start to lean and soon his entire body is going along for the ride, a roller coaster rounding the corner into a death plunge.

The defender follows, more out of duty than desire. It is a hopeless pursuit. But here's the funny thing: It's hopeless in a way he is not even aware of yet.

Look at the ball. The bodies are tumbling offstage, but the ball hasn't moved. It's been there this whole time, waiting patiently. It has seen all this before.

The defender is committed; momentum and gravity are now his enemies. He digs deep, ignores his complaining muscles, and hauls himself back to center. There's only one problem: His tormentor is already there, already departing. And this time he is taking the ball with him.

He could be going either way for all the difference it would make to the defender. Zoom out a little and it would probably make more sense to dart left, infield, since a handful of other opponents also bought the initial routine. But no, he's going right, going where he pretended to go before, where the defender has just returned from, back to the scene of the crime.

Why? That's the easy part. It's funnier this way.

One of the best things about football is the sheer variety of responses—rational, emotional, physical—it is capable of eliciting in the observer. Some of them are common and recurring. Those people running around in front of us or on our television screens make us swoon, make us tremble with nervous energy, make us tear our hair out.

One reaction, though, is rarer than it should be, at least when you reach the professional game. Football can be awfully po-faced; it hardly ever makes you laugh.

At which point enters Garrincha, the Little Wren, not quite the greatest Brazilian footballer of all time, but definitely, definitely the most hilarious.

We'll circle back to the tragic irony of that fact later and lament the tears of the clown, but when it comes to Garrincha, it really is worth just establishing a baseline appreciation of his oeuvre in all its wriggly, flippant glory.

The dribble described above—that full-bodied, Drunken Master feint—has always been my favorite. But Garrincha, not inappropriately, adhered to a version of the old Groucho Marx line, "This is my signature trick, and if you don't like it . . . well, I have others."

Watch the videos. Through the analog fuzz and the bad camera angles emerges an extraordinary catalog of dummies, flicks, and feints, a hodgepodge of silly tricks. There are fast dribbles and there are slow dribbles, when he seems to want to take in the view. There are slalom runs, all acute angles and twisted ankles, and there are direct bursts. There are hundreds of little forays into forests of legs, an eager little dog pursuing a rabbit, not even sure if he wants to catch it, just enjoying the sheer exhilaration of the chase.

There he goes, inside and out, outside and in, twisting, jerking, leaping, skipping. He nutmegs defenders. More often he just lures them in, makes them think the ball is there to be won, then flicks it away with a nonchalance that manages to be both cruel and cheerful. Occasionally, he just seems to teleport *through* them.

And so you laugh. You laugh because it's funny seeing football played like this. Funny to see the strategy and the superstructure stripped away for a moment, leaving only pure play. You laugh because you could easily be watching Charlie Chaplin or Stan Laurel, those other masters of slapstick. You laugh because sometimes you see something your brain doesn't quite know what to do with, something that is at once recognizably wonderful and not recognizable at all.

He was born into poverty in a town whose name translates as Big Stick and he had crooked legs. The left one was about two inches shorter than the right and turned outward. The right one turned in. When Garrincha reported for military service as a teenager, the local army chief took one glance at him and told him he wouldn't be needed. The notion that he would become a footballer was deeply illogical.

Garrincha—Mané to his friends—dribbled past logic. After doing well for the local factory team, he went for a trial at Botafogo, one of the big clubs in Rio de Janeiro. He was 19. He yanked Brazil full-back Nílton Santos into so many strange shapes during his first practice session that Botafogo fast-tracked him into their first team. Within months, the young winger was the talk of the city.

It is not hard to imagine a world in which Garrincha remained a darling of the provinces. His talent spoke for itself, but his outlook was blinkered: He liked to return to his hometown between games, knocking about with old friends. It wasn't immediately obvious that his matador skill set would translate beyond the local leagues. His unprofessionalism—to say that Garrincha liked to drink and womanize is akin to saying fish are partial to water—also appeared to make him a poor fit for genuine stardom.

He made Brazil's squad for the 1958 World Cup, but it looked like it was going to be a washout. Garrincha was characterized as childish and moronic in psychological tests commissioned by the Brazilian federation before the tournament and was then left out of Brazil's first two games.

His appearance in the starting lineup for the third, against the Soviet Union, owed much to his popularity among his fellow players, who had lobbied coach Vicente Feola for his inclusion. Garrincha repaid the favor with a display of almost ludicrous menace and never left the side as Brazil claimed their first World Cup.

He was doubly influential as Brazil defended their crown in Chile four years later. Garrincha was the best player at the World Cup, scoring four times and leading the attack after an injury sustained in the group phase ended Pelé's involvement. The image of Brazil's No. 7 running rings around opposition defenses—often literally—will forever be embedded in the nation's collective memory.

The wider football community, too, was now awake to Garrincha's otherworldly charms. "Garrincha," ran one headline in Chilean newspaper *El Mercurio*, "what planet are you from?"

The spontaneity and devil-may-care looseness of Garrincha's play did not only endear him to fans. He was also a gift to Brazil's writers, who were beguiled and fascinated by him.

"The joy of Garrincha's football is that he plays on pure inspiration, on magic, without reservations, without plans," wrote newspaper columnist Paulo Mendes Campos.

Playwright Nelson Rodrigues, one of Brazil's most celebrated cultural figures, was even more lyrical. "Garrincha doesn't think," he wrote in 1958. "He doesn't need to. Rationality is foolish, a horse-drawn cart up against the vertiginous agility of instinct.

"He teaches us that nothing is more beautiful than speed. Up against him, we are all slowcoaches, cattle, hippopotamuses. He doesn't kick the ball like others do. He cultivates it like it was a rare orchid. Even God must admire him from above."

Garrincha's appeal transcended the bounds of the pitch. Brazilians also identified with the man, imperfect of body and of mind, a mortal—so crushingly mortal—among the idols. The unavoidable comparison here is with Pelé, sporting excellence personified but also inscrutable, even a little remote. Garrincha was one of the gang and people loved him for it.

That only became more true as his flaws consumed him. Garrincha played at the 1966 World Cup, but his drinking had reached catastrophic levels by then. He was at the wheel—and likely inebriated—in a car crash that killed his mother-in-law in 1969. By that stage, his club career had fizzled out into a series of failed restarts. Already his story had begun to take on the grim pallor of tragedy.

The years after his retirement confirmed it. Garrincha, feeling increasingly abandoned and alone, bounced between the bar and the hospital, often on the same day. Alcohol's grip grew tighter, ever tighter, until it was impossible for even the great escape artist to squirm free.

"I ask myself if there was some deep reason that made him drink," wrote Nílton Santos, Garrincha's old Botafogo and Brazil teammate. "Maybe it was something so personal, so intimate, that he didn't want to tell anyone.

"I got tired of telling him, 'Mané, that's a slow death.' But I don't think I understood that his true, unconfessed desire was to die. He lived trying to destroy himself."

In his final years, Garrincha cut a ghostly figure. One of his final public appearances, on a parade float during the 1980 Rio Carnival, was so distressing that it moved those who observed it—Pelé included—to the brink of tears. "He was sitting there on a float, with no apparent notion of what was going on around him," wrote Pelé. "His face looked worn out like there was no life left. It was one of the saddest things I ever saw."

Garrincha died in January 1983. He was 49.

Grief enveloped Brazil. It was tempered only by a parallel movement to celebrate Garrincha's life and to restate, one last time and for future generations, the reasons for his status as a national emblem.

That task was best tackled by the great Brazilian poet Carlos Drummond de Andrade, whose tribute, published in the *Jornal do Brasil*, captured the nuances of the collective mood. He painted a picture of Garrincha as an antidote to—or, like Carnival, a distraction from—Brazilian ennui. A figure who, during those electric colt years, made an entire country lift its chin. "Joy of the People," they called him, and that was no empty sentiment.

"Fun, spontaneous, inconsequential, with an innocence that did not stop him from being street-smart . . . there could be no better model to seduce a public that, looking around, did not find serious heroes, the miraculous saints they needed in their day-to-day lives," Drummond de Andrade wrote.

"Garrincha asked nothing of his admirers; he didn't demand sacrifices or mental effort to follow him. He carried the weight on his shoulders with joy, giving us permission to do the same.

"He was a poor mortal who helped an entire country to sublimate its miseries. The sad thing is that the miseries return, but there is no other Garrincha available. We need a new one to feed our dreams."

Four decades have passed since Drummond de Andrade wrote those words. You can add on a couple more to get back to Garrincha's peak. It can be hard to appreciate the depth of feeling at such a remove. Emotion slowly bleeds out of history; there is no tourniquet.

We must be thankful, at least, for those blurry videos. They are a poor substitute for what it must have felt like being there, but they tell just enough of the story and evoke warm echoes of the sentiments.

There he is, the king of the playground, thrillingly unbound. There he is, giggling as he outruns his own shadow. There he is, legs askew, a living, breathing repudiation of common sense, dodging, ducking, throwing punch lines.

Go ahead, laugh. It is what Garrincha would have wanted.

Player name: Manuel Francisco dos Santos (Garrincha)
Born: October 28, 1933
Died: January 20, 1983 (aged 49)
Position: Right-winger
Debut: 1953
Main teams: Botafogo (1953–65); Brazil (1955–66)
Career highlights: Won the World Cup in 1958 and 1962 and was joint winner of the Golden Boot at the latter tournament.

13.

Gerd Müller

The prolific Müller scores West Germany's second against the Netherlands in the 1974 World Cup final.

Germany's greatest goalscorer

By Nick Miller

There is one thing every footballer in this book has in common. It's a bit technical, so apologies for blinding you with jargon here, and please don't feel too bad if you don't completely follow, but here it is: They're all really good at football.

Well, that's sort of true. It depends what you mean by "really good at football." One of them did not boast the same skill or grace or innovation or mystery or fantasy as the others. He wasn't so much really good at football, but *really good at scoring goals*. Are those two things different? Maybe not. But Gerd Müller made up for not being stellar at the other stuff, the things we often talk about when we talk about the "greats," by being maybe the best there ever was at the game's most fundamental task.

Here are a few statistics. He scored 365 goals in 427 Bundesliga games. He scored 40 in one season, a record that stood for five decades. He scored 85 for club and country in one calendar year. He scored 68 goals in 77 European games. He scored an astonishing 68 in 62 international games for West Germany and would have managed many more had he not retired from the national team in 1974 aged 28, after the German federation banned the players' wives from attending the post–World Cup victory celebration banquet.

Among those international goals, he scored 14 over 13 games at two World Cups, a record that stood for 32 years until it was broken by Ronaldo in 2006.

He scored 566 goals in 607 games for Bayern Munich, the club for whom he made his debut in 1964 when they were still playing in the German second tier and, along with Franz Beckenbauer, played as much of a role as anyone in making them the behemoth they are today. He made it into double figures for league goals in each of his 14 full seasons with Bayern. He can be forgiven for the only time he managed fewer than 10 league goals in a campaign—he scored nine in 19 games in the first half of the 1978–79 campaign before moving to the Fort Lauderdale Strikers in the United States.

Goals were his obsession and it was the *what* rather than the *how* that consumed him. The method of the conversion did not matter, but the result did.

He would score by whatever means necessary: tap-ins, scuffed shots, headers from three yards out, in off the thigh, the shins, the torso, scooped in from the floor, left foot, right foot, head—whatever body part could propel a football over that line.

If you watch clips of Müller's goals, one of the things you'll notice is how often he just seems to . . . emerge. And then score. The ball will disappear into a melee of defenders, only for Müller to suddenly appear, completely free, like a cartoon character calmly stepping out of a cloud of flailing arms and legs. He appeared to have an ability to be in the right position to score and often you weren't entirely sure how he arrived there.

It's pretty hard to explain how he did it. Some attribute it to his short, stocky frame, thus allowing him to have a low center of gravity to wriggle away from hulking defenders, but also with the strength to muscle his way into advantageous positions. He had thighs like beer barrels and calves like hams, giving him the sort of power you might not expect from a relatively diminutive man.

The most appealing, perhaps romantic, explanation for why he was so good is that it was something intangible. He could, in the traditions of the great goal poachers, smell opportunities. It all just happened. He just . . . knew. "You can't learn that," he said in a documentary produced by the Bundesliga. "You just have to have the instinct to score goals."

Müller's single-season Bundesliga scoring record of 40, set in 1971–72, was thought for decades to be insurmountable. In fact, between him setting that record and Robert Lewandowski establishing himself as an elite striker in the mid-2010s, the only other players even to break 30 goals, never mind come close to the record, were Jupp Heynckes in 1973–74 and Dieter Müller in 1976–77.

When it became clear that Lewandowski was going to break the record, as he did by scoring an extraordinary 41 in 2020–21, it felt like there was a move in the German footballing consciousness to preserve Müller's status as still the greatest striker the league had ever seen.

"Robert's definitely a great striker, but he didn't score goals like Gerd, with his shin, his chest, or his knee," Uli Hoeneß told the Bavarian newspaper *Münchner Merkur*. "Gerd didn't care less how he got the ball in. It just had to go in any which way it could. Robert hammers it into the back of the net, but, with Gerd, sometimes the ball would just stop an inch over the line."

That wasn't just an old friend of Müller trying to protect his legacy. "In terms of efficiency, he's second among the best-ever strikers of Bayern's history after Gerd Müller," Lewandowski's contemporary, Thomas Müller, told *Sport Bild*.

It felt like Lewandowski was as keen as anyone to defer to Müller:

When he scored his 40th, equaling the record, he lifted up his Bayern shirt to reveal a T-shirt with Müller's face and the message "4ever Gerd." There was a poignancy to the fact that, while Müller was alive when the record was broken, he was in a care home, suffering from the last few months of the Alzheimer's disease that would eventually claim his life.

Müller's record-setting season was part of a record-setting year: In 1972 he registered a whopping 85 goals in 60 games for club and country, a mark that held until no less a man than Lionel Messi managed 91 in 2012. Kids, if you're reading this having previously not known much about Müller and take just one thing away from this section of the book, let it be that it took 40 years and the greatest player of all time to eclipse the German.

He didn't just score goals in quantity, but also quality—not in terms of them being spectacular strikes that would make *golazo* compilations for years to come, but crucial goals, high-pressure goals, trophy-winning goals.

He scored four in various DFB-Pokal finals; three in two different European Cup finals; two in the 1972 European Championship final for West Germany; and, of course, the winner in the 1974 World Cup final. You can also throw in two in the "Game of the Century"—the 1970 World Cup semifinal that West Germany ultimately lost 4–3 to Italy, plus two in the 1972 Euros semifinal against Belgium and four in the two-legged 1967 European Cup Winners' Cup semifinal against Standard Liège, which Bayern would win and then go on to claim their first European trophy.

Which is to say that his goals didn't just make for impressive statistics, but made his country world and European champions and his club among the biggest in Europe. Or, as Beckenbauer put it while giving a speech at Müller's 50th birthday party: "Without Gerd Müller, we'd probably still be in the wooden hut that was once our clubhouse. He's the most important player in the history of Bayern."

The noble art of goal poaching is often treated a little sniffly, but consider the following: Müller scored 14 World Cup goals for West Germany, in 1970 and 1974.

Here are short descriptions of all of them: heads in a rebound off the crossbar from two yards out; turns home a low cross from about four yards; a penalty, high into the top corner; a header from a right-sided cross from about 10 yards; brings down a ball from deep on his chest, pokes in from seven yards; converts a low cross from six yards; header from seven yards; hooked in from three yards; bundled over the line from two yards; header from four yards; near-post header from five yards; miscontrol then scooped in while on the floor from four yards; low finish from 13 yards; miscontrol then steps back and scores from eight yards.

Obviously, the distances are all rough estimates, but from those descriptions the average gap from Müller to goal was about 6.2 yards. He barely needed to leave the six-yard box. Helmut Schön, the manager of West Germany at both of those World Cups, famously described him as being "a man of small goals." Again, that was not intended as an insult.

Take the winner in the 1974 final in Munich, which you can look at in a couple of ways: either as a stumble, a piece of opportunism, or a man mopping up his own mistake having allowed the low cross to skew off the side of his boot. But watch it again with softer eyes and you may instead see a man showing incredibly quick reactions, followed by extraordinary strength to change direction so rapidly, implausible balance to avoid falling on his backside, and then great poise and finishing ability to shoot low into the corner, giving the goalkeeper no chance.

And you could go through plenty of his goals and give them similar treatment. Just because they were from close in—or were not necessarily from chances created by him, or are not your typical screamers—does not mean they lack beauty or skill.

One thing that has sprung to mind repeatedly while considering all of the incredible names in this book is whether the great players from the past would be superstars today. Players like Johan Cruyff, Michel Platini, Pelé, Marco van Basten: It seems inconceivable that if they were born at the right time with the advantages of modern training, nutrition, and so forth, then they would have been just as great.

With Müller, though, you're not so sure. There isn't much space in the modern game for someone who does not offer a huge amount other than goals, as absurd as that sounds. Maybe he would have adapted, but it feels like he existed in an era suited to him.

Müller makes for a pretty lousy highlights reel. There aren't many stories about spectators lining up to gasp at his genius, few misty-eyed recollections of the time he made opponents look foolish. He wasn't a meme-able footballer, nor one for whom a compilation of his best skills will blow up on YouTube.

He didn't change the game. He didn't innovate in the way that his contemporaries, Beckenbauer or Cruyff, did. He didn't have a "move." There's a tendency toward overintellectualizing players like that, but not with Müller, which might explain why he often isn't mentioned in the same breath as some of those other greats.

Yet you could make a strong argument that he was the greatest pure footballer of all time because he was among the best at doing the purest thing the game has. There are so many things to find pleasurable in football: a brilliant piece of skill, a great pass, a crunching tackle, a player effortlessly controlling the game, a dummy, a subtle touch here and there. But ultimately, the point of it all is to score goals. You win games, and thus attain glory, by scoring goals. Müller scored goals.

In fact, his contribution to the language of football, in Germany at least, was to lend his name to a verb, but it wasn't something unique to him: to *müllern* means to score. Which says it all, really: He was so associated with the scoring of goals that his name was not given to a turn or a trick or a position. It was bestowed on the most fundamental element of the sport.

Player name: Gerhard Müller
Born: November 3, 1945
Died: August 15, 2021 (aged 75)
Position: Striker
Debut: 1963
Main teams: 1861 Nördlingen (1963–64), Bayern Munich (1964–79), Fort Lauderdale Strikers (1979–81); West Germany (1966–74)
Career highlights: Won the World Cup in 1974 and the Golden Boot at the 1970 edition of the tournament. Won the 1972 European Championship. Scored 68 goals in 62 games for West Germany. Won the European Cup three times in a row with Bayern Munich and scored a total of 566 goals for the club. Claimed the Ballon d'Or in 1970.

12.

Ronaldo

Ronaldo's year at Barcelona culminates in victory in the European Cup Winners' Cup against Paris Saint-Germain.

How Barcelona enjoyed the striker at his peak

By Nick Miller

When you picture Ronaldo, it probably isn't in a Barcelona shirt. He exists in the broader public consciousness in the white of Real Madrid, or the yellow of Brazil, or even the black and blue of Inter Milan. You think of him scoring twice in the 2002 World Cup final or that hat trick against Manchester United in the Champions League in 2003. Or perhaps even some of his darker moments; his face contorted in agony after his second knee injury at Inter or looking spaced-out before the 1998 World Cup final.

But his one season at Barcelona, 1996–97, was his peak.

Arguably, it was the peak of center-forwards, full stop. It was where he recorded his biggest single-season goal tally. It was where he announced himself as a true world great. It was where he did things that made people who had seen it all in football admit they had never seen anything quite like him.

The January 1997 edition of *World Soccer* magazine had Ronaldo on the cover under the headline "Best Ever?" It was a big question to ask about a 20-year-old halfway through his first season in one of Europe's top leagues, but they weren't wrong.

Most of the players in this book justified their inclusion through a whole career of excellence—or at least an extended spell. Ronaldo does, too, but even if we were to forget the other 17 seasons of his career—the club trophies, the World Cup, the Golden Boot, the many cabinets of individual awards, the 305 goals for Cruzeiro, PSV Eindhoven, Inter, Real Madrid, AC Milan, and Corinthians—and just concentrated on that year in Catalonia, he would still qualify as one of the greats.

Josep Lluís Núñez wasn't sure. The Barcelona president had asked Bobby Robson, appointed as their manager in the summer of 1996, for his preference as a new striker. He suggested Alan Shearer but was told in no uncertain terms by Blackburn Rovers that the Englishman was not for sale, a few weeks before he was sold to Newcastle United.

Robson's other option was Ronaldo.

Just about to turn 20 at the time, the Brazilian had scored a bagful of goals in two seasons at PSV, although a knee injury—which would turn out to be a ticking time bomb—had curtailed his second year in the Netherlands.

Robson thought he could be signed for $10 million, but Núñez went back to PSV over and over, incrementally increasing his bids and, after each rejected offer, returned to Robson to ask if he was certain about this kid. "At one point, Núñez wagged his finger at me and warned, 'Bobby, you know your job depends on this?'" Robson wrote in his autobiography.

Eventually, the deal was done for $20 million, an extraordinary sum at the time, the world transfer record (albeit one broken shortly afterward by Shearer), and a particular gamble given Ronaldo's youth and relative lack of pedigree. But Robson was sure.

Ronaldo's first goal came five minutes into his debut, in the Spanish Super Cup against Atlético Madrid. The first league goal was scored against Racing Santander three weeks later. Then he got two in the next game against Real Sociedad. Then another two against Real Zaragoza.

By this point, his teammates were convinced. "I'd seen him on television at PSV and thought: 'Wow,'" his Barca teammate Luis Enrique told *FourFourTwo* magazine in 2017. "Then he came to Barcelona. He's the most spectacular player I've ever seen. He did things I'd never seen before. We're now used to seeing [Lionel] Messi dribble past six players, but not then."

The seventh league game of the season came at SD Compostela. They are a small, relatively unremarkable side who have only spent four seasons in the Spanish top flight in their history. They haven't had many former players or managers of particular note. They've never won a major trophy. At the risk of being insulting or patronizing, what happened on October 12, 1996, might be the most notable event in the club's history.

This was the goal. *The Goal.* The most remarkable goal you will perhaps ever see. It starts before Ronaldo even touches the ball, his mere presence making two Compostela defenders crash into each other near the halfway line, like slapstick cartoon henchmen. Midfielder Saïd Chiba gives up on trying to tackle him and grabs a big handful of his jersey, but it's of absolutely no use. Ronaldo breaks away and the only shame is that Chiba isn't just left standing there with a ripped piece of shirt in his hand as his opponent speeds off into the distance.

Ronaldo then accelerates past two defenders and into the area, at which point the angle to the goal appears to have narrowed a little too much. So he cuts inside and his feet become a blur, whipping the ball back and forth at a speed that is difficult to pick up with the naked eye.

Briefly, Ronaldo seems to lose control of the ball. But no matter, he reacts to it before anyone else can. He sweeps it into the corner. Everyone in the stadium recognizes that they've seen something unforgettable.

On the touchline, Robson leaps to his feet, throws his hands in the air, and then clasps them to his head like a pilgrim overcome with religious fervor upon seeing a holy icon or relic. "You won't find a player who can score goals like that," he told the media after the game. "Can anybody, anywhere, show me a better player?"

No, they could not. Ronaldo finished that season with 47 goals in 49 games. He scored the only goal, a penalty amid another mesmerizing performance, in the European Cup Winners' Cup final against Paris Saint-Germain. Barcelona missed the league title by two points, broadly due to a 2–1 loss to Hércules in the closing weeks, a game Ronaldo missed while on international duty. Later in 1997, he became the youngest player to win the Ballon d'Or.

In 2017, Óscar García, who was in that Barcelona squad and later became a coach at the club, was asked by the journalist Graham Hunter for a *Bleacher Report* piece to compare a couple of the greats that he encountered at the Camp Nou.

"I've worked around Barcelona while Leo Messi's been there and at his best. I've never seen anything like Ronaldo."

Here's the weird thing about Ronaldo's season at Barcelona: By the latter stages of that campaign, he wasn't really that popular with the home supporters.

He annoyed some of them by swapping shirts with Roberto Carlos after a *Clásico* in which he had scored the opener in a 3–2 win. He missed crucial games toward the end of the campaign while playing for Brazil. His agents became minor public enemies as talk of him wanting to leave grew. He agreed to a nine-year contract with Barcelona before he and/or his representatives reneged on it and ultimately engineered the move to Inter.

But one of the main reasons he was not as popular as you would think in Barcelona was his habit of taking frequent trips back to Brazil.

The perception was that these were jollies—unprofessional transatlantic jaunts that were distracting him from the job at hand. While he did frequently visit his girlfriend Susana Werner, and the pictures of him fully and enthusiastically enjoying the Rio Carnival hardly helped, these trips did serve another purpose. Ronaldo was visiting a specialist named Nilton Petrone about his increasingly troublesome knee.

The warning lights had been flashing on that knee since his PSV days. The big problem was that it was not just one problem. He had been diagnosed with Osgood-Schlatter disease, a condition that causes inflammation in the knee and is common in young people who are still growing. He also had a condition called trochlear dysplasia, a problem that, as Dr. Petrone explained in an interview with *FourFourTwo* magazine in 2018, causes the kneecap to "dance on the femur."

Furthermore, they were both problems that were exacerbated by twisting and turning at speed and neither could, at the time at least, be corrected with surgery. They just had to be monitored closely in the hope that nothing too serious went wrong.

His first knee injury, while playing for Inter against Lecce in November 1999, was serious but looked like a relatively routine ligament tear. He was able to walk—limp—off the pitch on that occasion and it took a scan to reveal what was actually wrong.

The second was much more, for want of a more elegant description, spectacular. He was six minutes into his return, against Lazio in April 2000, when his foot stopped in the turf and the rest of his body continued to move forward, prompting him to scream in pain. "He ripped the kneecap tendon completely," Petrone told *FourFourTwo*. "His kneecap actually exploded and it ended up in the middle of his thigh."

After that, he was never quite the same again. The explosiveness was dulled. The pace a few clicks down. But it tells you how good he was that he could lose all of that and still be among the greatest players in the world.

He was just a genius now rather than an alien.

Ronaldo is unquestionably one of the greats, a footballer of extraordinary physical and technical gifts, perhaps the one that combined those two elements to the most devastating effect of them all.

But he does raise an interesting debate about what qualifies a footballer for a place among the pantheon. Is ability enough, or does one require longevity? And if the answer to that is yes, then for how long? What is the minimum length of time that a genius has to be at their peak to qualify?

Ronaldo arguably only stayed at the summit for two and a half years—the season at Barcelona and his first 18 months in Italy with Inter, the time between him joining an elite club and his first serious knee injury. That injury was sustained in November 1999. From that point, he wasn't the same, so it's not particularly controversial to say that his best years were done by the time he was only just 23.

But if we are to accept that his feats before the knee injury were enough to qualify him as one of the greatest, then we have to consider whether we would think the same if he had not played another game afterward. Had his career stopped in 1999, would he be in this book? If he had not played for Real Madrid or won the World Cup in 2002? If he had not been around for a few years afterward being merely one of the best strikers in the world rather than a glorious freak of nature?

Probably not. Those latter years gave us two things. First are the tangible achievements, most notably those goals in Japan and South Korea. Ronaldo scored eight in that tournament in 2002, finding the net in every game apart from the quarterfinal against England. He scored the only goal in the semifinal against Turkey and both in the final against Germany. It wasn't quite "Diego Maradona in 1986" levels of a player winning the World Cup on his own, but it was not far off.

Second is the physical reminder of his greatness. Had he disappeared completely, then we would not have been able to watch a version of what he could have become. Even though he wasn't at his absolute peak in those years, he was close enough to keep him in our collective consciousness, to make us think, If this guy is this good after his knee collapsed, then imagine what he could have been like.

"Ronaldo copied the classic journey of the mythological local hero who descends into hell then comes back to change history," wrote Luis Fernando Verissimo in the Brazilian newspaper *O Globo*.

The thing that is always said about Ronaldo, the unanswerable hypothetical, is what he could have been were it not for the injuries. But do we need to wonder? Do we need another six or seven years to appreciate how special he was? It would have been wonderful, but the time he was that good, particularly in the Barcelona season—the things he showed us then that we had not seen before and really haven't seen since—are surely enough.

Player name: Ronaldo Luís Nazário de Lima (Ronaldo)
Born: September 18, 1976
Position: Striker
Debut: 1993
Main teams: Cruzeiro (1993–94), PSV (1994–96), Barcelona (1996–97), Inter Milan (1997–2002), Real Madrid (2002–07), AC Milan (2007–08), Corinthians (2009–11); Brazil (1994–2011)
Career highlights: Won the 1994 (albeit he did not feature) and 2002 World Cups, as well as the Golden Boot at that tournament in Japan and South Korea. Won the Golden Ball at the 1998 World Cup and the Ballon d'Or twice.

11.

Eusébio

Eusébio (right) and Pelé embrace before Portugal plays Brazil at the 1966 World Cup.

The man who went head-to-head with Pelé

By Stuart James

> I've been the best player in the world, the top scorer in the world. I've done everything. I just haven't won a World Cup.
>
> —Eusébio to *Tribuna Expresso* in November 2011

Eusébio da Silva Ferreira only had one shot at the World Cup. Actually, that's not strictly true—he had 17 in one game against Brazil, a competition record that still stands and underlines his insatiable appetite for scoring goals. There were more than 700 scored in a Benfica shirt and another 41 for Portugal, including nine during an unforgettable month in England over the summer of 1966.

That was the first time Portugal had qualified for the World Cup finals, and unfortunately for Eusébio, it would be another 20 years until they did so again—something he could never have imagined when he was eating breakfast in bed at the Saxon hotel in Harlow, on the outskirts of London, and contemplating playing in a semifinal against the hosts at Wembley later that day.

Aged 24, Eusébio was in his pomp in July 1966. Quick, powerful, and blessed with a rocket of a shot, he was the reigning European Footballer of the Year and arrived in England with more than World Cup glory on his mind. Portugal's third and final group match, against the 1958 and 1962 World Cup winners Brazil, presented an opportunity for individual acclaim, too.

"For the first time, he was in competition with Pelé," Antonio Simões, who played alongside Eusébio for Portugal and Benfica and shared a room with him at the World Cup, told ESPN in 2014. "He wanted to be better than Pelé in this game. People already knew Eusébio's name in European football, but the World Cup was the consecration. It would be forever."

Two years younger than Pelé, Eusébio was born on January 25, 1942, in Mozambique, a Portuguese colony at the time. He signed for Benfica in 1960 and crossed paths with Pelé on a couple of occasions shortly afterward. There was the Intercontinental Cup in 1962, when Pelé inspired his Brazilian team Santos to victory over Benfica, and much more intriguingly, a close-season tournament in Paris the previous year.

Benfica were being thrashed by Santos when Béla Guttmann, their Hungarian coach, turned to a 19-year-old forward who had been picked up following a tip-off in a barbershop in Lisbon.

The player's name was Eusébio.

José Carlos Bauer, who had previously played under Guttmann, returned from a football tour in Mozambique convinced that the teenager playing up front for Sporting Clube de Lourenço Marques was a star in the making. "I wanted to get him for myself, but those fools are asking for $20,000 for him!" Bauer, who was managing a club side in Brazil at the time, told Guttmann.

The story behind Eusébio's eventual transfer to Benfica could be a film script. There were all sorts of wild allegations at the time, including claims that Benfica kidnapped Eusébio to prevent him from signing for Sporting Lisbon, their bitter rivals. Incredibly, Eusébio was still denying those rumors in 2008. "These are all lies, pure and simple," he said in an interview with *FourFourTwo*.

In Eusébio's eyes, it was always going to be Benfica for him. His father, Laurindo António, an Angolan railroad worker who passed away when Eusébio was only eight, was a Benfica fan. Indeed, Eusébio would have joined Benfica's feeder club in Mozambique had a coach not dismissed him for being too small.

Guttmann wasn't going to make the same mistake. Benfica offered Eusébio a deal worth about $1,000 for three years, his brother asked for double, and everything was quickly agreed. "They signed the contract with my mother and she got the money," Eusébio said. "She put it in a bank in Mozambique with a clause on it, saying that if her son didn't go to Portugal and become a great footballer, she would pay the money back because she had a good heart."

Benfica wanted to keep Eusébio under the radar until all the official (and unofficial) paperwork had gone through—and that took a while. Eusébio arrived in Lisbon as "Ruth"—"I never knew that I traveled under a woman's name, but that was so that no one from Sporting would know," he said in an interview in 2011—and ended up spending 12 days in the Algarve surrounded by three bodyguards.

"I told them my orders," Guttmann said. "Eusébio cannot be left alone, not for a minute, and he can only stay at the Benfica house."

Seven months later, Eusébio came on against Santos in his first overseas appearance for Benfica and stole the show. "He scored three goals, all of them from a 20 to 25-meter distance!" Guttmann said.

Guttmann was a little generous with his description of the distance of two of the goals, but the power in Eusébio's shooting for all three was astonishing—the ball exploded off his right boot. Benfica lost 6–3, but that wasn't the result everyone was talking about the next day. "Eusébio 3 Pelé 2," read the headline in French sports newspaper *L'Équipe*.

Eusébio and Benfica never looked back. The following year, in the 1962 European Cup final, Eusébio scored twice in a 5–3 victory over Real Madrid.

By the time the 1966 World Cup came around, it felt like Eusébio and Pelé were at the peak of their powers. At least that was the theory. In reality, Pelé was unable to show anything close to his best after being kicked from pillar to post against Bulgaria in Brazil's opening group game and then crudely targeted by João Morais, the Portugal right-back, in the match at Goodison Park.

Eusébio believed Pelé should never have lined up against Portugal in the first place. "Why did he start, knowing he wasn't fit to play? It was just to frighten us," he said.

Brazil, however, were desperate. The world champions had lost against Hungary in their second group game, leaving them on the brink of elimination, and they were already missing Garrincha, another star, through injury. Pelé simply had to play.

A Eusébio master class followed. He had three shots inside the first four minutes, took nearly every Portugal set piece (Eusébio thought nothing of trying to score from 45 yards), and at one point was skipping around Brazilian players in the Portugal left-back spot. Indeed, it was his run and cross that led to the opening goal for Simões, after a mistake from the Brazilian goalkeeper Manga, and he headed in the second shortly before the half-hour mark.

Brazil were in disarray and Morais's poor challenges on Pelé a few minutes later added insult to injury (literally). Eusébio always claimed Morais caught Pelé on his ankle rather than the knee that would be heavily strapped for the rest of the match. Either way, it seems incredible that the English referee George McCabe took no action against the Portugal defender.

As Pelé lay prone just outside the Portugal penalty area, Eusébio walked over and offered his hand. Many years later, he was asked what he said to Morais and Pelé. "I didn't say anything to Morais,"

Eusébio said. "I just showed my support to my friend Pelé—nothing more."

While Pelé returned to the pitch looking like he had just come out of an emergency room, Eusébio was setting off on another attack. He was, quite simply, unplayable.

David Coleman, the distinguished BBC commentator, marveled at everything Eusébio did against Brazil, not least the bouncing ball the forward emphatically dispatched to make it 3–1 after Rildo had pulled a goal back for Brazil. Eusébio's technique to keep the ball down was textbook, but it was the ferocity of the shot that took the breath away. "Oh my word," Coleman said. "Have you ever seen anything like that?"

Portugal were never going to relinquish their grip on the game after their third goal. In fact, Eusébio didn't even want to let go of the ball, with which he disappeared down the tunnel at the final whistle, only for the linesman to chase after him and ask for it back.

Four days later, Eusébio had the ball under his arm again at Goodison Park, only this time it was his to keep.

North Korea were Portugal's opponent in one of the all-time World Cup matches. The rank outsiders caused a huge surprise by beating Italy in the group stage and now, to the delight of the neutrals, threatened to pull off an even bigger shock against Portugal. With 25 minutes on the clock, North Korea were ahead 3–0.

What happened next cemented Eusébio's status as the best player in the world at the time. Eusébio scored four in the space of little more than half an hour to single-handedly turn the game around. The way he ran back with the ball after his first, casually bouncing it like a Harlem Globetrotter before placing it on the center spot, proved to be a sign of things to come. "That was the best game of my life in a Portugal jersey," he reflected in an interview with the Associated Press in 2010. "It left its mark on me."

It left a mark on others, too. In his autobiography, *My Name Is Eusébio,* he dedicated a page to the British newspaper reports of his performance against North Korea. Some of the language used is a product of the time—"The Black Panther of Mozambique" was a moniker that stuck and which Eusébio embraced—and naturally, comparisons were also made with you-know-who.

"Who is the most spectacular and brilliant footballer in the World Championship? Who has electrified thousands of spectators in the field and millions on television? Eusébio. Eusébio. The most spectacular player in the World Cup, who is now greater than Pelé."

Eusébio may have wanted to come out on top in that Brazil game, but he was never preoccupied with the Pelé debate outside of the 1966 World Cup. "I always said to him: 'Pelé, you're not better than me and I'm not better than you. There are no comparisons, that's for journalists. Garrincha is better than us and he has a crooked leg!'"

Unfortunately for Eusébio, his World Cup dream ended at the semifinal stage in a narrow loss to England and amid controversy that the venue was changed from Goodison Park to Wembley at short notice. Eusébio converted a late penalty and, famously, sportingly consoled Gordon Banks, England's goalkeeper, after he collected the ball. But when the final whistle sounded moments later, Portugal's talisman broke down in tears.

His nine goals at the World Cup (he went on to score another against the Soviet Union in the third-place playoff) won him the Golden Boot and the $1,300 in prize money that came with it. Much more significantly, Eusébio was now a global star and a trailblazer for African players, too.

He could (and would) have joined Inter Milan that summer and earned a fortune in the process, but António de Oliveira Salazar, the Portuguese dictator, had other ideas. "It was because he thought I was so important to the country that he wouldn't let me leave," Eusébio said.

Two years later, Eusébio was back at Wembley, this time with Benfica, for the 1968 European Cup final against Manchester United. Nobby Stiles was tasked with keeping him quiet again, just as he had in the World Cup semifinal, only this time the United player did so with a lot less grace.

"I felt sorry for Eusébio because Nobby Stiles was marking him and not in the way you're supposed to mark people," Paddy Crerand, the former Manchester United defender, told the BBC in 2014. "People kicked lumps out of him and he didn't care, he just carried on playing. What a player."

A gentleman, too. United won 4–1 after extra time but, in the closing minutes of normal time, Eusébio had a wonderful chance to score. Alex Stepney denied him and Eusébio made a point of applauding the United goalkeeper there and then. "On and off the pitch, I'm somebody who has always been a believer in fair play," he said.

Eusébio finally left Benfica in 1975 after winning 11 league titles in Portugal to play in the North American Soccer League. Pelé was there, too, and Eusébio never missed an opportunity to have a joke at his good friend's expense. "When we're in that group of the 10 best of the century, we like to poke fun at him: 'You should have played in Europe, to see what winter was like, to get your arse kicked by the cold and the mud!'" he said.

After returning to Portugal at the end of his playing career, Eusébio later took on an ambassadorial role for both the national team and Benfica, where a statue at the Estádio da Luz provides a permanent reminder of his contribution to the club that he fell in love with as a teenager—a lasting legacy of one of the world's greatest footballers.

Player name: Eusébio da Silva Ferreira (Eusébio)
Born: January 25, 1942
Died: January 5, 2014 (aged 71)
Position: Forward
Debut: 1961
Main teams: Sporting Lourenço Marques (1957–60), Benfica (1961–75), Boston Minutemen (1975), Toronto Metros-Croatia (1975–76), União de Tomar (1977–78); Portugal (1961–73)
Career highlights: Guided Portugal to the semifinals of the 1966 World Cup and won the Golden Boot at the tournament. At Benfica, he won the European Cup in 1962 as well as the Portuguese top flight 11 times. Claimed the Ballon d'Or in 1965.

10.

Michel Platini

Platini lifts the trophy after inspiring France to win Euro 1984 on home soil.

The ghost who set the *carré magique* apart

By Amy Lawrence

The game of *pelota* is a regional speciality most often played in the Basque Country. It is played on a narrow court, sometimes off a wall, and usually the ball is struck either with a bare hand or a rudimentary bat. The rules vary from place to place. In 1991, when Michel Platini found himself in Bayonne, in southwest France, while he was manager of the national team, he and some of his coaches were challenged to a game of *pelota* the night before the match. He did not know much about the sport but soon picked it up. Within minutes he was the best player out there.

Platini was blessed with innate sporting qualities of coordination, reading the flight of a ball, reacting, thinking quickly. These were hallmarks of his style of football and, naturally, he could put them to good use in any pursuit. Like many of history's most elusive footballers, it is the way they think early, anticipate, and calculate what is around them and how best to navigate any obstacles in the blink of an eye that truly elevates them. Pure skill is a gift, but how that gift is used separates the great from the good.

One of Platini's peers, who came up against him in his heyday, described him as a ghost on the pitch. You might think you know where he is or might think space is covered, but he would suddenly appear. As Platini himself explained in a column for *L'Équipe* in 1999, "Seeing the game is seeing before others."

All managers find the job is simpler when they have an exceptional talent around whom to build. Platini was everything a manager could wish for. A No. 10 with extra shooting prowess, he was often described as a nine and a half. Top scorer. Free-kick specialist. Captain. *Trequartista*. Responsibility taker. *Le Roi*. Apparition. There seemed to be no limits.

Michel Hidalgo was the manager of the French national team when Platini was in his pomp. What a blessing. "When you have a Platini with you, everything seems easier," Hidalgo said. "He appears to be playing with a remote-controlled ball. Even his feet are intelligent."

It was a French generation embellished with a multitude of luxuries in the midfield department. Hidalgo leaned into that and established the *carré magique*, the magic square; a quartet of high-caliber, creative players who became the beating heart of the team. Before long, he made a small adjustment, introducing a more combative ball winner to the base—making the square function even more magically still.

In 1984, as France hosted the European Championship, they peaked together. Platini was the axis, with Jean Tigana, Alain Giresse, and Luis Fernández placing themselves at the other points to complete the *carré magique*. Platini reflected back on that team some years later in an interview with *L'Équipe* in 2014. "In 1984, the debate was: 'Why put so many No. 10s together? They can't play together!' Well, yes, they can . . . It was like the great Ajax team, except that the Total Football of the French team was not the total physical, but the total technical."

With their blend of technique and tenacity, ambition and audacity, they signaled a new era for *Les Bleus*.

France had not even qualified for the World Cup in 1970 or 1974 and exited at the group stage in 1978. But by the time the *carré magique* was beginning to take shape in 1982, they had a team to make the French dream. Anyone who witnessed that World Cup semifinal against West Germany will instantly be able to summon the intense emotions from that infamous night. France played like marvels against mighty opponents but had to withstand several awful blows—first, the freakish shock of the goalkeeper, Harald Schumacher, plowing into Patrick Battiston in a way that was more assault than tackle, then the whittling away of a two-goal lead in extra time, and finally the heartbreak of defeat on penalties.

In the dressing room afterward, Hidalgo compared the scene to a group of weeping little ones being left at kindergarten by their moms. They were inconsolable.

"We called our midfield 'magic square,'" recalls Giresse. "It was sometimes a diamond . . . we had trouble finding a real geometric shape for it. It's true that there was a lot of freedom because the animation demanded it. If Michel dropped out, I moved up a notch and vice versa. There was a form of *sliding* depending on the situations . . . because the movement always had to be done while respecting a collective organization: All the zones had to be constantly occupied."

The *carré magique* became the identity of the French team. The symbol.

The thing about a square is that in a pure mathematical sense, all sides and all angles must be equal. While there was beautiful balance in the quartet France crafted in 1984, there was not absolute equality—one of the four elements sparkled brighter than the rest.

Platini's special status was already well established before the summer of 1984. Having caught the imagination domestically as an emerging player at Nancy, he moved to the more glamorous scene at Saint-Étienne and, in 1982, he was headhunted by Juventus. At the time, foreign players were extremely limited in Serie A and only the best from around the globe were imported. Italy was football's nirvana during that era, and being chosen by Juventus, home to so many of the players who won the World Cup that summer, was something that meant a lot not just to Platini, but also to France.

What he learned from being immersed in the winning culture of Italian football were lessons he took back to his homeland. Platini often arranged meetings and chats with the players, sometimes separately from the coaches, to inculcate some of the messages he had absorbed. "He communicated this thirst for victory to us," noted Maxime Bossis in Tom Williams's book *Va-Va Voom*. "In Italy, it's victory that counts. . . . It was important he went over there. He could tell us that we were playing well, that we weren't far away, but that now it was time to win."

Jean-François Domergue was one of the defenders in the squad. He recalled the impact Platini had on the rest of the group. "He impressed with his gaze. He is charismatic. When you are in the locker room and he speaks to you, it is still striking. You are happy. You say to yourself: 'Michel Platini told me this or that, he is not just anyone!' He was always focused on the group. At the time, we didn't have video analysis, we just watched tapes. Before or after dinner, we would meet in a living room to watch the opponent. Michel was in charge.

"When a match was average, he would go through it at high speed. We could dissect a game in 15–20 minutes maximum. The first time I saw that, I was dying of laughter. I said to myself: 'Fuck, he does what he wants!' But he was a great leader."

It was time to avenge all those feelings they retained from that semifinal in 1982.

Platini dominated the 1984 European Championship as if every football experience from his entire life snowballed toward that moment of truth. Could France be brilliant to watch, but could they also win?

He scored the winner in their opening game against Denmark and followed that up with two perfect hat tricks—left foot, right foot, header—in the remaining group games against Belgium and Yugoslavia. The wind was behind France's backs.

The semifinal in Marseille's sultry Vélodrome served up the game of the tournament. A topsy-turvy encounter was heading toward penalties in the 119th minute when Tigana surged toward the byline and sent a ball across to the one man that every single French supporter would wish to be in that position at that moment. It was intense and chaotic and there was a flurry of opponents in front of him hurling themselves in the way, but Platini found the time in his own mind to neatly control the ball and measure his shot into the net. He ran and ran in elated celebration.

No one knew it at the time, but some kind of legacy was passed directly from Platini that night. On the sidelines, on the periphery of the action, sat a ball boy. That 12-year-old was Zinédine Zidane.

The final in Paris had overtones of destiny for this group. Platini etched his name onto it with a free kick, helped in by a mistake from the Spanish goalkeeper, taking his scoring rate to a dazzling nine goals from five matches over the tournament. France made sure with a glory goal in the 90th minute, chipped in by Bruno Bellone. He had no doubt who the poster boy was from the triumphant Euros. "Platini was the boss," Bellone reckoned. "He was the sails of the boat. He was the one who made us move forward. And there he was on top of the world. He scored nine goals, the guy!"

During his peak years, Platini won the Ballon d'Or three times in a row. He was a stellar performer in the league that was undeniably the grandest on the world stage. For Platini to also be top scorer in Serie A for three consecutive seasons from his deeper No. 10 position was remarkable. Marco Tardelli was his teammate at Juventus and it impressed him how hard he was for opponents to smother. "You didn't take the ball from him! At the moment when you thought you were going to tackle him, he had already offered the ball to an unmarked teammate. He didn't seem fast, but he was elusive because he managed to give this twist of the hips to escape you.

"He had this impressive quality on free kicks that ensured a significant number of goals. Michel had a precise and powerful shot, hitting with both feet, on the volley, with a flick, at ground level. And what's more, he was skillful with his head. A complete player, à la Cruyff, even if it was in a different style. He knew how to play everywhere. If you put him in front of your defense, he made the difference as well as in attack. He didn't hesitate to come back into cover, to go and get the ball in his own half. His tactical intelligence was such that he shone everywhere."

When Michael Laudrup joined Juventus, he was able to observe Platini's specialities up close. "I think Platini was the best player in Europe at the time. He was another with vision. So clever. He had the short pass and the long pass and he had that ability to make up for his lack of speed. He could not take on players and go past them always, but he knew exactly where the ball was and where to be. His timing was incredible and to score so many in Serie A at that time as an attacking midfielder, with the strikers they had back then, was impressive. I learned a lot just from watching him."

Didn't we all.

We learned something else in the latter phase of Platini's football life. We learned that our relationship with our heroes is complicated, that those who are admired for one thing can be a huge disappointment in another.

Platini's postplaying career continued the thread of him being central, a prime mover, a leader. After a spell managing the national team, he took on a senior role in the game's administration. He became UEFA president in 2007 and it was initially a popular accession for those who felt reassured to have a top player, with all the know-how of having experienced so much on the field, in the corridors of power.

He dabbled with the idea of campaigning to become FIFA president in 2015 but before long was found guilty of ethics violations—relating to a $2.2 million payment of FIFA money made to Platini in 2011 for work as a presidential advisor from 1998 to 2002—and was suspended from any football-related activity. He was cleared in 2022 and acquitted for a second time in 2025.

But the resulting scars on his image did not easily fade. For all the years of legal cases that followed, it was hard for those who had perfect recall of the player in his pomp to reconcile that with the broader, besuited political figure who had been under the microscope for corruption.

The Platini of the distant past nonetheless remains a central figure in the pantheon of French football. But the ghost, when he looks in the mirror, perhaps haunts himself.

Most Goals Scored at One European Championship

Player	Country	European Championship	Goals Scored
Michel Platini	France	1984	9
Antoine Griezmann	France	2016	6
Marco van Basten	Netherlands	1988	5
Alan Shearer	England	1996	5
Savo Milošević	Yugoslavia	2000	5
Patrick Kluivert	Netherlands	2000	5
Milan Baroš	Czech Republic	2004	5
Cristiano Ronaldo	Portugal	2020	5
Patrik Schick	Czech Republic	2020	5

Player name: Michel Platini
Born: June 21, 1955
Position: Attacking midfielder
Debut: 1973
Main teams: Nancy (1973–79), Saint-Étienne (1979–82), Juventus (1982–87); France (1976–87)
Career highlights: Won the 1984 European Championship with France, scoring nine goals in five games. Won the European Cup with Juventus and the Italian league twice. Also won the French top flight once. He claimed the Ballon d'Or three times in a row.

9.

Ferenc Puskás

Puskás hands over Hungary's pennant to the England captain Billy Wright ahead of the sides' meeting in 1953.

The "little fat chap" who taught the world how to play

By Sarah Shephard

Fresh from inflicting the 6–3 defeat on England that stunned more than 100,000 spectators inside Wembley Stadium, Hungary's captain, Ferenc Puskás, returned to the team's Cumberland Hotel in London to be greeted by a small boy. Approaching the footballer in the hotel's grand foyer, the child pleaded with him: "Please, sir, take me to your country and teach me to play football."

Until that seismic day in November 1953, England, and all who sailed in her, believed wholeheartedly in her supremacy in a multitude of ways. Chief among them was her prowess on the football pitch.

Hungary were the reigning Olympic champions when they arrived in London, having triumphed in Helsinki the previous summer, but that counted for little in the minds of a nation that had never lost at home to a team from outside the British Isles. Before kickoff, they knew nothing of the "Magical Magyars" who were unbeaten in three years and had seen off Italy so impressively (3–0) in Rome a few months earlier that at the final whistle, Italy's own fans stood and applauded.

"We didn't know about Puskás," said future England manager Bobby Robson, then 20 and among the thousands in attendance to watch what the British press dubbed "The Match of the Century." "None of these players meant anything to us. We thought we would demolish this team. . . . We were the masters, they were the pupils."

When the two captains—Puskás and Billy Wright—walked out side by side at Wembley, the sight of the shorter, stockier Hungarian alongside his taller, leaner counterpart only served to bolster English confidence.

"Look at that little fat chap," one of the English players is said to have commented before kickoff.

Wright noted the lightweight boots worn by Hungary's players and scoffed to England's No. 9, Stan Mortensen, "We should be alright here, Stan, they haven't got the proper kit."

Within 50 seconds of the game starting, it was the "little fat chap" in the slippers who was laughing as Hungary went ahead courtesy of Nándor Hidegkuti, a player whose positioning as a deep-lying center-forward left England center-back Harry Johnston completely baffled. England equalized, but shortly afterward, Hidegkuti scored his second. Four minutes later, the ball fell to Puskás on the edge of England's six-yard box.

Aware of Wright charging straight at him, Puskás placed his left foot on the ball and dragged it back, leaving the England captain kicking at thin air—"like a fire engine going in the wrong direction for the blaze," wrote Geoffrey Green in the London *Times*—and gifting himself time to curl the ball into the back of the net. The skill and speed of Puskás left everyone watching in awe.

Who was this majestic left-footer with the slicked-back hair and barrel chest?

By the time of Hungary's historic mauling of England in 1953, Puskás was already a star in his home country and parts of Europe where his exploits for Kispest, his team since childhood, had attracted attention.

In May 1947, Juventus had offered him the huge sum of $100,000 to join them, but he felt he couldn't leave Hungary and, in particular, his parents and sister. The Puskás family had German ancestry and, in the postwar era, there was a very real prospect of retaliation in Hungary against suspected German sympathizers. Puskás knew that his rising profile and importance to his country as one of their highest-profile sportsmen would act as protection to those around him.

The following season, Puskás scored 50 goals for Kispest, making him Europe's top scorer. Starting in 1949–50, the team went on to win the Hungarian league in five of the following seven seasons. He was starring for his country, too, having made his debut at 18 in the first postwar internationals played in August 1945, scoring three goals in his two appearances. From then on, he was a firm fixture on the national team as they evolved into "The Golden Squad" under the guidance of staunch socialist Gusztáv Sebes.

Its emergence was strongly tied to the transformation of Puskás's Kispest club into Honvéd—the club of the Hungarian army—in 1949. Sebes believed that having the majority of Hungary's players come from one or two club teams was crucial to the success of the national team and this was his chance. The best young players in the country were conscripted into the army club, so Puskás was joined at Honvéd by Sándor Kocsis, Zoltán Czibor, László Budai, and goalkeeper Gyula Grosics, who all became key members of the Mighty/Magnificent/Magical Magyars. The other team chosen to house national team players was MTK. In 1949, they were taken over by Hungary's secret police, the ÁVH.

With the nucleus of Hungary's national team able to build relationships and get to know each other's games intimately, they became unbeatable.

Puskás and Kocsis formed one of the most formidable international striking partnerships of all time, scoring 159 goals for Hungary between them by October 1956—more than many national teams over the same period. The tactical advances brought in by Sebes were critical to unlocking that attacking prowess, including the use of the No. 9 in a deeper position, thereby creating a vacuum in the center-forward line. Puskás at inside left and Kocsis at inside right gratefully filled the void.

The fluidity of their play also left opposition teams flummoxed. The starting positions of Hungary's outfield players meant nothing because once the game began, they had the freedom to move wherever they wanted, each man knowing what he had to do to compensate for or complement a teammate's movement. Puskás was critical, according to teammate Jenő Buzánszky, who described him as one of the side's "computers," able to process information about the opposition within the first 15 minutes of the game and reorganize their tactics to suit.

Part of this ability was his unshakable focus, said Hungary coach Sebes. "It was as if the game took place within a closed room and nothing distracted him: It was just the ball, his teammates and the opposition. His eye encompassed the whole pitch and his passing revealed his insight."

Puskás was not a great header of the ball and was entirely left-footed, but it made no difference in his ability to influence what was happening on the pitch. "He was a natural, a grand master of the game," said Ron Greenwood, a center-back at Chelsea at the time of England's defeat and the national team's manager from 1977 to 1982. "No matter how the ball came, the old left foot went up and his control was instant and precise. It was as if he had glue on the toe of his boot. He seemed to glide rather than run and, a sure sign of a strong personality, he dictated the shape and pace of the game."

Hungary's demolition job at Wembley rendered Puskás and his

teammates heroes. They returned home to be greeted by crowds of more than 100,000 while Puskás received 300–400 letters a day from all over the world congratulating him and his team on their historic victory. England, meanwhile, were left to confront a harsh truth. They were no longer the ones setting the pace in world football.

A few months later, the outlook got even bleaker for Walter Winterbottom's side when they were demolished 7–1 in Budapest, with Puskás and Kocsis scoring two each. England's players left the pitch feeling like they'd been bamboozled by a side of "soccer sorcerers." "It was like playing people from outer space," said shell-shocked centerback Syd Owen, who was playing in just his second international.

With the 1954 World Cup looming and Hungary marked as strong favorites, Puskás was almost untouchable in his home country. Life under one of the most repressive regimes in Eastern Europe was typified by fear and paranoia for most—even those in positions of power—but the leader of the "Golden Squad" was able to scold politicians who he felt weren't delivering on their promises and make public jokes at their expense without fear of recrimination. And the general public loved him for it.

But by the end of the year, almost everything had changed.

Hungary were beaten 3–2 by West Germany in the World Cup final despite beating them 8–3 earlier in the tournament and going two goals up in the final. It was a huge shock to a nation of fans who had not seen their team lose in years. The reaction in Hungary was vitriolic.

Crowds overturned trams in Budapest and rumors spread that players had "sold the game for a Mercedes car each." When they returned home, Sebes and his team were warned by police not to leave their houses for a few days until feelings calmed. But even then, the tension was rife. Puskás was looked at in the streets as if he "had some kind of disease" and goaded by those who had idolized him just weeks earlier.

By the time of the next World Cup, in 1958, Puskás was no longer playing for Hungary. Not because of form or fitness. Because of politics.

On October 22, 1956, Puskás and his national teammates returned to Hungary after playing a series of matches in Europe and headed straight into a training camp for an upcoming game against Sweden, initially unaware of the developing unrest in Budapest. That unrest would swiftly develop into the Hungarian Uprising, a revolt against the pro-Soviet government and their repressive policies.

Amid chaotic scenes in the capital, Puskás was reported (by the BBC in London and elsewhere) to have been killed in the fighting. In reality he was 40 miles away from the violence with the rest of the national team, preparing for a game that, it quickly became clear, could not take place. The players returned home for a short time having missed the worst of the initial violence, but alternative arrangements were quickly made to ensure their safety.

For Puskás and his Honvéd teammates, that meant traveling to Bilbao for the first leg of a European Cup tie, making their way first by coach to Vienna. At the Austrian border, Puskás received strange looks from those who had read reports of his demise. He was very much alive, though it would be the last time for many years that he crossed a border involving his home country.

The Uprising was eventually (and brutally, with thousands killed and wounded) crushed by Soviet tanks and troops, leaving the players facing the difficult decision of what to do next: Return to a country where Hungarians were being arrested, imprisoned, and even executed amid ongoing unrest? Or stay away, get family members out of the country, and make new lives for themselves elsewhere in Europe?

Puskás's mind was made up after he was told that the Hungarian FA was planning to ban him from playing football for 18 months. After being knocked out of the European Cup by Bilbao, Puskás and his teammates had taken up an offer to play a series of matches in Brazil against the wishes of the Hungarian FA. When he returned to Vienna and discovered the punishment awaiting him in Hungary, Puskás decided he was not going home. He was almost 30 and felt that such a lengthy ban was "a virtual death sentence" for his career.

After scoring 84 goals in 85 international matches for Hungary, leading them to Olympic gold and a World Cup final, the man they called the "Galloping Major" would never play for his country again.

• • •

The closing of one chapter in Puskás's remarkable life led to the opening of another. The transition was not immediate, though. Having left his club without permission, Puskás was banned from playing professionally for 18 months, during which time he settled in Italy with his wife and daughter and indulged in his other great love alongside football: food.

He received some offers from clubs around Europe and eventually started training with Inter Milan, but he was about 40 pounds overweight and, two months before the ban was due to end, the club said they couldn't sign him. After turning down an offer from Portugal to coach there ("I'm not old enough to be a coach yet," he fumed; "I want to play"), Puskás started to panic. But then came a visit from an old friend that changed everything.

Emil Österreicher was financial secretary of Honvéd at the time of the Uprising and had also chosen not to return to Hungary, instead settling in Spain, where he was hired by Real Madrid as technical director. He made it his mission to bring Puskás to the European champions.

Puskás told Österreicher he needed time to lose weight when he was first approached, but he was convinced to visit Madrid anyway to meet with club president Santiago Bernabéu. That led to a comical scene, relayed in his book *Puskás on Puskás*, in which the forward (who described himself as "the size of a large balloon") and Bernabéu tried to converse in their different languages.

"In the end," Puskás recalled, "I threw up my arms and gestured, 'Listen, this is all very well but have you looked at me? I'm at least 18 kilos overweight.'"

"That's not *my* problem," replied Bernabéu. "It's *yours*."

Puskás signed a four-year deal worth nearly $100,000, plus wages and bonuses. "It wasn't much to pay for a fit Puskás," said Österreicher. "But it wasn't bad for a fat one."

Many believed it was too late for Puskás. That he was too old. Too fat. Too slow for the Spanish league. And too out of touch, having not kicked a ball in competition for nearly two years. But by the end of his first season in Spain (1958–59), no one believed those things anymore.

Puskás finished second-top scorer in the league behind his teammate Alfredo Di Stéfano. In *Puskás on Puskás*, the Hungarian recalled going into the final match of that campaign, apparently against Granada, level with his teammate on 21 league goals. Then, with the ball at his feet and the opposition goal gaping in front of him late on, he spurned the chance to edge ahead and instead squared for Di Stéfano to score and finish at the top of the standings.

Time may actually have played tricks on the mind; in reality, the pair did not score in the team's last two league fixtures, neither of which was against Granada that year, and Di Stéfano actually finished with 23 league goals to Puskás's 21. But the new man clearly recognized that Di Stéfano would not react well to being trumped. As it transpired, the pair became firm friends.

He stayed at Madrid for seven more seasons, scoring 242 goals in 262 competitive matches overall, during which time Madrid won three European Cups and five consecutive league titles—the latter a feat no other club has equaled in Spanish football. But there is one match that, much like the game against England in 1953, lingers longer in the memory than most: the 1960 European Cup final at Hampden Park in Glasgow, when around 130,000 fans witnessed one of the finest club matches of all time as Madrid beat Eintracht Frankfurt 7–3.

Puskás scored four times, showcasing the creative genius and wondrous left foot—"like a hand, he could do anything with it," said teammate Paco Gento—that marked him out as one of the most special players the game has ever seen. FIFA went on to establish the Puskás Award, given to the player judged to have scored the most beautiful goal of the year, in his honor in 2009.

His career was simultaneously complex and beautifully simple. He played for only three teams (disregarding the four caps he earned for Spain after becoming a Spanish citizen), was never bought or sold, and scored more than 200 goals for both of the clubs for whom he played.

But it is the legacy he left behind that marks out the "little fat chap" who first played football on the meadows of a small Hungarian village with a ball made from old stockings as something truly special: The role he played in Hungary's reimagination of how football could be played. The impact that had on English football and English mindsets. And the way he emerged from the darkness to become a hero of the Bernabéu.

It wasn't only the little boy in London who wanted Puskás to teach him how to play football. It was the entire footballing world.

Scoring a Hat Trick in the European Cup/Champions League Final

Player (Club)	Final	Goals
Ferenc Puskás (Real Madrid)	1960 vs. Eintracht Frankfurt	4
Alfredo Di Stéfano (Real Madrid)	1960 vs. Eintracht Frankfurt	3
Ferenc Puskás (Real Madrid)	1962 vs. Benfica	3
Pierino Prati (AC Milan)	1969 vs. Ajax	3

Player name: Ferenc Puskás
Born: April 1, 1927
Died: November 17, 2006 (aged 79)
Position: Forward, inside left
Debut: 1943
Main teams: Kispest/Budapest Honvéd (1943–56), Real Madrid (1958–66); Hungary (1945–56), Spain (1961–62)
Career highlights: Best player in the famous Hungarian team that reached the 1954 World Cup final and beat England 6–3 and 7–1 in consecutive years, scoring 84 goals for Hungary overall. Claimed an Olympic gold medal in 1952. Won the European Cup three times with Real Madrid and scored two hat tricks in European Cup finals. Won the Hungarian top flight five times with Kispest (later renamed Budapest Honvéd).

8.

Zinédine Zidane

Zidane, lining up a free kick against Brazil, enjoyed a resurgent tournament at the 2006 World Cup.

The summer of 2006 and the love of an old flame

By Amy Lawrence

> There is no great genius without some touch of madness.
>
> —Aristotle

Imagine Zinédine Zidane at home, in the dead of night, having a mysterious conversation with a person or force he has vowed to never name. This was the scenario that compelled him to come out of retirement for one last dance with *Les Bleus*. It makes sense that it happened this way—suitably enigmatic. It would not be right for a player of his supernatural style to suddenly rewrite his story in a mundane way. That wouldn't do.

Zidane had withdrawn from international football in the summer of 2004. His place in the pantheon of French football was supremely established as the man who epitomized the 1998 World Cup, bringing France's first star on their shirt, and followed it up with an imperious exhibition of his mastery as they won the European Championship two years later.

He was the symbol of an extraordinary era of French football, with his face illuminating the Arc de Triomphe as crowds sang for "Zizou Président." He had done enough, hadn't he?

No, intoned the voice to Zidane. With his country flailing in their pitiful attempts to qualify for the 2006 World Cup, at the age of 33, Zidane underwent his change of heart.

He explained it all to an astonished public on his website: "One night, at 3am, I suddenly woke up and I then spoke with someone. Until I die I will never tell. This is just too crazy. This is someone that you will probably never meet. During the hours that followed, I was on my own with that person, at home, and I took the decision to come back. I had never experienced that before, I felt pushed by this force which dictated my behaviour. It was a revelation for me, I had to obey that voice that was advising me."

Zidane and two of his experienced compatriots who had also said their farewells to international football, Lilian Thuram and Claude Makélélé, agreed to return together to fix France's broken team. The news was greeted like a religious happening. This second coming made those whose faith was waning find renewed belief. Even within the camp, the impact was extraordinary.

Thierry Henry did not hold back when asked how he felt about the return of Zidane. "What I am going to say may sound over the top, but it's the truth. God exists and he has returned to the France team."

These three prodigal sons helped to pull the team from a perilous position in the qualification table to finish as group winners. The re-kindling of an old love affair was aflame.

• • •

There is a reason that two artists, Douglas Gordon and Philippe Parreno, chose Zidane as the focus of their film in 2005. It was an interesting idea: to follow one player within a team game, in real time, for the duration of a match.

They used 17 synchronized cameras to capture every detail of their subject's performance during a La Liga match between Real Madrid and Villarreal to make *Zidane: A 21st Century Portrait.* Such is the nature of live art; there are no guarantees of any particular drama, depth, or outcome. As it happened, Zidane was observed jogging and scanning for much of the film. But because it zooms in on its central character, what the film does not easily transmit is the perspective of how he interpreted the game in relation to all the moving parts around him, which was a key part of his magic.

He did provide a chipped assist for Ronaldo, and for his part in a ruckus at the end of the game, he was sent off. But those things were almost incidental or accidental. The movie is more a study of a player who possesses a certain magnetism, a certain allure. That is why he was the obvious choice for this kind of project ahead of any of his skilled contemporaries. We could watch Zidane, we could study Zidane, we could love Zidane, but we couldn't easily get beneath the surface to understand what he was really like.

Zidane played with an inimitable kind of measured grace. A lot of great players capture the imagination with their dynamism or sparks of brilliance. Zidane seemed to be communing with the ball in a cerebral fashion—as if he identified how to tame it or manipulate it just ahead of time, which made it all the easier to bewilder an opponent with a clever movement or gossamer touch.

It's a fascination, really, to wonder how much of greatness is spontaneous and how much comes from intelligence and practice. Is there really time to think during the intense perpetual motion of a match? Zidane considered that during a chat with *The Athletic* in 2023. "When I am on the pitch, it is instinctive," he said. "I didn't have special rituals. I didn't feel the pressure. I was just happy to be there on the pitch and to play in front of 50 or 80,000 people. It was my dream since I was little. To come out and play in front of 80,000 people? Imagine that! That's what's incredible."

Germany, the World Cup host in 2006, was the destination for one last, captivating, summertime fling for Zidane and France.

He had already clarified that this would be the end, his finale, and that he would retire from the game completely at the end of the tournament. There were extra layers of scrutiny on him—Zidane in ordinary circumstances existed under a brighter spotlight than most anyway. Add the comeback story line and the swan song and it was impossible to watch France at this World Cup without focusing on the main man.

France began the group with two underwhelming draws against Switzerland and South Korea. Their football was slumbering, stuttering. *L'Équipe* caught the mood of the nation with a plaintive headline: "And Now What Do We Do?" A quarter of a million people replied to a poll in the newspaper querying whether France could reach the final and 88 percent replied in the negative. Oof.

The team did the necessary against Togo in their third match to qualify, but overall there was scant evidence during the group stage of a theatrical farewell, with a fitting flourish, for Zidane.

On to the knockouts and suddenly the dynamic changed. The reins were loosened and the horse began to gallop and flare its nostrils.

When Spain met France in the last 16 in Hanover, it was arguably the tie of the round. There was an energy in the stadium and the Spanish took the lead early. France looked deep into themselves—there was abundant talent in the squad to show far more than they had managed under their eccentric coach Raymond Domenech. It was on the players and they knew it. After a problematic qualification and a boring group stage, they were now losing in the first knockout round. They essentially took over from within, with Zidane the controller-in-chief.

The response was, well, *magnifique*. Franck Ribéry equalized. Then Zidane floated over a free kick that found its way to Patrick Vieira to head France into the lead. Next came the moment that transformed the collective belief. They didn't just win, they won with Zidane adding the maestro's touch. It was confirmation they could soar again.

In stoppage time, Zidane powered up the left wing and gathered the ball under his spell. The temperature inside the stadium spiked. Everyone's eyes widened, their breath quickened. He chopped the ball past Carles Puyol, leaned in, and thumped his strike past Iker Casillas. His face in celebration was the epitome of a wise old head showing the kids how it's done.

L'Équipe did another poll about final chances after the Spain game and the swing was impressive—90 percent reckoned yes, the resurrected France could make it after all.

Next? Brazil.

Frankfurt was the setting for a quarterfinal matchup with deep emotional resonance. Zidane and Ronaldo, whose fortunes had been entwined in such contrasting ways back in the 1998 World Cup final, met again. There was a picture for the ages as they faced each other just before kickoff. They shared a private joke and giggled like children without a care. When you live the life they do, there are not many who can empathize with your experience, but their shared history made for a moment to reflect that probably nobody outside the pair of them could quite grasp.

Zidane played like a dream. Like an actor in his last scene or a musician strumming his last chord, he loved it. He had fun—in a game of this magnitude. From the off, he pirouetted and eased away to roaring approval from the audience. He orchestrated French progress by carving open the decisive move of the game. His arcing free kick picked out Henry for the winner. It was a mythical performance, one to be always remembered.

A semifinal against Portugal in Munich connected with more powerful memories from Zidane's past. A penalty sealed it. Zidane made it look effortless. He had done the same from 12 yards at the same stage in the European Championship in 2000. That had been an extreme psychological test, as his opponents back then lost their heads and threatened to leave the pitch, such was their rage about the award of a penalty in the final moments of extra-time—a point of no return.

He had to wait several minutes and barely moved. When teammates came to talk to him to offer advice or encouragement, he shut them out. He stayed in his zone. Those moments are deeply personal. "I don't listen. I don't listen because I'm the one who's going to shoot. It's my responsibility. It's me who knows what I have to do. It's not for someone else to tell me what I have to do," he explained.

Those couple of weeks of the knockout rounds in Germany were like a holiday romance, where Zidane and France were entranced with one another. So when the final came around, it felt like destiny was watching.

Italy. The final hurrah with the World Cup at stake. Zidane's blue halo was intact when he stood over the penalty to give France the lead. He elected for a power Panenka off the crossbar. He made it look easy. It was Godfather of Football stuff. But then, infamously, devilry came into play.

The Italian Marco Materazzi was an agent provocateur, tossing out words about Zidane's family like a grenade set to spew forth a red mist. Zidane charged his head into the defender's chest. It was instinctive, emotional, and as a climax to a brilliant career, utterly shocking. The scene as Zidane brushed past the golden trophy on its plinth, taunting him as he exited toward the dressing room, had the impact of Shakespearean tragedy.

As the saying goes, there is no great genius without some touch of madness.

Naturally, some of the criticism was sharp and pained. How could France's beloved icon falter like that? How could it be explained? Won't anybody think of the children? Yet back in Paris, after the World Cup, thousands of ordinary fans flocked to the Place de la Concorde and chanted for their fallen hero: "Zizou!"

Zidane's summer of love ended with a dark act of passion.

The headbutt is a defining image, but it is craziness of another kind for that to in any way sum up Zidane's place in football. He was a wonder, a creator, a warrior, a poet on the pitch. He remains the footballing god to whom Henry referred; only he showed himself to be human after all.

Player name: Zinédine Zidane
Born: June 23, 1972
Position: Attacking midfielder
Debut: 1989
Main teams: AS Cannes (1989–92), Bordeaux (1992–96), Juventus (1996–2001), Real Madrid (2001–06); France (1994–2006)
Career highlights: Won the 1998 World Cup and Euro 2000 and captained France to the 2006 World Cup final. Won the Champions League with Real Madrid in 2002 after scoring a stunning volley in the final and won the league in Italy (twice) and Spain (once). Won the Ballon d'Or in 1998.

7.

Franz Beckenbauer

Beckenbauer, in his pomp, strides forward in possession for Bayern Munich.

Der Kaiser and the slap that helped make Bayern Munich a force

By Nick Miller

If you subscribe to the multiverse theory—the idea that every decision we make splits the world into different universes: one where we turn left, one where we turn right—then somewhere in the infiniteness there is another reality where the biggest club in Munich is not actually Bayern, but 1860.

The split may have occurred during a Bavarian junior football tournament in 1958.

A young striker was playing for his team, SC Munich 1906, but the word was that the club was struggling to find the money and coaches to continue with all their teams the following season. A group of the players thus planned to move to 1860, who were the biggest club in the region at that time and who they just happened to be playing in the final of the tournament.

The game was ill-tempered and the striker in question became embroiled in an altercation with an opponent. The 1860 player ended up giving the forward a slap around the face.

And that, the story goes, is how Franz Beckenbauer decided to snub his local side—the one he grew up supporting and whose forwards, Ludwig Zausinger and Kurt Mondschein, he so idolized—in favor of Bayern.

There is almost certainly a good degree of mythmaking to the tale. It was one Beckenbauer was fond of telling and a few different people have claimed to be the deliverer of the slap over the years. But whether the truth is that neat, or whether there was more nuance, his decision changed the course of German, European, and maybe even world football history.

Is that an exaggeration? Perhaps, but Beckenbauer's impact on the game shouldn't be underestimated.

He wasn't just a brilliant player. There are loads of brilliant players. Another 99 of them in this book, for starters. Very few are brilliant players *and* invent things that change the game. But Beckenbauer was and did.

Maybe it is also a slight stretch to say that he invented Bayern as we know them today. But when he made his first-team debut for them in 1964, they were the second-most-popular team in Munich and were in the German second tier. They were promoted the following season, won the DFB-Pokal the season after that, claimed the European Cup Winners' Cup in 1967 and their first Bundesliga title (along with the DFB-Pokal again) in 1969, and were three-time European champions by the mid-1970s.

Beckenbauer was captain for a lot of this, and although coaches like Udo Lattek and Branko Zebec were clearly influential and players like Gerd Müller, Sepp Maier, and Paul Breitner had comparable impacts on the pitch, only one of those men earned the nickname "Der Kaiser."

Correlation does not always equal causation, but before Beckenbauer arrived, Bayern had one German title in 1932—in the pre-Bundesliga days, the champions were decided through regional leagues that then fed into a playoff-type system—and one German cup to their name. By the time he left in 1977, they were the dominant force in German football and would remain so for the following generations.

Unless something implausible happens between the writing of this book and whenever you are reading it, they will almost certainly remain the biggest club in Germany for some time to come.

And he was always keen to take the credit for it. "Lattek should have been grateful to me," he wrote in one of his autobiographies, published in 1975, about the success that had been built at Bayern by the early 1970s. If you want an idea of how much he was deferred to at Bayern, regard what Müller, the greatest goalscorer in Bayern and German history, told *Bild* in 1971. "I will always be in Beckenbauer's shadow," he said. "At some other club, I would have the chance to be the number one."

Beckenbauer also invented a position.

The Italian interpretation of the sweeper, or *libero*, was purely as a prophylactic; the player who sat behind the defense and swept up any lingering attacking threats, the last, last line of defense after the last line of defense.

His version of the position was rather truer to the literal translation of the word *libero*, which is Italian for "free" or "independent." Beckenbauer was initially a slightly flighty forward who was moved back into midfield by a youth coach concerned about how often he was kicked up in the air by ruffian defenders. When he arrived at Bayern, he was moved even farther back in part because of his slightly bratty nature. The theory was to teach him some responsibility and teamwork. And it paid off.

Beckenbauer was initially more of what we would now term a

deep-lying midfielder, but back in the 1960s, the role was very much viewed as part of the defense. He realized that with nobody specific to mark, he could have a bit more freedom than most defenders. He took inspiration from the Italian left-back Giacinto Facchetti, who would often storm forward down the flank, but Beckenbauer realized that while Facchetti was limited by the constraints of his position on the flank, from the middle he could essentially go anywhere if he wanted to.

And he did, roaming forward and starting attacks at will; a defender with a forward's spirit.

The role became so closely associated with him that he starred in an odd 1973 film—called *Libero*—that was part fiction, part documentary about his life and career up to that stage. Alas, the film wasn't so much panned as utterly ridiculed when it came out and there were rumors that Beckenbauer tried to buy every copy of it so they could be destroyed. If he did try, he wasn't successful. You can watch all deeply curious 79 minutes of it on YouTube.

Still, while the film sank without a trace, the position after which it was named very much did not. It never really caught on properly in England, but it took hold in Germany to the extent the national team played with a *libero* pretty consistently until the early 2000s, with either specialists like Matthias Sammer or aging players who dropped back, like Lothar Matthäus.

And it made him one of the greats. The men's Ballon d'Or tends to be the preserve of the attacker, the *fantasista*, the player who gets us out of our seats. That is perfectly logical. The ultimate point of football is to score goals, so why should we heap praise on the nerds trying to stop them? As such, at the time of writing, only four goalkeepers or defenders have been bestowed *France Football*'s shiny orb since the first in 1956: Lev Yashin, Sammer, Fabio Cannavaro, and Beckenbauer. Der Kaiser is the only one to win it more than once.

This is partly because he was so good, but also partly because he had many of the elements of the attackers that more naturally catch the eye. He wasn't just some meat-and-potatoes center-back who headed and cleared and tackled. He was elegant and upright, a defender who incorporated the bits of football that we do find fun.

That's just the stuff he did as a player.

His career ended slightly limply. He moved to the United States in 1977 to join the nascent North American Soccer League, where he took over from Pelé as the jewel in the crown of the defining club of that era, the New York Cosmos. That move was not inspired by the spirit of invention, or to expand into football's new world, but was largely motivated by a need for money to pay a colossal tax bill.

The negotiations to take him to New York were tough and resulted in Beckenbauer having to give up some of his $2.8 million salary to grease the wheels with Bayern, who were stubbornly holding out for a decent transfer fee. That meant his farewell was low-key, as Uli Hesse outlined in his biography of the player, *The Three Lives of the Kaiser*. "There was not even a lap of honor, let alone plans for a testimonial. Beckenbauer had even declined the offer of a banquet in his honour with a scathing riposte: 'If you have to part with 350,000 deutsche mark to get away from the club, you can pay for your own dinner.'"

He returned to West Germany for an underwhelming spell at Hamburg, but his next significant contribution to the game would come on the international stage.

The failure to make it out of the group stage at the 1984 European Championship had produced mass national handwringing and a nation turned its lonely eyes to Der Kaiser. Coach Beckenbauer duly took West Germany to the final of the 1986 World Cup, where they lost to Argentina. But he went on to become the second man to lift the trophy as both a player and a manager (Mário Zagallo did it in 1970 and Didier Deschamps would join them in 2018) when Andreas Brehme's penalty won a truly turgid final in 1990 against the same opposition.

National treasure status assured, then? Well, yes. Mostly.

Beckenbauer was, broadly speaking, admired as not just his nation's greatest-ever player, but as a footballing statesman. The sort of person whose words could make even preeminent figures stop in their tracks. "It feels great he speaks positively about me," Jürgen Klopp told the media after Beckenbauer praised his work at Liverpool in 2019. "It is just like the king with his sword calling a man 'sir.'"

Yet, oddly, despite being widely admired and adored by the majority of the German public for most of his life, Beckenbauer still carried a minor chip on his shoulder. The sense that he could be loved more.

In his autobiography, Beckenbauer spoke about the affection given to many other German football heroes. "Even the fans in Munich never cheered me the way people in Hamburg cheered their Uwe Seeler . . . these are men everyone can relate to. People have the impression that this player is one of them. Sadly, this is not the case with me."

You can read this a few ways. One is that Beckenbauer really did never truly receive the adoration from the broader public. Or that his complaints are just human nature: People always want something they do not have and the different sort of affection the public held for those other players was what he wanted. Another is that this was just a thinly veiled excuse for a humblebrag, that he knew he was an impossible man to relate to because he was so otherworldly. He didn't exist on the same plane of reality as everyone else.

His nickname was Der Kaiser. How do you relate to an emperor?

He was also the symbol of Bayern, the most loved and the most hated club in Germany until RB Leipzig arrived on the scene to take ownership of the latter crown. Bayern's combination of arrogance, superiority, and unrelenting success made them a target for ire by the early 1970s and that has continued to this day.

Another, less generous interpretation of why perhaps not everyone loved Beckenbauer was his relationship with money. The tax bill in the 1970s was one thing, but in later years he was implicated in a few different scandals connected to various World Cup bids. In 2016 he was sanctioned by the FIFA Ethics Committee for initially not cooperating with a corruption inquiry. He was questioned over payments linked to South Africa's bid for the 2010 tournament, which he said were consultancy fees. He denied taking bribes from Qatar and Russia in connection to their World Cups, investigations that were curtailed in 2021 because the statute of limitations had expired.

The thing is, do you *really* think of those things when you contemplate Beckenbauer? Perhaps we should, but when he died in 2024, most of the obituaries glossed over any question of impropriety, partly because of the "don't speak ill of the dead" rule, but also because his contribution to the game over previous decades ensured that most people overlooked all of that.

Should that be the case? The pure of heart and soul might suggest not, but it was. It would take more than that to taint the name of Franz Beckenbauer.

Player name: Franz Beckenbauer
Born: September 11, 1945
Died: January 7, 2024 (aged 78)
Position: Defender, *libero*
Debut: 1964
Main teams: Bayern Munich (1964–77), New York Cosmos (1977–80, 1983), Hamburg (1980–82); West Germany (1965–77)
Career highlights: Captained West Germany to victory at the 1972 European Championship and 1974 World Cup. Won the European Cup three times in a row with Bayern Munich and four league titles. Instrumental in the invention of the sweeper position. Won the Ballon d'Or twice.

6.

Alfredo Di Stéfano

Alfredo Di Stéfano won the Ballon d'Or twice while at Real Madrid.

A player strike, a "pirate league," the Cold War . . . and frustration in the colors of three nations

By Michael Cox

Among the top 10 on this list, Alfredo Di Stéfano is the obvious outlier.

Five of the others—Lionel Messi, Diego Maradona, Pelé, Franz Beckenbauer, and Zinédine Zidane—won the World Cup. Another two, Ferenc Puskás and Johan Cruyff, came very close as the star players for celebrated sides defeated in the World Cup finals of 1954 and 1974, respectively.

Michel Platini never won the World Cup, but he did produce unquestionably the greatest individual European Championship campaign ever as his France side won the competition in 1984. Cristiano Ronaldo also won the European Championship, in 2016, and is the only male player to have scored in five World Cups.

Then there's Alfredo Di Stéfano. He never played at a World Cup, only won 37 official caps, spent nearly a decade in the international wilderness, and ended up representing three different nations. Yet here he is, almost solely on the strength of his club career at Real Madrid, for whom he helped win five straight European Cups from 1956 to 1960, theoretically playing as a center-forward but bamboozling opponents by dropping deep, almost as a prototype Messi.

It is no exaggeration to suggest that Di Stéfano's brilliance was the catalyst for the development of Europe's most famed rivalry, its most successful club, and its most prestigious competition. His arrival in Spain in 1953 prompted an extraordinary tug-of-war between Barcelona, the reigning Spanish champions, and Real Madrid, who at that stage had not won the title for two decades.

Having only won two titles upon Di Stéfano's arrival, his influence ensured that Madrid overtook Barcelona, Valencia, and neighbors Atlético and Athletic Bilbao to become the most successful club in Spanish history, a status they have never relinquished. Atlético had previously been considered Real Madrid's main rivals. It was only after the Di Stéfano transfer saga that Real Madrid versus Barcelona became the chief rivalry; the *Clásico*.

Those five European Cup–winning campaigns, meanwhile, were the first five seasons of the competition. Real have, from the outset, been the European Cup's most successful club. Establishing a new major tournament can be difficult—the early years of the World Cup, the European Championship, and the UEFA Cup were somewhat of a struggle—but the glamour of Real, and of Di Stéfano, meant the European Cup instantly became fabled.

Real completed that run of five with a 7–3 victory over Eintracht Frankfurt in Glasgow, perhaps the most celebrated team performance in the history of club football. Di Stéfano scored a hat trick; his teammate Puskás scored four.

All things considered, there's an argument that Di Stéfano is the greatest club footballer ever and an even stronger argument that he is the most influential club footballer ever. But what exactly went wrong at the international level?

Di Stéfano was born in Buenos Aires to a father of Italian descent and a mother of French and Irish descent.

If that hinted at a complex international football allegiance, his heritage ultimately played no part in him representing two further countries, as well as his native Argentina. His international career started in a fairly typical manner. After making a sole appearance for River Plate in 1945 and spending a fruitful season on loan with mid-table Huracán in 1946, Di Stéfano started up front for River throughout the 1947 season.

He finished top goalscorer in the Primera Division, with 27 in 30 games, as River won the title. Naturally enough, there was clamor for the 21-year-old to be selected by Argentina coach Guillermo Stábile for the Campeonato Sudamericano, the forerunner of the Copa América, in December 1947. Stábile was himself a former No. 9 for the national side and the first World Cup Golden Boot winner, having scored eight goals in four matches at the tournament in 1930. Bizarrely, that was the entirety of his international career. It was brief and it was spectacular. The same would apply to Di Stéfano's time with Argentina.

The 1947 Campeonato Sudamericano was compromised by the absence of Brazil owing to an ongoing dispute between the Brazilian and Argentine federations. The format was a simple league system featuring eight nations. What turned out to be Argentina's crucial game—against eventual runners-up Paraguay—was both sides' opening fixture and was won 6–0. Di Stéfano was, at this stage, not in the side. René Pontoni, a reliable penalty-box operator, started the campaign up front and scored three. He was seemingly assured of his place.

But Pontoni's downfall was the fact that—highly unusually at this time—the competition permitted the use of substitutes. Therefore, in a 7–0 win over Bolivia two days later, Pontoni, who had scored midway through the first half, was replaced by Di Stéfano later in the match. Di Stéfano scored and showcased an all-around game of which Pontoni could only dream.

Despite that, there were concerns among supporters that Di Stéfano would be a destabilizing force in Stábile's well-crafted Argentina. The side was based around the inside forward José Manuel Moreno. Pontoni's role was partly about sacrificing himself for Moreno, but Di Stéfano dropped deep to provide some of the qualities expected at the time of inside forwards rather than the center-forward, who was expected to stay up front and bang in the goals.

Still, Di Stéfano's all-around ability was irresistible and he took over from Pontoni as the No. 9. He ended Argentina's successful tournament with six goals from six games. Although the artful Moreno was named the tournament's best player, the youngster's talent was unquestionable. Yet at this stage, he was merely considered the next big thing, ready to take over when the 31-year-old Moreno's fondness for cigarettes and alcohol finally got the better of him.

Instead, after six goals in six caps, Di Stéfano never played for Argentina again.

That had nothing to do with his level of performance. In the late 1940s, Argentine football was prospering in terms of attendances, but players were still paid very badly—if they were paid at all. It was commonplace for top-flight footballers to go months without receiving their salaries, while directors enjoyed increasingly lavish lifestyles.

The Argentine FA refused to formally recognize the players' union and eventually a significant number of players decided enough was enough, and went on strike. It was a dramatic move and not entirely popular among the media or supporters. Di Stéfano, unhappy at his meager wages in comparison to established but less talented teammates, was one of those to withdraw his labor. Coming from a relatively comfortable background, he was not unduly troubled by his lack of income. As a gruff introvert, he did not care too much about pleasing fans, either.

He was more concerned by the stagnation in his career at precisely the moment he was set to explode into a world-class forward. Therefore, he opted to abandon Argentina and headed to Colombia.

This was a dramatic switch. Not only was Di Stéfano strongly attached to Buenos Aires, but he also had a fear of flying. Moreover, Colombia offered almost no football pedigree in the late 1940s. They had never even attempted to qualify for the World Cup and in both the 1947 and 1949 Campeonato Sudamericano, they finished bottom without winning a single match.

That wasn't entirely surprising considering that, in April 1948, Colombia was on the brink of civil war after the assassination of presidential candidate Jorge Gaitán. To improve the reputation of the country internationally and occupy the thoughts of its citizens, the Colombian government decided to form a new all-star league, the country's first professional football competition. The Colombian FA played no role in the formation of the division, which meant it was essentially banned by FIFA—which in turn meant international transfer regulations were not adhered to.

It was considered a "pirate league" by many. Back in Argentina, Di Stéfano was cast as an unpatriotic traitor for jumping ship, although around 60 others did the same.

Colombia could briefly claim to boast as many top-class footballers as any other league, especially at a time when, in many leading countries, signing foreign players was either frowned upon or explicitly banned. In Colombia, around 60 percent of the players were from abroad. "They offered financial terms 15 times higher than in Argentina," Di Stéfano later explained.

Reports on the quality of footballer varied. Di Stéfano's Millonarios side are considered among the finest South America has ever seen, although Englishman Neil Franklin, who also moved to Colombia, suggested the top sides were "no better than the average Third Division side back home."

But the presence of some top-class players was undeniable and therefore an all-star XI played sporadic exhibition games. Di Stéfano turned out in four of these matches against other national XIs during his four-year spell in the country and this is often considered to be him *playing for Colombia*. But these matches remain unofficial. They were not recognized by FIFA and most players were ineligible for the country even at a time when the criteria were somewhat loose.

Why did Di Stéfano not continue playing for Argentina? Well, take your pick from a variety of reasons.

First, he was unpopular back home, having fled the country for that pirate league. Second, the fact the Colombian league was outside FIFA's control meant he was banned from playing in FIFA competitions anyway.

Third, the Argentine FA's tendency to squabble with CONMEBOL and other federations meant they barely participated in any major competitions. They neglected to defend their Campeonato Sudamericano trophy in Brazil in 1949 and did not travel to Peru for the next tournament, either. They also withdrew from qualification for the 1950 World Cup, hosted by Brazil and won by their other great rivals, Uruguay, then did the same for the 1954 World Cup. There was, therefore, little to tempt Di Stéfano back.

Fourth, by the time Argentina got their act together and qualified for the World Cup in 1958, they had a policy of only selecting domestic-based players, which meant overlooking their best footballers who had moved abroad, mainly to Europe. That would have included Di Stéfano, who by then was playing his club football in Spain.

More significantly, he was playing his international football for Spain.

That hadn't been the plan. Di Stéfano moved to Real Madrid in 1953 and was an immediate success. For the first European Cup final in 1956, Madrid's 4–3 victory over French side Stade de Reims, Di Stéfano was regarded as the one permitted foreign player in the Madrid side. Reims had led 2–0 and 3–2 in that final, with their star performer the lively attacker Raymond Kopa. Madrid, on their way to assembling their first team of *galácticos*, wanted to sign Kopa for themselves, but they weren't permitted a second foreigner.

Therefore, four months after that 1956 final, Di Stéfano "gained citizenship primarily because Real Madrid pushed for it," in the words of his biographer, Ian Hawkey. For the second European Cup final in 1957, Real's 2–0 win over Fiorentina in Madrid, they were again regarded as having one foreign player, but now it was Kopa. Di Stéfano was a Spaniard in terms of citizenship and in terms of international representation, having made his debut in January, scoring a hat trick against the Netherlands. He was 30 and that was his first official international game in nine years.

Di Stéfano was one of a number of world-class players, including Hungarians Puskás and László Kubala and Uruguayan center-back José Santamaria, to make Spain their second national side. FIFA initially refused to sanction these "transfers" but eventually gave in. Rules around appearing for a second nation were significantly tightened in later years, before being loosened again recently, but Spain have always been more relaxed than most major nations at capping players who qualify through residency. That owes something to Di Stéfano's legacy.

Considering Real Madrid's abundance of talent and the presence of some top-class overseas players including Di Stéfano, Spain should have been among the favorites to win the 1958 World Cup. But, having failed to qualify for the 1954 tournament after drawing with Turkey and losing on the drawing of lots, they again failed to get past relatively weak opposition, dropping points in their three-team qualification group by drawing 2–2 at home to Switzerland and then losing 4–2 in Scotland, despite having led both matches.

The frustration for Di Stéfano was compounded by the fact his former side, Argentina, with Stábile still in charge, *did* once again enter and qualify for the tournament, although their self-inflicted international inexperience was obvious as they finished bottom of their group. Meanwhile, Brazil romped to victory and 17-year-old Pelé established himself as football's first truly global superstar. It could have been Di Stéfano.

• • •

It seemed Di Stéfano would have to wait another four years to play at a major tournament, but happily, in 1960 along came the European Nations' Cup—later the European Championship.

The competition was belittled in its formative years, with the likes of England, Italy, West Germany, Belgium, and the Netherlands all declining to enter the inaugural tournament—contested as a two-legged home-and-away competition until the semifinals and final, which were held in France. Spain looked fearsome and thrashed Poland 7–2 on aggregate in the round of 16, with Di Stéfano scoring two goals in the away game and then opening the scoring in the return leg at the Bernabéu. Afterward, Spain manager Helenio Herrera declared that Di Stéfano was the world's best player. The win set up a quarterfinal against the Soviet Union.

That was a problem. Both countries were terrified of one another.

Spain's XI was set to be drawn heavily from the Real Madrid team that had played in that 7–3 European Cup final win against Eintracht Frankfurt earlier that month. Meanwhile, the Soviet Union had demolished Poland 7–1 in a friendly, surpassing Spain's margin of victory in their two-legged clash against the same opposition. But the tensions were much less about football and much more about politics at the height of the Cold War.

The two countries had no diplomatic relations—Spanish passports explicitly stated they could not be used for entry into the Soviet Union, although this issue was expected to be momentarily waived for the sake of playing the match.

Still, Spanish head of state General Francisco Franco learned that the Soviet Union were set to send a large number of traveling fans to Madrid and that they were insisting on their flag being displayed and their anthem played. He could not stand the thought of this happening in Madrid and therefore demanded that both matches be played at a neutral ground. The Soviets refused, so Franco responded by ordering the Spanish federation to withdraw the team from the competition.

"The whole world is laughing at Franco's latest trick," said Nikita Khrushchev, First Secretary of the Communist Party of the Soviet Union, before launching into pun mode. "From his position as the right-sided defender of American prestige, he has scored an own goal."

As a result, the Soviet side received a bye to the final four, eventually winning the first edition of the Euros courtesy of victories over Czechoslovakia and Yugoslavia. Instead, Di Stéfano and Spain traveled to his hometown of Buenos Aires, where they lost 2–0 to Argentina in a friendly.

There was one final chance: the 1962 World Cup in Chile.

Spain qualified and were drawn in a tough group alongside Brazil, Czechoslovakia, and Mexico, but the presence of Di Stéfano, at last, in a World Cup squad was hugely exciting. "Happily for the health of the game, Di Stéfano has lost little of his mastery," wrote Roger Macdonald in *World Soccer* magazine on the eve of the tournament. "Di Stéfano in action is still without a peer. . . . Age is certainly catching up with him, but for the moment, he is the one man who could transform the Spanish national side from a collection of individuals into a cohesive unit."

But now, after his international career had been compromised by problems as outlandish as a player strike, a rebel league, and Cold War tensions, his last shot was ruined by something altogether more normal: injury.

Di Stéfano traveled to the tournament hoping he would be fit in time for the knockout stage, but Spain did not even progress that far, having been defeated by a single goal by the Czech and Brazilian sides who would eventually contest the final. Both Di Stéfano and Pelé were out—injured for the crucial final group match. What was constantly reported as a "magic liniment" for Di Stéfano's injury, given to him by his father, failed to produce a miraculous recovery.

At the age of 36, Di Stéfano conceded the game was up and retired from international duty. A year later, he captained the first-ever World XI, assembled at Wembley to celebrate the Football Association's 100th anniversary—a demonstration of how revered he was despite his lack of World Cup appearances.

Then came a cruel final twist. For the first major tournament after his international retirement, Euro 1964, Spain went and won it. Moreover, they won it by defeating the Soviet Union at the Bernabéu, the exact fixture Franco had refused to sanction four years earlier. Di Stéfano could still have made the side—he had spent the season playing up front for a Real Madrid team that won the league and reached the European Cup final, where they lost to Inter Milan. The star man in that Inter side, Luis Suárez, was also Spain's best player in their Euro 1964 success and the national hero.

Half a century later, shortly before Argentina defeated the Netherlands on penalties in the 2014 World Cup semifinal in São Paulo, there was a minute's silence. Back in Madrid, Di Stéfano had collapsed while walking near the Bernabéu and died at the age of 88. The players linked arms while his photo was displayed in the stadium and broadcast around the world.

It was, at long last, what Di Stéfano had always deserved: being center stage at a World Cup.

Player name: Alfredo Di Stéfano Laulhé (Alfredo Di Stéfano)
Born: July 4, 1926
Died: July 7, 2014 (aged 88)
Position: Forward
Debut: 1945
Main teams: River Plate (1945–49), Huracán (loan, 1945–46), Millonarios (1949–53), Real Madrid (1953–64), Espanyol (1964–66); Argentina (1947), Spain (1957–61)
Career highlights: Won the European Cup five times in a row at Real Madrid and La Liga eight times overall. Won the 1947 Campeonato Sudamericano with Argentina. Won the Ballon d'Or twice.

5.

Cristiano Ronaldo

Cristiano Ronaldo: prolific for club and country and a trophy machine.

The obsessions of a man made in Madeira

By Daniel Taylor

Over time, the locals of Quinta do Falcão, a village in the hills of Funchal, the capital of Portugal's Madeira Islands, have become accustomed to the sight of people trekking up the punishing slopes for what can feel at times like a football pilgrimage.

Some of the visitors wear Real Madrid shirts. Others prefer the colors of Manchester United, and for a while there were even a few in the black-and-white stripes of Juventus. They are all drawn here for one reason: Cristiano Ronaldo, superstar. And almost always, they underestimate the long, steep climbs that could sap the strength from even the most impressive calf muscles.

As a kid, this was Ronaldo's turf. He would use two stones to mark out a goal and, in the absence of a sports pitch, play football in the street, regardless of the gradient. If a bus came up or down the hill, the driver usually waited for him to take the stones away. Then the bus would continue its journey and Ronaldo would put the stones back down to resume his game. It was his daily routine—remove stones, replace stones, and on and on—for many years, until he moved from Madeira to mainland Portugal to take his chance with Sporting Lisbon, aged 12.

"The ball would invariably land in my neighbours' gardens," Ronaldo wrote in his 2007 book, *Moments*. "Many of them used to complain to my mother, others would threaten to keep the ball.

"Some of them would keep their promise and I would go home crying. Every day [my neighbor], Mr. Agostinho, who was very proud of his plants, would say to me: 'If the ball gets in here, I will puncture it!'

"I didn't take any notice because all I wanted to do was play football. I took chances and inevitably the ball would land in his garden. Every time that happened, I would run as fast as I could to get the ball out of there. He would complain to my mother, who would tell me off. But the following day, the same happened again. There was nothing he could do."

The family's house—Bairro da Quinta Falcão, Casa 29—was a tiny, ramshackle place with a washing machine perched on its roof. The walls were made from exposed bricks and wooden slabs. There were three small rooms to accommodate a family of six and not a great deal else in this part of the Santo António neighborhood other than a few shops and a bar where, on sunny days (and it's almost always sunny in Santo António), the Super Bock is served cold and Madeiran wall lizards cling to the whitewashed exteriors.

The older generation in Santo António will tell you these properties were built as social housing for families who had previously lived in shacks. It can feel a long way from the five-star hotels, infinity pools, and cruise ships that bring tourists to this holiday island. Ronaldo pretty much ticked every box for the classic story of the working-class footballer done good.

Today, though, there is nothing left of his old house other than an uneven patch of concrete where it once stood and the wall against which the skinny, curly-haired Ronaldo spent endless hours honing his first touch.

The council demolished the property in 2008, the same year Ronaldo won his first Ballon d'Or. The land is now a parking lot covered in weeds, with no blue plaque or any other clues about who lived here apart from the fading stickers that fans of various clubs—even one from Benfica—have attached to a surviving drainpipe.

It seems remarkable they would tear down the house where Madeira's most celebrated islander spent his formative years. Did the local authorities not realize its potential? Or the history? What a shame. What a wasted opportunity on the island that has turned Christopher Columbus's house into a popular tourist attraction.

Let's not be too harsh, though, when most visitors to Madeira get their first experience of the Ronaldo love-in even before setting foot on land.

Fly into Funchal and you will hear the pilot welcome you to Cristiano Ronaldo International Airport (the airport was renamed in 2017 in a ceremony attended by the country's prime minister and president). A bust of Ronaldo was put on display in the arrivals hall, and when it was widely mocked for looking nothing like him—including comparisons with former Republic of Ireland striker Niall Quinn and ex–Formula One driver David Coulthard—a replacement was made. "Even Jesus did not please everyone," Emanuel Santos, the original sculptor, lamented in an interview with *Globo Sports*.

Opposite the ferry terminal, meanwhile, the CR7 museum welcomes more than 100,000 visitors every year to celebrate the greater glory of you-know-who.

Outside, there is a statue of Ronaldo in the familiar pose—legs planted, fingers spread, sizing up another opportunity to bolster his goal statistics—that used to send electricity through crowds whenever he was standing over any free kick with the opposition goal within shooting range. His shoulders are Adonis-like, his torso reminiscent of an Olympic swimmer. The gold plaque by his feet reads: "Best Player in the World."

Through the double doors, it is a full, peacock-like spreading of Ronaldo's feathers featuring more than 200 gleaming trophies and medals, various life-sized models, and family album photographs.

One cabinet is filled with fan mail. Others display his 66 signed hat-trick footballs. There is even his lanyard from Portugal winning Euro 2016. And if all this hero worship makes you hungry, you can always pop around the corner in Praça CR7—yes, the square is also named in his honor—to the CR7 Corner restaurant and bar, where the menu includes Ballon d'Or chocolate mousse, a Hat Trick flavor ice cream (chocolate, passion fruit, and pistachio), and a pizza named after the local hero.

A vanity project? Yes. A shrine of self-love? Yes, again. A gold-plated, multimillion-euro temple to the glory of one man? Absolutely. Ronaldo, one imagines, would shout his own name during lovemaking.

As the *Daily Telegraph* noted in 2014, "You have to admire the chutzpah. Pelé, the greatest of them all, needed three World Cups, 1,281 goals, and another 31 years after his career finished before anyone felt it necessary to open a museum in his name."

What the author of that piece might not have realized was that Ronaldo would still be going strong a decade later and that as time passed, his career would be remembered almost as much for its longevity as it is for his goals and associated glories.

No other footballer in the history of the sport has played more games in international football, and that alone warrants genuine greatness. Ronaldo won his 200th cap for Portugal in June 2023 and, naturally, marked the occasion with an 89th-minute winner against Iceland.

So let's consider just a few of the other achievements on his CV. The Ballon d'Or (2008, 2013, 2014, 2016, 2017), UEFA Player of the Year (2014, 2016, 2017), Champions League Golden Boot (2008, 2013, 2014, 2015, 2016, 2017, 2018), Portuguese sportsman of the year (2011, 2012,

2014, 2015, 2016, 2017, 2018, 2019), Premier League player of the year (2007 and 2008), Alfredo Di Stéfano award for best player in Spain (2012, 2013, 2014, 2016), Pichichi award as La Liga's top scorer (2011, 2014, 2015), and Serie A player of the year (2019 and 2020).

Not a bad list, right? And this is just a selection of his individual prizes. We haven't even mentioned his team honors yet: the five Champions League wins, the three Premier League titles, two league titles in Spain, two in Italy, and all the cup competitions that have ended with him puffing out his chest for the victory photographs. The man is a trophy machine.

Not everyone approves of the way he has gone about his work and the occasional tantrums that were evident, for example, while he was pining for a move to Real Madrid during his final year in Manchester.

At one point, Ronaldo had the audacity to complain about the five-star prison otherwise known as Old Trafford and tell the Portuguese television station TVI, "I am a slave." He was desperate for the adventures that could be had at the Bernabéu and, having returned to Old Trafford 12 years later, his second spell as a United player ended in acrimony because of a television interview with Piers Morgan in which the player seemed hell-bent on making his position almost untenable.

Ronaldo, who had been left out of the team, claimed he had been "betrayed" by the club and then-manager Erik ten Hag. It was a naked attempt to force his way out and, Ronaldo being Ronaldo, he got his way. The move to Al Nassr of Saudi Arabia quickly followed.

Nobody, however, could ever question Ronaldo's dedication to his art, his work ethic, or his sheer bloody-mindedness to make sure his face needed no introduction wherever he was on the planet.

When he first arrived at Old Trafford in the summer of 2003, he wore braces on his teeth, he had pimples on his forehead, and there was work to be done to turn him into a far more accomplished package. Over time, however, he developed an adult intelligence about when to pass, when to keep it, and when to try the tricks and shiny pyrotechnics.

As for his obsession with winning the Ballon d'Or, that was perhaps best encapsulated in the 2015 film named *Ronaldo* (what else?), when viewers were given a rare insight into what it was like to walk in his shoes.

One scene showed his godson being baptized with a small gathering around the font. The baby's head had just been wet when the priest looked over to Ronaldo, standing beside the proud parents, and whipped out a cell phone to interrupt proceedings. "Any chance of a quick selfie?" he wanted to know.

The most revealing moment, however, was the sight of Ronaldo's agent, Jorge Mendes, and another of his associates in a Real Madrid executive suite muttering about the possibility that "the other guy might destroy everything."

The other guy, of course, was Lionel Messi of Barcelona. "It's a card inside an envelope that can change so much," said Ronaldo, describing how it felt to watch his old adversary beat him to the trophy. "To see Messi win four in a row was difficult for me. After he won the second and third, I thought to myself: 'I'm not coming here again.'"

So what is it like to coach such a player?

Paul Clement, formerly assistant manager to Carlo Ancelotti at Real Madrid, answered that question when he spoke to *The Athletic*, and recalled the player's almost 24/7 obsession with outperforming everyone else.

"We were coming back from a Champions League away game one night. You're always late leaving the ground after the doping tests. You get to the airport and it takes forever for the skips to be loaded onto the plane. So, by the time we get back to the training ground in Madrid, it is often 3 a.m. or 4 a.m.

"It's not a day off, the next day. The players are in for training in the afternoon because we are playing again in two days. So getting off the bus, they're grabbing their bags . . . you'd hear the vroom of the cars and they'd be off, screeching away through the gate. Fair enough, it's 4 a.m. Go and get some rest."

One player, though, had not finished. "I turn around," Clement continued, "and there's Cristiano, pulling Pepe and Fábio Coentrão towards the main building: 'We're going for an ice bath.' It's 4 a.m. and not only is he doing it, he's getting others to participate as well. It's ultra-professional. These are the things he does, over and over. And it's that compound effect of doing the little things really, really well that has got him to superhuman level."

László Bölöni, the manager at Sporting who gave a 17-year-old Ronaldo his debut, was also interviewed. "I was asked on the radio [after his first game] how good I thought he was going to be. I said I hoped Ronaldo would make [Portuguese people] forget Eusébio and Luís Figo.

"Within an hour, my lawyer was on the phone. My lawyer was a Benfica fan and had a role on the Benfica board. He told me I was crazy and that the Benfica fans were up in arms. For them, Eusébio was like the singer Amália Rodrigues, the 'Queen of Fado'—Portuguese royalty. If you disrespect one of them, everybody is against you.

"I told my lawyer that I thought Ronaldo could do it, barring injury. He told me I was making a big mistake. So we made a deal: if Ronaldo went on to do something really special, he had to buy me a nice bottle of Champagne. If not, I would buy him one. I spoke with my lawyer again after Ronaldo won his first Ballon d'Or. The Champagne tasted good!"

When Ronaldo's precious magic earned him his first Footballer of the Year award in England, Sir Alex Ferguson's verdict, imparted to the 22-year-old and an enthralled audience at the celebratory dinner, was that the player's "strokes of artistry put paint on the canvas."

Or how about the response of George Best—No. 15 on our list—when it was put to the legendary Manchester United player during Ronaldo's first season in England that the new kid on the block might become, well, the new George Best?

"There have been a few players described as the new George Best over the years," he replied. "But this is the first time it's been a compliment to me."

They certainly had similarities: courage, for the most part. Wherever they were on the pitch, they wanted the ball. No matter how many times they were kicked by opposition defenders, they wanted it again. Both understood that the best way to hurt their opponents was to have the ball.

There have also been times in Ronaldo's life that help to explain why his inner strength is a legacy, almost certainly, of his childhood years.

It took guts, just for starters, for a 12-year-old island boy to leave home by himself and step off a flight in Portugal's capital with a cardboard sign around his neck so that Sporting's executives could recognize him.

Hugo, his older brother, now runs the Ronaldo museum but, as a younger man, was spiraling into alcoholism. Their father, José Dinis Aveiro (Dinis, for short), had a drinking problem of his own. Together they resorted to selling Ronaldo's shirts so they could pay for more booze.

The story locally is that Dinis was never the same after being called up to fight in the Portuguese colonial war in Angola. His wife, Maria Dolores, confirms it is true in the *Ronaldo* documentary, recalling how he came back "very angry." His head was filled with images of the war and, though she says he always cared for his children, Dolores says she became "his victim." Dinis drank himself into an early grave, aged 51.

Ronaldo, then at Manchester United, was 20. "He was drunk nearly every day and when that happened it became hard to have a conversation," he told the filmmakers. "I didn't get to know my father for years."

Against that backdrop, it becomes easier to understand why Ronaldo—named after the former US President Ronald Reagan—regarded great football men such as Ferguson, Ancelotti, and Portugal's former national coach Luiz Felipe Scolari as father figures who meant more to him than just being the team manager.

• • •

Ronaldo may not have invented the art of dribbling, but he (and Messi) elevated the skill to its highest level. "I always had the belief that if you put five men in front of me," he told reporters as a 20-year-old, "I could go past them all."

Not many ex-United players are applauded off the pitch at Anfield, home of their archrivals Liverpool, as Ronaldo was when he returned to Merseyside to play for Real Madrid a few years later.

Liverpool's fans have always been good at recognizing greatness on a football field and that is really the only worthy description for a player who has amassed 900-plus career goals and, in the process, become the only player in history to score against 200 or more different teams.

The best goal, you might think, was the overhead kick for Madrid against Juventus in Turin, when again his brilliance warranted spontaneous applause from a usually partisan crowd.

There is stiff competition, however, if you remember the 40-yard shot for Manchester United in a Champions League tie against Porto in 2009.

That firecracker of a shot earned him the first-ever Puskás Award as the best goal scored by anyone that year. But perhaps we can conclude by going back a few more years to the 2006–07 season, when the Bolton Wanderers were the visitors to Old Trafford and lost 4–1 in a Ronaldo master class.

Henrik Pedersen, the Denmark international, was experimenting as Bolton's right-back that day, despite being better known as a striker. He was directly up against Ronaldo and it turned into such an ordeal for the visiting player that he had to be substituted after 28 minutes.

It was the ultimate indignity. Pedersen trudged off, looking as though he needed smelling salts to wake him from his nightmare. In the postmatch news conference, Bolton's manager, Sam Allardyce, was asked whether Ronaldo's superiority might have left his defenders with psychological scars.

"Scars?" Allardyce replied. "We're going to need a fucking plastic surgeon after that."

Cristiano Ronaldo's Goals for Club and Country by Season, in All Competitions

Up to the end of the 2023–24 campaign

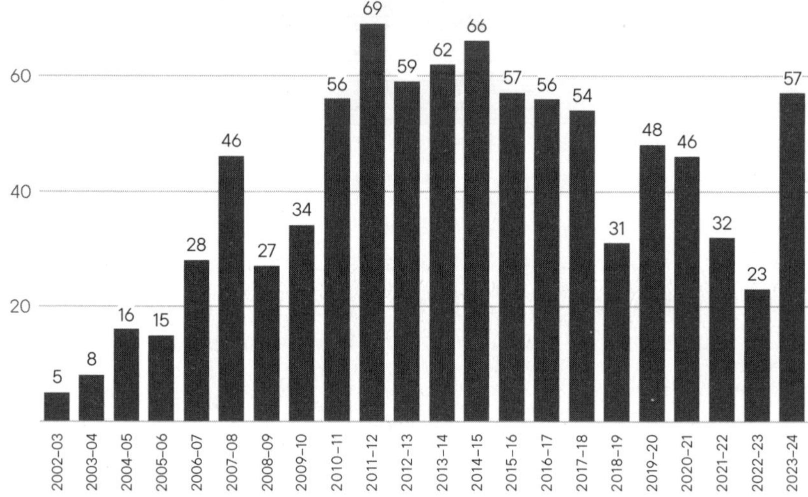

Player name: Cristiano Ronaldo dos Santos Aveiro
Born: February 5, 1985
Position: Forward
Debut: 2002
Main teams: Sporting Lisbon (2002–03), Manchester United (2003–09, 2021–22), Real Madrid (2009–18), Juventus (2018–21), Al Nassr (2023–); Portugal (2003-)
Career highlights: Top goalscorer in the history of international football and the European Cup/Champions League. Won Euro 2016 and has claimed the Champions League five times. Won the league in England (three times), Spain (twice), and Italy (twice). Won the Ballon d'Or five times and is on course to score 1,000 career goals.

4.

Johan Cruyff

Cruyff wearing the captain's armband for the Netherlands at the 1974 World Cup.

In search of Jan Olsson, the first victim of The Turn

By Phil Hay

You've come all the way from England? For what?"

The boy in front of me is a typical youth-team footballer: pleasant, chirpy, well groomed, and optimistic. He's a central midfielder for Åtvidabergs FF, a lower-league club in Sweden. For now he's training with the under-19s. "But I hope for the first team," he says. "Very soon."

I tell him I'm here, in his patch of Sweden, to write about the 1974

World Cup. I tell him I'm here to find Jan Olsson, an old Åtvidaberg warhorse, and compile a story about the grand master of Total Football, Johan Cruyff. "Ah," he says, "you mean . . ." and without missing a beat, he twists his left shoulder, flicks his right foot behind his other heel, and turns away. *Precisely.*

He smiles and walks off. Subconsciously, he has explained the purpose of my trip. Everybody knows the routine. Everybody can imitate it. Everybody knows what to type into YouTube if footage of the Cruyff Turn is what you're after: grainy highlights of a World Cup game between the Netherlands and Sweden. The original and the best.

The leaves are on the wane in Åtvidaberg, a small town 125 miles south of Stockholm. They're falling like Åtvidaberg's team, no longer contenders for Sweden's domestic title as they were in the 1970s, no longer even close. I've come to this region of autumnal, undulating farmland in pursuit of Cruyff's pièce de résistance, the moment in his career that outshone all others.

The roots of the Cruyff Turn are here, and so is the man who partnered him in that mesmerizing dance 50 years ago.

Even now, the colors are resplendent. The orange of Cruyff's Netherlands jersey gleams. Olsson, Sweden's right-back, is wearing a deep blue shirt, his short, stocky body contrasting with Cruyff's slender frame. The grass is a blend of green and yellow, vibrant at the height of summer.

This scene is burned in the memory. How many times has it been replayed? But still, without fail, there are shades of Houdini about Cruyff. You know what's coming, but the magic never gets old.

A cross-field pass comes his way. He almost loses the ball before retrieving it with his toe. Had it run away from him, football writers would not be tracking Olsson down to Åtvidaberg half a century later. History hinged on that outstretched touch.

Cruyff backs into Olsson and holds him off. Olsson goes left as Cruyff goes left, the Swede's eyes fixed on the spot where he and the watching world expect the ball to run. Without even glancing at him, Cruyff swivels in the other direction, using his right foot to feather the ball away from Olsson. Cruyff is gone. Olsson almost ends up on his back. The Turn is conceived.

Åtvidaberg's league season is finished but, down at their stadium, a group of players are completing bleep tests, sweating in the damp air as they run. Staff there tell me that Olsson, now 82, is in poor health. He is at home a few streets away but not well enough to chat about 1974. Instead, they put me in touch with his son, Micke, who meets me at a local coffee shop just as the lunchtime rush gets going.

Micke coaches Åtvidaberg's under-17s. He was born in the town and his father saw out some of the best years of his career here. The streets are steeped in sporting excellence. Seven members of the Sweden squad at the 1974 World Cup had spells on Åtvidaberg's books, many of them during the glorious championship years of 1972 and 1973. Once upon a time, the club ruled the Swedish roost. Those times have gone.

I wonder about the Cruyff Turn. It is football's greatest trick, or thereabouts. Olsson is famous because of it. But he's famous because he was the victim of it, outwitted by the sleight of hand wielded by a premium escape artist. Does that sting? Is being remembered primarily as Cruyff's prey a backhanded compliment? Would he rather be forgotten, or left in peace?

"Cruyff screwed him," Micke says, laughing, the comment dripping with affection.

Cruyff did screw him—into the ground and then a little further—but whenever Olsson has been quoted about The Turn (and media outlets flocked to him after Cruyff died in 2016), his tone is joyous. "I laughed then and I laugh now," Olsson told *The Guardian* as he reflected on Cruyff's death. "It was very funny. I still cannot understand. I loved everything about this moment."

Micke has heard Olsson talk about The Turn so many times. He says his father is genuinely magnanimous about it. "He's proud that it's him you see in those pictures, so proud of it," Micke says. "There was no bad feeling. In that moment, he found out what it means for a footballer to be world-class, like one of the best ever. It was right in front of him and it's my father who's against it, against Cruyff. It's crazy.

"My father didn't play for Sweden until he was 31. Maybe by then, before it happened, he thought he never would. It made him happy to be at a World Cup, to be in the same space as a player like Cruyff. He likes that people remember.

"His way of thinking is always 'try, try, try.' He had a game against Yugoslavia where a player did a tunnel through his legs [a nutmeg] three times. Three times! But then, when he figured it out, it wasn't going to happen again. It's how he thought about Cruyff. Cruyff beat him once. Now try to stop him beating you in the same way twice."

Cruyff was uncompromising and famously single-minded. Through his career and his life, he was a mixture of traits: sublime, majestic, stubborn, antagonistic. He sought perfection, he stood by his principles, and he spoke his mind without fear, making friends and enemies as a result. But the Cruyff Turn was not an attempt to belittle an opponent and less still an egotistical pitch for acclaim. The biggest myth about the trick is that it was in any way preconceived.

Cruyff's posthumous autobiography, *My Turn*, betrayed the randomness behind it. "It wasn't something I ever practised," he insisted. "It wasn't a move I ever really thought about." Olsson had him tightly marked, virtually locked down on one side of Sweden's box, and in retrospect, the full-back did everything right. He was sticking to Sweden's strategy. The twist was Cruyff's instinctive way out of Dodge.

"The idea came to me in a flash because at that particular moment, it was the best solution for the situation I was in," Cruyff's autobiography recorded. Genius often works in such ways.

The proof of Cruyff's comments is the fact Olsson wasn't duped by The Turn again. There is no evidence of Cruyff trying to fool him for a second time. The pair played against each other on four occasions, internationally and for their clubs. When Åtvidaberg met Cruyff's

Barcelona in the quarterfinals of the 1975 European Cup, Olsson came away with the forward's shirt—a shirt Micke would casually wear during kickabouts with his friends.

What Olsson didn't lay his hands on was the Dutch top Cruyff wore on the day of The Turn. He came home to Sweden with midfielder Willem van Hanegem's instead. "He couldn't have taken the one Cruyff was wearing," Micke says with a laugh. "It would have been like having him at home every day—like the turn and the No. 14 in front of his eyes forever!"

The shirt used by Cruyff for the Netherlands at the 1974 World Cup was an example of what he had become by then. Adidas provided the Dutch equipment, but Cruyff had a well-paid boot deal with Puma and, aware of the power of his profile and brand, he was reluctant to freely market a rival manufacturer.

As a compromise, his strip was adapted to display just two stripes down the arms rather than Adidas's traditional three the rest of the Dutch squad wore. It's not clear if the top he had on when he mugged Olsson is in good hands, or even in one piece. Given that Diego Maradona's "Hand of God" Argentina shirt sold for about $9.1 million at auction in 2022, Cruyff's 14 from June 19, 1974, could have made somebody very rich. Micke chuckles. "It's true," he says. "But never mind."

Ralf Edström, Sweden's striker in 1974, has a theory about where it went. "Ove Grahn," he says, confidently. "I think he got it."

Why does he think that? "Because when we played West Germany later in the tournament, I asked Franz Beckenbauer for his shirt. I'd been battling with Beckenbauer, his position against mine, so it would have been normal to swap. Beckenbauer said sorry, no. He'd already promised it to Ove. Ove asked for it after about one minute."

So Edström suspects his teammate was stockpiling priceless collectors' items? "Yes," he says with a broad smile. Grahn died in 2007, taking the truth with him.

Edström also has a theory about why the 1974 World Cup got away from Cruyff and the Netherlands and why they lost to West Germany in the final in Munich. It gets to the heart of who Cruyff was, how he thought, and how much influence he exerted. The Edström I meet is in his early 70s, his hair gray but his enthusiasm infectious. He's put off a session of walking football to chat about Cruyff close to his home near Gothenburg.

Edström spent more time on Cruyff's radar than the average footballer. A classic center-forward, he joined PSV Eindhoven in 1973 not long before Cruyff ended a celebrated, era-defining period with Ajax by joining Barcelona for a world-record fee. They played together in a Europe versus South America exhibition match at Camp Nou a few months later, rewarded for their attendance with gold watches. In the Ballon d'Or vote that same year, a vote Cruyff won, Edström made the top 10. The list is framed in his house.

"Cruyff was so clever," Edström says. "He's the best European player ever, I'm sure of that. But also, he was the chef, the boss. He was in charge. At that World Cup, in my opinion, they made a mistake.

"He was a king in Amsterdam, but in places like Eindhoven, where I played, they saw him differently. I liked him a lot. I liked his company, but I knew he had friends and [adversaries], lots of both. His reputation was that if he decided something, that was it.

"In 1974, the best goalie in Holland was Jan van Beveren at PSV. He was fantastic. I tell you this because I saw and I know. But at the World Cup, Holland used Jan Jongbloed, who was not so good. Jongbloed played for FC Amsterdam. From what I heard, Johan wanted him in the team, not Jan [van Beveren]. The coach thought the same, so Jongbloed played.

"I'll always believe that if Jan van Beveren is playing in the final against West Germany, Cruyff and Holland win the game. There's no doubt. The winning goal? It's a piece of cake for a goalie. Jan would have saved that."

Sweden played both finalists at the 1974 tournament. The Dutch had no way past them in an early goalless draw. West Germany needed two late goals to fight out a 4–2 win during the second group stage. And so the obvious question: Which team was better? Because when Cruyff retired in 1984, a World Cup was the glaring omission from his list of honors. It was there for him in 1974 and then it was gone. He would not appear at a World Cup again.

"The Dutch were better," Edström says. "Individually, it was definitely them. But in the end, it's what they say about the German machine. You can play better than them. You can be better than them. Eventually, the German machine comes and you cannot stop it. That's what happened."

In the mid-1970s, Germany was more than a decade away from reunification between East and West. West Germany hosted the 1974 World Cup, and Sweden versus the Netherlands in the city of Dortmund—a Group 3 fixture in the competition's initial stage—was a depiction of the Dutch philosophy.

It was, admittedly, no for-the-ages master class and an organized, disciplined Sweden side had their chances. But watch it back and Cruyff is here, there, and everywhere: appearing on the right to create from that flank, then popping up on the left to twist Olsson inside out. His flow is as smooth as an oil painter's brushstrokes. His poise is hypnotic. It's Cruyff in his prime and his prime seemed to go on forever: multiple league titles at Ajax, Barcelona, and Feyenoord, three European Cups, and three Ballon d'Or trophies, including in 1974.

Football was his art and it mattered to him that others saw the sport as art, too.

The variety in Cruyff's play was the essence of Total Football. The concept's origin is a matter of debate (many think it was nurtured in Austria and Hungary before the Netherlands), but in Cruyff's era, the Dutch and their national coach, Rinus Michels, were committed disciples of it. Total Football was the theory of space, or the theory of creating space on the field. No player in the system could be so limited as to have the skills for one position alone. Michels's squad was awash with talent—Johan Neeskens, Johnny Rep—but it helped that

Cruyff was a generational master of his craft, a sublime conductor of the orchestra.

Preparing to face him, in days when video analysis was a pipe dream, was not easy.

"We had a plan," Edström says. "The idea was that when Johan had the ball, we would stay close to him and make sure he had to run or pass back into midfield. If the ball is going into midfield, it's fine. If he's going forward, then it's not. He was so quick. Björn Nordqvist stopped him by wrapping his arms around him—a yellow card then and maybe a red these days. Björn's face just said: 'He's too fast. What am I supposed to do?'"

The advantage for Olsson, or so the Swedes thought, was the full-back's own burst of pace. Olsson was rapid off the mark and could recover well in situations where he briefly lost his man. "Speed was Jan's big strength," Edström says. "If a player went five yards past him, it didn't matter. Jan would get back and there was no problem.

"But if Cruyff does to you what he did to Jan, it's something else. It could have been anybody, not just Jan. There's nothing you can do."

I ask Edström if he sensed at the time, in the instant when Cruyff left Olsson trailing, that the forward had pulled off a stunt that would resonate for years. "It would be hard to say yes," he says. "We were in the middle of a big game. But I do know this: Afterwards, we laughed with Jan about it. 'Jan, come down, come down! Come down from wherever he left you!'

"Jan loved to joke about it, too. He's one of the nicest guys I know. It was a happy memory. But yes, we had fun with him when the game was over."

A theme among football's greatest exponents is the degree to which their brilliance comes naturally.

It is easy to accept that the Cruyff Turn was an improvised flash of inspiration because of the way his brain was wired. In an article published in June 2024, *The Athletic* reported that Cruyff never owned a cell phone. Every single number he needed was mentally stored and accessible. His memory, to some extent, was plainly photographic.

In the years leading up to his death, Cruyff had a plan to revamp Ajax and their youth production line. The entire blueprint was in his head—so much so that when it came to creating a hard copy one day, it was hastily scribbled down on a huge piece of wallpaper. Jasper van Leeuwen, who was head of talent recruitment for Ajax's academy and got to know Cruyff well, talked of him being a "mathematical genius." "He'd be constantly thinking about spaces and time and he saw them so quickly," Van Leeuwen told *The Athletic*. "Like Einstein."

No single aspect of Cruyff's life constitutes his legacy. He meant different things to different people and he would sacrifice anything on the altar of his footballing ideals. But The Turn was unique, an ageless encapsulation of his supreme control of a football.

In the decades that followed, child after child across the world attempted to mimic it. Under-19s in Åtvidaberg still know the drill as soon as Cruyff is mentioned. Micke's friends used to talk to him about it when he was growing up. He doesn't tire of watching replays. "It's my father I'm seeing," he says. "It's amazing to me, him and Johan Cruyff, right there together."

When Cruyff died, Olsson's phone began to ring. Journalists wanted to hear from the man who had been on the end of The Turn. Television companies talked about flying him abroad to interview him face-to-face and the world understood that it took two to tango; that the Cruyff Turn would not exist without Olsson's involvement.

"When he is about to kick the ball, I'm sure I'm going to take it," Olsson told *The Guardian*. Every time you replay the reel, you think exactly the same. That's the beauty of Cruyff's skill.

Much has changed in the 50 years since. Aspects of football have changed, some beyond all recognition. Cruyff is no longer with us. Olsson will not be around forever either. But history promises to remember them: Cruyff facing out toward the touchline, Olsson clamped to him, time appearing to freeze, and then Cruyff, with a magician's touch, slipping free of the chains.

A few seconds of football in Dortmund were destined to last for eternity.

Player name: Hendrik Johannes Cruyff
Born: April 25, 1947
Died: March 24, 2016 (aged 68)
Position: Forward, attacking midfielder
Debut: 1964
Main teams: Ajax (1964–73, 1981–83), Barcelona (1973–78), Los Angeles Aztecs (1979), Washington Diplomats (1980–81), Feyenoord (1983–84); Netherlands (1966–77)
Career highlights: Played a key role in the development of Total Football. Guided Netherlands to the 1974 World Cup final. Won the European Cup three times in a row with Ajax and another 15 trophies at the club. Won La Liga with Barcelona and the Ballon d'Or three times.

3.

Pelé

Pelé was a Brazilian icon.

Brazil's globetrotting ambassador—for his sport, his nation, and his own talent

By Jack Lang

The paper is yellowing. The pages, for all the effort that has gone into preserving them, are a little dog-eared. They contain black-and-white advertisements for a cabinet supplier, the local zoo ("Wife trouble Saturdays?"), and Ron Dewdney's pasties, plus a few outmoded stereotypes. It is a document of its time—1973—but also of its place: Plymouth, a faded jewel of England's southwest coast, about as worldly as a crisp sandwich and only slightly more glamorous.

It is that context that makes the rest of this little booklet all the more surreal and magical.

It is a souvenir program from a Plymouth Argyle match. The color scheme of its cover—green and an evocative sunshine gold—immediately signals that this was no run-of-the-mill Division Three fixture. The visitors to Home Park on that March evening were not Scunthorpe United or Southend United, but, as the program has it, "SANTOS of BRAZIL," capital letters nonnegotiable.

And there, above the text, gazing serenely out across the decades, is Edson Arantes do Nascimento—Pelé to all but his closest relatives—regarded almost unanimously at that juncture as the greatest footballer of all time.

The tone of the editorial a few pages later is, as you may well imagine, feverish. Pelé in Plymouth! Even at the time, there was a palpable sense of disbelief to it all. My dad attended the game aged 14—the program, now one of my prized possessions, was once his—and still talks about it like a Christian might about bumping into Jesus at a gas station.

Any account of Pelé's brilliance will alight on the big-ticket stuff: the controlled explosions of his teenage years, the four-figure goal tally, the indelible mark he left on the World Cup, culminating in the Technicolor dreamscape that was the 1970 edition. We will circle back around to all that. But there is another aspect that often gets lost when we assess his career from the pedestal of modernity. It is there in that program and in a million memories, lovingly passed down through the generations in Plymouth and Port of Spain, Casablanca and Cádiz, Bangkok and Baltimore.

The best footballers today have global reach as standard. They all play for the same handful of European clubs, whose matches are broadcast weekly on every continent. It was different for Pelé. Despite offers from abroad, he remained at Santos—a relatively small, provincial outfit, both then and now—for 18 years, only undertaking a new adventure, with the New York Cosmos, in the twilight of his career. The World Cup, yes, made him famous, but it was as a touring attraction that he really secured a place in people's hearts.

Pelé had never left Brazil before the 1958 World Cup in Sweden. Between that tournament and his retirement in 1977, he played matches in 74 different countries, as well as in every conceivable corner of Brazil. The vast majority of those were exhibition games for Santos, who—at least during their imperial phase, in the early to mid-1960s—could lay claim to being both the best team in the world and the busiest.

It is hard to underestimate the extent to which Santos spread the gospel of Brazilian football during that period. It was a miniature national team, full of World Cup winners—Zito, Pepe, Gilmar, Mauro Ramos, Coutinho, and Mengálvio in the early days, then Joel Camargo, Clodoaldo, Carlos Alberto, Edu—and their play lived up to that billing.

At the heart of it all was Pelé, gleaming goal emissary, the Platonic ideal of a Brazilian footballer made flesh before the eyes of a different public, night after night.

It stands to reason that there has always been an anecdotal, even mythical flavor to Pelé's genius. When it comes to placing him in the pantheon, that can work against him: Set against rigorous statistics and huge bodies of recorded footage, anecdotes and myths can be easy to dismiss.

But we should embrace them. The stories—even those that have been lovingly embellished—are the whole point. Sport exists to elevate our souls. It does that best when it is happening not on a screen, but right in front of your face. Pelé put himself in front of more faces than anyone.

He was, more than any player before or since, *available*.

This point extends beyond the never-ending fixture list. One of the first things that becomes evident when you go through some of the old newsreels is that Pelé existed in the center of a mob, forever being grabbed, hugged, yanked this way and that. People groped at his skin as if they expected it to confer magic powers.

This was not the strain of celebrity we know now, mediated by security guards, press officers, and social media strategies. Pelé was public property, a tangible public good. That he smiled his way through it all only added to the charm.

Pelé was not just the most gifted footballer of his generation, possibly ever; he also perfected the art of genuine connection. He was a globetrotting ambassador—for his sport, for his nation, for his own talent. Unlike any player before or since, he took the transcendental and made it local, in Plymouth and in countless other towns that have been dining out on the experience ever since.

To fully comprehend what Pelé means to Brazil and Brazilians, you have to understand "mongrel complex."

Coined by playwright Nelson Rodrigues, the phrase referred to an enduring inferiority felt by many Brazilians when they looked out into the world. Theirs was a young country, not long liberated from the tentacles of the Portuguese empire. From there, after a brief interregnum, Brazil had lurched into dictatorship, acquiring the attendant psychological scars. Democracy arrived in the wake of World War II, but it did not immediately spark an upturn in the nation's mood.

Even good things turned to rot. Brazil hosted the World Cup in 1950. It was a chance to display the country's feathers to European visitors and to make a statement on the field. But the national team fluffed its lines, losing to Uruguay in the final match when a draw would have secured the title. It was a historic embarrassment, made worse by the staggering levels of hubris that had preceded it; two newspapers and the mayor of Rio de Janeiro had declared Brazil champions before the game had even kicked off.

"Our Hiroshima," Rodrigues called it, a distasteful epithet that nonetheless captured the depths of the ensuing despair.

It is no great exaggeration to say that Pelé helped Brazil to feel good about itself again.

The 1958 tournament was the start of that process. Pelé was a late bolter for the squad, a 17-year-old wild card. He missed Brazil's first two games due to a knee injury, then missed his first two chances after being selected against the Soviet Union.

From that point, however, he was electric. Pelé set up Vavá's decisive second goal against the Soviets, then scored the only goal in the quarterfinal against Wales, prodding into the corner after a sumptuous turn inside the penalty area. He netted three more times against France in the semifinal, then twice in the 5–2 final victory against Sweden.

Brazil were mongrels no more. Pelé, young and fearless, did not so much represent his country's newfound self-confidence as embody it. Indeed, it is revealing that no less a cultural icon than Gilberto Gil, one of Brazil's most respected musicians, at home and abroad, has described Pelé as "the symbol of Brazilian emancipation."

It hardly needs restating, but he was also just a breathtakingly talented footballer. To watch those 1958 games now is to be struck by just how *inevitable* Pelé was, even in his rawest form. He was at once Mensa-smart, two-footed, technically faultless, a physical marvel—seriously, has anyone ever looked healthier than he did in those coltish early years?—and about as likely to take prisoners as a hurricane. His opponents never stood a chance.

He burnished his reputation at club level as Santos established themselves as South America's preeminent force in the years that followed. From 1960 to 1965, inspired by their talisman, the seasiders won five national championships, five São Paulo state trophies, and two Copa Libertadores titles. They also lifted the Intercontinental Cup twice, overcoming Benfica over two legs in 1962 and AC Milan over three the following year. Pelé scored seven times in those five matches.

His overall goal tally for Santos and Brazil has been the subject of significant debate over the years: There is no real consensus over whether to include goals scored in friendly matches and unofficial internationals or for the Brazilian military. Pelé himself famously counted them all—insert joke about backyard kickarounds with his grandkids here—and put the total close to 1,300. Even the most conservative quotes are well north of 700. But there can be no doubt that he was a finisher of the very highest order, with both feet and with his head.

Yet, in some ways, the focus on the raw numbers diminishes Pelé. He was a startlingly complete forward, a creator as much as a finisher. He could hold his own in the midfield battleground. In a pinch, his physique would probably have made him a decent stand-in defender, too. "I have gone through my memories looking for any kind of deficiency in his game, but I haven't found one," his former Brazil teammate Tostão once wrote.

It was really only injuries—or the timing of them—that threatened to slow Pelé down. He won his second World Cup in 1962, but it was a frustrating tournament on a personal level. He scored in Brazil's first game, against Mexico, but aggravated a long-standing groin injury in the following game against Czechoslovakia and missed the rest of the campaign.

He was still only 21, but already there was a sense that his exertions were catching up with him. Santos filled stadiums around the world, but there was little time for rest; Pelé played 80, 90, even 100 games a year as standard. "We were in demand and the suits were very keen to cash in," he once lamented. On one "ridiculous" tour of Europe, Santos played 22 matches in six weeks; little wonder Pelé ended it feeling "bruised and drained."

Worse was to come in 1966, when Pelé was kicked out of his third World Cup. After just about surviving a tetchy game against Bulgaria—"I was kicked to pieces, especially by [Dobromir] Zhechev, who seemed to mistake my ankles for the ball"—he was further targeted by Portugal, ending the match limping and helpless to prevent Brazil being knocked out of the tournament.

Pelé was so angry at the violence and at the lack of protection from referees that he vowed never to play at the World Cup again.

Pelé added at least two memorable phrases to the Brazilian football lexicon.

The first is "the goal Pelé didn't score," a reference to his audacious attempt from the center circle against Czechoslovakia in 1970. The best part about this is that the same description could easily have been used for—and, indeed, may even have better suited—the madcap, run-the-long-way-around-the-goalkeeper effort against Uruguay 14 days later. Pelé's misses were cooler than most people's goals.

The second dates back to 1961, when Pelé netted for Santos against Fluminense. No video exists of the goal, but reporters from local newspaper *O Esporte* named it the most beautiful ever to be scored at the Maracanã and installed a plaque to commemorate it. Even now, commentators are apt to describe a particularly fine strike as a *gol de placa*—a plaque-worthy goal.

Then there is the visual iconography. There is the Gordon Banks save, the embrace with Bobby Moore, the celebration atop a platform of shoulders at the Azteca—and that was all in a single summer.

In Brazil, a couple of others are up there on a similar level. One is a picture of Pelé holding a football high above his head, surrounded by radio aerials. He has just scored for Santos against Vasco da Gama, and although the match is not yet over, everything has stopped. There are reporters on the pitch. Soon the night sky will be full of white balloons. Pelé's facial expression is equal parts ecstasy and relief. He has just scored his 1,000th career goal.

The other is a photo from a charity match between the Brazil national team and club side Flamengo in 1976. Pelé, now moving inexorably toward retirement's embrace, is holding his right arm out, seemingly calling for a pass. There are three big patches of sweat on his canary-yellow jersey. One is around his armpit, another just below his collar. The third is the curious one. It adorns his chest. It is the shape of a heart.

By the end of the 1960s, the great tropical utopia—heralded by a wave of cultural expression as well as those two World Cup wins—had curdled into a nightmare. As an authoritarian military government tightened its grip on Brazil, Pelé's position as national treasure began to carry uncomfortable new connotations.

Images of him shaking hands with General Emílio Médici, the head of a regime that normalized the torture of its own citizens, were quietly damning. A footballer who had once represented progress—not least as a prominent Black athlete in a nation with a complex history of racial dynamics—came to be viewed in some quarters as part of the problem.

"He was a 'Yes-sir' Black man," former Brazil teammate Paulo Cézar Caju said in Netflix's 2021 documentary, *Pelé*. "One statement from Pelé would have gone a long way."

Pelé was always evasive on the topic. He would have been justified in fearing the consequences of speaking out at the time, but it is interesting that he did not hide behind easy excuses later in his life. "I was never forced to do anything," he admitted in the same documentary. "I always had an open door . . . even when things were bad."

That political neutrality might have tainted Pelé's legacy were it not for his 1970 World Cup campaign, a definitive statement of his excellence told in six chapters.

Even the most casual football fan will be familiar with those glorious images from Mexico, but the context adds to the emotional pull. Pelé had been persuaded to return to the Brazil setup after the trials of 1966, but the lead-up to the tournament was not straightforward. He clashed with the coach, João Saldanha, only settling when Saldanha was ousted and replaced by Mário Zagallo, a former teammate. Even then there were doubts over his fitness, plus mounting pressure on the team from the Médici regime.

A lesser player, a lesser character, would have caved. Pelé bore the weight with customary poise and inspired his team to victory. He did so with just the right amount of swagger, in the process cementing his place as the world's most beloved player.

Pelé died in December 2022. The public grief that ensued left little room for doubt about the degree to which he touched the lives of Brazilians. Hundreds of thousands of people lined up to pay their respects at his coffin, which was left open, at Santos's Vila Belmiro stadium. The funeral procession was broadcast in its entirety on multiple television channels—the kind of coverage usually reserved for heads of state.

In the days that followed, fresh eulogies jostled for space with quotes from Pelé's contemporaries, dating back to the 1970s and beyond. Many blended together, as can happen in these cases. A few stood out, cutting through the layers of cliché.

Johan Cruyff: "Pelé was the only footballer who surpassed the boundaries of logic."

Mário Zagallo: "Pelé was everything. Everything you could imagine."

Ferenc Puskás: "The greatest player in history was Alfredo Di Stéfano. I refuse to classify Pelé as a player. He was above that."

At this point, we are firmly back in mythic territory and not only because the precise origins of those Cruyff and Puskás lines seem to have been lost to history.

Some people will squirm at this way of paying tribute to a player, consider it imprecise or even cloying. Maybe Pelé—Brazilian football, even—is not for them.

The rest of us, though? We can luxuriate in the warm glow of the words, safe in the knowledge that their subject—the King, the first (and still only) man to win three World Cups as a player, a one-man memory factory and a globetrotting ambassador, both for his nation and for a romantic ideal of football—was worthy of the poetic license.

Player name: Edson Arantes do Nascimento (Pelé)
Born: October 23, 1940
Died: December 29, 2022 (aged 82)
Position: Forward
Debut: 1956
Main teams: Santos (1956–74), New York Cosmos (1975–77); Brazil (1957–71)
Career highlights: Won the World Cup in 1958, 1962, and 1970 and scored 77 times for Brazil. Won 24 trophies with Santos and scored a record 643 goals in competitive games for the club.

2.

Diego Maradona

Maradona scuttles away from England's Terry Butcher, Terry Fenwick, and Peter Reid on the way to scoring Argentina's second goal in the 1986 World Cup quarterfinal.

How the master showcased his brilliance, and resilience, in the frenzy of the Estadio Azteca

By Michael Cox

Can we quantify the most legendary individual sporting performance ever? It's impossible to compare goals to home runs, touchdowns, or three-pointers, but there is one viable, if somewhat reductive, measure: Diego Maradona's shirt from Argentina's 2–1 victory over England in the quarterfinal of the 1986 World Cup is the most valuable match-worn jersey in the history of sport.

In May 2022, Maradona's shirt from that historic contest at the Estadio Azteca was put up for auction by Sotheby's. It eventually sold for about $9.1 million, around a 60 percent increase on the previous record, Babe Ruth's New York Yankees top between 1928 and 1930. While Ruth wore his jersey for two years, Maradona only wore his for 45 minutes, having changed at halftime because of the sweltering conditions in Mexico City.

Sotheby's conducted "extensive diligence and scientific research" to verify it was the correct shirt—not the one Maradona used throughout a tame first half, but the one in which he scored two of the most famous goals in football history within the space of five minutes; more celebrated than any of his many goals in the colors of Argentinos Juniors or Boca Juniors back in Argentina, or in Europe as he elevated Napoli to unprecedented levels.

The first goal at the Azteca was blatant cheating. The second was indisputable brilliance. They served as a perfect microcosm of Maradona's character.

The shirt's previous owner, England midfielder Steve Hodge, was never in doubt. Last to leave the pitch because he was conducting a pitch-side television interview, he happened to be walking back down the tunnel alongside a jubilant Maradona, ambitiously proposed the swap, and was surprisingly handed a shirt he possessed for 36 years and eventually earned him several times his career earnings.

The shirt itself had essentially existed for less than a day.

With England wearing white, Argentina were unable to play in their traditional blue-and-white stripes. Therefore they were set to play in their away colors—solid blue—for the second game running, having done so for a 1–0 second-round win over neighbor Uruguay. But Argentina's players had been troubled by the heaviness of those shirts and worried they would be even more uncomfortable for a midday kickoff.

So, the day before the England quarterfinal, Argentina procured a lighter shirt, with faint vertical stripes, from a run-of-the-mill Mexico City sports shop. The Argentina crest was sewn on the night beforehand, alongside the logo of shirt manufacturer Le Coq Sportif—who, of course, had not actually made these shirts—while the shirt numbers were silver-gray, glittered, and designed for American football jerseys. Somewhat unexpectedly, this slapdash design process created the most valuable sporting item of clothing ever.

But all this was in keeping with the amateurish nature of the tournament. Mexico, who stepped in as replacement for Colombia as host in May 1983 largely due to economic issues, produced a finals featuring stadiums with poor facilities and dreadful pitches. Argentina manager Carlos Bilardo said his players were so exhausted from their club campaigns that he did not hold proper training sessions—the side effectively pretended to train to prevent criticism from journalists for not training at all.

As several Argentina players would later agree, while the conditions made the tournament unpleasant, it perhaps suited the plucky nature of their side.

The narrative in the buildup to Argentina's clash with England was heavily based around the Falklands War, the 10-week conflict in 1982 that began when Argentina invaded the Falkland Islands (or, as Argentinians refer to them, *las Islas Malvinas*), a British territory in the South Atlantic about 300 miles from the Argentine coast. The conflict cost the lives of 649 Argentinians, 255 Britons, and three islanders before Argentina surrendered.

Four years on, the meeting between the countries was inevitably framed in relation to that war. Both camps were under strict instructions not to engage with politically motivated questions in prematch press conferences. Most obeyed the order, although Argentina goalkeeper Nery Pumpido did veer off-message and declared that "beating the English would represent a double satisfaction for everything that happened in the Malvinas."

Argentina had breezed through the group stage, with routine 3–1 and 2–0 victories over South Korea and Bulgaria sandwiching a 1–1 draw with Italy, the nation where Maradona now played his club football with Napoli—and a team he would inspire to the first *Scudetto* in their 61-year history in 1987—before the win over Uruguay in the last 16.

The eternal debate about facing Maradona's Argentina was whether opposition managers should elect to man-mark him. A player of his talent necessitated special attention, yes, but the only match of the four in which Maradona had scored was the game against Italy, who were the only side who had man-marked him. It was thus far from certain that it was the right option.

Besides, Maradona had increasingly embraced a free role, moving deep or wide in search of space. England, accustomed to playing a 4-4-2 with zonal defending, simply weren't comfortable playing with a man-marker. Bilardo, meanwhile, made a significant tactical switch, scrapping his 4-3-1-2 and instead using a 3-5-2 formation to provide a spare man against England's strike duo, with Maradona playing off Jorge Valdano rather than behind two strikers. This was a hugely surprising decision because it involved dropping Pedro Pasculli, the striker who had scored the only goal against Uruguay. He did not play another minute at the World Cup.

Despite theoretically playing higher up the pitch, Maradona popped up everywhere against England. He dropped deep to collect short passes from Argentina's less technical players but remained between the lines when the ball was at the feet of Sergio Batista, whom Maradona trusted to thread the ball between opponents and toward him. He moved to the flanks to find space before prompting one-twos with teammates, particularly Valdano.

On four occasions, Valdano responded with a heavy touch, taking the ball into the air—presumably because of the bobbly pitch. Maradona, for his part, repeatedly backheeled the ball while sprinting at full pelt, leaving England defenders unsure whether to follow the player or the ball.

Maradona produced, even in an unmemorable first half, quite an individual performance. He boasted a peculiar, distinctive manner of striking the ball—a close-range free kick was whipped in such an understated way that it was remarkable the ball traveled over the wall, let alone nearly flew inside the near post. There were some wayward passes and a hopeless cross midway through the first half, but even if you had never watched a game of football beforehand, you would still understand that Maradona was the most talented of the 22 players on show.

There was room for an element of comedy, too. Midway through the first half, Maradona jogged across to take a corner from the right flank. Several photographers were in the way of his run-up, so he responded by picking up the corner flag and throwing it to the floor, allowing him to take a straighter run-up at the ball.

Costa Rican linesman Berny Ulloa wasn't having any of that. He ordered Maradona to replace it, an instruction that was only partly followed because Maradona replaced the pole, but left the flag itself on the ground. Ulloa insisted upon the flag, too, and stood in Maradona's way until it was replaced.

So Maradona picked up the flag and carefully, sarcastically balanced it on top of the pole. Ulloa still wasn't happy, so eventually Maradona reluctantly threaded the flag back onto the pole. It was a complete waste of time—Maradona being Maradona—but it was a small example of why he was so popular. He was a natural entertainer.

Clearly, this isn't the officiating incident everyone remembers from that game.

What is often overlooked in the controversy around Maradona's handballed opener, however, is the level of physical abuse dished out to Maradona throughout the game. Of the two sides, it was England who focused on a somewhat unsporting approach.

It started after just two minutes when Maradona, receiving the ball on the turn inside the center circle, was body-checked by defender Terry Fenwick right in front of the referee. Nothing too unusual about that; Argentina had the ball and played on. But it took just 30 seconds before Maradona was fouled for a second time, by midfielder Peter Reid, and this time he was awarded a free kick.

Of course, Maradona's constant determination to dribble meant he naturally invited challenges and fouls. He dribbled past an opponent 53 times at this World Cup, which was 37 more than any other player and the most at any World Cup according to Opta, who have statistics for every game going back to 1966. Remarkably, he was the most-fouled player at the World Cups in 1982, 1986, and 1990. Nevertheless, England brought him down repeatedly, often with considerable force, in a manner that is truly shameful when viewed today.

Nine minutes in, Maradona chested the ball down, dribbled inside left-back Kenny Sansom, and was chopped down with remarkable force by Fenwick—who was absolutely nowhere near the ball and went in with a scissor motion that ensured he hacked down Maradona as aggressively as possible. Having only just returned from a suspension for collecting two bookings in the group stage, Fenwick was booked again. For 81 minutes, he was playing against the world's best dribbler on a yellow card.

And for those 81 minutes, that initial yellow card should have proved irrelevant; not because Fenwick was composed enough to resist confrontations with Maradona, but because he could have been shown a straight red card at least twice afterward.

The most blatant occasion came five minutes before halftime. Maradona dribbled forward from an inside-left position and knocked the ball out to right-sided center-back José Luis Cuciuffo, who produced a terrible shot that was made to look even worse by the fact he was wearing the No. 9 shirt. (Argentina's squad was numbered not by position, but instead in alphabetical order—with the three exceptions being center-back Daniel Passarella, Maradona, and Valdano, who were allowed to wear their favored No. 6, No. 10, and No. 11 respectively.)

As Cuciuffo blazed over, Maradona had continued his run in behind Fenwick and been flattened with a blatant elbow. He received treatment from the Argentina physio for a couple of minutes afterward. Having finally clambered back to his feet, he went up to Fenwick and told him what he thought of the challenge, pointing to him and gesturing with an elbow. Fenwick claimed it was accidental. Maradona shook his head—he wasn't having any of it.

The second incident came two minutes before the opening goal and is laced with irony.

A big Argentina clearance bounced midway between Fenwick and Maradona in the center circle. The Argentina captain sprang up toward the ball while Fenwick launched himself into the air and led aggressively with his arm, a somewhat unusual manner of challenging for an aerial ball. It almost looked like he was trying to win the ball with his hand, although realistically he was surely just trying to smash Maradona's face with his elbow again.

But Fenwick, in trying to cheat, actually lost the challenge—Maradona got his head to the ball and knocked it past the defender, although he was unable to reach his own flick-on because he was again on the floor, holding his head. Fenwick had missed the ball, but he'd gotten the man.

All things considered, watching England repeatedly trying to injure Maradona, it is difficult to have too much sympathy when, two minutes after that second incident—and after Valdano yet again miscontrolled a Maradona pass, with Hodge nipping in to knock the ball into the air—Maradona went up for a challenge with goalkeeper Peter Shilton and led with his arm. Maradona, though, missed the man and got the ball. It bounced into the goal.

Was he inspired by Fenwick's challenge? Was he initially trying to match England's aggression and using his elbow for brute force, then ended up being in a position to handball it in?

Whatever the truth, the goal stood. The manner the ball traveled from Maradona suggested a feebler contact than a pure header. But Tunisian referee Ali Bennaceur did not spot a hand and neither did Bulgarian linesman Bogdan Dochev. If either of them suspected anything, it hardly helped that they did not share a common language, and so could not discuss the situation. Curiously, for the 2-2 group-stage draw between Paraguay and Belgium, they had also worked together—but on that occasion, Dochev was the referee and Bennaceur was the linesman.

Maradona reacted as if nothing untoward had happened, running across to celebrate in front of his father in the stand. Then, as England's defenders desperately appealed for handball, Maradona somewhat unwisely celebrated by repeatedly raising his left fist to the crowd, replicating his decisive touch. Valdano ran across and told him to stop in case the officials realized what had happened.

• • •

Then came arguably the most celebrated goal in football history.

As a general rule, there are three genres of great goal in football: a team move, a spectacular strike, and a solo dribble. Each has an almost "official" greatest ever: Carlos Alberto against Italy in 1970, Marco van Basten against the Soviet Union in 1988, and Diego Maradona against England in 1986. There is simply no arguing with this triumvirate.

This particular dribble was outstanding from the outset. Maradona produced a double dragback to evade Peter Beardsley and then Reid, which earned cheers from the crowd when he was still on the halfway line. Then came his typical change of pace, picking up speed before going past Terry Butcher on the inside, then Fenwick on the outside, and then rounding Shilton to score.

The manner in which he dribbled past Shilton feels entirely natural after he'd already beaten four England players, but Maradona later revealed that, in the moment, he had thought back to a similar incident against England six years earlier in a friendly at Wembley. On that occasion, he attempted to side-foot past goalkeeper Ray Clemence but put it wide of the far post.

The evening after that encounter, his younger brother Hugo had phoned him to rebuke him for shooting when Clemence had already committed himself and left space to dribble around. Maradona was, at the time, furious at his 11-year-old brother's armchair punditry. But he recalled that conversation when bearing down on an England goalkeeper half a decade later, and this time took Hugo's advice, rounded Shilton, and converted into an empty net under pressure from Butcher. There was no doubting the legitimacy of that one.

Even after both the goals, there was yet another incident when Fenwick threw his elbow at Maradona. This time, Valdano had flicked on a long pass, Maradona and Fenwick were again chasing the second ball, and Fenwick jumped and threw out an elbow into Maradona's face. This brought another free kick, although Maradona couldn't take it because he was off the field receiving treatment again for a couple of minutes.

Fenwick, in fairness, was far from the only offender. There was a two-footed foul from Beardsley, a strong challenge from Reid after he was beaten by Maradona's skill, and a trip from Hodge that sent Maradona headlong into a collision with Sansom, again leaving Argentina's No. 10 on the floor holding his head. Football was refereed differently all those years ago, but watch the entire 90 minutes here and the physical treatment handed out to Maradona should embarrass even the most partisan Englishman.

Afterward, it was that controversial first goal, rather than the glorious second, that dominated the discussion. Maradona initially claimed the goal was legitimate. "I swear on my life, but I hit it with my head," he said. "You could see [Shilton's] fist and that's why there's confusion. But it was a header. No doubt. I even have a bump on my forehead."

In fairness, that final part was probably true given how frequently Fenwick had clobbered him.

Nestor Ferrero, an Argentine journalist who worked for an Italian news agency and had covered Maradona's travails in Serie A, knew he was lying. "Well," said Ferrero, "it must have been the hand of God." Maradona liked that. "It must have been," he agreed.

The famous phrase was not actually Maradona's own and it didn't initially take off. As noted by Guillem Balague in his biography of Maradona, only one Argentina-based newspaper ran the phrase "the hand of God" the following day, although Maradona subsequently mentioned it frequently, often in relation to revenge for the conflict in the Falklands.

Arguably, Maradona's best was yet to come. He again scored twice in a stunning performance in the 2–0 victory over Belgium in the semifinal. Again, both his goals came shortly after the break. First, Maradona opened the scoring by running in behind and converting Jorge Burruchaga's outside-of-the-foot through-ball with an outside-of-the-foot clip over goalkeeper Jean-Marie Pfaff. Then he settled the game, receiving the ball between the lines, dribbling past four Belgium defenders, and firing home.

This was already being spoken about as possibly the greatest World Cup campaign any individual had ever produced.

Maradona failing to score in the 3–2 final victory over West Germany was, therefore, treated as something of a disappointment. Germany's key man Lothar Matthäus was handed the responsibility of marking him and largely did it well, although his unnecessary late foul after 21 minutes brought a booking and conceded the free kick that led to Argentina's opener, headed home by José Luis Brown. Maradona was involved in the passing move for Valdano to score the second and played the crucial through-ball for Burruchaga's winner. That was his fifth assist of the tournament, to go with his five goals, a neat summary of how he was both creator and provider.

Still, his goals against England live longest in the memory and feel even more unlikely in the context of watching the entire 90 minutes. Maradona was subject to disgraceful physical treatment and still won the match, well, single-handedly.

"I boshed him two or three times and tried to intimidate him, but I couldn't do that," conceded Fenwick in an interview with Sky after Maradona's death in 2020. "He was talking to me throughout the game, just chatting away to me, like this was a walk in the park."

But Fenwick's costliest error came after the final whistle. Maradona offered to swap shirts—and Fenwick said no.

Player name: Diego Armando Maradona Franco
Born: October 30, 1960
Died: November 25, 2020 (aged 60)
Position: Attacking midfielder
Debut: 1976
Main teams: Argentinos Juniors (1976–81), Boca Juniors (1981–82, 1995–97), Barcelona (1982–84), Napoli (1984–91), Sevilla (1992–93), Newell's Old Boys (1993); Argentina (1977–94)
Career highlights: Won the World Cup in 1986 and the tournament's Golden Ball. He twice claimed Serie A with Napoli, with their success in 1987 the first in the club's 61-year history, and the UEFA Cup in 1989 before eventually leaving in disgrace having served a 15-month ban for failing a drug test. A second ban followed in 1994, ending a 17-year international career.

1.
Lionel Messi

Messi decorated many a Barcelona win with his goalscoring brilliance.

The greatest of all time

By Oliver Kay

The pantheon of sporting greats is dominated by larger-than-life athletes and larger-than-life personalities, towering figures who looked like they were born to dominate and transcend the sporting landscape: Muhammad Ali, Michael Jordan, Michael Phelps, Tom Brady, Usain Bolt.

In that context, it feels all the more remarkable to say that the greatest living footballer—in our collective view, the greatest of all time—is someone who needed growth-hormone treatment to reach a height of 5'7", an introvert who regards fame and celebrity as the downside of his genius.

Lionel Messi doesn't look like a megastar. At one stage, he barely looked like a footballer.

Of all the footballers whose arrival in the big time is heralded in such excited terms—the next Pelé, the next Maradona, the next Cruyff—he looked the most unlikely. Emerging from Barcelona's academy as a 17-year-old, there was a profound teenage awkwardness about him, as if he had been on a stadium tour with a group of schoolmates, taken a wrong turn, and found himself on the touchline ready to come on as a substitute.

Seriously? Him?

Then you saw him with the ball at his feet and he took your breath away. The waif with the lank hair and the blank stare played football like you would not believe.

You don't forget your first time. I had already watched him on television as he established himself in the Barcelona team over the course of the 2005–06 season, but my first time watching him in the flesh came when Messi, still 18, emerged off the bench for Argentina in a group game against Serbia and Montenegro at the 2006 World Cup in Germany.

It is a day that sticks in the mind for a variety of reasons: an outstanding 6–0 Argentina victory, a sublime goal that saw Esteban Cambiasso provide the finishing touch to a sweeping 25-pass move, the theatrics of a delirious Diego Maradona in the stands threatening to steal the show.

But then came Messi's cameo—and the sense of quasi-religious fervor that swept the crowd in Gelsenkirchen as he appeared on the touchline. He hadn't played a competitive match for three months due to a hamstring injury, but that only increased the air of anticipation.

It was like we were preparing for the second coming. The sight of Maradona watching from high in the VIP area, clasping his hands together like a proud father and struggling to hold back the tears, only heightened that feeling. Nearby, Messi's image adorned a huge banner with his legend, *Este es mi sueño* (This is my dream).

In the press box, there was just a little cynicism. What number "next Maradona" was this? There had been Ariel Ortega, Pablo Aimar, Juan Román Riquelme, Marcelo Gallardo, Andrés D'Alessandro, and Javier Saviola, to name but six. Great talents all of them, and some had achieved great things, but none had come close to Maradona's level. And this kid was going to be different, was he? *Seriously? Him?*

Within two minutes, Messi had scampered down the left wing to set up Hernán Crespo for Argentina's fourth goal. He scored the sixth himself, threading the ball between the goalkeeper's legs. But even more than those contributions, it was his adhesive touch and the way he carried the ball. The speed with which he drifted between opponents and into space was something else. Every movement was perfect.

I remember writing in the London *Times* in early 2010, flying home from Barcelona the morning after watching him score four times in an astounding performance against Arsenal in the Champions League, that what Messi was doing at the age of 22 was of a level not seen since Maradona's heyday in the 1980s. I followed that with a note of caution, pointing out that even Maradona had not been able to sustain such standards throughout his career and that other true greats, such as Marco van Basten and the Brazilian forward Ronaldo, had been thwarted by injury at what proved to be the peak of their powers.

We should enjoy Messi's brilliance for as long as it lasts, I wrote, adding that "experience warns us that this could be as good as it gets."

Hmmm. Experience tells me I shouldn't have worried.

Where do you start when it comes to detailing what makes Messi so special?

If he was just a goalscorer, the record books at the International Federation of Football History and Statistics tell us he is the second greatest of all time behind Cristiano Ronaldo. But goals have never even been the main feature of Messi's game, which has instead been defined by his vision, his passing, his dribbling, his creativity.

By the time he made his 1,000th career appearance, which he marked with a goal for Argentina against Australia at the 2022 World Cup, he had scored 789 goals and registered 348 assists. At the time of writing, he has won 12 league titles—10 with Barcelona and two with Paris Saint-Germain (plus a Supporters' Shield with Inter Miami), as well as four Champions League titles (all with Barcelona), the Copa América twice, the World Cup once, and the Ballon d'Or award eight times, finishing as runner-up on another five occasions. The numbers are outrageous, but again, the trophy collection and the goal tally cannot begin to do justice to his talent.

Every great athlete has a moment that defines his or her excellence in the public consciousness.

In football, Pelé is best recalled for the goals he scored in the 1958 and 1970 World Cup finals; Maradona for the astonishing solo goals he scored against England and Belgium en route to World Cup glory in 1986; Van Basten for that stunning volley against the Soviet Union in the European Championship final in 1988; Zinédine Zidane for his volley for Real Madrid against Bayer Leverkusen in the 2002 Champions League final; Cristiano Ronaldo—though there are plenty of alternatives—for his overhead kick for Real Madrid against Juventus in a Champions League quarterfinal in 2018.

With Messi, though, where do you even begin? The goal he scored as a teenager for Barcelona against Getafe in April 2007, dribbling from inside his own half and beating six (seven? eight?) challenges, that in terms of pure technique surpassed even Maradona's "Goal of the Century" against England? The one against Athletic Bilbao in the Copa del Rey final eight years later in which he dribbled in and out of five challenges and thrashed the ball inside the near post? Was that peak Messi? Or was it another solo goal against Eibar, Girona, Real Zaragoza, or Real Madrid? Or against Manchester United in a Champions League final (take your pick from 2009 and 2011)? Or was it any one of the inspirational acts he produced en route to World Cup glory with Argentina—finally—in 2022?

There is something almost ethereal about Messi's talent. Watch any of those YouTube compilations that showcase his dribbling and his passing, set to classical music, and it looks like sport as an art form. It is a thing of beauty, poetry in motion.

But what doesn't always come across on television, what really strikes you when you are watching him in person, is the raw energy behind his genius. Like Ali, he floats like a butterfly but stings like a bee.

I have been privileged to witness some of his most acclaimed moments in person. One match that sticks in the mind was at Wembley in a Champions League group game in 2018 when he rattled the frame of the Tottenham Hotspur goal twice before adjusting his sights slightly and scoring two goals. It was a classic illustration of Messi as a force of nature, possessed of iron will as well as unearthly skill, but in truth, it was career-defining only in the sense that it was consistent with what was seen on innumerable occasions in the years before and since. Would it make his top 10 most memorable performances? Almost certainly not. Top 50? Possibly. For almost anyone else, it would be the performance of a lifetime.

I remember letting out a loud gasp in the press box at Camp Nou in May 2015 when, with a Champions League semifinal against Bayern Munich hanging in the balance, he gave Jérôme Boateng the slip and then dinked the ball over the advancing Manuel Neuer, leaving the great German goalkeeper grasping at thin air. It was stunning in both conception and execution, but by Messi's standards, it was, again, an ordinary day's work.

The venerable British sportswriter Paul Hayward was in the hospital at the time, between chemotherapy sessions after being diagnosed with cancer. He would later describe watching that match in the lowest of spirits "on a screen in a room short of cheer" and feeling himself "rise from my chair" in wonder when he saw Messi do that to Boateng and Neuer.

"That moment will not leave my memory," Hayward wrote, "because it made the world full of possibilities again."

• • •

So how did a tiny, painfully shy kid from Rosario, Argentina, overcome the odds to become the greatest footballer of all time?

The reference to his height is important. When he was 10 and already showing prodigious talent, he was sent to see a specialist because the coaches at his local club, Newell's Old Boys, were, like his parents, worried that at 4'2" he was so much smaller than his peers. He had barely grown in two years.

Dr. Diego Schwarzstein, a specialist in endocrinology, conducted tests over a period of six months before concluding that because of a growth hormone deficiency, he was unlikely to grow beyond five feet tall. He was prescribed a course of growth hormone drugs, injected into his legs every day. Slowly but surely, he started growing. By the age of 12, he was up to 4'10", well on the way to his adult height of 5'7".

The treatment cost about $1,000 a month. Even with a contribution from Newell's, that left a huge dent in the Messi family's finances. It was Barcelona's offer to cover the costs of the treatment—after Messi left their coaches enthralled during a trial—that persuaded the family to leave Argentina so he could begin an apprenticeship with the Catalan club at the age of 13.

Without that treatment, without Barcelona's willingness to cover the bill, it is highly doubtful whether even a player as talented as Messi could have coped with the physical demands of a top-level career, let alone scale the heights he has.

There was also an extreme reservedness about Messi. On the pitch, he was uniquely expressive. Off the pitch, he was—and to an extent still is—the opposite.

During the 2016 Copa América, Maradona declared that Messi had "no personality," that he was a nice guy but lacked "the character to be a leader." Maradona was an extreme personality at one end of the spectrum, Messi at the other. It was only in the later years of his career that Messi began to look comfortable with his role as captain of the Argentina team.

Messi is introverted in a way that seems at odds with his status. Off the pitch, he does not radiate anything like the aura of his great rival Cristiano Ronaldo. He has become a more confident public speaker as his career has gone on, but I am reminded of a line the author John Carlin wrote about interviewing a 21-year-old Messi, an experience he described as "so forgettable that I have no recollection of writing an article after it."

Watching him play football, on the other hand, is unforgettable.

Fernando Signorini, the former Argentina fitness coach, described Messi as a "genetic miracle." "Just like Diego (Maradona), his neuromuscular coordination has a cosmic power," Signorini said. "Almost unthinkable ability to control their body in time and space, defying gravity."

On the face of it, Messi never seemed to be blessed with extraordinary pace. Sure, he was fast, but not *that* fast. During the 2014 World Cup, at the age of 27, the highest speed he was clocked at was about 20 miles per hour. That is some way below Cristiano Ronaldo's top speed, let alone Kylian Mbappé's (23.5 miles per hour).

But where Messi is unequaled is his speed with the ball under control. Watching him, you would be excused for thinking he is quicker with the ball than without it. He looks terrifying in full flight: twisting, turning, feinting, swerving. Some players do tricks. Messi doesn't, really. There is an old-school element to his dribbling, but the speed at which he does it, twisting between challenges in the tightest of spaces, appears almost futuristic.

To study Messi in action is to witness an athlete whose perception of space and time—and how to use them—sets him apart. Opponents converge, but he is already two or three steps ahead. Even when you pause the action and zoom out for a wide-angle view, you wonder how on earth he has seen what he has seen.

"Leo always had the talent and personality, but he is also very intelligent," former Barcelona coach Jordi Roura says. "He quickly understood the way to play collectively and he took on the concepts of Barcelona. He knew the positions to take up on the pitch, how to approach the ball, to *perfilarse* (shape himself), what to do in each moment."

There is a line another former Barcelona coach, Robert Moreno, used about him in an interview with *The Athletic* in 2022. "He's like *The Matrix*," Moreno said. "Do you remember that scene where the character is moving his body and all the bullets go slowly? For me, Messi plays like this. All the things are happening slower in his mind than are happening for the rest of the world."

This analysis has been widely interpreted, in layman's terms, as "Messi's brain slows down time." Could that be true? Ask the man to explain his genius, as many have done in interviews over the years, and he struggles to put it into words. He just does what comes naturally.

David Sumpter is a professor of applied mathematics and the co-founder of Twelve Football, which uses data to help inform clubs not just about scouting, but about decision-making on the field. He worked with Barcelona during Messi's time there, studying patterns of play and analyzing players' decisions and their relationship with space and time.

"What we found," Sumpter says, "is that he and his teammates were finding pockets of space that didn't yet exist. It wouldn't exist as a space for another two or three seconds. In that respect, yes, these players could see two seconds into the future, five seconds into the future. But with Messi, it was almost like he could see 10 minutes into the future. I don't mean that literally because football is such a fluid game, but what he would do is map out early in the match where those spaces were likely to occur—and then he would make sure he found those spaces as the match went on."

It makes the whole thing sound scientific, as if Messi is walking around the pitch like the mathematician John Nash, as portrayed by Russell Crowe in *A Beautiful Mind*. "No, I'm not saying he's thinking in mathematical terms," Sumpter says. "But having studied the patterns he creates, I would say he is thinking constantly about space and the various angles. We don't know without scanning his brain, but there must be something mathematical going on in there.

"I would expect in spatial reasoning tests he would score higher than the average person and higher than the average footballer. He strikes me as one of those rare people who has something beautiful and unique in his head which allows him to do what he does."

"It's a different thing to the intelligence a 'normal' person has," Moreno added. "It's the knowledge that you can't explain. [Footballers] are able to do things, but they are not able to explain why they do them. Messi is the maximum expression of that situation. He finds solutions where mortal people aren't able to do so."

For years, it felt like the only thing holding Messi back in the GOAT debate was that, unlike Pelé and Maradona, he had never won the World Cup.

The argument underestimated how much the sporting landscape had changed. Through the 1960s, 1970s, and 1980s, greatness was viewed primarily through the prism of international football and the World Cup in particular. In the twenty-first century, the club game has become so all-consuming, dominated by a handful of "super clubs," that the final stages of the Champions League have come to be recognized as the highest form of the game, technically superior to the World Cup, albeit not quite as big a global spectacle.

Messi suffered defeats in the World Cup quarterfinal in 2006 and 2010, the final in 2014, and the round of 16 in 2018. Inspiration sometimes eluded him, but Argentina were beaten by better teams; on two occasions by the eventual winners. It was never a question of failing to make a step up in quality. The problem was that in what was often a dysfunctional team, Messi seemed to creak under the burden, with his nation's hopes resting on his slender shoulders.

Did he really have to win the World Cup to be considered the best of his generation, to join Maradona and Pelé at the top of the pantheon or indeed to be considered the greatest of them all? In a team sport, such an argument felt a little facile.

But in Qatar in 2022, Messi went and won it anyway, at the age of 35. He didn't quite "carry" the team in the way Maradona did in 1986, but he made huge contributions at every stage of the tournament: a fabulous goal in Argentina's hour of need against Mexico in the group stage; a precise finish to help beat Australia in the round of 16; a wonderful assist for Nahuel Molina and a high-pressure penalty (followed by another in the shootout) in the quarterfinal against the Netherlands; another high-pressure penalty and a mesmerizing run to set up Julián Alvarez in the semifinal against Croatia; two goals (one a penalty) and then another successful penalty in the shootout as an epic World Cup final against France came to a nerve-shredding denouement.

When victory was confirmed, he fell to his knees, overcome. This was his crowning glory, his Holy Grail. "It's any player's childhood dream," he told reporters afterward. "I am lucky enough to have achieved everything. This is what I was missing. Now it's here."

But there is something in what Pep Guardiola said subsequently. "If he had not won the World Cup, my opinion . . . would not have changed at all," the Manchester City and former Barcelona coach said. "For me, it's easy to say he's the best of all time. Maybe that's a lack of respect to Pelé and Maradona, but for me, he is."

There is no definitive answer. The debate is never-ending. Even now, there are many who regard Cristiano Ronaldo, by virtue of his goalscoring record, as superior to Messi. The football landscape is so different now to when Maradona played, let alone when Johan Cruyff, Pelé, and Alfredo Di Stéfano played. Messi has excelled in an era in which creative players have largely been spared the brutality faced by the great players of the past.

But he has also played in an era when the game is so much faster and more athletic, when technical levels across the board are so elevated. And Messi has consistently elevated those levels to almost preposterous heights.

There might, in time, be others who score more goals or more eye-catching goals than Messi, who spot a pass better than Messi, who weight a pass better than Messi, who dribble better than Messi, who understand space and time better than Messi. But . . . all of that in one player? We will be waiting a very long time before we see another player who does all those things to such an extraordinary level, week in and week out, season in and season out, for the best part of two decades.

As Guardiola once said, "Don't try to explain Messi, don't try to write about him, don't try to describe him. Watch him!"

Seriously. Him.

Lionel Messi's Barcelona Goals by Season, in All Competitions

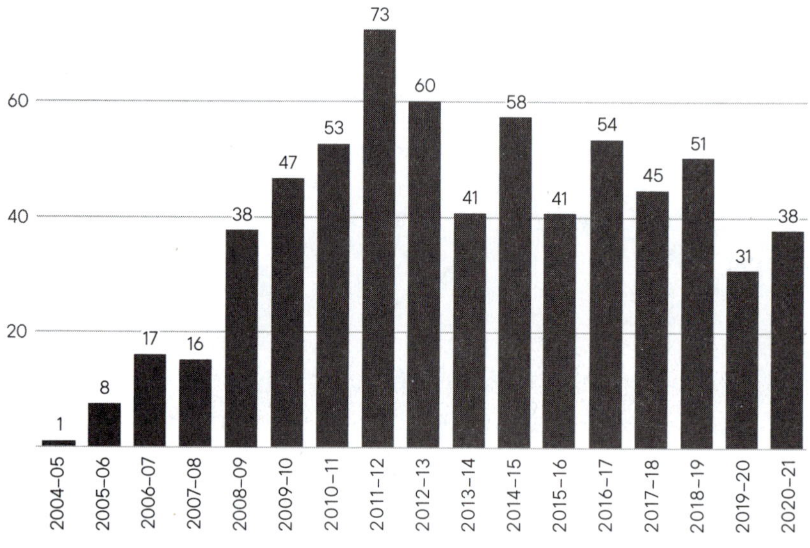

Player name: Lionel Messi
Born: June 24, 1987
Position: Forward
Debut: 2004
Main teams: Barcelona (2004–21), Paris Saint-Germain (2021–23), Inter Miami (2023–); Argentina (2005–)
Career highlights: Won the World Cup in 2022, the Copa América in 2021 and 2024, 10 La Liga titles with Barcelona, four Champions League titles, and the Ballon d'Or a record eight times. Scored a record 672 goals for Barca.

Appendix: Competition Explainer

Africa Cup of Nations: A competition for African national teams. It began in 1957 and is now usually held every two years. The most recent editions have seen 24 countries competing.
Argentine Primera División: The top league for clubs in Argentina. It has existed in various forms since 1891 and is currently contested by 30 teams. It is played every season and the winners are crowned champions of Argentina.
Ballon d'Or: An annual award given to the best player in the world. It launched in 1956 and was only open to European players until 1995, when non-Europeans playing club football in Europe became eligible. In 2007, it was expanded further so that any player in the world could win. It is currently voted for by journalists.
Brazilian Série A: The top league for clubs in Brazil. It has existed in various forms since 1937 and is currently contested by 20 teams. It is played every season and the winners are crowned champions of Brazil.
Bundesliga: The top league for clubs in Germany. Its first season was in 1963–64 and the winners of each campaign, in which 18 teams currently compete, are crowned champions of Germany. There was a German football championship, in various forms, before the introduction of the Bundesliga. It is played every season.
Campeonato Sudamericano / South American Championship / Copa América: A competition for South American national teams (though countries from outside the continent are occasionally also invited to play). It began in 1916 and is now held roughly every three years. It has been called Copa América since 1975.
***Clásico*:** Any football match between Spanish clubs Barcelona and Real Madrid.
Club World Cup: This competition has existed in various forms since its introduction in 2000 and is largely contested by the club champions of each continent. An expanded version, featuring

32 teams, took place in the United States in the summer of 2025. The winner is crowned world champions, but it has never been considered as prestigious as the World Cup or Europe's Champions League.

Copa del Rey: The main domestic cup competition for clubs in Spain. It began in the 1903 season and is held every year.

Copa Libertadores: The most prestigious competition in South American club football and played every season. It is contested by the best club sides from across the continent. It started in 1960 and is currently contested by 47 teams.

Coppa Italia: The main domestic cup competition for clubs in Italy. It began in 1922 and is held every year.

Coupe de France: The main domestic cup competition for clubs in France. It began in the 1917–18 season and is held every year.

DFB-Pokal: The main domestic cup competition for clubs in Germany. It began in the 1935 season and is held every year.

Domestic cup: This refers to the major cup competition within a country. For example, the FA Cup in England and the Copa del Rey in Spain.

Eredivisie: The top league for clubs in the Netherlands, its first season was 1956–57. The winners of each campaign, in which 18 teams currently compete, are crowned the champions of the Netherlands. There was a Dutch football championship, in various forms, before the introduction of the Eredivisie. It is played every season.

European Championship: A competition for European national teams. The first edition took place in 1960, when four countries played in the final stage. It is held every four years. The most recent edition, in 2024, had 24 teams competing. The name is often shortened to Euro 2000 or Euro 2004.

European Cup / Champions League: The most prestigious competition in European club football, played every season. It is contested by the best club sides from across the continent, with the strongest leagues being allocated more places for their clubs. It started in 1955 and was called the European Cup before being rebranded as the Champions League in 1992. The competition proper is currently contested by 36 teams.

European Cup Winners' Cup: A club competition that existed from 1960 to 1999 and was largely contested by the winners of the main domestic cup competitions across Europe. It was considered the secondary European club competition during its existence, behind the European Cup / Champions League and ahead of the UEFA Cup.

FA Cup: The main domestic cup competition for clubs in England, and the oldest knockout competition in the world. It began in the 1871–72 season and is held every year. It is eligible to all clubs down to level nine of the English football pyramid, with sides from level 10 acting as stand-ins if necessary. A record 763 clubs competed in 2011–12.

First Division / Premier League: The top league for clubs in England, and the oldest football league in the world. Its first season was in 1888–89 (it was called the Football League until 1892) and it was rebranded ahead of the 1992–93 campaign as the Premier League. The team that wins it are crowned champions of England. It is currently contested by 20 clubs and played every season.

French Division 1 / Ligue 1: The top league for clubs in France. Its first season was in 1932–33 and the winners of each campaign, in which 18 teams currently compete, are crowned champions of France. It was rebranded as Ligue 1 for the 2002–03 season. There was an amateur French football championship before the professional era began in 1932. It is played every season.

KNVB Cup: The main domestic cup competition for clubs in the Netherlands. It began in the 1898–99 season and is held every year.

La Liga: The top league for clubs in Spain. Its first season was in 1929 and the team that wins it are crowned champions of Spain. It is currently contested by 20 clubs and is played every season.

Serie A: The top league for clubs in Italy. Its first season was in 1929–30 and the winner of each campaign, in which 20 teams currently compete, are crowned the champions of Italy. "Winning the *scudetto*" is a synonym for "winning Serie A." There was an Italian football championship, in various forms, before the introduction of Serie A. It is played every season.

Top flight: This refers to the highest-ranked league within a country. For example, the Premier League is England's top flight and La Liga is the Spanish equivalent.

UEFA Cup / Europa League: The secondary competition in European club football, played every season. It is contested by the best-performing sides across the continent who have not qualified for the Champions League. It started in 1971 and was called the UEFA Cup before being rebranded as the Europa League in 2009. During the existence of the European Cup Winners' Cup (which was discontinued in 1999), the UEFA Cup was considered the tertiary European club competition. It is currently contested by 36 teams.

World Cup: The most prestigious competition in international football and contested by national teams. It began in 1930 when 13 countries played in it and is held every four years. There will be 48 teams playing at the 2026 edition in the United States, Canada, and Mexico.

World Cup Golden Ball: Awarded to the best player at each World Cup. It is currently voted for by journalists and was introduced in 1982.

World Cup Golden Boot: Awarded to the top goalscorer at each World Cup and was introduced in 1982.

Appendix: The 100 by Nationality

Brazil	15
Italy	14
France	10
England	10
Germany/West Germany	9
Argentina	6
Netherlands	6
Spain	5
Portugal	3
Wales	3
Hungary	2
Soviet Union	2
Scotland	2
Sweden	2
Northern Ireland	1
Croatia	1
Bulgaria	1
Liberia	1
Belgium	1
Egypt	1
Austria	1
Côte d'Ivoire	1
Denmark	1
Romania	1
Mexico	1

Appendix: Phonetic Spellings and Pronunciations

1: Lionel Messi
English pronunciation: **Lie**-nel Messy
Native pronunciation: Li-oh-**nel Mes**-si
Nationality: Argentinian
Note: Messi's surname is Italian in origin

2: Diego Maradona
English pronunciation: Dee-**ay**-go Ma-ra-**dun**-na
Native pronunciation: Dee-**ay**-go Ma-ra-**don**-na
Nationality: Argentinian
Note: Maradona's surname is also Italian

3: Pelé
English pronunciation: **Peh**-lay
Native pronunciation: Peh-**leh**
Nationality: Brazilian
Note: Full name is Edson Arantes do Nascimento

4: Johan Cruyff
English pronunciation: **Yo**-han **Kroiff**
Native pronunciation: **Yo**-hun **Cr-ra-uff**
Nationality: Dutch
Note: The Dutch spell his surname "Cruijff"

5: Cristiano Ronaldo
English pronunciation: Cris-ti-**ah**-no Ro-**nal**-doh
Native pronunciation: Crish-ti-**ah**-noo Kho-**nal**-doo
Nationality: Portuguese

6: Alfredo Di Stéfano
English pronunciation: Al-**fray**-doh Dee Ste-**fan**-oh
Native pronunciation: Al-**fray**-doh Dee **Ste**-fan-oh
Nationality: Argentinian
Note: Like a lot of Argentinians (including Messi), Di Stéfano had Italian roots: his father was Italian. His origins are reflected in his name.

7: Franz Beckenbauer
English pronunciation: **Frans Beh**-ken-bough-er

Native pronunciation: **Frants Beh**-ken-bough-er
Nationality: German

8: Zinédine Zidane
English pronunciation: Zin-eh-**deen** Zi-**dan**
French pronunciation: Zin-ay-**deen** Zee-**dan**
Arabic pronunciation: **Zeh**-neh-din Zi-**dan**
Nationality: French
Note: Zidane is of Algerian origin, hence the inclusion of the Arabic pronunciation

9: Ferenc Puskás
English pronunciation: **Fer**-enk **Pus**-kas
Native pronunciation: **Fer**-ents **Push**-kash
Nationality: Hungarian

10: Michel Platini
English pronunciation: Mi-**shell Pla**-tee-nee
Native pronunciation: Mi-**shell** Pla-tee-**nee**
Nationality: French
Note: Platini's family was originally from Piedmont, hence his Italian surname, but the pronunciation here is distinctively French

11: Eusébio
English pronunciation: Yu-**say**-bee-oh
Native pronunciation: Eh-oo-**sheh**-bee-oo
Nationality: Portuguese
Note: Full name is Eusébio da Silva Ferreira

12: Ronaldo
English pronunciation: Ron-**al**-doh
Native pronunciation: Kho-**nal**-doo
Nationality: Brazilian
Note: Full name is Ronaldo Luís Nazário de Lima

13: Gerd Müller
English pronunciation: Gerd **Mul**-ler
Native pronunciation: Gert **Meww**-ler
Nationality: German

14: Garrincha
English pronunciation: Ga-**rin**-cha
Native pronunciation: Ga-**hin**-sha
Nationality: Brazilian

15: George Best
English pronunciation: George Best
Native pronunciation: George Best
Nationality: Northern Irish

16: Marco van Basten
English pronunciation: **Mar**-ko van **Bas**-ten
Native pronunciation: **Marr**-ko van **Bas**-tn
Nationality: Dutch

17: Paolo Maldini
English pronunciation: **Pow**-lo Mal-**dee**-nee
Native pronunciation: **Pa**-oh-lo Mal-**dee**-nee
Nationality: Italian

18: Lev Yashin
English pronunciation: **Lev Ya**-shin
Native pronunciation: **Lyev Ya**-shin
Nationality: Russian (Soviet Union)

19: Franco Baresi
English pronunciation: **Fran**-ko Bar-**ez**-ee
Native pronunciation: **Fran**-ko Ba-**ray**-zee
Nationality: Italian

20: Bobby Charlton
English pronunciation: **Bob**-ee **Charl**-ton
Native pronunciation: **Bob**-ee **Charl**-ton
Nationality: English

21: Xavi Hernández
English pronunciation: **Za**-vi (or **Ha**-vi) Her-**nan**-des
Native pronunciation: **Cha**-bi Aer-**nan**-deth
Nationality: Spanish
Note: Xavi is from Catalonia, and his given name derives from Catalan, not Spanish

22: Ronaldinho
English pronunciation: Ron-al-**deen**-i-o
Native pronunciation: Khon-al-**deen**-nyu
Nationality: Brazilian

23: Thierry Henry
English pronunciation: **Tee**-air-ree On-**ree**
Native pronunciation: **Tee**-eh-**ree** On-**ree**
Nationality: French

24: Jairzinho
English pronunciation: Jar-**zin**-yo
Native pronunciation: Ja-ir-**zeen**-yuu
Nationality: Brazilian

25: Andrés Iniesta
English pronunciation: And-**res** In-ee-**es**-ta
Native pronunciation: And-**res** In-ee-**es**-ta
Nationality: Spanish

26: Lothar Matthäus
English pronunciation: **Lo**-tar Mat-**tee**-as
Native pronunciation: **Lo**-tar Mat-**tay**-us
Nationality: German

27: Zico
English pronunciation: **Zee**-ko
Native pronunciation: **Zee**-koo
Nationality: Brazilian

28: Bobby Moore
English pronunciation: **Bob**-ee Moor
Native pronunciation: **Bob**-ee Moor
Nationality: English

29: Kylian Mbappé
English pronunciation: **Kil**-ee-an Um-**ba**-pay
Native pronunciation: **Kil**-ee-**an Em**-ba-**pay**
Nationality: French

30: Carlos Alberto
English pronunciation: **Car**-los Al-**bur**-toh
Native pronunciation: **Car**-losh Al-**ber**-too
Nationality: Brazilian

31: Ruud Gullit
English pronunciation: Rood **Hul**-et
Native pronunciation: Rroot **Khool**-lit
Nationality: Dutch

32: Romário
English pronunciation: Ro-**mar**-ee-oh
Native pronunciation: Kho-**mar**-ee-oo
Nationality: Brazilian
Note: His full name is Romário de Souza Faria

33: Gianluigi Buffon
English pronunciation: Jan-loo-**ee**-gee **Boo**-fon
Native pronunciation: Jan-loo-**ee**-gee Boo-**fon**
Nationality: Italian

34: Dino Zoff
English pronunciation: **Dee**-no Zoff
Native pronunciation: **Dee**-no Zoff
Nationality: Italian

35: Jimmy Greaves
English pronunciation: **Jim**-me **Gree**vz
Native pronunciation: **Jim**-me **Gree**vz
Nationality: English

36: Luka Modrić
English pronunciation: Lu-ka **Mod**-rik
Native pronunciation: **Loo**ka **Mod**-ritch
Nationality: Croatian

37: Andrea Pirlo
English pronunciation: **An**-drey-a **Peer**-lo
Native pronunciation: An-**dreh**-a **Peer**-lo
Nationality: Italian

38: Manuel Neuer
English pronunciation: **Man**-well **Noy**-ur
Native pronunciation: **Man**-oo-el **Noy**-er
Nationality: German

39: Roberto Baggio
English pronunciation: Ro-**bur**-toh **Baj**-ee-o
Native pronunciation: Ro-**berr**-toh **Baj**-joh
Nationality: Italian

40: Paco Gento
English pronunciation: Pa-ko **Jen**-to
Native pronunciation: Pa-ko **Hen**-toh
Nationality: Spanish

41: Karim Benzema
English pronunciation: Kar-**eem** Ben-**zee**-ma (or **Ben**-zee-ma)
French pronunciation: **Kar**-eem **Ben**-zay-**ma**
Arabic pronunciation: Ka-**rihm** Bin-**zeh**-ma
Nationality: French

Note: Like Zidane, Benzema is of Algerian heritage and speaks some Arabic (as well as Spanish and English)

42: Luís Figo

English pronunciation: **Loo**-is (as in "Lewis") **Fee**-go
Native pronunciation: Lu-**eesh Fee**-gu
Nationality: Portuguese

43: Cafu

English pronunciation: Ka-**foo**
Native pronunciation: Ka-**foo**
Nationality: Brazilian
Note: Real name is Marcos Evangelista de Morais

44: Kaká

English pronunciation: **Ka**-kah
Native pronunciation: **Ka**-**ka**
Nationality: Brazilian
Note: Real name is Ricardo Izecson dos Santos Leite

45: Fabio Cannavaro

English pronunciation: **Fab**-ee-o Ca-na-**vah**-row
Native pronunciation: **Fab**-ee-o Can-na-**va**-ro
Nationality: Italian

46: Neymar Júnior

English pronunciation: **Nay**-mar **Ju**nior
Native pronunciation: Nay-**mar Jun**-i-**or**
Nationality: Brazilian
Note: His full name is Neymar da Silva Santos Júnior

47: Raymond Kopa

English pronunciation: **Ray**-mond **Ko**-pah
Native pronunciation: Ray-**mon Ko**-**pah**
Nationality: French
*Note: Kopa was of Polish origin; his actual surname was Kopaszewski [Ko-pa-**shev**-ski]*

48: Rivaldo

English pronunciation: Ree-**val**-doh
Native pronunciation: Khee-**val**-doo
Nationality: Brazilian
Full name: Rivaldo Vítor Borba Ferreira

49: Dennis Bergkamp

English pronunciation: Dennis **Burg**-kamp (or even "Bird-camp")

Native pronunciation: Dennis **Berkh**-kamp
Nationality: Dutch

50: Kenny Dalglish
English pronunciation: Kenny Dal-**gleesh**
Native pronunciation: Kenny Dal-**gleesh**
Nationality: Scottish

51: Sándor Kocsis
English pronunciation: **San**-door **Kok**-sis
Native pronunciation: **Shan**-door **Ko**-chish
Nationality: Hungarian

52: Toni Kroos
English pronunciation: Tony Croos
Native pronunciation: **Toe**-nee **Crohs**
Nationality: German

53: Wayne Rooney
English pronunciation: Wayn **Roo**-nee
Native pronunciation: Wayn **Roo**-nee
Nationality: English

54: Hristo Stoichkov
English pronunciation: **Hris**-toh **Stoich**-koff
Native pronunciation: **Hris**-toh **Stoich**-koff
Nationality: Bulgarian

55: Johan Neeskens
English pronunciation: **Yo**-han **Nee**-skins
Native pronunciation: **Yo**-hun **Nay**-skens
Nationality: Dutch

56: George Weah
English pronunciation: George **Way**-ah
Native pronunciation: George **Way**-ah
Nationality: Liberian

57: Giuseppe Meazza
English pronunciation: Ji-**sep**-ee **Me**-ats-a
Native pronunciation: Giu-**zepp**-eh **Meh**-ats-ah
Nationality: Italian

58: Sergio Busquets
English pronunciation: **Surg**-i-oh **Bus**-kets
Native pronunciation: **Ser**-hi-o Boos-**kets**

Nationality: Spanish
Note: Busquets's surname comes from Catalan, not Spanish

59: Stanley Matthews
English pronunciation: **Stan**-lee **Math**-hews
Native pronunciation: **Stan**-lee **Math**-hews
Nationality: English

60: Just Fontaine
English pronunciation: Joost Fon-**tayn**
Native pronunciation: Joost Fon-**tennn**
Nationality: French

61: Sócrates
English pronunciation: **Soc**-ra-tees
Native pronunciation: **Soo**-cra-tyesh
Nationality: Brazilian
Note: His full name is Sócrates Brasileiro Sampaio de Souza Vieira de Oliveira

62: Ryan Giggs
English pronunciation: **Rye**-ann Gigs
Native pronunciation: **Rye**-ann Gigs
Nationality: Welsh

63: Mario Kempes
English pronunciation: **Mar**-ee-o **Kem**-pez
Native pronunciation: **Mar**-ee-o **Kem**-pes
Nationality: Argentinian

64: Frank Rijkaard
English pronunciation: Frank **Rye**-kard
Native pronunciation: Frank **Rrrye**-kaard
Nationality: Dutch

65: Zlatan Ibrahimović
English pronunciation: **Zla**-tan Ib-ra-**him**-a-vich
Native pronunciation: **Zla**-tan Ee-bra-**heem**-oh-vich
Nationality: Swedish
Note: Ibrahimović was born in Sweden to a Bosnian father and a Croatian mother, so his name comes via Bosnian/Serbo-Croat. The pronunciation is fundamentally the same in both languages, although Swedish has a distinctive intonation.

66: Kevin De Bruyne
English pronunciation: **Kev**in Duh **Broi**-nuh

Native pronunciation: **Keh**-fin Duh **Bruh**-nuh
Nationality: Belgian
Note: Belgium has three official languages (Flemish, French, and German). De Bruyne's name comes from Flemish, which is a variety of Dutch.

67: Mohamed Salah
English pronunciation: Mo-**ham**-ed **Sa**-la
Native pronunciation: Mu-**humm**-ad Sa-**laaah**
Nationality: Egyptian

68: Gianni Rivera
English pronunciation: **Ja**-nee Ree-**vay**-ra
Native pronunciation: **Jan**-nee Ree-**veh**-ra
Nationality: Italian

69: Francesco Totti
English pronunciation: Fran-**ches**-co **To**-tee
Native pronunciation: Fran-**ches**-co **Tot**-tee
Nationality: Italian

70: Matthias Sindelar (German), Matěj Šindelář (Czech)
English pronunciation: Matt-**eye**-ass **Sin**-dee-lar
German pronunciation: Matt-**ee**-ass **Zin**-duh-lar
Czech pronunciation: **Mat**-ay Shin-de-**lar**
Nationality: Austrian
Note: Sindelaar represented Austria, but he was born into a Czech-speaking family in the days of the Austro-Hungarian Empire. He moved to Vienna when he was two, which led to his name being Germanized in school. The German rendering of his name is much more common.

71: Didier Drogba
English pronunciation: **Di**-dee-ay **Drog**-ba
Native pronunciation: **Di**-dee-ay **Drog-ba**
Nationality: Ivorian
Note: The official language of Côte d'Ivoire is French, so the "native" pronunciation reflects French conventions.

72: Alessandro Del Piero
English pronunciation: Al-ess-**an**-dro del Pee-**air**-oh
Native pronunciation: Al-ess-**an**-dro del Pee-**aer**-oh
Nationality: Italian

73: Karl-Heinz Rummenigge
English pronunciation: **Karl-Hainzz Room**-in-ig-grrr

Native pronunciation: **Karl-Haints Room**-eh-nig-guh
Nationality: German

74: Michael Laudrup
English pronunciation: **My-k**ul [Michael] **Loud**-drop
Native pronunciation: Mik-a-el **Loud**-drup
Nationality: Danish

75: Günter Netzer
English pronunciation: **Goon**-ter **Net**-zer
Native pronunciation: G-**eew**-n-ter **Net**-tser
Nationality: German

76: Gabriel Batistuta
English pronunciation: **Gabe**-ree-el Bat-ee-**stoo**-ta
Native pronunciation: Gab-ree-**el** Bat-ee-**stoo**-ta
Nationality: Argentinian

77: Roberto Carlos
English pronunciation: Ro-**bur**-toh **Car**-los
Native pronunciation: **Khroo**-ber-too **Car**-losh
Nationality: Brazilian
Full name: Roberto Carlos da Silva Rocha

78: Gordon Banks
English pronunciation: **Gor**-don **Banks**
Native pronunciation: **Gor**-don **Banks**
Nationality: English

79: Paul Gascoigne
English pronunciation: Paul **Gas**-coin
Native pronunciation: Paul **Gas**-coin
Nationality: English

80: John Charles
English pronunciation: John Charles
Native pronunciation: John Charles
Nationality: Welsh

81: Denis Law
English pronunciation: **Den**-is Law
Native pronunciation: **Den**-is Law
Nationality: Scottish

82: Gheorghe Hagi
English pronunciation: George **Ha**-ji

Native pronunciation: Gay-**or**-gay **Haa**-jee
Nationality: Romanian

83: Dixie Dean
English pronunciation: **Dix**-ee **Deen**
Native pronunciation: **Dix**-ee **Deen**
Nationality: English

84: Raúl
English pronunciation: Rowl
Native pronunciation: Ra-**ool**
Nationality: Spanish
Note: Full name is Raúl González Blanco

85: Philipp Lahm
English pronunciation: **Phil**-ip **Laam**
Native pronunciation: **Fil**-ip L**ah**m
Nationality: German

86: Paolo Rossi
English pronunciation: **Pow**-lo **Roz**-ee
Native pronunciation: **Pa**-oh-lo **Ros**-see
Nationality: Italian

87: Oleh Blokhin (Ukrainian), Oleg Blokhin (Russian)
English pronunciation: **O**-leg **Block**-in
Ukrainian pronunciation: Ol-**yeh** **Blo**-khin
Russian pronunciation: Al-**yeg** Bla-**khin**
Nationality: Ukrainian (then the Soviet Union)

88: Luigi "Gigi" Riva
English pronunciation: Loo-**ee**-gee "**Gee**-gee" **Ree**-va
Native pronunciation: Loo-**ee**-gee "**Gee**-gee" **Ree**-va
Nationality: Italian

89: Marcel Desailly
English pronunciation: **Mar**-sell **Des**-eye-eee
Native pronunciation: Mar-**sell** Deh-sigh-**eee**
Nationality: French

90: Tostão
English pronunciation: Tost-**oww**
Native pronunciation: Tosh-t**oww**
Nationality: Brazilian
Note: His full name is Eduardo Gonçalves de Andrade

91: Patrick Vieira
English pronunciation: **Pat**-rick Vi-**ay**-raa

Native pronunciation: Patr-**reek** Vi-ay-**raa**
Nationality: French

92: Eric Cantona
English pronunciation: **Er**-ic **Can**-toh-nah
Native pronunciation: Ay-**reek Con**-toh-**nah**
Nationality: French

93: Giacinto Facchetti
English pronunciation: Ja-**sin**-to Fa-ch-**eh**-ti
Native pronunciation: Ja-**chin**-to Fak-**ett**-ee
Nationality: Italian

94: Gareth Bale
English pronunciation: **Ga**-reth Bale
Native pronunciation: **Ga**-reth Bale
Nationality: Welsh

95: Hugo Sánchez
English pronunciation: **Hugh**-go San-**chez**
Native pronunciation: **Oo**-go **San**-cheth
Nationality: Mexican

96: Alan Shearer
English pronunciation: **Al**-an **She**-rer
Native pronunciation: **Al**-an **She**-rer
Nationality: English

97: Gunnar Nordahl
English pronunciation: Gunner **Nor**-del
Native pronunciation: **Goo**-nar **Nor**-dawl
Nationality: Swedish

98: Kevin Keegan
English pronunciation: **Kev**-in **Kee**-gan
Native pronunciation: **Kev**-in **Kee**-gan
Nationality: English

99: Javier Zanetti
English pronunciation: Ha-vi-**eh** Zan-**et**-ee
Native pronunciation: Ha-vi-**aer** Than-**eh**-ti
Nationality: Argentinian
Note: Like Maradona and Messi, Zanetti's surname is about as Italian as they come. The Italians would pronounce his name "Zan-eht-tee."

100: Uwe Seeler
English pronunciation: **Ooo**-vay **See**-ler
Native pronunciation: **Ooo**-vuh **Zay**-ler
Nationality: German

Notes

Where a syllable sounds the same as an English word, I have used the English word to transcribe it, for example: "Eye" is to be read the same as the letter *I*; "Lie" for the opening syllable of the English "Lionel" (as in Lionel Richie); "Loud" for the "Laud" in "Laudrup"; "Bough" (bough of a tree) in "Beckenbauer."

There are a few more specific sounds to be aware of:

- *Eh* should be read as a short *e*, as in "meh!"
- *Ah* (as in "Lahm") is a long *a*, as in "arch."
- *Ay* is like the letter *A* in "A, B, C."
- *Oh* is the sound at the end of the English word "toe."

Notes on individual languages:

French

The difficulty in transcribing French names is to do with stress (or the pattern according to which certain syllables are given more emphasis over others in the same word). There is a debate among linguists as to whether French has any linguistic stress at all, with some arguing that all syllables are given equal emphasis (as in, say, Japanese). In practice, the last audible syllable is always "stressed," but the first syllable is often emphasized almost as much. This is why some of the French names have been marked with two "stressed" syllables.

Italian

Some of the Italian transcriptions look like simple copies of the English, but there are differences even when the phonetic spellings look very similar. The key one is that Italians pronounce all consonants, so both *t*'s in the middle of "Totti" are pronounced ("Tot-ti," as opposed to the English slang term "totty").

Portuguese

The initial *r* is pronounced with an *h* sound, a bit like the *ch* in the Scots word "loch." I've used *Kh* to show this sound, which also appears frequently in German, Dutch, Russian, and Ukrainian, among others.

Dutch

The *r* can be rolled very heavily in Dutch, which is why I've transcribed it with *rr*. The letter *g* is pronounced with a *ch* sound that is a bit similar to "loch," hence "Berkh-kamp."

German

The umlaut (the two dots in the letters *ä*, *ö*, and *ü*) is sometimes replaced by the letter *e* for ease of typing, especially when typing (especially when working with an English-language keyboard) so you sometimes see "Lothar Matthaeus" or "Gerd Mueller." The spelling with the umlaut is far more common in German-language texts.

Russian

In Russian, the unstressed *o* sounds like an *a*, which is why Oleg Blokhin's name is pronounced "Al-**yeg** Bla-**khin**."

Spanish

If a Spanish word has an acute accent in it, the syllable with the accent is always stressed (hence Ra**úl**, **Sán**chez, **Pér**ez). This a useful trick commentators tend to miss—not least because English speakers often leave the accents out.

Finally, be aware that all these transcriptions are approximate. Dialects and accents can vary markedly within the same country or region, meaning there is often more than one "correct" way to pronounce any given name.

—Daniel Williams

Acknowledgments

How do you try to distill all the brilliant male players this wonderful game has given us into a list of our centurions? Challenge accepted!

The Soccer 100 has been a labor of love for those of us at *The Athletic*. From drawing up our long list, to our diverse panel of experts arguing over the rankings, to researching the profiles and coming up with new angles to explore, it has been challenging and rewarding in equal measure.

And then came the writing part, and a chance to bring what we do every day at *The Athletic* to a unique project like this. We sent journalists to a sleepy corner of Sweden, a trendy café in Copenhagen, and an island off the coast of west Africa in search of stories, had one pacing around a crematorium in east London, and, once he was done there, dispatched him to Mönchengladbach, Germany, to explore the site of a 1970s nightclub once owned by a World Cup–winning midfielder.

Our writers penned love letters, requested death certificates, pored over WyScout clips and grainy black-and-white footage of long-distant World Cup campaigns, and dug up newspaper clippings from the 1920s—all in an attempt to bring the careers of our 100 selections to life.

The result is a wonderfully eclectic mix, with everything from profiles to interviews to color pieces. We think it works, bringing together characters from around the world; each with his own distinct story to tell.

As ever, reaching the point where we have the book in hand has been a collaborative effort. My thanks go to our wonderful commissioning editor, Dominic Fifield, for the care, commitment, and diligence with which he has led this project. Thank you, Dom—we couldn't have done it without you. And to all 33 of the writers involved for diving in and making the pieces so fresh, interesting and informative. Then to our brilliant chief subeditor, Joseph Bentley, and his team who painstakingly fact-checked the copy before ensuring it sang. Joe was superbly assisted by Aimee Lewis, Will Jeanes—who also contributed the graphics to illustrate some of the more remarkable feats of the players involved—Justin Guthrie, and Peter Carline; Dan Williams provided an excellent pronunciation guide.

The project was overseen by Peter South and Isla Matthews in London. We leaned heavily on Hannah Eades, Andrew Pigott, Natalie Simmonds, and Lucie McCann, and on Rosalie Pisano, Trevor Gibbons, Jocelyn Chancellor, Luke Leissring, and Terri Ann Glynn in the United States. We would also like to thank Mauro DiPreta, Allie Johnston, and Andrew Yackira at HarperCollins.

We are confident *The Soccer 100* sits comfortably alongside *The Baseball 100*, *The Basketball 100*, and *The Football 100* in *The Athletic*'s library detailing the greatest players in the history of some of the world's most popular sports. This offering is a celebration of the beautiful game; we hope you enjoy it.

—Laura Williamson, Editor in Chief, *The Athletic*

Notes

98. KEVIN KEEGAN

"If Kevin Keegan fell into the Tyne": Daniel Taylor, "Past Is Another Country for Keegan," *Guardian*, August 11, 2001.

94. GARETH BALE

"The thing in Madrid is": Ben Machell, "Gareth Bale: I was never fussed about my price tag. I always wanted to be a normal person," *Times*, May 21, 2021.

91. PATRICK VIEIRA

"I was captain at Leeds and I'm walking": "Twenty Years On: What Was It Like to Play Against Arsenal's Invincibles," *Athletic*, August 21, 2023.

"Vieira gave as good as he got": Ibid.

"I loved playing against Vieira": Ibid.

90. TOSTÃO

"These doubtful, uncertain times": *Folha de São Paulo*, April 5, 1970.

"I felt like a charlatan": Bernardo Pombo, Márcio Mará, and Raphael Zarko, "Os 70 anos de Tostão: 'Fui Grande jogador, mas num Segundo ou terceiro escalão,'" *Globo Esporte*, January 24, 2017.

"I practically only used my left foot": Tostão, *Lembranças, Opiniões, Reflexões sobre Futebol* (DBA, 1997).

"Jean-Claude Killy, the famous French skier": Ibid.

"I wasn't the center-forward he wanted": Ibid.

"Younger people must watch the final": Pombo et al., "Os 70 anos de Tostão."

"I played for the collective": "'Fui o facilitador dos gols de uma Seleção revolucionária,' diz Tostão," *Lance!* June 17, 2020.

"He facilitated the work of others": Sam Kunti, *Brazil 1970* (Pitch publishing, 2022).

89. MARCEL DESAILLY

"That's when I took a big risk": Marcel Desailly, "Winning the World Cup Was Remarkable . . . and I Almost Missed It," *Guardian*, June 11, 2018.

France captain Didier Deschamps: Andrew Longmore, "French Art Enters Blue Period," *Independent*, October 25, 1998.

"Over the years, I knew I could not last": "Marseille 1993/AC Milan 1994 . . . with Marcel Desailly," James Richardson's *Kings of Europe* podcast, May 25, 2023.

85. PHILIPP LAHM

"At the beginning of the 2000s": Raj Chohan, "The Evolution of a Full-back: Philipp Lahm on How Position Has Changed," BBC, December 19, 2023.

83. DIXIE DEAN

"Well, that was before half-time": Interview with John Roberts for *Everton: The Official Centenary History* (Harper Collins, 1978), sportingintelligence.com.

"It was a scene beyond description": James Corbett, ed., *Faith of Our Families: Everton FC, an Oral History 1878–2018* (De Coubertin Books, 2017).

"Dixie Dean was Everton": Ibid.

"heard his own obituary": James Corbett, *The Everton Encyclopedia* (De Coubertin Books, 2012).

82. GHEORGHE HAGI

"It was the most difficult goal": "'I wanted to win the World Cup': Gheorghe Hagi on Romania's Incredible Run at USA '94 Including 'That' Touchline Goal Against Colombia," *FourFourTwo*, July 16, 2023.

"the greatest event celebrated by our people": "Hagi and Co Go Showtime in California," FIFA, July 11, 2024.

"I am convinced that with our style": "Gheorghe Hagi on USA '94: 'Whenever I lost at rummy, we'd play well the next day. I won and we lost to Sweden,'" *FourFourTwo*, June 4, 2014.

"I failed": M. J. Corrigan, "Gheorghe Hagi, the Master of Fantasy at USA 94," *These Football Times*, April 16, 2019.

81. DENIS LAW

"All some of his most brilliant interventions": Bobby Charlton, *My Manchester United Years* (Headline, 2008).

"Not only was it difficult": Denis Law, *The King: My Autobiography* (Bantam Press, 2003).

"greatest disappointment": Ibid.

79. PAUL GASCOIGNE

"He's still lovable": Paul Gascoigne, *Gazza, My Story* (Headline, 2005).

72. ALESSANDRO DEL PIERO

"Everyone wants it": Walter Veltroni, "Del Piero: In Italia ormai il calcio è diventato noioso, chi fa scommesse rovina il suo sogno. Il giorno che vorrei rivivere," *Corriera della Sera*, October 20, 2023.

"I never forgive myself": Ibid.

"I was club captain, a fan": Filippo Bonsignore and Timothy Ormezzano, "Juventus, festa e amarcord: Del Piero batte Zidane, la promessa di tornare grandi," *Corriera della Sera*, October 20, 2023.

"The unique link between the old Juventus": Rob Hughes, "Heart of Juventus, Unloved in the End," *New York Times*, October 25, 2011.

"I played for Juventus for so many years": Bonsignore and Ormezzano "Juventus, festa e amarcord."

71. DIDIER DROGBA

"I don't have the money": Didier Drogba, *The Autobiography* (Aurum Press, 2008).

70. MATTHIAS SINDELAR

"Sindelar's shot hit the back": Jonathan Wilson, *Inverting the Pyramid* (Seven Dials, 2014).

"inimitably elegant": "The Wunderteam and Its Paper Man," FIFA, June 3, 2024.

"I almost had the impression": Ulrich Hesse-Lichtenberger, *Tor! The Story of German Football* (WSC Books, 2013).

68. GIANNI RIVERA

"At his age, I didn't even dream": Marco Tarozzi, "Gianni Sessanta," *Calcio 2000*, September 2003.

66. KEVIN DE BRUYNE

"One assist. Zero goals.": "Kevin De Bruyne: Let Me Talk," *Players' Tribune*, April 15, 2019.

"It was so cool": Pol Ballús and Lu Martin, *Pep's City: The Making of a Superteam* (BackPage and Polaris, 2019).

64. FRANK RIJKAARD

"plug straight into the system": Nick Ames, "'A Volcano That Exploded': The '95 Ajax Side That Changed European Football," *Guardian*, May 24, 2020.

"never seen such intense rhythm": Ibid.

"We used to do 150-meter runs": Simon Hughes, *Men in White Suits: Liverpool in the 1990s* (Corgi, 2016).

62. RYAN GIGGS

"I remember the first time I saw him": Alex Ferguson with Hugh McIlvanney, *Managing My Life: My Autobiography* (Hodder and Stoughton, 1999).

"flat out": Ryan Giggs with Joe Lovejoy, *Giggs: The Autobiography* (Michael Joseph, 2005).

"having a nightmare": Ibid.

"his capacity to terrorize defenders": David Meek, *The Unique Treble* (Hodder and Stoughton, 2000).

"pass-and-move midfielder": Giggs, *Giggs: The Autobiography.* (Michael Joseph, 2005).

"It would be nice to say that I had": Ibid.

"the one I'd like to be remembered by": Ibid.

61. SÓCRATES

"An endless orgasm": *CartaCapital*, June 12, 2002.

"If you didn't accompany his thought": Walter Casagrande Júnior and Gilvan Ribeiro, *Sócrates & Casagrande: Uma História de Amor* (Globo Livros, 2016).

"organized chaos": Andrew Downie, *Doctor Sócrates: Footballer, Philosopher, Legend* (Simon & Schuster UK, 2017).

"That Brazil side was extraordinary": "Pablito Paints Over Futebol-Arte," FIFA, May 30, 2024.

"Football as we know it died": Fernando Duarte, "World Cup 1982: Brazil v Italy and 'the Day Football Died,'" BBC, November 11, 2022.

60. JUST FONTAINE

"Like Jesus": "A Tribute to Just Fontaine," FIFA, March 2, 2023.

"The sport taught me to pretend": Bernard Lions, "Just Fontaine: Mon record est comme le bon vin, plus il vieillit, plus il prend de la valeur," *L'Équipe*, June 26, 2014, republished on March 1, 2023.

"We shared a room": "A Tribute to Just Fontaine," FIFA.

"He told them: 'The day you score 13'": Lions, "Just Fontaine."

"We would have scored more goals": Ibid.

"I hope to do better": Jean-Philippe Cointot, "Machine à buts, légende des Bleus puis entraîneur: Fontaine, une vie de foot," *L'Équipe*, March 1, 2023.

"I know that today": Lions, "Just Fontaine."

"Afterwards, he came to see me": Cointot, "Machine à buts."

"One day, in 3050": Lions, "Just Fontaine."

"My record? It's like a fine wine": Ibid.

59. STANLEY MATTHEWS

"I hear some modern players": Stanley Matthews, *The Way It Was: My Autobiography* (Canelo, 2000).

"football has lost its greatest player": Ibid.

"The newspapers were generous": Ibid.

"I'd make for home and breakfast": Ibid.

56. GEORGE WEAH

"Weah was a real surprise": "Iconic Weah Is a True Great," FIFA, October 20, 2013.

55. JOHAN NEESKENS

"I didn't mind being the second greatest": Brian Davies, "Johan Neeskens: 'The Second Greatest Player in the World,'" *Ajax Daily*, 2017.

"But during the gym lessons": Frans van den Nieuwenhof, "Johan Neeskens: keihard en kwetsbaar," *Voetbal International*, October 7, 2024.

"I didn't dare to give interviews": Ibid.

"I never act softly": Ibid.

"kamikaze pilot": Jonathan Wilson, "The Great European Cup Teams: Ajax 1971–73," *Guardian*, May 22, 2013.

"If someone passes me": Michael Butler, "Johan Neeskens, the Most Complete Player of the Total Football Era," *Guardian*, October 8, 2024.

"I was completely devastated": Van den Nieuwenhof, "Johan Neeskens."

53. WAYNE ROONEY

"With the kind of physique": Sir Alex Ferguson, *Alex Ferguson: My Autobiography* (Hodder, 2014).

"This whole thing's potty": Jonathan Northcroft, "Was Rooney Selection Really Such a Gamble?" *Sunday Times*, April 6, 2003.

"He's not just a footballer": Michel Salgado, "My Debt to Margate," *Guardian*, November 16, 2004.

51. SÁNDOR KOCSIS

"They both wanted things their own way": Miklós Bocsák, *Kocsis és Czibor* (Sport Kiadás, 1983).

"There has never been anybody": "The Beginning of the Magyars' Magic," FIFA, June 3, 2020.

50. KENNY DALGLISH

"life-changing": *The Rest is Football* podcast, March 2024.

"In his best days at Liverpool": *Kenny: The Player, the Man, the Truth*, documentary, 2017.

48. RIVALDO

"too selfish": Gary Meenaghan, "Rivaldo: The Brazil and Barcelona Great Who, in Childhood Poverty, Never Dared to Dream," BBC, December 21, 2021.

"One day in training": Jordi Mestre, "The Cult: Rivaldo," *Vice*, April 25, 2016.

47. RAYMOND KOPA

"He's the one who showed us the path": "Zidane: Kopa nous a montré le chemin," *Le Parisien*, March 3, 2017.

"Eight hours a day in the depths of the earth": Raymond Kopa with Patrice Burchkalter, *Kopa* (Mareuil, 2017).

"He was an extraordinary teacher": "Kopa: Je représente ma génération," *France Football*, December 26, 2000.

"England, take heed": Desmond Hackett, "'Napoleon' Kopa Is England Menace," *Daily Express*, March 18, 1955.

"slaves": "Des mines du Nord au Real, six histoires de Raymond Kopa," *Libération*, March 7, 2017.

"Leaving Reims during such a difficult period": Kopa, *Kopa*.

45. FABIO CANNAVARO

"between cars, everywhere": "Fabio Cannavaro: The Street Urchin Who Became a World Cup Legend," CNN, June 6, 2014.

"You can be short and fast": Fabio Cannavaro, "From Ball Boy to Ballon d'Or," *Players' Tribune*, March 1, 2017.

found that transition "difficult": Ibid.

44. KAKÁ

"Innocently playing at the water park": Kaká, "Inside My Mind: 2007 Champions League Final," *Players' Tribune,* May 31, 2024.

43. CAFU

"At Roma, I was playing in midfield": Amy Lawrence, "Cafu Born to Win," *Observer,* May 22, 2005.

"I need to talk about a very special player": Ibid.

42. LUÍS FIGO

"Johnnie Walker, I think": Sid Lowe, *Fear and Loathing in La Liga: Barcelona vs Real Madrid* (Yellow Jersey, 2014).

"Maybe it was my lucky moment": Sergio Krithinas, "The Big Interview: Luís Figo—'Barca weren't treating me properly—it was too late when they did, so I joined Real Madrid,'" *FourFourTwo,* May 12, 2017.

something of a "bluff": Ibid.

"And then things took the direction": Lowe, *Fear and Loathing in La Liga.*

a "guinea pig": Sid Lowe, "Luís Figo: 'I Had Everything at Barcelona—Moving to Real Madrid Took Its Toll,'" *Guardian,* October 15, 2022.

39. ROBERTO BAGGIO

"The agony for the Italian public": Julie Cart, "World Cup '94: 1 Day and Counting: Keeping the Faith: Fans Aren't Sure What to Make of Italy's Roberto Baggio, a Soft-Spoken Buddhist Who Is the Best Player in Europe," *Los Angeles Times,* June 16, 1994.

"We won 5–1": "1990 Roberto Baggio," *FourFourTwo,* June 29, 2021.

37. ANDREA PIRLO

"cheese on spaghetti": Carlo Mazzone on his Instagram page, November 17, 2019.

36. LUKA MODRIĆ

"I was impressed by the atmosphere": Luka Modrić, *My Autobiography* (Bloomsbury Sport, 2021).

"I felt at peace—like a man": Ibid.

"Is there bigger recognition": Ibid.

"Modrić is still irreplaceable": Onze Mondial, June 21, 2018.

"a humble genius": Modrić, *My Autobiography.*

"I made him my target in 2011": Ibid.

35. JIMMY GREAVES

"someone closing the door": Richard Williams, "Jimmy Greaves Was a Genius, the Purest Finisher England Has Produced," *Guardian*, September 19, 2021.

"A good centre-forward will attack": Jimmy Greaves, *The Heart of the Game* (Sphere, 2006).

"cherish it forever": Ibid.

"It was the stuff of my dreams": Ibid.

"He was a sort of Dickensian": Guillem Balague, "Cristiano Ronaldo Is All Power; Greaves Was Just like Messi," *AS*, May 16, 2017.

"The only one who could compare": Michael Walker, *Green Shoots* (De Coubertin, 2017).

"You can't mark him": Football Hall of Fame official guidebook.

34. DINO ZOFF

"Don't talk for the sake": Dino Zoff, *Dura solo un attimo, la gloria. La mia vita* (Mondadori, 2015).

"You've got what it takes": Ibid.

"Like Rome, it's a liquid city": Ibid.

33. GIANLUIGI BUFFON

"Juventus went to see me play": Matt Barker, "The Big Interview: Gianluigi Buffon—'Goalkeepers are perverse. You're playing a game where everyone uses their feet, but you want to use your hands,'" *FourFourTwo*, July 2014.

"Everyone, whether they are a teammate": "Chiellini: Buffon Makes Difficult Things Look Easy," FIFA, October 18, 2017.

"black hole of the soul": Nicky Bandini, "Gianluigi Buffon: 'It's Important to Get Things Wrong in Life—and Pay the Price,'" *Guardian*, March 3, 2021.

"one of the most important": Barker, "The Big Interview."

"But I need to have my own experiences": Bandini, "Gianluigi Buffon."

32. ROMÁRIO

"I have scored against *every* team": Johnette Howard, "On and off Field, Romário Does as Romário Pleases," *Washington Post*, July 7, 1994.

"about 900 goals": Márcio Iannacca, "Romário lança DVD e diz que Ronaldo está cheinho, mas vai esvaziar," globoesporte.com, August 5, 2008.

Well, enough to be making phone calls: Simon Kuper, "Scoring Genius of Brazil's Selfish Giant," *Financial Times*, March 9, 2007.

"like a player from a cartoon": "Controversial Brazil Star Is as Singular as His Name," *Chicago Tribune*, June 10, 1994.

"I already know": "Reinstated Romário Saves Brazil," FIFA, September 19, 2023.

"Well, I saved it": Howard, "On and off Field."

"He can win the title": Francesco Rea, "Brasile, 24 anni di vigilia," *L'Unità*, July 17, 1994.

"I want a window seat": James Brooke, "Brazil: Prima Donna Image Lurks," *New York Times*, May 25, 1994.

"Romário's weakness": Randy Harvey, "The Goal Dust Twins: With Romário and Bebeto at forward, Brazil poses a big problem, but as many will attest, it's not always for the other team," *Los Angeles Times*, July 2, 1994.

"The fact that I lost the World Cup didn't change": Peter Speetjens, "The Return of Romário," *Blizzard*, September 2024.

"This is my World Cup": Ken Jones, "Lions Lie in Wait for Roaring Romário," *Independent*, June 23, 1994.

"I'm sure they'll understand": "Romário Snub to Barcelona Demands," *Independent*, July 31, 1994.

31. RUUD GULLIT

"Ruud Gullit" sounded more like a footballer: Ruud Gullit, *My Autobiography* (Century, 1998).

"Cruyff's will was law": Ruud Gullit, *How to Watch Football* (Penguin, 2017).

"someone special, the great footballer": Ibid.

"we felt bigger and stronger": Ibid.

"Adaptation": Ibid.

"Once again I had to adapt": Ibid.

"In the end, we managed": Ibid.

"Because Gullit is an extrovert": Frits Barend and Henk van Dorp, *Ajax, Barcelona, Cruyff* (Bloomsbury, 1998).

"My own role was modest": Gullit, *How to Watch Football.*

30. CARLOS ALBERTO

"If I had to choose one moment": "Captain's Clincher Earns Brazil Immortality," FIFA, November 2022.

29. KYLIAN MBAPPÉ

"king without a crown": François Verdenet, "Roi sans couronne," *L'Équipe*, December 19, 2022.

become his "heir": Alessandro Grandesso, "Mbappé da Pallone d'oro. Sarà il nuovo Pelé," *La Gazzetta dello Sport*, March 5, 2021.

"It must be something extraordinary": *France 98: nous nous sommes tant aimés,* France TV, June 5, 2018.

There were precious few proclamations: *Les Bleus 2018: au coeur de l'épopée russe,* TF1, July 17, 2018.

He was unable to find the net: José Barroso, Vincent Duluc, and François Verdenet, "J'ai eu le temps de faire le deuil de ce départ," *L'Équipe,* October 5, 2021.

"My ambition was to become European champion": Christophe Remise, "J'avais l'ambition d'être champion d'Europe et de faire un bon Euro, je n'ai fait ni l'un, ni l'autre: Mbappé ne se cache pas après Espagne-France," *Le Figaro,* July 10, 2024.

27. ZICO

"I was seen as a good prospect": "Zico: *Seleção* Genius, *Mengão* King," FIFA, March 2, 2010.

"I barely saw him": Cassius Leitão and Marcelo Pizzi, "Zico 60: o surgimento do Galinho de Quintino e a trajetória até o estrelato," *O Globo,* March 3, 2013.

"laboratory superstar": *Jornal da Tarde,* March 22, 1976.

"I made a pig's ear of that World Cup": Interview with *Placar* magazine on August 3, 1984.

"I've come to terms with it": Interview with *Placar* magazine on March 18, 1988.

"I'd like to be remembered as someone": "Zico: *Seleção* Genius, *Mengão* King," FIFA.

26. LOTHAR MATTHÄUS

"The sole broke": Simon Hart, *World in Motion: The Inside Story of Italia 90—The Tournament That Changed Football* (De Coubertin, 2018).

"What Maradona saw": Simon Kuper, *The Football Men: Up Close with the Giants of the Modern Game* (Simon & Schuster, 2012).

"What made me strong": Ibid.

25. ANDRÉS INIESTA

"I froze": Andrés Iniesta, *The Artist: Being Iniesta* (Headline, 2016).

"Andrés wanted a medical": Ibid.

"everything will be fine": Ibid.

"The torment is over": Ibid.

23. THIERRY HENRY

"I saw it as my duty": James McNicholas, "The Premier League 60: No 1, Thierry Henry," *Athletic,* September 9, 2020.

"Do you know the number": Ibid.

Vela compared Henry's "hard": Ryan Tolmich, "'Henry Tried Every Day to Be the Best'—Vela Says Jordan's Last Dance Documentary Conjured Memories of Arsenal Icon," *Goal,* May 21, 2020.

21. XAVI HERNÁNDEZ

"The football we played to win": John Atkin, "How Does It Feel to Win a EURO?" UEFA, January 28, 2019.

20. BOBBY CHARLTON

"with the grace of a ballet dancer": Quotes from Manchester United's official website, October 2022.

19. FRANCO BARESI

"Franchino, you'll come": Franco Baresi, *Libero di sognare* (Feltrinelli, 2021).

18. LEV YASHIN

"I was in disbelief": "Lev Yashin, the Impregnable Spider," FIFA, March 20, 2020.

"We were so calm": Ibid.

"He wanted to quit": Patrick Jennings, "Yashin," BBC, June 7, 2018.

17. PAOLO MALDINI

"Where do you want to play": Simon Kuper, "Maldini Finds Secret of Eternal Youth," *Financial Times,* May 20, 2005.

16. MARCO VAN BASTEN

"If I had the choice again": BBC Radio 5 Live's Euro League's podcast, November 5, 2020.

"Johan had two apples": Marco van Basten, *Basta* (Cassell, 2020).

"My father is traumatically dominant": Ibid.

"He was meteoropathic": Arrigo Sacchi, *The Immortals* (BackPage, 2021).

"I'll make a bargain with you": Van Basten, *Basta.*

"What they all found so wonderful": Ibid.

"Ultimately, maybe it was a kind of divine": Ibid.

"I will never forget it": *AS,* March 19, 2021.

15. GEORGE BEST

"That was one of the most important nights": *Goal* magazine interview, March 1996.

Denis Law called it "electric": Denis Law, *The King.*

"Before the noisiest crowd": George Best, *Best of Both Worlds* (Pelham, 1968).

"A tremendous roar greeted": Sir Bobby Charlton, *My Manchester United Years* (Headline, 2014).

"75,000 Portuguese screaming": Sir Matt Busby, *Soccer at the Top* (Weidenfeld & Nicolson, 1974).

Best did not know why: Best, *Best of Both Worlds.*

"for some reason": George Best, *Blessed: The Autobiography* (Ebury, 2002).

"It was a strange experience": Ibid.

"He had to climb a gate": Carol Best, *Our George* (Macmillan, 2008).

That year of 1968, aged 21: Germaine Greer, "The Best Year of My Life," *Independent,* November 27, 2005.

"I wish they had shot": Michael Walker, *Green Shoots.*

14. GARRINCHA

"The joy of Garrincha's football": Paulo Mendes Campos, *O Gol É Necessário* (Civilizacao Brasileira, 2000).

"He teaches us that nothing is more beautiful": *Manchete Esportiva,* November 14, 1958.

"I got tired of telling him": *Placar,* January 28, 1983.

"He was sitting there on a float": Pelé, *Pelé: The Autobiography* (Simon & Schuster, 2007).

"He was a poor mortal who helped": *Jornal do Brasil,* January 22, 1983.

11. EUSÉBIO

"I wanted to get him for myself": David Bolchover, *The Greatest Comeback: From Genocide to Football Glory, The Story of Béla Guttmann* (Biteback Publishing, 2017).

"They signed the contract with my mother": Interview with Eusébio by Paul Hayward in *The Observer,* June 6, 2010.

"I never knew that I traveled": Interview with *Tribuna Expresso,* November 2011.

"I told them my orders": Bolchover, *The Greatest Comeback.*

"He scored three goals": Ibid.

"Why did he start, knowing": Interview with Eusébio by Tom Kundert in *FourFourTwo*, July 2008.

"I didn't say anything": Ibid.

"Who is the most spectacular and brilliant": Eusébio, *My Name Is Eusébio* (Routledge & Kegan Paul, 1967).

"I always said to him": *Tribuna Expresso*, November 2011.

"It was because he thought": Ibid.

"On and off the pitch": Tom Kundert, *FourFourTwo*.

"When we're in that group": *Tribuna Expresso*, November 2011.

10. MICHEL PLATINI

"He appears to be playing": Jocelyn Lermusieaux, "Bon anniversaire, Platoche," *L'Équipe*, June 21, 2024.

"We called our midfield 'magic square'": Cédric Chapuis, "Michel Platini à l'Euro 1984, 9 buts et l'apogée d'un 10," *L'Équipe*, June 4, 2024.

"When a match was average": Robinson Martineau, "Jean-François Domergue raconte France-Portugal, demi-finale de l'Euro 84: Je dis: 'Je le sens' et Michel me dit: 'Vas-y!,'" *L'Équipe*, May 23, 2024.

"Platini was the boss": Jean-Christophe Bassignac, "Bruno Bellone sur l'Euro 84: Platini, c'était les voiles du voilier," *L'Équipe*, May 30, 2024.

"He had this impressive quality": Roberto Notarianni, "Marco Tardelli sur Michel Platini: 1983–84, c'est le top de sa carrière," *L'Équipe*, May 28, 2024.

9. FERENC PUSKÁS

"Please, sir, take me to your country": Ferenc Puskás, *Captain of Hungary* (The History Press, 2007).

"We didn't know about Puskás": "The Day Magic Wowed Wembley," FIFA, November 25, 2023.

"Look at that little fat chap": "England v Hungary—a Football Match That Started a Revolution," BBC, November 23, 2013.

"We should be alright here": Ferenc Puskás, *Puskás on Puskás* (Robson Books, 1998).

one of the side's "computers": Ibid.

"It was as if the game took place": Ibid.

"He was a natural": David Lacey, "Ferenc Puskás: A Man Who Changed the Game Forever," *Guardian*, November 18, 2006.

a side of "soccer sorcerers": Sir Tom Finney, *Finney on Football* (Sportsman Book Club, 1960).

"It was like playing people from outer space": Puskás, *Puskás on Puskás.*

"sold the game for a Mercedes": Ibid.

"had some kind of disease": Ibid.

"a virtual death sentence": Ibid.

"I'm not old enough to be a coach": Ibid.

"But it wasn't bad for a fat one": Ibid.

"like a hand, he could do anything": Lacey, "Ferenc Puskás."

8. ZINÉDINE ZIDANE

"What I am going to say": Amy Lawrence, "Zidane Lifts France but Irish Won't Lie Down," *Observer,* September 4, 2005.

"I don't listen": Amy Lawrence, "Zidane: A Study of 'The Master' Since 1996—and Finally an Interview," *Athletic,* July 12, 2023.

6. ALFREDO DI STÉFANO

"They offered financial terms": Jimmy Burns, *La Roja: A Journey Through Spanish Football* (Simon & Schuster, 2012).

"no better than the average": John Leonard, *Flight to Bogota: England's Football Rebel, Neil Franklin* (Pitch Publishing, 2020).

"The whole world is laughing": Miguel Delaney, "Franco vs Khrushchev: When Politics and Sport Certainly Mixed," *Independent,* June 30, 2018.

5. CRISTIANO RONALDO

"There have been a few players": "16 Quotes That Define the Life and Times of George Best," *Daily Telegraph,* November 25, 2015.

3. PELÉ

"the symbol of Brazilian": *Pelé,* Netflix documentary (2021), directed by David Tryhorn and Ben Nicholas.

"I have gone through my memories": Tostão, "Antes de a bola chegar, pelo olhar, Pelé já me dizia pretendia fazer," *Folha de São Paulo,* December 29, 2022.

"bruised and drained": Pelé, *Pelé: The Autobiography.*

"I was kicked to pieces": Ibid.

"Pelé was everything": *Pelé,* Netflix.

2. DIEGO MARADONA

"beating the English would represent": Jimmy Burns, *Maradona: The Hand of God* (Lyons Press, 1997).

"You could see [Shilton's] fist": Guillem Balague, *Maradona: The Boy, the Rebel, the God* (Seven Dials, 2022).

"It must have been the hand of God": Ibid.

1. LIONEL MESSI

"That moment will not leave my memory": Paul Hayward, "How the Genius of Lionel Messi and Dan Carter Gave Me Hope in Fighting Cancer," *Daily Telegraph,* November 3, 2015.

"so forgettable": John Carlin, "Inside the Mind of Lionel Messi—and What Next for Barcelona?" London *Times,* September 10, 2021.

"genetic miracle": Marcela Mora y Araujo, "Lionel Messi: Traitor to Some, Genius to All and Carrying the Heaviest Burden," *Guardian,* June 15, 2018.

"He's like *The Matrix*": Sarah Shephard, "How Lionel Messi's Body and Brain Help Make Him the World's Best Footballer," *Athletic,* December 16, 2022.

"If he had not won the World Cup": "Guardiola a Che Tempo Che Fa: 'Messi il più forte di tutti i tempi. Io via dal City? Non è vero, devo ancora riflettere,'" *Eurosport,* October 13, 2024.

"Don't try to explain Messi": Jeré Longman, "Messi's Brilliance Transcends His Numbers," *New York Times,* December 11, 2012.

Photograph Credits

All images are courtesy of Getty Images. Additional credit information is below.

p. 1 dpa/picture alliance; p. 6 Friedemann Vogel/Bongarts; p. 11 Liverpool FC; p. 15 Touring Club Italiano/Marka/Universal Images Group; p. 20 Shaun Botterill/Allsport/Hulton Archive; p. 25 Allsport/Hulton Archive; p. 30 Clive Mason; p. 35 Hulton Archive; p. 40 Anton Want/Allsport; p. 45 Stuart MacFarlane/Arsenal FC; p. 51 4Imagens; p. 56 Mark Leech/Offside; p. 60 Alessandro Sabattini; p. 65 Peter Robinson/EMPICS; p. 70 Mark Leech/Offside; p. 75 Adam Pretty/Bongarts; p. 80 MIGUEL RIOPA/AFP; p. 85 © Hulton-Deutsch Collection/CORBIS/Corbis; p. 90 Michael Kunkel/Bongarts; p. 95 Keystone; p. 100 Reg Burkett/Keystone Features/Hulton Archive; p. 107 David Cannon/Allsport; p. 114 STAFF/AFP; p. 121 Shaun Botterill; p. 128 DANIEL GARCIA/AFP; p. 135 Schirner/ullstein bild; p. 143 Ben Radford/Allsport; p. 151 Werner OTTO/ullstein bild; p. 158 Valerio Pennicino; p. 165 Ian MacNicol; p. 172 ullstein bild/ullstein bild; p. 180 Paolo Bruno; p. 187 Alessandro Sabattini; p. 194 John Powell/Liverpool FC; p. 202 Alex Livesey; p. 209 Michael Campanella; p. 216 VI Images; p. 223 Allsport; p. 229 Matthew Peters/Manchester United; p. 236 Mark Leech; p. 244 Keystone-France\Gamma-Rapho; p. 252 S&G/PA Images; p. 259 Alex Caparros; p. 266 -/AFP; p. 273 Stu Forster/Allsport; p. 281 Horstmüller/ullstein bild; p. 288 Neal Simpson/EMPICS; p. 295 Bryn Lennon; p. 303 David Ramos; p. 309 Keystone/Hulton Archive; p. 317 SSPL; p. 323 Mike Cooper/ALLSPORT; p. 330 Phil Cole /Allsport; p. 337 Universal/Corbis/VCG; p. 344 MARTIN BERNETTI/AFP; p. 351 PASCAL PAVANI/AFP; p. 359 DAMIEN MEYER/AFP; p. 366 Tim De Waele; p. 373 Yu Chun Christopher Wong/Eurasia Sport Images; p. 380 Alejandro Gonzalez/Real Madrid; p. 387 Barratts/PA Images; p. 394 Juventus FC - Archive/Juventus FC; p. 402 Diego Souto; p. 408

Matthew Ashton - PA Images; p. 415 KENZO TRIBOUILLARD/AFP; p. 422 S&G/PA Images; p. 429 Ferdi Hartung/ullstein bild; p. 436 KARIM JAAFAR/AL-WATAN DOHA/AFP; p. 443 Tony Marshall/EMPICS; p. 451 Etsuo Hara; p. 459 Mirrorpix; p. 466 Catherine Ivill; p. 473 Bettmann / Contributor; p. 481 Jean-Yves Ruszniewski/Corbis/VCG; p. 488 Bernd Wende/ullstein bild; p. 495 Jamie McDonald; p. 503 STAFF/AFP; p. 510 Matthew Ashton/EMPICS; p. 517 Henri Szwarc/ Stringer; p. 524 Etsuo Hara; p. 532 S&G/PA; p. 539 Alessandro Sabattini; p. 546 © Hulton-Deutsch Collection/CORBIS/Corbis; p. 553 Etsuo Hara; p. 560 Peter Robinson/EMPICS; p. 568 Mirrorpix; p. 576 ullstein bild/ullstein bild; p. 583 -/AFP; p. 590 Stu Forster/Allsport/Hulton Archive; p. 597 and p. 604 Alessandro Sabattini; p. 612 Barratts/PA Images; p. 621 Simon Bruty/Anychance; p. 628 Werner OTTO/ullstein bild; p. 635 STAFF/AFP; p. 645 JAVIER SORIANO/AFP; p. 656 Werner Baum/picture alliance; p. 666 Alessandro Sabattini; p. 675 STAFF/AFP; p. 686 JOSEP LAGO/AFP.

Index

NOTE: **Bold** page references indicate profiles of top 100 players; *italic* page references indicate photos and tables.